THE INSTITUTES OF GAIUS

TEXTS IN ROMAN LAW
General Editor: Peter Birks
Professor of Civil Law, University of Edinburgh

Justinian's Institutes
The Institutes of Gaius
A Commentary on the Institutes

The Institutes of Gaius

Translated with an Introduction by
W.M. Gordon
Douglas Professor of Civil Law
University of Glasgow

and O. F. Robinson
Senior Lecturer, Department of Legal History
University of Glasgow

with the Latin text of Seckel and Kuebler

Duckworth

First published in 1988 by
Gerald Duckworth & Co. Ltd.
The Old Piano Factory
43 Gloucester Crescent, London NW1

Introduction and translation © 1988 by W.M. Gordon
and O.F. Robinson

ISBN 0 7156 2504 7 (cased)
ISBN 0 7156 2505 5 (paper)

British Library Cataloguing in Publication Data

Gaius
   The Institutes of Gaius. (Texts in
   Roman Law).
   1. Roman Law.
   I. Title   II. Series
   343.706'02632   [LAW]

ISBN 0-7156-2504-7

Photoset in North Wales by
Derek Doyle & Associates, Mold, Clwyd
and printed in Great Britain by
Redwood Burn Limited, Trowbridge

Contents

Introduction

1. Gaius and his place in Roman Law

The major source of our knowledge of Roman law is the
collection, made by Justinian (Roman Emperor at
Constantinople, A.D. 527-65), which is known as the
Corpus Iuris Civilis. This consists of the *Digest*, the *Code*,
and the *Institutes*, as well as the *Novels*, which were
Justinian's own legislation and an addition to, rather than
part of, the mainstream of Roman law preserved in the
Corpus. A survey of these component parts is given in the
Introduction to the companion volume of Justinian's
Institutes. Here it is sufficient to say that the *Digest* is a
selection from the writings of the classical jurists, that is,
those who flourished between the later first century B.C.
and the mid-third century A.D. Each selection, or
fragment, is ascribed to its author and the relevant book.
The *Code* is a collection of imperial legislation, running
from the early second century up to Justinian's own time.
However, much is legislation almost of a judicial character,
with the emperor explaining the application of the law to
particular cases. This is especially so for the period of the
Roman Empire before the adoption of a new style of
government – and the official acceptance of Christianity –
by the Emperor Constantine in the early fourth century.

The *Institutes* was written specifically as a text-book for first-year law students. Like the other parts of the *Corpus*, it was a compilation rather than an original piece of writing, although it was drafted to give the appearance of a coherent work.

Not surprisingly, the process of compilation under Justinian involved editing. He was aiming to produce a compact law library for use by students and practitioners of his own day. Although he deliberately preserved fragments showing the development of earlier lawyers' thought, he excised the totally obsolete. The extent to which his editing altered the substance of what the classical jurists wrote has been a prolific field of research for modern scholars. Interpolation-hunting, as it has been called, is now much less radical, but there is no doubt that we often do not have the actual words and the original contexts of the passages in the *Corpus*. Yet almost all that we do know has come to us through Justinian. There are a few works which have survived independently and fully enough to show their original structure, but all but one of them are from the post-classical period and are themselves deliberate simplifications of previous material. Only one book (in the modern sense) has come down to us which is an original work of the classical period and, moreover, has not been revised by the compilers of the *Corpus Iuris Civilis*, and that book is the *Institutes* of Gaius.

Gaius is acknowledged as the main source for Justinian's *Institutes*, both in content and in structure. It was from Gaius that Justinian drew his division of the whole outline of private law under the headings of Persons, Things, and Actions. The importance of this scheme has been well explained in pages 10-16 of the Introduction to the companion translation of Justinian's *Institutes*. It must remain an open question whether Gaius invented this system, the institutional structure which came to influence all European legal systems to a greater or lesser extent. We certainly do not know of any predecessor, nor is there any inherent improbability in his having achieved this. The very fact that we know almost nothing about Gaius, that his contemporaries and their successors did not refer to him, that we think he spent his life as a teacher of law rather than in its practice or in senior administrative office, may indeed argue that he had time and energy to develop this intellectual system. He could well have done so just because he was able to look at the whole field of law, and perhaps even to reconsider it regularly for the benefit of his students. Furthermore, the close study of the text of his *Institutes* which is necessarily required for a translation confirms us in the belief that what we have is something based on a course of lectures (perhaps even actual lecture notes), tidied rather than polished.

We know almost nothing about Gaius himself. We do not even know his other names. We can assume that he lived from about A.D. 110 to at least 179, since he wrote on legislation passed in 178, and his output, which we know from extracts in the *Digest* as well as references he makes in the *Institutes*, suggests that his life was not particularly brief. All that is known and most that can reasonably be guessed about him is incorporated in Honoré's biography (A.M. Honoré, *Gaius*, Oxford, 1962). While it is generally agreed that Gaius had strong links with the provinces, his main concern was with the law of Rome, which in his day meant the law of Rome itself and of the Italian peninsula, even though its influence was already spreading in the western provinces. In his time, the Roman Empire (more especially its eastern half) was still in theory a collection of autonomous city states and former kingdoms under the military rule of Rome. But his references to various provincial legal practices, as in 1.193, are made in passing; the law of which he was expounding the outline was that of Rome. Moreover, he was interested in Rome's legal history – as we could tell from the *Institutes*, even if he had not also written a commentary on the Twelve Tables of the mid-fifth century B.C. Although Gaius was apparently not outstanding in his lifetime, his achievement in producing the pattern of a lucid introduction to Roman private law, arranged systematically so that the inter-relationships of the different areas of law could be traced, led to his recognition in later centuries. In the Law of Citations of the Emperor Theodosius II in A.D. 426 he was given a place along with the later and more distinguished Papinian, Paul, Ulpian and Modestinus as an authoritative juristic source. Justinian referred to him as 'Gaius noster', 'our own Gaius'. His place in the history of the development of the law in western civilisation rests on his originality in organisation; it was this which was perpetuated by Justinian.

But his place is also vital in the internal history of Roman law. Gaius is the only classical jurist who has left us a reasonably complete book untouched by Justinian's editors. From Gaius we learn the enormous importance of the forms of action in classical law. Perhaps it was his institutional scheme which made it easy thereafter to separate substantive law from procedure. He also tells us of legal rules which had been abolished, or had fallen into disuse, in Justinian's day. It is from him that we learn about the perpetual guardianship of women, about formal methods of conveyance, about the trust conveyance called 'fiducia', and the literal contract. He also gives us most of the information we have about the 'legis actiones', the legal procedure in use before the formulary system of his own day, and about interdicts, quasi-administrative preliminaries to bringing matters to trial. For those who want to know more of classical Roman law he is invaluable.

2. The text of the *Institutes*

'Until 1816 we had, apart from the excerpts in the *Digest*, only a Visigothic precis of Gaius' *Institutes*, known as the *Epitome*. This entirely omitted the crucially important book 4, on actions. In 1816 Niebuhr found and Savigny identified an almost complete fifth-century manuscript in the library of the cathedral at Verona. The text had been overwritten with letters of St. Jerome and of Gennadius. Later discoveries have filled some gaps, though in the meantime in the 1820s the Verona palimpsest was seriously damaged by the use of chemicals intended to improve its legibility' (P. Birks and G. McLeod, Introduction to the companion volume of Justinian's *Institutes*, p.14). The Verona manuscript was never entirely easy to read just because it is a palimpsest; that is, the surface of the parchment was scraped so that it could be used for the over-writing of quite different material. In some places the Gaian text was the third layer of writing. Something like a twelfth of the whole was illegible. The first edition of this manuscript was published by J.F.L. Goeschen in 1820; F. Bluhme also worked on it, but the chemicals he used have often made reading harder for later scholars. In 1874 G. Studemund's *Apographum*, or exact copy, was published at Leipzig; revised versions were published by Studemund and P. Krueger at Berlin over the next thirty years. In 1927 fragments of the fourth book were found among the Oxyrhynchite papyri; further fragments came to light in Cairo in 1938. These were published by V. Arangio-Ruiz at Florence and re-edited in *Bullettino dell' Istituto di Diritto Romano* 42 (1934) 571-624. All the additional material appears to date from the fourth century or even the later third. While there have been some Romanists, scholars such as Beseler, Albertario and

Solazzi, who have suspected the Verona text of corruption, the further fragments have vindicated the general authenticity of the main manuscript.

The text used for this translation is that produced for the Teubner series by E. Seckel and B. Kuebler, first published in 1903 but here in Kuebler's revised edition of 1935, including the new fragments preserved on papyrus. The modern critical edition is that of M. David and H.L.W. Nelson, publication of which began at Leiden in 1954. The Teubner text shows the pagination of the Verona manuscript in the margins. It normally follows that text where it can be read, but not quite always. The upper set of footnotes, the *apparatus criticus*, shows the textual variations. It indicates whether the main printed text is following the Verona manuscript (V) according to Studemund's exact copy, or where there is a difference between the scribe who worked on the manuscript (V^1) and another who made corrections (V^2). Material taken from the Oxyrhynchite papyri (0) and the Cairo folios (F) is also indicated. That the Gaius is a third layer is indicated by t.s. Square brackets [] in the body of the Teubner text mark what must have been written in error (as 'patron' for 'freedman' in 4.46) or what was inserted at a later date (such as the sprinkling of sub-headings). Straight lines ——— mark the places where the manuscript is illegible, and the Teubner edition indicates how many lines are missing; asterisks **** indicate illegible letters. Italics are used for parts of the text supplied from the excerpts in the *Digest* (*D.*) or from Justinian's *Institutes* (*I.* or *Inst.*). Other Roman law sources referred to in the footnotes of the *apparatus criticus* are Justinian's *Code* (*C.*), the Theodosian Code of A.D. 438 (*C.Th.*), and other legal sources, collected by P.E. Huschke and later edited by Seckel and Kuebler in the work entitled *Iurisprudentiae anteiustinianae reliquiae* (*Iurispr.*), or in the collection of C.G. Bruns, seventh edition by O. Gradenwitz, entitled *Fontes iuris romani antiqui* (*Bruns*[7]). Other papyrological sources are recorded as (*B G U*) and (*Chrest.*). (*C.I.L.*) is the *Corpus Inscriptionum Latinarum*, a vast collection of epigraphic source material, and (*V.I.R.*) is the *Vocabularium iurisprudentiae romanae*, a comprehensive word-list for the writings of the classical jurists, for thê most part taken from the *Digest*.

The names of the various scholars who have suggested emendations to the text of the Verona manuscript are also given in the upper footnotes. Many of them, such as Huschke (Hu.), Krueger or Goeschen, have themselves edited Gaius. Others are scholars whose general work in Roman law has led them to doubt particular words or phrases or to suggest material to fill the gaps. Sometimes the note gives the place where the arguments for such emendations are to be found, most frequently in the *Zeitschrift der Savigny-Stiftung, Romanistische Abteilung* (*ZS*). These footnotes also sometimes remark on the general topic which Gaius must have dealt with in the context. Comparisons are made with other legal texts, for instance, the *Epitome Ulpiani* (*Ulp.*), which will be found in the collections already mentioned.

The lower set of footnotes refer to the numbered sections into which each of the four books of the *Institutes* is divided. They relate the substance of Gaius' text to other sources, legal, literary and epigraphic. Reference to Gaius and other jurists in the form (*Gai.* 404) – which occurs in s.1 – describes the entry in the *Palingenesia* of O. Lenel (Leipzig, 1889), which offers a reconstruction of the books written by the classical jurists. It is in these footnotes too that the dates, where known, of statutes and similar things will be found. The *Oxford Classical Dictionary* should be able to provide identification of most of the literary sources cited.

3. This translation

Our translation of Gaius has been influenced by the need to co-ordinate with the translators of Justinian's *Institutes*, since we all wanted to bring out the debt owed to Gaius by Justinian. This is why the words of Gaius which have been lifted for use by Justinian are printed in **bold** type. Such an exercise cannot be perfectly accurate because all authors use neutral, commonplace words; to identify the texts a common theme must be discernible. Still less can it be accurate where it is the translation rather than the Latin original which is so picked out. But we hope it will be helpful since, as far as we know, there is no edition of Gaius using so graphic a device. Sometimes, even where the Latin words are the same, our translations have diverged; in these cases our translation is still printed in bold type. The reasons for divergence are normally based on a change in the nature of the institution described. 'Patria potestas', for example, was a much weaker thing in the sixth century than in the second; 'family authority' is fair enough for Justinian, but 'paternal power' seemed to us better to reflect the literal power of life and death over his children, and sometimes his grandchildren, which could be exercised lawfully during his whole lifetime by the 'paterfamilias', the 'head of the family', and by him alone within the family.

The aim, or one aim, of the whole project has been to provide a translation which does not merely echo the Latin. We have tried to avoid retaining any Latin words or phrases, and to use Latinate terms as sparingly as possible. There have inevitably been cases where this was impossible, for example, 'mancipation' or 'usucapion'. Occasionally it has not been possible to avoid using a term which has a rather different meaning or flavour in modern

Scots (or English) law, for instance, 'interdict'. Technical terms which are not fully explained by Gaius himself are to be found in the Vocabulary at the end of the translation. This also comments on the translation of those terms which we found difficult to render satisfactorily into English. An alphabetical list of Latin words is given at the end, but discussion of them is referred to the place in the Vocabulary where related topics are considered together; for example, 'fideiussor' (= 'guarantor') and 'sponsor' (= 'special surety') are described together in the context of personal security. The Commentary, which is the third volume of this project, will pick up difficulties of meaning rather than of translation and expound particular legal institutions.

As regards the grammar of the translation, we have sacrificed many of the particles used by Gaius, at the risk of losing the occasional fine nuance; but he is particularly prolix in their use – some seem hardly more than a clearing of the throat – and English anyway employs them much less than does Latin. We have tried to stay close to the plain style of Gaius. We have not had the same constraints on space as the translators of Justinian, and we have therefore been able to follow the original more faithfully when Gaius himself is repetitive. We have, however, broken up some of the longer sentences in an effort to avoid Latinate grammatical constructions. We have also broken up some of the longer apparent paragraphs in the Teubner text. In matters of singular and plural we have followed normal usage, rather than the literal accidence, just as the Latin future perfect is normally rendered in the present tense.

We have tried to come to the task of translation with fresh minds; O.F.R.'s first draft (of the first and fourth books) was made by her husband Sebastian, who is a civil servant with a classical background. He has also commented on various drafts of the whole work, and we are very grateful for his labours. However, we cannot have avoided all echoes from the translation of F. de Zulueta (Oxford, 1946), which we have used for so long that its cadences have become part of our understanding of Gaius. But we did avoid any deliberate and direct reference to it until the stage of the final draft. It is an excellent translation, but it does use many Latin terms and phrases.

We have normally translated directly what is on the facing page but, where there are gaps in the text, we have incorporated the suggestion in the footnotes where this seemed reasonably secure. We have put such suggestions in square brackets. If the suggested emendation would completely fill the gap in the Latin text, we give no other indication than the square brackets, but where we have not felt able to supplement completely from the footnotes we have put dots. Sometimes we have added a comment on the nature of the missing topic. These additions are distinguishable from the passages bracketed in the Gaian text by reference to the Latin on the facing page.

This is a translation, and we have simply given the reader what the Latin says, with perhaps some further explanation in the Vocabulary. The editorial Outline of Contents is very full and should be used in conjunction with the Vocabulary. The volume of Commentary to come will concentrate on Justinian's work, because this had the direct influence on the development of the legal systems of Europe, but it will also provide an opportunity for discussion of difficult points in Gaius, where the words are clear but their meaning is not; for example, noxal surrender of a dead body (4.81).

THE INSTITUTES OF GAIUS
text and translation

GAI INSTITVTIONVM
COMMENTARII QVATTVOR.

COMMENTARIVS PRIMVS.

[I. De iure ciuili et naturali.[1]]. **1.** *Omnes populi, qui legibus et moribus reguntur, partim suo proprio, partim communi omnium hominum iure utuntur: nam quod quis[2]-* C. Ver que populus ipse sibi ius constituit, id ipsius proprium est uocaturque ius ciuile, quasi ius proprium ciuitatis; quod uero naturalis ratio inter omnes homines constituit, id apud omnes populos peraeque custoditur uocaturque ius gentium, quasi quo iure omnes gentes utuntur. populus itaque Romanus partim suo proprio, partim communi omnium hominum iure utitur. quae singula qualia sint, suis locis proponemus.

2. Constant autem iura populi Romani ex legibus, plebiscitis, senatus consultis, constitutionibus princi-

---

1) I de iure ciuili et nat *correctoris manu* V.   2) *initium suppl. ex D.*

---

§ 1. = *I*. 1, 2, 1. *D*. 1, 1, 9 (*Gai*. 404). *cf. infra* 3, 154. *Dosith*. 1. *D*. 41, 1, 1 *pr*. (*Gai*. 491). *I*. 1, 2, 11. *Auct. ad Herenn*. 2, 13, 19. *Cic. de inv*. 2, 22, 67. *de off*. 3, 17, 69. *Isidor. orig*. 5, 4, 1. quae singula qualia sint] *i. e. utrum iuris gentium an iuris civilis sint etc. cf infra* 1, 52. 55. 78. 82. 83. 84. 85. 86. 89. 108. 119. 189. 193. 197. 2, 65. 67. 69. 70. 73. 77. 79. 3, 93. 132.

§ 2. *cf. 1*. 1, 2, 3. *D* 1, 2, 2, 12 (*Pomp*. 178). 1, 1, 7 (*Pap*. 46). *Cic. top*. 5, 28. *Isidor. orig*. 5, 9, 2.

THE INSTITUTES OF GAIUS
FOUR COMMENTARIES

BOOK ONE

[I On state* and natural law*] 1. **All peoples who are governed by laws and customs use law which is partly theirs alone and partly shared by all mankind. The law which each people makes for itself is special to itself. It is called 'state law', the law peculiar to that state. But the law which natural reason makes for all mankind is applied in the same way everywhere. It is called 'the law of all peoples'* because it is common to every nation. The law of the Roman people is also partly its own and partly common to all mankind. Which parts are which we will explain below.**

2. **The laws of the Roman people are based upon acts*, plebeian statutes*, resolutions of the**

pum, edictis eorum, qui ius edicendi habent, responsis
prudentium.   3. Lex est, quod populus iubet atque
constituit. plebiscitum est, quod plebs iubet atque
constituit. plebs autem a populo eo distat, quod populi appellatione uniuersi ciues significantur, connume-
ratis et patriciis; plebis autem appellatione sine patriciis ceteri ciues significantur; unde olim patricii
dicebant plebiscitis se non teneri, quae sine auctoritate
2 eorum facta essent; sed postea | lex Hortensia lata
est, qua cautum est, ut plebiscita uniuersum populum
tenerent: itaque eo modo legibus exaequata sunt.
4. Senatus consultum est, quod senatus iubet atque
constituit; idque legis uicem optinet, quamuis *de ea re*[1]
fuerit quaesitum.   5. Constitutio principis est, quod
imperator decreto uel edicto uel epistula constituit.
nec umquam dubitatum est, quin id legis uicem opti-
neat, cum ipse imperator per legem imperium accipiat.[2]
6. Ius autem edicendi habent magistratus populi Romani. sed amplissimum ius est in edictis duorum
praetorum, urbani et peregrini, quorum in prouinciis

---

1) de ea re *addidimus*. *cf.* 2, 236.   2) nec umquam —
accipiat *a Gaio abiudicat Kreller ZS* 41, 270.

§ 3. *cf. I.* 1, 2, 4.   *D.* 1, 2, 2, 8 (*Pomp.* 178). 50, 16, 238 *pr.*
(*Gai.* 442). *Liv.* 1, 17, 9. 3, 55, 3. 4, 49, 6. 6, 42, 10. 8, 12, 14; 15.
Capito ap. Gell. 10, 20, 2; 5; 6 (*Iurispr.* I, 69). *Plin. n. h.* 16, 37.
Laelius Felix ap. Gell. 15, 27, 4 (*Iurispr.* I, 94). *Fest. v. populi*
p. 233 (*Bruns* II[7], 24). *v. scita* p. 293 (*Bruns* II[7]. 36). *v. scitum*
p. 330 (*Bruns l. c.*). *Isidor. orig.* 5, 10, 11. *Boethius l. 3 ad*
Cic. top. 5, 28 *p.* 321 *Or.* lex Hortensia] *a.* 289—286 *a. Chr.*
§ 4. *cf I.* 1, 2, 5.   *D.* 1, 2, 2, 9 (*Pomp.* 178). 1, 3, 9 (*Ulp.*
541). *Isidor. orig.* 5, 12. *Boeth. l. c.*
§ 5. *cf. I.* 1, 2, 6.   *D.* 1, 3, 11 (*Iul.* 842). 1, 2, 2, 11 (*Pomp.*
178). 1, 4, 1 *pr.* 1 (*Ulp.* 1916). *Isidor. orig.* 5, 13.
§ 6. *cf. I.* 1, 2, 7.   *D.* 1, 2, 2, 10 (*Pomp.* 178). 1, 1, 7, 1 (*Pap.*
46). 1, 1, 8 (*Marcian.* 42).   *Plaut. Capt.* 4, 2, 43 = 823. *Poen.*
11 *sq. Cic. ad Att.* 6, 1, 15. *divin.* 17, 56. *in Verr.* 2, 1, 41, 106.
45, 116. *Corn. Nep. Cat.* 2, 3. *Ascon. in Cornel. p.* 52, 5 *Kiessl.*
(*Bruns* II[7], 69). *Tacit. ann.* 12, 60. *Gell.* 13, 15, 1. 15, 11, 2.
Boeth. l. 3 ad Cic. top. 5, 28 *p.* 321 *Or. Bruns* I[7] *p.* 211.

Senate*, **imperial** enactments*, **edicts*** of those
having the right to issue them, and **answers given by
jurists***. 3. **An act is law which the people** decide
and enact. **A plebeian statute is law which the
plebeians*** decide and enact. **Plebeians and people**
differ **in that the people is the whole citizen body,
including the patricians***; **but the plebeians are the
citizens without the patricians.** This is why formerly
the patricians used to say that they were not bound by
plebeian statutes, which were made without their
authorisation. Subsequently, however, the **Hortensian Act** was passed providing that plebeian
statutes should bind the whole people; and so they
were placed on the same level as acts. 4. **A resolution
of the Senate is law decided and enacted by the
Senate;** this also has the status of an act, although
this point has been questioned. 5. An imperial
enactment is law which the Emperor enacts in a
decree, edict or **letter**. It has never been doubted that
it has the status of an act, since it is by means of an
act that the Emperor himself assumes his imperial
authority. 6. The magistrates of the Roman people
have the right to issue edicts. The right is found most
fully in the **edicts of the** two **Praetors**, Urban* and
Peregrine* (whose jurisdiction in the provinces* is

iurisdictionem[1] praesides earum habent; item in edictis
aedilium curulium, quorum iurisdictionem in prouinciis
populi Romani quaestores habent; nam in prouincias
Caesaris omnino quaestores non mittuntur, et ob id
hoc edictum in his prouinciis non proponitur. 7. Responsa prudentium sunt sententiae et opiniones eorum,
quibus permissum est iura condere. quorum omnium
si in unum sententiae concurrunt[2], id, quod ita sentiunt,
legis uicem optinet; si uero dissentiunt, iudici licet
quam uelit sententiam sequi; idque rescripto diui
Hadriani significatur.

[II. De iuris diuisione.] 8. Omne autem ius, quo
utimur, uel ad personas pertinet uel | ad res uel ad 3
actiones. sed[3] prius uideamus de personis.

[III. De condicione hominum.] 9. Et quidem summa
diuisio de iure[4] personarum haec est, quod omnes homines aut liberi sunt aut serui. 10. Rursus liberorum
hominum alii ingenui sunt, alii libertini. 11. Ingenui
sunt, qui liberi nati sunt; libertini, qui ex iusta seruitute manumissi sunt. 12. Rursus libertinorum *tria
sunt genera: nam aut ciues Romani aut Latini aut*

---

1) in prouinciis iurisdictionem] iurisdictionem in prouinciis
Polenaar. 2) concurrant V. 3) ac *Inst Iust.; an ex Gaio?*
cf. § 12. 51. 125. 143. 2, 99. 4) de iure *del. Beseler ZS* 46, 268.

---

§ 7. cf. *I.* 1, 2, 8. *D.* 1, 2, 2, 47 (*Pomp.* 178). *Cic. p. Mur.*
18, 28. *p. Caec.* 23, 65. *Senec. ep.* 94, 27. *Gell.* 13, 10, 1. 13, 13, 1.
Isid. orig. 5, 14.
§ 8. = *D.* 1, 5, 1. *I.* 1, 2, 12. cf. *D.* 1, 5, 2 (*Herm.* 3).
Donat. ad Terent. Adelph. 2, 3, 1 (254).
§ 9. = *D.* 1, 5, 3. *I.* 1, 3 *pr.* cf. *D.* 1, 1, 4 (*Ulp.* 1912).
Gai epit. 1, 1 *pr.*
§ 10. cf. *I.* 1, 3, 5. *Dosith.* 4. *D.* 1, 5, 5 *pr.* (*Marcian.* 45).
Gai epit. 1, 1 *pr.*
§ 11. libertini] = *D.* 1, 5, 6. cf. *D.* 1, 5, 5, 2 (*Marcian.* 45).
I. 1, 4 *pr.* 1, 5 *pr. Gai epit.* 1, 1 *pr.*
§ 12. cf. *Ulp.* 1, 5. *Dosith.* 4. *Gai epit.* 1, 1 *pr. Auson.*
Griph. v. 65 p. 203 *ed. Peiper. I.* 1, 5, 3.

exercised by provincial governors) and again in the
edicts of the curule aediles (whose jurisdiction in the
provinces of the Roman people is exercised by
quaestors – quaestors are never posted to the Imperial
provinces, and on that account this edict is not
published in those provinces). 7. **Juristic answers
are the opinions and advice of those entrusted with
the task of building up the law.** If the **opinions of all
of them** agree on a point, what they thus hold has the
status of an act; if, however, they disagree, a judge*
may follow which opinion he wishes. This is made
known in a written reply* of the Emperor* Hadrian.

[II On the division of law] 8. **All our law is about
persons, things or actions. We turn to persons first.**

[III On status] 9. **The main classification in the
law of persons is this: all men are either free or
slaves.** 10. Again, among free men, some are
free-born while others are **freed***. 11. Free-born are
those who were born free; **freedmen, those who have
been manumitted* from lawful slavery.** 12. Again,
there are three classes of freedmen; for they are either
Roman citizens, or **Latins*** or in **the category of**

dediticiorum[1] numero sunt. de quibus singulis dispiciamus; ac prius *de* dediticiis.

[IIII. De dediticiis uel lege Aelia Sentia.] 13. Lege
itaque Aelia Sentia cauetur, ut, qui serui a dominis
poenae nomine uincti sunt[2], quibusue stigmata inscripta
sunt[2], deue quibus ob noxam quaestio tormentis habita
sit et in ea noxa fuisse conuicti sunt[2], quiue ut[3] ferro
aut cum bestiis depugnarent traditi sint, inue ludum
custodiamue coniecti fuerint, et postea uel ab eodem[4]
domino uel ab alio manumissi, eiusdem condicionis
liberi fiant[5], cuius condicionis sunt peregrini dediticii.
[V. De peregrinis dediticiis.] 14. Vocantur autem peregrini dediticii hi, qui quondam aduersus populum
Romanum armis susceptis pugnauerunt, deinde[6] uicti
se dediderunt. 15. Huius ergo turpitudinis seruos quocumque modo et cuiuscumque aetatis manumissos, etsi
pleno iure dominorum fuerint, numquam aut ciues
Romanos aut Latinos fieri dicemus, sed omni modo
dediticiorum numero constitui intellegemus.

16. Si uero in nulla tali turpitudine sit seruus,
manumissum modo ciuem Romanum modo Latinum
4 fieri dice mus. 17. Nam in cuius personam tria haec
concurrunt, ut maior sit annorum triginta et ex iure

---

1) tria—dediticiorum *suppl. Goeschen ex Epit.* 1, 1 *pr.*
2) sint *Goeschen.* 3) quiue ut] quique aut V. 4) ab eodem]
auem V[1]. ab eo? V[2]. 5) fiunt V. 6) deinde V[2]. et V[1].

---

§ 13. *cf. Ulp.* 1, 11. *Paul.* 4, 12, 5 *sq. Gai epit.* 1, 1, 3.
infra 1, 26. 3, 74. *D.* 50, 16, 204 (*Ven.* 65). 50, 16, 216 (*Ulp.*
1933). *Suet. Aug.* 40. *Isid. orig.* 9, 4, 49 (*Bruns* II[7], 84), 50.
C. 7, 5, 1 (*a.* 530). *Gnom. Id. Log.* § 20. lex Aelia Sentia] *lata
a Sex. Aelio Cato C. Sentio Saturnino consulibus a.* 4 *p. Chr.*
§ 15. *cf. infra* 1, 17; 26; 68.
§ 16. *cf. Dosith.* 5. 13.
§ 17. *cf. Ulp.* 1, 6; 10; 12; 16. *Gai epit.* 1, 1, 1; 2. *Plaut.
Cas.* 2, 8, 68 = 504. *Cic. top.* 2, 10. *Boeth. ad h. l.* (*Bruns*
II[7], 73). *Plut. de ser. num. vind.* p. 550 (*ed. Bernardakis* III 422).
C. 7, 6, 1, 6 (*a.* 531). *Gnom. Id. Log.* § 19.

capitulated aliens*. Let us examine each of these in turn, beginning with capitulated aliens.

[IV On capitulated aliens or the Aelian-Sentian Act] 13. It is provided in the Aelian-Sentian Act that slaves who have been chained by their owners as a punishment, or those who have been branded, or interrogated under torture concerning some wrongdoing and convicted of that offence, or handed over to fight in gladiatorial combat with swords or with the beasts, or sent to the games or thrown into custody, and who have afterwards been granted freedom, whether by that owner or by another, shall be free men of the same status as foreigners* who have capitulated.

[V On foreigners who have capitulated] 14. Those foreigners are described as 'capitulated' who have in the past taken up arms and fought against the Roman people and then surrendered after defeat. 15. We may state that slaves of such wickedness, no matter in what form they were granted their freedom or at what age, and even if in the full ownership of their masters, never become Roman citizens or Latins; but we shall understand that in all respects they are counted in the category of capitulated aliens.

16. If, on the other hand, a slave was not as wicked as this, we may state that once granted freedom he becomes either a Roman citizen or a Latin. 17. For any person who fulfils three conditions – that he is above the age of thirty, that he is in the quiritary

Quiritium domini et iusta ac legitima manumissione
liberetur, id est uindicta aut censu aut testamento, is
ciuis Romanus fit; sin uero aliquid eorum deerit, Latinus erit.

[VI. De manumissione uel causae probatione.] 18. Quod
autem de aetate serui requiritur, lege Aelia Sentia in-
troductum est. nam ea lex minores xxx annorum
seruos non aliter uoluit manumissos ciues Romanos
fieri, quam si uindicta, apud consilium iusta causa
manumissionis adprobata, liberati fuerint. 19. Iusta
autem causa manumissionis est, ueluti si quis filium
filiamue aut fratrem sororemue naturalem aut alum-
num aut paedagogum aut seruum procuratoris habendi
gratia aut ancillam matrimonii causa apud consilium
manumittat.

[VII. De consilio adhibendo.] 20. Consilium autem
adhibetur in urbe Roma quidem quinque senatorum
et quinque equitum Romanorum puberum[1], in prouinciis autem uiginti recuperatorum ciuium Romanorum. idque fit ultimo die conuentus; sed Romae certis
diebus apud consilium manumittuntur. maiores uero
triginta annorum serui semper manumitti solent, adeo
ut uel in transitu manumittantur, ueluti cum praetor
aut pro consule in balneum uel in theatrum eat.

---

1) equo publico *Karlowa*.

---

§ 18. *cf. Ulp.* 1, 12. *Dosith.* 13. *D.* 40, 2, 16 *pr.* (*Ulp.* 1935).
40, 4, 27 (*Paul.* 914). *Suet. Aug.* 40. *Dio Cass.* 55, 13, 7. *lex
Salpens. c.* 28 (*Bruns* I[7], 146). *C. I. L.* VI 1877 (*Dessau* 1910).
32881 (*Dessau* 1985). XIV 1437 (*Dessau* 1984). *Gnom. Id. Log.*
§ 21. *BGU* 326 *col.* I *l.* 4. 5 (*Bruns* I[7] *p.* 312). *infra* 1, 29 *sq.*
§ 19. *cf. infra* 1, 39.
§ 20. *cf. infra* 1, 38. *Ulp.* 1, 13 a. *I.* 1, 5, 2. *Theophil.*
1, 5, 2; 4. 1, 6, 4. *D.* 40, 9, 7, 1 (*Iul.* 903). 40, 2, 16 *pr.* (*Ulp.*
1935). 1, 10, 1 *pr.* (*Ulp.* 2055). 1, 21, 2 *pr.* (*Ulp.* 2268). 40, 2, 24
(*Paul.* 1037). *C.* 7, 1, 1 (*a.* 211). recuperatores] *cf. infra* 4, 105.
ultimo die conuentus] *cf. Suet. Galb.* 10. *Plut. Galb.* 5. in
transitu] *cf. D.* 40, 2, 8 (*Ulp.* 256). *Plin. ep.* 7, 16, 3.

ownership* of his master, and that he is freed by means of a lawful and legally recognised manumission (that is, by rod*, by inclusion in the census, or by will) – becomes a Roman citizen; but if any of those conditions is lacking he will be a Latin.

[VI On the grant of freedom or the proof of his case] 18. The requirement as to the age of the slave was introduced by the Aelian-Sentian Act. For the intention of that statute was that slaves under the age of thirty should become Roman citizens on manumission only if they were freed by rod, after it had been proved to a committee that there was good reason for the grant of freedom. 19. Now, a good reason for the grant of freedom exists, for instance, if a person frees before the committee his **son or daughter or his real brother or sister**, his foster-child or his teacher, or **a slave to be made a general agent***, or **a female slave for the purpose of marriage**.

[VII On the summoning of a committee] 20. In the City of Rome the committee is formed of five senators and five Romans of the equestrian order* of full age*. In the provinces it consists of twenty assessors* who must be Roman citizens; its session takes place on the final day of the assize*. In Rome, however, manumissions take place before the committee on stated days. The practice is that **slaves** over thirty **are readily manumitted; it is such an everyday matter that manumissions are performed even en route from one place to another, for instance, when the praetor or proconsul is on the way to the baths or the theatre**. 21. Moreover, a slave below the age of

21. Praeterea minor triginta annorum seruus manumissus potest ciuis Romanus fieri, si ab eo domino, qui soluendo non erat, testamento eum liberum et[1] 5 heredem relictum[2] ＊＊＊＊ | —— *vv. 24 nunc legi non* 6 *possunt* —— | [3] **22.** homines Latini Iuniani appellantur; Latini ideo, quia adsimulati sunt Latinis coloniariis; Iuniani ideo, quia per legem Iuniam libertatem acceperunt, cum olim serui uiderentur esse. **23.** Non tamen illis permittit[4] lex Iunia uel ipsis testamentum facere uel ex testamento alieno capere uel tutores testamento dari. **24.** Quod autem diximus ex testamento eos capere non posse, ita intellegemus, ne quid inde[5] directo hereditatis legatorumue nomine eos posse capere dicamus; alioquin per fideicommissum capere possunt.

25. Hi uero, qui dediticiorum numero sunt, nullo modo ex testamento capere possunt, non magis quam quilibet peregrinus; quin[6] nec ipsi testamentum facere possunt secundum id quod magis[7] placuit.[8] **26.** Pessima

---

1) ei? V.　　2) *cf. apographum.*　　3) *videtur Gaius in pagina quinta primum ea, quae de servo creditoribus satisfacturo exponere iam coeperat, ad finem perduxisse, deinde dominium ex iure Quiritium verbo tetigisse (cf.* § *17), infra* (2, 40) *accuratius expositurus, porro de tribus legitimae manumissionis modis egisse (cf.* 1, 126), *denique ad Latinos transiisse (vid.* § 16). *cf. Inst. Iust.* 1, 6, 1. *Ulp.* 1, 12; 14. *Gai epit.* 1, 1, 2. *Gai.* 3, 56. *Theoph.* 1, 5, 4. *Lex Rom. Burg* 44, 5. *Salvian. ad eccl.* 3, 7, 31—34.　　4) promittit V.　　5) inde *Goudsmit.* in V. 6) quia V.　　7) magis〕 m̄ḡn̄ V.　　8) secundum — placuit *del. Beseler Z. S.* 47, 357. *totam paragr.* 25 *del. Solazzi.*

---

§ 21. *cf. infra* 2, 154. 276. *Ulp.* 1, 14. *Dosith.* 16. *I.* 1, 6, 1. *D.* 28, 5, 61 (*Cels.* 240). 40 4, 27 (*Paul.* 914).

§ 22. *cf.infra* 3, 56. *Ulp.* 1, 10; 12. *Dosith.* 5; 6. *Gai epit.* 1, 1, 2.

§§ 23. 24. *cf. infra* 2, 110; 275. *Ulp.* 20, 14. 22, 3; 8. 17, 1. 25, 7. 11, 16. *Fr. Vat.* 172 (*Paul. Sent.* 2, 27, 6). *Gai epit.* 1, 1, 4. *Gnom. Id. Log.* § 22.

§ 25. *cf. infra* 3, 75. 2, 285. *Ulp.* 22, 2. 20, 14. *Gai epit.* 1, 1, 4. *Gnom. Id. Log.* § 20.

§ 26. *cf. I.* 1, 5, 3. *infra* 1, 67. *Coll.* 4, 3, 4 (*Paul.* 19) *Gai epit.* 1, 1, 4. *Suet. Aug.* 40.

thirty can become a Roman citizen, if he is made free and heir **in the will of an owner who** was **insolvent** ... [24 lines illegible in the MS: the passage presumably went on to deal with the satisfaction of the creditors, and then turned to the other conditions for receiving citizenship, quiritary ownership and correct form of procedure]. 22. ... men are called Junian Latins: Latins because they are assimilated to the Latins of the colonies, Junian because they received freedom under the Junian Act, though formerly they were regarded as slaves. 23. The Junian Act does not, however, permit them either to make a will for themselves or to take under the will of another, nor to be appointed as guardians in a will. 24. When we have said that they cannot take under a will, we shall understand this in the sense that they cannot take anything from that source directly under the heading of inheritance or legacies; but they can take through a trust*.

25. On the other hand, those who are in the category of capitulated aliens can in no way take under a will, any more than any foreigner can; indeed, according to received opinion, they themselves cannot make a will. 26. So those who are in the category of capitulated

itaque libertas eorum est, qui dediticiorum numero
sunt; nec ulla lege aut senatus consulto aut constitutione principali aditus illis ad ciuitatem Romanam
datur. 27. Quin etiam in urbe Roma uel intra centesimum urbis Romae miliarium morari prohibentur;
et si qui contra ea fecerint, ipsi bonaque eorum publice
uenire iubentur ea condicione, ut ne in urbe Roma
uel intra centesimum urbis Romae miliarium seruiant
neue umquam manumittantur; et si manumissi fuerint,
serui populi Romani esse iubentur. et haec ita lege
Aelia Sentia conprehensa sunt.

[*Quibus modis* Latini ad ciuitatem Romanam perueniant.] |
28. Latini uero multis modis ad ciuitatem Romanam 7
perueniunt. 29. Statim enim ex lege Aelia Sentia[1]
minores triginta annorum manumissi et Latini facti si
uxores duxerint uel ciues Romanas uel Latinas colo-
niarias uel eiusdem condicionis, cuius et ipsi essent,
idque testati fuerint adhibitis non minus quam septem
testibus ciuibus Romanis puberibus et filium procrea-
uerint, cum is filius anniculus esse coeperit, datur eis
potestas per eam legem adire praetorem uel in prouinciis praesidem prouinciae et adprobare se ex lege
Aelia Sentia uxorem duxisse et ex ea filium annicu-
lum habere: et si is, apud quem causa probata est, id
ita esse pronuntiauerit, tunc et ipse Latinus[2] et uxor
eius, si et ipsa eiusdem *condicionis sit, et filius eius,
si et ipse eiusdem* condicionis sit, ciues Romani esse
iubentur. 30. Ideo autem in *persona filii*[3] adiecimus

---

1) *quod addit h. l.* V: cautum est ut, *nunc apparet glossema esse. om. etiam Polen. et Krueger. edd.* 2) iunianus
add. V[2] *supra lineam.* 3) persona filii *Polenaar. vide apogr.*

---

§ 27. *cf. Isid. orig.* 9, 4, 52 (*Bruns* II[7], 84). *D.* 29, 1, 29, 1
(*Marcell.* 134).
§ 28. *cf. Ulp.* 3, 1. *Gai epit.* 1, 1, 4. *C.* 7, 6, 1 (*a.* 531).
§ 29. *cf. Ulp.* 3, 3.
§ 30. *cf. infra* 1, 32; 66; 80. *Ulp.* 3, 3.

aliens enjoy the very lowest sort of freedom; there is no statute or resolution of the Senate or imperial pronouncement* which gives them the means of attaining Roman citizenship. 27. They are even forbidden to remain in the City of Rome, or within one hundred miles of the City. Those who contravene these rules are ordered to be put up for public sale together with their property, with the condition that they shall not serve as slaves within the City of Rome or within one hundred miles of the City, and that they shall never be manumitted; if they should be manumitted, it is ordered that they be slaves of the Roman people. These matters are covered in the Aelian-Sentian Act.

[The ways in which Latins may achieve Roman citizenship] 28. Latins achieve Roman citizenship in many ways. 29. For, right away according to the Aelian-Sentian Act, men freed under thirty and made Latins may marry wives who are either Roman citizens or colonial Latins, or of the same status as themselves, in front of not less than seven Roman citizens of full age as witnesses. If they beget a son, then, when that son reaches the age of one year, they are empowered by the Act to go to the praetor (or, in the provinces, to the provincial governor), and to prove that they have, as prescribed in the Act, married a wife and had by her a child of the age of one year. If the magistrate before whom the proof is brought pronounces that it is so, it is laid down that the Latin himself, and his wife and son, if they are of his status, are Roman citizens. 30. Our reason for adding 'if they are of his status' is that, under a recent

'si et ipse eiusdem condicionis sit', quia si uxor Latini ciuis Romana est, qui ex ea nascitur, ex nouo
senatus consulto, quod auctore diuo Hadriano factum
est, ciuis Romanus nascitur. 31. Hoc tamen ius adipiscendae ciuitatis Romanae etiamsi soli[1] minores triginta annorum manumissi et Latini facti ex lege Aelia
Sentia habuerunt, tamen postea senatus consulto, quod
Pegaso et Pusione consulibus factum est, etiam maioribus triginta annorum manumissis Latinis factis concessum est. 32. Ceterum etiamsi ante decesserit Latinus, quam anniculi filii causam probarit[2], potest mater
eius causam probare, et sic et ipsa fiet | ciuis Romana,
8 si Latina fuerit ——— | ——— *vv. 2 paucis litteris exceptis legi nequeunt* ——— *etiamsi* | ipse filius ciuis Romanus sit, quia ex ciue Romana matre natus est,
tamen debet causam probare, ut suus heres patri fiat.
32ᵃ. *Quae uero diximus de filio anniculo, eadem et de
filia annicula* dicta intellegemus. **32ᵇ.** *Praeterea ex
lege Visellia tam maiores quam minores* xxx *annorum
manumissi et Latini facti ius Quiritium adipiscuntur,*[3]
id est fiunt ciues Romani, si Romae inter uigiles sex
annis militauerint. postea dicitur factum esse senatus
consultum, quo data est illis ciuitas Romana, si triennium militiae expleuerint. 32ᶜ. Item edicto Claudii[4]
Latini ius Quiritium consecuntur, si nauem marinam
aedificauerint, quae non minus quam decem milia mo-

---

1) socii V¹, *del.* V².   2) *sic* V². probet V¹.   3) praeterea—adipiscuntur *ad sententiam supplevit Hu. cf. Ulp.* 3, 5.
4) diui Claudii *Hu. cf. Ulp.* 3, 6.

---

§ 31. *cf. Ulp.* 3, 4. Peg. et Pus.] *cf. infra* 2, 254. *I.* 2,
23, 5 'Vespasiani Aug. temporibus'.
§ 32. *cf. Coll.* 16, 3, 7; 15. *infra* 3, 5.
§ 32ᵃ. *cf. infra* 1, 72.
§ 32ᵇ. *cf. Ulp.* 3, 5. *C. I L.* VI 220 (*Dessau* 2163). lex
Visellia] *a.* 24 *p. Chr.*
§ 32ᶜ. *cf. Ulp.* 3, 6. *Suet. Claud.* 18; 19. *D.* 50, 5, 3
(*Scaev.* 202).

resolution of the Senate passed on the proposal of the Emperor Hadrian, if the Latin's wife is a Roman citizen her baby is born a Roman citizen. 31. Although the Aelian-Sentian Act gave this right of acquiring Roman citizenship only to men freed under thirty and made Latins, yet it has since been granted, by a resolution of the Senate passed when Pegasus and Pusio were consuls, to men freed over thirty who have become Latins. 32. But even if the Latin dies before having proved the claim of his year-old son, the child's mother can prove the claim. In this way she also will become a Roman citizen if she was a Latin ... [2 largely illegible lines] ... although the son himself is a Roman citizen, because he is born of a mother who is a Roman citizen; yet he must prove the claim in order to become immediate heir* to his father. 32a. We are to understand that what we have said about a one-year-old son applies also to a one-year-old daughter. 32b. Moreover, according to the Visellian Act those freed over as well as under thirty and becoming Latins achieve quiritary rights, that is, they become Roman citizens, if they serve six years in the night watch at Rome. It is said that later a resolution of the Senate granted Roman citizenship to those who completed three years such service. 32c. Again, by an edict of Claudius, Latins acquire the right of citizenship if they build a sea-going ship with a capacity of not less than ten thousand bushels of

dior*um frumen*ti capiat, eaque nauis uel quae in eius
locum substituta *sit, sex* annis frumentum Romam
portauerit. 33. Praeterea *a Nero*ne *constitutum est*[1], ut
si Latinus, qui patrimonium sestertium CC milium
plurisue habebit, in urbe Roma domum aedificauerit,
in quam[2] non minus quam partem dimidiam patrimonii
sui impenderit, ius Quiritium consequatur. 34. Denique Traianus[3] constituit, ut si *Latinus* in urbe triennio
pistrinum exercuerit, *quod in*[4] dies singulos non minus
quam centenos m*odios* frumenti pinseret[5], ad ius Qui-
ritium perueni|*at*[6] ———*vv. 1—3* ——— | 35. *Praeterea* 9
possunt maiores triginta annorum manumissi et Latini

---

1) '*Goeschenus quidem initium huius §i ita restituendum
censuit:* "*lege Iulia cautum est, ut Latinus, si in perficiendo*
aedificio *Romae* non *minus*" etc. *ex Dig.* 50, 16, 137 (*Ulp. lib.* 7
ad l. Iul. et Pap.). *cetera tunc egregie; sed de lege Iulia nec
apparet, qua ratione ea de hoc Latinorum beneficio, qui tum
nondum erant, quicquam cautum esse potuerit, et Dig.* 24, 3, 64
maxime § 7 *ostendit, quid in causa fuerit, ut Ulpianus hoc
libro de libertis dotalibus Latinis vel facto mariti vel suo iure
civitatem adeptis exponeret. praeterea cum Gaius ordinem temporis secutus esse videatur*, *non dubito ex Tacit. A.* 15, 43 *ad
a.* 65 "*addidit praemia pro cuiusque ordine et rei familiaris
copiis*" *Neronis edicto hoc beneficium adscribere. nam Vespasianus alia sanxit. Suet. Vesp.* 8. *Lex Flav. Mal.* 62. *sed
et senatus nec Tacitus meminit nec eius partes in re lege non
constituta solebant esse'. haec Hu., qui* 'constitutum est edicto'
in textu posuerat. edicto ut parum certum delevimus.
2) quo V. qua *Stud.; sed Gaius dicere solet impendere in aliquid.*   3) diuus Traianus *Hu.*   4) quod in *Hu.* in quo in
Stud.; sed ipsum pistrinum est centenarium (Fr. Vat. 233) *et cf.
antea eaque nauis . . . portauerit.*   5) cf. apogr. eiusque supplementum.   6) cf. apograph. et supplem; videtur Gaius *in
vv.* 1—3 *fere dixisse ex SCto mulierem Latinam ter enixam,
beneficio principali omnes Latinos ius Qu. consequi posse (cf.
Ulp.* 3, 1; 2), *deinde ad iterationem, qua ipse patronus hoc beneficium tribuit, transiisse.*

---

§ 33. cf. *Ulp.* 3, 1. *D.* 50, 16, 139 (*Ulp.* 2012). *Tacit. ann.*
15, 43. *Suet. Vesp.* 8.
§ 34. cf. *Ulp.* 3, 1. *Fr. Vat.* 233. 235 (*Ulp.* 2133. 2135).
§ 35. cf. *Ulp.* 3, 4. 1, 12. *Fr. Vat.* 221 (*Ulp.* 2129). *Gai*

grain, and that ship, or any replacement for it, carries corn to Rome for six years. 33. Moreover, it was enacted by Nero that if a Latin worth 200,000 sesterces* or more builds a house in the City of Rome on which he spends at least half his capital, he is to obtain the right of citizenship. 34. Finally, Trajan enacted that if a Latin operates a mill in the City for three years, in which he grinds not less than one hundred bushels of corn each day, he attains the right of Roman citizenship. ... [3 illegible lines, perhaps mentioning other modes of acquiring citizenship]. 35. Moreover, men manumitted over thirty who have become Latins are able to obtain the right of

facti *iteratione* ius Quiritium consequi. quo —— *triginta*
annorum manumittant —— *vv. 1½* —— | manumissus
uindicta aut censu aut testamento *et ciu*is Romanus |
et eius libertus fit, qui *e*um iter*a*uerit. ergo si seruus
in bonis tuis, ex iure Quiritium meus erit, Latinus
quidem a te solo fieri potest, iterari autem a me, non
etiam a te potest et eo modo meus libertus fit. sed
et ceteris modis ius Quiritium consecutus meus libertus fit. bonorum autem, quae ——[1], cum is morietur[2],
reliquerit, tibi possessio datur, quocumque modo ius
Quiritium fuerit consecutus. quod si cuius et in bonis
et ex iure Quiritium sit, manumissus ab eodem scilicet
et Latinus fieri potest et ius Quiritium consequi.

36. *Non tamen cuicumque uolenti manumittere licet.*
37. *Nam is, qui* in fraudem creditorum uel in fraudem
patroni manumittit, nihil agit, quia lex Aelia Sentia
inpedit libertatem. **38.** Item eadem lege .minori xx
annorum domino non aliter manumittere permittitur,
10 quam si [uindicta][3] apud con silium iusta causa manumissionis adprobata fuerit. **39.** Iustae autem causae
manumissionis sunt, ueluti si quis patrem aut matrem

---

1) n̄a V   2) morientur V.   3) si uindicta] uindicta
si *Savigny.* uindicta *del.* **Hu.**

epit. 1, 1, 4. *Dosith.* 14. *Plin. ep.* 7, 16, 4. *Tacit. ann.* 13, 27.
bonorum possessio] *cf. infra* 2, 88 *ibiq. cit.*
§§ 36. 37. = *I.* 1, 6 *pr. cf. Ulp.* 1, 15. *Gai epit.* 1, 1, 5; 6.
Dosith. 16. *D.* 28, 5, 61 (*Cels.* 240). 42, 8, 15 (*Iul.* 678). 40, 9,
23 (*Pomp.* 822). 40, 9, 8 (*Afr.* 20). 40, 9, 10 (*Gai.* 489). 40, 9, 24
(*Terent. Clem.* 24). 42, 8, 23 (*Scaev.* 127). 40, 9, 25 (*Pap.* 532).
40, 9, 16, 2 (*Paul.* 918). 28, 5, 56 (*Paul.* 913). 28, 5, 58 (*Paul.*
701). 40, 9, 27 *pr.* (*Herm.* 10). *C.* 7, 11, 1 (*a.* 223). in fraudem
patroni] *cf. D.* 40, 12, 9, 2 (*Gai.* 38). 38, 5, 11 (*Paul.* 919).
§ 38. = *I.* 1, 6, 4. *cf. Ulp.* 1, 13. *Dosith.* 13. *lex Salpens.*
c. 28 (*Bruns* I[7], 146). *D.* 40, 9, 7, 1 (*Iul.* 903). 40, 4, 3 (*Pomp.*
386). 40, 1, 1 (*Ulp.* 2468). 40, 2, 16, 1 (*Ulp.* 1935). 1, 10, 1, 2
(*Ulp.* 2057). 40, 2, 24 (*Paul.* 1037). 40, 1, 16 (*Mod.* 177). *C.* 6,
21, 4 (*a.* 222). 7, 4, 5 (*a.* 222?). 7, 11, 4 (*a.* 224). *Dio Cass.* 55, 13, 7.
§ 39. *cf. supra* 1, 19. *I.* 1, 6, 5. *Gai epit.* 1, 1, 7. *D.* 40,
2, 19 (*Cels.* 241). 40, 2, 25 (*Gai.* 477). 40, 2, 11; 13 (*Ulp.* 2180).

citizenship by repetition. ... of thirty years, they may manumit ... a person manumitted by rod, by inclusion in the census, or by will becomes a Roman citizen and the freedman of the one who repeated the manumission. Therefore, if a slave is part of your estate* but mine by quiritary right he can become a Latin by act of you alone; but the manumission can only be repeated by me, not by you, and in this way he becomes my freedman. Also, if he acquires the right of citizenship in other ways he becomes my freedman. On his death, however, estate-possession* of the property which ... he leaves is granted to you, whatever the method by which he obtained citizen's rights. But if he is freed by a person who both has him in his estate and owns him by quiritary right he can both become a Latin and also obtain the right of citizenship from one and the same person.

36. **The law does not allow complete freedom of manumission.** 37. **A manumission in fraud of creditors** or of a patron **is void, because the Aelian-Sentian Act bars the grant of liberty.** 38. **The same Act also forbids manumission by an owner under twenty except [by rod] when a good reason for manumission has been shown to the committee.** 39. **Such reason exists where, for instance, the grantee is the grantor's real father or mother, his teacher or foster-sibling.** Those grounds

aut paedagogum aut conlactaneum manumittat. sed
et illae causae, quas superius[1] in seruo minore XXX
annorum exposuimus, ad hunc quoque casum, de quo
loquimur, adferri possunt. item ex diuerso hae causae,
quas in minore XX annorum domino rettulimus, por-
rigi possunt et ad seruum minorem XXX annorum.
40. Cum ergo certus modus manumittendi minoribus
XX annorum dominis per legem Aeliam Sentiam constitutus sit, euenit, ut qui XIIII annos aetatis exple-
uerit, licet testamentum facere possit et in eo heredem
sibi instituere legataque relinquere possit, tamen si
adhuc minor sit annorum XX, libertatem seruo dare
non possit.[2] 41. Et quamuis Latinum facere uelit minor XX annorum dominus, tamen nihilo minus debet
apud consilium causam probare et ita postea inter
amicos manumittere.[3]

42. Praeterea lege Fufia Caninia certus modus constitutus est in seruis testamento manumittendis. 43. Nam
ei, qui plures quam duos neque plures quam decem
seruos habebit, usque ad partem dimidiam eius numeri
manumittere permittitur; ei[4] uero, qui plures | quam
X neque plures quam XXX seruos habebit, usque ad

11
t. s.

---

1) superius id ē V, id *expunctum*.   2) potest V.
3) *paragraphum* 41 *del. Solazzi.*   4) si V.

40, 2, 12; 16 (*Ulp.* 1934). 40, 2, 20 (*Ulp.* 2056). 40, 2, 15 (*Paul.*
911). 40, 2, 9 (*Marcian.* 151). 40, 2, 14 (*Marcian.* 267). 40, 9, 21
(*Mod.* 96).

§ 40. *cf. I.* 1, 6, 7. *infra* 2, 113. *Gai epit.* 1, 1, 7.

§ 41. *cf. Dosith.* 13. inter amicos] *cf. Dosith.* 6 *sq. Ulp.* 1, 10.
Bruns I[7], 164 (*Chrest.* 362). *Pap. Oxy.* 9, 1205.

§ 42. *cf. infra* 2, 228. *Paul.* 4, 14. *I.* 1, 7. *C.* 7, 3. *Script.*
Hist. Aug. Tacit. 10, 7. *D.* 35, 1, 37 (*Paul. libro singulari ad*
legem Fufiam Caniniam; 925). 50, 16, 215 (*Paul.* 926). *C. Th.*
16, 8, 28 (a. 426). lex Fufia Caninia] *lata a L. Caninio Gallo*
C. Fufio Gemino consulibus a. 2 a. Chr., *cf. Bull. dell' Ist. di*
dir. Rom. XVIII, 115 = *Dess.* 9250. *Pap. Hamb.* 72.

§ 43. *cf. Ulp.* 1, 24. *Paul.* 4, 14, 4. *Gai epit.* 1, 2 *pr. D.*
40, 5, 22, 1 (*Pap.* 303).

which we have set out above in the case of a slave aged less than thirty can also be applied to the case of which we are now speaking. Again, to put it the other way round, those grounds which we have set out as applying to an owner of less than twenty can be extended to a slave of less than thirty. 40. **When the Aelian-Sentian Act restricted the rights of owners under twenty to grant freedom, a consequence for someone over fourteen was that, despite having capacity to make a will, appoint an heir and leave legacies, he** cannot till twenty give freedom to a slave. 41. And although an owner below twenty may wish to make a Latin, yet he must nevertheless prove the case before the committee, and thereafter grant him his freedom among friends.

42. **Furthermore, the Fufian-Caninian Act has restricted manumissions in wills**. 43. Someone who has more than two but not more than ten slaves is permitted to free up to half their number; someone who has more than ten but not more than thirty is permitted to free up to one-third. Someone who has

tertiam partem eius numeri manumittere permittitur.
at ei, qui plures quam XXX neque plures quam centum habebit, usque ad partem quartam potestas manumittendi datur. nouissime ei, qui plures quam C habebit nec plures quam D, non plures manumittere[1]
permittitur quam[2] quintam partem; neque plures *quam
D habentis ratio habetur, ut ex eo numero pars defi-
ni*atur[3], sed praescribit lex, ne cui plures manumittere
liceat quam C. quod[4] si quis unum seruum omnino
aut duos habet, ad hanc legem non pertinet[5] et ideo[6]
liberam habet potestatem manumittendi. 44. Ac ne
ad eos quidem omnino haec lex pertinet, qui sine
testam*ento* manumittunt.[7] itaque licet iis, qui uindicta
aut censu aut inter amicos manumittunt, totam familiam suam liberare, scilicet si alia causa non inpediat
libertatem. 45. Sed quod de numero seruorum testamento manumittendorum diximus, ita intellegemus, ne
umquam ex eo numero, ex quo dimidia aut tertia aut
quarta aut quinta pars liberari potest, *pauciores* manu-
mittere liceat quam ex antecedenti numero licuit. et
hoc ipsa *ratione*[8] *pro*uisum est: erat enim sane absurdum, ut X seruorum domino quinque liberare liceret,
quia usque ad dimidiam partem eius numeri manumittere ei concedit*ur*, XII seruos habenti non plures
liceret manumittere quam IIII; at eis, qui plures quam
X neque |

12
t. s.   ——————————— *vv. 1—24.*[9] ———————————— |
13   ——————

1) ei manumittere V.   2) quam ut V.   3) quam—definia-
tur *suppl. Hu.*   4) cq V. contra *Polenaar.*   5) *nihil mutandum, cf. V. I. R.* I *p.* 154.   6) ad hanc — ideo *del. Beseler Z. S.*
45, 456.   7) manumittuntur V.   8) ratione *Polenaar; cf. Paul.*
2, 1, 1.   9) *de paginae* 12 *lectione desperandum est. conferenda est
Gai epit.* 1, 2 §§ 2—4: *Nam si aliquis testamento plures manumittere uoluerit, quam quot continet numerus supra scriptus,
ordo seruandus est: ut illis tantum libertas ualeat, qui prius*

——————

§ 44. *Gai epit.* 1, 2, 1. *Dionys.* 4, 24. inter amicos] *cf.
ad* § 41.

more than thirty but not more than one hundred is allowed to free up to a quarter. Finally, someone who has more than one hundred but not more than five hundred is permitted to free not more than one-fifth; nor does the Act take account of someone owning more than five hundred to select a proportion from that number, but it prescribes that no one may lawfully free more than one hundred slaves. But if someone has only one slave in all, or two, this Act does not apply and so he has full power to free. 44. This Act also has no relevance for those who grant freedom otherwise than in a will. So they who manumit by rod, or by inclusion in the census, or among friends, may free their entire household, that is, provided that there is no other bar to their freedom. 45. What we have said about the number of slaves who may be freed in a will we are to understand in this way: it is not the requirement of the law that out of a given number, of whom a half, a third, a quarter or a fifth can be freed, one is not allowed to free as many as one could have done from the preceding number. This is established by simple common sense. It was quite absurd that the owner of ten slaves might lawfully free five (since he is allowed to manumit up to half), but that he who has twelve might not lawfully free more than four; again those who have more than ten but not ... [24 lines illegible in the MS, presumably making the same point about other numbers, and perhaps giving further details of the Fufian-Caninian Act.] 46.

46. nam et si testamento scriptis in orbem seruis
libertas data sit, quia nullus ordo manumissionis inuenitur, nulli liberi erunt, quia lex Fufia Caninia, quae
in fraudem eius facta sint, rescindit. sunt etiam spe-
cialia senatus consulta, quibus rescissa sunt ea, quae
in fraudem eius legis excogitata sunt.

47. In summa sciendum est, *quod* lege Aelia Sentia
cautum sit, ut[1] creditorum fraudandorum causa manumissi liberi non fiant, hoc etiam[2] ad peregrinos pertinere, [senatus ita censuit ex auctoritate Hadriani][3]

*manumissi sunt, usque ad illum numerum, quem explanatio
continet superius comprehensa: qui uero postea supra constitutum numerum manumissi leguntur, in seruitute eos certum est
permanere. quod si non nominatim serui uel ancillae in testamento manumittantur, sed confuse omnes seruos suos uel ancil-
las is, qui testamentum facit, liberos facere uoluerit, nulli peni-
tus firma esse iubetur hoc ordine data libertas, sed omnes in
seruili condicione, qui hoc ordine manumissi sunt, permanebunt.
nam etsi ita in testamento seruorum manumissio adscripta fuerit,
id est in circulo, ut qui prior, qui posterior nominatus sit, non
possit agnosci, nulli ex his libertatem ualere manifestum est, si
agnosci non potest, qui prior, qui posterior fuerit manumissus.
3. Nam si aliquis in aegritudine constitutus in fraudem huius
legis facere noluerit testamentum, sed epistolis aut quibuscumque
aliis rebus seruis suis pluribus, quam per testamentum licet, con-
ferre uoluerit libertates et sub tempore mortis hoc fecerit, hi, qui
prius manumissi fuerint, usque ad numerum superius constitutum liberi erunt, qui uero post statutum numerum manumissi
fuerint, serui sine dubio permanebunt. 4. Nam si incolumis
quoscumque diuerso tempore manumisit, inter eos, qui per testamentum manumissi sunt, nullatenus computentur. 'Ex his
tamen Epitomator ea, quae §§ 3. 4. continentur, aliunde quam
ex Gaio sumpsisse videtur'. Hu.* 1) aut V. *cf. apographi
supplementum.* ut aut patroni aut *suppl. Hu. 'certe non dubi-
tandum etiam apud peregrinos, etiamsi non omnes, patronis aliquod ius in bonis libertorum fuisse'. Hu.* 2) hoc etiam
Goeschen. etiam hoc V. 3) senatus—Hadriani *del. Mommsen.*

§ 46. *cf. infra* 2, 239. *D.* 35, 1, 37 (*Paul.* 925). *Gai epit.*
1, 2, 2. *Auson. lud. VII sapient.* 80 (*Solon* 8). *D.* 40, 5, 24, 17
(*Ulp.* 1887).

§ 47. *cf. supra* 1, 37.

... For if freedom is granted in a will to slaves whose names are written in a circle, because no order in which they are to be manumitted can be found, none of them will be free, because the Fufian-Caninian Act makes void anything done to evade it. There are also specific resolutions of the Senate by which things devised to evade the Act are made void.

47. Finally, it must be known that the Aelian-Sentian Act lays down that persons manumitted in fraud of creditors do not become free; this applies also to foreigners [as the Senate resolved, on the proposal of Hadrian]. Other sections of this Act, on the other

cetera uero iura eius legis ad peregrinos non pertinere.

48. Sequitur de iure personarum alia diuisio. nam quaedam personae sui iuris sunt, quaedam alieno iuri sunt subiectae. 49. Sed rursus earum personarum, quae alieno iuri subiectae sunt, aliae in potestate, aliae in manu, aliae in mancipio sunt. 50. Videamus nunc de iis, quae alieno iuri subiectae sint: *nam* si cognouerimus, quae istae personae sint[1], simul intellegemus, quae sui iuris sint. 51. Ac prius dispiciamus de iis, qui in aliena potestate sunt.

52. In potestate itaque sunt serui dominorum. quae quidem potestas iuris gentium est: nam apud omnes peraeque gentes animaduertere possumus dominis in seruos uitae necisque potestatem esse, et quodcumque per seruum adquiritur, id domino adquiritur.[2] 53. Sed 14 hoc tempore neque ciuibus | Romanis nec ullis aliis hominibus, qui sub imperio populi Romani sunt, licet supra modum et sine causa in seruos suos saeuire: nam ex constitutione **sacratissimi**[3] imperatoris Anto-

---

1) sunt $\bar{V}$.　2) et $\bar{-}$ adquiritur *del. Solazzi.*　3) s V, 'in quo *Stud. apogr. p.* 300 *literam* s *mero calami lapsui tribuit. sed collata D.* 38, 17, 9 *etiam h. l., ubi Gaius sui imperatoris primum mentionem facit,* sacratissimi *cum prior. edd. retinere malui'. Hu. cf. C. I. L.* $\bar{V}$ 875 (*Dessau* 1374). IX 23. 5833 (*Dessau* 6472). XII 594 (*Dessau* 6988). *Dessau* 4052. 6468. *Bruns* I[7], 294 *l.* 6.

---

§§ 48—51. = *D.* 1, 6, 1 *pr. I.* 1, 8 *pr. cf. Gai epit.* 1, 3 *pr.*
§ 49. *cf. Fr. Vat.* 298. 300 (*Paul.* 796). *lex Salpens. c.* 22 (*Bruns* I[7], 143).
§ 52. = *D.* 1, 6, 1, 1. *I.* 1, 8, 1. *cf. Gai epit.* 1, 3, 1. *D.* 1, 5, 4, 1 (*Flor.* 25, *unde I.* 1, 3, 2). 12, 6, 64 (*Tryph.* 21). 1, 1, 4 (*Ulp.* 1912). *Isid. orig.* 5, 6. uitae necisque potestatem] *cf. Senec. de benef.* 3, 23, 3. per seruum adquiritur] *cf. infra* 2, 86 *sq.*
§ 53. = *D.* 1, 6, 1, 2. *I.* 1, 8, 2. *cf. Paul. Coll.* 3, 2, 1. *Coll.* 3, 3 = *D.* 1, 6, 2 (*Ulp.* 2213). *Coll.* 3, 4 (*a.* 285). *D.* 1, 12, 1, 1; 8 (*Ulp.* 2079). 48, 8, 11, 1; 2 (*Mod.* 230). *C.* 9, 14, 1 (*a.* 319). *Senec. de clem.* 1, 18. *Suet. Claud.* 25. *Script. Hist. Aug. Hadr.* 18, 7. sine causa] *cf. D.* 45, 1, 96 (*Marcell.* 152). 30, 53, 3 (*Ulp.* 2678). ad statuas principis] *cf. Senec. de clem.* 1, 18, 2.

hand, do not apply to foreigners.

48. **We come to another classification in the law of persons. Some people are independent* and some are subject to others. 49. Again, of those** persons **who are dependent, some are in power*,** some in marital subordination* and some in bondage*. 50. **Let us examine the dependent category. If we find out who is dependent, we cannot help seeing who is independent. 51. We turn first to the ones in** the **power** of another.

52. **Slaves are in the power of their owners. This power rests on the law of all peoples, for we can observe the same thing everywhere; owners hold the power of life and death over slaves and owners get whatever slaves acquire. 53. But nowadays** neither Roman citizens nor any other **men who live under the rule** of the Roman people **may lawfully inflict immoderate or groundless cruelty on their slaves. A pronouncement of the Emperor Antoninus** Pius of blessed memory **makes a man**

nini, qui sine causa seruum suum occiderit, non minus teneri iubetur, quam qui alienum seruum occiderit.
sed et maior quoque asperitas dominorum per eiusdem
principis constitutionem coercetur: nam consultus a
quibusdam praesidibus prouinciarum de his seruis, qui
ad fana deorum uel ad statuas principum confugiunt,
praecepit, ut si intolerabilis uideatur dominorum sae-
uitia, cogantur seruos suos uendere. et utrumque recte
fit: male[1] enim nostro iure uti non debemus; qua ratione et prodigis interdicitur bonorum suorum administratio. 54. Ceterum cum apud ciues Romanos duplex sit dominium (nam uel in bonis uel ex iure
Quiritium uel ex utroque iure cuiusque seruus esse
intellegitur[2]), ita demum seruum in potestate domini
esse dicemus, si in bonis eius sit, etiamsi simul ex iure
Quiritium eiusdem non sit: nam qui nudum ius Quiritium in seruo habet, is potestatem habere non intellegitur.

55. Item in potestate nostra sunt liberi nostri, quos
iustis nuptiis procreauimus. quod ius proprium ciuium
Romanorum est (fere enim nulli alii sunt homines,
qui talem in filios suos habent potestatem, qualem nos
habemus) idque diui Ha|driani edicto, quod proposuit 15
de his, qui sibi liberisque suis ab eo ciuitatem Romanam petebant, significatur.[3] nec me praeterit Galata-
rum gentem credere in potestate[4] parentum liberos esse.

---

1) regula male V.   2) intellegatur V.   3) significauit V.
4) potestatem V.

---

seruos suos uendere] cf. D. 48, 18, 1, 27 (Ulp. 2212). prodigis] cf. D.
27, 10, 1 pr. (Ulp. 2423). Paul. 3, 4ᵃ, 7. Pap. Flor. 99 (Chrest. 368).
§ 54. cf. supra 1, 35. infra 2, 40; 88. 3, 166.   Ulp. 1, 16.
Theoph. 1, 5, 4 (Ferr. p. 25).
§ 55. = D. 1, 6, 3. I. 1, 9 pr.; 2. cf. infra 1, 93; 64; 128;
189. 2, 135a. 3, 20. Gai epit. 1, 3, 2. Ulp. 5, 1. C. 8, 46, 3
(a. 227). 8, 46, 10 = C. Th. 4, 8, 6 (a. 323). C. Th. 3, 3 (a. 391).
lex. Salp. c. 22 (Bruns I⁷, 143). Dionys. 2, 26; 27. Plut. Num. 17
i. f. Boeth. l. 2 ad Cic. top. 4, 20 (ed. Baiter p. 304). Isid. orig. 9,
5, 17; 18. Galatarum] cf. Caes. Bell. Gall. 6, 19, 3.

who kills his own slave without good grounds no less liable **than one who kills someone else's slave. Excessive severity on the part of owners is curbed by a pronouncement of the same Emperor. He was consulted by some provincial governors about slaves who take refuge** at the shrines of the gods **or at statues of the emperors; he ordered that if the cruelty of the owner was found to have been intolerable, such slaves should be compulsorily sold.** Both these are **quite right**. We ought not to abuse our rights; that is also the reason why spendthrifts are forbidden to administer their own property. 54. Since, however, among Roman citizens there is a double form of ownership (the slave of any man is understood to be either in his estate or held by quiritary right or both), we may state that a slave is in the power of an owner only if he is part of his estate, even if he is not at the same time the slave's quiritary owner. For one who has the bare quiritary right over a slave is not regarded as having power over him.

55. **Again, we have in our power our children*, the offspring of a Roman law marriage. This right is one which only Roman citizens have; there are** virtually **no other peoples who have such power over** their sons **as we have over ours.** This was made known by the Emperor Hadrian in an edict which he issued concerning those who applied to him for Roman citizenship for themselves and their children. I have not forgotten that the Galatians believe that children are in the power of their parents. 56. Roman

56. *Iustas autem nuptias contraxisse liberosque iis pro-
creatos in potestate habere ciues Romani ita intelleguntur*[1], si ciues Romanas uxores duxerint uel etiam Latinas peregrinasue, cum quibus conubium habeant:
cum enim conubium id efficiat, ut liberi patris condicionem sequantur, euenit, ut non *solum* ciues Romani fiant, sed et in potestate patris sint. **57.** Unde
et[2] ueteranis quibusdam concedi solet principalibus constitutionibus conubium cum his Latinis peregrinisue,
quas primas post missionem uxores duxerint; et qui
ex eo matrimonio nascuntur, et ciues Romani et in
potestatem parentum fiunt. **58.** *Nec tamen omnes nobis uxores ducere licet:*[3] nam a quarundam nuptiis abstinere debemus. **59.** Inter eas enim personas, quae
parentum liberorumue locum inter se optinent, nuptiae
contrahi non possunt, nec inter eas conubium est, uelut
inter patrem et filiam uel inter matrem et filium uel inter
auum et neptem *uel inter auiam et nepotem*[4]; et si tales
16 personae inter se coierint, nefarias | et incestas nuptias
contraxisse dicuntur. et haec adeo ita sunt, ut quamuis
per adoptionem parentum liberorumue loco sibi esse
coeperint, non possint[5] inter se matrimonio coniungi, in

---

1) iustas—intelleguntur *suppl. Hu.*, *in* V *duo versus vacui
relicti sunt.*   2) unde et] und cc V. *cf. apographum.* unde causa
cognita *Polenaar.*   3) *duorum versuum lacuna a librario relicta ex Institutionibus Iustin. suppleta est.*   4) *suppl. Knicp
ex epitoma.*   5) possunt V.

§ 56. *cf. Ulp.* 5, 2 *sq. Gai epit.* 1, 4 *pr. D.* 1, 5, 19 (*Cels.*
239). 1, 5, 24 (*Ulp.* 2698).

§ 57. *cf. diplomata militum a Mommseno collecta in Corporis inscriptionum Latinarum volumine tertio, quorum non-
nulla exempla edidit Bruns* I[7], 274 *sq. Gnom. Id. Log.* § 54.

§§ 58. 59. = *I.* 1, 10, 1. *cf. Ulp.* 5, 6 = *Coll.* 6, 2, 1. *Paul.
Coll.* 6, 3, 1. *D.* 23, 2, 8 (*Pomp.* 480). 23, 2, 53 (*Gai.* 249). 23,
2, 68 (*Paul.* 1910). *C.* 5, 4, 17 (*a.* 295). incestas nuptias] *cf.
D.* 23, 2, 39, 1 (*Paul.* 1122). *Ulp.* 5, 7 = *Coll.* 6, 2, 4. *Coll.* 6, 4
(*a.* 295). quamuis per adoptionem] *cf. Paul. Coll.* 6, 3, 2.
D. 23, 2, 55 *pr.* (*Gai.* 249). etiam dissoluta adoptione] *cf. D.*
1, 7, 13 (*Pap.* 377).

citizens are understood to have contracted a Roman law marriage and to have the children of it in power if they take Roman citizens as wives. This also applies to Latin or foreign women with whom they have capacity to enter a Roman law marriage, for the effect of such capacity is that the children follow the status of the father; the result is that not only do they become Roman citizens but are also subject to their father's power. 57. Hence it has been customary for imperial pronouncements to grant to certain veterans* the capacity to enter a Roman law marriage with those Latin or foreign women whom they first marry after discharge from the service. Any offspring of that marriage are Roman citizens and in paternal power*. 58. Next, **we cannot marry any and every woman; for there are certain women whom we must refrain from marrying. 59. Marriage cannot be contracted between people in the relations of parent and child,** nor does the capacity to enter a Roman law marriage exist between them – **for instance, father and daughter, or mother and son, or grandfather and granddaughter or grandmother and grandson. A union within these degrees is evil and incestuous. If their relationship as parent and child is based on adoption*, they still cannot marry; the same applies even after the**

tantum, ut etiam dissoluta adoptione idem iuris maneat; itaque eam, quae mihi per adoptionem filiae seu[1]
neptis loco esse coeperit, non potero[2] uxorem ducere,
quamuis eam emancipauerim.[3] 60. Inter eas quoque
personas, quae ex transuerso gradu cognatione iunguntur, est quaedam similis obseruatio, sed non tanta.
61. Sane inter fratrem et sororem prohibitae sunt
nuptiae, siue eodem patre eademque matre nati fuerint
siue alterutro eorum: sed si qua per adoptionem soror
mihi esse coeperit, quamdiu quidem constat adoptio,
sane inter me et eam nuptiae non possunt consistere;
cum uero per emancipationem adoptio dissoluta sit,
potero eam uxorem ducere; sed et si ego emancipatus
fuero, nihil inpedimento erit nuptiis. 62. Fratris
filiam uxorem ducere licet: idque primum in usum
uenit, cum diuus Claudius Agrippinam, fratris sui
filiam, uxorem duxisset: sororis uero filiam uxorem
ducere non licet. et haec ita principalibus constitu-
tionibus significantur. | 63. Item amitam et mater- 17
teram uxorem ducere non licet. item eam, quae

---

1) filiae seu *Polenaar.* filia sed (sed *per compendium scriptum*) V.   2) potero eam V.   6) emancipauerimus V.

---

§§ 60. 61. = *I.* 1, 10, 2. *cf. Ulp.* 5, 6 = *Coll.* 6, 2, 2. *Gai
epit.* 1, 4, 2. *D.* 23, 2, 8 (*Pomp.* 480). 23, 2, 54 (*Scaev.* 196).
23, 2, 68 (*Paul.* 1910). *Gnom. Id. Log.* § 23. sed si qua *etc.*]
cf. D. 23, 2, 17 *pr.* (*Gai.* 248). *Paul. Coll.* 6, 3, 2. cum uero
per emancipationem] *cf. D.* 23, 2, 17, 1 (*Gai.* 248). 23, 2, 55, 1
(*Gai.* 249). 28, 2, 9, 4 (*Paul.* 1601). 45, 1, 35, 1 (*Paul.* 1844).
   § 62. *cf. I.* 1, 10, 3; 5. *Gai epit.* 1, 4, 3; 4.   *Ulp.* 5, 6
= *Coll.* 6, 2, 2. *Paul. Coll.* 6, 3, 3. *Coll.* 6, 4, 5 *fere* = *C.* 5, 4,
17 (*a.* 295). *Gnom. Id. Log.* § 23. cum diuus Claudius] *cf. Tacit.
ann.* 12, 5 *sq.* 13, 2. *Suet. Claud.* 26. 39. 43.   *Dio Cass.* 68,
2, 4. 71, 1, 3. *Script. Hist. Aug. M. Aurel.* 7, 7. sororis uero
filiam] *cf. D.* 12, 7, 5 *pr.* (*Pap.* 186).
   § 63. *cf. I.* 1, 10, 6; 7. *Ulp.* 5, 6 = *Coll.* 6, 2, 3. *Paul.
Coll.* 6, 3, 3. *Gai epit.* 1, 4, 5. *Coll.* 6, 4, 5. *D.* 23, 2, 40 (*Pomp.*
340). 24, 3, 16 (*Pomp.* 626). 23, 2, 15 (*Pap.* 494). 12, 7, 5, 1
(*Pap.* 186). 25, 7, 1, 3 (*Ulp.* 1985). 23, 2, 14, 1; 4 (*Paul.* 526.

adoptive tie is broken. I cannot marry a girl who has become my daughter or granddaughter by adoption, not even if I have emancipated* her. 60. A similar but less stringent regime applies to collaterals. 61. **Marriage is obviously forbidden between brother and sister, whether they have the same father and mother or are siblings with one common parent. There can be no marriage during the currency of the adoptive relationship between** me and my **adopted sister, but** I **can marry her once the adoptive tie is broken by her emancipation. If** I myself am **emancipated the bar to marriage also goes**. 62. It is lawful to marry one's brother's daughter; this practice was introduced when the Emperor Claudius married Agrippina, the daughter of his brother. **It is not**, on the other hand, **lawful to marry one's sister's daughter**. This is made known in imperial pronouncements. 63. **Again, a man may not marry his paternal or maternal aunt.** Again, I

mihi quondam socrus aut nurus aut priuigna aut nouerca fuit. ideo autem diximus 'quondam', quia, si
adhuc constant eae nuptiae, per quas talis adfinitas
quaesita est, alia ratione mihi nupta esse non potest,
quia neque eadem duobus nupta esse potest neque
idem duas uxores habere. 64. Ergo si quis nefarias
atque incestas nuptias contraxerit, neque uxorem habere uidetur neque liberos: itaque hi, qui ex eo coitu
nascuntur, matrem quidem habere uidentur, patrem
uero non utique, nec ob id in potestate eius sunt,
quales sunt ii, quos mater uulgo concepit: nam et hi
patrem habere non intelleguntur, cum is etiam[1] in-
certus sit; unde solent spurii filii appellari uel a
Graeca uoce quasi σποράδην concepti uel quasi sine
patre filii.

    65. *Aliquando autem euenit, ut liberi, qui statim ut*
nati[2] *sunt, parentum in potestatem*[3] *non fiant, ii postea*
tamen redigantur in potestatem. 66. *Velut si Latin*us
ex lege Aelia Sentia uxore ducta filium procreauerit
aut Latinum ex Latina aut ciuem Romanum ex ciue
Romana, non habebit eum in potestate; *sed si postea*
causa probata ciuitatem Romanam consecutus fuerit,

---

    1) et V.   2) aliquando—nati *suppl. ex Inst.*   3) pot V.
cf. § 57. *aliter* § 93. 94. 95. 107.

---

528). *Cic. p. Cluent.* 5, 12—14. *Verg. Aen.* 10, 389. idem duas
uxores] *cf. Ed. D.* 3, 2, 1. *D.* 3, 2, 13, 4 (*Ulp.* 285). *C.* 9, 9, 18
(*a* 258). 5, 5, 2 (*a.* 285). 1, 9, 7 (*a.* 393). *Cic. de orat.* 1, 40,
183. *Suet. Caes.* 52. *Plut. comp.. Demetr. c. Ant.* 4. *Socrat. Hist.*
Eccl. 4, 31 (*Tom.* 67 *p.* 548 *ed. Migne*). *Niceph. Hist. Eccl.* 11,
33 (*Tom.* 146 *p.* 689 *ed. Migne*).
    § 64. *cf. I.* 1, 10, 12. *Gai epit.* 1, 4, 8. *Ulp.* 4, 2. 5, 7
= *Coll.* 6, 2, 4. *D.* 1, 5, 19 (*Cels.* 239). 50, 1, 1, 2 (*Ulp.* 190).
1, 5, 23 (*Mod.* 89). *C.* 5, 5, 6 = *C. Th.* 3, 12, 3 (*a.* 396). *Isid.*
orig. 9, 5, 24; 25. *Auct. inc. de praenom.* 6 (*in Val. Max. ed.*
Kempf[2] *p.* 590, 22). *Plut. q. R.* 103. *Z. S.* 49, 261.
    § 65. = *I.* 1, 10, 13.
    § 66. *cf. Ulp.* 7, 4. *supra* 1, 29.

may not marry a woman who was previously my **mother-in-law** or **daughter-in-law** or **step-daughter** or **step-mother**. We have said 'previously', because if the marriage establishing such a relationship is still in being **there is another reason** why she cannot be married to me; **the same woman cannot be married to two men**, nor the same man **have two wives**. 64. Therefore, if someone has contracted an evil and incestuous union, he is regarded as having neither a wife nor children. **Children born of such a relationship** are regarded as having a mother certainly, a father, on the other hand, not at all; for this reason **they are not in** his **power but in the same position as those conceived casually. These too are considered fatherless, their fathers being unknown. Such sons are called 'spurious'. The word comes from the Greek 'sporaden', meaning 'scattered around' or perhaps from the initial letters of the Latin 'sine patre filii' (sons without a father).**

65. **Sometimes children excluded from paternal power at birth are brought into power later.** 66. For instance, if a Latin marries a wife under the Aelian-Sentian Act and begets a son – a Latin if the mother is Latin or a Roman citizen if the mother is a Roman citizen – he will not have him in power; but if he subsequently proves his case and obtains Roman citizenship, he will at the same time come to have the

simul eum[1] in potestate | sua habere incipit.   **67. Item** 18
si ciuis Romanus Latinam aut peregrinam uxorem
duxerit per ignorantiam, cum eam ciuem Romanaṁ
esse crederet, et filium procreauerit, hic non est in
potestate eius, quia ne quidem ciuis Romanus est, sed
aut Latinus aut peregrinus, id est eius condicionis,
cuius et mater fuerit, quia non aliter quisque ad
patris condicionem accedit, quam si inter patrem et
matrem eius conubium sit: sed ex senatus consulto
permittitur causam erroris probare, et ita uxor quoque et filius ad ciuitatem Romanam perueniunt, et ex
eo tempore incipit filius in potestate patris esse. idem
iuris est, si eam per ignorantiam uxorem duxerit, quae
dediticiorum numero est, nisi quod uxor non fit ciuis
Romana.   **68. Item** si ciuis Romana per errorem nupta
sit peregrino tamquam ciui Romano, permittitur ei
causam erroris probare, et ita filius quoque eius et
maritus ad ciuitatem Romanam perueniunt, et aeque
simul incipit filius in potestate patris esse. idem iuris
est, si peregrino tamquam Latino ex lege Aelia Sentia
nupta sit; nam et de hoc specialiter senatus consulto
cauetur. idem iuris est aliquatenus, si ei, qui dediticiorum numero est, tamquam ciui Romano aut Latino
e[2] lege Aelia Sentia nupta sit; nisi quod scilicet qui
dediticiorum numero est, in sua condicione permanet,
et ideo filius, quamuis fiat ciuis Romanus, in potestatem patris non redigitur.   **69. Item** si Latina peregrino,
cum eum Latinum esse cre|deret, *e lege Aelia Sentia*[3]   19
                                                              t. s

---

1) simul ergo eum *sched. Goesch.*   2) a. se V.   3) e lege
Aelia Sentia *inseruit Hu., opinatus litteras a. s., quae in* V
leguntur § 68 post Latino (*vid. not.* 2), *per errorem illuc il-
lapsas revera huc pertinere.*

---

§ 67. *cf. Ulp.* 7, 4. 5, 9. *infra* 2, 142. 3, 5; **73.** *Coll.* 16,
3, 7; 15. *supra* 1, 26. *Gnom. Id. Log.* § 46. 'hoc *senatus consultum
antiquius fuisse alio sub Hadriano facto apparet ex* 2, 142. 144'. *Hu.*
§ 68. *cf. Ulp.* 7, 4. *supra* 1, 15; 26.

child in his power. 67. Again, if a Roman citizen marries a Latin or foreign wife through ignorance, believing her to be a Roman citizen, and begets a son, this child is not in his power because he is not in fact a Roman citizen but either a Latin or a foreigner according to the status of his mother. No one takes his father's status unless there is capacity to enter a Roman law marriage between his mother and father. However, a resolution of the Senate allows proof of the grounds for the mistake, and in this way both the wife and the son achieve Roman citizenship and the son at the same time comes into his father's power. The rule is the same if a man through ignorance marries a wife who is in the category of capitulated aliens, except that the wife does not become a Roman citizen. 68. Again, if a female Roman citizen has mistakenly married a foreigner as though he were a Roman citizen, she is permitted to prove the grounds for her mistake, and in this way both her son and her husband attain Roman citizenship; equally the son at the same time comes into his father's power. The rule is the same if under the Aelian-Sentian Act she has married a foreigner as though he were a Latin; a resolution of the Senate expressly provides for this. The rule is the same, up to a point, if under the Aelian-Sentian Act she has married a man in the category of capitulated aliens as if he were a Roman citizen or a Latin; that is to say, a man in the category of capitulated aliens remains, of course, in that status, and therefore his son, although becoming a Roman citizen, is not brought into his father's power. 69. Again, if under the Aelian-Sentian Act a female Latin marries a foreigner because she believed him to be a Latin, she can on the birth of a son prove the

nupserit, potest ex senatus consulto filio nato causam
erroris probare: *et ita* omnes fiunt ciues Romani, et
filius in potestate patris esse incipit. 70. Idem constitutum est et[1] si Latinus per errorem peregrinam
quasi Latinam aut ciuem Romanam e lege Aelia Sentia
uxorem duxerit. 71. Praeterea si ciuis Romanus, qui
se credidisset Latinum esse[2], ob id Latinam *uxorem
duxerit*[3], permittitur ei[4] filio nato erroris causam probare, tamquam si[5] e lege Aelia Sentia uxorem duxisset[6]:
item his[7], qui cum ciues Romani essent, peregrinos
se esse credidissent et peregrinas uxores duxissent,
permittitur ex senatus consulto filio nato causam erroris probare. quo facto fiet uxor ciuis Romana, et
filius * * * * * * *[8] non solum ad ciuitatem Romanam
peruenit, sed etiam in potestatem[9] patris redigitur.
72. Quaecumque de filio esse[10] diximus, eadem et de
filia dicta intellegemus. 73. Et quantum ad erroris
causam probandam attinet, nihil interest, cuius aetatis
filius sit | ——— *vv. 2* ———[11]| si minor anniculo sit
filius filiaue, causa probari non potest. nec me praeterit in aliquo rescripto diui Hadriani ita esse consti-
tutum, tamquam quod ad erroris q * | ——— *vv. 3*
——— dedit. | 74. Si peregrinus ciuem Romanam
uxorem duxerit, an ex senatus consulto *causam*[12] pro-

20
t. s.

---

1) ut V? 2) esse et V. 3) uxorem duxerit *suppl. Krueger.*
4) eis V. 5) modo V. 6) duxissent V. *Hu. verba* tamquam—duxissent (duxerit) *transposita ratus locum (fortasse
recte) sic constituit:* Praeterea si ciuis Romanus, qui se credidisset Latinum esse, ob id Latinam tamquam modo e lege
Aelia Sentia uxorem duxerit, permittitur ei filio nato erroris
causam probare. 7) hi V. 8) *septem fere litterae legi nequeunt;* quoque natus *Kniep. alii aliter supplent.* 9) potestate
V. 10) *videtur cum Polenaario delendum esse.* 11) *Kniep
supplet:* filia(ue cum) sen(atus consultum) sic i(ntellegere debeamus. sed si) Latinus e (lege Aelia Sentia ius) Qui(ritium
uult) consequi. 12) causam] b V.

§ 72. *cf. supra* 1, 32ᵃ. *cf.* filio filiaue *Ulp.* 3, 3. liberi
Ulp. 7, 4. § 73. *cf. supra* 1, 29. § 74. *cf. supra* 1. 68.

grounds for her mistake in accordance with the resolution of the Senate; in this way all of them become Roman citizens and the son comes into his father's power. 70. The same is enacted if a male Latin under the Act takes a foreign wife in error as if she were a Latin or a Roman citizen. 71. Moreover, if a Roman citizen, who believed himself a Latin, has therefore married a Latin woman, on the birth of a son he may prove the grounds for the mistake as if he had married her under the Aelian-Sentian Act. Again, Roman citizens who believed themselves foreigners and married foreign wives may, according to the resolution of the Senate, on the birth of a son prove the grounds for their mistake. The wife then becomes a Roman citizen and the son ... not only attains Roman citizenship but also falls into his father's power. 72. Whatever we have said about sons is to be understood as applying similarly to daughters. 73. So far as relates to proving the grounds for the mistake, it makes no difference how old the son has grown ... if the son or daughter is below the age of one year, it is not possible for the grounds to be proved. I have not forgotten that in a written reply of the Emperor Hadrian it was enacted as to the ... of the mistake ... [3 illegible lines] gave. 74. If a foreigner marries a female Roman citizen, it has been questioned whether he can prove the grounds under the resolution of the

bare possit, quaesitum est. | -―――― *vv. 1½* ―――― | hoc
ei specialiter concessum est. sed cum peregrinus ciuem
Romanam uxorem duxisset et filio nato alias ciuitatem
Romanam consecutus esset, deinde cum quaereretur,
an causam probare posset, rescripsit imperator Antoninus proinde posse eum causam probare, atque si
peregrinus mansisset. ex quo colligimus etiam peregrinum causam probare posse. 75. Ex iis, quae diximus, apparet, siue ciuis Romanus peregrinam siue
peregrinus ciuem Romanam uxorem duxerit, eum qui
nascitur peregrinum *esse, sed* si quidem per errorem
tale matrimonium contractum fuerit, emendari uitium
eius ex senatus consulto[1] *secundum*[2] ea, quae superius
diximus. si uero nullus error interuenerit, *sed* scientes
suam condicionem ita coierint, nullo casu emendatur
uitium eius matrimonii.

76. Loquimur autem de his scilicet, *inter* quos conubium non sit; nam alioquin si ciuis Romanus peregrinam, cum qua ei conubium est, uxorem duxerit,
sicut supra quoque diximus, iustum matrimonium contrahitur[3], et tunc ex iis qui nascitur, ciuis Romanus
est et in potestate patris erit. 77. Item[4] si ciuis Romana peregrino, cum quo ei conubium est, nupserit,
peregrinus[5] sane procreatur et is iustus patris filius
est, tamquam si ex peregrina eum procreasset. | hoc 21
tamen tempore *e* senatus consulto, quod auctore diuo
Hadriano sacratissimo[6] factum est, etiamsi non fuerit
conubium inter ciuem Romanam et peregrinum, qui

---

1) senatus consulto *Krueger.* c V.　　2) l. **V.** *cf. apogr.*
p. 300 l. 16.　　3) contrahitur *Krueger, Polenaar.* contrahi **V.**
4) itaque? **V.**　　5) nupserit peregrinus] nupserit | erit pere-
grinum **V.**　　6) s **V.** *cf. supra p.* 14 *n.* 2.

---

§ 75. *cf. supra* 1, 68.
§ 76. *cf. supra* 1, 56.
§ 77. *cf. infra* 1, 92. *Liv.* 23, 2, 6. 31, 31, 11. 38, 36, 6.

Senate. ... this has been specially granted him. But when a foreigner had married a female Roman citizen and after the birth of a son had attained Roman citizenship by other means, and the question was then raised whether he could prove the grounds, the Emperor Antoninus Pius gave a written reply that he could prove the grounds just as if he had remained a foreigner. From this we gather that a foreigner too can prove the grounds. 75. It is clear from what we have said that, whether a Roman citizen marries a foreign wife or a foreigner a Roman wife, the child born to them is a foreigner. But if indeed such a marriage is contracted by mistake, its defect can be made good under the resolution of the Senate, as we have said above. If, on the other hand, there was no mistake but their union was in full knowledge of their status, in no case can the defect of such a marriage be made good.

76. We are speaking of persons between whom indeed there is not the capacity to enter a Roman law marriage. Otherwise, if a Roman citizen marries a foreigner with whom he has this capacity, a Roman law marriage is contracted, just as we have said earlier. Any child born of them is a Roman citizen and will be in his father's power. 77. Again, if a female Roman citizen marries a foreigner with whom she has this capacity, the child she conceives is a foreigner and the lawful son of his father, just as if he had begotten him on a foreign wife. Yet, at the present time, under a resolution of the Senate passed on the proposal of the Emperor Hadrian of blessed memory, even if there is no capacity between the Roman citizen and her foreign husband, any child is the lawful son of

nascitur, iustus patris filius est. | 78. Quod autem diximus inter ciuem Romanum peregrinamque¹ *nisi conubium sit, qui* | nascitur, peregrinum esse, *lege Minicia cauetur, ut is quidem deterioris*² parentis condicionem *sequatur.* eadem lege *autem* ex diuerso cauetur, *ut* si peregrinus, *cum* | qua ei conubium non sit, uxorem *duxerit ciuem Romanam,* peregrinus ex eo coitu nascatur. sed hoc maxime casu necessaria lex Minicia *fuit;* nam remota ea lege diuersam condicionem sequi de- *bebat, quia* ex eis, inter quos non est conubium, qui nascitur, iure gentium matris condicioni accedit. qua parte autem iubet lex ex ciue Romano et peregrina peregrinum nasci, superuacua uidetur; nam et remota ea lege hoc utique iure gentium futurum erat. 79. Adeo autem hoc ita est, ut ex *ciue Romano et Latina qui nascitur, matris condicioni accedat; nam in lege Minicia quidem peregrinorum nomine comprehenduntur non*³ solum exterae nationes et gentes, sed etiam qui Latini nominantur; sed ad alios Latinos pertinet, qui proprios populos propriasque ciuitates habebant et erant peregrinorum numero. 80. Eadem ratione ex contrario ex Latino et ciue Romana, siue ex lege Aelia Sentia siue aliter *contractum* fuerit matrimonium, ciuis Romanus 22 nascitur. fuerunt | tamen, qui putauerunt ex lege Aelia Sentia contracto matrimonio Latinum nasci, quia uidetur eo casu per legem Aeliam Sentiam et Iuniam⁴ conubium inter eos dari, et semper conubium efficit, ut qui nascitur, patris condicioni accedat; aliter uero contracto matrimonio eum, qui nascitur, iure gentium

---

1) peregrinuque? V.   2) *cf. suppl. apogr., cuius lectio incerta est.*   3) *suppl. Hu.*   4) et Iuniam *del. F. Schulz ad Ulp.* 3, 3.

---

§ 78. *cf. supra* 1, 75.   *Ulp.* 5, 8.   *D.* 1, 5, 24 (*Ulp.* 2698) *C. Th.* 14, 7, 1 (*a.* 397).

§ 79. *cf. supra* 1, 29; 22.   *Ulp.* 3, 3.   *infra* 1, 96; 131 *et ibi citatos.*

§ 80. *cf. supra* 1, 30.

his father. 78. Our statement that the child of a
Roman citizen and a foreign wife is a foreigner, unless
there was capacity to enter a Roman law marriage, is
provided in the Minician Act, that a child follows the
parent of inferior status. On the other hand, the same
Act provides that if a foreigner marries a female
Roman citizen with whom he does not have capacity,
the child of that union is a foreigner. In this event
there is a particular need for the Minician Act;
without that Act the child should follow a different
status, because by the law of all peoples a child born
of parents between whom there is no capacity to
marry takes the status of the mother. Where, then,
the Act commands that the child of a Roman citizen
and a female foreigner is a foreigner, it appears
entirely unnecessary; for this would be the effect of
the law of all peoples even without the Act. 79. It is
also thus that the child of a Roman citizen and a
female Latin takes the status of his mother. For the
Minician Act classes as foreigners not only foreign
races and peoples but also those called Latins; it also
applies to the other Latins, who had their own
communities and cities and were in the category of
foreigners. 80. Conversely, by the same reasoning the
child of a male Latin and a female Roman citizen,
whether married under the Aelian-Sentian Act or
otherwise, is born a Roman citizen. Yet there were
those who considered that the child of an Aelian-
Sentian marriage was born a Latin, because it appears
that in that event capacity to enter a Roman law
marriage is granted them by the Aelian-Sentian and
Junian Acts, and the effect of this capacity is always
that the child takes his father's status; but otherwise,
once a marriage has been contracted, a child born
would by the law of all peoples follow the status of his

matris condicionem sequi et ob id esse ciuem Romanum. sed hoc iure utimur ex senatus consulto, quod auctore diuo Hadriano significat[1], ut quo*quo*modo[2] ex Latino et ciue Romana natus ciuis Romanus nascatur. 81. His conuenienter[3] et illud senatus consultum diuo Hadriano auctore[4] significauit, ut ex Latino et peregrina, item contra ex peregrino et Latina *qui* nascitur, is matris condicionem sequatur. 82. Illud quoque his consequens est, quod ex ancilla et libero iure gentium seruus nascitur, et contra ex libera et seruo liber nascitur. 83. Animaduertere tamen debemus, ne iuris gentium regulam uel lex aliqua uel quod legis[5] uicem optinet, aliquo casu commutauerit. 84. Ecce enim ex senatus consulto Claudiano poterat ciuis Romana, quae alieno seruo uolente domino eius coiit, ipsa ex pactione libera permanere, sed seruum procreare; nam quod inter eam et dominum istius serui conuenerit, ex[6] senatus consulto ratum esse iubetur. sed postea diuus Hadrianus iniquitate rei et inelegantia iuris motus restituit iuris gen|tium regulam, ut cum ipsa mulier libera permaneat, liberum pariat. 85. *Item e lege* —[7] ex ancilla et libero poterant liberi nasci; nam ea lege cauetur, 23

---

1) significatur **V**. *ante h. v.* factum est quo *inserit Polenaar.* 2) qm **V**. quo(*quo*)modo *Polen.* 3) conueniuntur **V** (?). 4) Hadriano auctore] Hadrianos (*sed* s *expunctum*) auctor **V**. 5) lege **V**. 6) eo *Hu.* 7) *nomen legis periit. hanc legem, quae Romana fuit, de peregrinis cuiusdam regionis aut condicionis egisse ex eo sequi videtur, quod Gaius §§ 85. 86 non cives Romanos Romanasve, sed liberos liberasve dicit. verbis* 'ea lege cauetur' *SC. Claudianum significari non potuit.*

---

§ 82. *cf. infra* 1, 88; 89. *Ulp.* 5, 9. *Paul.* 2, 24, 1—3. *I.* 1, 4 *pr.* *D.* 1, 5, 5, 2; 3 (*Marcian.* 45). *C.* 5, 18, 3 (*a.* 215). 5, 5, 3 *pr.* (*a.* 319). *Isid. orig.* 9, 5, 18.
§ 83. *cf. D.* 1, 5, 24 (*Ulp.* 2698).
§ 84. *cf. Paul.* 2, 21 a. 4, 10, 2. *infra* 1, 91; 160. *Tacit. ann.* 12, 53. *Suet. Vesp.* 11. *C. Th.* 4, 12 (11), 4 (5) (*a.* 331).
§ 85. *cf D.* 40, 15, 2 *pr.* (*Pap.* 716). *C.* 5, 18, 3 (*a.* 215).

mother and therefore be a Roman citizen. But our
current law, according to a resolution of the Senate
passed on the proposal of the Emperor Hadrian,
makes known that a child of a Latin father and a
Roman citizen mother is in all circumstances born a
Roman. 81. In conformity with these principles, that
resolution of the Senate passed on the proposal of the
Emperor Hadrian made known that the child of a
Latin father and a foreign mother, and, the other way
round, of a foreign father and a Latin mother, follows
the mother's status. 82. A further consequence of
these principles is that, by the law of all peoples, the
child of a female slave and a free man is born a slave,
while, the other way round, the child of a free woman
and a male slave is born free. 83. Yet we must consider
whether there are any circumstances in which some
statute or other thing having the force of statute has
modified the rule of the law of all peoples. 84. We see
that under the Claudian Resolution of the Senate a
female Roman citizen who has intercourse with
another person's slave with the consent of the owner
could remain free herself under their agreement but
conceive a slave; for the agreement reached between
her and the owner of that slave is by resolution of the
Senate ratified. Subsequently the Emperor Hadrian,
moved both by the injustice of the case and the
awkwardness of the law, restored the rule of the law of
all peoples, that since the woman herself remained
free, she should bear a free child. 85. Again, under the
… Act [some unknown Act, perhaps dealing with a
particular region of the Empire] children of a female
slave and a free man could be born free; for it is
provided in the Act that if a man had intercourse with

ut si quis cum aliena ancilla, quam credebat liberam
esse, coierit, siquidem masculi nascantur, liberi sint,
si uero feminae, ad eum pertineant, cuius mater ancilla fuerit. sed et in hac specie diuus Vespasianus
inelegantia iuris motus restituit iuris gentium regulam,
ut omni modo, etiamsi masculi nascantur, serui sint
eius, cuius et mater fuerit. 86. Sed illa pars eiusdem
legis salua est, ut ex libera et seruo alieno, quem
sciebat seruum esse, serui nascantur. itaque apud
quos talis lex non est, qui nascitur[1], iure gentium
matris condicionem sequitur et ob id liber est.

87. Quibus autem casibus matris et non patris condicionem sequitur qui nascitur, iisdem casibus in potestate eum patris, etiamsi is ciuis Romanus sit, non
esse plus quam manifestum est. et ideo superius rettulimus quibusdam casibus per errorem non iusto con-
tracto matrimonio senatum interuenire et emendare
uitium matrimonii eoque modo plerumque efficere, ut
in potestatem patris filius redigatur.[2]   88. Sed si ancilla ex ciue Romano conceperit[3], deinde manumissa
ciuis Romana facta sit et tunc pariat, licet ciuis Ro-
24 manus sit qui nascitur, | sicut pater eius, non tamen
in potestate[4] patris est, quia neque ex iusto coitu conceptus est, neque ex ullo senatus consulto talis coitus
quasi iustus constituitur.

89. Quod autem placuit, si ancilla ex ciue Romano
conceperit, deinde manumissa pepererit[5], qui nascitur,

---

1) nascantur V.   2) et ideo — redigatur del. Beseler Z. S.
45, 456.   3) concepit V.   4) potestatem V.   5) peperit V.

---

§ 86. cf. D. 1, 5, 24 (Ulp. 2698). C. 5, 18, 3 (a. 215). Cic.
de nat. deor. 3, 18, 45.
§ 87. cf. supra 1, 66 sq. 68.
§ 89. cf. Gai epit. 1, 4, 9. Ulp. 5, 10. D. 50, 1, 9 (Ner. 26).
38, 17, 2, 3 (Ulp. 2517). 1, 5, 5, 2; 3 (Marcian. 45) = I. 1, 4 pr.
C. 9, 47, 4 (211—217). Paul. 2, 24, 1—3. Quintil. inst. orat.
3, 6, 25

another's slave in the belief that she was free, any male children are free, but, if female, they belong to the owner of their slave mother. But in this situation too the Emperor Vespasian, moved by the awkwardness of the law, restored the rule of the law of all peoples so that in all cases, even if those born were males, they should be slaves of their mother's owner. 86. But that section of the same Act has been preserved, that children of a free woman and some person's slave, whom she knew to be a slave, are born slaves. Among those who do not have a statute of this kind, a child therefore follows his mother's status in accordance with the law of all peoples and is on that account free.

87. In those cases where the child follows his mother's not his father's status, it is more than abundantly clear that he is not in his father's power, even if he is a Roman citizen. This is why we have explained above that in certain cases of error, when a Roman law marriage has not been contracted, the Senate has stepped in and made good the defect in the marriage; in this way it has often ensured that a son is brought into his father's power. 88. If a female slave conceives a child by a Roman citizen, then is manumitted and becomes a Roman citizen and thereafter bears the child, although the child is a Roman citizen, just like his father, yet he is not in his father's power, because he was not conceived in legal intercourse and there is no resolution of the Senate which brings such intercourse so to speak within the law.

89. The received opinion that, if a female slave conceives by a Roman citizen and then gives birth following manumission, the child is free-born is a

liberum nasc*i*, *n*aturali ratione fit; nam hi. qui illegi-
time concipiuntur, statum sumunt ex eo tempore, quo
nascuntur; itaque si ex libera nascuntur, liberi fiunt,
nec interest, ex quo mater eos conceperit[1], cum ancilla
fuerit: at hi, qui legitime concipiuntur, ex conceptionis
tempore statum sumunt. 90. Itaque si cui mulieri
ciui Romanae praegnati aqua et igni interdictum fuerit,
eoque modo peregrina *facta*[2] tunc pariat, conplures
distinguunt et putant, si quidem ex iustis nuptiis conceperit[1], ciuem Romanum ex ea nasci, si uero uolgo
conceperit[1], peregrinu*m* ex ea nasci.[3] 91. Item si qua
mulier ciuis Romana praegnas ex senatus consulto
Claudiano ancilla facta· sit ob id, quod alieno seruo
inuito et denuntiante domino eius *coierit*, conplures
distinguunt[4] et existimant, si quidem ex iustis nuptiis
conceptus sit, ciuem Romanum ex ea nasci, si uero
uolgo conceptus sit, *seruum* nasci eius, cuius mater
facta esset ancilla. 92. Peregrina quoque si uolgo conceperit, deinde ciuis Romana *facta* tunc pariat, ciuem
Romanum parit; si uero ex peregrino | secundum leges 25
moresque peregrinorum conceperit[1], ita uidetur ex senatus consulto, quod auctore diuo Hadriano factum
est, ciuem Romanum parere, si et patri eius ciuitas
Romana donet*ur*.[5]
   93. Si peregrinus sibi liberisque suis ciuitatem Romanam petierit, non aliter filii in potestate eius fiunt,

---

1) concepit V.   2) *vide apographon*.   3) nascitur V.
4) *cf. apographon*.   5) 'rectius pro donet scriptum foret
donata sit'. *Hu.*

---

§ 90. *cf. infra* 1, 161. *D.* 1, 5, 18 (*Ulp.* 2698).
   § 91. *cf. supra* 1, 84. *infra* 1, 160. *Ulp.* 11, 11. *Paul.*
2, 21a. 2, 24, 2; 3. *D.* 16, 3, 27 (*Paul.* 1494). *C.* 7, 16, 3
(*a.* 225). 6, 59, 9 (*a.* 294). 7, 24, 1 (*a*, 531—534). *C. Th.* 4,
12 (11), 2 (*a.* 317) *cum interpret.* 4, 12 (11), 5 (6) (*a.* 362). *I.* 3,
12, 1 *cum Theoph.* (*Ferr. p.* 316). *Tert.* *ad uxor.* 2, 8.
   § 92. *cf. supra* 1, 77. *infra* 1, 94.
   § 93. *cf. infra* 2, 135ᵃ. 3, 20. *supra* 1, 55. *Plin. ep. ad*

matter of natural reason; for those who are conceived illegitimately take their status from the time when they are born. Thus the children of a free woman are born free, and it does not matter that their mother was a slave when she conceived them. Those who are legitimately conceived, however, take their status from the time of conception. 90. Therefore, if a female Roman citizen, while pregnant, is banished from home and hearth and so gives birth as 'a foreigner, many authorities make a distinction and think that, if she conceived the child in Roman law marriage, her child is a Roman citizen, but if she conceived as a result of promiscuity her child is a foreigner. 91. Again, if a female Roman citizen while pregnant becomes a slave under the Claudian Resolution of the Senate on the grounds that she has cohabited with someone else's slave against the will and formal notification of the owner, many authorities make a distinction and hold that, if the child was conceived in Roman law marriage, her child is a Roman citizen; if, on the other hand, she conceived as a result of promiscuity, he is born the slave of his mother's owner. 92. Also, if a foreign woman conceives as a result of promiscuity, then becomes a Roman citizen and thereafter gives birth, she gives birth to a Roman citizen; if, on the other hand, she conceived by a foreign man in accordance with their laws and customs she is regarded as giving birth to a Roman citizen if and only if Roman citizenship is granted to the father; this is in accordance with the resolution of the Senate passed on the proposal of the Emperor Hadrian.

93. If a foreigner seeks Roman citizenship for himself and his children, his sons will come into his power only if the Emperor brings them into power; he

quam si imperator eos in potestatem redegerit: quod
ita demum is facit, si causa cognita aestimauerit hoc
filiis expedire: diligentius autem exactiusque causam
cognoscit de impuberibus absentibusque: et haec ita
edicto diui Hadriani significantur. 94. Item si quis
cum uxore praegnante ciuitate Romana donatus sit,
quamuis is, qui nascitur, ut supra dixi[1], ciuis Romanus sit, tamen in potestate patris non fit: idque sub-
scriptione diui sacratissimi[2] Hadriani significatur. qua
de causa, qui intellegit uxorem suam esse praegnatem,
dum ciuitatem sibi et uxori ab imperatore petit, simul
ab eodem petere debet, ut eum, qui natus erit, in
potestate sua habeat. 95. Alia causa est eorum, qui
Latii iure cum liberis suis ad ciuitatem Romanam
perueniunt; nam horum in potestate fiunt liberi.
96. Quod ius quibusdam peregrinis ciuitatibus datum
est uel a populo Romano uel a senatu uel a Caesare
— — — —[3] aut maius est Latium aut minus; maius
est Latium, cum et hi, qui decuriones leguntur, et ei,
26 qui honorem aliquem aut | magistratum[5] gerunt, ciui-
tatem Romanam consecuntur; minus Latium est, cum
hi tantum, qui uel[4] magistratum uel[5] honorem gerunt,

---

1) diximus *Goeschen*.   2) s V. *cf.* 1, 53; 77.   3) *'talia
fere suppleri posse videntur:* huius autem iuris duae species sunt;
nam' *Krueger*   4) qui uel *Hu.* uel qui V.   5) aut magistratum *et* uel magistratum uel *del. Solazzi.*

Trai. 11 (6), 2. *panegyr.* 37. *D.* 1, 6, 11 (*Mod.* 90). *Coll.* 16, 7, 2
(*Ulp.* 1927).

§ 94. *cf. supra* 1, 92.

§ 96. *cf. Ascon. in Cic. Pison. p.* 3 (*Bruns* II[7], 67). *Cic. ad
Att.* 5, 11, 2. *Strab.* 4, 1, 12 *p.* 186. *Suet. Aug.* 47. *Plin. n. h.*
3, 18; 20; 23; 24; 30; 133. *Tacit. ann.* 15, 32. *hist.* 3, 55. *Plin.
paneg.* 37. 39. *Appian. bell. civ.* 2, 26. *Script. Hist. Aug. Hadr.*
21, 7. *lex Salp. c.* 21. 22. 23 (*Bruns* 1[7], 143). *C. I. L.* V 532
(*Dessau* 6680), *l.* 45. II 1945 (*Dessau* 1982). 2096. 1631. 1610
(*Dessau* 1981). I 1635. VIII 1269 = 14763 (*Dessau* 6781).

does so only if, having heard the case, he judges this to be in the sons' interest. He hears the case with more care and more searchingly where the children are under puberty and absent; this is made known in an edict of the Emperor Hadrian. 94. Again, if someone is granted Roman citizenship together with his pregnant wife, although the child is born a Roman citizen (as I have said above) yet he does not come under his father's power; this is made known in a written reply of the Emperor Hadrian of blessed memory. For this reason, a man who is aware that his wife is pregnant at the time when he is seeking citizenship from the emperor for them both, should at the same time seek to have in his power the child which is due. 95. The case is different with those who attain Roman citizenship, together with their children, by Latin right; for their children become subject to power. 96. This right has been granted to certain foreign cities, either by the Roman people or by the Senate, or by the emperor. [There are two kinds of this right; for there is] either the greater or the lesser Latin right. The greater Latin right is when those chosen as local councillors, as well as those who hold some office or magistracy, obtain Roman citizenship. The lesser Latin right is when only those who hold magistracy or office attain citizenship. This is made known in

ad ciuitatem Romanam perueniunt. idque conpluribus
epistulis principum significatur.

97. *Non solum tamen naturales liberi secundum ea,
quae* diximus, in potestate nostra sunt, uerum et[1] hi,
quos adoptamus. 98. Adoptio autem duobus modis
fit, aut populi auctoritate aut inperio magistratus uel*ut*
praetoris. 99. Populi auctoritate adoptamus eos, qui
sui iuris sunt: quae species adoptionis dicitur adrogatio,
quia et is, qui adoptat, rogatur, id est interrogatur,
an uelit eum, quem adoptaturus sit, iustum sibi filium
esse; et is, qui adoptatur, rogatur, an id fieri patiatur; et populus rogatur, an id fieri iubeat. imperio
magistratus adoptamus eos, qui in potestate parentium
sunt, siue primum gradum liberorum optineant, qualis
est filius et filia, siue inferiorem, qualis est nepos
neptis, pronepos proneptis. 100. Et quidem illa adoptio,
quae per populum fit, nusquam nisi Romae fit; at
haec etiam in prouinciis apud praesides earum fieri
solet. 101. Item per populum feminae non adoptantur,
nam id magis placuit; apud | praetorem[2] uero uel in 27
prouinciis apud proconsulem[3] legatumue etiam feminae
solent adoptari. 102. Item inpuberem apud populum
adoptari aliquando prohibitum est[4], aliquando permissum

---

1) etiam *Inst.*   2) p. r. (*id est* populum Romanum) V.
3) proconsules V   4) aliquando prohibitum est] olim prohibitum
fuit *Beseler Subsec. 1, delens* aliquando permissum est.

16914. 16915. 16916. 16919 (*Dessau* 1983). 18218 (*Dessau* 6848).
22737 (*Dessau* 6780). XII 83.
§ 97. = *I.* 1, 11 *pr. cf. Gai epit.* 1, 5 *pr. Ulp.* 8, 1. *D.* 1,
7, 1 *pr.* (*Mod.* 186).
§§ 98. 99. = *D.* 1, 7, 2 *pr. I.* 1, 11, 1. *cf. Gai epit.* 1, 5, 1.
Ulp. 8, 2; 3. *infra* 2, 138. *D.* 1, 7, 1, 1 (*Mod.* 186). *Gell.* 5, 19.
Cic. pro domo 29, 77. *Suet. Aug.* 65. *Appian. bell. civ.* 3, 94.
§ 100. *cf. Ulp.* 8, 4. *D.* 1, 18, 2 (*Ulp.* 2695).
§ 101. *cf. Gai epit.* 1, 5, 2. *Ulp.* 8, 5. *Gell.* 5, 19, 10. *D.*
1, 7, 21 (*Gai.* 485). *C.* 8, 47 (48), 8 (*a.* 294).
§ 102. *cf. Ulp.* 8, 5. *I.* 1, 11, 3. *Gell.* 5, 19, 10. *D.* 1, 7, 17, 1
(*Ulp.* 2691). *C.* 8, 47 (48), 2 (*a.* 286). *Tacit. ann.* 15, 19.

numerous imperial letters.

97. **We have just set out the rules under which our real children fall into our power. This also happens with those whom we adopt.** 98. **Adoptions can be done in two ways, either by** authority of the people **or through the jurisdiction of a magistrate,** for instance, a praetor. 99. The authority of the people **is used when we adopt someone who is an independent person. This kind of adoption is called adrogation***, because the adopter is asked, that is, interrogated, whether he wishes the person whom he is about to adopt to be his lawful son; and he who is being adopted is asked whether he allows this to be done; and the people are asked whether they command it to be done. **Adoption before a magistrate is used for those still within paternal power. This applies to descendants* in the first degree, sons or daughters, and to those below, grandchildren or great-grandchildren.** 100. That form of adoption effected by the people takes place nowhere except Rome; but the latter form commonly takes place in the provinces before the provincial governors. 101. Women are not adopted by the authority of the people; this is the received opinion. On the other hand, women too are commonly adopted before the praetor, or in the provinces before the proconsul or legate. 102. Again, for **a person below the age of puberty** adoption effected by the people has sometimes been forbidden and sometimes

est: nunc ex epistula optimi imperatoris Antonini,
quam scripsit pontificibus, si iusta causa adoptionis
esse uidebitur, cum quibusdam condicionibus permissum
est. apud praetorem uero et in prouinciis apud proconsulem legatumue cuiuscumque aetatis adoptare possumus. 103. Illud[1] uero utriusque adoptionis commune
est, quod[2] et hi, qui generare non possunt, quales sunt
spadones, adoptare possunt. 104. Feminae uero nullo
modo adoptare possunt, quia ne quidem naturales liberos in potestate habent. 105. Item si[3] quis per populum siue apud praetorem uel apud praesidem prouinciae adoptauerit, potest eundem alii in adoptionem
dare. 106. Sed *et* ill*ud, de quo*[4] quaestio est, an minor
natu maiorem natu adoptare possit, utriusque adoptionis commune est. 107. Illud proprium est eius adoptionis, quae per populum fit, quod is, qui liberos in
potestate habet, si se adrogandum dederit, non solum
ipse potestati adrogatoris subicitur, sed etiam liberi
eius in eiusdem fiunt potestate tanquam nepotes. |

28　　　108. [5]*Nunc de his personis uideamus, quae in manu
nostra sunt.* *quod* et ipsum ius proprium ciuium Ro-

---

1) illi V.　　2) quod *Dig. et Inst.* quia V.　　3) siue
Polenaar.　　4) et illud de quo *Polenaar.* illa V.　　5) *duos
versus rubricae causa vacuos reliquisse librarius videtur, ex
quibus unum Goesch. explevit.*

---

§ 103. = *D.* 1, 7, 2, 1. *I.* 1, 11, 9. *cf. Gai epit.* 1, 5, 3.
Ulp. 8, 6. *D.* 28, 2, 6 *pr.* (*Ulp.* 2445). 1, 7, 40, 2 (*Mod.* 2). *Cic.
pro domo* 13, 34.
§ 104. = *I.* 1, 11, 10. *cf. Gai epit.* 1, 5, 2. *Ulp.* 8, 8a. *D.*
1, 5, 9 (*Pap.* 362). 5, 2, 29, 3 (*Ulp.* 2349). *C.* 8, 47 (48), 5 (*a.* 291);
8 (*a.* 294). *Suet. Galb.* 4. quia ne quidem] *cf. supra* 1, 67.
infra 2, 161; 218. 3, 51.
§ 105. *cf. I.* 1, 11, 8. *D.* 1, 7, 37, 1 (*Paul.* 1953).
§ 106. *cf. I.* 1, 11, 4. *D.* 1, 7, 16 (*Iav.* 21). 1, 7, 40, 1
(*Mod.* 2). *Cic. pro domo* 13, 34. 14, 36. *Suet. Tib.* 2.
§ 107. = *D.* 1, 7, 2, 2. *I.* 1, 11, 11. *cf. Gai epit.* 1, 5, 4.
Ulp. 8, 8. *D.* 1, 7, 15 *pr.* (*Ulp.* 2680). 1, 7, 40 *pr.* (*Mod.* 2).
§ 108. *cf. supra* 1, 55. *Dionys.* 2, 25. *Gell.* 10, 23, 5.

permitted. At present, according to a letter written to the pontiffs by the excellent Emperor Antoninus Pius, it is permitted **under certain conditions**, if there appears to be a good **reason** for the adoption. On the other hand, we can adopt persons of any age before the praetor, and in the provinces before the proconsul or legate. 103. **Another feature common to both kinds of adoption is that people unable to have children, eunuchs, can adopt.** 104. **But women cannot adopt** by any method, **because they do not have power even over their real children.** 105. Then, too, someone adopted, whether by the people or before the praetor or provincial governor, can be given in adoption to someone else. 106. The question of whether a younger person can adopt an older is, indeed, common to both forms of adoption. 107. **A characteristic peculiar to adoption effected** by the people **is that if the person adrogated has children in his power, not only himself but the children too are taken into the power of the adrogator, as grandchildren.**

108. Now let us examine those persons who are subordinate to us in marriage. This also is a right peculiar to Roman citizens. 109. While it is customary

manorum est. 109. Sed in potestate quidem et masculi
et feminae esse solent; in manum autem feminae tantum conueniunt. 110. Olim itaque tribus modis in manum conueniebant: usu, farreo, coemptione. 111. Usu
in manum conueniebat, quae anno continuo nupta
perseuerabat; *quia*[1] enim uelut annua possessione usu
capiebatur, in familiam uiri transibat[2] filiaeque locum
optinebat. itaque lege duodecim tabularum cautum
est, ut si qua nollet eo modo in manum mariti conuenire, ea quotannis trinoctio abesset atque eo modo
cuiusque anni *usum* interrumperet. sed hoc totum
ius partim legibus sublatum est, partim ipsa desuetu-
dine obliteratum est. 112. Farreo in manum[3] conueniunt per quoddam genus sacrificii, quod Ioui Farreo fit;
in quo farreus panis adhibetur, unde etiam confar-
reatio[4] dicitur; complura praeterea huius iuris ordinandi
gratia cum certis et sollemnibus uerbis praesentibus
decem testibus aguntur et fiunt. quod[5] ius etiam
nostris temporibus in usu est: nam flamines maiores,
id est Diales, Martiales, Quirinales, item | reges sacro- 29
rum, nisi ex farreatis nati non leguntur: ac ne ipsi
quidem sine confarreatione sacerdotium habere possunt.
113. Coemptione uero in manum conueniunt per mancipationem, *id est* per quandam imaginariam uendi-

---

1) perseuerabat quia] pseuerabant *litteris* nt *fortasse per
correcturam in* tq *mutatis* V.   2) transiebat V.   3) manus V.
4) conferratio V.   5) quos V.

§ 110. cf. *Serv. ad Georg.* 1, 31 (*Bruns* II[7], 78). *Corp. Gloss.*
VI, 253. *Boeth. ad Cic. top.* 3, 14 (*Bruns* II[7], 73). *Arnob.* 4, 20.
§ 111. cf. *Cic. pro Flacco* 34, 84. *Serv. l. c. Boeth. l. c.*
Qu. Muc. ap. Gell. 3, 2, 12; 13 *et Macrob. Sat.* 1, 3, 9 (*Iurispr.*
I, 18). *infra* 1, 115 b; 118. legibus] cf. *Tacit. ann.* 4, 16.
§ 112. cf. *Ulp.* 9. *Serv. l. c.; idem ad Aen.* 4, 103; 374
(*Bruns* II[7], 76). *Dionys.* 2, 25. *Plin. n. h.* 18, 10. *Tacit. ann.*
4, 16. *Script. Hist. Aug. Alex. Sev.* 22, 3 (ius confarreationis
ex coni. Madvigii). *Ambros. de lapsu virginis* 5, 20. *C. I. L.* X
6662 (*Dessau* 1455).
§ 113. cf. *Cic. pro Flacc.* 34, 84. *de orat.* 1, 56, 237. *Serv.
ad Aen.* 4, 103 (*Bruns* II[7], 76). 214. *ad Georg.* 1, 31 (*Bruns*

for both men and women to be in power, only women fall into marital subordination. 110. Formerly there used to be three methods by which they fell into subordination: by usage, by sharing of bread, and by contrived sale*. 111. A woman used to fall into marital subordination by usage if she remained in the married state for a continuous period of one year: for she was, as it were, usucapted* by a year's possession, and would pass into her husband's kin in the relationship of a daughter. The Twelve Tables* therefore provided that if any woman did not wish to become subordinate to her husband in this way, she should each year absent herself for a period of three nights, and in this way interrupt the usage of each year. But this whole legal state was in part repealed by statute, in part blotted out through simple disuse. 112. Women fall into marital subordination through a certain kind of sacrifice made to Jupiter of the Grain, in which bread of coarse grain is employed, for which reason it is also called the sharing of bread. Many other things, furthermore, have to be done and carried out to create this right, together with the saying of specific and solemn words in the presence of ten witnesses. This legal state is still found in our own times; for the higher priests, that is the priests of Jupiter, of Mars and of Quirinus, as also the Sacred Kings, are chosen only if they have been born in marriage made by the sharing of bread, and they themselves cannot hold priestly office without being married by the sharing of bread. 113. Women fall into marital subordination through contrived sale, on the other hand, by means of mancipation*, that is, by a sort of imaginary sale; for in the presence of not less

tionem: nam adhibitis non minus[1] quam v testibus
ciuibus Romanis puberibus, item libripende, emit[2] uir[3]
mulierem, cuius in manum conuenit. 114. Potest[4] autem
coemptionem facere mulier non solum cum marito suo,
sed etiam cum extraneo; scilicet aut matrimonii causa
facta coemptio dicitur aut fiduciae; quae enim cum
marito suo facit coemptionem, *ut* apud eum filiae loco
sit, dicitur matrimonii causa fecisse coemptionem;
quae uero alterius rei causa facit coemptionem aut
cum uiro suo aut cum extraneo, uelut tutelae euitan-
dae causa, dicitur fiduciae causa fecisse coemptionem.
115. Quod est tale: si qua uelit quos habet tutores deponere[5] et alium nancisci, illis auctoribus[6] coemptionem
facit; deinde a coemptionatore remancipata ei, cui ipsa
30 uelit, et ab eo uindicta | manumissa incipit eum ha-
bere tutorem, *a* quo manumissa est; qui tutor fiduciarius dicitur, sicut inferius[7] apparebit. 115ᵃ. Olim
etiam testamenti faciendi gratia fiduciaria fiebat coemptio:
tunc enim non aliter feminae testamenti faciendi ius
habebant, exceptis quibusdam personis, quam si coemptionem fecissent remancipataeque et manumissae fuissent; sed hanc necessitatem coemptionis faciendae ex
auctoritate diui Hadriani senatus remisit. | ——— *vv.* 1½·

---

1) manu V.   2) libripendaemit V.   3) eum V. is
Krueger. nummo *Goeschen.*   4) poste V.   5) deponere
Krueger. reponere V.   6) tutoribus V.   7) inferioribus V.

II[7], 78). *Non.*(*Varro*) *p.* 531 *Merc.* (*Bruns* II[7], 65). *Boeth. ad*
Cic. top. 3, 14 (*Bruns* II[7], 73). *Isid. orig.* 5, 24, 26 (*Bruns* II[7],
81). 9, 5, 8. adhibitis ... libripende] = *Priscian.* 6, 96 *p.* 282
ed. Hertz.

     § 114. *cf. Cic. pro Mur.* 12, 27. filiae loco] *cf. infra* 1, 136.
2, 159. *Dionys.* 2, 25 (ὡς θυγάτηρ πατρός). *Boeth. et Serv. loc.*
cit. Gell. 18, 6, 9. *cf. etiam Ter. Andr.* 1, 5, 60 = 295 *sq.*

     § 115. *cf. infra* 1, 166a; 195a. 3, 84. *Fest. v. remancipa-*
tam p. 277 (*Bruns* II[7], 31).

     § 115ᵃ. *cf. Cic. top.* 4, 18. *Liv.* 39, 9. *Gell.* 1, 12, 9. *Plut.*
Num. 10. *infra* 2, 112. *Gnom. Id. Log.* § 33.

than five adult Roman citizens as witnesses, and also a scale-holder, the man to whom the woman becomes subordinate 'buys' her. 114. A woman, however, can make a contrived sale not only with her husband but also with a third party. A contrived sale is indeed said to be made either for the purpose of marriage or of a formal trust*. For when she makes a contrived sale with her husband, so as to take the status of a daughter, she is said to have made a contrived sale for the purpose of marriage. On the other hand, the woman who makes a contrived sale for some other purpose, whether with her husband or with a third party — for instance, for the purpose of evading a guardianship* — is said to have made a contrived sale for a fiduciary purpose. 115. This last is as follows: if a woman wishes to set aside the guardians she has and to get another, she makes a contrived sale of herself with their authorisation*; then she is remancipated by the other party to the contrived sale to the person whom she wishes, and, when she has been formally manumitted by him, she comes to have this man as guardian. He is called the 'fiduciary guardian' as will appear below. 115a. Formerly a contrived sale used also to take place for the purpose of making a will; for at one time women, with certain exceptions, had no right to make a will unless they had made a contrived sale and been remancipated and manumitted. But, on

—— | ¹ 115ᵇ. fiduciae causa *cum uiro suo fecerit coemptionem*, nihilo minus filiae loco incipit esse: nam si omnino qualibet ex causa u*xor* in manu uiri sit, placuit eam filiae iura nancisci.

116. Superest, ut exponamus, quae personae in mancipio sint. 117. Omnes igitur liberorum personae, siue masculini siue feminini sexus, quae in potestate parentis sunt, mancipari ab hoc eodem ² modo possunt, quo etiam serui mancipari possunt. 118. Idem · iuris est in earum personis, quae in manu sunt: *nam feminae a* coemptionatoribus eodem modo possunt *mancipari, quo liberi a parente possunt*, adeo quidem, *ut quamuis ea sola* apud coemptionatorem filiae loco sit. *quae ei* nupta sit, *tamen* nihilo minus etiam | quae ei 31 nup*ta* non sit³ nec ob id filiae loco sit, ab eo mancipari possit. 118ᵃ. *Sed*⁴ plerumque solum⁵ et a parentibus et a coemptionatoribus mancipantur, cum uelint parentes coemptionatoresque *ex* suo iure eas personas dimittere, sicut inferius euidentius apparebit. 119. Est autem mancipatio, ut supra quoque diximus, imaginaria quaedam uenditio: quod⁶ et ipsum ius proprium

---

1) *Krueger putat Gaium hacc fere dixisse:* eam feminam, quae fiduciae causa cum extraneo coemptionem fecerit, filiae loco apud eum non fieri; sed quae fi d u ci a e c a u s a *etc.*
2) eodem hoc V.   3) est V.   4) *suppl. Hu.*   5) tum solum *Kalb.*   6) quia V.

---

§ 115ᵇ. *cf. supra* 1, 114. *infra* 1, 118. 2, 139. 3, 14.
§ 117. *cf. Dionys.* 2, 27. *Plut. Num.* 17 *fin. infra* 1, 132. C. 8, 46 (47), 10 (*a.* 323).
§ 118. *cf. supra* 1, 114 *sq. infra* 1, 123; 137.
§ 118ᵃ. *cf. infra* 1, 132 *sq.*
§ 119. = *Boeth. l.* 3 *ad Cic. top.* 5, 28 (*p.* 322 *ed. Baiter*). *cf. Gai epit.* 1, 6, 3. *supra* 1, 113. *Ulp.* 19, 3; 4. *Varro de l. l.* 5, 163. 9, 83. *Theoph.* 1, 12, 6 (*Ferr. p.* 60). *Fest. v. rodus* p. 265 *M.* (*Bruns* II⁷, 32). *C. Aelius*(?) *apud Priscian.* 8, 16 *p.* 382 *Hertz* (*Iurispr.* I, 38 *n.* 6). *Hor. ep.* 2, 2, 158 *et Porphyr. ad h. l.* qui libram ... libripens] = *Priscian.* 6, 96 *p.* 282 *Hertz.*

the proposal of the Emperor Hadrian, the Senate remitted this requirement of making a contrived sale. [A woman who makes a fiduciary contrived sale with an outsider does not stand as a daughter to him, but 115b. she who] makes a contrived sale with her husband for a fiduciary purpose nevertheless comes to stand as a daughter. For if for any reason at all a wife should become subordinate to her husband, the received opinion is that she acquires the rights of a daughter.

116. It remains for us to describe what persons are in bondage. 117. All children, whether male or female, who are in the power of their father can be mancipated by him in the same way as slaves can. 118. The same rule applies to persons in marital subordination; for women can be mancipated by the other parties to the contrived sale in the same way as children by their father. This is so to the extent that, although she stands as a daughter to the other party only in that she is married to him, yet when she is not married and therefore does not stand as a daughter to the other party, she can nevertheless be mancipated by him. 118a. For the most part people are mancipated, both by their father and by other parties to a contrived sale, only when the fathers and other parties wish to release them from their control, as will appear more fully below. 119. Mancipation, then, as we have also said earlier, is a sort of imaginary sale; it is also part of the law peculiar to Roman citizens. It is carried out as follows. There are brought together not

ciuium Romanorum est; eaque res ita agitur: adhibitis
non minus quam[1] quinque testibus ciuibus Romanis
puberibus et praeterea alio eiusdem condicionis, qui
libram aeneam teneat, qui appellatur libripens, is, qui
mancipio accipit, rem[2] tenens ita dicit: HVNC EGO HÒ-
MINEM EX IVRE[3] QVIRITIVM MEVM ESSE AIO ISQVE MIHI
EMPTVS ESTO HOC AERE AENEAQVE LIBRA; deinde
aere percutit libram idque aes dat ei, a quo mancipio
accipit, quasi pretii loco. 120. Eo modo et seruiles
et liberae personae mancipantur; animalia quoque, quae
mancipi sunt, quo in numero habentur boues, equi,
muli, asini; item praedia tam urbana quam rustica,
quae et ipsa mancipi sunt, qualia sunt Italica, eodem
modo solent mancipari. 121. In eo solo praediorum
mancipatio a ceterorum mancipatione differt, quod personae seruiles et liberae, item animalia, quae mancipi
sunt, nisi in praesentia sint, mancipari non possunt;
32 adeo quidem, | ut eum, *qui* mancipio accipit[4], adpre-
hendere id ipsum, quod ei[5] mancipio datur, necesse sit;
unde etiam mancipatio dicitur, quia manu res capitur:
praedia uero absentia solent mancipari. 122. Ideo
autem aes et libra adhibetur, quia olim aereis tantum
nummis utebantur; et erant asses, dipundii, semisses,

---

1) quod V.   2) aes *Boethius. cf. Ihering, Geist d.
röm. Rechts* II⁵, 572, 776ᵃ. *Mommsen, Staatsr.* III, 23, 1.
3) ius͞t V.   4) accepit V.   5) et (?) in V.

---

§ 120. *cf. Ulp.* 19, 1. *supra* 1, 113; 117. *infra* 2, 19; 21;
27; 35. *Cic. pro Flacc.* 32, 80. *Tac. ann.* 1, 73.
§ 121. *cf. Ulp.* 19, 6. *Isid. orig.* 5, 25, 31 (*Bruns* II⁷, 82).
Varro de l. l. 6, 85.
§ 122. *cf. Plin. n. h.* 33, 42; 43. *Dionys.* 9, 27. *Varro de
l. l.* 5, 169. *infra* 4, 14. *Plin. n. h.* 17, 7. *Gell.* 15, 13, 11. 16,
10, 8. 20, 1, 12. *Fest. v. viginti quinque* p. 371 (*Bruns* II⁷, 46).
Isid. orig. 15, 5, 3. 16, 18, 5. 16, 25, 3. *Priscian.* 6, 66 *p.* 251
ed. Hertz. Maecian. ass. distrib. 44. *Fest. v. pendere* p. 208 *M.*
(*Bruns* II⁷, 23). *v. grave aes* p. 98 *M.* (*Bruns* II⁷, 10). *Schol.
Pers.* 2, 59. dispensatores] *cf. Fest s. h. v.* p. 72 (*Bruns* II⁷, 7).
Varro de l. l. 5, 183 (*Bruns* II⁷, 55). *Isid. orig.* 10, 67.

less than five witnesses, adult Roman citizens, together with another of the same status, who holds bronze scales* and is called the 'scale-holder'. The person who is taking by mancipation, while holding the object says the following words: 'I declare that this man is mine by quiritary right and let him be bought to me with this bronze and bronze scales.' Then he strikes the scales with the bronze, and gives it to him from whom he is taking by mancipation by way of a price. 120. Both slaves and free persons are mancipated in this way, as also animals which are capable of mancipation*. In this category are counted cattle, horses, mules and donkeys; again, any land, urban and rustic, which is itself capable of mancipation as is Italian land, is customarily mancipated in this way. 121. The mancipation of land differs from the mancipation of other things in this alone, that persons, slaves and free, and animals which are capable of mancipation, cannot be mancipated unless they are physically present. This is so true that it is necessary for the person who is accepting by mancipation to take hold of whatever is being transferred to him; this, too, is why it is called mancipation, because the thing is taken (in Latin, 'capitur') by hand (in Latin, 'manu'). Land, on the other hand, is customarily mancipated in its absence. 122. The reason, then, for the use of the bronze and the scales is because in earlier times men used only copper monies; there were the 'as'*, the double-'as', the half-'as' and the quarter-'as' and no gold or silver

quadrantes, nec ullus aureus uel argenteus nummus in usu erat, sicut ex lege XII tabularum intellegere possumus; eorumque nummorum uis et potestas non in numero erat, sed in pondere; | ——— *12 fere litt.* ——— | asses librales erant, et dipondii | ——— *12 fere litt.* ——— | unde etiam dupondius dictus *est*, *qua*si duo pondo: quod nomen adhuc[1] in usu retinetur. semis*ses* *quo*que et quadrantes pro rata scilicet portione ad pondus examinati erant. *tunc igitur et* *q*ui dab*at alicui*[2] pecuniam, non numerabat[3] eam, sed appendebat; unde serui, quibus permittitur admini*s*tratio pecuniae, dis*pe*nsatores appellati sunt. **123.** | ——— *2 vcrs.* ——— |[4] *illa* quidem, quae coemptionem fac*it*, *non* de*ducitur* *in* seruilem condicionem, *at a parentibus et a coemptionatoribus* mancipati mancipataeue seruorum loco constituuntur, adeo quidem, ut ab eo, cuius in mancipio | sunt, neque hereditates neque legata aliter capere possint[5], quam si *si*mul eodem testamento liberi esse iubeantur, sicuti iuris est in persona seruorum. sed differentiae ratio manifesta est, cum a parentibus et a coemptionatoribus isdem uerbis mancipio accipiantur[6], quibus serui; quod non similiter *fit* *i*n coemptione.

124. Videamus nunc, quo modo *ii*, qui alieno iuri *subi*ecti sunt, eo iure liberentur.

125. Ac prius de his dispiciamus, qui in potestate

(margin) 33

---

1) adhunc V. 2) *'possis etiam facere:* conuenienter qui dabat olim.' *Hu.* 3) adnumerabat *Hu.* 4) Si tamen quaerat aliquis, quare, si qua coemptionem fecit, differat a mancipatis *suppl. Hu., ad sensum recte.* 5) possunt V. 6) accipiunt V.

---

§ 123. *cf. supra* 1, 113. 117. *infra* 1, 138. 2, 160. 3, 114 *et Gell.* 18, 6, 9, *unde apparet quosdam uxorem, quae coemptionem fecerat, in manu mancipioque viri esse dixisse.* sicuti iuris est in persona seruorum] *cf. infra* 2, 186.

§ 124. = *I.* 1, 12 *pr.*

§ 125. *cf. supra* 1, 13 *sq.*

coin was in use, as we can understand from the Twelve Tables. The force and power of those monies lay not in their number but in their weight; ... 'asses' weighed one pound and double-'as' pieces ... this, too, is why it was called a 'dupundius', as it were, twice the weight, a name which is still kept in use. Half and quarter-'asses' also were tested for weight in due proportion. In those times, a person paying money would not count it but weigh it. This is why slaves who are permitted the administration of money are called in Latin 'dispensatores', that is, weighers-out. 123. ... certainly the woman who makes a contrived sale of herself does not fall into a servile status, but those, male and female, mancipated by fathers and by other parties to a contrived sale are in the relationship of a slave to the extent in fact that they cannot take an inheritance or legacies from the man in whose bondage they are, unless at the same time they are made free in the same will, as is the legal position in the case of slaves. The reason for the difference is obvious, since people are taken in mancipation by their fathers and other parties with the same words as are used for slaves; the same is not the case in a contrived sale.

124. **Let us now examine how dependent persons are freed from another's control.**

125. We turn first to those who are in power. 126.

sunt. 126. Et quidem serui *quem*admodum potestate
liberentur, ex his intel*legere* possumus, quae de seruis
manumittendi*s s*uperius exposuimus. 127. ¹Hi uero,
qui *in potestate* parentis sun*t, mortuo eo sui iuris fiunt.
sed hoc dis*tinctionem recipit; nam *mortuo patre* sane
omni modo filii filiaeue sui iuris efficiun*tur;* mortuo
uero auo *non omni* modo nepotes *neptes*ue *sui iuris
fiunt, sed ita si post mortem aui* in patris sui potestatem recasuri non s*unt. itaque* si moriente auo *pater
eorum et uiuat et in potestate* patris fuerit, tunc post
obi*tum aui in patris* sui potestate fiunt; si uero is,
quo tempore au*us* moritur, aut iam mor*tuus est aut
exiit de potestate *patris, tunc hi, quia in potestatem*²
eius cadere non possunt, sui iuris fiunt. 128. Cum
autem is, cui [ob aliquod maleficium ex lege Cornelia]³
aqua et igni interdicitur, ciuitatem Romanam amittat,
sequitur, ut quia⁴ eo modo ex numero ciuium Romanorum tollitur, proinde ac mortuo eo desinant liberi
in potestate eius esse: nec enim ratio patitur, ut pere-
grinae condicionis homo ciuem Romanum in potestate
habeat. pari ratione et si ei, qui in potestate parentis
sit, aqua et igni interdictum fuerit, desinit in potestate
parentis esse, quia aeque ratio non patitur, ut pere-
grinae condicionis homo in potestate sit ciuis Romani

In left margin: 34

---

1) *supplementa debentur Inst.* 2) patris *usque ad* potestatem *om.* V. 3) ob aliquod — Cornelia *del. Levy, Heidelb.
Sitz.-Ber.* 1931, 5, 38, *Solazzi.* ob aliquod maleficium *del. Albertario.* ex lege Cornelia *del. Krueger.* 4) qui V.

---

§ 126. = *I.* 1, 12 *pr.* superius] *cf. supra* 1, 21 *et quae ibi
notata sunt.*
§ 127. = *I.* 1, 12 *pr. cf. Gai epit.* 1, 6 *pr. Ulp.* 10, 2. *infra*
1, 146. 2, 156. *D.* 26, 2, 1, 2 (*Gai.* 263). 1, 6, 5 (*Ulp.* 2829).
25, 3, 3, 2 (*Ulp.* 982). 1, 7, 41 (*Mod.* 189). 1, 7, 40 *pr.* (*Mod.* 2).
Gell. 1, 12, 4. *Apul. apol. c.* 68.
§ 128. = *I.* 1, 12, 1. *cf. Gai epit.* 1, 6, 1. *Ulp.* 10, 3.
infra 1, 161. *D.* 38, 10, 4, 11 (*Mod.* 148). proinde ac mor-
tuo] *D.* 37, 4, 1, 8 (*Ulp.* 1099). 38, 2, 4, 2 (*Paul.* 595). *infra* 3, 153.

For slaves these ways can be gathered from what we have already said about manumission. 127. By contrast, people in paternal power become independent on the head of the family's death. But distinctions must be made. The death of a father who is head of the family makes his sons and daughters completely independent at once. The death of a grandfather does not always do so, but only if the grandchildren do not fall into their father's power on their grandfather's death. If at the time of their grandfather's death their father is alive and in his power, they then pass into the power of their father. If at the grandfather's death their father is already dead or has emerged from paternal power, the grandchildren cannot pass into their father's power; they become independent. 128. Then, since someone who is banished from home and hearth [under the Cornelian law for some crime] loses his Roman citizenship, it follows that his removal from the Roman citizen body releases his children from his power just as though he had died; for it is contrary to reason that a man whose status is that of a foreigner should have a Roman citizen in his power. The same logic means that a dependent person who is banished from home and hearth passes out of the power of the head of his family, because it would be equally contrary to reason for a man of foreign status to be in the power of a parent who is a Roman citizen. 129. But if the head of

parentis. 129. Quod si ab hostibus captus fuerit parens, quamuis seruus[1] hostium fiat, tamen pendet ius liberorum propter ius postliminii, quo[2] hi, qui ab hostibus capti sunt, si reuersi fuerint, omnia pristina iura recipiunt; itaque reuersus habebit liberos in potestate: si uero illic mortuus sit, erunt quidem liberi sui iuris; sed utrum ex hoc tempore, quo mortuus est apud hostes parens, an ex illo, quo[2] ab hostibus captus est, dubitari potest. ipse quoque filius neposue si ab hostibus captus fuerit, similiter dicemus propter ius postliminii potestatem quoque parentis in suspenso esse. 130. Praeterea exeunt liberi uirilis sexus de parentis potestate, si flamines Diales inaugurentur, et | feminini 35 sexus, si uirgines Vestales capiantur. 131. Olim quoque, quo tempore populus Romanus in Latinas regiones colonias deducebat, qui iussu parentis in coloniam Latinam nomen dedissent, desinebant in potestate parentis esse, quia efficerentur alterius ciuitatis ciues. 132. *Praeterea* emancipatione desinunt liberi in potestate[3] parentum esse. sed filius quidem tribus man-

---

1) seruo V.   2) quod V.   3) potestatem V.

---

§ 129. = *I*. 1, 12, 5. *cf. Gai epit.* 1, 6, 2. *Ulp.* 10, 4. *Paul.* 2, 25, 1.   seruus hostium] *cf. I.* 1, 3, 4.   *D.* 1, 5, 5, 1 (*Marcian.* 45).   pendet ius] *cf. D.* 14, 6, 1, 1 (*Ulp.* 874). 38, 7, 2, 3 (*Ulp.* 1198).   ius postliminii] *cf. D.* 49, 15, 19 (*Paul.* 1893). *Boeth. l.* 4 *ad Cic. top.* 8, 36 (*p.* 336 *ed. Baiter*).   *Fest. s. v.* *postliminium p.* 218 (*Bruns* II[7], 25).   *Isid. orig.* 5, 27, 28. dubitari potest] *cf. D.* 49, 15, 22, 2 (*Iul.* 761). 49, 15, 12, 1 (*Tryph.* 13). 49, 15, 18 (*Ulp.* 2799).   similiter *etc.*] *cf. D.* 49, 15, 14 *pr.* (*Pomp.* 424). 28, 2, 31 (*Paul.* 1626).

§ 130. *cf. Ulp.* 10, 5. *infra* 1, 145. 3, 114. *Tac. ann.* 4, 16. *Gell.* 1, 12, 9. *Plut. Num.* 10 (*Bruns* I[7], 9).   *Ambros. de virgin.* 1, 4, 15. *epist. ad Valentin. I.* 18, 11.

§ 131. *cf. Cic. pro Caec.* 33, 98. *pro domo* 30, 78. *pro Balbo* 11, 27—13, 31. *Dosith.* § 6.   *Boeth. l.* 2 *ad Cic. top.* 4, 18 (*p.* 302 *ed. Baiter*).

§ 132. *cf. Gai epit.* 1, 6, 3. *Ulp.* 10, 1. *I.* 1, 12, 6. *infra* 1, 135. 2, 141. 3, 6. 4, 79. *D.* 28, 3, 8, 1 (*Ulp.* 2510). *C.* 8, 48

the family is captured by enemies, although he becomes the slave of the enemy, the status of the children is in suspense because of his right of rehabilitation*. By this, **prisoners of war who come back recover all their former rights. He will have his children in his power again when he gets back. If** he dies as a prisoner, his children will be **independent**; but there is room for doubt as to whether this dates from the time of the father's death in enemy hands or from the moment of his capture. **Similarly, if a son or grandson is captured by the enemy, his potential for rehabilitation puts the head of the family's power into suspense. 130.** Moreover, male children leave paternal power if they are ordained as priests of Jupiter, females if they are chosen as Vestal Virgins. 131. In former times, at the period when the Roman people were founding colonies in the districts of Latium, those who at the command of a parent submitted their names for membership of a Latin colony ceased to be in paternal power, because they were made citizens of another state. 132. **Moreover, children also emerge from paternal power by emancipation.** A son leaves paternal power after three mancipations; other children, on the other

cipationibus, ceteri uero liberi siue masculini sexus
siue feminini una mancipatione exeunt de parentium
potestate: lex enim XII tabularum tantum in persona
filii de tribus mancipationibus loquitur his uerbis: 'si
pater *ter*[1] filium uenum du*it*, a patre filius liber esto'.
eaque res ita agitur: mancipat pater filium alicui; is
eum uindicta manumittit: eo facto reuertitur in potestatem patris; is eum iterum mancipat uel eidem uel
alii (sed in usu est eidem mancipari) isque eum postea
similiter uindicta manumittit; eo facto rursus in potestatem patris reuertitur[2]; tertio pater eum mancipat
uel eidem uel alii (sed hoc in usu est, ut eidem man-
cip*etur*) *eaque* mancipatione *des*init *in* potestate patris
esse, etiamsi nondum manumissus sit, sed adhuc in
causa mancipii.[3] ─────────────────────────────── 4

³⁶
t. s.

133. [5]*Admonendi autem sumus liberum esse arbitrium
ei, qui filium et ex eo nepotem in potestate habebit, filium
quidem de potestate dimittere*[6], *nepotem uero in potestate
retinere: uel ex diuerso filium quidem in potestate retinere, nepotem uero manumittere, uel omnes sui iuris efficere. eadem et de pronepote dicta esse intellegemus.*

---

1) ter *post* pater *verisimilius exidit quam post* filium; *quamquam Ulp.* 10, 1 *obstat.*   2) fueri reuertitur V.   3) eaque —
mancipii *del. Solazzi, Athenaeum* 1927, 129.   4) *in pag.* 36 *paucissimis exceptis nihil legi potuit; videtur Gaius hic primum
adiecisse filium tertia manumissione sui iuris effici; cf. Theoph.*
1, 12, 6. *haec quae exceperint, apparet ex Gai epit.* 1, 6, 3 *med.:*
'Tamen cum . . . . in hereditate succedit'. *cf. Inst.* 1, 12, 6 *verba*
'Et tunc ex edicto praetoris' *etc.*   5) *suppl. a Goesch. ex
Inst.* 1, 12, 7 *et Dig.* 1, 7, 28.   6) de potestate dimittere *Inst.*
potestate dimittere *Dig. cf.* § 134.

---

(49), 6 (*a.* 531). *Dionys.* 2, 27. *Boeth. l.* 2 *ad Cic. top.* 4, 19
(*p.* 303, 17 *sq. ed. Baiter). C. I. L.* VI 1527 *l.* 16 (*Bruns*
1[7], 321). *P. Lips. Inv.* 136 *ed. Mitteis Lips.* 1912 (*P. M. Meyer,
Iur. Papyr. nr.* 9; *Girard, Textes*[4] *p.* 824).

§ 133. *cf. Gai. epit.* 1, 6, 3. D. 37, 4, 7 (*Gai.* 281). 37, 8, 3
(*Marcell.* 121). 38, 6, 6 (*Ulp.* 1101). 37, 8, 1, 4 (*Ulp.* 1124).
37, 4, 6, 3 (*Paul.* 579). 37, 8, 4 (*Mod.* 117). 37, 4, 21 (*Mod.* 116).

hand, whether male or female, after one; for the Twelve Tables speaks of mancipation only for a son as follows: 'If a father puts his son up for sale three times, the son is to be free of the father'. The process is as follows. The father mancipates his son to someone, who manumits him by rod; by this act, the son returns into the power of his father. He again mancipates him, either to the same person or to someone else (but it is usual for him to be mancipated to the same person) who then again manumits him by rod, and by this act he again returns into the power of his father. The father mancipates him for a third time, either to the same person or to someone else (but it is usual that he be mancipated to the same person), and by that mancipation he ceases to be in the power of his father, although he has not yet been manumitted but is still in a state of bondage. ... [Whole page is largely illegible.]

133. **We should note that where the head of the family has a son and by that son a grandchild, it is a matter entirely for him whether to discharge the son from his power but keep the grandchild or, vice versa, to discharge the grandchild and keep the son, or to make them all independent. It is the same for great-grandchildren.**

134. *Praeterea parentes etiam liberos in adoptionem datos in potestate habere desinunt. et in filio quidem, si in adoptionem datur, tres mancipationes*[1] | et duae 37 intercedentes manumissiones proinde fiunt, ac fieri solent, cum ita eum pater de potestate dimittit, ut sui iuris efficiatur. deinde aut patri remancipatur, et ab eo is, qui adoptat, uindicat apud praetorem filium suum esse, et illo contra non uin*di*cante *a* praetore uindicanti filius addicitur, aut non remancipatur patri, *sed* ab eo uindicat is, qui adop*tat, apud* quem *in tertia*[2] mancipatione est: sed sane commodius est patri remancipari.[3] in ceteris uero liberorum personis, seu masculini seu feminini sexus, una scilicet mancipatio sufficit, et aut remancipantur[4] parenti aut non remancipantur.[4] eadem et in prouinciis apud praesidem prouinciae solent fieri. 135. Qui ex filio semel iterumue mancipato conceptus est, licet post tertiam mancipationem patris sui nascatur, tamen in aui potestate est, et ideo ab eo et emancipari et in adoptionem dari potest. at is, qui ex eo filio conceptus est, qui in tertia mancipatione est, non nascitur in aui potestate: sed eum Labeo quidem existimat in eiusdem mancipio esse, cuius et pater sit: utimur autem hoc iure, ut quamdiu pater eius in mancipio sit, pendeat ius eius, et si quidem pater eius ex mancipatione manumissus erit, cadat in eius potestatem, si uero is, dum in man-

---

1) *ex Goescheni fere restitutione ad sensum demonstrandum* supplevit *Hu.* 2) sed — tertia *partim Scheurl, partim Hu.* 3) *sc. ab eo, cui in adoptionem daturus est, ne aliam personam, cui mancipetur, adhibere necesse sit. cf. Scheurl, de modis liberos in adopt. dandi, Erlang.* 1851. sed sane — remancipari *del. Solazzi, l. c.* 118. 4) remancipatur V.

---

§ 134. *cf. Plin. ep.* 8, 18, 4. *Gell.* 5, 19, 3. *Suet. Aug.* 64. *Cic. de fin.* 1, 7, 24. *Tert. apolog.* 9, 7. *I.* 1, 12, 8. *C.* 8, 47 (48), 11 (a. 530). *infra* 2, 141. 3, 6. 4, 79.
§ 135. *cf. I.* 1, 12, 9. *supra* 1, 132; 89.

134. Moreover, parents cease to have in their power those children whom they give in adoption. In the case of giving a son in adoption, three mancipations and two intermediate manumissions accordingly take place (as is the practice when the father releases him from power so as to make him independent). He may then be remancipated to his father, from whom the person making the adoption claims him as his son before the praetor; on the father's not making a counter-claim, he is assigned by the praetor as son to the claimant. If he is not remancipated to his father the person making the adoption claims him from the man to whom he was mancipated for the third time. It is, however, a good deal more convenient for him to be remancipated to his father. But for other children in power, whether male or female, one mancipation is enough, and they are either remancipated to the father or not. In the provinces the practice is the same before the provincial governor. 135. A child begotten by the son in power after the first or second mancipation, although he is born after his father's third mancipation, is still in the power of his grandfather and can therefore be emancipated and given in adoption by him. However, a child begotten by the son after the third mancipation is not born in the power of his grandfather. Labeo certainly judges him to be in bondage to the same man as his father is; however our current law is that as long as the father is in bondage his legal state is in suspense; if indeed the child's father is manumitted from bondage, the child falls into his power but if the father dies while in bondage the child becomes independent. 135a. The

38 cipio sit, de|cesserit, sui iuris fiat. 135ª. Eadem sci-
licet | —— — *vv. 2* —— |¹ ut supra diximus, quod in
filio faciunt tres mancipationes, hoc facit una manci-
patio in nepote. 136. | —— *vv. 2¾* —— |² Maximi et
Tuberonis³ cautum est, u*t* haec quod ad sacra tantum
uideatur in manu esse, quod uero ad ceteras causas
proinde habeatur, atque si in manum non conuenisset.
*eae uero mulieres, quae in manum conueniunt per
coemptionem*⁴, potestate parentis liberantur; nec interest,
an in uiri sui manu sint an extranei, quamuis hae
solae loco filiarum habeantur, quae in uiri manu *sunt*.

137. | —— *vv. 3* —— |⁵ desinunt in manu esse, et
si ex ea mancipatione manumissae fuerint, sui iuris
effici*untur*. 137ª. | —— *vv. 3½* —— |⁶ nihil*o* magis
39 potest cogere, | quam et⁷ filia patrem. sed filia quidem

---

1) *Krueger Huschkium secutus ita supplet:* dicemus de eo,
qui ex nepote semel mancipato necdum manumisso conceptus
fuerit. nam. 2) *Krueger ita fere ad sensum suppleri posse
censet:* Praeterea mulieres, quae in manum conueniunt, in
patris potestate esse desinunt. sed in confarreatis nuptiis de
flaminica Diali senatus consulto ex relatione. 3) *Paulus Fabius
Maximus et Q. Aelius Tubero css. a. 743 u. = 11 a. Chr.; de ICtis
Cornelio Maximo et Q. Aelio Tuberone (Pomp. Dig. 1, 2, 2, 45; 46)
cogitavit Hu.* 4) eae—coemptionem *ad sensum suppl. Hu.*
5) *Krueger ex parte Huschkium secutus ita fere suppl.:* In manu
autem esse mulieres desinunt iisdem modis, quibus filiae familias potestate patris liberantur; sicut igitur filiae familias una
mancipatione de potestate patris exeunt, ita eae, quae in manu
sunt, una mancipatione. 6) *in* V *legitur lin.* 21 quae; *lin.*
22/23 cogere coemptionatorem; *lin.* 23/24 et cui ipsa velit.
Krueger sic fere ad sensum supplet: inter eam uero, qu a e
cum extraneo, et eam, quae cum uiro suo coemptionem fecerit,
hoc interest, quod illa quidem cogere coemptionatorem
potest, ut se remancipet, c u i i p s a u e l i t, haec autem uirum
suum. *Hu. similiter.* 7) et *delendum*?

---

§ 135ª. *cf. supra* 1, 132; 134.
§ 136. *cf. supra* 1, 112; 114; 115ᵇ. *Tac. ann.* 4, 16.
§ 137. *cf. supra* 1, 127.
§ 137ª. *cf. supra* 1, 118; 118ª. *I.* 1, 12, 10. *Fest. v. reman-
cipatam p.* 277 (*Bruns* II⁷, 31).

same, indeed, [we may say about the child who is begotten by a grandson after one mancipation but before manumission. For,] as we have said above, one mancipation does for a grandson what three mancipations do for a son. 136. [Moreover, women who fall into marital subordination cease to be in the power of their father. But for those married by sharing of bread as the wife of a priest of Jupiter,] it is provided [by a resolution of the Senate moved by] Maximus and Tubero that such a woman is regarded as being in marital subordination only so far as religious observances are concerned; in other matters, on the other hand, she is viewed just as if she had not fallen into marital subordination. However, women who have fallen into subordination by a contrived sale are freed from their parent's power; nor does it matter if they are subordinate to their husband or to some other person, although only those women who are subordinate to a husband are viewed as standing to him as a daughter.

137. [Women cease to be in subordination in the same ways as daughters are freed from paternal power. Just as daughters emerge from power by one mancipation so, by one mancipation, do women] cease to be subordinate; if such women should be manumitted after that mancipation they are made independent. 137a. [The difference between a woman who has made a contrived sale with a third party and her who has made one with her husband is that the former can compel the other party to remancipate her to whomever she wishes, but] the latter can no more compel [her husband] than can a daughter her father. A daughter certainly cannot in any manner compel

nullo modo patrem potest cogere, etiam si adoptiua
sit: haec autem *uirum* repudio misso proinde compel-
lere potest, atque si ei numquam nupta fuisset.
138. Ii, qui in causa mancipii sunt, quia seruorum
loco habentur, uindicta, censu, testamento manumissi
sui iuris fiunt. 139. Nec tamen in hoc casu lex Aelia
Sentia locum habet: itaque nihil requirimus, cuius
aetatis sit is, qui manumittit et qui manumittitur; ac
ne illud quidem, an patronum creditoremue manumis-
sor habeat; ac ne numerus quidem lege Fufia Caninia[1]
finitus in his personis locum habet. 140. Quin etiam
inuito quoque eo, cuius in mancipio sunt, censu libertatem consequi possunt, excepto eo, quem pater ea
lege mancipio dedit, ut sibi remancipetur; nam quodam modo tunc pater potestatem propriam reseruare
sibi uidetur eo ipso, quod[2] **mancipio recipit.**[3] ac ne is
quidem dicitur inuito eo, cuius in mancipio est, censu
libertatem consequi, quem pater ex noxali causa mancipio dedit, ueluti quod furti eius nomine damnatus
est et eum mancipio actori dedit: nam hunc actor
pro pecunia habet. 141. In summa admonendi sumus
aduersus eos, quos in mancipio habemus, nihil nobis |
contumeliose facere licere; alioquin **iniuriarum** tene- 40
bimur. ac ne diu quidem in eo iure detinentur homines, sed plerumque hoc fit **dicis gratia**[4] uno momento[5];
nisi scilicet ex noxali causa **mancipantur.**[6]
142. Transeamus nunc ad aliam diuisionem. nam
ex his personis, quae neque in potestate neque in

---

1) legis Fuf. Can. V.   2) quo V.   3) nam — recipit
del. Grosso. 4) gratiam V.   5) sed — momento *del. Solazzi.*
Glosse a Gaio 165. *De* §§ 138—141 *cf. Beseler, Studi Albertoni*
1, 435.   6) manciparentur V.

§ 138. *cf. supra* 1, 123. *infra* 2, 160. 3, 114.
§ 139. *cf. supra* 1, 38; 18; 42: 47.
§ 140. *cf. infra* 4, 75; 79. *Coll.* 2, 3 (*Pap.* 62). *I.* 4, 8, 7.
D. 43, 29, 3, 4 (*Ulp.* 1616).
§ 141. *cf. supra* 1, 118[8]; 132. *infra* 4, 79. *Paul. sent.* 2, 25, 2.
§ 142. = *I.* 1, 13 *pr.*

her father, even if she is an adoptive daughter; but once a woman has sent notice of divorce, she can compel her husband just as if she had never been married to him.

138. Those who are in bondage, because they stand in the relationship of slaves, become independent after being manumitted, whether by rod, by inclusion in the census or by will. 139. The Aelian-Sentian Act, however, has no place in this situation. And so we do not inquire into the ages of the persons granting freedom and freed, nor indeed whether the grantor has a patron or creditor. And the limits on numbers in the Fufian-Caninian Act have no place for these people. 140. Indeed, they can obtain freedom by inclusion in the census even against the wishes of the person in whose bondage they are, with the exception of someone whose father gave by mancipation with the provision that he be remancipated to himself. The father is then regarded as, in a certain sense, keeping for himself his own, because he is taking him back by mancipation. Nor, indeed, may someone whose father has handed him over by mancipation on account of a noxal action*, for instance, because the father was condemned in his son's name for theft and gave him in bondage to the pursuer*, be said to obtain freedom by inclusion in the census against the wishes of the person in whose bondage he is; for the pursuer is holding him instead of money compensation. 141. In brief, we must note that we have no right to abuse those whom we hold in bondage; otherwise, we are liable for contempt*. Men are in fact not held long in this legal condition, but generally it is only for the moment, for form's sake, unless indeed they are mancipated on noxal grounds.

142. **Let us now pass on to another classification. Among those who are not in the power** of father or owner, nor in marital subordination, nor in bondage,

manu neque in mancipio sunt, quaedam uel in tutela
sunt uel in curatione, quaedam neutro iure tenentur.
uideamus igitur, quae in tutela, quae in curatione sint:
ita enim intellegemus ceteras[1] personas, quae neutro
iure tenentur. 143. Ac prius dispiciamus de his, quae
in tutela sunt.

144. Permissum est itaque parentibus liberis, quos
in potestate sua habent, testamento tutores dare: masculini quidem sexus inpuberibus, *feminini uero inpuberibus puberibus*que, *uel*[2] cum nuptae sint. ueteres enim
uoluerunt feminas, etiamsi perfectae aetatis sint, propter
animi leuitatem in tutela esse. 145. Itaque si quis
filio filiaeque testamento tutorem dederit et ambo ad
pubertatem peruenerint, filius quidem desinit habere
tutorem, filia uero nihilo minus in tutela permanet:
tantum enim ex lege Iulia et Papia Poppaea[3] iure liberorum a tutela liberantur feminae. loquimur autem |
41 exceptis uirginibus Vestalibus, quas etiam ueteres in
honorem[4] sacerdotii liberas esse uoluerunt: itaque etiam
lege XII tabularum cautum est. 146. Nepotibus autem
neptibusque ita demum possumus testamento[5] tutores
dare, si post mortem nostram in patris sui potestatem
iure[6] recasuri non sint. itaque si filius meus mortis

---

1) intellegemus ceteras *Inst. Iust.* intellegimus de ceteris V. intellegemus deinde ceteras *Polenaar.*   2) feminini—uel *suppl. Hu.*   3) Popeia V.   4) honores V.
5) testes V.   6) *om. Inst. Iust.; del. Hu., Krueger.*

§ 143. = *I.* 1, 13 *pr.*
§ 144. *cf. infra* 1, 190. *Gai epit.* 1, 7, 2. *Ulp.* 11, 1; 15.
Fr. Vat. 229 (*Paul.* 2057). *D.* 26, 2, 1 *pr.* (*Gai.* 263). 26, 2,
20, 1 (*Paul.* 557). *I.* 1, 13, 3. *infra* 1, 190. 2, 240; 289. *Liv.*
34, 2. *Cic. pro Mur.* 12, 27. *Boeth. l.* 2 *ad Cic. Top.* 4, 18
(*p.* 302 *B.*). *l.* 4 *ad top.* 11, 46 (*p.* 341 *B.*). *Isid. orig.* 9, 7, 30.
C. I. L. VI 10231 (*Bruns* I⁷, 336).
§ 145. *cf. infra* 1, 194. 3, 44. *Ulp.* 11, 14; 15. *Plut. Num.*
10 (*Bruns* I⁷, 9). *Dio* 56, 10, 2; 3. lege Iulia] *a.* 736 *u.* = 18 *a.*
Chr. Papia Poppaea] *a.* 9 *p. Chr.*
§ 146. = *I.* 1, 13, 3. *cf. Gai epit.* 1, 7, 2. *D.* 26, 2, 1, 2
(*Gai.* 263). *supra* 1, 127.

some are under guardianship or supervision* and others are free from both these restraints. We must look first at those under guardianship and supervision; in that way we will also see which persons are free from both these restraints. 143. We start with those under guardianship.

144. **Where the head of a family has children in his power he is allowed to appoint guardians for them by will.** That is, for males while under puberty but for females however old they are, even when they are married. For it was the wish of the old lawyers* that women, even those of full age, should be in guardianship as being scatterbrained. 145. And so if someone appoints a guardian in his will for his son and his daughter and both of them reach puberty, the son ceases to have a guardian but the daughter still continues in guardianship. It is only under the Julian and Papian-Poppaean Acts that women are released from guardianship by the privilege of children*. We speak, however, with the exception of the Vestal Virgins, whom even the old lawyers wished to be free of restraint in recognition of their priesthood; this is also provided in the Twelve Tables. 146. **We can appoint guardians by will for our grandsons and granddaughters only if our death will not put them into the power of their father. And so, if my son is**

meae tempore in potestate mea sit, nepotes[1] ex eo non
poterunt[2] ex testamento meo habere tutorem, quamuis
in potestate mea fuerint; scilicet quia mortuo me in
patris sui potestate futuri sunt.[3] 147. Cum tamen in
compluribus aliis causis postumi pro iam natis habeantur, et in hac causa placuit non minus postumis
quam iam natis testamento tutores dari posse, si
modo in ea causa sint, ut si uiuis nobis nascantur[4],
in potestate nostra fiant. hos *enim* etiam heredes instituere possumus, cum extraneos postumos heredes instituere permissum non sit.[5] 148. *Vxori,* quae in manu
est, proinde ac[6] filiae, item nurui, quae in filii manu
est, proinde ac nepti tutor dari potest. 149. Rectissime
autem tutor sic dari potest: LVCIVM TITIVM LIBERIS
MEIS TVTOREM DO *uel* VXORI MEAE[7] TVTOREM DO. sed
et si ita scriptum sit: LIBERIS MEIS uel VXORI MEAE
TITIVS TVTOR ESTO, recte datus intellegitur. 150. In
persona tamen | uxoris, quae in manu est, recepta est 42
etiam tutoris optio, id est ut liceat ei permittere,
quem uelit ipsa, tutorem sibi optare, hoc modo:
TITIAE VXORI MEAE TVTORIS OPTIONEM DO. quo
casu licet uxori *tutorem optare*[8] uel in omnes res uel

---

1) nepotes quos V. quos *om. Inst.*   2) potesint V. pote-
rint *Lachmann.*   3) sint V.   4) nascuntur V.   5) sint V.
6) ac si V.   7) uel uxori meae *Hu.* lic V.   8) tutorem
optare *suppl. Lachmann.*

§ 147. = *I.* 1, 13, 4.   *cf. D.* 26, 2, 1, 1 (*Gai.* 263).   pro
iam natis] *cf. D.* 38, 16, 7 (*Cels.* 235). 1, 5, 7 (*Paul.* 1263). 50,
16, 231 (*Paul.* 1908). postumis tutores dari] *cf. I.* 1, 14, 5 =
D. 26, 2, 5 (*Ulp.* 2533) *et* 6 (*Ulp.* 2831). *D.* 3, 5, 28 (29) (*Call.* 69).
26, 2, 16, 5 (*Ulp.* 2850). 26, 2, 19, 2 (*Ulp.* 1016). *Suet. Caes.* 83.
hos enim etiam heredes] *cf. infra* 2, 130; 242; 287.
§ 148. *cf. supra* 1, 110 *sq. infra* 2, 159.
§ 149. *cf. infra* 2, 289. *Fr. Vat.* 229 (*Paul.* 2057). *D.*
26, 2, 23 (*Afr.* 106). 26, 2, 33 (*Iav.* 228). 26, 2, 8, 3 (*Ulp.* 2671).
26, 2, 10, 4 (*Ulp.* 2830). 26, 2, 16 *pr.* (*Ulp.* 2850). 26, 2, 32, 2
(*Paul.* 1528).
§ 150. *cf. Liv.* 39, 19. *Plaut. Truc.* 4, 4, 6 = 859. *lex
Salp.* 22 (*Bruns* I[7], 143).

in my **power at the time of** my **death** my
grandchildren by him cannot be given guardians in
my **will, despite being in** my **power; for obviously**
on my **death they will be in the power of their own**
father. 147. **Since for many other intents and**
purposes posthumous children are treated as
though born before the death, it is received opinion
that guardians should be appointed by will for
them just as for those already born. This applies
where, had they been born during our **lifetime, they**
would have come into our **power.** For we can
institute these children our heirs, even though we may
not institute as heirs the posthumous children of
outsiders*. 148. A guardian can be appointed for a
wife in marital subordination just as if she were a
daughter, as also for a daughter-in-law who is
subordinate to one's son, just as if she were a
granddaughter. 149. The most correct form of
appointment as guardian is: 'I appoint Lucius Titius
as guardian to my children' or 'as guardian to my
wife'. But if it is written as: 'Let Titius be guardian to
my children' or 'to my wife', he is taken as correctly
appointed. 150. In the case of a wife in marital
subordination, a choice of guardians is also accepted;
that is, so that she may lawfully be allowed to choose
whom she herself wishes as her tutor, in this form: 'I
give my wife Titia choice of guardian'. In that event,
it is lawful for the wife to choose a guardian, either for
all purposes or perhaps for one or two. 151. The choice

in unam forte aut duas.[1] 151. Ceterum aut plena optio
datur aut angusta. 152. Plena ita dari solet, ut proxime supra diximus. angusta ita dari solet: TITIAE
VXORI MEAE TVTORIS OPTIONEM DVMTAXAT[2] SEMEL DO,
aut DVMTAXAT BIS DO. 153. Quae optiones plurimum
inter se differunt[3]: nam quae plenam optionem habet,
potest semel et bis et ter et saepius tutorem optare;
quae uero angus*tam* habet optionem, si dumtaxat semel
data est optio, amplius quam semel optare non potest[4],
si tantum bis, amplius quam bis optandi facultatem
non habet.[5] 154. Vocantur autem hi, qui nominatim
testamento tutores dantur, datiui, qui ex optione su-
muntur, optiui.

155. Quibus testamento quidem tutor datus non
sit, iis ex lege XII *tabularum* agnati sunt tutores, qui
uocantur legitimi. 156. Sunt autem agnati per uirilis
sexus personas cognatione iuncti, quasi a patre cognati,
uelut i frater eodem patre natus, fratris filius neposue

43
t. s.

ex eo, item patruus et patrui | filius et nepos ex eo.
at hi, qui per feminini sexus personas cognatione con-
iunguntur, non sunt agnati, sed alias naturali iure
cognati. itaque inter auunculum et sororis filium non
agnatio est, sed cognatio. item amitae, materterae
filius non est mihi agnatus, sed cognatus, et inuicem
scilicet ego[6] illi eodem iure coniungor, quia qui nascun-

---

1) quo casu—duas *del. Solazzi, Aegyptus* 2, 177.   2) tutoris
optionem dumtaxat *Hu.* dumtaxat tutoris optionem V.   3) differant V.   4) poten̄ V.   5) habetis V.   6) scilicet ego *Hu.*
scilicet sic eo V. *Poeschmann coni.*: et inuicem. scilicet
etsi ego illi agnatus sum, non tamen filio illius eodem iure
etc. collato Theoph. 1, 15, 1; *Polenaar delet* scilicet—coniungor.

---

§ 154. *cf. Ulp.* 11, 14.
§ 155. = *I.* 1, 15 *pr. cf. Gai epit.* 1, 7, 1. *Ulp.* 11, 3. *D.*
26, 4, 1 *pr.* (*Ulp.* 2529). 26, 4, 5 *pr.* (*Ulp.* 1000). *C.* 5, 30, 2
(*a.* 293). *Nov. Iust.* 118, 5.
§ 156. = *I.* 1, 15, 1. *D.* 26, 4, 7. *cf. Gai epit.* 1, 7, 1. *Ulp.*
11, 4. *Isid. orig.* 9, 6, 1; 2. *infra* 3. 10.

given may, however, be full or restricted. 152. Full choice is usually given in the form set out just above. Restricted choice is normally given as follows: 'I give my wife Titia one choice only of guardian' or 'two choices only'. 153. There is a great difference between these types of choice. The woman who has full choice can choose a guardian once, twice, three times and again and again; on the other hand, she who has restricted choice, if she has been given one choice only cannot choose more than once; if only two choices, she has no opportunity of choosing more than twice. 154. Guardians who are appointed by name in a will are called appointed guardians, those taken as a result of choice 'optative'.

155. **Under the Twelve Tables agnates* are made guardians when there is no appointment by will. We call them statutory guardians. 156. Agnates are relatives through the male sex, loosely relations through the father, as for instance his brother (if born of the same father), that brother's son, and a grandson through that son, also his father's brother, that uncle's son, and a grandson through that son. People related through females are not agnates. They are related in a way which is recognised by the law of nature, as cognates*. And** so between an uncle and the son of his sister there is not agnation but cognation. **Again, if my father's or** mother's **sister has a son he is not** my **agnate. To me he is a cognatic relative, as, of course, in the same system I am to him. On birth, babies enter the**

tur, patris, non matris familiam secuntur. 157. Sed
olim quidem, quantum ad legem XII tabularum attinet,
etiam feminae agnatos habebant tutores. sed postea
lex Claudia lata est, quae[1], quod ad feminas attinet,
agnatorum[2] tutelas sustulit: itaque masculus quidem
inpubes fratrem puberem aut patruum habet tutorem;
femina uero talem habere tutorem non potest. 158. Sed
adgnationis quidem ius kapitis diminutione perimitur,
cognationis uero ius eo modo non commutatur, quia
ciuilis ratio ciuilia quidem iura corrumpere potest,
naturalia uero non potest.[3] 159. Est autem kapitis diminutio prioris *status*[4] permutatio: eaque tribus modis·
accidit: nam aut maxima est kapitis diminutio[5] aut
minor, quam quidam mediam uocant, aut minima.
160. Maxima est kapitis diminutio, cum aliquis simul
et ciuitatem et libertatem amittit; quae accidit in-
censis, qui ex forma censua|li uenire[6] iubentur: quod
ius | ——— vv. 1½ ——— |[7], qui contra eam legem in
urbe Roma domicilium habuerint; item feminae, quae
ex senatus consulto Claudiano ancillae fiunt eorum dominorum, quibus inuitis et denuntiantibus[8] cum seruis

44
t. s.

---

1) q. V.   2) *add. Goeschen.*   3) utique *Inst. Iust. cf.*
§ 64.   4) capitis V.   5) dimidia V.   6) ueniri V.
7) *post* ius *legitur* p, *in sequenti versu* ex leg.   8) denuntiantibus dominis V. denuntiantibus nihilo minus *Hu.*

---

§ 157. *cf. infra* 1, 171. *Ulp.* 11, 8. *C. Th.* 3, 17, 2 (*a.* 326).
C. 5, 30, 3 (*a.* 472). *C. I. L.* VI 1527 *l.* 14. 15 (*Bruns* I', 322).
  § 158. = *I.* 1, 15, 3. *cf. infra* 3, 27; 51. *Ulp.* 11, 9.
D. 26, 4, 5, 5 (*Ulp.* 1012). 26, 4, 3, 9 (*Ulp.* 2838). 4, 5, 7 *pr.*
(*Paul.* 222). ciuilis ratio] *cf. D.* 50, 17, 8 (*Pomp.* 430). 4, 5, 8
(*Gai.* 107).
  § 159. = *I.* 1, 16 *pr. cf. Ulp.* 11, 10. *D.* 4, 5, 1 (*Gai.* 106). 4, 5, 11
(*Paul.* 1628). *Cic. top.* 6, 29. *Fest. v. deminutus capite p.* 70 (*Bruns*
II', 7). *Boeth. l.* 2 *ad Cic. top.* 4, 18 (*p.* 302 *B.*). *Auson. Griph.* 65.
  § 160. *cf. I.* 1, 16, 1. *Ulp.* 11, 11. incensis] *cf. Dionys.* 4, 15 *in*
fine. 5, 75. *Liv.* 1, 44, 1. *Cic. p. Caec.* 34, 99. qui contra eam legem]
cf. supra 1, 27. senatus consulto Claudiano] *cf. supra* 1, 84; 91.

family of their father, not of their mother. 157.
Certainly in former times, under the regime of the
Twelve Tables, women also had their agnates as
guardians. Subsequently, however, a Claudian Act
was passed which abolished the guardianship of
agnates so far as it applies to women. And so a male
below puberty can certainly have his adult brother or
his paternal uncle as guardian but a woman cannot
have such a guardian. 158. **The agnatic tie is broken
by status-loss*. Cognatic relationship, by contrast,
is not affected by status-loss. While the logic of
state law can destroy rights founded on the state
law, it cannot affect rights founded on the law of
nature.** 159. **Status-loss is the** exchange **of one
status for another, and happens in three ways,
namely in the first, the second – also called
intermediate – or the third degree.** 160. **Status-loss
in the first degree happens when a person loses his
citizenship and his liberty together;** this happens to
those who evade the census, who in accordance with
the census regulations are ordered to be sold. This rule
… [applies to capitulated aliens under the Aelian-
Sentian Act] who contrary to that statute make their
home in Rome; again, women who under the Claudian
Resolution of the Senate become the slaves of the
owners of those slaves with whom they have cohabited
against the will and formal notification of the owners.

eorum coierint. **161.** Minor siue media est kapitis diminutio[1], cum ciuitas amittitur, libertas retinetur[2]; quod accidit ei, cui aqua et igni interdictum fuerit. **162.** Minima est capitis diminutio, cum et ciuitas et libertas retinetur[2], sed status hominis conmutatur; quod accidit in his, qui adoptantur, item in his, quae coemptionem faciunt, et in his, qui mancipio dantur quique ex mancipatione manumittuntur; adeo quidem, ut quotiens quisque mancipetur aut[3] manumittatur, totiens capite diminuatur. **163.** Nec solum maior*ibus capitis* diminutionibus ius adgnationis corrumpitur, sed etiam minima; et ideo si ex duobus liberis alterum pater emancipauerit, post obitum eius neuter alteri agnationis iure tutor esse poterit. **164.** Cum autem ad agnatos tutela pertineat, non simul ad omnes per-

45 tinet, sed ad eos tantum, qui proximo gradu sunt. |
t. 8. ————————————— *vv. 17.* ————————————— 4

165. Ex eadem lege XII tabularum libertarum[5] et inpuberum libertorum[6] tutela ad patronos liberosque eorum pertinet; quae et ipsa tutela legitima uocatur,

---

1) dimidia V. 2) retineretur V. 3) ut *Solazzi, Athenaeum* 1927, 104; 125. 4) *Hollweg statuit in his 17 versibus Gaium primum egisse de legitima gentilium tutela, ad quam lector remittatur infra* 3, 17. *quid secutum sit, ignoratur.* 5) iibera-rum V. 6) liberorum V.

---

§ 161. = *I.* 1, 16, 2. *cf. Ulp.* 11, 12. *D.* 4, 5, 5 *pr.* (*Paul.* 221). *supra* 1, 128.

§ 162. = *I.* 1, 16, 3. *cf. Ulp.* 11, 13. *D.* 4, 5, 3, 1 (*Paul.* 220). *infra* 3, 83. 4, 38. adoptantur] *cf. supra* 1, 97 *sq.* coemptionem] *cf. supra* 1, 113 *sq.* mancipio dantur] *cf. supra* 1, 117 *sq.* ex mancipatione manumittuntur] *cf. supra* 1, 132 *sq.*

§ 163. *cf. Ulp.* 11, 9. *I.* 1, 15, 3. *D.* 26, 4, 2 (*Ulp.* 2832). *C.* 5, 30, 4 (*a.* 498).

§ 164. = *I.* 1, 16, 7. *cf. Gai epit.* 1, 7, 1. *D.* 26, 4, 9 (*Gai.* 264). *lex Salp. c.* 29 *in fine* (*Bruns* I[7], 146).

§ 165. = *I.* 1, 17. *cf. Gai epit.* 1, 7, 1. *Ulp.* 11, 3. *D.* 26. 4, 3 *pr.* (*Ulp.* 2838). 26, 4, 5 (*Ulp.* 1000). *Schol. Bob. ad Cic. p. Flacco* 34, 84 (*p.* 244 *B.*). *Script. Hist. Aug. M. Anton.* 11, 8. *Boeth. l.* 4 *ad Cic. top.* 8, 33 (*p.* 335 *B.*).

161. **Second degree or intermediate status-loss means loss of citizenship but not liberty, as where a man is banished from home and hearth.** 162. **Third degree status-loss occurs where a man keeps both citizenship and freedom but alters his personal standing.** This happens with those who are adopted, also with those who make a contrived sale of themselves and those who are transferred by mancipation and manumitted from this state of bondage. Whenever any person is mancipated or manumitted he loses his status. 163. The agnatic tie is destroyed not only by first or second degree status-loss but even by the third; accordingly if a father has emancipated one of two children, on his death neither can by agnatic right be guardian for the other. 164. **Though guardianship belongs to the agnatic relations, it does not devolve on all of them at once but only on the closest. ...** [17 lines largely illegible, presumably on other aspects of statutory guardianship.]

165. **Again by virtue of the Twelve Tables, guardianship of freedmen below puberty and of freedwomen is vested in their patrons* and their patrons' descendants. This too is called statutory guardianship, not because provisions for it are**

non *quia nominatim* ea lege de hac tutela *cauetur, sed*
quia proinde accepta est per interpretationem, atque
si uerbis legis *introducta*[1] esset: eo enim ipso, *quod*
*hereditat*es libertorum libertarumque, si | intestati de- 46
cessissent, iusserat lex ad patronos liberosue eorum t. s.
pertinere, crediderunt ueteres uoluisse legem etiam tutelas ad eos pertinere, quia et agnatos, quos ad hereditatem uocauit, eosdem et tutores esse iusserat.
[De fiduciaria *tutela.*[2]] **166.** Exemplo patronorum re-
cepta est[3] *et alia tutela, quae et ipsa legitima uocatur.*
nam si quis filium nepotemue aut pronepotem inpuberes,
uel filiam neptemue aut proneptem tam puberes quam
inpuberes alteri ea lege mancipio dederit, ut sibi reman-
ciparentur, remancipatosque manumiserit, legitimus eorum
tutor erit. **166ᵃ.** Sunt et aliae tutelae, quae fiduciariae
uocantur, id est quae ideo nobis competunt, quia liberum caput mancipatum nobis uel a parente uel a
coemptionatore manumiserimus.[4] **167.** Sed Latinarum et
Latinorum impuberum *tutel*a non omni modo ad manumissores libertinorum[5] pertinet, sed ad eos, quorum

---

1) introducta *Inst.* accepta V.   2) de fiduciaria *in* V
spatio relicto scriptum est post sequens patronorum.   3) re-
cepta est] rectae V. *hic inseruit Krueger paragraphum com-*
positam ex Inst. Iust. 1, 18 *et Gai.* 1, 172 *eumque secutus est*
Hu.; quam nos leviter mutavimus. nam 'deinceps' *vice adiectivi*
fungens, quod ex Inst. Iust. receperunt et Kr. et Hu., inter
classicos auctores unus Ulpianus usurpavit. cf. E. Th. Schulze,
Ztschr. d. Sav. Stiftg. VIII, 290.   4) 'cum Gaius de tutelis
fiduciariis plurali numero loquatur, dubitari potest, num eam
quoque, quae in Inst. 1, 19 sola remansit, commemoravit. nec
tamen hoc loco iniuria ei a librario facta esse videtur. cf
1, 175'. *Hu.*   5) liueris | in̨eorum V. liberosque eorum *Kniep.*

---

§ 166. *cf. I.* 1, 18. *infra* 1, 172; 175. *D.* 26, 4, 3, 10 (*Ulp.*
2838). *C.* 2, 20 (21), 5 (*a.* 293). 5, 61, 2 (1) (*a.* 294).
§ 166ᵃ. = *I.* 1, 19. *supra* 1, 115. *infra* 1, 172; 175; 195ᵃ.
Ulp. 11, 5. *D.* 26, 4, 4 (*Mod.* 14).
§ 167. *cf. Ulp.* 11, 19. *supra* 1, 35. *infra* 3, 56. *lex Salp.*
23 (*Bruns* I⁷, 144). lege Iunia] *cf. supra* 1, 22.

spelled out in that code, but because it has been evolved by an interpretation which treats it as though there were express provisions for it. **The old lawyers held that the fact that the code vested the estates of intestate freedmen and freedwomen in their patrons and their patrons' descendants meant that it intended to vest the guardianship in them too. They inferred this from its treatment of agnates; the code made them heirs and also imposed guardianship upon them.**

[On fiduciary guardianship] 166. **Modelled on the case of patrons, another kind of guardianship, also called statutory, has been evolved. For if someone** mancipates **his son, or his grandson by a son and so forth** while they are under age, **or his daughter, or granddaughter by a son and so forth**, whether she be adult or under age, to a third party with the condition that they be remancipated to himself, and when they have been remancipated he manumits them, **he will be their statutory guardian**. 166a. There are yet **other cases of guardianship, called fiduciary**, that is, those which come to us because we have manumitted a free person who has been mancipated to us either by a father or by the other party to a contrived sale. 167. But in the case of male and female Latins below puberty, guardianship does not always vest in those who granted them liberty, but in those to whom they belonged by quiritary right

ante manumissionem ex iure Quiritium *fuerunt: unde
si ancilla ex iure Quiritium*[1] tua sit, in bonis mea, a
me quidem solo, non etiam a te manumissa Latina
fieri potest, et bona eius ad me pertine*t*, sed eius
tutela tibi competit; nam ita lege Iunia cauetur. itaque si ab eo, cuius et in bonis et ex iure Quiritium
ancilla fuerit, facta sit Latina, ad eundem et bona et
tutela pertinent.[2]

168. Agnatis et patronis et liberorum capitum ma-
numissoribus permissum est feminarum tutelam alii in
iure cedere; pupillorum autem tutelam non est per-
47 missum cedere, quia non uidetur one|rosa, cum tem-
pore pubertatis finiatur.[3] 169. Is. autem, cui ceditur
tutela, cessicius tutor[4] uocatur. 170. Quo mortuo aut
kapite diminuto reuertitur ad eum tutorem tutela, qui
cessit[5]; ipse quoque, qui cessit, si mortuus aut kapite
diminutus sit, a cessicio[6] tutela discedit et reuertitur
ad eum, qui post eum, qui cesserat, secundum gradum
in ea tutela habuerit. 171. Sed quantum ad agnatos
pertinet, nihil hoc tempore de cessicia tutela quaeritur,
cum agnatorum tutelae in feminis lege Claudia sublatae sint. 172. Sed fiduciarios quoque quidam putauerunt cedendae tutelae ius non habere, cum ipsi se
oneri subiecerint. quod etsi placeat, in parente tamen,
qui filiam neptemue aut proneptem alteri ea lege mancipio dedit, ut sibi remanciparetur, remancipatamque
manumisit, idem dici non debet, cum is et legitimus
tutor habeatur et non minus huic quam patronis honor
praestandus sit.[7]

---

1) fuerunt — Quiritium *suppl. Hu.* 2) pertinet V. 3) pupillorum—finiatur *del. Solazzi.* 4) tutor *Goeschen.* uocator V. 5) *corr.
ex* cessauit V. 6) a cessicio *Goeschen.* accessio V. 7) est V.

---

168. *cf. Ulp.* 11, 6; 8; 17. *Boeth. l. 4 ad Cic. top.* 11, 46
(*p.* 342 *Bait.*). *infra* 1, 196.
§§ 169. 170 *cf. Ulp.* 11, 7. *C. I. G.* 2941 (= *Dessau* 8875).
§ 171. *cf. Ulp.* 11, 8. *supra* 1, 157.
§ 172. *cf. supra* 1, 166. *infra* 1, 175. *I.* 1, 18.

before their manumission. For this reason, if a female slave is yours by quiritary right but is a part of my estate, my grant of freedom alone makes her a Latin, without any grant by you, and her property vests in me, but her guardianship goes to you; this is a provision of the Junian Act. And so, if a female slave is made a Latin by someone who both has her in his estate and has quiritary ownership, both her property and her guardianship vest in the same person.

168. Agnates, patrons and those who manumit free persons are permitted to transfer the guardianship of women to someone else by assignment in court*. It is not, however, permitted to assign the guardianship of young children, because this is not seen as burdensome, finishing as it does with puberty. 169. The person to whom guardianship is assigned is called the assignatory guardian. 170. On his dying or suffering status-loss, guardianship reverts to the guardian who assigned it; if he too has died or suffered status-loss, the guardianship passes from the assignatory guardian and reverts to whoever is in the next degree in relation to the guardianship after the man who assigned it. 171. As regards agnates, however, no question of assignatory guardianship arises at the present time, since agnatic guardianship for women was abolished by the Claudian Act. 172. Certain jurists have thought that fiduciary guardians too do not have the right to assign their guardianship, since they placed the burden on themselves. Even if this opinion is accepted, yet the same principle should not be said to apply to a parent who has given his daughter, granddaughter or great-granddaughter to another by mancipation on the condition that she be remancipated to himself and has then manumitted her after the remancipation, since he is viewed as a statutory guardian, whose position is no less deserving of respect than that of patrons.

173. Praeterea senatus consulto mulieribus permissum est in absentis tutoris locum alium petere, quo petito prior desinit[1]; nec interest, quam longe absit[2] is tutor. 174. Sed excipitur, ne in absentis patroni locum liceat libertae tutorem petere. 175. Patroni | autem loco habemus etiam parentem, qui ex eo, quod 48 ipse sibi remancipatam[3] filiam neptemue aut proneptem manumisit, legitimam tutelam nanctus est. sed[4] huius quidem liberi fiduciarii tutoris loco numerantur; patroni autem[5] liberi eandem tutelam adipiscuntur, quam et pater eorum habuit. 176. Sed aliquando etiam in patroni absentis locum permittitur tutorem petere, ueluti ad hereditatem adeundam. 177. Idem senatus censuit et in persona pupilli patroni filii. 178. Nam et[6] lege Iulia de maritandis ordinibus ei, quae in legitima tutela pupilli sit, permittitur dotis constituendae gratia a praetore urbano tutorem petere. 179. Sane patroni filius, etiamsi inpubes sit, tamen[7] libertae efficietur tutor, quamquam in nulla re auctor fieri potest, cum ipsi nihil permissum sit sine tutoris auctoritate agere. 180. Item si qua in tutela legitima furiosi aut muti sit, permittitur ei senatus consulto dotis constituendae gratia tutorem petere. 181. Quibus casibus saluam manere tutelam patrono patronique filio manifestum est. 182. Praeterea senatus censuit, ut si tutor

---

1) quo — desinit del. Solazzi.   2) absit Krueger. aberit V.
3) rem mancipatam V.   4) add. Polenaar.   5) patroni autem]
autem patroni V.   6) e V.   7) addidit Hu.

---

§§ 173. 174. cf. Ulp. 11, 22. D. 50, 16, 199 (Ulp. 2291).
Schol. Sin. 37.
    § 175. cf. supra 1, 166; 172. I. 1, 19 cum Theophilo.
§§ 176. 177. cf. Ulp. 11, 22.
    § 178. cf. Ulp. 11, 20. D. 23, 3, 61 pr. (Clem. 5). 26, 5, 3
(Ulp. 2018). 26, 5, 7 (Ulp. 2255). lege Iulia] cf. supra 1, 145.
    § 179. cf. I. 1, 25, 13.
    § 180. cf. Ulp. 11, 21. D. 26, 1, 17 (Paul. 1781). 26, 4,
10, 1 (Herm. 51). 26, 1, 1, 2; 3 (Paul. 556).
    § 182. cf. Ulp. 11, 23. D. 40, 5, 41, 2 (Scaev. 287). 26, 2,
11, 1—3 (Ulp. 2835). C. 5, 36, 2 (a. 228). 5, 36, 4 (a. 260).

173. Furthermore, women are permitted by a resolution of the Senate to apply for another guardian in place of one who is absent. On the application, the previous guardian lapses; nor does it matter how long his absence is. 174. An exception is, however, made so that a freedwoman is not allowed to apply for a guardian in place of her absent patron. 175. We also regard a parent as being in the same position as a patron, deriving his statutory guardianship as he does from the fact that he has manumitted his daughter, granddaughter or great-granddaughter after she has been remancipated to him. Yet his descendants are counted as being in the position of fiduciary guardian; the children of a patron, however, obtain the same guardianship as their father held. 176. But sometimes it is permissible to apply for a guardian in place even of an absent patron, for instance, in order to enter upon an inheritance. 177. The Senate has ruled that the same holds good when the patron's son is a young child. 178. For under the Julian Act on the regulation of marriages a woman who is in the legitimate guardianship of a young child is permitted to apply to the Urban Praetor for a guardian for the purpose of constituting a dowry. 179. A patron's son, even if he is under puberty, will still become the guardian of his father's freedwoman, although he cannot give authorisation in any matter, since he himself is not permitted to act at all without the authorisation of his own guardian. 180. Again, if a woman is in the statutory guardianship of someone who is mad or dumb, she is permitted by a resolution of the Senate to apply for a guardian for the purpose of constituting a dowry. 181. It is obvious that in these cases the guardianship remains preserved for the patron and his son. 182. Moreover, the Senate has ruled that if the guardian of a male or female child has been removed

pupilli pupillaeue suspectus a tutela remotus sit siue
ex iusta causa fuerit excusatus, in locum eius alius
tutor detur, quo facto prior tutor amittit tutelam.
49 183. Haec omnia similiter et Romae et in pro|uinciis
obseruantur, scilicet ut[1] in prouinciis a praeside prouinciae tutor pe*ti debeat*.

184. Olim cum legis actiones in usu erant, etiam
ex illa causa tutor dabatur, si inter tutorem et mulierem pupillum*ue* lege[2] agendum erat: nam quia ipse
tutor in re sua auctor esse non poterat, alius dabatur, quo auctore legis actio perageretur: qui dicebatur praetorius tutor[3], quia a[4] praetore urbano dabatur.[5] sed post sublatas legis actiones quidam putant
hanc speciem dandi tutoris in usu esse desisse; ali*is
autem* placet adhuc[6] in usu esse, si legitimo iudicio
agatur.

185. Si cui nullus omnino tutor sit, ei datur in
urbe Roma ex lege Atilia a praetore urbano et maiore
parte tribunorum plebis, qui Atilianus tutor uocatur;
in prouinciis uero a praesidibus prouinciarum *ex lege*

---

1) et V. scilicet — debeat *del. Solazzi.*   2) pupillumue
lege] pupillumqe legem V.   3) tutelae V.   4) aut V.
5) datur V.   6) athunc V.

---

§ 183. *cf. Ulp.* 11, 20. *lex Salp. c.* 29 (*Bruns* I[7], 146).
§ 184. *cf. Ulp.* 11, 24. *I.* 4, 10 *pr.* 1, 21, 3. *D.* 26, 1, 5
(*Pomp.* 641). 26, 1, 3, 2—4 (*Ulp.* 2837). 27, 3, 9, 4 (*Ulp.* 1014).
26, 1, 4 (*Paul.* 1780). *C.* 5, 44. quia ipse tutor *etc.*] *cf. D.* 26.
8, 22 (*Lab.* 216). 26, 8, 1 *pr.* (*Ulp.* 2425). 26, 8, 5 *pr.* (*Ulp.* 2854).
legitimo iudicio] *cf. infra* 4, 103 *sq.*
§ 185. = *I.* 1, 20 *pr. cf. Gai epit.* 1, 7, 2. *Ulp.* 11, 18.
infra 1, 195. lex Atilia] *cf. Liv.* 39, 9, 7. *Cic. Verr.* 2, 1, 56,
146. *Boeth. l.* 4 *ad Cic. top.* 8, 33 (*p.* 335, 2 *Bait.*; urbani praetoris iurisdictione formatur). *Schol. Sin.* 45. 54. l. Iulia et
Titia] *cf. Diod.* 37, 8, 4 *Dind.* (*Excerpt. Vales. p.* 397). *Theoph.*
1, 20 (*p.* 76 *Ferr.*). *Schol. Sin.* 54. *lex Salp.* 29 (*Bruns* I[7], 146).
Pap. Oxy 4, 720 (*Bruns* I[7], 421). 12, 1466. *Zeitschr. Sav. Stiftg.*
40, 359. 54, 312.

from the guardianship as suspect, or if he has been excused on lawful grounds, another guardian is appointed in his place; on this, the earlier guardian loses his guardianship. 183. All these practices are observed in the same manner in Rome and in the provinces, save that in the provinces the application for a guardian must be made to the provincial governor.

184. In former times, when procedure by actions in the law* was in use, a guardian was also appointed on the grounds **that a matter between the guardian and the** woman or **child** had to go to court; **for a guardian could not give his authorisation where his own interest was involved**. Another guardian was appointed with whose authorisation the action in the law could be concluded. He was called the 'praetorian' guardian, because he was appointed by the Urban Praetor. But after the abolition of the actions in the law, some jurists think that this kind of appointment of guardian has fallen into disuse; it is accepted by others, however, that it is still in use if an action is brought in a statutory court*.

185. **If someone** has **no guardian at all, the practice in the City of Rome** is **for him to be given one under the Atilian Act by the Urban Praetor and a majority of the tribunes of the people;** he is called an Atilian guardian. **In the provinces this is done by the provincial governors under the**

Iulia et Titia. 186. Et ideo si cui testamento tutor
sub condicione aut ex die certo datus sit, quamdiu
condicio aut dies pendet, tutor dari potest; item si
pure datus fuerit, quamdiu nemo heres existat[1], tamdiu
ex his legibus tutor petendus est; qui desinit tutor
esse, posteaquam aliquis ex testamento tutor esse coeperit. 187. Ab hostibus quoque tutore capto ex his
legibus tutor peti debet; qui desinit tutor esse, si is,
qui captus est, in ciuitatem reuersus fuerit: nam re-
uersus recipit tutelam iure postliminii. |

188. Ex his apparet, quot sint species[2] tutelarum. 50
si uero quaeramus, in quot genera hae[3] species diducantur[4], longa erit disputatio: nam de ea re ualde
ueteres dubitauerunt. nos qui diligentius hunc tracta-
tum exsecuti sumus et in edicti interpretatione et in his
libris, quos ex Quinto Mucio fecimus, hoc totum *omitti-
mus.*[5] *hoc solum*[6] tantisper sufficit admonuisse, quod
quidam quinque genera esse dixerunt, ut Quintus Mucius, alii tria, ut Seruius Sulpicius; alii duo, ut Labeo;
alii tot genera esse crediderunt, quot etiam species essent.

189. Sed inpuberes quidem in tutela esse omnium
ciuitatium iure contingit; quia id naturali rationi[7] conueniens est, ut is, qui perfectae aetatis non sit, alterius tutela regatur, nec fere ulla ciuitas est, in qua

---

1) **exstat** *vel* existit *Polenaar. sed cf. Inst. Iust.* 2) spe-
ciesins V. 3) haec V. 4) deducantur V. 5) *suppl. Kniep.*
6) hoc solum *supplevimus; cf. infra 3, 33.* 7) ratione V.
iure *Inst. Iust.*

§ 186. = *I.* 1, 20, 1. *cf. I.* 1, 14, 3. *D.* 26, 2, 10 *pr.* (*Ulp.*
2824). 26, 2, 10, 3; 4 (*Ulp.* 2830). 26, 2, 11 *pr.* (*Ulp.* 2835). 27,
3, 9, 2 (*Ulp.* 1014).
§ 187. = *I.* 1, 20, 2. *cf. D.* 26, 4, 1, 2 (*Ulp.* 2529). 27, 3, 8
(*Pap.* 347). 26, 1, 15 (*Ulp.* 2844).
§ 188. *cf. Ulp.* 11, 2. *Boeth. l.* 4 *ad Cic. top.* 8, 33 (*p.* 334 *sq.*
Bait.).
§ 189. = *I.* 1, 20, 6. supra] 1, 55.

Julian-Titian Act. 186. If there is **a guardian appointed by will, but subject to a condition or from a specified day, an appointment** can **be made to cover the interval till the condition is satisfied or the day comes. Even if there was an unconditional appointment, a guardian is needed under** these **Acts until the position of heir is accepted. Such a person ceases to act** after someone has begun to be guardian under the will. 187. **Another case for a petition under these Acts arises if a guardian becomes a prisoner of war. Here the appointee ceases to act if the prisoner comes back and resumes his guardianship by virtue of his right of rehabilitation.**

188. From this it can be seen how many kinds of guardianship there are. If indeed we were to inquire into how many classes these kinds may be divided, the debate would be long, for the old lawyers had serious doubts about the subject. We omit all this since we have dealt with this field quite thoroughly, both in our interpretation of the Edict and in those books which we wrote on Quintus Mucius. It is sufficient to have noted that some, like Quintus Mucius, have said that there are five classes; others, like Servius Sulpicius, that there are three; others, like Labeo, two; while others again have believed that there are as many classes as kinds.

189. **The institution of guardianship for those who are still children** is provided for in the law of all states, because **it is in accordance with natural reason for a young child to be ruled by a guardian.** There is virtually no state in which it is not lawful for

non licet parentibus liberis suis inpuberibus testamento[1]
tutorem dare; quamuis, ut supra diximus, soli ciues
Romani uideantur tantum[2] liberos suos in potestate
habere. 190. Feminas uero perfectae aetatis in tutela
esse fere nulla pretiosa ratio suasisse uidetur: nam
quae uulgo creditur, quia leuitate animi plerumque
decipiuntur et aequum erat eas tutorum auctoritate
regi, magis speciosa[3] uidetur quam uera; mulieres enim,
quae perfectae aetatis sunt, ipsae[4] sibi negotia tractant,
51 et in quibusdam | causis dicis gratia tutor[5] interponit
auctoritatem suam; saepe etiam inuitus auctor fieri a
praetore cogitur. 191. Unde cum tutore nullum ex
tutela iudicium mulieri datur[6]: at ubi pupillorum pu-
pillarumue negotia tutores tractant, eis[7] post pubertatem tutelae iudicio[8] rationem reddunt.[9] 192. Sane
patronorum et parentum legitimae tutelae uim aliquam
habere intelleguntur eo, quod hi neque ad testamentum faciendum neque ad res mancipi alienandas neque
ad obligationes suscipiendas auctores fieri coguntur,
praeterquam si magna causa alienandarum rerum mancipi[10] obligationisque suscipiendae interueniat.[11] eaque

---

1) co. st. V.   2) tant V   3) hispeciosa V.   4) ipsi V.
5) tutele V.   6) datum V.   7) tractant eis Cramer. trac-
tans ei V.   8) iudici V.   9) at — reddunt del. Beseler, Beitr.
4, 110.   10) mancipio V.   11) interueniant V.

§ 190. cf. supra 1, 144. infra 2, 122. Ulp. 11, 25; 27. D.
26, 5, 26 (Scaev. 245). Cic. top. 11, 46 c. Boeth. ad h. l. (p. 342,
20 Bait.).
§ 191. = I. 1, 20, 7.
§ 192. cf. Ulp. 11, 27. Cic. pro Flacco 34, 84. ad testam.
fac.] cf. infra 2, 112; 118; 122. 3, 43. Ulp. 20, 15. 29, 3. ad
res manc. al.] cf. infra 2, 47; 80. Fr. Vat. 1 (Paul. 1782). 45
(Paul. 1011). 259 (Pap. 693). oblig. susc.] cf. infra 3, 91:
108; 176. supra 1, 176; 178; 180. Fr. Vat. 110 (Paul. 1517).
D. 23, 3, 60 (Cels. 92). Cic. pro Caec. 25, 72. pro Flacco 35, 86.
C. I. L. IV Suppl. 154 (Bruns I⁷, 332, 8). C. I. L. VI 10231
(Bruns I⁷, 336). C. I. L. XIII 7521 (Dessau 7473). eaque
omnia] cf. D. 26, 4, 1 pr. (Ulp. 2529). C. I. L. VI 1527 l. 14.
15. 21 (Bruns I⁷, 322).

parents to appoint a guardian by will for their young children, although, as we said above, Roman citizens are regarded as unique in having their children in power. 190. There seems, on the other hand, to have been no very worthwhile reason why women who have reached the age of maturity should be in guardianship; for the argument which is commonly believed, that because they are scatterbrained they are frequently subject to deception and that it was proper for them to be under guardians' authority, seems to be specious rather than true. For women of full age deal with their own affairs for themselves, and while in certain instances the guardian interposes his authorisation for form's sake, he is often compelled by the praetor to give authorisation, even against his wishes. 191. For this reason, a woman is not granted any action against her guardian on account of the guardianship; but **where guardians are dealing with the affairs of male or female children, when the wards grow up the action on guardianship calls the guardians to account**. 192. Of course, the statutory guardianships of patrons and parents are understood to have some efficacy. These persons are not compelled to give their authorisation, whether for making a will or for alienating things capable of mancipation or for undertaking obligations, unless very significant grounds arise for the alienation of things capable of mancipation and the undertaking of an obligation. All these matters are so arranged for the

omnia ipsorum causa constituta sunt, ut quia ad eos
intestatarum mortuarum hereditates pertinent[1], neque
per testamentum excludantur ab hereditate neque alie-
natis pretiosioribus rebus susceptoque aere alieno minus loc*u*ples ad eos hereditas *per*ueniat. 193. Apud
peregrinos non similiter, ut apud nos, in tutela sunt
feminae; sed tamen plerumque quasi in tutela sunt:
ut ecce[2] lex Bithynorum, si quid mulier contra*hat*[3],
maritum auctorem esse iubet aut filium[4] eius puberem.
194. Tutela autem liberantur ingenuae quidem trium
liberorum iure, libertinae uero quattuor, si in patroni[5]
liberorumue eius legitima tut*ela*[6] sint; nam ceterae,[7]
quae alterius generis tutores habent, uelut Atilianos
aut fiduciarios, trium liberorum | iure tutela liberantur. 52
195. Potest autem pluribus modis libertina *tutorem*
alterius generis habere, ueluti si a femina manumissa
sit; tunc enim e lege Atilia petere debet tutorem, uel
in prouincia *e lege Iulia* et Titia: nam in patronae
tutela esse non potest. 195ᵃ. Item si *sit a* masculo
manumissa et auctore eo coemptionem fecerit, deinde
remancipata et manumissa sit, patronum quidem habere tutorem desinit. incipit autem habere eum tutorem, a quo manumissa est, qui fiduciarius dicitur.

---

1) pertinet V.　2) ut ecce *Hollweg*. ui haecce V.　3) con-
trahat *Lachm*.　hat V.　4) filius V.　5) liberorum — patroni
suppl. Hollweg.　6) tutum V.　7) et ceterae V.　et *del. Hu*.

§ 193. *cf. Cic. pro Flacco* 30, 74. *Ter. Andr.* 1, 5, 60 = 295.
§ 194. *cf. supra* 1, 145. *infra* 3, 44. *Ulp.* 29, 3. *Dosith.* 15.
D. 50, 60, 137 (*Paul.* 938). *Plut. Num.* 10. *Pap. Oxy.* XII 1467.
C. I. L. VI 10246. 10247 (*Bruns* I⁷, 336). 1877 (*Dessau* 1910).
VIII 4573. *papyris saepe legitur*: χωρὶς κυρίου χρηματίζουσα
(τέκνων δικαίῳ) κατὰ τὰ ʿΡωμαίων ἔθη (*BGU*. 94. 96. 131. 717.
863. 920. 1069. *CPR.* 3. 9. 63. 140. 176. 227. *Pap. Lond.* II 171 b.
Pap. Grenf. II 85. *Pap. Lips.* 3 I 3; 7. II, 6. 4, 8. 5 II 5. 29, 2.
Pap. Straßb. 29, 29. *Pap. Oxy.* 909, 6. 1199, 7. 1276, 2. 24. 1277, 2.
1460, 4. 1463, 9. 1475, 12. *P. Freib.* 9, 4. *P. Hamb.* 15, 6. 16, 5.
P. S. I. 187, 10. *P. Ryl.* 165, 10. *Arch. f. Papyrusforsch.* I, 299, 17).
§ 195. *cf. supra* 1, 185. *Liv.* 39, 9, 7.
§ 195ᵃ *cf. supra* 1, 115.

sake of the guardians themselves, because the inheritances of women who die intestate vest in them; they cannot be excluded from the inheritance by a will, nor may the value of the inheritance be diminished before it reaches them by selling off the more valuable property and incurring debts. 193. Among foreigners, women are not in guardianship in the same way as with us, yet they are for the most part in a sort of guardianship; see, for example, the statute of the Bithynians which orders that if a woman enters into a contract her husband or her adult son must give authorisation.

194. Free-born women are released from guardianship by the privilege of three children. Freedwomen, however, need four if they are in the statutory guardianship of a patron or his children; others, who have guardians of another sort, such as Atilian or fiduciary, are released from guardianship by the privilege of three children. 195. There are many ways in which a freedwoman can have a guardian of another sort, for instance, if she has been manumitted by a woman. She must then apply for a guardian under the Atilian Act, or in the provinces under the Julian-Titian Act, because she cannot be in the guardianship of a female patron. 195a. Again, if she was manumitted by a man and at his proposal made a a contrived sale of herself, and was then remancipated and manumitted, she ceases to have her patron as guardian. She comes instead to have the man by whom she was manumitted as guardian, who is termed fiduciary. 195b. Again, if the patron or his son

195ᵇ. Item si patron*us* *eiusue* *filius* in adoptionem se
dedit, debet liberta *e* *lege* *Atilia* *uel* *Iulia* *et* Titia tutorem petere. 195ᶜ. Similiter ex iisdem legibus petere
debet tutorem liberta[1], si patronus decesserit nec
ullum uirilis sexus liberorum in familia re*liquerit*.
196. Masculi *autem* *cum*[2] puberes esse coeperint, tutela
liberantur: *puberem* *autem* Sabinus quidem et Cassius
ceterique nostri praeceptores eum esse putant[3], qui
habitu corporis pubertatem ostendit, id est eum, qui
generare potest; sed in his, qui pubescere non possunt,
quales sunt spadones, eam aetatem esse spectandam,
cuius aetatis puberes fiunt; sed diuersae scholae auctores annis putant pubertatem aestimandam, id est eum

53
t. s. puberem esse existimant, *qui* | *xiiii* *annos* *expleuit.* |[4]

———————————— *tota* *pag.* ————————————— |

54
t. s. 197. . . . . | aetatem peruenerit, in qua res suas tueri
possit, sicuti apud peregrinas gentes custodiri superius
indicauimus. 198. Ex iisdem causis et in prouinciis a
praesidibus earum curatores dari uolunt.[5]

———————

1) busta V.   2) autem cum *verisimile* *Studemundo* *visum*
est.   3) *librarius* *alteram* *syllabam* *errore* *bis* *scripsisse* *videtur.*
4) *in* *p.* 53 *Gaius* *primum* *de* *pubertate* *Neratii* *Prisci* *senten-*
tiam (*Ulp.* 11, 28) *addidisse,* *deinde* *ad* *eas* *personas,* *quae* *in*
curatione *sunt* (*cf.* 1, 142. 143), *transiisse* *videtur,* *cf.* *Epit.* 1, 8.
quid *postea* *specialiter* *Gaius* *tractaverit,* *in* *incerto* *relinquimus.*
5) *uoluit* *Hu.* *solent* *Lachmann.*

———————

§ 195ᵇ. *cf.* *I.* 1, 22, 4. *Ulp.* 11, 9.
§ 195ᶜ. *cf.* *supra* 1, 179. *Liv.* 39, 9, 7.
§ 196. *cf.* *supra* 1, 168; 189; 103. *Ulp.* 11, 28. *Paul.* 3,
4ᵃ, 1; 2. *I.* 1, 22 *pr.* *D.* 27, 3, 4 *pr.* (*Paul.* 1786). 28, 6, 2 (*Ulp.*
2469). 28, 1, 5 (*Ulp.* 2468). *C.* 6, 22, 4 (a. 294). 5, 60, 3 (a. 529).
Senec. *cons.* *ad* *Marciam* 24, 1. *Quintil.* *inst.* *or.* 4, 2, 5. *Cass.*
Dio 54, 16, 7. *Fest.* *s.* *v.* *pubes* *p.* 250. 251. *Censorin.* 7, 4. *Tertull.*
de *anima* 38. *de* *virg.* *veland.* *c.* 11. *Macrob.* *Somn.* *Scip.* 1, 6, 71.
Saturn. 7, 7, 6. *Serv.* *ad* *Verg.* *Bucol.* 8, 40. *ad* *Aen.* 7, 53. *Isid.*
orig. 11, 2, 13. *lex* *col.* *Iul.* *Gen.* *c.* 98 (*Bruns* I⁷, 132).
§ 197. *cf.* *supra* 1, 189. *Gai* *epit.* 1, 8. *Ulp.* 12, 4. *I.* 1,
23 *pr.* *Script.* *Hist.* *Aug.* *M.* *Anton.* 10, 12. *Isid.* *orig.* 10, 53.
§ 198. *cf.* *D.* 26, 5, 8, 3 (*Ulp.* 2293). 27, 10, 2 (*Paul.* 1061)

gives himself in adoption, the freedwoman should apply for a tutor under the Atilian Act or the Julian-Titian Act. 195c. Similarly, a freedwoman should apply for a tutor under the same Acts if her patron dies, leaving no male descendants in his family. 196. **Guardianship ends** for boys **when they reach puberty**. Sabinus, Cassius and others of our teachers certainly think that a boy shows he has reached puberty **by physical development**: that is, he is capable of begetting. However, in the case of those who cannot reach puberty such as eunuchs, regard must be had to the age at which puberty is normally reached. The authorities of the other school* think that puberty should be reckoned in years: that is, they judge anyone who has reached the age of fourteen as having reached puberty. [On the illegible page Gaius presumably went on to discuss persons under supervision.] ... 197. ... reaches the age at which he can look after his own affairs; a custom which, as we have indicated above, is observed among foreign peoples. 198. On the same grounds, the practice **in the provinces** is for their **governors** to **appoint supervisors**.

199. Ne tamen et pupillorum et eorum, qui in curatione sunt, negotia a tutoribus curatoribusque consumantur aut deminuantur, curat praetor, ut et tutores *et* curatores eo nomine satisdent. **200.** Sed hoc non est perpetuum; nam et tutores testamento dati satisdare non coguntur, quia fides eorum et diligentia ab ipso testatore probata est; et curatores, ad quos non e[1] lege curatio[2] pertinet, sed *qui* uel a consule uel a praetore uel a praeside prouinciae *dan*tur, plerumque non coguntur satisdare, scilicet quia satis hon*esti electi s*unt.[3]

---

1) non e] nonne V.   2) curato V.   3) scilicet — snnt *del. Kniep et Solazzi.*

---

§§ 199. 200. = *I.* 1, 24 *pr. cf. infra* 4, 99. *D.* 26, 4, 5, 1; 3 (*Ulp.* 1000). 2, 8, 8, 4 (*Paul.* 259). *Tit.* 27, 7. 46, 6. *C.* 2, 40 (41), 4 (*a.* 294). *Tit.* 5, 57. 5, 42. a consule] *cf. Suet. Claud.* 23. *Plin. ep.* 9, 13, 16. *Script. Hist. Aug. M. Anton.* 10, 11. *I.* 1, 20, 8.

199. **To prevent guardians and supervisors from wasting and depleting the estates of wards and others under them, the praetor takes steps to make them give security.** 200. **But the practice is not uniform. Guardians appointed by will are not compelled to give security. It is assumed that the testator will have satisfied himself of their honesty and application.** Supervisors whose duty does not arise under statute but who have been appointed by a consul or praetor or provincial governor, are for the most part not compelled to give security, **because** of course **they were chosen** for their probity.

COMMENTARIVS SECVNDVS.

1. *Superiore commentario de iure personarum* exposuimus; modo uideamus de rebus: quae uel in
nostro patrimonio sunt uel extra nostrum patrimonium
habentur. **2.** Summa itaque rerum diuisio in duos articulos
diducitur: nam aliae sunt diuini iuris, aliae humani.
3. Diuini iuris sunt ueluti res sacrae et religiosae.
4. Sacrae sunt, quae diis superis consecratae sunt;
religiosae, quae diis Manibus relictae sunt. **5.** Sed
sacrum quidem hoc solum existimatur, quod *ex* auctoritate populi Romani consecratum est, ueluti lege de
ea re lata aut senatus consulto facto. **6.** Religiosum
uero nostra uoluntate facimus mortuum inferentes in
locum nostrum, si modo eius mortui funus ad nos
pertineat. **7.** Sed in prouinciali solo placet plerisque
solum religiosum non fieri, quia in eo solo dominium

---

§ 1. = *I.* 2, 1 *pr. cf. Gai epit.* 2, 1 *pr. supra* 1, 8.

§§ 2. 3. = *D.* 1, 8, 1 *pr. cf. Gai epit.* 2, 1, 1. *D.* 43, 1, 1 *pr*
(*Ulp.* 1459).

§ 4. *cf. I.* 2, 1, 7. *Fest. v. religiosus p.* 289. *religiosum
p.* 281 (*Bruns* II[7], 31). *Macrob. Sat.* 3, 3. *Gromat. ed. Lachm.
p.* 22.

§ 5. *cf. I.* 2, 1, 8. *D.* 36, 4, 15 (*Val.* 1). 1, 8, 9 *pr.* 1; 2
(*Ulp.* 1483). 1, 8, 6, 3 (*Marcian.* 74). *Cic. de harusp. resp.* 6,
11 *sq. ad Att.* 4, 2, 3. *Fest. v. sacratae leges p.* 318 (*Bruns*
II[7], 34). *sacer mons p.* 318 (*Bruns* II[7], 33). *Gell.* 4, 9, 8.

§ 6. *cf. I.* 2, 1, 9. *D.* 36, 4, 15 (*Val.* 1). 11, 7, 2, 5 (*Ulp.*
728). 24, 1, 5, 9 (*Ulp.* 2765). 11, 7, 40. 44 (*Paul.* 1293. 1294).
1, 8, 6, 4 (*Marcian.* 74). *Fest. v. fulguritum p.* 12 (*Bruns* II[7], 10).

§ 7. *cf. supra* 1, 6. *infra* 2, 21; 27; 46. *Gromat. ed. Lachm.
p.* 36 (*Bruns* II[7], 86). 63. *Plin. ad Trai.* 49. 50 (58. 59). *Theoph.*
2, 1, 40 (*p.* 115 *Ferr.*). *Dio Cass.* 41, 43, 2.

BOOK TWO

1. **After persons in the previous** commentary **we turn to things. They are either in the category of private wealth or not.**

2. Now the main division of things has two limbs; some things are **under divine law**, others **under human law. 3. Sacred* and religious* things**, for instance, are **under divine law. 4. Sacred things are those consecrated** to the gods above; religious things those left to the gods below. 5. But note that to be considered sacred land must have been consecrated by authority of the Roman people, by a statute* on the matter, for instance, or by a Senate resolution*. 6. On the other hand, we can ourselves **make land religious by deciding to bury a dead body in** our **land**, provided that it is our responsibility to see to the dead person's funeral. 7. But in the case of land in the provinces* most people accept that it is not made religious, because ownership of such land is held by

populi Romani est uel Caesaris, nos autem possessionem tantum et[1] usumfructum habere uidemur; utique
tamen, etiamsi non sit religiosum[2], pro religioso habetur: item quod in prouinciis[3] non ex auctoritate
populi Romani consecratum est, proprie sacrum non
est, tamen pro sacro habetur. 8. Sanctae quoque res,
uelut muri et portae, quodam modo diuini iuris sunt.
9. Quod autem diuini iuris est, id nullius in bonis est:
id uero, quod humani | *iuris est, plerumque alicuius in
bonis est; potest autem et nullius in bonis esse: nam
res hereditariae, antequam aliquis heres existat, nullius
in bonis sunt*[4] |——— *vv. fere 8* ——— | ue domino.
10. [5]Hae autem *res*, quae humani iuris sunt, *aut publicae* sunt aut priuatae. 11. Quae publicae sunt, nul-
l*ius* *u*identur in bonis esse; ipsius enim uniuersitatis
esse creduntur.[6] priuatae sunt, quae singulorum homi-
n*um sunt.*

12. Quaedam praeterea res corporales sunt, quaedam incorporales. 13. *Corporales* hae *sunt*, quae tangi
possunt, uelut fundus, homo, uestis, aurum, argentum
et denique aliae res innumerabiles. 14. Incorporal*es
sunt*, quae tangi non possunt, qualia sunt ea, quae *in*[7]

1) et *Goudsmit*. uel V. et usumfructum *del*. *Sol*. 2) religiosus V. 3) 'in prouinciis *noli cum Momms. pro glossemate
habere'*. *Hu*. 4) iuris — sunt *suppl*. *ex D*. 1, 8, *pr*.
5) §§ 10—14 *restitutae partim ex Dig*. 1, 8, 1. 6) ipsius - creduntur *del*. *Schnorr v. Carolsfeld*. 7) in *add*. *Hu. ex Inst*. (*cf. Theoph*.

§ 8. = *D*. 1, 8, 1 *pr*. *I*. 2, 1, 10. *cf. Gai epit*. 2, 1, 1. *D*.
1, 8, 11 (*Pomp*. 318). 1, 8, 9, 3; 4 (*Ulp*. 1486). 43, 6, 3 (*Paul*.
Sent. 5, 6, 1ª). 1, 8, 8, 2 (*Marcian*. 256). 43, 6, 2 (*Herm*. 89).
Isid. orig. 15, 4, 2 *in fin*.
§ 9. = *D*. 1, 8, 1 *pr*. *cf. Gai epit*. 2, 1, 1. *I*. 2, 1, 7. *infra*
3, 97. *D*. 1, 8, 6, 2 (*Marcian*. 74). 41, 3, 9 (*Gai*. 110). 6, 1, 23, 1
(*Paul*. 328). *C*. 3, 44, 4 (a. 223). res hereditariae] *cf. infra* 2,
52 *sq*. 3, 201.
§§ 10. 11. *cf. D*. 43, 1, 1 *pr*. (*Ulp*. 1459). 50, 16, 15 (*Ulp*.
343). 43, 1, 2, 1 (*Paul*. 745). 1, 8, 6, 1 (*Marcian*. 71) = *I*. 2, 1, 6.
§§ 12—14. = *I*. 2, 2. *D*. 1, 8, 1, 1. *cf. Gai epit*. 2, 1, 2;

the Roman people or by the Emperor; we are regarded
as having only possession or a usufruct; all the same,
although not in fact religious, it is treated as religious.
Again, anything in the provinces not consecrated by
authority of the Roman people is not sacred properly
speaking, yet it is treated as sacred. 8. **Sanctified
things such as city walls and gates, are also in a
certain sense under divine law.** 9. Now, **what is
under divine law, cannot be private property;** what
is under human law, on the other hand, is generally
someone's property but may also be no one's; for
things in an inheritance are no one's property until
someone emerges as heir ... [the remainder of this
section is illegible apart from the words 'or to/from the
owner.'] 10. Now things which are under human law
are either public or private. 11. Public things are
regarded as no one's property; for they are thought of
as belonging to the whole body of the people. Private
things are those belonging to individuals.

12. **Moreover, some things are corporeal, some
incorporeal. 13. Corporeal things can be touched –
land, a slave, clothes, gold, silver and of course
countless others. 14. Incorporeal things cannot be
touched. They consist of legal rights – inheritance,**

iure consistunt, sicut hereditas, ususfructus, obligationes quoquo modo contractae. nec ad rem per*tinet,
quod in hereditate res corporales continentur[1], et fructus, qui ex fundo percipiuntur, corporales *sunt*, et *id,*
quod ex aliqua obligatione nobis debe*tur*, | plerumque
corporale est, ueluti fundus, homo, pecunia: nam ipsum
ius successionis et ipsum iu*s utendi* fruendi et ipsum
ius obligationis incorporale est. eodem numero sunt
iura praediorum urbanorum et rusticorum. |———
vv. 2¼——— |[2] non extollendi, ne luminibus uicini offi-
ciatur: item fluminum et stillicidiorum idem[3] ius ut
|——— 5 *vv.* ——— | —

14ᵃ. Res *praeterea aut mancipi sunt aut* nec man-
cipi.[4] |——— *vv.* 5 ——— | *seruitutes* praediorum urba-
norum nec mancipi *sunt.* item stipendiaria praedia et

2, 2, 1); *exhibent Dig. quoque et Gai epit. cf. infra* 3, 131; 141.
aliter infra 3, 182.　　1) nam, *quod addunt Inst. et Dig., melius abest.*　　2) *ad sensum praeeunte Kruegero suppleri potest:*
Praediorum urbanorum iura sunt uelut ius altius tollendo
aedes suas officiendi luminibus uicini aedium aut.
3) *Krueger partim Epitomam secutus optime ita supplevit:* ius
id est (*pro* idem ius) ut uicinus flumen uel stillicidium in
aream uel in aedes suas recipiat; item cloacae immittendae
et luminum immittendorum. praediorum rusticorum iura sunt
uelut uia, iter, actus, item pecoris ad aquam adpulsus, item
ius aquae ducendae. haec iura tam rusticorum quam urbanorum praediorum seruitutes uocantur (*cf. Dig.* 1, 8, 1, 1 *in
fine et Inst.* 2, 2, 3). *sed cf. Solazzi, Glosse a Gaio* 2, 348.
4) *abhinc Krueger supplet:* mancipi sunt uelut fundus in Italico
solo, item aedes in Italico solo, item serui et ea animalia,
quae collo dorsoue domari solent, uelut boues, equi, muli,
asini, item seruitutes praediorum rusticorum. nam.

---

3. *D.* 8, 2, 2 (*Gai.* 175). *Cic. top.* 5, 27 *et Boeth. ad h. l.* (*p.* 319
Bait.). *Quint inst.* 5, 10, 116.
§ 14. obligationes quoquo modo contractae] *cf. infra* 2, 38.
iura praed. urb.] *cf. Cic. de orat.* 1, 39, 179. iura praed. rust.]
cf. infra 2, 17.
§ 14ᵃ. *cf. Ulp.* 19, 1. *supra* 1, 120. *Fr. Vat.* 259 (*Pap.*
693). *C.* 7, 31, 1, 5 (*a.* 531). *Boeth. l.* 3 *ad Cic. top.* 5, 28
(*p.* 321 *Bait.*).

usufruct, obligations however contracted. It is irrelevant that an inheritance may include corporeal things, that what a usufructuary takes from the land will also be corporeal, and that what is owed to us by virtue of an obligation is usually corporeal, such as land, a slave, or money. The point is that the actual right of inheritance is incorporeal, as is the actual right to the use and fruits of a thing, and the right inherent in an obligation. The rights which belong to urban and rustic estates also come under this heading. [**Rights of urban land** are such as the right of raising a building higher and obstructing a neighbour's light] or **of not raising it higher to prevent obstruction of a neighbour's light**; again, a right of streams or run-offs [that is, **that a neighbour receive a stream or run-off on to his buildings or his site**; again a right to insert a sewer and to have light. **The following are rights belonging to rustic land; way, passage, drive**; also **driving cattle to water, or aqueduct. These rights** whether belonging to rustic or to urban land **are called servitudes**].

14a. Moreover, things are capable of mancipation* or they are not. [The former are such as an estate on land in Italy or a house on such land, and again, slaves and animals usually broken in as beasts of draught or burden, such as oxen, horses, mules, donkeys; again servitudes belonging to rustic land], for servitudes belonging to urban lands are not. Stipendiary* and

tributaria nec mancipi sunt. 15. Sed quod diximus *ea*
animalia, quae domari solent[1], mancipi esse, n ————
| ———— *v.* 1¾ ———— |[2] statim ut nata sunt, mancipi esse
putant[3]; Nerua uero et Proculus et ceteri diuersae
scholae auctores non aliter ea mancipi esse putant
quam si domita sunt; et si propter nimiam feritatem
domari non possunt, tunc uideri mancipi esse incipere,
cum ad eam aetatem peruenerint, in qua[4] domari solent. 16. *At* ferae bestiae nec mancipi sunt, uelut ursi,
leones, item ea animalia, quae ferarum[5] bestiarum
numero sunt, uelut elefanti et cameli, et ideo ad rem
non pertinet, quod haec animalia etiam collo dorsoue
domari *solent*; nam ne *notitia* quidem eorum animalium
illo tempore fuit, qu*o* constituebatur quasdam res mancipi esse, quasdam ne*c*[6] mancipi. 17. Sed item fere
omnia, quae incorporalia sunt, nec mancipi sunt, exceptis seruitutibus praediorum rusticorum; nam eas
mancipi esse constat, quamuis sint ex numero rerum
incorporalium.

18. Magna autem differentia est inter mancipi res
et nec mancipi. 19. Nam res nec mancipi ipsa traditione pleno iure alterius fiunt, si modo corporales
sunt et ob id recipiunt traditionem. 20. Itaque si tibi

58
t. s

---

1) ea—solent *suppl. Krueger.*   2) nostri quidem praeceptores haec animalia *Hu. fere suppl., conatus etiam cetera,*
quae in lacuna fuerint, divinare. sed haec nimis incerta.
3) putantur V.   4) in qua] quia V. *cf. supra* 1, 197.
5) ferarum *Goeschen.* fere V. *cf. Kalb, Arch. Lexicogr.* I, 83.
6) non V. — *ceteras res mobiles* (§§ 20. 81) *praeter animalia*
Gaius omittit etiam § 32.

---

§ 15. *cf. Isid. orig.* 9, 4, 45 (*Bruns* II[7], 83).
§ 16. *cf. Varro r. r.* 2, 6, 3. 2, 9, 7 (*Ed. Aedil. D.* 21, 1, 40).
§ 17. *cf. supra* 1, 120. *infra* 2, 27; 29. *Ulp.* 19, 1. *Fr.*
Vat. 45 (*Paul.* 1011).
§ 19. *cf. infra* 2, 28. *D.* 41, 1, 43, 1 (*Gai.* 159). *I.* 2, 1, 40
cum Theoph. (*p.* 115 *Ferr.*). *Ulp.* 19, 7. *Boeth. l. c. p.* 322.
§ 20. *cf. D.* 41, 1, 31 *pr.* (*Paul.* 482).

tributary* lands are not capable of mancipation. 15. But when we say that animals which are usually broken in are capable of mancipation, [the authorities of our school* think that they are so] as soon as they are born; on the other hand Nerva, Proculus and the rest of the authorities of the other school think that they are not capable of mancipation unless they have been broken in; and if they cannot be broken in because they are too wild, they are to be regarded as becoming capable of mancipation when they have reached the age at which they are usually broken in. 16. Again, wild beasts such as bears and lions, and also those animals which are to be counted as wild, such as elephants and camels, are not capable of mancipation. It is irrelevant that the latter are also commonly broken in for use as beasts of draught or burden; they were not even known about when it was determined that some things were capable of mancipation and some were not. 17. Again, more or less all incorporeal things are incapable of mancipation, the exception being servitudes belonging to rustic lands; for it is settled that they are capable of mancipation although they are counted as incorporeal.

18. Now, there is a great difference between things capable of mancipation and those which are not. 19. For the latter become the full property of someone else by the very act of delivery, provided that they are corporeal and so capable of delivery. 20. And so, if I deliver to you clothing or gold or silver, whether on the

uestem uel aurum uel argentum tradidero siue ex uen-
ditionis causa siue ex donationis siue quauis alia ex
causa, statim tua fit ea res, si modo ego eius dominus
59
t. s. sim.   21. In¹ eadem | causa sunt prouincialia praedia,
quorum alia stipendiaria, alia tributaria uocamus:
stipendiaria sunt ea, quae in his prouinciis sunt, quae
propriae populi Romani esse intelleguntur; tributaria
sunt ea, quae in his prouinciis sunt, quae propriae
Caesaris esse creduntur.   22. Mancipi uero res sunt,
quae² per mancipationem ad alium transferuntur; unde
etiam mancipi res sunt dictae.   quod autem ualet mancipatio, *idem ualet et in iurc cessio.*   23. *Et mancipatio*³ quidem quemadmodum fiat, superiore commentario tradidimus.   24. In iure cessio autem hoc modo
fit: apud magistratum populi Romani uel*ut* praetorem
urbanum [aut praesides prouinciae]⁴ is, cui res in iure ceditur, rem tenens ita dicit: HVNC EGO HOMINEM EX IVRE
QVIRITIVM MEVM ESSE AIO; deinde postquam hic uin-
dica*uerit, praetor inter*rogat eum, qui cedit, an contra
uindicet; quo negante aut tacente tunc ei, qui uindi-

---

1) *ante* in *duae litterae* ic *vel* io *vel una* m *fuerunt in* V,
quibus iure ciuili *significari putaverunt Hu., Polen., Muirh. sed
cf. Studemundi supplementum. fortasse ante* in *fuit* fere *vel
simile quid. neque enim provincialia praedia* pleno iure (2, 19),
*sicut ceterae res nec mancipi, traditione alterius fieri possunt,
quoniam eorum proprietas est populi Romani aut Caesaris.
cf.* 2, 7.   2) sunt quae *del. Hu.*   3) idem — mancipatio *suppl.
Goeschen, Savigny.*   4) uelut — prouinciae] ū p̄r. ū a p̄r. praesides prouinciae V.

---

§ 21. *cf. supra* 1, 6. 2, 7. *Fr. Vat.* 61. 259. 288. 285. 289.
293. 315. 316. *I.* 2, 1, 40 *cum Theoph.* (*p.* 115 *Ferr.*).
§ 22. *cf. supra* 1, 119; 120. *infra* 2, 204. *Ulp.* 19, 3. *Fr.
Vat.* 311 (*Paul.* 41). *Diocl. et Const. Fr. Vat.* 313 (*a.* 296).
Boeth. l. 3 *ad Cic. top.* 5, 28 (*p.* 322 *Bait.*). *Varr. r. r.* 2, 10, 4
(*Bruns* II⁷, 63).
§ 23. *cf. supra* 1, 119.
§ 24. = *Boeth. l.* 3 *ad Cic. top.* 5, 28 (*p.* 322 *Bait.*). *cf.
Ulp.* 19, 9; 10. *supra* 1, 134. *infra* 2, 65.

basis of a sale or a gift or on any other basis, it immediately becomes yours, provided that I am owner of it. 21. **Land in the provinces**, which we **call either stipendiary or tributary land**, is in the same situation. **Stipendiary** land means land in the provinces which are regarded as belonging to the Roman people; **tributary** means land in the provinces which are understood to belong to the Emperor. 22. On the other hand, things capable of mancipation are those which are transferred to someone else by mancipation, which is just why they are so called. But an assignment in court* has the same effect as a mancipation. 23. We explained in the previous commentary how a mancipation takes place. 24. Assignment in court, however, is done in this way: in the presence of a magistrate of the Roman people such as the Urban Praetor* [or provincial governors] the assignee takes hold of the thing and says 'I say that this slave is mine by quiritary right*'; and then after he has made his vindication* the praetor asks the assignor whether he is making a counter-vindication. If he says that he is not or is silent the magistrate

cauerit, eam rem addicit; idque legis actio uocatur.
hoc fieri potest etiam in prouinciis apud praesides
earum. 25. Plerumque tamen et fere semper mancipationibus utimur: quod enim ipsi per nos praesentibus amicis agere possumus, hoc non interest *nec* necesse[1] cum maiore difficultate apud praetorem aut
apud praesidem prouinciae agere. 26. Quod si neque
mancipata neque in iure cessa sit res mancipi[2] | ——— 60 t. s.

————————————————| ——————— *vv. 8* —————————|[3] 61 t. s.

27. *Praeterea admo*nendi sumus, *quod ueteres dicebant soli
Italici nexum* esse, prouincialis soli nexum non *esse, hanc
habere* significationem: solum *Italicum* mancipi *esse*, pro-
uinciale nec mancipi es*se*. aliter enim ueteri lingua a*ctus
uocatur, et quod illis nexus, idem nobis est* mancipa*tio*.[4]

28. *Res* incorporales traditionem non recipere manifestum est. 29. Sed iura praediorum urbanorum in
iure cedi *tantum* possunt; rusticorum uero etiam man-

---

1) nec *duplicavit Hu.*   2) '*puta secutum esse:* sed tantum tradita. *ceterum* V *ex hac pag. pauca tantum continet
verba initio quorundam versuum, velut v.* 7 m plena possessio
concessa, *v.* 8 ex formula quamquam (*pro hoc sed dubie* qua hi
qui *Suppl.*), *v.* 11 fructus na, *v.* 12 Item adhuc i, *v.* 17 non
fuissent. *suspicari licet Gaium in hac pag. primum dixisse rem
mancipi tantum traditam non effici accipientis ex iure Quir.,
donec usucapiatur (in bonis fieri postea demum dicit* § 41);
*deinde exposuisse de iure commercii, et plenius quidem quam
Ulp.* 19, 4; 5'. *Hu.*   3) *reliquias vide in apographo.*
4) *suppl. Beseler Z. S.* 45, 414; *similiter Bonfante, Corso* II
2, 314, 1.

---

§ 26. *cf. infra* 2, 41; 204.
§ 27. *cf. supra* 1, 120. 2, 7; 21. *C.* 7, 31, 1 (*a.* 531). *Gromat. ed. Lachm. p.* 36 (*Bruns* II[7], 86). 62 *Cic. pro Flacc.* 32, 80
('Illud quaero, sintne ista praedia censui censendo, habeant
ius ciuile, sint necne sint mancipi'). *Sozom. hist. eccl.* 7, 9.
§ 28. *cf. supra* 2, 19. *D.* 41, 1, 43, 1 (*Gai.* 159).
§ 29. *cf. supra* 2, 17. *D.* 8, 2, 39 (*Paul.* 998). *Fr. Vat.*
45 (*Paul.* 1011).

awards the thing to the person who vindicated; and this is called an action in the law*. This can also take place in the provinces in the presence of the governor. 25. But generally, in fact more or less always, we mancipate. For there is no point and no need to do with greater difficulty in the presence of a praetor or the governor of a province what we can do ourselves in the presence of friends. 26. But if a thing capable of mancipation has neither been mancipated nor assigned in court ... [in the missing passage Gaius probably said that the effect was that the thing did not become the full property of the transferee until it had been usucapted*; he may have gone on to explain the so-called right of commerce held by Roman citizens and by others to whom it was given as a privilege.] 27. We may also notice that when the old lawyers* said that there was binding (in Latin 'nexus') of Italian land and not of provincial land this means that Italian land was capable of mancipation and that provincial land was not. For in the old language there was a different name for the act and what they called 'nexus' we call mancipation.

28. Obviously, incorporeal things are incapable of delivery. 29. Urban praedial servitudes can be dealt with only by assignment in court; rustic ones, on the other hand, can also be mancipated. 30. A usufruct

cipari possunt. 30. Ususfructus in iure cessionem tantum recipit: nam dominus proprietatis alii usumfructum in iure cedere potest, ut ille usumfructum habeat et ipse nudam proprietatem *retineat.* ipse usufructuarius in iure cedendo domino proprietatis usumfructum efficit, ut a se discedat et conuertatur in proprietatem; alii uero in iure cedendo nihilo minus ius suum retinet: creditur enim ea cessione nihil agi. 31. Sed haec scilicet in Italicis praediis ita sunt, quia 62 et ipsa praedia mancipationem | et in iure cessionem recipiunt. alioquin in prouincialibus praediis siue quis usumfructum siue ius eundi agendi aquamue ducendi uel altius tollendi aedes aut non tollendi, ne luminibus uicini officiatur, ceteraque similia iura[1] constituere uelit, pactionibus et stipulationibus id efficere potest; quia ne ipsa quidem praedia mancipationem aut *in* iure cessionem recipiunt. 32. Sed[2] cum ususfructus et hominum et ceterorum animalium constitui possit, intellegere debemus horum[3] usumfructum etiam in prouinciis per in iure cessionem constitui posse. 33. Quod autem diximus usumfructum in iure cessionem tantum recipere, non est temere dictum, quamuis[4] etiam per mancipationem constitui possit eo, quod iu mancipanda proprietate detrahi potest; non enim ipse ususfructus mancipatur, sed cum in mancipanda proprietate deducatur, eo fit, ut apud[5] alium ususfructus, apud alium proprietas sit.

---

1) uel — iura *del. Solazzi.*   2) recipiunt. Sed] recipiunt' et V. quia — recipiunt *glossam esse censet Rabel.*   3) honorum V.   4) quamuis *Goeschen.* quod iis V.   5) apυtut V.

---

§ 30. *cf. Paul.* 3, 6, 32. *Fr. Vat.* 45. 47. 48. 49. 50. 54. 75, 4. *Ulp.* 19, 11. *infra* 2, 33. *I.* 2, 4, 3. *D.* 23, 3, 66 (*Pomp.* 254).
§ 31. *cf. Gai epit.* 2, 1, 3. *I.* 2, 4, 1. 2, 3, 4. *D.* 7, 1, 3 *pr.* (*Gai.* 494). 7, 1, 25, 7 (*Ulp.* 2587).
§ 32. *cf. D.* 7, 1, 3, 1 (*Gai.* 494).
§ 33. *cf. supra* 2, 30. *Fr. Vat.* 47 (*Paul.* 985). 50 (*Paul.* 989) *D.* 7, 1, 32 (*Pomp.* 775).

can only be assigned in court. For the person in whom the property is vested can assign a usufruct to someone else so that the latter has a usufruct and he himself retains the bare property. The effect of the **usufructuary's assigning to the person in whom the property is vested** is that the usufruct leaves him and becomes part of the property again. If, on the other hand, he assigns to anyone else he still retains his right; **for by such an assignment he** is regarded as **achieving nothing at all.** 31. That is to say, this is what happens in the case of Italian land because the land itself can be mancipated and assigned in court. It is a different thing in the case of provincial land. **If someone wishes to constitute a usufruct or a right of way or a right of drive or aqueduct** or of raising a house higher or **of not raising it higher to prevent obstruction of a neighbour's light** and other similar rights **he can do it by pacts and stipulations,** because even the land itself cannot be mancipated or assigned in court. 32. But as there can be a usufruct both of slaves and of the other animals, we must understand that even in the provinces it can be constituted by assignment in court. 33. Now, when we said that a usufruct can only be assigned in court this was not a slip of the tongue, although it can be constituted by mancipation also, in the sense that it can be excepted in mancipating the property. It is not the usufruct as such which is mancipated; when it is deducted in the course of a mancipation the result is that one party holds a usufruct and another the property.

34. Hereditas quoque in iure cessionem tantum recipit. 35. Nam si is, ad quem ab intestato legitimo iure pertinet hereditas, in iure eam alii ante aditionem cedat, id est antequam heres extiterit, proinde fit heres is, cui in iure cesserit, ac si ipse per legem ad hereditatem uocatus esset: post obligationem uero si cesserit, nihilo minus ipse | heres permanet et ob id 63 creditoribus[1] tenebitur, debita uero pereunt, eoque modo debitores hereditarii lucrum faciunt; corpora uero eius hereditatis proinde transeunt ad eum, cui cessa est hereditas, ac si ei singula in iure cessa fuissent. 36. Testamento autem scriptus heres ante aditam quidem hereditatem in iure cedendo eam alii nihil agit[2]; postea uero quam adierit si cedat, ea accidunt, quae proxime diximus de eo, ad quem ab intestato legitimo iure pertinet hereditas, si post obligationem in iure cedat. 37. Idem et de necessariis heredibus diuersae scholae auctores existimant, quod nihil uidetur interesse, utrum *aliquis* adeundo hereditatem[3] fiat heres an inuitus existat.[4] quod quale sit, suo loco apparebit: sed nostri praeceptores putant nihil agere necessarium heredem, cum in iure cedat hereditatem.[5]

38. Obligationes quoquo modo contractae nihil eorum recipiunt: nam quod mihi ab aliquo debetur, id si uelim tibi deberi, nullo eorum modo, quibus res corporales ad alium transferuntur, id efficere possum[6];

---

1) acreditoribus V.   2) agi V.   3) hereditatemstatem V.
4) existant V.   5) §§ 35—37 *a Gaio abiudicat Solazzi*.
6) possumus V.

---

§ 34. cf. Ulp. 19, 11. Serv. ad Verg. Aen. 3, 297.
§ 35. cf. infra 3, 85. Ulp. 19, 12—14. D. 44, 4, 4, 28 (Ulp. 1681). C. 7, 75, 1 (a. 213). Senec. de benef. 6, 5, 3. cesserit] 'sive ipse heres, sive is, cuius is iuri postea subiectus est, velut si sua heres filia in manum eius convenerit (3, 84)'. Hu. Varr. r. r. 3, 16, 2.
§ 36. cf. infra 3, 86. Ulp. 19, 13; 14. Plin. ep. 5, 1, 3.
§ 37. cf. infra 3, 87. suo loco] infra 2, 152 sq.
§ 38. cf. supra 2, 14; 19; 22. infra 3, 176.

34. An inheritance also can be dealt with only by assignment in court. 35. For if someone who has a statutory title to an inheritance on intestacy assigns the inheritance to someone else before he accepts it, that is before he has become heir, the person to whom he has assigned it becomes heir just as if he himself were entitled to the inheritance by statute; but if the heir makes the assignment in court after he has become bound he himself still remains heir and so is liable to the creditors. On the other hand debts owed are extinguished and so the debtors to the inheritance gain; but the physical things in the inheritance pass to the person to whom the inheritance was assigned just as if the individual things had been assigned to him in court. 36. However, if a person who has been appointed heir in a will assigns the inheritance in court to someone else before accepting it he achieves nothing at all; on the other hand, if he assigns it after acceptance the same effects follow as we have just explained in the case of someone with a statutory title to an inheritance on intestacy who assigns the inheritance in court after he has become bound. 37. The authorities of the other school consider that the same applies also in the case of compulsory heirs*, because it does not seem to matter whether someone becomes heir by accepting an inheritance or becomes heir against his own wishes. How that comes about will appear in due course. But our teachers think that when a compulsory heir assigns the inheritance in court he achieves nothing at all.

38. None of this applies to obligations, however contracted; for if I want something owed by someone to me to be owed to you, I cannot achieve this in any of the ways by which corporeal things are transferred to someone else, but you must stipulate from him on my

sed opus est, ut iubente me tu ab eo stipuleris; quae
res efficit, ut a me liberetur et incipiat tibi teneri.
quae dicitur nouatio obligationis. 39. Sine hac uero
nouatione non poteris[1] tuo nomine agere, sed debes
64 ex persona mea quasi cognitor | aut procurator meus
experiri.

40. Sequitur, ut admoneamus apud peregrinos
quidem unum esse dominium; nam aut dominus quisque est aut dominus non intellegitur. quo iure etiam
populus Romanus olim utebatur: aut enim ex iure
Quiritium unusquisque dominus erat aut non intellege-
batur dominus. sed postea diuisionem accepit dominium, ut alius possit esse ex iure Quiritium dominus,
alius in bonis habere. 41. Nam si tibi rem mancipi
neque mancipauero neque in iure cessero, sed tantum
tradidero, in bonis quidem tuis ea res efficitur, ex
iure Quiritium uero mea permanebit, donec tu eam
possidendo usucapias: semel enim impleta usucapione
proinde pleno iure incipit, id est et in bonis et ex
iure Quiritium tua res esse, ac si ea mancipata uel in
iure cessa *esset*. 42. *Vsucapio autem*[2] mobilium quidem
rerum anno completur, fundi uero et aedium biennio;
et ita lege XII tabularum cautum est.

43. Ceterum[3] etiam earum rerum usucapio nobis
conpetit, quae non a domino nobis traditae fuerint,

---

1) poterit V.   2) esset—autem *suppl. Lachmann.*
3) ceterarum V.

§ 39. *cf. infra* 4, 82; 86.
§ 40. *cf. supra* 1, 54; 35; 167. *infra* 2, 88. 3, 166. *Theoph.*
1, 5, 4 (*p.* 25 *Ferr.*).
§ 41. *cf. supra* 2, 26. *infra* 2, 204. 3, 80. *Ulp.* 1, 16. *D.*
40, 12, 38, 2 (*Paul.* 1573).
§ 42. *cf. Ulp.* 19, 8. *I.* 2, 6 *pr. cum Theoph.* (*p.* 129 *Ferr.*).
infra 2, 54; 204. *C.* 7, 31, 1 (*a.* 531). *Cic. pro Caec.* 19, 54.
topic. 4, 23. *Plin. ep.* 5, 1, 10. *Boeth. l.* 2 *ad Cic. top.* 4, 23,
unde Isid. orig. 5, 25, 30 (*Bruns* II[7], 74).
§§ 43. 44. *cf. infra* 2, 49. *Ulp.* 19, 8. *I.* 2, 6 *pr. D.* 41,
10, 5 (*Ner.* 36). 41, 3, 1 (*Gai.* 333).

instructions. The result is that he is released from his obligation to me and becomes liable to you; this is called novation of the obligation. 39. Without this novation you will not be able to sue in your own name but you must raise the action in my name as if you were my representative in court* or my agent*.

40. Next we must note that among foreigners* there is only one type of ownership; for with them a person either is owner or is not understood to be owner. At one time the Roman people had the same rule; for everyone was either owner by quiritary right or he was not understood to be owner at all. But afterwards a division was made of ownership, so that one person can be owner by quiritary right and another can have the thing in his estate*. 41. For if I have neither mancipated a thing capable of mancipation nor assigned it to you in court but have merely delivered it, the thing certainly becomes part of your estate; on the other hand it will remain mine by quiritary right, until you usucapt it by possessing it. With usucapion once completed, the thing becomes fully yours, that is both as part of your estate and by quiritary right, just as if it had been mancipated or assigned in court. 42. Now, in the case of **moveables**, usucapion is completed **in one year**, in the case of land and houses on the other hand, **in two years;** and this is provided by the Twelve Tables*.

43. But we can also usucapt things which have not been delivered to us by the owner, whether they are

siue mancipi sint eae res siue nec mancipi, si modo eas[1] bona fide acceperimus, cum crederemus eum, qui traderet, dominum esse. 44. Quod ideo receptum uidetur, ne rerum dominia diutius in incerto essent, cum sufficeret domino ad inquirendam rem suam anni aut | biennii spatium, quod tempus ad usucapionem posses- 65 sori tributum est.

45. Sed aliquando etiamsi maxime quis bona fide alienam rem possideat, non tamen illi usucapio procedit, uelut si quis[2] rem furtiuam aut ui possessam possideat[3]; nam furtiuam lex XII tabularum usucapi prohibet, ui possessam lex Iulia et Plautia. 46. Item prouincialia praedia usucapionem[4] *non* recipiunt. 47. *Item olim*[5] mulieris, quae in agnatorum tutela erat[6], res mancipi usucapi non poterant, praeterquam si ab ipsa tutore *auctore* traditae essent: id ita lege[7] XII tabularum *cautum erat.*[8] 48. Item liberos homines et res sacras et religiosas usucapi non posse manifestum est. 49. Quod ergo uulgo dicitur furtiuarum rerum et ui possessarum[9] usucapionem per legem[10] XII tabularum prohibitam esse, non eo pertinet, ut ne *ipse fur quiue* per uim *possidet*[11], usucapere *possit* (nam huic alia ratione usucapio non competit, quia scilicet mala fide

---

1) ea V.   2) qui V.   3) possideatur V.   4) usucapio V.
5) item olim *Goeschen.* res V.   6) erant V.   7) legem V.
8) m (*rel* ca?) f V.   9) et ui possessarum *del. Appleton.*
10) lege V. 11) quiue — possidet *del. Appleton.*

§ 45. cf. *infra* 2, 49. *I.* 2, 6, 1; 2.   *D.* 47, 8, 6 (*Ven.* 75). 41, 3, 33 *pr.* (*Iul.* 614). 41, 3, 4, 6 (*Paul.* 673), *Gell.* 17, 7. lex Iulia et Plautia] cf. *D.* 41, 8, 33, 2 (*Iul.* 614). 41, 3, 4, 22; 23 (*Paul.* 674).
§ 46. cf. *supra* 2, 7; 21. *I.* 2, 6 *pr.* *C.* 7, 31, 1, 2 (*a.* 531).
§ 47. cf. *supra* 1, 192. *infra* 2, 80. *Fr. Vat.* 259 (*Pap.* 693). *Fr. Vat.* 1 (*Paul.* 1782). *Cic. ad Att.* 1, 5, 6. *pro Flacco* 34, 84.
§ 48. cf. *I.* 2, 6, 1.   *D.* 41, 3, 9 (*Gai.* 110).   *C.* 7, 14, 6 (*a.* 293). 7, 22, 3 (*a.* 314). *Cic. de harusp. resp.* 14, 32. *Gromat.* ed. *Lachm. p.* 56.
§ 49. = *I.* 2, 6, 3. cf. *D.* 41, 3, 24 (*Pomp.* 289).

capable of mancipation or not, provided that we receive them **in good faith, in the belief that the person who delivered them was owner.** 44. And this appears to have been accepted **to prevent** too lengthy **uncertainty over title,** because the period of one or two years granted to the possessor for usucapion **gave the owner long enough to discover his property.**

45. **But sometimes usucapion will not work to the advantage of the possessor of** another's **thing, even although his possession is definitely in good faith. Examples are where he possesses something stolen or taken by force; the reason is that the Twelve Tables** prohibit **usucapion of a stolen thing and the Julian-Plautian Act does the same for a thing taken by force.** 46. Again, land in the provinces is not usucapted. 47. And at one time things capable of mancipation belonging to a woman* who was under the guardianship* of her agnates* could not be usucapted, except where they had been delivered by her with her guardian's authorisation*; this was provided by the Twelve Tables. 48. Again, **free persons** and **sacred and religious things** obviously **cannot be usucapted.** 49. **And so the point of the** common **saying** that the Twelve Tables **prohibited usucapion of things stolen and taken by force is not to exclude the thief or the violent taker himself from the right to usucapt. He is excluded anyhow for another reason: he possesses in bad faith. It is**

possidet), sed nec ullus alius, quamquam ab eo bona
fide emerit, usucapiendi ius habeat. 50. Vnde in rebus
mobilibus non facile p*rocedit, ut bonae fidei possessori
usucapio c*ompetat, quia qui alienam rem uendidit et
tradidit, furtum committit; idemque accidit etiam, si
ex alia causa tradatur. sed tamen hoc aliquando aliter
se habet; nam si heres rem defuncto commodatam aut
locatam uel apud eum depositam[1] existimans eam esse
66 here|ditariam, uendiderit aut donauerit, furtum non
committit; item si is, ad quem ancillae ususfructus
pertinet, partum etiam[2] suum esse credens uendiderit
aut donauerit, furtum non committit; *f*urtum enim sine
affectu furandi non committitur. aliis quoque modis
accidere potest, ut quis sine uitio furti rem alien*am
ad aliquem transferat et efficiat, ut a possessore usucapiatur. 51. Fundi quoque alieni potest aliquis s*ine
ui[3] possessionem nancisci, quae uel ex neglegentia domini uacet, uel quia dominus sine successore decesserit uel longo tempore afuerit: quam[4] si ad alium
bona fide accipientem transtulerit, poterit usucapere
possessor; et quamuis ipse, qui uacantem possessionem
nactus est, intellegat alienum esse fun*d*um, *tamen* nihil
*hoc bonae fidei p*ossessori ad usucapionem nocet, *cum
inprobata sit eorum sententia, qui putauerint furt*iuum
fundum fieri posse.

---

1) eum depositam *Inst.* eundem positam V.   2) et V.
eius *coni. Hu. cf. Dig.*   3) sine ui] ine ui *corr. ex* in eum V.
4) quam *Goeschen.* nam V.

---

§ 50. = *I.* 2, 6, 3 *med.* — 6. *cf. D.* 41, 3, 36 (*Gai.* 492).
furtum non committit — committitur] = *D.* 41, 3, 37 *pr.* quia
qui alienam] *cf. C.* 7, 26, 1 (*a.* 213). 7, 26, 7 (*a.* 294). ancillae ususfructus] *cf. Paul.* 3, 6, 19. furtum enim] *cf. infra*
3, 197. aliis modis] *cf. D.* 17, 1, 57 (*Pap.* 639). 41, 8, 4 (*Paul.* 668).
§ 51. Fundi — afuerit] = *D.* 41, 3, 37, 1. *cf. I.* 2, 6, 7. *D.*
41, 3, 38 (*Gai.* 493). furtiuum fundum fieri posse] *cf. Sabin.
ap. Gell.* 11, 18, 13 (*Iurispr.* I, 74). *D.* 41, 3, 38 (*Gai.* 493). 47,
2, 25 *pr.* (*Ulp.* 2862).

rather that a third party has no right to usucapt even after buying from him in good faith. 50. And so with moveable things such a possessor cannot often rely on usucapion, because someone who sells and delivers another's property commits theft; the same applies even if the delivery is on some other basis. Yet sometimes the result is different. Suppose that an heir, in the belief that it forms part of the inheritance, sells or gifts something that had in fact been given on loan* or hired to or deposited with the deceased; he does not commit theft. Again, a person with a usufruct in a female slave who sells or gives away the offspring in the belief that they are his does not commit theft. Theft is not committed without intent to steal. There are also other ways that someone can transfer a third party's property to another without the taint of theft and leave it possible for the recipient to usucapt the thing. 51. A person can also acquire possession of another's land without using force, if it is lying unoccupied through the neglect of its owner or because the owner has died with no successor or has been away for a long time; if he transfers it to another who receives in good faith, the possessor can usucapt. Although the person who took possession of the unoccupied land knows that it belongs to someone else this does not prejudice the usucapion of the possessor in good faith at all, because the opinion of those who thought that land could be stolen has been discarded.

52. Rursus ex contrario accidit, ut qui sciat alienam rem se possidere, usucapiat, uelut si rem hereditariam, cuius possessionem heres nondum nactus est, aliquis possederit[1]; nam ei concessum *est usu*capere, si modo ea res est, quae recipit usucapionem. quae species possessionis et usucapionis pro herede uocatur. 53. Et in tantum haec usucapio concessa est, | ut et 67 res, quae solo continentur, anno usucapiantur. 54. Quare autem hoc casu etiam[2] soli rerum annua constituta sit usucapio, illa ratio est, quod olim rerum hereditariarum possessione[3] ipsae hereditates usucapi credebantur, scilicet anno: lex enim XII tabularum soli quidem res biennio usucapi iussit, ceteras uero anno: ergo hereditas in ceteris rebus uidebatur esse, quia soli non est [quia neque corporalis est][4]; *et* quamuis postea creditum sit ipsas hereditates usucapi non posse, tamen in omnibus rebus hereditariis, etiam quae solo tenentur[5], annua usucapio remansit. 55. Quare autem omnino tam inproba possessio et usucapio concessa sit, illa ratio est, quod uoluerunt ueteres maturius hereditates adiri, ut essent, qui sacra facerent, quorum illis temporibus summa obseruatio fuit, ut et creditores haberent, a quo suum consequerentur. 56. Haec autem species possessionis et usucapionis etiam lucratiua uocatur: nam sciens quisque rem alienam lucri-

---

1) posiderit V.　　2) hoc casu etiam] etiam hoc casu V. 3) possessionesut V.　　4) *uncis inclusa del. Polenaar tamquam glossema. cf. etiam Kalb, Archiv. Lexicogr. Latin.* I, 88. 5) teneantur V.

§ 52. *cf. infra* 3, 201. *supra* 2, 9. *D.* 41, 3, 29 (*Pomp.* 696). *Plin. ep.* 5, 1, 10. si modo ea res est] *cf. supra* 2, 45 *sq.*

§§ 53. 54. *cf. Cic. pro Flacco* 34, 85. *ad Att.* 1, 5, 6. *top.* 6, 29. *Senec. de benef.* 6, 5, 3. *supra ad* 2, 42 *cit.*

§ 55. *cf. Cic. de leg.* 2, 19, 47 *sq. pro Mur.* 12, 27. *Fest. v. sacer p.* 318 (*Bruns* II[7], 38). *v. sine sacris p.* 290 (*Bruns* II[7], 39). *Paul* 4, 3, 3. *Plaut. Capt.* 4, 1, 7 = 775. *Trin.* 2, 4, 83 = 484.

§ 56. *cf. D.* 47, 2, 72 (71), 1 (*Iav.* 61). 41, 5, 2, 1 (*Iul.* 620). 41, 3, 33, 1 (*Iul.* 614).

52. Then, conversely, there are cases where someone who knows that he is in possession of another's thing will usucapt it. For instance, if someone has taken possession of a thing belonging to an inheritance before the heir has done so, he is permitted to usucapt it, provided that the thing is capable of usucapion; this kind of possession and usucapion is called 'as heir'. 53. This kind of usucapion even allows immoveables to be usucapted in a year. 54. Now the reason why in this case a one year usucapion has been admitted even for immoveables is that at one time it was believed that inheritances themselves were usucapted through possession of things belonging to the inheritance, namely in a year. For the Twelve Tables authorised the usucapion of immoveables in two years, but for other things it was one. And so an inheritance was regarded as comprised in other things, because it is not a form of land; [because it is not even corporeal]. And although the view was later taken that inheritances themselves could not be usucapted, usucapion in a year stayed for everything belonging to an inheritance, even what is immoveable. 55. Now, why such an improper possession and usucapion was allowed at all is that the old lawyers wanted inheritances to be accepted more quickly so that there would be someone to perform the sacred rites, which was done meticulously in those days, and so that the creditors would have someone from whom to claim their debts. 56. This kind of possession and usucapion is also called lucrative; for each taker knowingly makes gain from another's property. 57. But these days it is no longer

facit. 57. Sed hoc tempore iam[1] non est lucratiua:
nam ex auctoritate *diui*[2] Hadriani senatus consultum
factum est, ut tales usucapiones reuocarentur; et ideo
potest heres ab eo, qui rem usucepit, hereditatem
petendo proinde[3] eam rem consequi, atque si usucapta
68 non esset. | 58. *Suo*[4] et necessario tamen herede extante
nihil ipso iure pro herede usucapi potest. 59. Adhuc etiam
ex aliis causis sciens quisque rem alienam usucapit: nam
qui rem alicui fiduciae causa mancipio dederit uel in iure
cesserit, si eandem ipse possederit, potest usucapere, anno
scilicet, *si mobilis sit, biennio*[5], soli si sit. quae species usucapionis dicitur usureceptio, quia id, quod aliquando habuimus, recipimus per usucapionem. 60. Sed
cum fiducia contrahitur aut cum creditore pignoris
iure aut cum amico, quo[6] tutius nostrae res apud eum
essent, si quidem cum amico contracta sit fiducia, sane
omni modo conpetit usus receptio; si uero cum creditore, soluta quidem pecunia omni modo conpetit, nondum uero soluta ita demum competit, si neque con-
duxerit eam rem a creditore debitor neque precario
rogauerit, ut eam rem possidere liceret; quo casu lucratiua usus capio conpetit. 61. Item si rem obligatam

---

1) etiam V.   2) *add. Hu.*   3) p̄. inde V.   4) *add. Solazzi
Dir. her.* 2, 10.   5) *suppl. Beseler Beitr.* 2, 1; etiam *Lachmann.*   6) quod V.

§ 57. *cf. D.* 4, 6, 17 *pr.* (*Ulp.* 432)? 43, 2, 1 *pr.* (*Ed. Ulp.* 1460).
§ 58. *cf. infra* 3, 201. *C.* 7, 29, 2 (*a.* 293).
§ 59. *cf. Paul.* 2, 13. 3, 6, 16. 5, 1, 1.   *Plaut. Bacchid.* 3,
3, 9 = 413. *Trinumm.* 1, 2, 79 = 116 *sq. Cic. de off.* 3, 17, 70.
pro Flacco 21, 51. *Boeth. libr.* 4 *ad Cic. top.* 10, 41 (*p.* 340
Bait.; Bruns II[7], 74). *Isid. orig.* 5, 25, 23 (*Bruns* II[7], 82). *C.
I. L.* II, 5042. 5406 (*Bruns* I[7], 334). *C. I. L.* IV *Suppl.* 154
(*Bruns* I[7], 332).
§ 60. neque precario rogauerit] *cf. D.* 44, 7, 16 (*Iul.* 217).
13, 7, 22, 3 (*Ulp.* 903). *Isid. orig.* 5, 25, 17 (*Bruns* II[7], 82).
neque conduxerit] *cf. D.* 13, 7, 22, 3 (*Ulp.* 903). 13, 7, 37
(*Paul.* 1111).
§ 61. *cf. D.* 23, 3, 54 (*Gai* 48; *ad edictum praetoris titulo
de praediatoribus*). 18, 5, 9 (*Scaev.* 11). *Varro de l. l.* 5, 40. 6, 74.

lucrative, for on the proposal of the Emperor*
Hadrian a resolution of the Senate was passed so that
such usucapion might be set aside. And so the heir, by
bringing an action to claim the inheritance, can
recover the thing from the person who usucapted it,
just as if it had never been usucapted. 58. But if there
is an immediate and compulsory heir* in existence, as
a matter of law nothing can be usucapted as heir. 59.
But there are still some other situations in which a
person can knowingly usucapt another's property. For
where someone who has mancipated a thing or
assigned it in court to another, in trust*, has himself
obtained possession of the thing he can usucapt it,
that is to say in a year, if it is moveable, or two years if
it is classed as land. This kind of usucapion is called
recovery by use because what we once had we recover
by usucapion. 60. When a trust is entered into – either
with a creditor as a right of pledge or with a friend so
that our property may be safer with him – if the trust
is entered into with a friend, recovery by use is, of
course, always competent. On the other hand, if it is
with a creditor, it is always competent if the money
owed has in fact been paid, but if the money has still
to be paid, recovery by use is only competent if the
debtor has neither leased nor hired the thing from the
creditor nor obtained possession from him by licence;
in that case lucrative usucapion is competent. 61.
Again, if the Roman people have sold a thing over

sibi populus uendiderit eamque dominus possederit[1], concessa est usus receptio: sed *et*[2] hoc casu praedium biennio usurecipitur: et hoc est, quod uolgo dicitur ex praediatura possessionem usurecipi: nam qui mer-- catur a populo, praediator appellatur.

62. Accidit aliquando, ut qui dominus sit, alie- nandae rei potestatem non habeat, et qui dominus non sit, | *ali*enare possit. 63. Nam dotale praedium 69 maritus inuita mulie*re* per leg*e*m Iuliam prohibetur alienare, quamuis ipsius *si*t uel mancipatum ei dotis causa uel in iure cessum uel usucaptum. quod quidem ius utrum ad Italica tantum praedia an etiam ad pro- uincialia pertineat, dubitatur.[3] 64. Ex diuerso agnatus furiosi curator rem furiosi alienare potest ex lege XII tabularum; item procurator | —— *versus dimidius legi nequit* —— |[4] est; item creditor pignus ex pactione, quamuis eius ea res non sit. sed hoc forsitan ideo

---

1) possiderit V.   2) *add. Beseler l. c.*   3) quod — dubi- tatur *del. Solazzi.*   4) *Mommsen suppl.:* si quid, ne corrumpa- tur, distrahendum. *Krueger:* rem absentis, cuius negotiorum libera administratio ei permissa.

Cic. ad Att. 12, 14, 2. 12, 17. *pro Balb.* 20, 45 (= *Val. Max.* 8, 12, 1). *Liv.* 22, 60, 4. *Suet. Claud.* 9. *Fest. s. v. manceps* p. 151 (*Bruns* II[7], 13). *s. v. praes* p. 233 (*Bruns* II[7], 26). *Schol. Bob. ad. Cic. pro Flacc.* 32, 4 p. 244 *Bait. Ps. Ascon. in Cic. Verr.* 2, 1, 54, 142 p. 196 *Bait.* (*Bruns* II[7], 72). *lex Malac.* c. 64 (*Bruns* I[7], 153).

§ 62. = *I.* 2, 8 *pr.*

§ 63. *partim* = *I.* 2, 8 *pr. cf. Paul.* 2, 21[b], 2. *D.* 29, 1, 16 (*Paul.* 599). *de fundo dotali D. tit.* 23, 5. *C. tit.* 5, 23. *C.* 5, 13, 15 (*a.* 530). *Schol Sinait.* § 9.

§ 64. ex lege XII tab.] *cf. Ulp.* 12, 2. *Auct. ad Herenn.* 1, 13, 23. *Cic. de inv.* 2, 50, 148. *D.* 47, 2, 57, 4 (*Iul.* 343). procurator] *cf. D.* 17, 1, 60, 4 (*Scaev.* 234). 41, 1, 9, 4 (*Gai* 491) *fere* = *I.* 2, 1, 42; 43. *C.* 2, 12, 16 (*a.* 293). item creditor pignus] *cf. I.* 2, 8, 1. *Paul.* 2, 5, 1. *D.* 41, 1, 46 (*Ulp.* 1447). 10, 3, 6, 8 (*Ulp.* 640). 10, 2, 29 (*Paul.* 391). *tit.* 20, 5. *C. tit.* 8, 28. *Syr. röm. Rechtsb. ed. Bruns-Sachau* § 95 L. § 130 *Arm.* p. 272. olim pactus] *cf. D.* 47, 2, 71 (*Iav.* 62). 44, 3, 14, 5 (*Scaev.* 192). 13, 7, 4 (*Ulp.* 2874).

which they hold security and the owner has obtained possession of it, recovery by use is allowed; and in this case also land is recovered by usucapion in two years. This is the origin of the common saying that possession is recovered by usucapion in a case of land-dealing with the people (in Latin 'praediatura') for a person who purchases from the people is called a land-dealer.

62. **It sometimes happens that an owner does not have power to alienate and that a non-owner does.** 63. **For under the Julian Act a husband may not alienate land forming part of the dowry without his wife's consent. Yet it is his,** having been mancipated to him **as dowry** or assigned in court or usucapted. But note that there is a doubt whether this rule applies only to **Italian land** or to **provincial land** as well. 64. Against this, under the Twelve Tables the agnatic supervisor* of an insane person can alienate the insane person's property; again a general agent* ... [a gap in the text makes it uncertain what power was mentioned]. Again, **a creditor, under his contract**, has power **to alienate a pledge despite not being its owner. But here the explanation is**

uideatur fieri, quod uoluntate debitoris intellegitur
pignus alienari, qui olim pactus est, ut liceret creditori pignus uendere, si pecunia non soluatur.[1]

65. Ergo ex his, quae diximus, adparet quaedam
naturali iure alienari, qualia sunt ea, quae traditione
alienantur, quaedam ciuili; nam mancipationis et in
iure cessionis et usucapionis ius proprium est ciuium
Romanorum.

66. Nec tamen ea tantum, quae traditione nostra
fiunt, naturali nobis ratione adquiruntur, sed etiam
quae[2] occupando ideo *adepti erimus*[3], quia *antea* nullius essent, qualia sunt omnia, quae terra mari[4] caelo
capiuntur. 67. Itaque si *feram* bestiam aut uolucrem
aut piscem *ceperimus*, *simul atque* captum *fuerit hoc
animal*, *statim nostrum fit*[5], *et eo us*que nostrum esse
70 intellegitur, | donec nostra custodia coerceatur; cum
uero custodiam nostram euaserit et in naturalem se
libertatem receperit[6], rursus occupantis fit, quia nostr*um*
esse desinit: naturalem autem libertatem recipere uidetur, cum aut oculos nostros euaserit, aut licet *in* con-
spectu sit nostro, difficilis tamen eius[7] persecutio sit.
68. In iis autem animalibus, quae ex consuetudine

---

1) sed — soluatur *del. Kniep, Beseler Beitr.* 3, 83, *Albertario;
sed cf. Rotondi, Studii* 2, 580.   2) quae *Goeschen.* ū V (?)
3) *ad sensum supplevimus.*   4) marique V.   5) ceperimus — fit
suppl. Hu. cf. Instit. l. c.   6) perceperit V.   7) eius *Dig.
Inst.* in | rei V.

---

§ 65. *cf. I.* 2, 1, 11. *D.* 41, 1, 1 *pr.* (*Gai.* 491). *Fr. Vat.* 50
(*Paul.* 989). traditione] *cf. supra* 2, 19; 20. *D.* 41, 1, 9, 3 (*Gai.*
491). mancipationis] *cf. supra* 1, 113; 119. 2, 22; 23. in iure
cessionis] *cf. supra* 2, 24 *sq.* usucapionis] *cf. supra* 2, 41 *sq.*
§§ 66—68. *cf. D.* 41, 1, 1, 1; 3 *pr.*; 2; 5 *pr.*; 5 (*Gai.* 491).
I. 2, 1, 12; 15.
§ 66. *cf. D.* 41, 2, 1, 1 (*Paul.* 656). 41, 2, 3, 21 (*Paul.* 659).
occupando] *cf. D.* 41, 1, 30, 4 (*Pomp.* 796). 41, 7, 1 (*Ulp.* 432).
§ 67. *cf. D.* 41, 1, 14 *pr.* (*Ner.* 85). 41, 1, 44 (*Ulp.* 630).
Plaut. Rud. 4, 3, 31 = 971 *sq.*
§ 68. *cf. Coll.* 12, 7, 10 = *D.* 9, 2, 27, 12 (*Ulp.* 623). *D.*
10, 2, 8, 1 (*Ulp.* 632).

perhaps that he alienates the pledge with the debtor's authority, previously given by a term of the contract allowing the creditor the right to sell on failure to repay.

65. And so it is apparent from what we have said that some forms of alienation fall under the law of nature*, for example, alienation by delivery, and some fall under state law*. For the right to use mancipation, assignment in court and usucapion is specific to Roman citizens.

66. But it is not only by delivery that we acquire things as a matter of natural reason; this applies also to things which we get by **first taking** and which become ours because previously they belonged to no one, for example, **everything** caught **on land, in the sea or in the sky.** 67. And so, if we **catch a wild animal** or **bird** or **fish** it becomes ours **as soon as we have caught** it **and it remains** ours **so long as we keep** it **under our control. If it escapes our control and recovers its natural liberty the next taker can have it because it ceases to be ours. It is** thought **to have regained its natural freedom when it** has gone **out of** our **sight or when, though still in sight, it is difficult to reach it. 68. However, in the case of those animals which regularly come and go,** such

abire et redire solent, ueluti columbis et apibus, item
ceruis, qui in siluas ire et redire solent, talem habemus regulam traditam, ut si reuertendi animum habere desierint, etiam nostra esse desinant et fiant
occupantium: reuertendi autem animum uidentur desinere habere, cum reuertendi consuetudinem deseruerint.
69. Ea quoque, quae ex hostibus capiuntur, naturali
ratione nostra fiunt.

70. Sed et id, quod per alluuionem nobis adicitur,
eodem iure nostrum fit: per alluuionem autem id[1]
uidetur adici, quod ita paulatim flumen agro nostro
adicit, ut aestimare non possimus, quantum quoquo
momento temporis adiciatur: hoc est, quod uolgo dicitur per adluuionem id adici uideri, quod ita paulatim adicitur, ut oculos nostros fallat. 71. Itaque si
flumen partem aliquam ex tuo praedio resciderit et
ad meum praedium pertulerit, haec pars tua ma|net. 71
72. At si in medio flumine insula nata sit, haec eorum
omnium communis[2] est, qui ab utraque parte fluminis
prope ripam praedia possident[3]; si uero non sit in
medio flumine, ad eos pertinet, qui ab ea parte, quae
proxuma est, iuxta ripam praedia habent. 73. Praeterea id, quod in solo nostro ab aliquo aedificatum

---

1) ita V.   2) commune V.   3) possidentur V.

---

§ 69. *cf. I.* 2, 1, 17. *D.* 41, 1, 5, 7 (*Gai.* 491). *infra* 4, 16
in fine. D. 41, 1, 51, 1 (*Cels.* 15).
§ 70. *cf. I.* 2, 1, 20. *D.* 41, 1, 7, 1 (*Gai.* 491). 41, 1, 38
(*Alf.* 65). 41, 1, 56 *pr.* (*Proc.* 29). *Cod.* 7, 41, 1 (*de alluvionibus*).
Nov. Theodos. II. tit. 20. *Gromat. ed. Lachm. p.* 16. 49. 82. 124
(*Iurispr.* I, 79). *Isid. orig.* 14, 8, 42. 15, 13, 10.
§ 71. *cf. I.* 2, 1, 21. *D.* 41, 1, 7, 2 (*Gai.* 491).
§ 72. *cf. I.* 2, 1, 22. *D.* 41, 1, 7, 3 (*Gai.* 491). 41, 1, 30 *pr.*;
2 (*Pomp.* 796). 43, 12, 1, 6 (*Ulp.* 1510). 41, 1, 29 (*Paul.* 1892).
§ 73. *cf. Gai epit.* 2, 1, 4. *I.* 2, 1, 30. *D.* 41, 1, 28 (*Pomp.*
781). 41, 1, 7, 12 (*Gai.* 491). 43, 18, 2 (*Gai.* 856). 43, 17, 3, 7
(*Ulp.* 1540). 9, 2, 50 (*Ulp.* 2355). 46, 3, 98, 8 (*Paul.* 1398). *Cod.
Greg.* 3, 6(2), 2 (*a.* 244?). *Cod. Iust.* 3, 32, 2 (*a.* 213); 16 (*a.* 293).
8, 10, 5 (*a.* 290).

as **pigeons** and **bees** and also **deer which go back and forth to the woods**, we have **this rule** handed down: **if they lose their homing instinct, then they stop being** ours. **They then vest in the next taker. They are judged to lose the homing instinct when they stop coming back.** 69. By natural reason **we also become owners of things captured from enemies.**

70. **What is added to** our **property by alluvial accretion** also becomes ours by the same legal principle. **Now, an alluvial accretion is one which a river makes so gradually** to our land **that we cannot** judge **at any one moment what is being added.** Hence the common saying that an alluvial accretion is one so gradual that it deceives our eyes. 71. And so **if a river** cuts **away a piece of your land** and carries it down on to my land **this piece remains yours.** 72. But if **an island is formed in the middle of the river it becomes the common property of all those with land on each side with a frontage along the river;** if, on the other hand, it is not in the middle of the river, it goes to the owners of land **with a frontage to the river** on the nearest side. 73. Moreover, by the law of nature **what has been built** by someone on our **land** becomes ours although he built on his own

est, quamuis[1] ille suo nomine aedificauerit, iure naturali nostrum fit, quia superficies solo cedit.[2] 74. Mul-
toque magis id accidit et in planta, quam quis in solo
nostro posuerit, si modo radicibus terram complexa
fuerit. 75. Idem contingit et in frumento[3], quod in
solo nostro ab aliquo satum fuerit. 76. Sed si ab eo
petamus fundum[4] uel aedificium et inpensas in aedificium uel in seminaria uel in sementem factas ei
soluere nolimus, poterit nos per exceptionem doli
mali repellere, utique si bonae fidei possessor fuerit.
77. Eadem ratione probatum est, quod in cartulis siue
membranis meis aliquis scripserit, licet aureis litteris,
meum esse, quia litterae cartulis siue membranis ce-
dunt[5]: itaque si ego eos libros easue[6] membranas petam nec inpensam scripturae soluam, per exceptionem
doli mali summoueri potero. 78. Sed si in tabula
mea aliquis pinxerit ueluti imaginem, contra probatur:|
72 magis enim dicitur tabulam picturae cedere. cuius
diuersitatis uix idonea ratio redditur: certe secundum
hanc regulam si me possidente petas imaginem tuam
esse nec soluas pretium tabulae, poteris per exceptionem doli mali summoueri; at si tu possideas, con-
sequens est, ut utilis mihi actio aduersum te dari de-

---

1) qui V.   2) ceditur V.   3) p‾m‾to V.   4) fundum *Hu.*
fructum V.   5) ceduntur V.   6) easue *Lachm.* easque V.

---

§ 74. *cf. Gai epit.* 2, 1, 4. *I.* 2, 1, 31. *D.* 41, 1, 7, 13 (*Gai.*
491). 6, 1, 5, 3 (*Ulp.* 549). 41 1, 26,1 (*Paul.* 1868). *Cod. Greg.*
3, 6 (2), 1 (*a.* 242). *Cod. Iust.* 3, 32, 11 (*a.* 293).

§ 75. *cf. Gai epit.* 2, 1, 4. *I.* 2, 1, 32. *D.* 41, 1, 9 *pr.*
(*Gai.* 491).

§ 76. *cf. Gai epit.* 2, 1, 6. *I.* 2, 1, 3; 32. *D.* 41, 1, 7, 12;
9 *pr.* (*Gai.* 491). 6, 1, 37 (*Ulp.* 576). 44, 4, 14 (*Paul.* 1166). *C.*
8, 10, 5 (*a.* 290).

§ 77. *cf.* ⟨*Gai epit.* 2, 1, 4; 6. *I.* 2, 1, 33. *D.* 41, 1, 9, 1
(*Gai.* 491). 10, 4, 3, 14 (*Ulp.* 719). 6, 1, 23, 3 (*Paul.* 328).

§ 78. *cf. I.* 2, 1, 34. *D.* 41, 1, 9, 2 (*Gai.* 491). 6, 1, 23, 3
(*Paul.* 328). diuersitatis ratio] *cf. infra* 3, 98. utilis actio] *cf. D.*
6, 1, 5, 3 (*Ulp.* 549). furti actio] *cf.* 3, 203.

account, because the superstructure **becomes part of the land**. 74. Much more so is this the case where a person **has put a plant into** our **land, provided that the roots** are bound into the soil. 75. It is the same with **corn which has been sown** by someone **in** our **land**. 76. But if we **vindicate** the farm or **building** from him and refuse to pay him the cost laid out on the building, the plant-beds or the sowing, he will be able to counter us **by the defence* of deceit;** this assumes that he was a possessor **in good faith**. 77. On the same reasoning it has been held that what someone has written **on** my **paper or parchment** is mine **even if it is in letters of gold,** because **the letters become part of the paper or parchment;** and so if I **vindicate the books or parchment and do not pay the expenses of the writing** I can be met **by the defence of deceit**. 78. But **if someone has painted something on** my **board**, such as a portrait, the opposite rule holds; the preferred view is that **the board accedes to the painting**. The reason given for this difference is scarcely adequate. Mind you, according to this rule, if I am **in possession** and you **vindicate the portrait** as yours **without paying the price of the board** you **can be** met **by the defence of deceit;** but if you are **in possession it is logical that a policy action* be given to** me **against** you; **in that**

beat[1]; quo casu nisi soluam inpensam picturae, poteris
me per exceptionem doli mali repellere, utique si
bonae fidei possessor fueris. illud palam est, quod
siue tu subripueris[2] tabulam siue alius, conpetit mihi
furti actio.

79. In aliis quoque speciebus naturalis ratio requiritur: proin*de* si ex uuis *aut oliuis aut spicis* meis
uinum aut oleum aut frumentum feceris, quaeritur,
utrum meum sit id uinum aut oleum aut frumentum
an tuum. item si ex auro aut argento[3] meo uas aliquod feceris uel ex tabulis meis nauem aut armarium
aut subsellium fabricaueris, item si ex lana mea uesti-
mentum feceris uel si ex uino et melle meo mulsum
feceris siue ex medicamentis meis emplastrum aut
collyrium feceris, *quaeritur, utrum tuum sit id, quod
ex meo effeceris*[4], an meum. quidam materiam et substantiam spectandam esse putant, id est, ut cuius materia sit, illius et res, quae facta sit, uideatur esse, idque maxime placuit Sabino et Cassio; alii uero *eius
rem* esse putant, qui fecerit, idque maxime diuersae
scholae auctoribus uisum est: | sed eum quoque, cuius 73
materia et substantia fuerit[5], furti aduersus eum, qui
subripuerit, habere actionem; nec minus aduersus eundem condictionem ei competere, quia[6] extinctae[7] res,

---

1) debet V.   2) subripueris *Polenaar.* subripuisse V.
3) argumento V.   4) quaeritur—efteceris *suppl. Lachmann.*
5) fuit V.   6) qui V.   7) extincta V.

---

§ 79. *cf. Gai epit.* 2, 1, 5. *I.* 2, 1, 25. *D.* 41, 1, 7, 7 (*Gai.*
491). 50, 16, 13, 1 (*Ulp.* 300). ex uuis] *cf. D.* 10, 4, 12, 3 (*Paul.*
414). ex auro arg.] *cf. D.* 41, 1, 24 (*Paul.* 1868). ex tabulis
meis] *cf. D.* 41, 1, 26 (*Paul.* 1868). 13, 7, 18, 3 (*Paul.* 449).
ex lana mea] *cf. D.* 24, 1, 29, 1; 31 *pr.*; 1; 2 (*Pomp.* 599). 30,
44, 2 (*Ulp.* 2628). 10, 4, 12, 3 (*Paul.* 414). 41, 1, 26 (*Paul.* 1868).
ex uino et melle] *cf. D.* 6, 1, 5, 1 (*Ulp.* 549). ex medicamen-
tis] *cf. D.* 41, 1, 27, 1 (*Pomp.* 750). sed eum quoque] *cf. D.*
47, 2, 52, 14 (*Ulp.* 1042). extinctae res] *cf. D.* 13, 1, 16 (*Pomp.*
321). 13, 7, 22, 2 (*Ulp.* 902). 47, 2, 46 *pr.* (*Ulp.* 2877).

case, **assuming good faith** on your part, you **will be able to counter** me **with the defence of deceit if** I **fail to pay the expenses of the painting. Finally, an obvious point: where** you **or a third party stole the board** I have **the action for theft**.

79. Natural reason comes into play in other situations also. Thus, **suppose** you **make wine or oil or grain from** my **grapes or olives or corn, there is a question whether the wine, oil or grain** is mine or yours. Again, suppose you **make a pot of some kind from** my **gold or silver, or a ship or chest or chair from** my **planks, or clothes from** my **wool, or mead from** my **wine and honey, or a plaster or ointment from** my **drugs, there is a question whether** what you made from my property is yours or mine. Some people think that one should look to the materials and substance, that is, whoever **owns the materials** owns what was made from them; this view was taken especially by Sabinus and Cassius. On the other hand, others think the thing belongs to **the person who made it**, and this appealed especially to the authorities of the other school; but they also think that the person who owned the materials and substance has an action for theft against the person who stole it, without prejudice to an action of debt* against him, because **when something has ceased to exist it is no longer possible to bring a vindication,**

licet uindicari non possint[1], condici tamen furibus et
quibusdam aliis possessoribus possunt.

[V. De pupillis an aliquid a se alienare possunt.] 80. Nunc
admonendi sumus neque feminam neque pupillum sine
tutoris auctoritate rem mancipi alienare posse; nec
mancipi uero feminam quidem posse, pupillum non
posse. 81. Ideoque si quando mulier mutuam pecuniam alicui sine tutoris auctoritate dederit, quia facit
eam accipientis, cum scilicet[2] pecunia res nec mancipi
sit, contrahit obligationem. 82. At si pupillus idem
fecerit, quia non *facit accipientis sine tutoris auctoritate
pecuniam,* nullam contrahit obligationem: unde pupillus
uindicare qui*dem* nummos suos potest, sicubi extent,
id est *eos* petere, | ————————— *vv.* 5½ ——————— |[3]
83. Et[4] ex contrario *omnes res tam mancipi quam*[5]
nec mancipi mulieri*bus* | et pupillis sine tutoris aucto-
ritate[6] solui possunt, quoniam meliorem condicionem
suam facere eis etiam sine tutoris auctoritate concessum est. 84. Itaque si debitor pecuniam pupillo soluat,
facit quidem pecuniam pupilli, sed ipse non liberatur,
quia[7] nullam obligationem pupillus sine tutoris aucto-

---

1) possit V.   2) *sequuntur in* V *duae litterae evanidae.*
3) *haec frustula certo lecta sunt in* V: — | — repetere potest
s — | — de pupillo quidem quaeritur — | — mutuos dedit ab
eo qui accipit — | — actione eos persequi possit quoniam — |
— potest. *inde quid Gaius scripserit, divinari non potest. cf. Siber,
Nat. obl.* 49.   4) at *Inst.; sed cf. infra* 3, 93. *V. I R.* I, 1006, 42.
1007, 3.   5) *suppl. Goeschen.*   6) pupillis sine tut. auct.] pupilli spta V.   7) quia—potest *del. Solazzi, Ist. Lomb.* 59, 359.

---

§ 80. *cf. supra* 1, 192. 2, 47. *infra* 2, 85. *Ulp.* 11, 27. *Fr.
Vat.* 1 (*Paul.* 1782). 45 (*Paul.* 1011). 259 (*Pap.* 693). *D.* 26,
8, 9 (*Gai.* 267).
§ 82. *cf. I.* 2, 8, 2. *D.* 12, 1, 19, 1 (*Iul.* 150). 46, 3, 14, 8
(*Ulp.* 2737).
§ 83. *cf. I.* 2, 8, 2. 1, 21 *pr. D.* 2, 14, 28 *pr.* (*Gai.* 62).
C. 5, 37, 25 (*a.* 531).   ex contrario] ex diverso *D. l. c.*
§ 84. *cf. I.* 2, 8, 2 *ibiq. Theoph.* (*p.* 146 *Ferr.*). *D.* 46, 3,
15 (*Paul.* 1727). *Cic. top.* 11, 46.

but the action of debt can still be used against thieves and certain other types of possessor.

[V Whether wards* can alienate anything]

80. **Next we must note that** neither a woman **nor a ward can alienate a thing** capable of mancipation **without a guardian's authorisation;** but with things not so capable, a woman can alienate but a ward cannot. 81. **And so** when a woman **lends money** to someone without that authorisation, because she passes the property in it to the recipient, she contracts an obligation, because, of course, money is not mancipated. 82. But **if a ward does this, because, in the absence of his guardian's authorisation, he fails to make the money the property of the recipient, he does not contract any obligation;** and so note that the ward **can vindicate his coins wherever they are,** that is, claim that ... [some words can be read in the following lines but the passage cannot be reconstructed]. 83. **Conversely, anything,** whether capable of mancipation or not, **can be paid over to** women and **wards in discharge of an obligation without a guardian's authorisation,** because they are allowed to improve their position even without authorisation. 84. And so note that **if a debtor pays money to a ward** he passes the property in the money to the ward but **he** himself is **not discharged** because a ward cannot discharge any obligation without **his guardian's authorisation,**

ritate dissoluere potest, quia nullius rei alienatio ei
sine tutoris auctoritate concessa est[1]; sed tamen si ex
ea pecunia locupletior factus sit et adhuc petat, per
exceptionem doli mali summoueri potest. 85. Mulieri
uero etiam sine tutoris auctoritate recte solui potest:
nam qui soluit, liberatur obligatione, quia res nec
mancipi, ut proxume diximus, a se dimittere mulieres[2]
etiam sine tutoris auctoritate possunt[3]: quamquam hoc
ita est, si accipiat pecuniam; at si non accipiat, sed[4]
habere se dicat et per acceptilationem uelit debitorem
sine tutoris auctoritate liberare, non potest.

86. Adquiritur autem nobis non solum per nosmet
ipsos, sed etiam per eos, quos in potestate manu mancipioue habemus; item per[5] eos seruos, in quibus usumfructum habemus; item per homines liberos et seruos
alienos, quos bona fide possidemus: de quibus singulis
diligenter dispiciamus. 87. Igitur *quod* liberi nostri,
quos in potestate habemus, item quod serui *nostri*
mancipio accipiunt uel ex traditione nanciscuntur siue
quid stipulentur uel ex aliqualibet[6] causa adquirunt,
id nobis adquiritur: ipse enim[7], | qui in potestate 75
nostra est, nihil suum habere potest; et ideo si heres
institutus sit, nisi nostro iussu hereditatem adire non
potest; et si iubentibus[8] nobis adierit, hereditas[9] nobis

---

1) quia—est *del. Kniep.*   2) mulier V.   3) quia—possunt
del. Kniep.   4) et V.   5) pro V.   6) qualibet alia *Dig.*
Inst.   7) * * enim V.   8) ibonitibus V.   9) hereditate V.

§ 85. *cf. infra* 3, 171. *Cic. top.* 11, 46. *Pap. Lond.* 470
(II *p.* 212 = *Chrest.* 328 = *Bruns* I⁷ 361 = *Meyer, Iur. Pap.*
ur. 16). proxume] § 80.
§ 86. = *D.* 41, 1, 10 *pr. I.* 2, 9 *pr. cf. Gai epit.* 2, 1, 7.
Ulp. 19, 18. *infra* 2, 96.
§ 87. = *D.* 41, 1, 10, 1. *I.* 2, 9, 1. *cf. Ulp.* 19, 18; 19.
infra 3, 167ᵃ. *Fr. Vat.* 51 (*Paul.* 990). 71, 2 = *D.* 7, 1, 21
(*Ulp.* 2560). *Paul.* 5, 8. *Dosith.* 5. *D.* 41, 1, 53 (*Pomp.* 270).
29, 2, 79 (*Ulp.* 1986). *Cic. ad Attic.* 13, 50, 2. nihil suum
habere potest] *cf. infra* 2, 96. *I.* 2, 9, 3. *Senec. de benef.* 7,
4, 4. et ideo] *cf. D.* 29, 2, 6 *pr.* (*Ulp.* 2472). 36, 1, 67 *pr.* (*Marcian.* 30).

because he is not allowed to alienate anything without that authorisation; all the same **if he has been enriched** through the money **and still sues for it he can be countered by the defence of deceit**. 85. On the other hand, payment may properly be made to a woman even without her guardian's authorisation, for the payer is discharged because, as we have just said, women can dispose of things which are not capable of mancipation even without their guardian's authorisation. This is so if she actually receives the money; she cannot do so if she has not received it but declares that she has done so, and proposes to use a verbal release to discharge her debtor without her guardian's authorisation.

86. Now, **property passes to us not only through our own acts but through those of the people within our paternal power***, or in marital subordination* or bondage* to us. **This is true of slaves in whom we have a usufruct, also of free people and slaves belonging to others whom we possess in good faith. We must consider each of these closely. 87. First we acquire things which descendants* within** our **power** and **also** our **slaves obtain by** mancipation or **delivery, or when they take stipulations for anything or when things come to them on any other basis. Someone in** our **power can have nothing of his own. And so where he is instituted heir he cannot accept the inheritance except when we tell him to do so. When he does accept on** our **command** we **acquire the inheritance, just as if we had been**

adquiritur, proinde atque si nos ipsi heredes instituti
essemus; et[1] conuenienter scilicet legatum per eos nobis
adquiritur.   88. Dum tamen sciamus: si alterius in
bonis sit seruus, alterius ex iure Quiritium, ex omnibus causis ei soli per[2] eum adquiritur, cuius in bonis
est.   89. Non solum autem proprietas per eos, quos
in potestate habemus, adquiritur nobis, sed etiam possessio; cuius enim rei possessionem adepti fuerint, id
nos possidere uidemur; unde etiam per eos usucapio
procedit.   90. Per eas uero personas, quas in manu
mancipioue habemus, proprietas quidem adquiritur
nobis ex omnibus causis sicut per eos, qui in potestate
nostra sunt; an autem possessio adquiratur, quaeri
solet, quia ipsas non possidemus.   91. De his autem
seruis, in quibus tantum usumfructum habemus, ita
placuit, ut quidquid ex re nostra uel ex operis suis
adquirunt[3], id nobis adquiratur; quod uero extra eas
causas[4], id ad dominum proprietatis pertineat: itaque
si iste seruus heres institutus sit legatumue quid ei aut
donatum[5] fuerit, non mihi, sed domino proprietatis adquiritur.   92. Idem placet de eo, qui a nobis bona fide
76 possidetur, | siue liber sit siue alienus seruus: quod

---

    1) et his *Dig. cf. supra* 1, 81.   2) pro V.   3) adquirant
Dig. Inst.   4) persecuti sunt *add. Inst.*, persecuti sint *Dig.*
5) legatumue quid ei aut donatum *Inst.* legatumue quod ei
datum V. legatumue quid aut ei donatum *Dig.*

---

    § 88. *cf. Ulp.* 19, 20. *Paul.* 1, 7, 6. *supra* 1, 54. 2, 40.
infra 3, 166.
    § 89. = *D.* 41, 1, 10, 2.   *I.* 2, 9, 3.   *cf. D.* 41, 2, 1, 5
(*Paul.* 657).
    § 90. *cf. Fr. Vat.* 298 (*Paul.* 796). *D.* 41, 2, 1, 12 (*Paul.*
657). *Plaut. Cas.* 199–202 = 2, 2, 26—29.
    § 91. = *D.* 41, 1, 10, 3.   *I.* 2, 9, 4.   *cf. Ulp.* 19, 21. *infra*
3, 165. *Gai epit.* 2, 1, 7. *D.* 45, 3, 39 (*Pomp.* 285). 29, 2, 25 *pr.*
(*Ulp.* 2491).   41, 1, 47 (*Paul.* 645).
    § 92. = *D.* 41, 1, 10, 4.   *I.* 2, 9, 4.   *cf. Ulp.* 19, 21.   *infra*
3, 164. *D.* 29, 2, 45, 4 (*Iul.* 884). 45, 3, 39 (*Pomp.* 285). 41, 1,

made heirs ourselves. **Correspondingly, a legacy to him accrues to** us. 88. But remember that if a slave is in the estate of one person but belongs to another by quiritary right, the person in whose estate he is acquires through him in every case. 89. **Now, it is not only ownership but also possession that comes to** us **through those in power. Whatever things they possess** we **possess. And so usucapion also runs in** our **favour through them.** 90. On the other hand, while we acquire ownership in every case through persons in marital subordination or in bondage to us as we do through those in power, there is a standing question whether we acquire possession, because we do not possess them. 91. **With slaves in whom** we **only have a usufruct, the received opinion is that whatever they get through** our **property or by their work accrues to** us **but what they get by other means goes to their owners. Thus, if such a slave is instituted heir or is given a legacy or gift, it is the owner not** I **who acquires.** 92. **The law solves the problem in the same way in the case of someone possessed by** us **in good faith, whether free or another's slave. The solution adopted for the**

enim placuit de usufructuario, idem probatur etiam de
bonae fidei possessore: itaque quod extra duas istas
causas adquiritur, id uel ad ipsum pertinet, si liber
est, uel ad dominum, si seruus est.[1] 93. Sed[2] bonae
fidei possessor cum usucepit[3] seruum, quia eo modo
dominus fit, ex omni causa per eum sibi adquirere
potest. usufructuarius uero usucapere non potest; primum quia non possidet, sed habet ius utendi fruendi[4];
deinde quia scit alienum seruum esse. 94. De illo
quaeritur: an per eum seruum, in quo usumfructum
habemus, possidere aliquam rem et usucapere possumus, quia ipsum non possidemus? per eum uero, quem
bona fide possidemus, sine dubio et possidere et usucapere possumus. loquimur autem in utriusque persona secundum definitionem, quam proxume exposuimus; id est, si quid ex re nostra uel ex operis suis
adquirant, id nobis adquiritur. 95. Ex his[5] apparet per
liberos homines, quos neque iuri nostro subiectos habemus neque bona fide possidemus, item per alienos
seruos, in quibus neque usumfructum[6] habemus neque
iustam possessionem, nulla ex causa nobis adquiri
posse. et hoc est, quod uulgo dicitur per extraneam

---

1) sit V.   2) sed *Inst. Dig.* se si V. sed sano *Polenaar.*   3) usuceperit *Inst. Dig.*   4) et fruendi V.   5) iis V.
6) item—usumfructum *bis scripta in* V.

---

19 (*Pomp.* 414). 41, 1, 21 *pr.* (*Pomp.* 574). 41, 1, 54 (*Pomp.* 308).
41, 1, 43 *pr.* (*Gai.* 159). 12, 6, 67 *pr.* (*Scaev.* 14). 29, 2, 25 *pr.*
(*Ulp* 2491). 17, 1, 8, 5 (*Ulp.* 908). 41, 1, 23 *pr.*; 2 (*Ulp.* 2906).
41, 1, 57 (*Paul.* 1129). 45, 3, 20, 1 (*Paul.* 1396). *C.* 3, 32, 1
(*a.* 210).

§ 93. = *D.* 41, 1, 10, 5. *I.* 2, 9, 4. usufructuarius uero]
cf. C. 3, 33, 8 (*a.* 293). quia non possidet] *cf. D.* 41, 2, 12 *pr.*
(*Ulp.* 1546). 43, 26, 6, 2 (*Ulp.* 1607). *Cic. p. Caec.* 7, 19. 32, 94.

§ 94. *cf. I.* 2, 9, 5. *D.* 41, 2, 49 *pr.* (*Pap.* 53). 41, 2, 1, 8
(*Paul.* 657). 41, 2, 1, 6 (*Paul.* 657). proxume] § 91.

§ 95. = *I.* 2, 9, 5. *cf. Paul.* 5, 2, 2. *D.* 41, 3, 41 (*Ner.* 54).
41, 2, 23, 2 (*Iav.* 73). 13, 7, 11, 6 (*Ulp.* 809). *C.* 4, 27, 1 *pr.* (*a.*
290). 7, 32, 1 (*a.* 196).

usufructuary is also applied to the possessor in good faith; this means that acquisitions outside the two named cases accrue to the man himself if he is free or to his owner if he is a slave. 93. The possessor in good faith becomes owner of the slave when usucapion is completed and then has power to take all types of acquisition through him. By contrast the usufructuary cannot usucapt, first because he does not possess but has a right to the use and fruits, and secondly because he knows the slave belongs to another. 94. There is a question whether we can possess and usucapt anything through a slave in whom we have a usufruct, because we do not possess him; but we can undoubtedly both possess and usucapt through one whom we possess in good faith, but only in the cases just mentioned, that is, only what they obtain through our property or their work. 95. It is apparent from this that we never acquire through a free person except where we have power over him or possess him in good faith, nor through a third party's slave unless we have a usufruct in him or possess him in good faith. That justifies the common maxim 'no acquisition to us

personam nobis adquiri non posse; tantum de possessione quaeritur, an per *liberam personam*[1] nobis ad-
quiratur. 96. In summa sciendum est his, qui in |
77 potestate manu mancipioue sunt, nihil in iure cedi
posse; cum enim istarum personarum nihil suum esse
possit, conueniens est scilicet, ut nihil suum esse[2] in
iure uindicare possint.

97. *Hactenus* tantisper admonuisse sufficit, quemadmodum singulae res nobis adquirantur: nam legatorum ius, quo et ipso singulas res adquirimus, oppor-
tunius alio loco referemus. uideamus itaque nunc,
quibus modis per uniuersitatem res nobis adquirantur.
98. Si cui heredes facti sumus siue cuius bonorum
possessionem petierimus siue cuius bona emerimus
siue quem adoptauerimus siue quam[3] in manum ut
uxorem receperimus, eius res ad nos transeunt. 99. Ac
prius[4] de hereditatibus dispiciamus, quarum duplex
condicio est: nam uel ex testamento uel ab intestato
ad nos pertinent. 100. Et prius est, ut de his dispiciamus, quae nobis ex testamento obueniunt.

101. Testamentorum autem genera initio duo fuerunt:
nam aut calatis comitiis testamentum faciebant, quae
comitia bis in anno testamentis faciendis destinata
erant, aut in procinctu, id est, cum belli causa arma

---

1) liberam personam] *in* V *octo fere litterae legi nequeunt.*
cf. Inst. procuratorem *Goudsmit.*   2) esse posse V.
3) quem V.   4) primus V.

---

§ 96. *cf. supra* 2, 87.
§§ 97—100. = *I.* 2, 9, 6. *cf. Gai epit.* 2, 2 *pr.*
§ 97. alio loco] *infra* 2, 191 *sq.*
§§ 101—103. *cf. I.* 2, 10, 1 *cum Theoph.* (*p.* 154 *ed. Ferr.*).
Ulp. 20, 2. *Lael. Fel. ap. Gell.* 15, 27, 3 (*Iurispr.* I, 94).
Plut. Coriol. 9. *de sera num. vind. p.* 550 (*ed. Bernardakis* III, 422).
Cic. de orat. 1, 53, 228. *de natur. deor.* 2, 3, 9. *Ovid. ex Pont.*
1, 8, 10. *Vellei. Pat.* 2, 5, 3. *Frontin. Strateg.* 4, 1, 23. *Fest.*
v. procincta p. 225. 249 (*Bruns* II[7], 27). *endo procinctu p.* 77
(*Bruns* II[7], 8). *Serv. ad Verg. Aen.* 7, 612. *Schol. Veron. ad*
Verg. Aen. 10, 241 (*Bruns* II[7], 77). *Isid. orig.* 10, 218.

through an outsider'. Only for possession is there a question whether we may acquire through a free person ['general agent' may be a better suggestion]. 96. Finally note that nothing can be assigned in court to those who are in our power, or in marital subordination or bondage to us. As they can own nothing, it of course follows that they can vindicate nothing as theirs in court.

97. **No more need be said for the moment about acquiring single things. It is convenient to cover legacies, which also involve acquisition of individual things,** elsewhere. **We are now going to deal with the ways in which we acquire a man's property in its entirety. 98. Suppose we are made someone's heir, or we petition to be his estate-possessor*,** or we purchase his bankrupt estate* **or** we adopt* **someone or** we take a woman into marital subordination as our wife. **Their whole estate goes to** us. 99. **We must deal first with inheritance. This happens in two ways. The estate comes to us either by will or on intestacy. 100. Let us start with that which comes by will.**

101. Now, originally **there were two kinds of will**; for testators made a will **either before the convocation***, which was called together twice a year for that purpose, **or in battle-line**, that is when they took up arms for war; for the battle-line refers to an

sumebant: procinctus est enim expeditus et armatus
exercitus. alterum itaque in pace et in otio faciebant,
alterum in proelium exituri. 102. Accessit deinde ter-
tium | genus testamenti, quod per aes et libram agitur: 78
qui *enim*[1] neque calatis comitiis neque in procinctu
testamentum fecerat, is, si subita morte urguebatur,
amico familiam suam, id est patrimonium suum, mancipio dabat eumque rogabat, quid cuique post mortem
suam dari uellet.[2] quod testamentum dicitur per aes
et libram, scilicet quia per mancipationem peragitur.
103. Sed illa quidem duo genera testamentorum in
desuetudinem abierunt; hoc uero solum, quod per aes
et libram fit, in usu retentum est. sane nunc al*i*ter
ordinatur, quam olim solebat; namque olim familiae
emptor, id est, qui a testatore familiam accipiebat
mancipio, heredis locum optinebat, et ob id ei man-
dabat testator, quid cuique post mortem suam dari
uellet; nunc uero alius heres testamento instituitur, a
quo etiam legata relinquuntur[3], alius dicis gratia
propter ueteris iuris imitationem familiae emptor adhibetur. 104. Eaque res ita agitur: qui facit *testa-*
mentum, adhibitis, sicut in ceteris mancipationibus,
v testibus ciuibus Romanis puberibus et libripende,
postquam tabulas testamenti scripserit, mancipat alicui
dicis gratia familiam suam; in qua re his uerbis familiae emptor utitur: FAMILIAM PECVNIAMQVE TVAM
ENDO MANDATELA TVA[4] CVSTODELAQVE MEA *ESSE AIO*,

---

1) *add. Hu.*   2) dari uellet] dare uelletur V.   3) legata
relinquuntur] legato reliquantur V.   4) tuam V.   tutela *Hu.*

§ 104. *cf. Ulp.* 20, 2; 9. *D.* 28, 1, 20, 8 (*Ulp.* 2430). *Nov.*
Theod. II. 16, 1. *Isid. orig.* 5, 24, 12. *Quintil. decl.* 308. *Gell.*
15, 13, 11 (*Bruns* I[7] 33). *Suet. Ner.* 4. *Apul. Metam.* 2, 24. *Clem.*
Alex. Strom. 8, 8. *B G U* 326 (*Bruns* I[7] 311). 1655. *Pap. Ham-*
burg. 73. *P. Berol. Inv.* 7124 (*ed Castelli, Studi della scuola*
papirolog. II *p.* 80 *sq.*). *Ang. Segré, Stud. Bonfante* 3, 430. in
ceteris mancipationibus] *cf. supra* 1, 119. SECVNDVM LEGEM
PVBLICAM] *cf. infra* 3, 174. HOC AERE] *cf. D.* 50, 16, 159 (*Ulp.*
2429). TABVLIS CERISQVE] *cf. Liv.* 1, 24, 7.

army drawn up in arms. And so **they** made **one kind in times of peace and leisure and the other when battle was imminent, 102. Later a third kind of will developed, made by bronze and scales***. Someone facing the prospect of imminent death who had neither made a will before the convocation nor in battle-line would mancipate his 'family', that is his property, to a friend and ask him to distribute it according to his instructions after his death. **This will** is **said to be made by bronze and scales because, of course, it** is **done by mancipation. 103. But note that the two former kinds of will have gone out of use; only the one by bronze and scales** has been kept. But the present procedure is quite different from former practice. Formerly the **'property-purchaser'***, that is, the person who received the property from the testator by mancipation, had the position of heir and so the testator gave him instructions on the distribution of his estate after his death. Nowadays, however, one person is appointed heir by the will, and the legacies are charged on him; another is brought in as **property-purchaser** in name only, in imitation of the old law. 104. The procedure is as follows: as in other mancipations the person making the will assembles **five adult Roman citizens as witnesses and another to hold a pair of scales** and after writing out his will* he mancipates his property to somebody in name only. In these proceedings the property-purchaser says: 'I declare that your family and property are in my administration and custody; let them be bought to me with this

79 *EAQVE,* QVO TV IVRE TESTAMENTVM | FACERE POSSIS
SECVNDVM LEGEM PVPLICAM, HOC AERE, et ut quidam
adiciunt, AENEAQVE LIBRA, ESTO MIHI EMPTA; deinde
aere percutit libram idque aes dat testatori uelut
pretii loco; deinde testator tabulas testamenti manu[1]
tenens ita dicit: HAEC ITA VT IN HIS TABVLIS CERIS-
QVE SCRIPTA SVNT, ITA DO ITA LEGO ITA TESTOR[2],
ITAQVE VOS, QVIRITES, TESTIMONIVM MIHI PERHIBE-
TOTE[3]; et hoc dicitur nuncupatio: nuncupare est enim
palam nominare, et sane quae testator specialiter in
tabulis testamenti scripserit, ea uidetur generali sermone nominare atque confirmare. 105. In testibus
autem non debet is esse, qui in potestate[4] est aut
familiae emptoris aut ipsius testatoris, quia propter
ueteris iuris imitationem totum hoc negotium, quod
agitur testamenti ordinandi[5] gratia, creditur inter
familiae emptorem agi et testatorem; quippe olim, ut
proxime diximus, is, qui familiam testatoris mancipio
accipiebat, heredis loco erat; itaque reprobatum est
in ea re domesticum testimonium. 106. Unde et si is,
qui in potestate patris est, familiae emptor adhibitus
sit, pater eius testis esse non potest; ac ne is quidem,
qui in eadem potestate est, uelut frater eius. sed *et*[6]
si filius familias ex castrensi peculio post missionem
80 faciat testamentum, nec pater eius recte testis | adhi-
betur nec is, qui in potestate patris est.[7] 107. De
libripende eadem, quae et de testibus, dicta esse in-

---

1) testamenti manu *Hu.* test manti V.　　　2) testator V.
3) perhibitote V. *cf. Lachmann Kleinere Schriften p.* 234.
4) potestat·ēē V.　　　5) ornandi V.　　　6) sed et] sed V. et
Polenaar.　　　7) sit V. est *Inst.*

---

§ 105. *cf. Ulp.* 20, 3. *I.* 2, 10, 9; 10. *D.* 22, 5, 6 (*Lic. Ruf.* 4).
C. 4, 20, 3 (*a.* 255). proxime] § 103.
§ 106. *cf. Ulp.* 20, 4; 5. *I.* 2, 10, 9. *D.* 28, 1, 20, 2 (*Ulp.*
2430). 22, 5, 9 (*Paul.* 1598).
§ 107. *cf. Ulp.* 20, 3. *supra* 1, 119.

bronze, and (as some add) the bronze scales, so that you can lawfully make a will according to the public statute'. Then he strikes the scales with the bronze and gives it to the testator as if it were the price; then the testator, holding the will in his hand, says: 'These things, as they have been written on these wax tablets, I thus convey, I thus bequeath, I thus attest; and so you Roman citizens stand witness for me'. This is called the declaration. For to declare means to announce openly and this means that the testator is regarded as specifying and confirming by his general statement what he has written in detail in his will. 105. **But among the witnesses there should not be anyone who is within the paternal power** either of the property-purchaser or **of the testator himself, because,** as we are **imitating** the old law, **the whole procedure of making a will is looked on as a transaction between the testator and** the property-purchaser. Formerly, of course, as we have just said, the person who received the testator's property by mancipation functioned as heir, **and so in this context there are objections to evidence from within the family.** 106. Thus even if someone who is in his father's power is used as property-purchaser his father cannot be a witness; nor even someone in the same power, such as his brother. Even **if a son* within power wants to make a will after his demobilisation in respect of his military fund*, it is wrong for his father or any person in his father's power to be a witness.** 107. What has been said of witnesses is to be understood as applying to the holder of the scales as well; he is counted among the

tellegemus: nam et is testium numero est. 108. Is
uero, qui in potestate heredis aut[1] legatarii est, cuiusue
heres ipse aut legatarius in potestate est, quique in
eiusdem potestate est, adeo[2] testis et libripens adhi-
beri potest, ut ipse quoque heres aut[3] legatarius iure
adhibeantur. sed tamen quod ad heredem pertinet
quique in eius potestate est cuiusue is in potestate
erit, minime hoc iure uti debemus.

[De testamentis militum.[4]] 109. Sed haec diligens
obseruatio in ordinandis testamentis militibus propter
nimiam inperitiam constitutionibus[5] principum remissa
est: nam quamuis neque legitimum numerum testium
adhibuerint neque uendiderint familiam neque nuncu-
pauerint testamentum, recte nihilo minus testantur.
110. Praeterea permissum est iis et peregrinos et Latinos instituere heredes uel iis legare; cum alioquin
peregrini quidem ratione ciuili prohibeantur capere
hereditatem legataque, Latini uero per legem Iuniam.
111. Caelibes quoque, qui lege Iulia hereditates legataque capere uetantur, item orbi, id est qui liberos
non habent, quos lex[6] | ——————— fol. deperd. ————
| ——— vv. 21 exceptis frustulis paucis legi nequeunt ——— 81
t. s.

---

1) aut in V.　　2) ab eo V.　　3) ut V.　　4) milium V.
5) mentistutionibus V.　　6) *post* lex *unum folium in* V *periit
nec in margine numeratum est. extremam sententiam Hu. ita
supplevit:* Papia plus quam dimidias partes hereditatis legato-
rumque capere uetat, ex militis testamento solidum capiunt.

---

§ 108. *cf. I.* 2, 10, 10; 11. *Cic. pro Mil.* 18, 48. legatarius]
cf. D. 28, 1, 20 *pr.* (*Ulp.* 2430). 34, 5, 14 (*Marcian.* 109). *C. Th.*
4, 4, 3, 3 (*a.* 396; *Scaev.* 344 *Lenel*). *C.* 6, 23, 22 (*a.* 480). *Plin.*
ep. 2, 20, 10. *Symmach. relat.* 41, 3 *sq.* (*p.* 313 *ed. Seeck*).
§ 109. = *I.* 2, 11 *pr. cf. Ulp.* 23, 10. *infra* 2, 114. *D. tit.*
29, 1. *C. tit.* 6, 21. *Gnom. Id. Log.* § 34.
§ 110. *cf. supra* 1, 23 *sq. infra* 2, 218; 275. *Ulp.* 17, 1.
22, 2; 3. *D.* 29, 1, 13, 2 (*Ulp.* 1132). *C.* 6, 21, 5 (*a.* 224).
Pausan. 8, 43, 5. *Pap. Cattaoui col.* IV, 1—15 (*Chrest.* 372
p. 421). *Gnom. Id. Log.* §§ 22. 34.
§ 111. *cf. infra* 2, 144; 286. *Ulp.* 17, 1. 22, 3.

witnesses. 108. On the other hand, a person in the power of the heir or of a legatee, or a person in whose power the heir or legatee is and anyone in the same power, can be used as witness and as holder of the scales as lawfully as can the heir himself or the legatee. All the same, where the heir is concerned or a person in his power or one in whose power he is, we should make minimal use of this rule.

[Military wills] 109. But this **detailed scheme for making wills has been relaxed for soldiers by imperial pronouncements*. Soldiers know little of such matters. Their wills are good despite defects in number of witnesses** or absence of a sale to a property-purchaser or the declaration of their wills. 110. Moreover, they are allowed to appoint foreigners and Latins* as heirs or to leave them legacies, although otherwise foreigners are prevented from taking inheritances and legacies by the principles of state law, and Latins by the Junian Act. 111. Also, the unmarried, who are excluded from inheritances and legacies by the Julian Act, and the childless (in Latin 'orbi'), that is those who have no children, who under the [Papian] law [may not take more than half of an inheritance or legacy can take the whole under a soldier's will]. [This conclusion of the sentence is a probable reconstruction of the beginning of a long section in which the text is missing or illegible. In this section Gaius seems to have dealt with other special rules affecting military wills and with capacity to make a will, referring, for example, to the incapacity of persons in power, under the age of puberty or insane.] 112. ... On the proposal of the Emperor

112. — *ex auc*toritate diui Hadriani senatus consultum factum est, quo permissum est ＊＊＊＊＊＊＊＊s[1] feminis etiam sine coemptione testamentum facere, si modo 82 non minores essent | annorum[2] XII[3]; scilicet ut quae tutela liberatae non essent, tutore auctore[4] testari deberent.[5] **113.** Videntur ergo melioris condicionis esse feminae quam masculi; nam masculus minor annorum[6] XIIII testamentum facere non potest, etiamsi tutore auctore testamentum facere uelit, femina uero potest; *facta enim* XII annorum testamenti faciundi[7] ius nanciscitur.[8]

114. Igitur si quaeramus, an ualeat testamentum, inprimis aduertere debemus, an is, qui id fecerit, habuerit testamenti factionem: deinde si habuerit, requiremus, an secundum iuris ciuilis regulam *te*status sit, exceptis militibus, qui*bus* propter nimiam *inp*eritiam, ut diximus, quomodo uelint uel quomodo *poss*int, permittitur testamentum facere.

115. Non tamen, ut iure ciuili *uale*at testamentum, sufficit ea obseruatio, quam supra exposuimus de familiae uenditione et de testibus et de nuncupatione.[9]

---

transiit deinde Gaius ad testamentifactionem activam; cf. Ulp. 20, 10—16, *tit. Inst.* 2, 12; *Gai epit.* 2, 2, 1—3.   1) sui iuris *vel* ingenuis *suppl. Krueger;* capite non minutis *suppl. Hu. cf. supra* 1, 115ᵃ.   2) annorum *Krueger.* anni V.   3) XII tab. V. 4) tutore auctore *Krueger.* ita V.   5) debent V.   6) minor annorum *Goeschen.* minori anni V.   7) faciunt diis V. 8) etiamsi — nanciscitur *del. Solazzi.*   9) nuncupatione *Hu.* nunccupationib. V.   de familiae — nuncupatione *del. Polenaar.*

---

§ 112. *cf. supra* 1, 115ᵃ. *infra* 2, 118; 121; 122. *Paul.* 3, 4ᵃ, 1.
§ 113. *cf. Gai epit.* 2, 2, 2. *supra* 1, 40. *I.* 2, 12, 1. *Ulp.* 20, 12; 15. *Paul.* 3, 4ᵃ, 1. *D.* 49, 15, 10, 1 (*Pap.* 357). 28, 1, 5 (*Ulp.* 2468). 28, 1, 19 (*Mod.* 119). *C.* 7, 64, 2 (*Imp. Alex.*). 6, 22, 4 (*a.* 294).
§ 114. ＝ *D.* 28, 1, 4. *cf. infra* 3, 75. *Cic. ad fam.* 7, 21. ut diximus] *supra* 2, 109. *cf. D.* 29, 1, 1 *pr.* (*Ulp.* 1178). *Pap. Fayum towns nr.* 10.
§ 115. ＝ *I.* 2, 13 *pr. cf. supra* 2, 104. *Ulp.* 20, 9.

Hadrian a resolution of the Senate was passed allowing [independent*] women to make a will even without a contrived sale*, provided that they were not under the age of twelve; and, of course, those who had not been released from guardianship were to need their guardian's authorisation to make a will. 113. Females, therefore, appear to be in a better situation than males; for a male under the age of fourteen cannot make a will, even if he wants to and has his guardian's authorisation, but a female can. Once she is twelve she acquires the right to make a will.

114. And so, if we are asking whether a will is valid, we must first of all consider whether the person who made it had the capacity to make a will; if he did we next inquire whether he followed the rules of the state law, except in the case of soldiers, who, as we have said, are allowed to make a will in any way they want to and can, because they know little of such matters.

115. **A will's validity** under state law **is not determined by the conditions which we set out above** regarding property-sale, witnesses and a declaration. 116. The very first question must be

116. *Sed* ante omnia requirendum est, an institutio
heredis sollemni more facta sit; nam aliter facta institutione nihil proficit familiam testatoris ita uenire
testesque ita adhibere et[1] *ita* nuncupare testamentum,
ut supra diximus.   **117.** Sollemnis autem institutio *haec*
est: TITIVS[2] HERES ESTO; sed et illa[3] iam conprobata
uidetur: TITIVM HEREDEM ESSE | IVBEO; at illa non 83
est conprobata: TITIVM HEREDEM ESSE VOLO; sed et
illae a plerisque inprobatae sunt: TITIVM HEREDEM
INSTITVO[4], item: HEREDEM FACIO.

118. Obseruandum praeterea est, ut si mulier, quae
in tutela est, faciat testamentum, tutore auctore[5]
facere debeat: alioquin inutiliter iure ciuili testabitur.
119. Praetor tamen, si septem signis testium signatum
sit testamentum, scriptis heredibus secundum tabulas
testamenti bonorum *possessionem* pollicetur, *et* si nemo
sit, ad quem ab intestato iure legitimo pertineat hereditas, uelut frater eodem patre natus aut patruus aut
fratris filius, ita poterunt scripti heredes retinere
hereditatem: nam idem iuris est et si alia ex causa[6]
testamentum non ualeat, uelut quod familia non
uenierit aut nuncupationis uerba testator locutus non
sit.[7] **120.** Sed uideamus, an etiam[8] si frater aut patruus
extent, potiores scriptis heredibus habeantur; rescripto

---

1) aut V.   2) Titus V.   3) illam V.   4) institutio V.
5) tutore auctore] tutores habet V.   6) SCto V.   7) nam
— sit *del. Solazzi.*   8) *del. idem.*

---

§ 116. *cf. D.* 29, 7, 10 (*Pap.* 240). *I.* 2, 20, 34. *C.* 6, 23,
15 (*a.* 339); 24 (*a.* 528).
§ 117. *cf. Ulp.* 21. *D.* 29, 7, 13, 1 (*Pap.* 279). *Theoph.* 1,
14, 1 (*p.* 65 *Ferr.*).
§ 118. *cf. supra* 1, 192. 2, 112. *infra* 3, 43. *Ulp.* 20, 15.
§ 119. *cf. infra* 2, 147 *sq. Ulp.* 23, 6. 28, 6. *I.* 2, 10, 2. *D.*
28, 3, 12 (*Ulp.* 83). 38, 6, 3 (*Ulp.* 2496). *C.* 6, 11, 2 *pr.* (*a.* 242).
Cons. 6, 18 (*Cod. Hermog. tit. de successionibus*). *Cic. Verr.* 2,
1, 45, 117. *top.* 4, 18 c. *Boeth. p.* 302 *Bait. B. G. U.* 361 III 12; 13.
§ 120. *cf. infra* 2, 149ᵃ. *Paul. Coll.* 16, 3, 1 (*Sent.* 4, 8, 1).
D. 37, 11, 11, 2 (*Pap.* 221). 44, 4, 4, 10 (*Ulp.* 1678).

whether the appointment of the heir was made in solemn form; if it was done in any other way, sale of the testator's property, adducing witnesses and making a testamentary declaration as described above is a waste of time. 117. Now, the solemn form of appointment is: 'Let Titius be heir'; but: 'I instruct Titius to be heir' is also regarded as acceptable now; however, 'I wish Titius to be heir' is not acceptable, and most authorities also reject 'I appoint Titius as heir' or 'I make [Titius] heir'.

118. Moreover, notice that if a woman under guardianship makes a will, she should have her guardian's authorisation; otherwise the will is not effective by state law. 119. Yet if the will is sealed with the seals of seven witnesses the praetor promises estate-possession in support of the will to the heirs appointed in it; and if there is no one with a statutory title to the inheritance on intestacy, such as a brother born of the same father or a paternal uncle or a brother's son, the appointed heirs will thus be able to keep the inheritance. The law is the same even if the will is invalid for some other reason, such as that the property was not sold or that the testator did not speak the words of the declaration. 120. But we need to see whether, even if there is a brother or paternal uncle, they should be preferred to the appointed heirs; for there is a written reply* by the Emperor Antoninus

enim imperatoris Antonini significatur[1] eos, qui secundum tabulas testamenti non iure factas bonorum
possessionem petierint, posse aduersus eos, qui ab intestato uindicant hereditatem, defendere se per exceptionem doli mali. 121. Quod sane quidem ad
masculorum testamenta pertinere certum est; item ad
feminarum, quae ideo non utiliter testatae sunt, quod
uerbi gratia familiam non uendiderint aut nuncupa-
84 tionis uerba locutae non sint: | an autem et ad ea
testamenta feminarum, quae sine tutoris auctoritate
fecerint, haec constitutio pertineat, uidebimus. 122. Loquimur autem de his scilicet feminis, quae non in
legitima parentium aut patronorum tutela sunt, sed [de
his][2] quae alterius generis tutores[3] habent, qui etiam
inuiti coguntur auctores fieri. alioquin parentem et
patronum[4] sine auctoritate eius facto testamento non
summoueri palam est.

123. Item qui filium in potestate habet, curare
debet[5], ut eum uel heredem instituat uel nominatim
exheredet; alioquin si eum silentio praeterierit, inutiliter testabitur: adeo quidem, ut nostri praeceptores
existiment, etiam si uiuo patre filius defunctus sit,
neminem heredem ex eo testamento existere posse, scilicet[6] quia statim ab initio non constiterit institutio;
sed diuersae scholae auctores, si quidem filius mortis
patris tempore uiuat, sane impedimento eum esse
scriptis heredibus et illum[7] ab intestato heredem fieri

---

1) significat V.　　　2) de his *del. Mommsen.*　　　3) tutorem V.　　4) patronorum V.　　5) debetur V.　　6) quod scilicet V. quod sciiicet non ualet *Kniep.*　　7) suum *Hu.*

---

§ 121. *cf. supra* 2, 104 *sq.*; 115; 118; 119.
§ 122. *cf. supra* 1, 190; 192.
§ 123. = *I.* 2, 13 *pr. Gai epit.* 2, 3 *pr.*; 1. *Ulp.* 22, 16.
Papiniani fr. Berolin. 14 (*Iurispr.* I 433). *D.* 28, 2, 8 (*Pomp.*
384). 28, 2, 30 (*Gai.* 300). 28, 3, 17 (*Pap.* 527). 34, 7, 3 (*Pap.*
242). 34, 7, 4 (*Ulp.* 2506). 28, 2, 7 (*Paul.* 1600). 28, 2, 31 (*Paul.*
1626). 50, 17, 210 (*Lic. Ruf.* 6). *Cic. de orat.* 1, 38, 175.

Pius making known that, where a will has not been properly made, claimants to estate-possession in support of the will can plead the defence of deceit against anyone vindicating the inheritance on intestacy. 121. And you may note that this certainly applies to wills made by males; and again to women whose will is not effectively made, because, for example, they have not sold their property or spoken the words of declaration. But we shall see whether this pronouncement also applies to wills made by women without their guardian's authorisation. 122. Now here, of course, we are speaking not of women in the statutory guardianship of their parents or their patrons but of those with guardians of some other kind, who must give their authorisation even when they do not want to. Obviously in the other case a parent or patron cannot be displaced by a will made without authorisation.

123. Again, **someone with a son within his power must be sure to appoint him heir or to disinherit him specifically. If he passes him over in silence, his will becomes a nullity. Even if the son** predeceases **the father**, our teachers consider that **it will be impossible for anyone to become heir under that will, for the obvious reason that** the appointment as heir **failed from the outset to come into existence.** The authorities of the other school acknowledge that, if the son is alive when his father dies, he indeed bars the appointed heirs and himself becomes heir on intestacy. On the other hand, they

confitentur; si uero ante mortem patris interceptus sit,
posse ex testamento hereditatem[1] adiri putant, nullo
iam filio impedimento; quia scilicet existimant *non*
statim ab initio inutiliter fieri testamentum filio praeterito. **124.** Ceteras uero liberorum personas si **prae-**
terierit testator, ualet testamentum: *sed* praeteritae istae
personae scriptis heredibus in | partem adcrescunt, si
sui heredes sint, in uirilem, si extranei, in dimidiam:
id est, si quis tres uerbi gratia filios heredes instituerit et filiam praeterierit, filia adcrescendo pro quarta
parte fit heres et ea ratione id consequitur, quod ab
intestato patre mor*tuo* habitura esset; at si extraneos
ille heredes instituerit et filiam praeterierit, filia adcrescendo ex dimidia parte fit heres.[2] quae de filia
diximus, eadem et de nepote deque omnibus *cete-*
ris[3] liberorum personis seu masculini seu *f*eminini
sexus dicta intellegemus. **125.** Quid ergo est? licet
hae secundum ea, quae diximus, scriptis heredibus[4]
dimidiam partem modo detrahant, tamen praetor eis
contra tabulas bonorum possessionem promittit[5], qua
ratione extranei heredes a tota hereditate repellun-
tur et efficiuntur sine re heredes. **126.** Et hoc iure
uteb*amur, quas*i nihil inter feminas et masculos in-
teresset; sed nuper imperator Antoninus significauit
rescripto suas[6] non plus nancisci feminas per bonorum
possessionem, quam quod[7] iure adcrescendi conseque-
rentur. quod in emancipatarum quoque personis[8] obseruandum est, ut[9] *nimirum hae quoque, quod* adcre-

85
t. s.

---

1) heredem V.   2) heret V.   3) *addidimus. cf.*
§ 124. 128. 131.   4) heredibus *in* V *legitur post* modo.
5) promittitur V.   6) suas *Hu.* suo V.   7) quam quod]
quodquam? V.   8) personis *Polen.* persona V.   9) est ut
Hu. osset V.

---

§ 124. *cf. Gai epit.* 2, 3, 1.   *Ulp.* 22, 17.   *Paul.* 3, 4[b], 8.
I. 2, 13 *pr. Nov. Maior.* 6, 3. *Lex Rom. Burgund.* 45, 4.
§ 126. *cf. C.* 6, 28, 4 (*a.* 531).

think that if he is carried off before his father the inheritance can be accepted under the will as the son is no longer a bar; in other words, they consider that passing over a son does not make the will radically ineffective. 124. On the other hand, if a testator passes over the other descendants in his power the will is valid but those persons who have been passed over **come in for a share** along with the appointed heirs. If these are the testator's immediate heirs they get a proportional share; if they are outside heirs* they get a half. To take an example, if, say, someone appoints three sons as heirs and passes over a daughter, the daughter comes in as heir and has a quarter and thus gets the same as she would have had on intestacy on her father's death; but if he appoints outsiders as heirs and passes over his daughter, the daughter comes in as heir and has a half. What we have said of a daughter applies equally to a grandson and all other descendants, male or female. 125. What then? Although according to what we have said they take only a half-share away from the appointed heirs, the praetor promises them estate-possession counter to the will, and thus the outside heirs are excluded from the whole inheritance and become heirs without an estate. 126. And this was the law applied, with no distinction made between female and male; but recently the Emperor Antoninus Pius made known in a written reply that a man's immediate female heirs should not get more by estate-possession than they would get by coming in as heirs. And this was to operate in the case of emancipated* females also, to the effect that they should get exactly the same by estate-possession as they would have had by coming

scendi iure habiturae essent[1], si in potestate fuissent,
id ipsum etiam per bonorum possessionem habeant.
127. Sed si quidem filius a patre exheredetur, nominatim exheredari *debet*; alioquin non prodest eum[2]
86 exheredari. nominatim autem *ex*heredari uidetur, siue
t. s. ita exhere|detur: TITIVS FILIVS MEVS EXHERES ESTO,
siue *ita:* FILIVS MEVS EXHERES ESTO, non adiecto proprio nomine. 128. Ceterae uero liberorum personae
uel feminini sexus uel masculini[3] satis inter ceteros
exheredantur, id est his *uerbis:* CETERI OMNES EXHERE-
DES SVNTO, quae *uerba statim post in*stitutionem heredum adici solent. sed hoc ita *est iure ciuili.* 129. Nam
praetor omnes uirilis sexus lib*erorum personas*, id est
nepotes quoque et pronepotes | ——————————
—————————— *2⅓ versus legi nequeunt* ——————————|[4]
130. Postumi quoque liberi nominatim[5] *uel heredes
insti*tui debent uel exheredari. 131. Et *in* eo[6] par
omnium condi*cio est, quod et in* filio *postumo et in
quolibet ex ceteris li*beris siue *feminini sexus siue masculini*[7] praeterito ualet *quidem testamentum, sed postea
adgnatione postumi si*ue postumae rumpitur, et ea ra-
*tione totum infir*matur. ideoque si mulier, ex qua

1) habiturae essent] habituresse V.   2) prodest eum
Polen. prosiet *vel* possiet? V.   3) uel feminini — masculini
del. Solazzi.   4) *Hu. ita supplevit:* nominatim exheredari iubet,
feminini uero sexus liberos, id est filias et neptes et proneptes
exheredari aut nominatim aut inter ceteros satis habet.   5) *om.
Inst.*   6) in eo *Inst.* ideo V.   7) siue feminini — masculini *del. Solazzi.*

§ 127. *cf. I.* 2, 13 *pr.* 1. *Ulp.* 22, 20. *supra* 2, 123. *infra*
2, 132. *D.* 28, 2, 1. 3 (*Ulp.* 2432. 2433 *pr.*). 28, 2, 2 (*Ulp.* 2377).
Cic. de orat. 1, 38, 175. *Quint. decl.* 2, 14 *i. f.*
§ 128. *cf.I.* 2, 13 *pr. Ulp.* 22, 20. *C.* 6, 28, 4 (*a.* 531)- *BG U* 7, 1696.
§ 129. *cf. infra* 2, 135.
§§ 130—132. = *I.* 2, 13, 1. *cf. Gai epit.* 2, 3, 2. *Ulp.* 22,
15; 18—21. 23, 2. *D.* 28, 3, 3 (*Ulp.* 2446). *C.* 6, 12, 2 (*a.* 224).
6, 29, 2 (*a.* 294). *Cic. de inv.* 2, 42, 122. *de or.* 1, 57, 241. *pro Caec.*
25, 72. *Isid. or.* 5, 24, 10. *Liv.* 1, 34, 3. *I.* 2, 13, 6. *Pap. Hamb.* 72.

in as heirs if they had been in power. 127. But if a son is to be disinherited by his father he should be disinherited specifically; otherwise it is no good disinheriting him. **Now, the requirement for specific removal is satisfied by: 'Let Titius my son be disinherited' and also by: 'Let my son be disinherited' with his actual name omitted.** 128. Other descendants in power, on the other hand, male or female, can be excluded by a general clause: 'Let all others be disinherited'. These words are usually added immediately after the appointment of the heirs. But this represents the state law. 129. In the case of all male descendants, that is, including grandsons and great-grandsons, the praetor ... [in the following passage, which is illegible, Gaius probably said that the praetor required all these male descendants to be disinherited specifically but allowed female descendants to be disinherited either specifically or by a general clause.]

130. **Posthumous children* must also be appointed heirs or disinherited** specifically. 131. **The rules are the same for all: if a posthumous son or any other posthumous offspring, male or female, is passed over, the will is good, but the birth of the posthumous child then nullifies it, overthrowing it completely. This means that if a woman carrying a**

*postumus aut postu*ma sperabatur, abor*tum fecerit, nihil impedimento est scriptis hered*ibus *ad hereditatem adeun-dam.* **132.** *Sed feminini* quidem sexus personae *uel* nomi*natim uel inter ceteros exheredari solent, dum tamen, si inter ceteros exheredentur, aliquid eis legetur, ne uideantur per obliuio*nem praeteritae *esse: masculini uero sexus liberorum person*as placuit non aliter recte exheredari, nisi[1] no¦minatim exheredentur, hoc scilicet modo* QVICVMQVE MIHI FILIVS GENITVS FVERIT EXHERES ESTO. ─────── *vv. 9½* ──────[2] **133.** *Postumo-rum autem loco sunt et hi, qui in sui heredis locum succedendo quasi adgnascendo fiunt parent*ibus sui here-des: ut ecce si filium et *ex eo nepotem neptemue in* potestate habeam, quia filius gradu praecedit, *is solus iura sui heredis habet, quamuis nepos quo*que et neptis *ex eo in eadem potestate sint; sed si filius meus me uiuo moriatur aut qualibet alia ratione exeat de po-testate mea, incipit nepos neptisue in eius locum succe-dere, et* eo modo iura suorum here*dum quasi adgnatio*ne nanciscuntur. **134.** Ne ergo eo modo rumpatur mihi testa*mentum, sicut ipsum filium uel heredem in*stituere uel exheredare[3] debeo, ne no*n iure faciam testamen-tum, ita et n*epotem neptemue ex eo necesse est mihi uel *heredem instituere uel exheredare, ne forte, me uiuo filio mortuo, succedendo in locum eius nepos neptisue*[4] | quasi adgnatione rumpat testamentum: idque lege Iunia

---

1) nisi *Inst.* quam si *Eisele, Grupe.*   2) *de lacuna sup-plenda cf. Gai. epit. 2, 3, 2 in fine. paragraphum* 132 *a Gaio abiudicat Solazzi, Gaio e la legge Iunia Vellaea.*   3) exhere-dare V. nominatim exheredare *Inst.* exheredare nominatim *Dig., vix ex Gaio.*   4) *quae ex Inst. et Dig. suppleta sunt, non sufficiunt ad explendos* V *vv.* 22—24.

§§ 133. 134. = *D.* 28, 3, 13. *I.* 2, 13, 2. *cf. Ulp.* 23,. 3. *Paul.* 3, 4b, 10. *D.* 28, 2, 29 (*Scaev.* 157). 28, 6, 2 *pr.* (*Ulp.* 2469). 28, 3, 6, 4 (*Ulp.* 2505). 28, 2, 9, 2 (*Paul.* 1601). *C.* 6, 28, 2 (*a.* 225). 3, 28, 34 (*a.* 531).

§ 134. lege Iunia Vellaea] *sub Claudio aut Nerone lata. cf. Mommsen Jur. Schr.* I, 285. *Hülsen, Mitteilungen des Ar-chaeol. Instituts* XIX (1904), 322. *cf. Bruns* I[7], 116.

posthumous child happens to miscarry, nothing
prevents the heirs appointed in the will from
accepting the inheritance. 132. In the case of
females the practice is to remove them either by a
specific or by a general exclusion. If a general
exclusion is used they are then given something by
way of legacy in order to show that they had not
simply been forgotten; but in the case of males, it is
held that any removal must be specific. Of course,
it has to be of this kind: 'Let any son begotten
hereafter by me be disinherited' ... [in the illegible
passage which follows Gaius may have pointed out
that the effect of passing over a posthumous female
was more serious than passing over one already born
because it nullified the will.] 133. Next, the rules on
posthumous children also apply to those who by
succeeding to the immediate heir of the head of
family become his immediate heirs in, as it were,
the second rank. Suppose, for example, that I have
a son within my power and through him a
grandchild also within power. Here the son is a
degree higher and he alone has the rights of the
immediate heir, despite the fact that they are
within power together. If my son dies before me, or
leaves my power for some other reason, the
grandchild succeeds to his place and assumes the
rights of immediate heir in, as it were, the second
rank. 134. To guard against the nullification of my
will, just as I must appoint or remove my son, I
must also appoint or remove my grandchildren by
him. That way I will avoid making an ineffective
will. The danger is that my son may die in my
lifetime and let in these second-ranked heirs,
whose succession will overthrow the will. This was
anticipated in the Junian-Vellaean Act which also

Vellaea[1] prouisum est, in qua simul exheredationis
modus notatur, ut uirilis sexus nominatim, feminini
uel nominatim uel inter ceteros exheredentur, dum
tamen iis, qui inter ceteros exheredantur, aliquid lege-
tur. 135. Emancipatos liberos iure ciuili neque heredes instituere neque exheredare necesse est, quia non
sunt sui heredes: sed praetor omnes tam feminini
quam masculini sexus[2], si heredes non instituantur, exheredari iubet, uirilis sexus nominatim, feminini uel[3]
nominatim uel inter ceteros: quod si neque heredes instituti fuerint neque ita, ut supra diximus, exheredati,
praetor promittit eis contra tabulas bonorum possessionem. 135ᵃ. In potestate patris non sunt, qui cum
eo ciuitate Romana donati sunt[4] nec[5] in accipienda
ciuitate Romana pater *petiit statim* a principe, ut eos
in potestate *haberet*[6], aut si *petiit*, non impetrauit;
nam qui *in* potestatem[7] patris ab imperatore redi-
guntur, nihil differunt a*b* his, *qui ita nati sunt*.
136. Adoptiui filii, quamdiu manent in adoptione[8], naturalium loco sunt; emancipati uero *a* patre adoptiuo
neque iure ciuili neque quod ad edictum praetoris
pertinet inter liberos numerantur. 137. Qua ratione
accidit, ut ex diuerso, quod ad naturalem parentem
pertinet, quamdiu quidem sint in adoptiua familia,
extraneorum numero habeantur; si uero emancipati
89 fuerint ab adoptiuo patre, tunc incipiant | in ea causa
esse, qua futuri essent, si ab ipso naturali patre *emancipati* fuissent.

---

1) lege Iunia Vellaea] legem iun. ūlea V.   2) omnes — sexus
del. Solazzi l.c. 50   3) u (*i. e.* uel) V. uero *Inst.*   4) sint V.   5) si nec
Polenaar. si non *Hu.*   6) habere V.   7) potum V.   8) adoptionem V.

§ 135. = *I.* 2, 13, 3. *cf. Ulp.* 22, 23. 28, 2—4. *supra* 2,
129. *infra* 3, 20. *Coll.* 16, 7, 2 (*Ulp.* 1927). *I.* 3, 1, 12. *C. I. L.*
VI 1527 *l.* 15. 16 (*Bruns* I⁷, 373).
   § 135ᵃ. *cf. supra* 1, 55; 93; 94. *infra* 3, 20. *Coll.* 16, 7, 2
(*Ulp.* 1927).
   §§ 136. 137. = *I.* 2, 13, 4. *cf. I.* 3, 1, 10—12. *Ulp.* 22, 14.
D. 37, 4, 1, 6 (*Ulp.* 1099). *C.* 8, 47 (48), 10 *pr.* (*a.* 530).

contains **a model exclusion**, specific for males and specific or general for females, with the proviso that those excluded by a general clause be left a legacy.

135. **Children who have been emancipated do not, according to the law of the state, have to be appointed or excluded, because they are not immediate heirs. But the praetor requires that all of them, male and female, must be disinherited, if they are not appointed. He requires males to be excluded specifically but allows** specific or **general exclusion of females. If they are neither appointed nor excluded in the way described above, the praetor gives them estate-possession counter to the will.** 135a. Where children are granted Roman citizenship along with their father, and in petitioning for citizenship the father either did not ask the emperor to have them in his power or, if he did, he was not successful in his petition, the children are not in their father's power; for those brought within their father's power by the emperor are in no way different from those born in power. 136. **Adoptive** sons **still in** their adoptive family are in the same legal position as real sons. **On the other hand, when emancipated by their adoptive father they no longer count as descendants either in state law or under the praetor's Edict*.** 137. **The logic of this applies conversely to the real father. His** sons while in the **adoptive family count as outsiders. But if the sons are emancipated by the adoptive father they assume the position that they would have had if emancipated by their own father.**

138. Si quis post[1] factum testamentum adoptauerit sibi filium aut per populum eum, qui sui iuris est, aut per praetorem eum, qui in potestate parentis fuerit, omni modo testamentum eius rumpitur quasi agnatione sui heredis. 139. Idem iuris est, si cui post factum testamentum uxor in manu*m* conueniat, uel quae in manu fuit, nubat: nam eo modo filiae loco esse incipit et quasi sua.[2] 140. Nec prodest, s*i*ue haec siue ille, qui adoptatus est, in eo testamento sit institutus institutaue: nam de exheredatione eius superuacuum uidetur quaerere, cum testamenti faciundi tempore suorum heredum numero non fuerint. 141. Filius quoque, qui ex prima secundaue mancipatione manumittitur, quia reuertitur in potestatem patriam, rumpit[3] ante factum testamentum; nec prodest[4], *si* in eo testamento heres institutus u*e*l exheredatus fuerit. 142. Simile ius olim fuit in eius persona, cuius nomine ex senatus consulto erroris causa[5] probatur[6], quia forte ex peregrina uel Latina, quae per errorem quasi ciuis Romana uxor ducta esset, natus esset: nam siue heres institutus esset a parente siue exheredatus, siue uiuo patre causa proba*ta* siue post mortem eius, omni modo quasi adgna|tione 90 rumpebat testamentum. 143. Nunc uero ex nouo se-

---

1) potest V.   2) suai V.   3) rumpitur V.   4) prode est V.   5) *an* causa erroris? *cf. Kalb, Archiv. Lexicogr.* I, 86. 6) prouatum? V.

---

§ 138. = *I.* 2, 17, 1. *cf. supra* 1, 98 *sq. Gai epit.* 2, 3, 3. *Ulp.* 23, 3. *D.* 28, 3, 8 *pr.* (*Ulp.* 2510).
§ 139. *cf. supra* 1, 114. *infra* 2, 159. 3, 3. *Ulp.* 23, 3. *Gell.* 18, 6, 9. *C. I. L.* VI 1527 *l.* 13. 14 (*Bruns* I[7], 322).
§ 140. *cf. D.* 28, 3, 18 (*Scaev.* 152). 28, 2, 28, 1 (*Tryph.* 70). 28, 2, 23 (*Pap.* 215) = 37, 4, 8, 7 (*Ulp.* 1105). 37, 4, 8, 8 *sq.* (*Ulp.* 1105).
§ 141. *cf. Ulp.* 23, 3. *supra* 1, 132; 135. *infra* 3, 6. *Paul. Coll.* 16, 3, 7 (*Sent.* 4, 8, 7). *D.* 28, 3, 8, 1 (*Ulp.* 2510).
§ 142. *cf. supra* 1, 32; 66. *infra* 3, 5.
§ 143. *cf. supra* 1, 32, *ubi tamen de intestato patre agitur.*

138. **Suppose that after making his will the testator adopts a son,** before the people **if the adoptee is independent, or through the praetor if he is not. Here the will is nullified. It is** totally **destroyed just as if a new immediate heir had been born.** 139. The law is the same if someone makes his will and then takes a wife into marital subordination or marries a woman who was subordinate to him; in this way she acquires the position of a daughter and is treated as his immediate heir. 140. And it does not help that she or the adoptee is appointed heir in the will. It is pointless to look for their exclusion when they were not counted among the immediate heirs when the will was made. 141. A son manumitted after a first or second mancipation also nullifies a will already made because he reverts to his father's power; it does not help that he was appointed heir or disinherited in the will. 142. The same rule used to be applied in the case of a person in whose favour a case of error was proved under a Senate resolution, say, where he was born of a foreign or Latin woman who had been married in the erroneous belief that she was a Roman citizen; whether he had been appointed heir by his father or disinherited and whether the error was proved in his father's lifetime or after his death, the will was nullified in every case just as if a new immediate heir had been born. 143. But now under a recent Senate resolution, passed on the proposal of the

natus consulto, quod auctore diuo Hadriano factum
est, si quidem uiuo patre causa probatur, aeque ut
olim omni modo rumpit testamentum; si uero post
mortem patris, praeteritus quidem rumpit testamentum,
si uero heres in eo scriptus est uel exheredatus, non
rumpit testamentum, ne scilicet diligenter facta testamenta rescinderentur eo[1] tempore, quo renouari non
possent.

144. Posteriore quoque testamento, quod iure factum[2] est, superius rumpitur; nec interest, an extiterit
aliquis ex eo heres an non extiterit: hoc enim solum
spectatur, an existere potuerit: ideoque si quis ex
posteriore testamento, quod iure factum est, aut noluerit heres esse aut uiuo testatore aut post mortem eius,
antequam hereditatem adiret, decesserit aut per cretionem[3] exclusus fuerit aut condicione, sub qua heres
institutus est, defectus sit aut propter caelibatum ex
lege Iulia summotus fuerit ab hereditate, [quibus casibus pater familias intestatus moritur: nam][4] et prius
testamentum non ualet ruptum a posteriore, et poste-
rius aeque nullas uires habet, cum ex eo nemo heres
extiterit.

145. Alio quoque modo testamenta iure facta infir-
mantur[5], uelut *cum* is, qui fecerit testamentum, kapite
deminutus[6] sit; quod quibus modis accidat, primo

---

1) eos V.   2) facturum V.   3) per cretionem *Goeschen.*
perceptionem V.   4) quibus — nam *del. Solazzi; cf. infra* 3, 72.
5) infirmatur V.   6) kapite deminutus] kd ā V.

---

§ 144. = *I.* 2, 17, 2. *cf. Gai epit.* 2, 3, 4.   *Ulp.* 23, 2. *I.*
2, 17, 7 (8). *D.* 28, 3, 2 (*Ulp.* 2439). *C.* 6, 23, 27 (*a.* 530). noluerit heres esse] *cf. Paul. Coll.* 16, 3, 1. *D.* 26, 2, 9 (*Pomp.*
227). 50, 17, 181 (*Paul.* 2065). per cretionem] *cf infra* 2, 166 *sq.*
condicione defectus sit] *cf. Paul. Coll.* 16, 3, 1. . lege Iulia] *cf.*
supra 2, 111. *infra* 2, 286.
    § 145. = *I.* 2, 17, 4. *cf. Gai epit.* 2, 3, 5. *Ulp.* 23, 4. *D.*
28, 1, 8, 1 *sq.* (*Gai.* 299). 37, 11, 11, 2 (*Pap.* 221). 28, 3, 6, 5 *sq.*
(*Ulp.* 2507). 29, 7, 8, 3 (*Paul.* 895). *Isid. orig.* 5, 24, 8. primo
comm.] *cf. supra* 1, 159 *sq.*

Emperor Hadrian, if the case is proved in the father's lifetime this still nullifies the will in every case, exactly as before. If it is proved after the father's death, on the other hand, a child passed over still nullifies the will but one appointed heir or disinherited in it does not; the idea is that wills carefully made should not be set aside when they can no longer be revised.

144. **Also, a later will, properly made, nullifies an earlier one. It does not matter whether an heir actually takes under it or not, since the only relevant question is whether an heir could do so. Suppose the heir** under the later, properly made will **declines, or he dies before the testator, or he dies after the testator but before he can accept the estate,** or he fails to make formal acceptance* in time, **or a condition of his appointment fails,** or he is excluded from the inheritance under the Julian Act because he is unmarried. **In these cases the head of the family* dies intestate: his earlier will is invalid, nullified by the later; and the later will is ineffective because it produces no heir.**

145. **Another way in which a will, good when made, can become invalid is by the testator's status-loss*. We discussed how this happens in the**

commentario relatum est. 146. Hoc autem casu in|rita 91
fieri testamenta dicemus, cum alioquin et quae rum-
puntur, inrita fiant, *et quae statim ab initio non iure
fiunt, inrita sint; sed et ea, quae iure facta sunt et
postea propter capitis deminutionem inrita fiunt,* possunt
nihilo minus rupta dici. sed quia sane commodius
erat singulas causas singulis appellationibus distingui,
ideo quaedam non iure fieri dicuntur, quaedam iure
facta rumpi uel inrita fieri.

147. Non tamen per omnia inutilia sunt ea testamenta, quae uel ab initio non iure facta sunt uel iure
facta postea inrita facta *aut* rupta sunt. nam si septem
testium signis signata sint testamenta, potest scriptus
heres secundum tabulas bonorum possessionem petere,
si modo defunctus testator et ciuis Romanus et suae
potestatis mortis tempore fuerit. nam si ideo inritum
factum sit[1] testamentum, quod puta ciuitatem uel
etiam libertatem testator amisit aut quia[2] in adoptionem se dedit *et* mortis tempore in adoptiui patris
potestate fuit, non potest scriptus heres secundum tabulas bonorum possessionem pet*ere*. 148. *Qui autem*
secundum tabulas testamenti, quae aut statim ab initio
non iure factae sunt[3] aut iure factae postea ruptae[4]
uel inritae erunt, bonorum possessionem accipiunt, si
modo possunt hereditatem optinere, habebunt bonorum
possessionem cum re; si uero ab his auocari hereditas potest, habebunt bonorum possessionem sine re.
149. Nam si quis heres iure ciuili institutus sit uel ex

---

1) factum sit *Inst.* fic? V.   2) aut quia *Inst.* uut his V.
3) sint V.   4) nuptae V.

---

§ 146. = *I.* 2, 17, 5 (4). *cf. Ulp.* 23, 1. *Paul. Coll.* 16, 3, 2.
D. 28, 3, 1 (*Pap.* 40). 38, 16, 1 *pr.* (*Ulp.* 2512).
§ 147. = *I.* 2, 17, 6 (5). *cf. Ulp.* 23, 6. 28, 6. *supra* 2, 119
et ibi citatos.
§ 148. *cf. Ulp.* 23, 6. 28, 13. *infra* 3, 35 *sq. Paul. Coll.*
16, 3, 1 (*Sent.* 4, 8, 1).

first commentary. 146. **In this case the will is said to be frustrated, although nullified wills could equally be referred to as frustrated, as could those bad from the beginning. Similarly, wills which are good as made but are subsequently frustrated by status-loss could also be described as nullified. All the same, because it is useful to have different terms for different things, we say some are invalid when made, others nullified, and others frustrated.**

147. **Wills which are invalid as made, or which are valid as made and then frustrated** or nullified, **are not absolutely ineffective for all purposes. If** the will **bears the seal of seven witnesses the appointed heir can** seek **estate-possession in support of the will. There are conditions: the deceased must have been a Roman citizen and independent at the time of his death. If the will was frustrated, say, by a status-loss which deprived the testator of citizenship or liberty as well, or which happened because he was adopted and at the time of his death he was within the power of his adoptive father, the appointee cannot seek estate-possession in support of the will.** 148. Now those who receive estate-possession in support of a will which either was never valid as made or was valid as made but subsequently nullified or frustrated, will have effective estate-possession provided that they can keep the inheritance; if on the other hand the inheritance can be taken away from them they will have provisional estate-possession. 149. For anyone appointed heir in accordance with state law under the

primo uel ex posteriore testamento uel ab intestato
iure legitimo heres sit, is potest ab *i*is hereditatem
92 auocare; si uero nemo | sit alius iure ciuili heres, ipsi
retinere hereditatem possunt, nec ullum ius aduersus
eos habent cognati, *qui* legitimo iure deficiuntur.
149ª. Ali*quando tamen, sicut su*pra quoque notauimus,
etiam legitimis[1] quoque *heredibus* potiores scripti habentur, u*eluti* si ideo n*on iure* factum sit testamentum,
quod familia non uenierit aut nuncupationis uerba
testator locutus non sit; ∗ ∗ ∗ ∗[2] *si* adgnati petant
hered*itatem* — 150. ——— *vv. 3½* ———[2] *ea* lege bona
caduca fiunt et ad populum deferri iubentur, si defuncto nemo *heres uel bonorum possessor sit*.[3]

151. Potest, ut iure facta testamenta *contraria uoluntate* infirmentur.[4] apparet *autem* non posse e*x eo s*olo
in*firma*ri testamentum, quod postea testator id noluerit ualere, usque adeo, ut si linum eius inciderit, nihilo minus iure ciuili ualeat. quin etiam si deleuerit
quoque aut combus*serit* tabulas testamenti, non ideo
minus[5] desinent ualere, *quae* ibi fuerunt scripta, licet
eorum probatio diff*icilis* sit. 151ª. Quid ergo est? si
quis ab intestato bonorum possessionem petieri*t et* is,

---

1) legitimus V.   2) *sic fere sententiam suppleas:* tum
enim, si adgnati petant hereditatem, per exceptionem
doli mali ex constitutione imperatoris Antonini summoueri
possunt. (*hucusque secundum Hu., sequentia secundum Kruege-
rum*) § 150. sane lege Iulia scriptis non aufertur hereditas,
si bonorum possessores ex edicto constituti sint. nam ita
demum ea lege *etc.*   3) heres—sit *suppl. Hu.*   4) infirme-
tur V.   5) *rectius Gaius scripsisset* magis.

---

§ 149ª. supra] 2, 120; 121.
§ 150. *cf. Ulp.* 28, 7. *D.* 30, 96, 1 (*Iul.* 553). 1, 5, 26 (*Iul.*
781). *infra* 3, 78.
§ 151. *cf. Paul. Coll.* 16, 3, 1 (*Sent.* 4, 8, 1). *D.* 28, 4, 3
(*Marcell.* 263). 34, 9, 12 (*Pap.* 251). 28, 4, 4 (*Pap.* 533). 29, 1,
36, 3 *et* 34, 4, 22 (*Pap.* 540). 34, 9, 16, 2 (*Pap.* 595). 28, 4, 2
(*Ulp.* 81). 38, 6, 1, 8 (*Ulp.* 1196). 44, 4, 4, 10 (*Ulp.* 1678). 28,
4, 1, 3 (*Ulp.* 2581).

first or a later will or anyone with a statutory title on
intestacy can take the inheritance away from them;
on the other hand, if there is no one else who is heir
under state law they themselves can keep the
inheritance; cognates*, who lack a statutory title,
have no right against them. 149a. Yet sometimes, as
we noted above, the appointed heirs are preferred
even to the statutory heirs, for instance, if the reason
why the will was not valid as made is that the
property was not sold or that the testator did not
speak the words of the declaration and the agnates
claim the inheritance [they can be countered by the
defence of deceit in terms of the pronouncement of the
Emperor Antoninus Pius] ... 150. ... [the paragraph
begins with an illegible passage which contained some
reference to the Julian Act] under that Act the estate
is forfeited and given to the people if no one is heir or
estate-possessor to the deceased.

151. Wills properly made may be invalidated if the
testator changes his mind. But it is clear that **a will
does not become invalid merely because the
testator wants to rescind it**. Why, even if he cuts the
thread holding it together it is still valid by state law.
Indeed even if he destroys or burns the will, what was
written in it is no less valid, although proof of what
that was may be difficult. 151a. What then? If anyone
claims estate-possession on intestacy and the person

qui ex eo testamento heres *est,* petat h*ered}tatem,*
—— *vv.* $2\frac{1}{4}$ ——[1], | perueniat hereditas: et hoc ita 93
*re*scripto imperatoris Antonini significatur.
152. Heredes autem aut necessarii dicuntur aut sui
et necessarii aut extranei. 153. Necessarius heres est
seruus cum libertate heres institutus, ideo sic appel-
latus, quia siue uelit siue nolit, omni modo post
mortem testatoris protinus liber et heres est. 154. Unde
qui facultates suas suspectas habet, solet seruum suum
primo aut secundo uel etiam ulteriore gradu liberum
et heredem instituere, ut si creditoribus satis non
fiat, potius huius heredis quam ipsius testatoris bona
ueneant[2], id est, ut ignominia, quae accidit[3] ex uenditione bonorum, hunc potius heredem quam ipsum
testatorem contingat; quamquam apud Fufidium Sabino
placeat eximendum eum esse ignominia, quia non suo
uitio, sed necessitate iuris bonorum uenditionem pate-
retur; sed alio iure utimur. 155. Pro hoc tamen in-
commodo illud ei commodum praestatur, ut ea, quae
post mortem patroni sibi adquisierit, siue ante bonorum uenditionem siue postea, ipsi reseruentur; et

---

1) *sic fere sententiam supplet Krueger:* per exceptionem doli
mali repelletur. si uero nemo ab intestato bonorum possessionem **petierit,** populus (*sic Girard*) scripto heredi quasi in-
digno auferet hereditatem, ne ullo modo ad eum, quem testator
heredem habere noluit. *Hu. vestigiis V insistens supplementa
(minus probabilia) proposuit haec:* potest eum per exceptionem
doli mali repellere, si modo ea mens testatoris fuisse pro-
betur, ut ad eos, qui ab intestato uocantur. 2) ueneantur V.
3) accidit *Lachmann.* accedit V.

§ 152. = *I.* 2, 19 *pr.* cf. *Gai epit.* 2, 3, 6.
§ 153. = *I.* 2, 19, 1. cf. *Gai epit.* 2, 3, 6. *infra* 2, 157;
160; 188. *Ulp.* 22, 24. *I.* 1, 6, 1. 2, 15 *pr.* = *D.* 28, 6, 36 *pr.*
(*Marcian.* 93). *Cod. tit.* 6, 27.
§ 154. = *I.* 2, 19, 1. *cf. infra* 3, 79. 4. 102. *D.* 28, 5, 89
(88) (*Gai.* 2). 42, 8, 23 (*Scaev.* 127). *C. Th.* 2, 19, 3 (*a.* 332).
C. 7, 71, 6 (*a.* 386). *lex Iul. municip. v.* 117 *sq.* (*Bruns* I[7], 108).
Cic. pro Quinct. 15, 49 *sq.*
§155. = *I.* 2, 19, 1. *cf. D.* 4, 4, 7, 5 (*Ulp.* 399). 42, 6, 1, 18 (*Ulp.*
1444). etiam saepius] cf. *D.* 42, 3, 4 *pr.* (*Ulp.* 1380). 42, 3, 6 (*Ulp.*
1440). 42, 3, 7 (*Mod.* 101). *C.* 7, 72, 3 (*Gordian.*). 7, 71, 1 (*a.* 223)

who is heir under the will claims the inheritance ... [in the illegible passage which follows and which ends with a reference to the destination of the inheritance, Gaius probably explained that measures were taken to prevent the heir under the will from obtaining the inheritance against the apparent wishes of the testator]; and this is made known in a written reply of the Emperor Antoninus Pius.

152. **There are compulsory heirs, immediate and compulsory heirs, and outside heirs.** 153. **A slave appointee** with a grant of freedom* **is a compulsory heir, so called because the testator's death automatically makes him free and heir whether he likes it or not.** 154. Someone **who doubts** his **solvency makes an appointment in the first or second rank or lower down, to one of** his **slaves,** along with a grant of freedom. **If the creditors' claims cannot be met, it is then his property and not the testator's** which is sold up. The result is that the ignominy associated with sale of one's property falls on him rather than on the testator himself; according to Fufidius, Sabinus holds that the slave should be spared this ignominy because he has his property sold up not because of his own failing but by necessity of law. But we apply a different rule. 155. **An advantage is given to him to balance this disadvantage: acquisitions after his patron's death are his,** whether made before or after the sale of his property and, **even if his property** is sold for part of

quamuis pro portione[1] bona uenierint, iterum ex hereditaria causa bona eius non uenient, nisi si quid ei
94 ex hereditaria causa fuerit adquisitum, | uelut si *ex eo,
quod*[2] Latinus adquisierit, locupletior factus sit; cum
ceterorum hominum, quorum bona uenierint pro portione, si quid postea adquirant, etiam saepius eorum
bona uenire[3] soleant.[4] 156. Sui autem et[5] necessarii
heredes sunt uelut filius filiaue, nepos neptisue ex filio
et deinceps ce*t*eri, qui modo in potestate morientis
fuerunt: sed uti nepos neptisue su*us* heres sit, non
sufficit eum in potestate aui mortis tempore fuisse,
sed opus est, ut pater quoque eius uiuo patre suo desierit suus heres esse aut morte interceptus aut qualibet ratione liberatus potestate[6]; tum enim nepos
neptisue in locum sui patris succedunt. 157. Sed sui
quidem heredes ideo appellantur, quia domestici heredes sunt et uiuo quoque parente quodam modo[7] domini
existimantur[8]; unde etiam si quis intestatus mortuus
sit, prima causa est in successione liberorum. necessarii uero ideo dicuntur, quia omni modo, *siue* uelint
siue nolint, tam ab intestato quam ex testamento[9]
heredes fiunt. 158. Sed his praetor permittit abstinere
se ab heredi*tate*, ut potius parentis bona ueneant.
159. Idem iuris est et *in* uxoris persona, quae in manu

---

1) pro portione *Heise.* propter contractione V.   2) ex eo
quod *suppl. Savigny.*   3) uenieri V.   4) soleant *Goeschen.*
solent V.   5) ut V.   6) aut morte — potestate *del. Bes.
Beitr.* 5, 4.   7) quodam modo] ꝙadmodo V.   8) et uiuo
— existimantur *del. Sol., Dir. ered.* 1, 163.   9) testat m̊ V.

---

§§ 156—158. = *I.* 2, 19, 2. *cf. infra* 3, 2. *Gai epit.* 2, 3, 6.
Ulp. 22, 24.   *Paul. Coll.* 16, 3, 6 (*Sent.* 4, 8, 6).   *D.* 28, 2, 11
(*Paul.* 1631). 38, 16, 1, 2; 4 (*Ulp.* 2512).   *Priscian.* 17, 121 (II
170 *ed. Hertz*). *Plaut. Trin.* 329 = 2, 2, 48.   *Plin. Paneg.* 37.
Auson. de herediolo (*p.* 16 *ed. Peiper*).

§ 158. parentis] *cf. D.* 29, 2, 57 *pr.* (*Gai.* 346). 50, 16, 51
(*Gai.* 349). *Cic. Phil.* 2, 42.

§ 159. *cf. infra* 3, 3. *supra* 2, 131. 1, 111. in manu est] *cf.
D.* 40, 5, 14 (*Mod.* 325). in nuru] *cf. D.* 50, 16, 50 (*Ulp.* 1402).

the debts, **it will not be sold again on account of the inheritance**, unless he acquires something on that account, for instance, if he has benefited from a Latin's acquisition; if the property of other men is sold for part of their debts and they later acquire anything, their property is normally sold again, even several times.

156. **The immediate and compulsory heirs are**, for instance, **a son or a daughter, also grandchildren through a son and so on down the line, who were within the paternal power of the deceased on his deathbed. But grandchildren do not qualify on that condition alone; their father must** also **have vacated the position of immediate heir in his father's lifetime, either through death or through some other discharge from power. It is then that the grandchild steps into his father's place.** 157. **These heirs are called immediate, the testator's own heirs, because they come from inside the family and are in a certain sense thought of as owners even while their parent is alive. That is why, in the event of intestacy, these descendants have the first entitlement. They are called compulsory because they have no choice in the matter. Whether under a will or not, they become heirs automatically.** 158. **But the praetor gives them a right to stand off from the estate so that it is the parent's property** which is sold up. 159. The law is the same for a wife in marital subordination,

est, quia filiae loco est, et in nuru[1], quae in manu
filii est, quia neptis loco est. 160. Quin etiam simi-
liter abstinendi potest|atem facit praetor etiam ei, qui 95
in causa [id est mancipato] mancipii est, *si* cum libertate[2] heres institutus sit, cum[3] necessarius, non etiam
suus heres sit, tamquam seruus. 161. Ceteri, qui testatoris iuri subiecti non sunt, extranei heredes appellantur: itaque liberi quoque nostri, qui in potestate
nostra non sunt, heredes a nobis instituti sicut extranei uidentur; qua de causa et qui a matre heredes
instituuntur, eodem numero sunt, quia feminae liberos
in potestate non habent. serui quoque, qui cum libertate[4] heredes instituti sunt et postea a domino manumissi, eodem numero habentur. 162. Extraneis autem
heredibus deliberandi potestas data est de adeunda
hereditate uel non adeunda.[5] 163. Sed siue is, cui abs-
tinendi potestas est, inmiscuerit se bonis hereditariis,
siue is, cui[6] de adeunda[7] deliberare licet, adierit, postea
relinquendae hereditatis facultatem non habet, nisi si
minor sit annorum[8] XXV: nam huius aetatis hominibus[9], sicut in ceteris omnibus causis deceptis, ita etiam
si temere damnosam hereditatem susceperint, praetor
succurrit. scio quidem diuum Hadrianum etiam maiori
XXV annorum[8] ueniam dedisse, cum post aditam here-

---

1) nurus *Hu.*   2) libertate *Hu.* lib. et V.   3) quamuis
Hu.   4) liberi et V.   5) de — adeunda *del. Solazzi.*   6) ui V.
7) de adeunda *del. Solazzi, Dir. ered.* 2, 6.   8) ann. V.   9) hominibus permissum est V.

§ 160. *cf. supra* 1, 123; 138. *infra* 3, 114. *D.* 50, 16, 52
(*Ulp.* 1403).

§ 161. = *I.* 2, 19, 3. *cf. Gai epit.* 2, 3, 6. *Ulp.* 22, 25.
26, 7. quia feminae] *cf. supra* 1, 104. *Ulp.* 26, 7. serui quo-
que] *cf. infra* 2, 188.

§§ 162. 163. == *I.* 2, 19, 5. *cf. Paul.* 3, 4[b], 11. *D. tit.* 28, 8
et C. tit. 6, 30 (*de iure deliberandi*). *D.* 29, 2, 11 (*Pomp.* 406).
29, 2, 57, 1 (*Gai.* 346). 29, 2, 87 *pr.* (*Pap.* 644). 29, 2, 12 (*Ulp.*
399). 4, 4, 7, 5; 9 (*Ulp.* 399). 29, 2, 38 (*Ulp.* 1154). 12, 6, 5
(*Ulp.* 2545). *C.* 2, 38 (39), 1 (a. 198). 6, 31, 4 (*a.* 293). nam huius
etc.] *cf. infra* 4, 57.

because she is in the position of a daughter, and for a daughter-in-law in marital subordination to a son, because she is in the position of a granddaughter. 160. More than that, the praetor gives the same power of standing off even to a person in bondage [that is, mancipated] if he has been appointed heir with a grant of freedom; being like a slave he is a compulsory heir but he is not an immediate heir.

161. **All other heirs, not being within the testator's paternal power, are called outsiders. The appointment of one of our own children, if outside our power, makes even him an outside heir; the same with every appointment by a mother, since women never have children within their power. If an owner appoints slaves** with a grant of freedom **and then frees** them, they **too are outside heirs. 162. Outsiders have a choice whether to accept the estate or not. 163. If an heir with a right to decline meddles in the estate, or** someone **entitled to take time to think it over does accept, he loses the power to renounce. The exception is someone under twenty-five. The praetor relieves people under that age who rashly accept a debt-ridden inheritance just as he helps them when they make mistakes in all other contexts. All the** same I know that **the Emperor Hadrian absolved even someone over twenty-five when large debts**

ditatem grande aes alienum, quod aditae hereditatis
tempore latebat, apparuisset. |

96 **164.** Extraneis heredibus solet cretio dari, id est
finis deliberandi, ut intra certum tempus uel adeant
hereditatem uel, si non adeant, temporis fine summo-
ueantur: ideo autem cretio appellata est, quia cernere
est quasi decernere et constituere. **165.** Cum ergo ita
scriptum sit: HERES TITIVS ESTO, adicere debemus:
CERNITOQVE IN CENTVM DIEBVS PROXVMIS, QVIBVS
SCIES POTERISQVE. QVOD NI ITA CREVERIS, EXHERES
ESTO. **166.** Et qui ita heres institutus est, si uelit
heres esse, debebit intra diem cretionis cernere, id est
haec uerba dicere: QVOD ME PVBLIVS MEVIVS[1] TESTA-
MENTO SVO HEREDEM INSTITVIT, EAM HEREDITATEM
ADEO CERNOQVE. quod si ita non creuerit, finito tempore cretionis excluditur; nec quicquam proficit, si
pro herede gerat, id est, si rebus hereditariis tamquam
heres utatur. **167.** At is, qui sine cretione heres insti-
tu*tus* sit aut qui ab intestato legitimo iure ad hereditatem uocatur, potest aut cernendo aut pro herede
gerendo uel etiam nuda uoluntate suscipiendae hereditatis[2] heres fieri: eique liberum est, quocumque tem-

---

1) Titus V.   2) uel—hereditatis *pro glossemate habet Kniep.*

---

§ 164. *cf. Ulp.* 22, 27. *Varro de l. l.* 7, 5, 98. *Isid. orig.*
5, 24, 15 *sq.* (*Bruns* II[7], 81). *Cic. de leg. agr.* 2, 15, 40. *Plin.
n. h.* 2, 95. *Senec. fgm.* 88 *ed. Haase* III, 434. *C. Th.* 4, 1, 1
(*a.* 426). 8, 18, 8, 1 = *C. Iust.* 6, 30, 17 (*a.* 407).

§ 165. *cf. infra* 2, 171. *Varro de l. l.* 6, 8, 81. *Cic. de orat.* 1, 22,
101. *B G U* 7, 1696. *cf. San Nicoló, Orient. Literaturztg.* 1927, 479.

§ 166. *cf. Ulp.* 22, 25; 26; 28. *Fest. ep. v. crevi p.* 53.
Cons. 6, 19 (*Cod. Hermog. a.* 294). *I.* 2, 19, 7. *diptycha duo
Arsinoitica, quae edidit Seymour de Ricci Nouv. Revue histor.*
XXX (1906), 480. 482 (*Bruns* I[7], 319).

§ 167. *cf. infra* 3, 87. *Ulp.* 22, 25. *I.* 2, 19, 7. *C. Th.* 2,
16, 2, 4 (*a.* 315 *seu* 319). 4, 1, 1 (*a.* 426). *Tit.* 8, 18. *D.* 28,
5, 23, 2 (*Pomp.* 390). 28, 8, 1, 1; 2 (*Ulp.* 1396). 28, 8, 3 (*Ulp.*
1396). 28, 8, 5 *pr.* (*Ulp.* 1397). 28, 8, 8 (*Ulp.* 1407). *C.* 6, 30, 9
(*a.* 293). 6, 30, 10 (*a.* 294).

appeared **which lay hidden at the time of his acceptance**.

164. Outside heirs are usually required to make a formal declaration of acceptance (in Latin a 'cretio'), that is, a limit is imposed on the time they have to think the matter over; either they accept within the fixed time, or if not, at the end of that time they are displaced. The requirement is called a 'cretio' because it comes from the Latin 'cernere', to decide and settle. 165. And so after writing 'Let you, Titius, be heir', we should add 'and make solemn declaration of acceptance within the hundred days next after you know and can do so. And if you have not made such a declaration let you be disinherited'. 166. Anyone so appointed who wants to be heir will have to make the declaration within the period allowed for it, that is, he will have to say: 'Whereas Publius Mevius appointed me heir in his will I accept that inheritance and make this declaration of acceptance'. But if he does not do so he is excluded once the time specified for the declaration has passed; it is no help **that he acts as heir**, that is, **that he behaves towards the assets of the estate as though he were heir**. 167. But someone **appointed heir** without a requirement to make a declaration, or **someone with a statutory title to the inheritance on intestacy, can become heir either** by making a declaration or **by acting as heir or merely by showing an intention to accept the estate**; and he is free to accept the inheritance at any time he wishes.

pore uoluerit, adire hereditatem; *sed* solet praetor
postulantibus hereditariis creditoribus tempus constituere, intra quod, si uelit, adeat[1] hereditatem, si minus, ut liceat creditoribus bona[2] defuncti uendere.
168. Si*cut* autem *qui*[3] cum cretione | heres institutus 97
est, nisi creuerit hereditatem, non fit heres, ita non
aliter excluditur, quam si non creuerit intra id tempus, quo cretio finita si*t*; itaque licet ante diem cretionis constituerit hereditatem non adire, tamen paeni-
tentia actus[4] superante die cretionis cernendo heres
esse potest. 169. At is, qui sine cretione heres institutus est quiue[5] ab intestato per legem uocatur, sicut
uoluntate nuda heres fit, ita et contraria destinatione
statim ab hereditate repellitur. 170. Omnis autem
cretio certo tempore constringitur. in quam rem
tolerabile tempus uisum est centum dierum: potest
tamen nihilo minus iure ciuili aut longius aut breuius
tempus dari; longius tamen interdum praetor coartat.
171. Et quamuis omnis cretio certis diebus constrin-
gatur, tamen alia cretio uulgaris uocatur, alia certorum dierum: uulgaris illa, quam supra exposuimus, id
est, in qua adiciuntur[6] haec uerba: QVIBVS S*C*IET PO-
TERITQVE: certorum dierum, in qua detractis his
uerbis cetera scribuntur. 172. Quarum cretionum magna
differentia est: nam uulgari cretione data nulli dies

---

1) uelit adeat] uelint hadeant V.   2) bona *Goeschen.*
ū V.   3) sicut autem qui *Lachmann.* si qui autem V.
4) actus V. *firmat Ulp.* 22, 30. *num* acta? *cf. V. I. R. s.* ago
p. 315, 11.   5) quique V. .   6) dicuntur V.

---

§ 168. *cf. Ulp.* 22, 30. *supra* 2, 144; 166.
§ 169. *cf. Ulp.* 22, 29. *I.* 2, 19, 7. *D.* 29, 2, 13 *pr.* (*Ulp.*
2479).
§ 170. *cf. D.* 28, 8, 2 (*Paul.* 699). *Cic. ad Att.* 13, 46, 3.
15, 2, 4 ('*diem testamenti*' *i. e. cretionis spatium*).
§ 171. *cf. Ulp.* 22, 31. *supra* 2, 164; 165. *Cic. ad Att.* 11,
12, 4. *de orat.* 1, 22, 101. *Testam. Dasumii* (*Bruns* I⁷, 304).
§ 172. *cf. Ulp.* 22, 32. *infra* 2, 190.

If, however, the creditors of the inheritance apply to the praetor he normally settles a time within which the heir must accept the inheritance if he intends to do so; if he does not accept the creditors are allowed to sell up the deceased's estate. 168. However, just as someone who has been instituted heir with a requirement to make a declaration does not become heir unless he makes the declaration, so he is not excluded except by failing to make the declaration within the time-limit for doing so; and so, even though he may have decided not to accept the inheritance before the time has passed, he can still become heir by making the declaration if he changes his mind while there is still time left. 169. But someone appointed heir without a requirement to make a declaration or someone entitled on intestacy by statute, **as he makes himself heir simply by coming to that decision, so a decision against accepting makes for an immediate exclusion from the estate**.

170. Now, all declarations have a fixed time-limit. A tolerable period for this has been taken as a hundred days. Despite this, by state law a longer or shorter period can be set; but if it is too long the praetor sometimes cuts it down. 171. And although all declarations set a fixed number of days for acceptance, one kind of declaration is called ordinary and the other is called a declaration with fixed days. The ordinary one is the one we explained above, that is, containing the words: 'In which he knows and can do so'; the one with fixed days has the rest of the formula without these words. 172. These kinds of declaration are very different; if there is a declaration in ordinary form the days begin to be counted against

conputantur, nisi quibus scierit quisque se heredem
esse institutum et possit cernere; certorum uero dierum
cretione[1] data etiam nescienti[2] se heredem institutum
98 esse numerantur dies con|tinui; item ei quoque, qui
aliqua ex causa cernere prohibetur, et eo amplius ei,
qui sub condicione heres institutus est, tempus numeratur; unde melius et aptius est uulgari cretione uti.
173. Continua haec cretio uocatur, quia continui dies
numerantur; sed quia tamen dura est haec cretio,
altera magis in usu[3] habetur; unde etiam uulgaris
dicta est.[4]

[De substitutionibus.] 174. Interdum duos pluresue
gradus heredum facimus, hoc modo: L. TITIVS HERES
ESTO CERNITOQVE IN DIEBVS CENTVM PROXIMIS, QVIBVS
SCIES POTERISQVE. QVOD NI ITA CREVERIS, EXHERES
ESTO. TVM MEVIVS[5] HERES ESTO CERNITOQVE IN
DIEBVS CENTVM et reliqua; et deinceps in quantum
uelimus, substituere possumus. 175. Et licet nobis uel
unum in unius locum substituere pluresue, et contra
in plurium locum uel unum uel plures substituere.
176. Primo itaque gradu scriptus heres hereditatem
cernendo fit heres, et substitutus excluditur; non cernendo summouetur, etiamsi pro herede gerat, et in
locum eius substitutus succedit; et deinceps si plures

---

1) cretione *Goeschen*. cretio V.   2) nescienti *Goeschen*.
nesciente V.   3) magis in usu *Goeschen*. minus V.   4) *Hu.*
proponit: ... tempus numeratur; unde *etiam* continua haec
cretio uocatur, quia continui dies numerantur. [sed] quia tamen
dura est haec cretio, melius et aptius est uulgari cretione uti *eaque*
magis quam altera in usu habetur, unde etiam uulgaris dicta est.
alii alia temptaverunt. cf. *Beseler ZS* 47, 356.   5) Maeuius V.

---

§ 174. *cf. Ulp.* 22, 33.   *Gai epit.* 2, 4 *pr.*; 1.   *I.* 2, 15 *pr.*
= *D.* 28, 6, 36 *pr.* (*Marcian.* 93).   *D.* 28, 6, 1 *pr.*; 1 (*Mod.* 100).
Paul. 3, 4[b], 4.   *Cic. ad Att.* 15, 2, 4.   *Tac. ann.* 1, 8.   *Suet. Aug.*
101.   *Appian. b. c.* 2, 143.   *Isid. orig.* 9, 5, 2.
§ 175. *cf. I.* 2, 15, 1 == *D.* 28, 6, 36, 1 (*Marcian.* 93).
§ 176. *cf. supra* 2, 168.

the heir only from the time he knows of his appointment as heir and can make a declaration; if there is a declaration with fixed days, on the other hand, the days are counted continuously, even against an heir who does not know of his appointment. Again, the time is also counted against someone who is prohibited from making a declaration for some reason and, not only that, against someone appointed heir under a condition. And so it is better and more suitable to use the ordinary form of declaration. 173. This declaration with fixed days is called continuous because the days are counted continuously; but because it does operate harshly, the other is more usual. This is precisely why it is called ordinary.

[Substitutions] 174. Sometimes we appoint **heirs** in two **or more ranks** in this way: 'Let you, L. Titius, be heir and make formal declaration of acceptance within the next one hundred days after you know and can do so and if you have not made such a declaration let you be disinherited. Then let you Mevius be heir and make formal declaration of acceptance in one hundred days', **and so forth**; and we **can go on to make as many of these substitutions as** we **want.** 175. And we are **allowed to substitute one person in place of one or several people** and, contrariwise, either one or several in place of several. 176. And so the heir appointed in the first rank becomes heir by declaring his acceptance of the inheritance and the substitute is excluded. If he does not make the declaration he is kept out, even if he acts as heir; the substitute takes his place. And, on the same principle,

gradus sint, in singulis simili ratione idem contingit.
177. Sed si cretio sine exheredatione sit data, id est
in[1] haec uerba: SI NON CREVERIS[2], TVM PVBLIVS ME-
VIVS HERES ESTO, illud diuersum inuenitur[3], quod[4]
si prior omissa cretione pro herede gerat, substitutum
in partem admittit, et fiunt ambo aequis partibus |
heredes[5]; quod si neque cernat neque pro herede gerat, 99
tum sane in uniuersum[6] summouetur, et substitutus
in totam hereditatem succedit. 178. Sed Sabino quidem
placuit, quamdiu cernere et eo modo heres fieri possit
prior, etiamsi pro herede gesserit, non tamen admitti
substitutum; cum uero cretio finita sit, tum pro herede
gerentem admittere[7] substitutum: aliis uero placuit
etiam superante cretione posse eum pro herede gerendo in partem substitutum admittere et amplius ad
cretionem reuerti non posse.

179. Liberis nostris inpuberibus, quos in potestate
habemus, non solum ita, ut supra diximus, substituere
possumus[8], id est, ut si heredes non extiterint, alius
nobis heres sit; sed eo amplius ut, etiamsi heredes
nobis extiterint et adhuc inpuberes mortui fuerint, sit
iis aliquis heres, uelut hoc modo: TITIVS FILIVS MEVS
MIHI HERES ESTO. SI FILIVS MEVS MIHI *HERES NON
ERIT, SIVE HERES MIHI* ERIT ET IS[9] PRIVS MORIATVR
QVAM IN SVAM TVTELAM VENERIT, TVNC[10] SEIVS HERES
ESTO. 180. Quo casu si quidem non extiterit heres

---

1) si V.   2) crerit V.   3) inuenit V.   4) quia V.   5) et —
heredes del. Beseler Z. S. 46, 268. cf. Stud. Riccob. 1, 302.
6) uniuerso V.   7) gerentem admittere Hu. gerente(?) admittit V.   8) possimus V.   9) hic *litteris pallidis* V. *fuitne*
his (= is)?   10) tunc esto V.

---

§§ 177. 178. cf. Ulp. 22, 34. D. 28, 5. 41 (40) (Iul. 440).
§ 179. = I. 2, 16 pr. cf. Ulp. 23, 7. Gai epit. 2, 4, 2. D.
28, 6, 2 pr. (Ulp. 2469). Hor. sat. 2, 5, 48 sq.
§ 180. = I. 2, 16 pr.; 2. duo quodam modo sunt testa-
menta] cf. D. 37, 11, 8, 4 (Iul. 387). 35, 2, 79 (Gai. 320). 28,
6, 20, 1 (Ulp. 2547). 35, 3, 1, 1 (Ulp. 1711). aut certe unum

this continues for each rank if there are several. 177.
But if a declaration is imposed with no disherison,
that is to say, like this: 'If you have not made formal
declaration of acceptance then let Publius Mevius be
heir' the result is different. If the appointee acts as
heir without making a declaration, he lets the
substitute in for a share and both become heirs in
equal shares; if he neither makes a declaration nor
acts as heir he is kept out entirely and the substitute
succeeds to the whole inheritance. 178. But note that
Sabinus took the view that, so long as the appointee
can make a declaration and become heir in this way,
the substitute is not let in even although the
appointee acts as heir; but if he acts as heir once the
time for the declaration has passed, he lets in the
substitute. On the other hand, others took the view
that he could let the substitute in for a share by acting
as heir even if there was still time left for the
declaration and could no longer fall back on the
declaration.

179. We **can draft one of these ordinary
substitutions for young children within our power,
that is, if they do not become our heirs let so and so
be heir. But we can also put in a substitute in case
the children become heir but die before puberty, in
effect: 'Let my son Titius be my heir. If he does not
become my heir or if, being heir, he dies before
taking control of his own affairs, let Seius be heir'.
180. Here if the son fails to become heir, the**

filius, substitutus patris¹ fit her*es; si uero* heres extiterit filius et ante pubertatem decesserit, ipsi filio fit
heres substitutus. quam ob rem duo quodam modo
100 sunt testamenta, | *aliud* patris, aliud fil*ii*, tamquam si
ipse filius sibi heredem instituisset; aut certe unum
est testamentum duarum hereditatum. 181. Ceterum
ne post obitum parentis periculo insidiarum subiectus
uideretur² pupillus, in usu est uulgarem quidem sub-
stitutionem palam facere, id est eo loco, quo pupillum
heredem instituimus; *nam* uulgaris substitutio ita uocat
ad hereditatem substitutum, si omnino pupillus heres
non extiterit; quod accidit, cum uiuo parente moritur,
quo casu nullum substituti maleficium suspicari possumus, cum scilicet³ uiuo testatore omnia, quae in
testamento scripta sint, ignorentur⁴: illam⁵ autem sub-
stitutionem, per quam, etiamsi⁶ heres extiterit pupillus
et intra pubertatem decesserit, substitutum uocamus,
separatim in inferioribus tabulis scribimus easque tabulas proprio lino propriaque cera consignamus et in
prioribus tabulis cauemus, ne inferiores tabulae uiuo
filio et adhuc inpubere aperiantur. sed longe *tutius*
est utrumque genus substitutionis separatim in inferioribus tabulis consignari, quia si ita⁷ consignatae
uel separatae fuerint substitution*es*, ut diximus, ex⁸
priore potest intellegi in altera⁹ quoque idem esse
101 substitutus.⁴| 182. Non solum autem¹⁰ heredibus insti-

---

1) patri *Inst.*   2) uideatur *Goeschen.*   3) scilicet et V.
4) uulgaris—ignorentur *et* sed longe—substitutus *del. Vassalli,
Misc.* 1, 28.   5) at illa V.   6) si etiam V.   7) quia si ita]
quaesita V.   8) et V.   9) altera alter V.   10) aut V.

est testamentum *etc.*] cf. *D.* 42, 5, 28 (*Iav.* 75). 29, 3, 11 (*Gai.*
463). 35, 2, 11, 5 *in fin.* (*Pap.* 353). 28, 6, 2, 4 (*Ulp.* 2469).
28, 6, 20 *pr.* (*Ulp.* 2547). 18, 4, 2, 2 (*Ulp.* 2962). 28, 6, 38, 3
(*Paul.* 1895).
    § 181. *cf. Gai epit.* 2, 4, 2. *I.* 2, 16, 3 *cum Theoph.* (*p.* 188
Ferr.). *D.* 29, 3, 8 (*Ulp.* 1224).
    § 182. = *I.* 2, 16, 4. *cf. Ulp.* 23, 8. *D.* 28, 6, 6 (*Clem.* 11).
28, 6, 10, 4 *sq.* (*Ulp.* 2456). 28, 6, 1, 2 (*Mod.* 100).

substitute comes in as the father's heir; if the son does become heir but dies in childhood the substitute takes as the son's heir, with the result that **there are in a sense two wills, the father's and the son's, as though the son had appointed an heir himself. Alternatively there is one will with two estates.** 181. But in case our **young son should seem to be exposed to foul play after his** father's **death, note that** the practice is to **make the ordinary substitution openly**, that is, at the point where we appoint him heir. This means that the ordinary substitution brings the substitute in if the child does not become heir at all. This happens when he dies in his parent's lifetime, in which case we cannot suspect any malpractice on the part of the substitute, as, of course, the contents of the will are not known during the testator's lifetime. **Then** we **make the substitution for** our **son's becoming heir but dying in childhood** at the back of the will, **sewn up and sealed independently. And** we **provide** on the top **that the back must remain sealed so long as** our **son lives and remains under age.** But it is far safer to seal both substitutions separately at the back, because if the substitutions are sealed in the way we said, even separately, it can be gathered from the former document that the same substitute also appears in the latter. 182. **By one of these substitutions against**

tutis inpuberibus liberis ita substituere possumus[1], ut
si ante pubertatem mortui fuerint, sit is heres, quem
nos uoluerimus, sed etiam exheredatis: itaque eo casu
si quid pupillo ex hereditatibus legatisue aut donationibus propinquorum adquisitum fuerit, id omne ad[2]
substitutum pertinet. 183. Quaecumque diximus de
substitutione inpuberum liberorum uel heredum institutorum uel exheredatorum, eadem etiam de postumis
intellegemus.[3] 184. Extraneo uero[4] heredi instituto ita
substituere non possumus[5], ut si heres extiterit et intra
aliquod tempus decesserit, alius ei heres sit; sed hoc
solum nobis permissum est, ut eum per[6] fideicommissum obligemus, ut hereditatem nostram totam uel *ex*
parte restituat; quod ius quale sit, suo loco trademus.

185. Sicut autem liberi homines, ita et serui tam
nostri quam alieni heredes scribi possunt. 186. Sed
noster seruus simul et liber et heres esse iuberi debet,
id est hoc modo: STICHVS SERVVS MEVS LIBER HERES
QVE ESTO, uel: HERES LIBERQVE ESTO.[7] 187. Nam si
sine libertate heres institutus sit, etiamsi postea manumissus fuerit a domino, heres esse non potest, quia
institutio in persona eius[8] non constitit[9]; ideoque licet
alienatus sit, non potest iussu domini noui cernere
hereditatem. 188. Cum libertate uero heres | institutus 102

---

1) possimus V.   2) ab V.   3) *num* dicta intellegemus?
4) uero uel filio puberi *Inst*.   5) possum V.   6) pro V.
7) ē esto V.   8) persona eius] personae V.   9) constit V.

---

§ 183. = *I*. 2, 16, 4. *cf. D*. 48, 19, 39 (*Tryph*. 40). 28, 6,
2 *pr*. (*Ulp*. 2469). 28, 6, 46 (*Paul*. 1552). *Cic. p. Cluent*. 11, 32.
de orat. 1, 39, 180. 2, 32, 141. *de inv*. 2, 21, 62. 2, 42, 122.
    § 184. = *I*. 2, 16, 9. *cf. Gai epit*. 2, 4, 3. *D*. 28, 6, 7
(*Pap*. 554). 28, 6, 41, 3 (*Pap*. 558). *C*. 6, 26, 5 (*a*. 290). suo
loco] 2, 277 *sq*.
    §§ 185. 186. *cf. I*. 2, 14 *pr*. *Ulp*. 22, 7. *Paul*. 3, 4ᵇ, 7.
supra 2, 153. 1, 21; 123.
    § 187. *cf. Ulp*. 22, 12 *i. f*.
    §§ 188. 189. = *I*. 2, 14, 1. *cf. Ulp*. 22, 11—13.

death in childhood we **can impose** our **choice of heir on children whom** we **appoint as** our **heirs if they should die before reaching full age.** We **can also do it for children whom** we **disinherit.** The **effect is to pass all the boy's acquisitions – inheritances, legacies and gifts from his relatives – to the substitute.** 183. **These rules about grafting substitutions for children on to appointments and exclusions also apply to posthumous issue.** 184. On the other hand, when an outsider is appointed heir we cannot make a substitution which makes someone else heir to him if he becomes heir and then dies within some space of time; all we are permitted to do is to impose an obligation on him by a trust to hand on the whole or part of our inheritance. We shall explain how the law stands on this at the appropriate point.

185. Now, just as we can appoint **free men as heirs,** we **can appoint slaves, both** our **own and another's.** 186. We should order our own slave to be simultaneously free and heir, like this: 'Let Stichus my slave be free and heir' or 'be heir and free'. 187. If he is appointed heir without a grant of freedom, he cannot be heir even if he is later freed by his master because the appointment does not take effect in his person; and so even if he is conveyed to another he cannot declare his acceptance of the inheritance on the orders of his new master. 188. On the other hand, if he is appointed heir with a grant of freedom, if his

si quidem in ea*dem* causa durauerit, fit ex testamento
liber et inde necessarius heres: si uero ab ipso testatore manumissus fuerit, suo arbitrio hereditatem adire
potest; quod si alienatus sit, iussu noui domini adire
hereditatem debet, qua ratione per eum dominus fit
heres: nam ipse neque heres neque liber esse potest.
189. Alienus quoque seruus heres institutus, si in eadem
causa durauerit, iussu domini hereditatem adire debet;
si uero alienatus ab eo fuerit aut uiuo testatore aut
post mortem eius, antequam cernat, debet iussu noui
domini cernere: si uero manumissus est, suo arbitrio
adire hereditatem potest. 190. Si autem seruus alienus
heres institutus est uulgari cretione data, ita *intellc-*
gitur dies cretionis cedere, si ipse seruus scierit se
heredem institutum esse nec ullum impedimentum sit,
quo minus certiorem dominum faceret, ut illius iussu
cernere possit.

191. Post haec uideamus de legatis. quae pars iuris
extra propositam quidem materiam uidetur: nam loquimur de his iuris figuris, quibus per[1] uniuersitatem res
nobis adquiruntur: sed cum omni modo de testamentis
deque heredibus, qui testamento instituuntur[2], locuti
103 simus[3], non sine causa sequenti loco | poterit haec iuris
materia tractari.

[De legatis.]

192. Legatorum itaque genera sunt quattuor: aut
enim per uindicationem legamus aut per damnationem
aut sinendi modo aut per praeceptionem.

---

1) pro V.   2) instituunt V.   3) sumus V.

§ 188. *cf. supra* 2, 153. *D.* 28, 5, 9, 16 *sq.* (*Ulp.* 2465). 28,
5, 52 (51) (*Marcian.* 247).
§ 189. *cf. infra* 2, 245. *D.* 29, 2, 62, 1 (*Iav.* 166). 37, 11,
2, 9 (*Ulp.* 1147). 28, 8, 1 *pr.* (*Ulp.* 1396).
§ 190. *cf. supra* 2, 172. *D.* 38, 15, 5 (*Marcell.* 125).
§ 191. = *I.* 2, 20 *pr. cf. supra* 2, 97.
§ 192. *cf. Gai epit.* 2, 5 *pr. I.* 2, 20, 2. *Ulp.* 24, 2.

position stays unchanged the will operates to make him free and so compulsory heir. **But if he has been freed by the testator** himself **he has a choice whether to accept the inheritance or not. Suppose he is conveyed to another. He must accept the inheritance if his new owner tells him to; his owner then becomes heir through him. He himself cannot become either heir or free. 189. Where the testator appoints as heir a slave belonging to another and that slave's position** stays **unchanged, he must accept the estate if his owner tells him to. If he has been transferred in the testator's lifetime, or after the latter's death but before his** declaration of **acceptance of the inheritance, his** declaration of **acceptance depends on his new owner's order. If he has been manumitted, the choice to accept is his own.** 190. However, if another's slave has been appointed with the ordinary form of declaration of acceptance, the time for making the declaration is regarded as beginning to run as soon as the slave himself knows that he has been appointed heir and there is nothing to stop him telling his master, so that he can make the declaration on his orders.

191. **We next turn to legacies*. This area of law might appear to be a digression from our theme, namely the rules on acquisition of entire estates. But the discussion has been all about wills and heirs appointed under wills. That gives a reason for going on to legacies.**

[Legacies]

192. **There** are **four kinds of legacy: proprietary, obligatory, permissive, and preceptive**.

193. Per uindicationem hoc modo legamus: TITIO
uerbi gratia HOMINEM STICHVM DO LEGO; sed *et* si
alteru*m* uerbum positum sit, ueluti DO aut LEGO,
aeque per uindicationem legatum est: item, ut magis
uisum est, *et* si ita legatum fuerit: SVMITO uel ita:
SIBI HABETO *uel* ita: CAPITO, aeque per uindicationem
legatum est. 194. Ideo *aut*em per uindicationem legatum appellatur, qui*a* post aditam hereditatem statim
ex iure Quiritium res legatarii fit; et si eam rem legatarius uel ab herede uel ab alio quocumque, qui eam
possidet, petat, uindicare debet, id est intendere suam
rem ex iure Quiritium esse. 195. In eo solo dissentiunt prudentes, quod Sabinus quidem et Cassius ceterique nostri praeceptores, quod ita legatum sit, statim
post aditam hereditatem putant fieri legatarii, etiamsi
ignoret sibi legatum esse[1], sed[2] postea quam scierit et
spreuerit[3] legatum, proinde esse atque si legatum non
esset; Nerua uero et Proculus ceterique illius scholae
auctores non alite*r* putant rem legatarii fieri, quam
si uoluerit eam ad se pertinere: sed hodie ex diui
Pii Antonini | constitutione hoc magis iure uti uide-
mur[4], quod Proculo placuit; nam cum legatus fuisset   104

1) esse *Hu.*   esse dimissum V.   2) et V.   3) spreuerit
Niebuhr. V *lectio incerta.*   4) uideuidemur V.

§ 193. *cf. Gai epit.* 2, 5, 1. *Ulp.* 24, 3. *Paul.* 3, 6, 6. *supra*
1, 149. *Fr. Vat.* 47 (*Paul.* 985). 57 (*Paul.* 996). 64 = *D.* 7,
4, 3 (*Ulp.* 2551). 83 = *D.* 7, 2, 3, 2 (*Ulp.* 2566). 87 (*Ulp.* 2570).
D. 33, 5, 20 (*Lab. ap. Iav.* 179). 32, 29, 4 (*Lab. ap. Iav.* 171).
32, 100, 2 (*Iav.* 173). 32, 79, 1 (*Cels.* 160). 30, 81, 2 *et* 40, 4,
15 (*Iul.* 458). 30, 84, 12 (*Iul.* 478). 33, 7, 15 *pr.* (*Pomp.* 490).
30, 65 *pr.*; 1 (*Gai.* 14). 31, 88, 3; 8 (*Scaev.* 258). 32, 91, 3 (*Pap.*
572). *Serv. ad Aen.* 5, 533.
§ 194. *cf. Gai epit.* 2, 5, 1. *Theoph.* 2, 20, 2 (*p.* 206 *Ferr.*).
infra 2, 204. *D.* 30, 69 *pr.* (*Gai.* 16). intendere *etc.*] *cf. infra*
4, 41.
§ 195. *cf. Paul.* 3, 6, 7. *D.* 30, 81, 6 (*Iul.* 461). 30, 86, 2
(*Iul.* 489). 8, 6, 19, 1 (*Pomp.* 770). Nerua *etc.*] *cf. D.* 31, 20
(*Cels.* 158). 47, 2, 65 (64) (*Ner.* 7). 30, 65, 1 (*Gai.* 14). 35, 1, 69
(*Gai.* 469). *infra* 2, 200. Latinus] *cf. Plin. ad Trai.* 107.

193. This is how we make a proprietary legacy: 'To Titius I give and bequeath' for example 'the slave Stichus'; but even if either word is used, for instance, 'I give' or 'I bequeath', this is equally a proprietary legacy; again, the majority would consider 'let him take' or 'let him have for himself' or 'let him accept' as being equally a proprietary legacy. 194. Now, this legacy is called proprietary because the thing becomes the property of the legatee by quiritary right immediately after the inheritance is accepted. If the legatee is claiming the thing either from the heir or from anyone else in possession of it he ought to vindicate it, that is, state in his principal pleading* that the thing is his by quiritary right. 195. Jurists* differ on only one point; Sabinus and Cassius and our other teachers think that something left by this kind of legacy becomes the property of the legatee immediately after acceptance of the inheritance, even if he does not know that the legacy has been left to him; but if he knows of the legacy and rejects it, it is just as if no legacy had been left. On the other hand, Nerva and Proculus and the other authorities of that school think that the thing does not become the legatee's property unless he indicates his intention to have it. But nowadays, after the pronouncement of the Emperor Pius Antoninus we seem to follow the rule approved by Proculus; for in a case where a Latin had left a proprietary legacy to a colony he says: 'Let

Latinus per[1] uindicationem coloniae, 'Deliberent', inquit, 'decuriones, an ad se uelint pertinere, proinde
ac si uni legatus esset'.[2] 196. *Eae* autem solae res per
uindicationem legant*ur* recte, quae ex iure Quiritium
ipsius testatoris sunt; sed eas quidem res, quae pon-
·dere, numero, mensura constant, placuit sufficere,
si mortis tempore sint ex iure Quiritium testatoris,
ueluti uinum, oleum, frumentum, pecuniam numera-
tam; ceteras res uero placuit utroque tempore testatoris ex iure Quiritium esse debere, id est, et quo faceret
*t*estamentum, et quo moreretur; alioquin inutile est
legatum. 197. Sed sane hoc ita est iure ciuili. postea
uero auctore Nerone Caesare senatus consultum factum
est, quo[3] cautum est, ut si eam rem quisque legauerit, quae eius numquam fuerit, proinde utile sit legatum, atque si optimo iure relictum esset. optumum
autem ius est per damnationem legati[4], quo genere
etiam aliena res legari potest, sicut inferius apparebit.[5]
198. Sed si quis rem suam legauerit, deinde post testamentum factum eam alienauerit, plerique putant non
solum iure ciuili inutile esse legatum, sed nec ex se-
105 natus consulto confirmari. quod ideo dictum | est,
quia et si per damnationem aliquis rem suam legauerit eamque postea alienauerit, plerique putant, licet
ipso iure debeatur legatum, tamen legatarium petentem
posse per exceptionem doli mali repelli, quasi contra
uoluntatem defuncti petat.[6] 199. Illud constat, si duo-

---

1) pro V.   2) sed hodie — esset *del. Ferrini, Beseler, Beitr*.
2, 105.   3) quod V.   4) legatum V.   5) optumum — apparebit
del. Ciapessoni, Stud. Bonfante 3, 661.   6) quod ideo — petat
del. ïdem l. c. 672.

---

§ 196. *cf. infra* 2, 222. *Gai epit.* 2, 5, 1; 3. *Ulp.* 24, 7.
D. 30, 22 (*Pomp.* 442). 30, 21 (*Ulp.* 2537).
§ 197. *cf. Ulp.* 24, 11ᵃ. *Fr. Vat.* 85 (*Ulp.* 2569). inferius]
2, 202.
§ 198. *cf. I.* 2, 20, 12. *Paul.* 3, 6, 16.
§ 199. *cf. Gai. epit.* 2, 5, 1; 4, 5. *Ulp.* 24, 12. *infra* 2, 206.

the members of the local council consider whether they wish to have it, just as if the legacy had been left to one of them'. 196. Now, only things belonging to the testator himself by quiritary right can properly be left by proprietary legacy. But note that for things consisting in weight, number or measure, such as wine, oil, corn, money, it is accepted that it is enough if they belong to the testator by quiritary right at the time of his death. On the other hand, it is accepted that other things should belong to the testator by quiritary right at both times, that is, both when he made the will and when he died; otherwise the legacy is ineffective. 197. But, of course, this is state law. Later, a Senate resolution was passed on the proposal of the Emperor Nero, providing that if anyone bequeaths a thing which never belonged to him the legacy is as effective as if it had been left in what is legally the best way; now, the best way is by obligatory legacy. By this kind even something belonging to someone else can be left, as will appear below. 198. But if someone bequeaths his own property and then conveys it away after making his will, most people think that the legacy is not only ineffective by state law but is not confirmed even by this Senate resolution. The reason for saying this is that even if someone leaves an obligatory legacy of his own property and conveys it away thereafter, most people think that, although the legacy is due as a matter of law, the legatee can still be met by the defence of deceit if he sues, inasmuch as he is suing against the deceased's wishes. 199. It is settled that **if**

bus pluribusue per uindicationem eadem res legata
sit, siue coniunctim siue disiunctim, et omnes ueniant
ad legatum, partes ad singulos pertinere et deficientis
portionem collegatario adcrescere. coniunctim autem
ita legatur: TITIO ET SEIO HOMINEM STICHVM DO
LEGO; disiunctim ita: LVCIO TITIO HOMINEM STICHVM[1]
DO LEGO. SEIO EVNDEM HOMINEM DO LEGO. 200. Illud
quaeritur, quod sub condicione per uindicationem legatum est, pendente condicione cuius esset: nostri praeceptores heredis esse putant exemplo statuliberi, id
est eius serui, qui testamento sub aliqua condicione
liber esse iussus est, quem constat interea[2] heredis
seruum esse; sed diuersae[3] scholae auctores putant
nullius interim eam[4] rem esse; quod multo magis di-
cunt de eo, quod sine condicione pure legatum est,
antequam legatarius admittat legatum.

201. Per damnationem hoc modo legamus: HERES
MEVS STICHVM[5] SERVVM MEVM DARE[6] DAMNAS ESTO;
sed et si DATO | scriptum fuerit, per damnationem 106
legatum est. 202. Eoque genere legati etiam aliena
res legari potest, ita ut heres rem redimere et prae-

---

1) istichum V.   2) interex V.   3) diuerso V.   4) ea V.
5) isticum V.   6) darem V. dare L. Titio Hu.

Paul. 3, 6, 26. l. 2, 20, 8. D. 32, 80 (Cels. 249). 35, 1, 30 (Iul.
848). 30, 16 pr.; 2 (Pomp. 440). 7, 2, 1, 3 = Fr. Vat. 77 (Ulp.
2563). 30, 33 (Paul. 1429). 30, 85 (Paul. 1181). 50, 16, 142
(Paul 966). 7, 9, 8 i. f. (Paul. 815). C. 6, 51, 1, 11 (a. 534).
§ 200. cf. supra 2, 195. Ulp. 2, 1; 2. D. 35, 1, 105 (Pomp.
187). 40, 9, 29, 1 (Gai. 478). 8, 6, 11, 1 (Marcell. 34). 10, 2,
12, 2 (Ulp. 652). 29, 5, 1, 4 (Ulp. 1235). 40, 7, 9 pr. (Ulp. 2701).
40, 7, 16 (Ulp. 2373). quod sine condicione] cf. D. 31, 80 (Pap.
44). 30, 44, 1 (Ulp. 2627).
§ 201. cf. Gai epit. 2, 5, 2. Ulp. 24, 4. Theoph. 2, 20, 2
(p. 206 Ferr.). Serv. ad Aen. 12, 727. Agroecius Gramm. Lat.
ed. Keil VII, 120, 16. C. I. L. VI 10229 l. 125 (Bruns I⁷, 308).
dato] cf. ex. gr. Cic. de inv. 2, 40, 116. V. I. R. II, 297, 42.
§ 202. cf. Gai epit. 2, 5, 2. Ulp. 24, 8. supra 2, 197. I. 2,
20, 4. D. 32, 30, 3 (Lab. ap. Iav. 172). 35, 2, 61 (Iav. 91). 30,
71, 3 (Ulp. 1246; cf. infra 4, 9).

one thing is left by proprietary legacy **to two** or more **people, jointly or severally**, and all come forward to claim it, each has a share and the share of one who fails to take goes to his **co-legatee. A joint example is: 'I give and bequeath the slave Stichus to Titius and Seius'. A several example is: 'I give and bequeath the slave Stichus to Lucius Titius. I give and bequeath** this same slave **to Seius'**. 200. If something is left conditionally by proprietary legacy, to whom does it belong before the condition is fulfilled? Our teachers think that it belongs to the heir, on the model of the potentially free slave, that is, a slave who is granted freedom by will under some condition; it is settled that he is the heir's slave in the meantime. But the authorities of the other school think that the thing belongs to no one in the meantime; they state this all the more strongly of a thing which is bequeathed absolutely, without conditions, before the legatee acknowledges the legacy.

201. This is how we make an obligatory legacy: 'Let my heir be bound to give my slave Stichus'; but even if: 'Let him convey' is written, this is an obligatory legacy. 202. **Even a third party's property can be left** by this kind of legacy. **Then the heir must buy the thing and hand it over, or pay its value.** 203. An

stare aut aestimationem eius dare debeat. 203. Ea
quoque res, quae in rerum natura non est, si modo
futura est, per damnationem legari potest, uelut fructus,
qui in illo fundo nati erunt, aut quod ex illa ancilla
natum erit. 204. Quod autem ita legatum est, post
aditam hereditatem, etiamsi pure legatum est, non, ut
per uindicationem legatum, continuo legatario adquiritur, sed nihilo minus heredis est: et ideo legatarius
in personam agere debet, id est intendere heredem
sibi dare oportere, et tum heres *rem*, si mancipi sit,
mancipio dare aut in iure cedere possessionemque tra-
dere debet; si nec mancipi sit, sufficit, si tradiderit.
nam si mancipi rem tantum tradiderit nec mancipauerit, usucapione *demum*[1] pleno iure fit legatarii. completur autem usucapio, sicut alio quoque loco diximus,
mobilium quidem rerum anno, earum uero, quae solo
teneantur, biennio. 205. Est et illa differentia huius
et per uindicationem legati, quod si eadem res duobus
pluribusue per damnationem[2] legata sit, si quidem coniunctim, plane singulis partes debentur, sicut in per
uindicationem legato diximus[3]; *si uero* disiunctim, sin-
107   gulis solida debetur[4]; ita fit, | ut scilicet heres alteri
rem, alteri aestimationem eius praestare debeat; et in
coniunctis deficientis portio non ad collegatarium pertinet, sed in hereditate remanet.[5]

---

1) usucapione demum *Goeschen*. usucapionem V.   2) damni
contractionem V.   3) in per uindicationem legato diximus
Kalb, Juristenlatein[2] *p.* 52. in illo uindicaii ✱ ✱ ✱ ✱ ✱ ✱ V.
4) solida debetur] solidae deuentur V.   5) remanetur V.

---

§ 203. = *I.* 2, 20, 7. *cf. Gai epit.* 2, 5, 3. *D.* 30, 24 *pr.*
(*Pomp.* 444). 35, 1, 1, 3 (*Pomp.* 229). 32, 17 *pr.* (*Marcian.* 9).
33, 6, 13 (*Ulp.* 2651).
§ 204. *cf. supra* 2, 194; 41; 42; 44; 54. *infra* 2, 213. *D.*
30, 82, 1 (*Iul.* 475). alio loco] 2, 44.
§ 205. *cf. Gai epit.* 2, 5, 4; 5. *supra* 2, 199. *Ulp.* 24, 13.
Fr. Vat. 85 (*Ulp.* 2569). 87 = *D.* 7, 2, 8 (*Ulp.* 2570). *D.* 30,
84, 8 (*Iul.* 478). 30, 82, 5 (*Iul.* 475). 30, 16 *pr.* (*Pomp.* 440).

obligatory **legacy of non-existent things is valid if they are likely to come into being, as crops from that land, or the offspring of that slave-woman.** 204. Now, something left by this kind of legacy is not acquired immediately by the legatee on acceptance of the inheritance, as is a proprietary legacy, even if the legacy has been left unconditionally; it is still the property of the heir. And so the legatee must bring a personal action*, that is, state in his principal pleading that the heir ought to convey to him; then if it is a thing capable of mancipation the heir must mancipate it or assign it in court and hand over possession; but if it is not capable of mancipation it is enough to hand it over. If he merely delivers a thing capable of mancipation instead of mancipating it, it becomes the legatee's property fully only by usucapion; as we said elsewhere, usucapion of moveable property is completed in one year, but in the case of immoveables in two years. 205. There is another difference between this kind of legacy and a proprietary legacy. If the same thing is left to two or more people by an obligatory legacy and it is left jointly, of course each is owed a share just as in the case of something left by a proprietary legacy; if it is left severally the whole is owed to each. This means that what the heir must do is to make the thing over to one and its value to the other; and in the case of joint legacies the share of any legatee who fails to take does not go to his co-legatee but remains in the inheritance.

206. Quod autem diximus deficientis portionem *in*
per damnationem quidem legato in hereditate retineri[1],
in per uindicationem uero collegatario accrescere, admonendi sumus ante legem Papiam *hoc* iure ciuili ita
fuisse; post legem uero Papiam deficientis portio caduca fit et ad eos pertinet, qui in eo testamento liberos habent. 207. Et quamuis prima causa sit in ca-
ducis uindicandis heredum liberos habentium, deinde
si heredes liberos non habeant, legatariorum liberos
habentium, tamen ipsa lege Papia significatur, ut col-
legatarius coniunctus, si liberos habeat, potior sit heredibus, etiamsi liberos habebunt. 208. Sed plerisque
placuit, quantum ad hoc ius, quod lege Papia coniunctis
constituitur, nihil interesse, utrum per uindicationem
an per damnationem legatum sit.

209. Sinendi modo ita legamus: HERES MEVS DAM-
NAS[2] ESTO SINERE LVCIVM TITIVM HOMINEM STICHVM
SVMERE SIBIQVE HABERE. 210. Quod genus legati plus
quidem habet *quam* per[3] uindicationem legatum, minus
autem quam per damnationem[4]: nam eo modo non
solum suam rem | testator utiliter legare potest, sed 108
etiam heredis sui, cum alioquin per uindicationem nisi
suam rem legare non potest, per damnationem autem

---

1) retinere V.   2) dare damnas V.   3) pro V.
4) damnacont·nem V.

31, 13, 1 (*Pomp.* 359). 31, 88, 6 (*Scaev.* 258). 31, 7 (*Paul.*
1153).

§§ 206. 207. *cf. supra* 2, 199; 205. *infra* 2, 286. *Ulp.* 24,
12; 13. 17, 2. 18. 19, 17. 1, 21. 25, 17. *Fr. de iur. fisci* § 3
(*Iurispr.* II 177). *Fr. Vat.* 195 (*Ulp.* 2109). *D.* 32, 80 (*Cels.* 249).
35, 1, 26 (*Iul.* 816). 28, 6, 5 (*Gai* 450). 32, 89 *et* 50, 16, 142
(*Paul.* 966). 31, 7 (*Paul.* 1153). *Iuven.* 9, 87 *sq. Tac. ann.* 3, 28.
Isid. Orig. 5, 15, 1.

§ 209. *cf. Gai epit.* 2, 5, 6. *Ulp.* 24, 5. *Excerpt. Prob.
Einsidl.* 40 (*Iurispr.* I 90). *Theoph.* 2, 20, 2 (*p.* 207 *Ferr.*). *D.*
32, 30, 1 (*Lab. ap. Iav.* 172). 33, 5, 20 (*Lab. ap. Iav.* 179). 33,
1, 2 (*Pomp.* 501). 50, 16, 164, 2 (*Ulp.* 2543).

§ 210. *cf. Gai epit.* 2, 5, 6. *Ulp.* 24, 10; 8. *Paul.* 3, 6, 11.

206. However, notice that when we said that, in the case of an obligatory legacy, the share of a legatee who fails to take is retained in the inheritance but in the case of a proprietary legacy the share goes to his co-legatee, this is what applied by state law before the Papian Act; since the Papian Act the share of a legatee who fails to take is forfeited and goes to beneficiaries of the will who have children. 207. And although in claims for forfeited property first place is given to heirs with children and then, failing such heirs, legatees with children come in, the Papian Act itself states that if a joint co-legatee has children he is in a stronger position than the heirs, even if they have children. 208. But most people accept that so far as concerns the right created for joint legatees by the Papian Act, it does not matter whether the legacy is left by proprietary or obligatory legacy.

209. This is how we make a permissive legacy: 'Let my heir be bound to permit Lucius Titius to take the slave Stichus and have him as his'. 210. Note that this kind of legacy is more than a proprietary legacy but less than an obligatory one. A testator can use it to bequeath effectively not only his own property but even his heir's property, whereas by proprietary legacy he can bequeath only his own property and by an obligatory legacy he can bequeath the property of

cuiuslibet extranei rem legare potest. **211.** Sed si quidem mortis testatoris tempore res uel ipsius testatoris
sit uel heredis, plane utile legatum est, etiamsi testamenti faciendi tempore neutrius fuerit. **212.** Quod si
post mortem testatoris ea res heredis esse coeperit,
quaeritur, an utile sit legatum: et plerique putant
inutile esse. quid ergo est? licet aliquis eam **rem**
legauerit, quae neque eius umquam fuerit neque postea
heredis eius umquam esse coeperit, ex senatus consulto
Neroniano proinde uidetur, ac si per damnationem relicta esset. **213.** Sicut autem per damnationem legata
res non statim post aditam hereditatem legatarii efficitur, sed manet heredis eo usque, donec is[1] tradendo
uel mancipando uel in iure cedendo legatarii eam fecerit, ita et in sinendi modo legato iuris est; et ideo
huius quoque legati nomine in personam actio est
QVIDQVID HEREDEM EX TESTAMENTO DARE FACERE
OPORTET. **214.** Sunt tamen, qui putant ex hoc legato
non uideri obligatum heredem, ut mancipet aut in
109 iure cedat | aut tradat, sed sufficere, ut legatarium rem
sumere patiatur; quia nihil ultra ei testator imperauit,
quam ut sinat, id est patiatur, legatarium rem sibi
habere. **215.** Maior illa dissensio in hoc legato interuenit, si eandem rem duobus pluribusue disiunctim
legasti; quidam putant utrisque[2] solidam deberi, sicut
per *damn*ationem[3]: nonnulli occupantis esse meliorem
condicionem aestimant, quia, cum eo genere legati
damnetur heres patientiam praestare, ut legatarius rem
habeat, sequitur, ut si priori patientiam praestiterit

---

1) is heres V.   2) utrique *Polenaar*.   3) damnationem
Goeschen. uindicationem V. *Kniep inter* per *et* uindicationem
inserit: damnationem legatam, alii partes ad singulos pertinere
sicut in legato per, *speciose aliter Beseler ZS* 46, 268.

§§ 211. 212. *cf. Gai epit.* 2, 5, 6. *Fr. Vat.* 85 (*Ulp.* 2569).
§ 213. *cf. supra* 2, 204. QVIDQVID *etc.*] *cf. infra* 4, 41.
§ 214. *cf. Gai epit.* 2, 5, 6. *infra* 2, 280. *D.* 19, 2, 29
(*Alf.* 27). 34, 3, 16 (*Paul.* 1172).
§ 215. *cf. D.* 33, 2, 14 (*Cels.* 153). *C.* 6, 51, 1, 11 (*a.* 534).

any third party. 211. If the thing belongs to the testator or to his heir at the testator's death, of course the legacy is effective even if it belonged to neither when the will was made. 212. But if the thing comes to be the heir's property after the testator's death, is the legacy effective? Most people think it is ineffective. What then? Even if someone bequeaths a thing which never was his and never became the heir's property thereafter, under the Neronian Resolution it is treated as if it had been left by an obligatory legacy. 213. However, just as a thing left by obligatory legacy does not become the legatee's property immediately on acceptance of the inheritance but remains the heir's property until the heir transfers it to the legatee by delivery or by mancipation or by an assignment in court, the law is the same for a permissive legacy; and so the action for this legacy is also a personal action: 'Whatever the heir ought to convey or perform under the will'. 214. Yet some people think that by this kind of legacy the heir is not to be regarded as bound to mancipate or assign in court or deliver; all he need do is allow the legatee to take the thing. This is because the testator's instructions do not go beyond permitting, that is allowing, the legatee to take the thing. 215. There is greater dispute in relation to this kind of legacy where you have bequeathed the same thing to two or more people severally. Some think that the whole is owed to each as in the case of an obligatory legacy; some consider that the first to take has the better position. The reasoning is that with this kind of legacy the heir is bound to provide the legatee with an opportunity to take the thing; it follows that if he gives the opportunity to one and he takes the thing,

et is rem sumpserit, securus[1] sit aduersus eum, qui
postea legatum petierit, quia neque habe*t* rem, ut patiatur eam ab eo sumi, neque dolo malo fecit, quo
minus eam rem haberet.

216. Per praeceptionem hoc modo legamus: LVCIVS
TITIVS HOMINEM STICHVM PRAECIPITO. 217. Sed nostri
quidem praeceptores nulli alii eo modo legari posse
putant nisi ei, qui aliqua ex parte heres scriptus esset.[2]
praecipere enim esse praecipuum sumere; quod tantum
in eius persona[3] procedit, qui aliqua ex parte heres
institutus est, quod is extra portionem hereditatis
praecipuum legatum habiturus sit. 218. Ideoque si extraneo legatum fuerit, inutile est legatum, adeo ut
Sabinus | existimauerit ne quidem ex *senatus* consulto 110
Neroniano posse conualescere: 'nam eo', inquit, 'senatus
consulto ea tantum confirmantur, quae uerborum uitio
iure ciuili non ualent, non quae propter ipsam personam legatarii non deberentur'. sed Iuliano et Sexto
placuit etiam hoc casu ex senatus consulto confirmari
legatum; nam ex uerbis etiam hoc casu accidere, ut
iure ciuili inutile sit legatum, inde[4] manifestum esse[5],
quod eidem aliis uerbis recte legaretur[6]. uelut per[7]
uindicationem, per[8] damnationem, sinendi modo[9]; tunc

---

1) secuturus V. 2) esset *Heffter*. esse V. sit *Hu*.
3) personam V. 4) inde *Goeschen*. unde V. 5) esse *Goeschen*.
est V. 6) legatur V. 7) pro V. 8) et per V. 9) inde
— modo *del. Ciapessori, Stud. Bonf*. 3, 695, 156.

---

§ 216. *cf. Ulp.* 24, 6. *Theoph*. 2, 20, 2 (*p*. 207 *Ferr*.). *Excerpt. Prob. Einsidl*. 41 (*Iurispr*. I 90). *D*. 31, 88 *pr*.; 1; 2; 3
(*Scaev*. 258). 31, 89 *pr*. (*Scaev*. 278). 33, 7, 27, 3 (*Scaev*. 56). 31,
77, 19 (*Pap*. 599). 32, 92 *pr*. (*Paul*. 1554). *C. I. L*. VI 10230
l. 8 (*Bruns* I[7], 327).

§ 217. *cf. Gai epit*. 2, 5, 7. *D*. 32, 32 (*Scaev*. 42). 31, 75, 1
(*Pap*. 560). 34, 1, 10 *pr*. (*Pap*. 615). 30, 17, 2 (*Ulp*. 2534). *Suet.
Galb*. 5. *Plin. ep*. 5, 7.

§ 218. *cf. Ulp*. 24, 11[a]. *Fr. Vat*. 85 (*Ulp*. 2569). *D*. 30,
18 (*Iul*. 451). peregrino] *cf. infra* 2, 285.

the heir is safe against anyone who sues for the legacy thereafter, for he neither has the thing and can let it be taken nor has he parted with it in bad faith.

216. This is how we make a preceptive legacy: 'Let Lucius Titius take the slave Stichus as a preference'. 217. But note that our teachers think that this kind of legacy can be left only to someone who has been appointed heir for some share; for to take preceptively is to take some preference. This only applies to someone who has been appointed heir for some share, because he is to have a preferential legacy beyond his share of the inheritance. 218. And so, if such a legacy is left to a third party, the legacy is ineffective; so much so that Sabinus considered that even the Neronian Resolution could not validate it. He says: 'This resolution of the Senate only confirms legacies which are invalid by state law through some fault in the wording, not those which would not be due because of an objection to the legatee.' But Julian and Sextus took the view that even in this case the Senate resolution confirms the legacy. They say that it is obvious that even in this case it is as a result of its wording that the legacy is invalid by state law, because the legacy could properly be left to the same person using other wording, such as by a proprietary, an obligatory or a permissive legacy; a legacy invalid

autem uitio personae legatum non ualere, cum ei legatum sit, cui nullo modo legari possit uelut peregrino, cum quo testamenti factio non sit. quo plane casu senatus consulto locus non est. 219. Item nostri praeceptores, quod ita legatum est, nulla *alia* ratione putant posse consequi eum[1], cui ita fuerit legatum, quam[2] iudicio familiae erciscundae, quod inter heredes de hereditate erciscunda, id est diuidunda, accipi solet: officio enim iudicis id contineri, ut ei, quod per praeceptionem legatum est, adiudicetur. 220. Unde intellegimus nihil aliud secundum nostrorum praeceptorum opinionem per praeceptionem legari posse, nisi quod testatoris sit. nulla enim alia res quam hereditaria deducitur in hoc iudicium. itaque si non suam rem
111 eo modo testator legauerit, | iure quidem ciuili inutile erit legatum, sed ex senatus consulto confirmabitur. aliquo[3] tamen casu etiam alienam rem *per* praeceptionem legari posse fatentur: ueluti si quis eam rem legauerit, quam creditori fiduciae causa mancipio dederit; nam officio iudicis coheredes cogi posse existimant soluta pecunia luere[4] eam rem, ut possit praecipere is[5], cui ita legatum sit. 221. Sed diuersae scholae[6] auctores putant etiam extraneo per praeceptionem legari posse, proinde ac si ita scribatur: TITIVS HOMINEM STICHVM CAPITO, superuacuo adiecta PRAE syllaba; ideoque per uindicationem *eam rem* legatam uideri: quae sententia dicitur diui Hadriani consti-

---

1) cum V.   2) quod V.   3) aliquod V.   4) soluta pecunia luere *Lachmann.* solutam pecuniam soluere V.
5) praecipere is *Goeschen.* percipere ei V.   6) sed diuersae scholae] et diuelse soles V.

---

§ 219. *cf. Theoph.* 2, 20, 2 (*p.* 207 *Ferr.*).   *Paul.* 3, 6, 1. *D.* 10, 2, 22, 1 (*Ulp.* 635). 30, 17, 2 (*Ulp.* 2534).
§ 220. *cf. Ulp.* 24, 11. *D.* 10, 2, 28 (*Gai.* 195). *C.* 6, 42, 6 (*a.* 224). ex senatus consulto] *cf. supra* 2, 197. fiduciao] *cf. supra* 2, 60.

through a fault affecting the person means a legacy left to someone to whom a legacy could not be left in any way, such as a foreigner, who has no capacity to take under a will. In such a case there is plainly no room for the Senate resolution. 219. Again, our teachers think that the person to whom a legacy of this sort has been left can claim the legacy only by the action for splitting an inheritance, which is normally brought between heirs for the splitting, that is, the division of the inheritance; it is part of the judge's* function to adjudicate to an heir what has been left to him by preceptive legacy. 220. From this we understand that in our teachers' opinion nothing can be left by preceptive legacy unless it belongs to the testator; for in this action only what forms part of the inheritance is brought into account. And so, if a testator bequeaths something which does not belong to him by this kind of legacy, note that the legacy will be ineffective by state law, but it will be confirmed by the Senate resolution. All the same they do admit that there are cases where even someone else's property can be bequeathed by preceptive legacy, for instance, if a person bequeaths something which he mancipated to his creditor under a trust; for they consider that it is part of the judge's function to compel the co-heirs to pay the money and release the thing so that the legatee may take it as a preference. 221. But the authorities of the other school think that a preceptive legacy can be left even to a third party, as if the wording were: 'Let Titius take the slave Stichus', the phrase 'as a preference' being superfluous; and so the thing is regarded as left by proprietary legacy. This view is said to have been confirmed by a pronouncement of the Emperor Hadrian. 222. And so,

tutione[1] confirmata esse. **222.** Secundum hanc igitur opinionem, si ea res ex iure Quiritium defuncti fuerit, potest[2] a legatario uindicari, siue is unus ex heredibus sit siue extraneus; quod si in bonis tantum testatoris fuerit, extraneo quidem ex senatus consulto utile erit legatum, heredi uero familiae herciscundae iudicis officio praestabitur; quod si nullo iure fuerit testatoris, tam heredi quam extraneo ex senatus consulto utile erit. **223.** Siue tamen heredibus secundum nostrorum opinionem siue etiam extraneis secundum illorum opinionem duobus pluribusue eadem res coniunctim aut disiunctim legata fuerit, singuli | partes habere debent. 112

[Ad legem Falcidiam. ·R] **224.** Sed olim quidem licebat totum patrimonium legatis atque libertatibus erogare nec quicquam heredi relinquere praeterquam inane nomen heredis; idque lex XII tabularum permittere uidebatur, qua cauetur, ut quod quisque de re sua testatus esset, id ratum haberetur, his uerbis: 'VTI LEGASSIT[3] SVAE REI[4], ITA IVS ESTO'. qua de causa[5], qui scripti heredes erant, ab hereditate se abstinebant, et idcirco plerique intestati moriebantur. **225.** Itaque lata est lex Furia, qua[6] exceptis personis quibusdam

---

1) constitutionem V.   2) posse V.   3) legasset V.
4) res V.   5) qua de causa *Kalb.* quaae V.   6) quae **V.**

---

§ 222. *cf. supra* 2, 40; 196; 197.
§ 223. *cf. Gai epit.* 2, 5, 7. *C.* 6, 51, 1, 11 (*a.* 534).
§ 224. *cf. I.* 2, 22 *pr. cum Theoph.* (*p.* 232 *Ferr.*). *XII tab.* 5, 3 (*Bruns* I[7], 23). *Ulp.* 11, 14. *D.* 50, 16, 120 (*Pomp.* 248). 50, 16, 53 *pr.* (*Paul.* 721). *Nov.* 22, 2 *pr. Rhet. ad Her.* 1, 13, 23. *Cic. de inv.* 2, 50, 148.
§ 225. *cf. I.* 2, 22 *pr. cum Theoph.* (*p.* 233 *Ferr.*). *infra* 4, 23; 109. *Ulp.* 1, 2. 28, 7. *Fr. Vat.* 301 (*Paul.* 796). *Varro libro III de vita pop. Rom.*: Plebisque scito cautum, ne qui legaret caussaue mortis donaret supra assis mille, *quod fragmentum ex Calpurnii Pisonis libro II de Continentia Veterum Poetarum attulit Paulus Merula in editione Annalium Ennii* (*Lugd. Batav.* 1595) *atque inde receptum est in Varronis editionem a Popma curatam et in Bipontinam* (*a.* 1788, *p.* 247),

according to this opinion, if the thing belonged to the deceased by quiritary right, it can be vindicated by the legatee, whether he is one of the heirs or a third party; but if it was held by the testator only as part of his estate, while the legacy will have effect in favour of a third party as a result of the Senate resolution, it will be made over to the heir in exercise of the judge's function in the action for splitting the inheritance. If, however, the testator had no right in it at all, it will have effect in favour both of the heir and of a third party as a result of the Senate resolution. 223. However, if the same thing has been bequeathed to two or more people, jointly or severally, that is to heirs according to our supporters' opinion or even to third parties according to theirs, each ought to have a share.

[The Falcidian Act] 224. **But note that at one time it was permissible to use up one's whole estate in legacies** and grants of freedom and not leave anything to one's heir except the empty name of heir. This was thought to be permitted **by the Twelve Tables**, which **provide** that whatever will a man has made of his estate, it should be ratified, by its words: **'As a man bequeaths his own, so let the law be'.** The effect was that the appointed heirs did not take up inheritances and so **most people died intestate.** 225. And so, **the Furian Act** was passed under which, with certain exceptions, no one was permitted to take

ceteris plus mille assibus legatorum nomine mortisue
causa capere permissum non est. sed [et] haec lex non
perfecit, quod uoluit: qui enim uerbi gratia quinque
milium aeris[1] patrimonium habebat, poterat quinque
hominibus singulis millenos asses legando totum patrimonium erogare. 226. Ideo postea lata est lex Voco-
nia, qua cautum est, ne cui plus legatorum nomine
mortisue causa capere liceret, quam heredes caperent.[2]
ex qua lege plane quidem aliquid utique heredes
habere uidebantur; sed tamen fere uitium simile nasce-
batur.[3] nam in multas legatariorum personas distributo
patrimonio poterat *testator* adeo heredi minimum relin
113 quere, ut non expediret heredi huius lucri gra|tia to-
tius hereditatis onera sustinere. 227. Lata est itaque
lex Falcidia, qua cautum est, ne plus ei legare liceat
quam dodrantem: itaque necesse est, ut heres quartam
partem hereditatis habeat: et hoc nunc[4] iure utimur.
228. In libertatibus quoque dandis nimiam licentiam
conpescuit lex Fufia Caninia, sicut in primo conmen-
tario rettulimus.

---

1) assium *Beseler.*   2) caperentur V.   3) nascebantur V.
4) nec V.

---

fictum esse videtur. cf. *Lawicki, de Fraude Pauli Merulae
Ennianorum Annalium editoris* (Bonn. 1852) *et Kettner, M. Te-
renti Varronis de vita populi Romani quae exstant* (Halis 1863)
p. 40. *Cic. in Verr.* 2, 1, 42, 109 *cum Ps. Asc.* (p. 190 B.). *pro
Balb.* 8, 21.
    § 226. *cf. I.* 2, 22 *pr. cum Theoph.* (p. 233 *Ferr.*). lex Vo-
conia] *a. u.* 585 = *a. Chr.* 169. *cf. Cic. in Verr.* 2, 1, 43, 110.
infra 2, 274.
    § 227. lex Falcidia] *a. u.* 714, *a. Chr.* 40. *cf. Gai epit.*
2, 6. *I.* 2, 22 *pr. Ulp.* 24, 32. *Paul.* 3, 8, 1. *D.* 35, 2, 1 *pr.*
(*Paul.* 921; *Bruns* I[7], 110). *Dio Cass.* 48, 33, 5. *Hieronym. ad
Euseb. Chronic. ad a. Abrah.* 1977 (*Olymp.* 185, 1 = *a. u.* 714
= *a. Chr.* 40) *ed. Schoene* 2, 139: C. Falcidius tribunus plebis
legem tulit, ne quis plus testamento legaret, quam ut quarta
pars heredibus superesset. *Isid. orig.* 5, 15, 2. *Suidas v.* Φαλ-
κίδιος. *C. I. L.* XI 419 (*Bruns* I[7], 351. *Dessau* 6663). *Plin. ep.*
5, 1, 9.
    § 228. *cf. supra* 1, 42 *sq.*

more than a thousand 'asses'* by way of legacy or in consequence of someone's death. This law also failed to achieve the full effect intended; someone who had an estate of 5,000, for example, could use up his whole estate by leaving 1,000 each to five people. 226. And so, later, **the Voconian Act** was passed. This provided that no one was to take more by way of legacy or in consequence of someone's death than the heirs took. Under this law, of course, it seemed quite clear that the heirs would at least have something; yet almost the same fault developed. By distributing his estate among many individual legatees a testator could leave very little for the heir, so that it was not worth his while to take on the whole burdens of the inheritance in order to get this benefit. 227. And so **the Falcidian Act was passed. This made it unlawful for him to give legacies of more than nine-twelfths**, and so the heir must necessarily have a quarter share of the inheritance. This is now the law. 228. Again, the Fufian-Caninian Act checked excessive grants of freedom, as we explained in the first commentary.

[℞ De inutiliter relictis legatis. ℞] **229.** Ante heredis
institutionem *in*utiliter legatur, scilicet quia testamenta
uim ex institutione heredis accipiunt, et ob id uelut
caput et fundamentum intellegitur totius testamenti
heredis institutio. **230.** Pari ratione nec libertas ante
heredis institutionem dari potest. **231.** Nostri prae-
ceptore*s* nec tutores eo loco dari posse existimant[1]:
sed Labeo et Proculus tutorem posse dari, quod nihil
ex hereditate erogatur tutoris datione.[2] **232.** Post mortem quoque heredis inutiliter legatur, id est hoc modo:
CVM HERES MEVS MORTVVS ERIT, DO LEGO, aut DATO.
ita autem recte legatur: CVM HERES *MEVS* MORIETVR[3],
quia non post mortem heredis relinquitur, sed ultimo
uitae eius tempore. rursum ita non potest legari:
PRIDIE QVAM HERES MEVS MORIETVR; quod non pre-
tiosa ratione receptum uidetur. | **233.** Eadem et de 114
libertatibus dicta intellegemus. **234.** Tutor uero an
post mortem heredis dari possit, quaerentibus eadem
forsitan[4] poterit esse quaestio, quae[5] de *eo* agitatur,
qui ante heredum institutionem datur.[6] [De poenae causa
relictis legatis.] **235.** Poenae quoque nomine inutiliter
legatur. poenae autem nomine legari uidetur, quod
coercendi heredis causa relinquitur, quo magis heres

---

1) existimantur V.   2) § 231 *del. Solazzi, Confer.* 86.
3) moriatur V.   4) forsitam V.   5) quam V.   6) § 234
del. Beseler Beitr. 3, 83, *Kniep, Albertario, Solazzi.*

§ 229. = *I.* 2, 20, 34. *cf. Ulp.* 24, 15. 25, 8. quia testamenta *etc.*] *cf. D.* 28, 4, 3 (*Marcell.* 263). 29, 7, 10 *i. f.* (*Pap.*
240). 28, 6, 1, 3 (*Mod.* 100).
§ 230. = *I.* 2, 20, 34. *cf. Ulp.* 1, 20.
§ 281. *cf. I.* 1, 14, 3.
§ 232. *cf. I.* 2, 20, 35. *Ulp.* 24, 16. 25, 8. *Paul.* 3, 6, 5; 6.
4, 1, 11. *infra* 3, 100. *C.* 8, 37 (38), 11 (*a.* 528).
§ 283. *cf. Ulp.* 1, 20.
§ 234. *cf. supra* 2, 231. *D.* 26, 2, 7 (*Paul.* 1637).
§ 285. *cf. I.* 2, 20, 36. *Ulp.* 24, 17. 25, 13. *D.* 34, 6, 1
(*Afr.* 122). 34, 6, 2 (*Marcian.* 110). 35, 1, 12 (*Ulp.* 2662). *C.*
6, 41, 1 (*a.* 528). *Script. Hist. Aug. Anton. Pius* 8, 5.

[Ineffective legacies] 229. **A legacy ahead of the heir's appointment** is **bad; the force of the will flows from the heir's appointment, which is its foundation or corner-stone.** 230. **Similarly a grant of freedom** can **not precede his appointment.** 231. Our teachers consider that a guardian's appointment is out of place there as well; but Labeo and Proculus allow a guardian's appointment because appointing a guardian takes nothing away from the inheritance. 232. **Legacies designed to take effect after the death of the heir** are **also bad,** such as: **'I give and bequeath'** or: **'I give, after my heir's death'. However, a legacy in the form: 'When my heir dies'** is good because it takes effect not after the heir's death but at the last moment of his life. On the other hand, it is not possible to leave a legacy in the form: **'On the day before my heir dies'.** There does not seem to be any very worthwhile reason for this. 233. What has been said applies equally to grants of freedom. 234. On the other hand, those who wonder whether a guardian can be appointed for after the death of the heir are perhaps raising the same question as is discussed in the case of a guardian appointed before the heir is named. [Penal legacies] 235. **Penal legacies are also ineffective. A penal legacy is one calculated to compel an heir to do or not to do something. For**

aliquid faciat aut non faciat, uelut quod ita legatur:
SI HERES MEVS FILIAM SVAM TITIO IN MATRIMONIVM
COLLOCAVERIT, X *MILIA* SEIO DATO, uel ita: SI FILIAM
TITIO IN MATRIMONIVM NON COLLOCAVERIS, X MILIA
TITIO DATO; sed et si heredem, *si*[1] uerbi gratia intra
biennium monumentum sibi non fecerit, x *milia* Titio
dari[2] iusserit *testator*[3], poenae nomine legatu*m est.* et
denique ex ipsa definitione multas similes species *cir*-
cumspicere possumus. 236. Nec libertas quidem poenae
nomine dari potest, quamuis de ea re fuerit quaesitum.
237. De tutore uero nihil possumus quaerere, quia non
po*test* datione tutoris heres conpelli quidquam facere
aut non facere. ideoque — datur[4] poenae *nomi*ne
tutor datus fuerit, magis sub condicione quam poenae
nomine datus uidebitur.[5]

238. Inceͧrtae personae legatum inutiliter relinquitur.
incerta autem uidetur persona, quam per incertam opi-
115 nionem | animo suo testator subicit[6], uel*ut cum* ita
legatum sit: QVI PRIMVS AD FVNVS MEVM VEN*E*RIT, *EI*
HERES MEVS X *MILIA* DATO; idem iuris est, si genera-
liter omnibus legauerit: QVICVMQVE AD FVNVS MEVM
VENERIT; i*n* eadem causa est, quod ita relinquitur:
QVICVMQVE FILIO MEO IN MATRIMONIVM FILIAM SVAM
CONLOCAVERIT, EI HERES MEVS X MILIA DATO; illud
quoque [in eadem causa est][7], quod ita relinquitur:
QVI POST TESTAMENTVM *SCRIPTVM PRIMI*[8] CONSVLES DE-
SIGNATI ERVNT, aeque incertis personis legari uidetur;

---

1) *add. Hu.*　　2) dare *Hu.*　　3) *add. Goeschen.*　　4) ideoque — datur] ideoquae datur V. ideoque etsi secundum men-
tem testatoris is, qui tutor datus est *Mommsen suppl.*　　5) § 237
del. Solazzi.　　6) subicitur V.　　7) in — est *del. Hu.,* om.
Inst. Kniep. coll. Cod. 6, 48, 1, 27 *supplet:* quod ita relinquitur 'qui post testamentum scriptum gener mihi erit'. item.
8) scriptum primi *ex Inst. add. Hu.*

---

§ 236. *cf I.* 2, 20, 36.
§ 237. *cf D.* 34, 6, 2 (*Marcian.* 110).
§ 238. *cf. I.* 2, 20, 25. *Ulp.* 24, 18. *Paul.* 3, 6, 13. *infra*
2, 287.

instance, a legacy in the form: **'If my heir marries his daughter to Titius let him pay** 10,000 **to Seius'** or 'if you do **not marry** your **daughter** to Titius pay 10,000 to Titius'. Even if the testator instructs his heir to give 10,000 to Titius if, say, he does not erect a monument to the testator within two years, this is a penal legacy; in short, we can think up many similar cases on the basis of the definition. 236. And note that there cannot be a penal grant of freedom either, although this was questioned. 237. On the other hand, we cannot raise this question about the appointment of a guardian because the heir cannot be compelled to do or not to do something by the appointment of a guardian; and so [even if the testator thinks that where a guardian is] appointed he is appointed as a penalty, the appointment will be regarded as conditional rather than as penal.

238. A legacy in favour of an unidentifiable person is ineffective. **A beneficiary counts as unidentifiable when the testator leaves his identity open to guesswork, for instance,** suppose a legacy reads: 'Let my heir give 10,000 to the person who comes first to my funeral'. The law is the same if the legacy is quite general: 'To whomsoever comes to my funeral'. The following legacy is in the same situation: **'Let my heir give** 10,000 **to the person who marries his daughter to my son'.** Also one like this: **'To the first persons designated consuls after the making of the will'** is **equally regarded as left to unidentified persons. And many other examples**

et denique aliae multae huiusmodi species sunt. sub
certa uero demonstratione incertae personae recte legatur, uelut: EX COGNATIS MEIS, QVI NVNC SVNT, QVI
PRIMVS AD FVNVS MEVM VENERIT, EI X MILIA HERES
MEVS DATO. 239. Libertas quoque non uidetur incertae personae dari posse, quia lex Fufia Caninia iubet
nominatim[1] seruos liberari. 240. Tutor quoque certus
dari debet.[2] 241. Postumo quoque alieno inutiliter
legat*ur*. *est* autem alienus postumus, qui natus inter
suos heredes testatori futurus non est: ideoque ex
emancipato *quo*que filio conceptus nepos extraneus
post*umus est; item qui* in utero est eius, quae iure[3]
ciuili ncn intellegitur uxor, extraneus postumus patris
intelle|git*ur*. 242. Ac ne heres quidem potest institui 116
postumus alienus: est enim incerta persona. 243. Cetera
uero, quae supra diximus, ad legata proprie pertinent;
quamquam non inmerito quibusdam placeat poenae
nomine heredem institui non posse. nihil enim interest, utrum legatum dare iubeatur heres, si fecerit aliquid aut non fecerit, an coheres ei adiciatur, quia tam
coheredis adiectione quam legati datione compellitur,
ut aliquid contra propositum suum faciat aut non faciat.

244. An ei, qui in potestate sit eius, quem heredem
instituimus, recte legemus, quaeritur. Seruius recte
legari putat, sed euanescere legatum, si quo tempore
dies legatorum cedere solet, adhuc in potestate sit;

---

1) nominatum V.   2) § 240 *del. Solazzi.*   3) in iure V.

---

§ 239. *cf. I.* 2, 20, 25. *supra* 1, 46. *Ulp.* 1, 25. *Paul* 4,
14, 1. *D.* 40, 4, 24 (*Gai.* 487). 40, 4, 51 (*Pap.* 714).
§ 240. = *I.* 2, 20, 25. *cf. I.* 2, 20, 27. *Ulp.* 11, 14. *D.* 26,
2, 20 *pr.* (*Paul.* 557).
§ 241. *fere* = *I.* 2, 20, 26 *in.*; *cf. infra* 2, 287. *C.* 6, 48, 1
(*a.* 528—529).
§ 242. *cf. I.* 2, 20, 28. 3, 9 *pr. supra* 1, 147. *infra* 2, 287.
§ 243. *cf. I.* 2, 20, 36. *supra* 2, 235.
§ 244. *cf. I.* 2, 20, 32. *Ulp.* 24, 23. *D.* 34, 7, 1 *pr.* (*Cels.*
250). 31, 82, 2 *i. f.* (*Paul.* 1360).

could be given. **But it is possible to give a legacy to an unidentified person within an identified group, as: 'Let my heir give** 10,000 **to anyone among my relatives now living who comes first to my funeral'.** 239. **Freedom** can **not be given to unidentifiable persons either**, because the Fufian-Caninian Act requires **the grant to be made to specified slaves.** 240. **The appointment of a guardian** must **also satisfy the requirement of certainty.** 241. **A legacy to a posthumous outsider** is also **void. Within this description falls one who when born will not count as an immediate heir of the testator. Thus a grandson of an emancipated son** is **a posthumous outsider; again, an unborn child of a woman who is not** regarded as **a wife** by state **law** is regarded as a posthumous outsider to his father. 242. Note that **a posthumous outsider can** not be **appointed heir** either; he is an unidentified person. 243. On the other hand, the rest of what we have said above properly relates to legacies; although some people hold, with some justice, that an appointment of **an heir cannot be made** effectively if it is made **as a penalty.** It does not matter whether the penalty imposed is that the heir is ordered to give a legacy or that a co-heir is added along with him if he has done or not done something; both **the addition of a co-heir** and **the imposition of a legacy** compel him to do or not do something against his own inclination.

244. **Can we leave a legacy** to someone in the paternal power of the person whom we appoint as **heir?** Servius thinks that the legacy is good but is extinguished if he is still in power when the legacy usually vests; and so an unconditional legacy is due if

ideoque siue pure legatum sit et uiuo testatore in
potestate heredis esse desierit, siue sub condicione et
ante condicionem id acciderit, deberi legatum. Sabinus
et Cassius sub condicione recte legari, pure non recte
putant; licet enim uiuo testatore possit desinere in
potestate heredis esse, ideo tamen inutile legatum intellegi oportere, quia quod nullas uires habiturum foret,
si statim post testamentum factum decessisset testator,
hoc ideo ualere, quia uitam longius traxerit, absurdum
117 esset. sed | diuersae scholae auctores nec sub condi-
cione recte legari, quia quos in potestate habemus, eis
non magis sub condicione quam pure debere possumus.
245. Ex diuerso constat ab eo, qui in potestate *tua*[1]
est, herede instituto recte tibi legari; sed si tu per
eum heres extiteris, euanescere legatum, quia ipse tibi
legatum debere non possis; si uero filius emancipatus
aut seruus manumissus erit uel in alium translatus, et
ipse heres extiterit aut alium fecerit, deberi legatum.
    246. Nunc[2] transeamus ad fideicommissa.
    247. Et prius de hereditatibus uideamus. 248. In-
primis igitur sciendum est opus esse, ut aliquis heres
recto iure instituatur eiusque fidei committatur[3], ut
eam hereditatem alii restituat; alioquin inutile est
testamentum, in quo nemo recto iure heres instituitur.
249. Verba autem utilia[4] fideicommissorum haec [recte][5]
maxime in usu esse uidentur: PETO, ROGO, VOLO, FIDEI

---

    1) tua *add. Goeschen.*   2) nunc *Goeschen ex Inst.* hinc V.
3) committabatur V.   4) *glossema esse censet Segré.*   5) *del.*
Boecking; om. Inst.

    § 245. *cf. I.* 2, 20, 33. *Ulp,* 24, 24. *supra* 2, 189. *D.* 30,
91 *pr.* (*Iul.* 520). 36, 2, 17 (*Iul.* 522). 35, 2, 30, 8 (*Marcian.* 41).
35, 2, 20 (*Scaev.* 164). alium fecerit] *cf. D.* 28, 5, 41 (40)
(*Iul.* 440).   §§ 246. 247. = *I.* 2, 23 *pr.*
    § 248. *fere* = *I.* 2, 23, 2. *cf. Gai epit.* 2, 7 *pr.*
    § 249. = *I.* 2, 24, 3. *cf. Ulp.* 25, 2. 2, 7. *Paul.* 4, 1, 5; 6.
D. 30, 115 (*Ulp.* 1923). *C.* 6, 43, 2 (*a.* 531). *C. I. L.* VI 10229
(*Bruns* I⁷, 304) *l.* 30. 34. 55. 83. 89. 104. 117. *BGU* 326 *col. I*
l. 11 *sq.* (*Bruns* I⁷, 312). *Papyr. Oxy.* VI 907, 7. *Charis.* 191, 27 *K.*

he ceases to be in the heir's power while the testator is alive, while a conditional legacy is due if this happens before the condition is fulfilled. Sabinus and Cassius think that **a conditional legacy is good** but **not** an **unconditional** one; although he may **cease** to be **in the heir's power while the testator is alive, the legacy should still be** regarded as **ineffective** because it would be absurd that something which would have no force **if the testator died straight after making the will should be made good by** an extension of the span of his life. But the authorities of the other school think that even a conditional legacy is void, because we can no more come under a conditional obligation to persons in our power than an unconditional one. 245. **Conversely**, it is settled that **where** someone in your power **is appointed heir** a legacy can validly be left to you. But if you become heir through him **the legacy is extinguished** because you cannot owe a legacy to yourself. If, on the other hand, your son is emancipated or your **slave** is **granted freedom** or **transferred** to someone else and **himself** becomes **heir** or makes someone else heir, the legacy is due.

246. **We now move on to trusts*.**

247. **And first we consider whole estates.** 248. **The crucial starting point is a valid appointment of an heir charged as trustee to hand over the estate to a third person. Without a proper appointment of an heir the will is void.** 249. **In creating** effective **trusts the following words seem to be most commonly used: 'I call upon; I ask; I wish; I rely on your**

COMMITTO, quae proinde firma singula sunt, atque si omnia in unum congesta sint. 250. Cum igitur scripserimus: *LVCIVS TITIVS HERES ESTO*, possumus adicere: ROGO TE, LVCI TITI, PETOQVE A TE, VT CVM PRIMVM POSSIS HEREDITATEM MEAM ADIRE, GAIO SEIO REDDAS REST*I*TVAS. possumus autem et de parte restituenda rogare; et liberum est uel sub condicione uel pure relinquere | fideicommissa uel ex die certa. 251. Restituta autem hereditate[1] is, qui restituit, nihilo minus heres permanet; is uero, qui recipit hereditatem, aliquando heredis loco est, aliquando legatarii. 252. Olim autem nec[2] heredis loco erat nec legatarii, sed potius emptoris. tunc enim in *u*su erat ei, cui restituebatur hereditas, nummo uno eam hereditatem dicis causa uenire; et quae stipulationes inter *uenditorem hereditatis et emptorem interponi solent, eaedem interponebantur inter*[3] heredem et eum, cui restituebatur hereditas, id est hoc modo: heres quidem stipulabatur ab eo, cui restituebatur hereditas, ut quidquid hereditario nomine condemnatus fuisset[4] siue quid alias bona fide dedisse*t*, eo nomine indemnis *e*sset, et omnino si quis cum eo hereditario nomine ageret, ut recte defenderetur; ille uero, qui recipiebat hereditatem, inuicem stipulabatur, ut si quid ex hereditate ad heredem peruenisset, id sibi restitueretur, ut etiam pateretur eum hereditarias actiones procuratorio aut cognitorio nomine exequi. 253. Sed posterioribus temporibus Tre-

118

---

1) hereditatem V.　　2) ne V.　　3) uenditorem—inter *suppl. Goeschen. cf. Gai. Augustodun.* 67.　　4) soluisset *Krueger, quod non esse necessarium iudicat Hu. coll. Dig.* 18, 4, 2, 20.

§ 250. = *I.* 2, 23, 2 *med. cf. Gai epit.* 2, 7 *pr. Cic. in Verr.* 2, 1, 47, 123. *C. I. L.* V 2834. VI 15237. XIV 331.

§ 251. = *I.* 2, 23, 3. *cf. infra* 2, 255.

§ 252. *cf. Theoph.* 2, 23, 3 (*p.* 239 *sq. Ferr.*). *D.* 32, 95 (*Maecian.* 12). *infra* 2, 257. nummo uno] *cf. D.* 5, 3, 13, 5 (*Ulp.* 512). *Cic. p. Rab. Post.* 17, 45. *Hor. Sat.* II 5, 109. quae stipulationes] *cf. D.* 50, 16, 97 (*Cels.* 245). 15, 1, 37 *pr.* (*Iul.* 199). 45, 1, 50, 1 (*Ulp.* 1229). 45, 3, 20, 1 (*Paul.* 1396). proc. aut cognit. nom.] *cf. infra* 4, 86 *sq.*

§ 253. = *I.* 2, 23, 4. *cf. Ulp.* 25, 14. *Paul.* 4, 2. 4, 3, 2.

**honour'. Using them all achieves no more than
using one. 250. Once** we have **written: 'Let Lucius
Titius be heir'** we can **then add: 'And I ask you,
Lucius Titius**, and I call upon you, **as soon as you
can accept the estate, to give it to Gaius Seius'.**
Alternatively, we **can ask the heir to hand over
part of the estate.** We are **free to make the trust
absolute or conditional or post-dated. 251. After the
transfer, the heir remains heir. The recipient is
treated sometimes as heir, sometimes as legatee.**
252. At one time, however, he was treated neither as
heir nor as legatee but rather as a purchaser. For at
that time the practice was that the recipient of the
inheritance made a nominal purchase of the
inheritance for a penny; and the stipulations which
are normally required between the seller of an
inheritance and its purchaser were required in the
same way between the heir and the recipient of the
inheritance. That is to say, on the one hand, the heir
stipulated from the recipient of the inheritance that
he, the heir, would have indemnity in respect of any
judgment-debts relating to the inheritance, and any
other disposals which he had made in good faith, and
that if any action at all were brought against him in
respect of the inheritance he would be properly
defended. The recipient of the inheritance, on the
other hand, stipulated in turn that anything coming
to the heir from the inheritance would be handed over
to himself and that the heir would also allow him to
bring the actions in respect of the inheritance as agent
or as representative in court. 253. But subsequently,

bellio Maximo et Annaeo Seneca consulibus senatus
consultum factum est, quo cautum est, ut si cui hereditas ex fideicommissi causa restituta sit, actiones, quae
iure ciuili heredi et in heredem conpeterent, *ei* et in
eum darentur, cui ex fideicommisso restituta esset
hereditas; per[1] quod senatus consultum desierunt illae
119 cautiones in usu haberi. | praetor enim utiles actiones
ei et in eum, qui recepit hereditatem, quasi heredi
et in heredem dare coepit, eaeque[2] in edicto proponuntur.　254. Sed rursus quia heredes scripti, cum aut
totam hereditatem aut paene totam plerumque restituere rogabantur, adire hereditatem ob nullum aut
minimum lucrum recusabant atque ob id extingue-
bantur fideicommissa, p*ostea* Pegaso et Pusione *consu-*
libus senatus censuit, ut ei, qui rogatus esset hereditatem restituere, proinde liceret quartam partem retinere, atque e lege Falcidia in legatis retinendi ius[3]
conceditur: ex singulis quoque rebus, quae per fideicommissum relincuntur, eadem retentio permissa est.
per quod senatus consultum ipse *heres* onera hereditaria sustinet; ille autem, qui ex fideicommisso reliquam partem hereditatis recipit, legatarii partiarii loco
est, id est eius legatarii, cui pars bonorum legatur;
quae species legati partitio uocatur, quia cum herede
legatarius partitur hereditatem.　unde effectum est, ut
quae solent stipulationes inter heredem et partiarium
legatarium interponi, eaedem interponantur inter eum,

---

1) post *Inst.*　　2) eacque *Goeschen.* aeque V.　　3) retinendi ius *Hu.* retinendis V. retinere *Inst.*; *cf.* 3, 75.

D. 36, 1, 1, 1; 2 (*Ulp.* 1871; *Bruns* I[7], 202). 36, 1, 41 (40) (*Paul.*
327). temporibus] *Neronis a.* 56 (?).
　§ 254 = *I.* 2, 23, 5. *cf. Gai. epit.* 2, 7 *pr. Ulp.* 25, 14; 15.
Paul. 4, 3.　Pegaso et Pusione consulibus] *Vespasiani temporibus.*
partitio] *cf. Ulp.* 24, 25. *Theoph.* 2, 23, 5 (*p.* 241 *Ferr.*). *Cic. p.*
Caec. 4, 12. 5, 15. *p. Cluent.* 7, 21. *de leg.* 2, 20, 50 (*Iurispr.* I, 21).
Plut. Cat. 11. *infra* 2, 257. *D.* 28, 2, 39 *pr.* (*Iav.* 164). 32, 29, 1
(*Iav.* 171). 30, 104, 7 (*Iul.* 888). 30, 26, 2 (*Pomp.* 448). 36, 1, 23, 5
(*Ulp.* 109). 50, 16, 164, 1 (*Ulp.* 2539). 36, 1, 20 (19), 1 (*Paul.* 1638)
31, 9 (*Mod.* 268). *C. I. L.* VI 10230, 4 (*Bruns* I[7], 327).

in the consulship of Trebellius Maximus and Annaeus Seneca, a resolution was passed by the Senate providing that after transfer of a trust estate the transferee should be entitled to and liable under the actions which by state law lay for or against an heir. As a result of this resolution those undertakings fell out of use. The praetor began to allow policy actions by and against the transferee as though by and against the heir, and they are set out in his Edict. 254. However, appointed heirs who were asked to give up all or most of the estate then saw little or no prospect of profit to themselves and began to refuse inheritances. The effect was to bring down the trusts. Consequently, in the consulship of Pegasus and Pusio, the Senate resolved that an heir required to transfer the estate should have the same right to retain a quarter as the Falcidian Act allows in relation to legacies. The same retention is allowed where a single thing is caught by the trust. Under this resolution, the burdens of an heir are again shouldered by the heir, but the beneficiary under the trust, as recipient of part of the estate, is placed in the position of a cut-in legatee. That kind of legatee is one who is left a share of the whole estate. Such a legacy is called a cut (in Latin 'partitio') because the legatee is cut in for a share of the estate with the heir. The result achieved is that the stipulations customarily required between heir and cut-in legatee are required between the heir

qui ex fideicommissi causa recipi*t* hereditatem, et heredem, id est, ut et[1] lucrum et damnum hereditarium
pro rata parte inter eos commune sit. 255. Ergo si
quidem non plus qua*m* dodrantem | hereditatis scriptus 120
heres rogatus sit restituere, tum ex Trebelliano senatus
consulto restituitur hereditas, et[2] in utrumque actiones
hereditariae pro rata parte dant*ur*, in heredem quidem
iure ciuili, in eum uero, qui recipit hereditatem, ex
senatus consulto Trebelliano; quamquam heres etiam
pro ea parte, quam restituit, heres permanet[3] eique
et in eum solidae actiones competunt; sed non ulterius
oneratur, nec ulterius illi dantur actiones, quam apud
eum commodum hereditatis remanet. 256. At si quis
plus quam dodrantem uel etiam totam hereditatem
restituere rogatus sit, locus e*st* Pegasiano senatus consulto. 257. Sed is, qui s*e*mel adierit hereditatem, si
modo sua uoluntate adierit, siue retinuerit quartam
partem siue noluerit retinere, ipse uniuersa onera hereditaria sustinet[4]; sed quarta quidem retenta quasi
partis et pro parte stipulationes interponi debent tamquam inter partiar*i*um legatarium et heredem; si uero
totam hereditatem restituerit, ad exemplum emptae et
uenditae hereditatis stipulationes interponendae sunt.
258. Sed si recuset scriptus heres adire hereditatem ob
id, quod dicat eam sibi suspectam esse quasi damnosam, cauetur *Peg*asiano senatus consulto, ut deside-
rante eo, cui restituere rogatus est, iussu | praetoris 12?
adeat et restituat, proindeque ei et in eum, qui rece-

---

1) est V.   2) set V.   3) permanent V.   4) susti-
netur V.

---

§ 255. = I. 2, 23, 6. cf. Ulp. 25, 14. D. 35, 2, 93 (Pap. 294).
§ 256. = I. 2, 23, 6. cf. Ulp. 25, 14.
§ 257. = I. 2, 23, 6. cf. supra 2, 254. Ulp. 25, 15. Paul.
4, 3, 2. D. 36, 1, 22 (21) (Pomp. 695). 36, 1, 47 (45) (Mod. 79).
45, 1, 50, 1 (Ulp. 1229).
§ 258. cf. Ulp. 25, 16. Paul. 4, 4, 2—4. D. 29, 4, 17 (Gai.
306). 36, 1 passim. Nov. 1, 1, 1 (a. 535).

and the beneficiary under the trust. These undertakings bind the parties to share profit and loss from the estate in proportion to their interests. 255. And so, suppose the appointed heir is required to transfer no more than nine-twelfths of the estate. Here the transfer falls under the Trebellian regime. The actions for and against heirs are proportionally distributed, to the heir under state law, to the recipient under the Trebellian Resolution. Although the heir remains heir even in respect of the share which he hands over and the actions are available to and against him in full, he does not bear the burdens nor does he have the actions beyond the extent to which he retains the benefit of the inheritance. 256. Suppose instead that the heir is to make over more than nine-twelfths or even the whole estate. Here the Pegasian regime applies. 257. Once the heir accepts, provided it is by his own wish, he has to bear all the burdens of an heir, whether he retains his quarter or chooses not to. If he does keep his quarter, the share-and-share stipulations ˉare required, as between heir and cut-in legatee. If he makes over the whole estate, the undertakings used between buyer and seller of an estate are required. 258. Suppose again that the appointed heir refuses to accept, claiming that the estate is unsound and likely to bring him loss. Here the Pegasian Resolution requires him to accept and to make over if the praetor so decrees, on the petition of the trust beneficiary, and the distribu-

perit[1], actiones dentur, ac iuris esset ex senatus consulto Trebelliano. quo casu nullis stipulationibus opus
est, quia simul et huic, qui restituit, securitas datur,
et actiones hereditariae ei et in eum transferuntur,
qui receperit[2] hereditatem. 259. Nihil autem interest,
utrum aliquis ex asse heres institutus[3] aut totam hereditatem aut pro parte restituere rogetur, an ex parte
heres institutus aut totam eam partem aut partis
partem restituere rogetur. nam et hoc casu de quarta
parte eius partis ratio ex Pegasiano senatus consulto
haberi solet.

260. Potest autem quisque etiam res singulas per
fideicommissum relinquere, uelut fundum, hominem,
uestem[4], argentum, pecuniam, et uel ipsum heredem
rogare, ut alicui restituat, uel legatarium, quamuis a
legatario legari non possit. 261. Item potest non solum propria testatoris res per fideicommissum relinqui,
sed etiam heredis aut legatarii aut cuiuslibet alterius.
itaque et legatarius non solum de ea re rogari potest,
ut eam alicui restituat, quae ei legata sit, sed etiam
de alia, siue ipsius legatarii siue aliena sit. [sed][5] hoc
solum obseruandum est, ne plus quisquam rogetur aliis
restituere, quam ipse ex testamento ceperit; nam |
122 quod amplius est, inutiliter relinquitur. 262. Cum

---

1) recipit hereditatem *Inst.*   2) recepit *Polenaar.*
3) institutus *Inst.* instituatur V.   4) uestem *Inst.* ucteste V.
5) sed *om. Inst.*

---

§ 259. = *I.* 2, 23, 8. *cf. D.* 36, 1, 28 (27), 8 (*Iul.* 569). 36,
1, 46 (44), 1 (*Marcell.* 178). 36, 1, 17 (16), 4 (*Ulp.* 1880). *C.* 6,
49, 2 (*a.* 244).
    § 260. = *I.* 2, 24 *pr. cf. Gai epit.* 2, 7, 1—3. uel legata-
rium] *cf. infra* 2, 271. *Ulp.* 24, 20.
    § 261. = *I.* 2, 24, 1. *cf. Gai epit.* 2, 7, 4; 5. *Ulp.* 25, 5.
Paul. 4, 1, 7; 8. *D.* 30, 114, 3 (*Marcian.* 132).
    § 262. = *I.* 2, 24, 1. *cf. Gai epit.* 2, 7, 6. *Ulp.* 25, 5. *Paul.*
4, 1, 7. *D.* 32, 30, 6 (*Lab. ap. Iav.* 172). 32, 14, 2 (*Gai.* 390).
C. 6, 42, 6, 1 (*a.* 224).

tion of actions is then controlled as though the Trebellian applied. Here there is no need for any stipulations. The trustee is instantly protected; at the same moment the transferee acquires the claims and liabilities belonging to an heir. 259. There is no difference for these purposes between an heir appointed to the whole pound* and asked to make over the whole or part, or an heir appointed to a share and asked to make over that whole share or part of it. In the second case the practice is to apply the Pegasian Resolution in respect of a quarter of that share.

260. It is also possible for specific things to be left on trust, for example, land, a slave, clothes, silver or money. The trust can be imposed on the heir or on a legatee. That is despite the rule that one legacy cannot be grafted on another. 261. It is not only the testator's own property which can be left on trust, but also that of the heir, a legatee, or anyone at all. The legatee can be called upon to transfer not just what the testator leaves him but also something else, something belonging to himself or a third party. The limit to be watched is this: nobody can be subjected to a trust to transfer more than he receives under the will. The disposition is void as to the excess. 262. In a trust of

autem aliena res per fideicommissum relinquitur, necesse est ei, qui rogatus est, aut ipsam[1] redimere et
praestare aut aestimationem *eius* soluere, s*icut iuris
est, si*[2] per damnationem aliena[3] res legata sit. sunt
tamen, qui putant, si rem per fideicommissum relictam
dominus non uendat, extingui fideicommissum; sed
aliam esse causam per damnationem legati.

263. Libertas quoque seruo per fideicommissum dari
potest, ut uel heres rogetur manumittere uel legatarius.
264. N*ec interest, utrum de suo proprio* seruo testator
roget an de eo, qui ipsius heredis aut legatarii uel
etiam extranei sit. 265. Itaque et alienus seruus redimi
et manumitti debet. quòd si dominus eum non uendat,
sane extinguitur fideicommissa libertas, quia hoc *casu*[4]
pretii computatio nulla interuenit. 266. Qui autem ex
fideicommisso manumittitur, non testatoris fit libertus,
etiamsi testatoris seruus *fuerit*[4], sed eius, qui man*u-
mitt*it. 267. At qui directo testamento liber esse iubetur, uelut hoc modo: STICHVS SERVVS *MEVS* LIBER
ESTO, uel hoc: STICHVM SERVVM MEVM LIBERVM
ESSE IVBEO, is *ipsius testat*oris fit libertus. nec alius
ullus directo ex testamento libertatem habere potest,
quam qui utroque tempore testatoris ex iure *Qui-*

---

1) ipsum V.   2) sicut iuris est si *Goeschen.* s * * umi*ri*
* * * es V *ex lectione Bluhmii. cf. apogr.*   3) alienam V.
4) *suppl. Studemund.*

§§ 263—267. = *I.* 2, 24, 2.   *cf. Gai epit.* 2, 7, 7. *Theoph.*
1, 14, 1 (*p.* 65 *sq. Ferr.*).
    § 263. *cf. Ulp.* 25, 18. 2, 7. *Paul.* 4, 12, 4. 4, 13. *D. tit.*
40, 5. *C. tit.* 7, 4. *C. I. L.* X 7457 (= *Bruns* 1[7], 316). XII 4335
(*Dessau* 3789).
    § 264. *cf. supra* 2, 261. *infra* 2, 272. *Ulp.* 2, 10. *D.* 31,
14, 1 (*Paul.* 2091). 32, 8, 1 (*Paul.* 858).
    § 265. *cf. Ulp.* 2, 11. *C.* 7, 4, 6 (*Imp. Alex.*).
    § 266. *cf. Ulp.* 2, 8. *D.* 38, 2, 29 *pr.* (*Marcian.* 139). *C.* 7,
4, 7 (*a.* 225).
    § 267. *cf. Ulp.* 2, 7; 8. 1, 23. *infra* 2, 272. *D.* 40, 4, 35
(*Serv. ap. Paul.* 641). 40, 4, 58 (*Maecian.* 19).

**property belonging to a third party the trustee
must either buy it and hand it over or pay its value,**
as the law stands where a third party's property is left
by an obligatory legacy. Still, some people think that
if the owner will not sell the thing left by a trust the
trust is extinguished, but that the case is different
with an obligatory legacy.

263. **A slave can be given his freedom under a
trust, as where an heir or legatee is called upon to
manumit him. 264. It makes no difference whether
the trust obligation is imposed in relation to the
testator's own slave, the heir's, legatee's, or a
third party's. 265. And so he can have an obligation
to buy and free someone else's slave. Suppose the
owner will not sell.** The freedom given by trust is
certainly nullified because there can be no com-
putation of a price in this case. 266. **A slave freed**
through **a trust does not become the freedman of the
testator but of the person who does the manumission, even if he was the testator's slave.** 267. **By
contrast one made free by the will itself,** like this:
'Let Stichus my slave be free' or: 'I order my slave
Stichus to be free' **does become the testator's
freedman. But the will itself can directly free only
one belonging to the testator** by quiritary right at

ritium fuerit, et quo faceret testamentum et quo more-
retur. |

123 ¹268. Multum autem diff*erunt ea*, quae per fidei
commissum reli*ncuntur*, ab his, quae² directo iure
legantur. 269. Nam ecce per fideicommissum ———
heredis relinqui potest: cum alioquin legatum ———
inutile sit.³ 270. Item intestatus moriturus potest ab
eo, ad quem bona eius pertinent, fidei*commissum* alicui
relinquere; cum alioquin ab eo legari non possit.
270ª. *Item legatum codicillis*⁴ relictum non aliter ualet,
quam si a testatore confirmati fuerint, id est, nisi in
testamento caue*rit* ——— testator, ut quidquid in
codicillis scripserit, id ratum sit; fideicommissum
uero etiam non confirmatis codicillis relinqui potest.
271. Item a legatario legari non potest, sed fideicommissum relinqui potest. quin etiam ab eo quoque,
cui per fideicommissum relinquimus, rursus alii per
fideicommissum relinquere possumus. 272. Item seruo
alieno directo libertas dari non potest, sed per fideicommissum potest. 273. Item codicillis nemo heres
institui⁵ potest neque⁶ exheredari, quamuis testamento

---

1) *praecedunt duae fere lineae vacuae, rubricae destinatae.*
2) qui V? 3) *alii aliter suppleverunt, nemo satis probabiliter.*
post legatum *Studemund legisse sibi visus est:* nisi(?) testamento
facto. 4) item—codicillis *suppl. Goeschen ad epitomen.*
5) instituti V. 6) *in forma* neque *offendit Kalb, Arch. Lexicogr. Lat.* I, 88.

§ 268. cf. *Gai epit.* 2, 7, 8. *infra* 2, 284.
§ 270. cf. *Gai epit.* 2, 7, 8. *Ulp.* 25, 4. *Paul.* 4, 1, 4. *I.*
2, 23, 10. *D.* 5, 2, 13 (*Scaev.* 257). 29, 7, 8, 1 (*Paul.* 895). *C.*
6, 42, 29 (*a.* 294).
§ 270ª. cf. *Gai epit.* 2, 7, 8. *Ulp.* 25, 8. *Paul.* 4, 1, 10.
Consult. 6, 12 (*Diocl. et Maxim. a.* 294, *ex cod. Hermog.*). *I.* 2
25, 1. *Cic. de finib.* 2, 17, 55. *C. I. L.* X 7475 (*Bruns* I⁷, 316).
B G U 326 col. II, 2; 8; 15; 16 (*Bruns* I⁷, 312). *Pap. Hamb.* 72
§ 271. cf. *supra* 2, 260; 261. *Gai epit.* 2, 7, 8. 2, 7, 2. *Ulp.*
24, 20. *I.* 2, 24 *pr.*; 1.
§ 272. cf. *supra* 2, 264; 267. *Gai epit.* 2, 7, 8. *I.* 2, 24, 2.
§ 273. cf. *Gai epit.* 2, 7, 8. *Ulp.* 25, 11. *I.* 2, 25, 2. 2, 23, 10.

**both of two critical times, when the will is made
and when the testator dies.**

268. Now, there is a great difference between trusts
and direct legacies. 269. To start with, a trust can be
left [?without appointment] of an heir; a legacy, on
the other hand, is ineffective [without a will]. 270.
Again, **someone about to die intestate** can impose a
trust in favour of another person which is charged on
the person to whom his estate goes, despite the rule
that he cannot impose **a legacy** on him. 270a. Again, a
legacy left in a codicil* is not valid unless the codicil
has been confirmed by the testator, that is, unless the
testator has provided in his will ... that whatever he
puts in a codicil is ratified; on the other hand, a trust
can be left even by an unconfirmed codicil. 271.
Again, a legacy cannot be imposed on a legatee; but a
trust can. Indeed, when we leave something to
someone by a trust we can in turn impose a trust on
him in favour of someone else. 272. Again, freedom
cannot be given directly to someone else's slave; but it
can by a trust. 273. Again, no one can be appointed
heir or disinherited by a codicil, even if the codicil is

confirmati sint; at is[1], qui testamento heres institutus
est, potest codicillis rogari, ut eam hereditatem alii
totam uel ex parte restituat, quamuis testamento codi-
cilli confirmati non sint. | 274. Item mulier, quae ab 124
eo, qui centum milia[2] aeris census est, per legem Vo-
coniam heres institui[3] non potest, tamen fideicommisso
relictam sibi hereditatem capere potest. 275. Latini
quoque, qui hereditates legataque[4] directo iure lege
Iunia capere prohibentur, ex fideicommisso capere
possunt. 276. Item cum senatus consulto prohibitum
sit proprium seruum minorem annis[5] xxx liberum et
heredem instituere, plerisque placet posse nos iubere
liberum esse, cum annorum xxx erit, et rogare, ut
tunc illi restituatur hereditas. 277. Item quamuis non
possimus[6] post mortem eius, qui nobis heres extiterit,
alium in locum eius heredem instituere, tamen possumus eum rogare, ut, cum morietur, alii eam hereditatem totam uel ex parte restituat; et quia post mor-

---

1) at is] aut his V.   2) mil. V.   3) heres institui
Goeschen. heredes instituti V.   4) legataque] legata quia V.
5) annorum *mavult Cramer; sed verba senatus consulti sequitur
Gaius. cf. V. I. R.* I, 457, 33.   6) *add. Goeschen.*

D. 36, 1, 78 (76) (*Scaev.* 79). 29, 7, 10 (*Pap.* 240). 29, 7, 13, 1
(*Pap.* 279). 28, 5, 78 (77) (*Pap.* 260). 28, 7, 10 (*Ulp.* 147). 28,
7, 27, 1 (*Mod.* 312). *C.* 6, 35, 4 (*a.* 223). 6, 36, 2 (*a.* 244). 6,
23, 14 (*a.* 294). 6, 36, 7 (*a.* 332). 6, 27, 5, 1 d (*a.* 531).
   § 274. *cf. supra* 2, 226. *Paul.* 4, 8, 20 (22). *Polyb.* 32,
14, 8. *Diod.* 31, 27, 7. *Cic. in Verr.* 2, 1, 42, 107 *sq. cum Schol. ed.
Bait. p.* 189. *pro Balb.* 8, 21. *de sen.* 5, 14. *de leg.* 2, 20, 49 *sq. de rep*
3, 10, 17. *de fin.* 2, 17, 55. *Liv. ep.* 41. *Quintil. decl.* 264. *Plin.
paneg.* 42. *Gell.* 6 (7), 13, 3. 17, 6, 1. 20, 1, 23 (*Iurispr.* I, 101).
Plut. Cic. 41. *Dio Cass.* 56, 10, 2. *August. de civ. dei* 3, 21.
   § 275. *cf. supra* 1, 23 *sq.* 2, 110. *Ulp.* 25, 7. 22, 3. *D.* 26,
5, 13 *pr.* (*Pap.* 194). *Fr. Vat.* 259 (*Pap.* 693).
   § 276. *cf. supra* 1, 18; 21. *D.* 40, 7, 13, 5 (*Iul.* 600). 40, 4,
46 (*Pomp.* 825). 34, 5, 29 (30) (*Scaev.* 73). 10, 2 39, 2 (*Scaev.* 223).
40, 4, 38 (*Paul.* 1187). *BGU* 326 (*Bruns* I[7], 312) *l.* 4. 5
   § 277. *cf. supra* 2, 184. *Gai epit.* 2, 7, 8. *BGU* 326 (*Bruns*
I[7], 312).

confirmed by a will. But someone appointed heir by a will can be asked in a codicil to make over the whole or part of the inheritance to someone else, even if the codicil is not confirmed by a will. 274. Again, a woman who, under the Voconian Act, cannot be appointed heir by a testator who is assessed in the census at 100,000 sesterces*, can still take an inheritance left to her by a trust. 275. Also, Latins, who are prohibited from taking inheritances or legacies directly by the Junian Act, can take through a trust. 276. Again, although there is a Senate resolution which prohibits us from freeing one of our own slaves under the age of thirty and appointing him heir, most people accept that we can order him to be free when he is thirty and ask that the inheritance be handed over to him then. 277. Again, although we cannot appoint someone else as heir to take the place of our heir on his death, we can ask our heir to hand over the whole or part of the inheritance to a third party when he dies. And because a trust can be created taking effect after the

tem quoque heredis fideicommissum dari potest, idem
efficere possumus et si ita scripserimus: CVM TITIVS
HERES MEVS MORTVVS ERIT, VOLO HEREDITATEM
MEAM AD PVBLIVM MAEVIVM PERTINERE. utroque
autem modo, tam hoc quam illo, Titius[1] heredem
suum obligatum relinquit[2] de fideicommisso restituendo.[3]
278. Praeterea legata *per*[4] formulam petimus; fideicommissa uero Romae quidem apud consulem uel apud
eum praetorem, qui praecipue de fideicommissis ius
dicit, persequimur, in prouinciis uero apud praesidem
prouinciae. 279. Item de fideicommissis semper | in
urbe ius dicitur, de legatis uero, cum res agun*tur*.
280. Item fideicommissorum usurae et fructus debentur, si modo moram solutionis[5] fecerit, qui fideicommissum debebit; legatorum uero usurae non debentur,
idque rescripto diui Hadriani significatur. scio tamen
Iuliano placuisse in eo legato, quod sinendi modo
relinquitur, idem iuris esse, quod in fideicommissis;
quam sententiam et his temporibus magis optinere
uideo. 281. Item legata Graece scripta non ualent;

125 (margin)

---

1) Titius *Rohrscheidt*. Titium V.　　2) relinquitur V.
3) utroque —restituendo *del. Beseler Beitr.* 4, 110.　　4) *add.*
Goeschen.　　5) *an* solutioni? *cf. Paul.* 5, 5ᵃ, 2.

---

§ 278. *cf. Ulp.* 25, 12. *Paul.* 4, 1, 18. *I.* 2, 23, 1. *D.* 31,
29 *pr.* (*Cels.* 251). 1, 2, 2, 32 *fin.* (*Pomp.* 178). 50, 16, 178, 2
(*Ulp.* 2964). 35, 1, 92 (*Ulp.* 1895). 2, 1, 19 *pr.* (*Ulp.* 1897). 32,
78, 6 (*Paul.* 2078). 40, 13, 4 (*Paul.* 1382). *C.* 8, 17 (18), 2 (*a.* 212).
8, 36, 7 (*a.* 239 *vel* 241). 6, 42, 16, 1 (*a.* 294). *Suet. Claud.* 23.
Quint. inst. or. 3, 6, 70. *C. I. L.* VI 1383. X 1123. 1254 (*Dessau*
1063. 1086. 1179; *cf.* 1050).

§ 279. *cf. D.* 36, 3, 15 *pr.* (*Paul.* 818).

§ 280. *cf. Gai epit.* 2, 7, 8. *Paul.* 3, 8, 4. *D.* 22, 1, 34
(*Ulp.* 530). 30, 39, 1 (*Ulp.* 2619). 35, 1, 92 *i. f.* (*Ulp.* 1895). 36, 3,
1, 13 (*Ulp.* 1727). 36, 4, 5, 21 (*Ulp.* 1255). 50, 10, 5 *pr.* (*Ulp.* 2075).
22, 1, 17, 3 (*Paul.* 2058). 31, 87, 1 (*Paul.* 1562). *C. tit.* 6, 47.

§ 281. *cf. Ulp.* 25, 9. *Paul.* 3, 4ᵃ, 13. *D.* 32, 11 *pr.* (*Ulp.* 1857).
32, 37, 5 (*Scaev.* 68). 32, 101 *pr.* (*Scaev.* 55). 31, 34, 7 (*Mod.* 318).
C. 6, 23, 21, 6 = *Nov. Theod.* 16, 8 (*a.* 439). *C. I. L.* III *suppl.*
12283. 14203, 15 (*Dessau* 7784). *Pap. E. R.* 1502 (*Mitteis,*
Privatr. I, 282, 60). *P. Oxy.* VI, 907. 990. *Gnom. Id. Log.* § 8.

heir's death we can achieve the same effect even by writing: 'When Titius my heir is dead I wish my inheritance to go to Publius Maevius'. Either way, the former and the latter, he leaves his heir Titius under an obligation to hand over the trust. 278. Moreover, we use the formulary procedure* to sue for legacies; for trusts, on the other hand, we use a special judicature*; we pursue our claim in Rome before the consul or before the praetor whose main jurisdiction relates to trusts; in the provinces it is before the governor of the province. 279. Again, in the City, cases concerning trusts are dealt with at all times; those concerning legacies only on business days. 280. Again, interest and fruits are due in respect of trusts if the person under obligation makes delay in performance, while interest is not owed on legacies; this is made known in a written reply of the Emperor Hadrian. All the same, I know that Julian took the view that with a permissive legacy the rule is the same as for trusts; and I see that this view is now gaining currency. 281. Again, legacies written in Greek are invalid, while

fideicommissa uero ualent. 282. Item si legatum per damnationem relictum heres infitietur, in duplum cum eo[1] agitur; fideicommissi uero nomine semper in simplum persecutio est. 283. Item *quod*[2] quisque ex fideicommisso plus debito per errorem soluerit, repetere potest; at[3] id, quod ex causa falsa[4] per damnationem legati plus debito solutum sit, repeti non potest. idem scilicet iuris est de eo legato[5], quod non debitum uel ex hac uel ex illa causa per errorem solutum fuerit.

284. Erant etiam aliae differentiae, quae nunc non sunt. 285. Ut ecce peregrini poterant fideicommissa[6] capere[7], et fere[8] haec[9] fuit origo fideicommissorum.[10] sed postea id prohibitum est, et nunc ex oratione diui[11] Hadriani senatus consultum[12] factum est, ut ea fideicommissa fisco uindicarentur. 286. Caelibes | quo- 126 que, qui per legem Iuliam[13] hereditates legataque capere prohibentur, olim fideicommissa uidebantur[14] capere posse. 286ᵃ. Item orbi, qui per legem Papiam ob id, quod liberos non habent[15], dimidias partes hereditatum[16] legatorumque perdunt, olim solida fideicom-

1) ego V.   2) *add. Goeschen.*   3) ad V.   4) *del. Beseler ZS* 46,268.   5) *del. Savigny; totam sententiam* idem scilicet—fuerit *del. Solazzi, min. età* 293 *sq. improbante Vassallio, Iuris et facti ignor.* 1,36.   6) fidemcommissam V.   7) facere V.   8) ferre V.   9) hac *vel* hae V.   10) fidecommissa V.   11) diui sunt V.   12) consultus V.   13) Iulianas V. Iuliam *alienas Polenaar.*   14) uidebatur V.   15) habebant V.   16) hereditarium V.

§ 282. *cf. Gai epit.* 2, 7, 8. *infra* 4, 9; 171. *Paul.* 1, 19, 1. *I.* 3, 27, 7. 4, 6, 19; 23; 26. 4, 16, 1. *C.* 1, 3, 45, 7 (*a.* 530).

§ 283. *cf. Ulp.* 24, 33. *Paul.* 3, 6, 92. *I.* 3, 27, 7. 2, 20, 25. *D.* 4, 3, 23 (*Gai.* 100). 12, 6, 62 (*Maecian.* 20). 12, 6, 2; 5 (*Ulp.* 2544. 2545). 35, 3, 3, 10 (*Ulp.* 1718). 19, 1, 5, 1 (*Paul.* 1636). 22, 6, 9, 5; 6 (*Paul.* 908). *C.* 6, 50, 9 (*a.* 238). 4, 5, 4 (*a.* 293). 6, 50, 19 (*a.* 532).

§ 284. *cf. supra* 2, 268.

§ 285. *cf. Theoph.* 2, 23, 1 (*p.* 238 *Ferr.*). *Cic. in Verr.* 2, 1, 47, 123. *Plin. ad Trai.* 75 76 (79. 80). *Paus.* 8, 43, 5. *Gnom. Id. Log.* § 18.

§ 286. *cf. supra* 2, 111; 144; 150; 206; 207. *Ulp.* 17, 1. 22, 3. *C. Th.* 8, 16, 1 = *C. I.* 8, 57 (58), 1. *Sozom. h. eccl.* 1, 9 (*p.* 881 *sq. ed. Migne*).

§ 286ᵃ. SC. Pegas.] *cf. supra* 2, 254. *Gnom. Id. Log.* § 27.

trusts are valid. 282. Again, if an heir denies liability for an obligatory legacy, there is an action for double against him; with trusts, on the other hand, the claim is always for the single value. 283. Again, if anyone in error pays more than is due under a trust, it can be recovered; but in the case of an obligatory legacy anything paid beyond what is due, on the basis of a mistake, cannot be recovered. Of course, the law is the same for this kind of legacy if something which is not due at all is paid in error for this or that reason.

284. There used to be other differences which no longer exist. 285. To start with, foreigners could take trusts; this was more or less how they started. But later this was prohibited; and now, following an address* of the Emperor Hadrian, a resolution of the Senate was passed that such trusts should be claimed for the Imperial Treasury. 286. Unmarried persons also, who are prohibited by the Julian Act from taking inheritances and legacies, were formerly regarded as being able to take trusts. 286a. Again, childless people, who lose half their share of inheritances and legacies as a result of the Papian Act because they have no children, were formerly regarded as being

missa uidebantur capere posse. sed postea senatus
consulto Pegasiano proinde fideicommissa quoque ac
legata[1] hereditatesque capere posse[2] prohibiti sunt;
eaque translata sunt ad eos, qui *in eo*[3] testamento liberos habent, aut si nulli[4] liberos habebunt[5], ad populum, sicuti iuris est in legatis et in hereditatibus, quae
eadem aut simili[6] ex causa *caduca fiunt.* 287. *Item*[7]
olim incertae personae uel[8] postumo alieno per fideicommissum relinqui poterat, quamuis neque heres
institui neque legari ei posset.[9] sed senatus consulto,
quod auctore diuo[10] Hadriano factum est, idem[11] in
fideicommissis, quod in legatis hereditatibusque constitutum est. 288. Item poenae nomine iam non dubitatur nec per fideicommissum quidem relinqui posse.

289. Sed quamuis in[12] multis iuris partibus longe
latior causa sit fideicommissorum quam eorum, quae
directo relincuntur, in quibusdam tantundem ualeant[13],
tamen tutor non aliter testamento dari potest quam
directo, ueluti hoc modo: LIBERIS MEIS *TI*TIVS TVTOR[14]
ESTO, uel ita: LIBERIS MEIS TITIVM TVTOREM DO; per
fideicommissum uero dari[15] non potest.

---

1) legatum V.   2) possem V. *del. Beseler ZS* 46, 268.   pro
semisse *Hu.*   3) in eo *add. Polenaar ex* 2, 206.   4) nulli *Savigny,*
Polenaar. nullos V.   5) habebint V.   6) simile V.   7) causa
—item *restituit Polenaar.* cautem V.   8) *num* velut? *cf. supra*
2, 242.   9) possit V.   10) diro V.   11) id V.   12) ui
vel ut V.   13) ualent V.   14) tutores V.   15) uero dari]
dari uero V.

---

§ 287. *cf. Ulp.* 25, 13. *D.* 34, 5, 5 (6); 7 (8) *(Gai.* 392).
34, 5, 4 (5) *(Paul.* 1593). neque heres institui] *cf. supra* 2, 242.
Ulp. 22, 4. *I.* 2, 14, 12.   neque legari] *cf. supra* 2, 238; 241.
   § 288. *cf. supra* 2, 235 *sq.* 243. *Ulp.* 25, 13.
   § 289. *cf. supra* 1, 149. *D.* 26, 2, 33 *(Iav.* 228). 26, 2, 3 *pr*
(Ulp 994). 26, 2, 7 *(Paul.* 1637). 26, 3, 1, 1 *(Mod.* 691).

able to take the whole of a trust. But afterwards the Pegasian Resolution of the Senate prohibited them from taking trusts as well, just like legacies and inheritances. The benefit is transferred to beneficiaries of the will who have children, or if no one has children, to the Roman people, just as is the law for legacies and inheritances which are forfeited for the same or a similar reason. 287. Again, at one time it was possible to leave something through a trust to an unidentifiable person or to a posthumous outsider, although such a person could neither be appointed heir nor left a legacy; but by a resolution of the Senate passed on the proposal of the Emperor Hadrian the same rule was established for trusts as for legacies and inheritances. 288. Again, there is no longer any doubt that nothing can be left by way of penalty, even through a trust.

289. Although in many areas of the law there is much greater scope for trusts than for direct bequests, in certain respects they have the same validity; but a guardian cannot be created by will except directly, for instance: 'Let Titius be guardian to my children', or: 'I make Titius guardian to my children'. A guardian cannot be created through a trust.

1. ¹*Intestatorum hereditates ex² lege* XII *tabularum primum ad suos heredes pertinent.* 2. *Sui autem heredes existimantur liberi, qui in potestate morientis fuerunt, ueluti filius filiaue, nepos neptisue ex filio³, pronepos proneptisue ex nepote filio nato prognatus prognataue. nec interest, utrum⁴ naturales sint⁵ liberi an adoptiui. ita demum tamen nepos neptisue et pronepos proneptisue suorum heredum numero sunt, si praecedens persona desierit in potestate parentis esse, siue morte id acciderit⁶ siue alia ratione, ueluti emancipatione; nam si per id tempus, quo quis⁷ moriatur⁸, filius in potestate*

---

1) "*primum huius commentarii folium deperditum ex Coll. 16, 2, 1—5 et Inst. aliquatenus tantum sarciri potuit: nam suppleta uni fere tantum sufficiunt codicis Veron. paginae et dubium non est, quin primum aliqua praecesserint transitus faciendi gratia. cf. 2, 99; 100. deinde pr. I. h. t. ex Gaio videtur petitum esse. et postremo is more suo praemonuisse putandus est interesse, utrum ingenuus an libertus decesserit. cf. §§ 18. 39. prius se de ingenuorum hereditatibus acturum.* 'Ingenuorum intestatorum' *etc. de siglis vid. ad Coll. notata.*" *ita fere Hu.* 2) ex *Inst.; om. Coll.* 3) ex filio *Inst.; om. Coll.* 4) utrum *Inst.; om. Coll.* 5) sint] sunt *Inst.; om. Coll.* 6) in potestate — acciderit *Inst.; om. Coll.* 7) quis *Inst.* quisque *Coll.* 8) moriatur *Verc.* morietur *BW.* moreretur *Inst.*

---

§ 1. = *I.* 3, 1, 1. *Coll.* 16, 2, 1. *cf. Gai epit.* 2, 8 *pr. Ulp.* 26, 1 (= *Coll.* 16, 4, 1). *Coll.* 16, 3, 3 (*Paul.*). *D.* 28, 2, 9, 2 *i. f.* (*Paul.* 1601). *C.* 6, 55, 4 (*a.* 293). — lege XII tab.] 5, 4.
§ 2. = *I.* 3, 1, 2; 2 b. *Coll.* 16, 2, 2. *cf. supra* 2, 156. *Gai epit., Ulp. ll. cc. Ulp.* 22, 14. *Coll.* 16, 3, 4; 8 (*Paul. Sent.* 4, 8, 4; 8). *D.* 50, 16, 220 *pr.* (*Call.* 108). 38, 16, 1, 2; 4 (*Ulp.* 2512). *C.* 6, 55, 5 (*a.* 293).

BOOK THREE

1. The Twelve Tables* give the estate of an intestate first to his immediate heirs*. 2. The immediate heirs are those in his power* at the time of his death: son or daughter, grandchild by the son, great-grandchild by a grandson through the son. It makes no difference whether they are real or adoptive*. Grandchildren or great-grandchildren only count as immediate heirs if people ahead of them have left the power of the head of the family*. This can happen by death, or for some other reason, like emancipation*. If a man has a son in his power on his death, a

eius sit, nepos ex eo suus heres esse non potest. idem[1]
et in ceteris deinceps liberorum personis dictum intellege-
mus.[2] 3. *Vxor quoque, quae in manu eius, qui mori-*
tur[3], *est, ei*[4] *sua heres est, quia filiae loco est.* item
nurus, quae in filii manu est, nam et haec neptis loco
est. sed ita demum erit sua heres, si[5] filius, cuius in
manu fuerit[6], *cum pater moritur, in potestate eius non*
sit. idemque dicemus[7] et de ea, quae in[8] nepotis manu
matrimonii causa sit, quia proneptis loco est. 4. Postumi
quoque, qui[9] *si uiuo parente nati essent, in potestate*
eius futuri forent, sui heredes sunt. 5. *Idem iuris est*
127 *de*[10] *his, quorum nomine ex lege Aelia Sentia uel ex sena-*
t. s. *tus consulto post |* mortem patris causa probatur: nam
et hi uiuo patre causa probata in potestate eius futuri
essent. 6. Quod etiam de eo filio, qui ex prima se-
cundaue[11] mancipatione[12] post mortem patris manumittitur, intellegemus. 7. Igitur cum filius filiaue et
ex altero filio nepotes neptesue extant, pariter ad
hereditatem uocantur; nec qui gradu proximior est,
ulteriorem excludit. aequum enim uidebatur nepotes
neptesue in patris sui locum portionemque succedere.

---

1) idque *Inst.*   2) intellegemus *Inst.* intellegimus *Coll.*
3) qui moritur *ins. Hu.*   4) ei *Inst.;* is *B.* in *Verc.; om. W.*
5) *om. Coll.*   6) fuerit *Krueger.* eius *Coll.*   7) dicimus *Coll.*
8) in] de *Verc.; om. BW.*   9) *om. Coll.*   10) in *Solazzi.*
11) secundaque V. *Coll.*   12) mancipationem V.

---

§ 3. = *Coll.* 16, 2, 3. *cf. supra* 1, 114; 115b; 118. 2, 139;
159. *Ulp.* 22, 14. 23, 3. 29, 1. *Gell.* 18, 6, 9. *Serv. ad Aen.*
7, 424. *Dionys.* 2, 25.
§ 4. = *I.* 3, 1, 2b *fin. Coll.* 16, 2, 4. *cf. Gai epit.* 2, 8, 1.
Ulp. 22, 15. *C.* 6, 55, 4 (a. 293).
§ 5. = *Coll.* 16, 2, 5. *cf. Coll.* 16, 3, 7; 15 (*Paul. Sent.* 4,
8, 7; 15). *supra* 1, 32. 2, 142 *sq.* 1, 66; 95. *Ulp.* 7, 4.
§ 6. = *Coll.* 16, 2, 6. *cf. Coll.* 16, 3, 7. *Ulp.* 23, 3. *supra*
1, 132. 2, 141.
§§ 7. 8. = *Coll.* 16, 2, 7; 8. *I.* 3, 1, 6. *cf. Gai epit.* 2, 8, 2.
Ulp. 26, 2. *D.* 38, 16, 1, 4—6 (*Ulp.* 2512). *C.* 6, 55, 2 (a. 290).
3 (a. 293).

grandson by that son cannot be an immediate heir. The same applies to other descendants*. 3. A wife in marital subordination* to her husband is also his immediate heir on his death, because she is like a daughter. So, too, is a daughter-in-law in marital subordination to a son, for she is like a granddaughter. But she will be immediate heir only if the son, to whom she is in subordination, is not in his power when the father dies. And the same applies to a woman in marital subordination to a grandson, because she is married to him; she is like a great-granddaughter. 4. **Posthumous children count as immediate heirs if, had the father been alive at their birth, they would have been in his power.** 5. The law is the same for children where a case is proved under the Aelian-Sentian Act or a Senate resolution after the father's death; if the case had been proved in the father's lifetime they too would have been in his power. 6. We are to understand this as applying also to a son who, following a first or second mancipation*, is manumitted after his father's death. 7. **And so, suppose the survivors are a son or daughter and a grandson or granddaughter by the other son. They take equally. The nearer degree does not displace the more remote. Justice required grandchildren to be placed in their father's shoes. The same reasoning**

pari ratione et si nepos neptisue[1] sit ex filio et ex
nepote pronepos *pro*neptisue, simul omnes uocantur ad
hereditatem. 8. Et quia placebat nepotes neptesue,
item pronepotes proneptesue in parentis sui locum
succedere, conueniens esse uisum est non in capita,
sed *in*[2] stirpes hereditatem[3] diuidi, ita ut filius partem dimidiam hereditatis ferat et ex altero filio duo
pluresue nepotes alteram dimidiam, item si ex duobus
filiis nepotes extent et ex altero filio unus forte uel
duo, ex altero tres aut quattuor, ad unum aut ad
duos dimidia pars pertineat et ad tres aut quattuor
altera dimidia.

9. Si nullus sit suorum heredum, tunc hereditas
pertinet | ex eadem lege XII tabularum ad adgnatos.[4]
10. Vocantur autem adgnati, qui legitima cognatione
iuncti sunt. legitima autem cognatio est ea, quae p*er*
*ui*rilis sexus persona*s coniungitur. itaque eodem p*atre*
nati fratres agna*ti sibi sunt, qui etiam consanguinei*
uocantur, nec requiritur, an etiam matrem eandem
habuerint. item patruus fratris filio et inuicem is illi
agnatus est. eodem numero sunt fratres patrueles inter
se, id est qui ex duobus fratribus progenerati sunt,
quos plerique eti*am* consobrinos uocant; qua ratione

(marginal: 128 t. s.)

---

1) neptisue *Coll.* neptisque V. *Inst.*   2) in *Coll. Inst.;*
om. V. 3) hereditatem *W Inst.* hereditates V. 4) gnatos V.

---

§ 9. = *Coll.* 16, 2, 9. *cf. Gai epit.* 2, 8, 3. *I.* 3, 2 *pr.*
Ulp. 26, 1. *Coll.* 16, 3, 13 (*Paul. Sent.* 4, 8, 13). *D.* 38, 16, 1, 9
(*Ulp.* 2513). *C.* 6, 58, 6 (*a.* 293). lege XII tab.] 5, 4. *D.* 50,
16, 195, 1 (*Ulp.* 1203).
  § 10. = *Coll.* 16, 2, 10; *inde a verbis* itaque eodem = *I.*
3, 2, 1 *med. cf. supra* 1, 156. *I.* 3, 2, 1 *in.* 3, 5, 4. *Gai epit.*
2, 8, 3. *Ulp.* 26, 1. *Coll.* 16, 3, 13; 15 (*Paul. Sent.* 4, 8, 13; 15).
16, 6, 1 (*Ulp.* 1926). *D.* 38, 16, 2, 1 (*Ulp.* 2524). 38, 16, 1, 10
(*Ulp.* 2513). 38, 10, 10, 4 (*Paul.* 876). 38, 7, 5 *pr.* (*Mod.* 105).
legitima cognatione] *cf. D.* 23, 2, 12, 4 (*Ulp.* 2688). 38, 10, 4, 2
(*Mod.* 148). consobrinos] *cf. I.* 3, 6, 4. *D.* 38, 10, 1, 6 (*Gai*
200). 38, 10, 10, 15 (*Paul.* 876).

applies if the survivors are a grandson or
granddaughter by one son and a great-grandson or
great-granddaughter by a grandson: they all take
the inheritance equally. 8. Since grandchildren and
great-grandchildren stand in their ascendants'*
places, the estate is correspondingly divided by
stems, not by heads: the son takes half, the two or
more grandsons by the other son take the other
half. If the survivors from two sons are, say, one or
two grandsons from one, and three or four from the
other, a half goes to the one or two, the other half to
the three or four.

9. If there is no immediate heir the same Twelve
Tables give the inheritance to the agnates*. 10.
'Agnates' means relatives with a statutory
relationship, which means in turn a relationship in
the male line. Two brothers born to one father are
agnatically related – they are also called full
agnates – and it is immaterial whether they also
have the same mother. An uncle and his brother's
son are agnatically related to one another. So are
the sons of two brothers, whom most people call
cousins. We could run through many degrees on

scilicet etiam ad plures gradus agnationis peruenire
poterimus. 11. Non tamen omnibus simul agnatis dat
lex XII tabularum hereditatem, sed his, qui¹ tum, cum
certum est aliquem intestatum decessisse, proximo
gradu sunt. 12. Nec in eo iure successio est. ideoque
si agnatus proximus hereditatem omiserit uel, antequam adierit, decesserit, sequentibus nihil iuris ex lege
competit. 13. Ideo autem non mortis tempore quis
*proxim*us fuerit², requirimus, sed eo tempore, quo
certum fuerit aliquem intestatum decessisse, quia si
quis *testamento facto* decesserit, melius esse uisum est
tunc ∗∗∗∗³ requiri proximum, cum certum esse coeperit neminem ex eo testamento fore heredem. 14. Quod
129 ad feminas tamen attinet, in hoc iure aliud in | ipsa-
rum hereditatibus capiendis placuit, aliud in ceterorum [bonis]⁴ ab his capiendis. nam feminarum *hereditate*s proinde ad nos agnationis iure redeunt atque
masculorum, nostrae uero hereditates ad feminas ultra
consanguineorum gradum non pertinent. itaque soror
fratri sororiue legitima heres est, amita uero et fratris
filia legitima heres esse *non potest; sororis autem nobis
loco est*⁵ etiam mater aut nouerca, quae per in manum
conuentionem apud patrem nostrum iura filiae nancta

---

1) quibus V.   2) fuerit *Polenaar*. erit V. *Coll.*
3) *quattuor litterae in* V *non satis certe legi possunt*. an eius?
om. Coll.   4) om. *Coll.*   5) non—est *suppl. ex Coll.*

---

§ 11. = *Coll.* 16, 2, 11. *I.* 3, 2, 1 *fin. cf. Gai epit.* 2, 8, 4.
Coll. 16, 3, 17 (*Paul. Sent.* 4, 8, 17). *I.* 3, 2, 6. 3, 1, 7.
§ 12. = *Coll.* 16, 2, 12. *cf. infra* 3, 22; 28. *Ulp.* 26, 5.
Paul. 4, 8, 21 (23); 24 (26). *I.* 3, 2, 7.
§ 13. = *Coll.* 16, 2, 13. *cf. I.* 3, 2, 6. 3, 1, 7. *D.* 28, 2, 16.
(*Afr.* 25). 38, 16, 1, 8 (*Ulp.* 2512). 38, 16, 2, 5 *sq.* (*Ulp.* 2524).
38, 16, 5 (*Ulp.* 1199). *C.* 6, 11, 1 (*a.* 223).
§ 14. = *Coll.* 16, 2, 14. *infra* 3, 23. *cf. Gai epit.* 2, 8, 5; 6.
Ulp. 26, 6. *Paul.* 4, 8, 22. *Coll.* 16, 3, 16; 20 (*Paul. Sent.* 4, 8, 16;
20). 16, 7, 1 (*Ulp.* 1927). *I.* 3, 2, 3; 3a; 3b. *C.* 6, 58, 4 (*a.* 250).
9 (*a.* 294). 14 (*a.* 531).

the same principle. 11. The Twelve Tables **do not give the estate to them all, only to the closest at the time when intestacy is certain.** 12. And **the right does not pass** from one to the other and so, if the **nearest** agnate does not take up **the inheritance or dies before accepting it, the statute** gives **no right to those who come next.** 13. Now, the reason why we ask who is **nearest,** not at the time of death, but at the time when it becomes certain that there is an intestacy, is that **if someone dies after making a will** it seems better to **ask** who is nearest **once it has become certain that there will be no heir under the will.** 14. But **where women* are concerned,** there is a difference between the law on taking inheritances in succession to them and the law on their succeeding to others. Inheritances of women come to us by agnatic right just like those of men; but our inheritances do not go to women further away in degree than agnatic sisters. And so a sister is statutory heir to her brother or sister, while an aunt or the daughter of a brother cannot be statutory heir. However, a mother or a step-mother who has acquired the rights of a daughter through marital subordination to our father is also like a sister to us. 15. Suppose the survivors of the

est. 15. Si ei, qui defunctus erit, si*t* frater et alterius
fratris filius, sicut ex superioribus intellegitur, frater
prior¹ est, quia gradu praecedit. sed alia facta est
iuris interpretatio inter suos heredes. 16. Quod si defuncti nullus frater extet, *sed*² sint liberi fratrum, ad
omnes quidem hereditas pertinet; sed quaesitum est,
si dispari forte numero sint nati, *uel*ut ex uno unus
uel duo, ex altero tres uel quattuor, utrum in stirpes
diuidenda sit hereditas, sicut inter suos heredes iuris
est, an potius in capita. iam dudum tamen placuit
in capita diuidendam esse hereditatem. itaque quotquot erunt ab utraque parte personae, in tot portiones
hereditas diuidetur, ita ut singuli singulas portiones
ferant.

17. Si nullus agnatus sit, eadem lex XII tabularum
gentiles ad hereditatem uocat.³ qui sint autem gen-
tiles, primo com|mentario rettulimus; et cum illic ad-   130
monuerimus totum gentilicium ius in desuetudinem
abisse, superuacuum est hoc quoque loco de eadem re
*iterum*⁴ curiosius tractare.

18. Hactenus lege XII tabularum finitae sunt intestatorum hereditates. quod ius quemadmodum stric-
tum fuerit, palam est intellegere. 19. Statim enim

---

1) potior *Coll.; cf. etiam Paul. Dig.* 20, 4, 15.   2) *suppl.*
ex Coll.   3) uocant V.   4) iterum *Hugo.* tisi V.

§ 15. ＝ *Coll.* 16, 2, 15. *cf. Gai epit.* 2, 8, 6. *Coll.* 16, 3,
18 (*Paul. Sent.* 4, 8, 18). *I.* 3, 2, 5. superioribus] § 11. alia] § 7.
§ 16. = *Coll.* 16, 2, 16. *cf. Gai epit.* 2, 8, 6. *Ulp.* 26, 4.
Coll. 16, 3, 17; 19 (*Paul. Sent.* 4, 8, 17; 19). *I.* 3, 2, 4. *D.* 38, 16,
2, 2 (*Ulp.* 2524).
§ 17. = *Coll.* 16, 2, 17. *cf. Coll.* 16, 3, 3 (*Paul. Sent.* 4,
8, 3). 16, 4, 2 (*Ulp.*). *Catull.* 68, 123. *Cic. Verr* 2, 1, 45, 115.
de orat. 1, 39, 176. *de domo* 13, 35. *Plin. paneg.* 37. lex XII tab.]
5, 5. *Auct. ad. Herenn.* 1, 13, 23. *Cic. de invent.* 2, 50, 148.
C. I. L. VI 1527 (*Bruns* I⁷, 323) col. I, 22. 24. primo commen-
tario] 1, 164? *cf. supra p.* 44 *not.* 4.
§ 18. *cf. I.* 3, 3 *pr.* 3, 9, 2.
§ 19. *cf. I.* 3, 1, 9. *D.* 37, 1, 6, 1 (*Paul.* 575).

deceased **are a brother and another brother's son**. It
will be clear from what is said above that **the brother**
is preferred because he is nearer in degree but the law
is differently interpreted in the case of immediate
heirs. 16. But if the deceased has no surviving brother
but there are children of brothers, note that the
inheritance goes to all of them; but where it happens
that their numbers are unequal, for instance, one
brother had one or two children and the other three or
four, there was a question whether the inheritance
should be divided by stems, as is the law where
immediate heirs are concerned, or rather by heads.
But it has been settled for some time now that the
inheritance should be divided by heads. And so,
whatever the number of persons on either side, the
inheritance will be divided into the same number of
shares, so that each gets one of the shares.

17. If there are no agnates the same Twelve Tables
give the inheritance to the members of the clan*.
Now, we explained who the members of the clan are in
the first commentary; since we pointed out there that
the whole law relating to the clan has fallen out of use,
it is a waste of time to go into any details here again.

18. Here we come to the end of the provisions of the
Twelve Tables on intestate succession and it is
obvious how restricted that law was. 19. For a start, it

emancipati liberi nullum ius in hereditatem parentis
ex ea lege habent, cum desierint sui heredes esse.
20. Idem iuris est, si ideo liberi non sint in potestate
patris, quia sint cum eo ciuitate Romana[1] donati nec
ab imperatore in potestatem[2] redacti fuerint. 21. Item
agnati kapite deminuti non admittuntur ex ea lege ad
hereditatem, quia nomen agnationis capitis deminutione
perimitur. 22. Item proximo agnato non adeunte hereditatem nihilo magis sequens iure legitimo admittitur.
23. Item feminae agnatae, quaecumque consanguineorum gradum excedunt, nihil iuris ex lege habent.[3]
24. Similiter non admittuntur cognati, qui per feminini sexus personas necessitudine iunguntur, adeo quidem, ut nec inter matrem et filium filiamue ultro
citroque hereditatis capiendae ius conpetat, praeterquam si per in manum conuentionem consanguinitatis
iura inter eos constiterint.[4]

25. Sed hae iuris iniquitates edicto praetoris emen-
131 datae | sunt. 26. Nam eos omnes, qui legitimo iure
deficiuntur, uocat ad hereditatem[5], proinde ac si in
potestate parentis mortis tempore fuissent, siue soli
sint, siue etiam sui heredes, id est qui in potestate

---

1) p m · V.   2) potestate V.   3) habentur V.   4) *sequitur linea vacua in* V.   5) *quaedam excidisse videntur. Polenaar
supplet:* sed liberos quidem emancipatos primo gradu uocat
ad hereditatem. *fortasse melius sic:* ac primo quidem gradu
liberos emancipatos uocat ad hereditatem.

---

§ 20. *cf. supra* 1, 55; 93; 94. 2, 135 a. *Coll.* 16, 7, 2 (*Ulp.* 1927).
§ 21. *cf. I.* 3, 5, 1. *Ulp.* 27, 5. *infra* 3, 27. *supra* 1, 158.
§ 22. *cf. supra* 3, 12. *infra* 3, 28.
§ 23. *cf. supra* 3, 14.
§ 24. *cf. Ulp.* 26, 7; 8. *I.* 3, 3 *pr. supra* 3, 3. *Quintil.
inst. orat.* 4, 2, 5.
§ 25. *cf. I.* 3, 9 *pr.* 3, 9, 2 *fin.* 3, 3 *pr.;* 1 *in.* 3, 1, 9. *D.* 38,
8, 2 (*Gai.* 295). *infra* 3, 41.
§ 26. *cf. supra* 3, 19; 20. *Coll.* 16, 7, 2 (*Ulp.* 1927). *Ulp.*
28, 8. *I.* 3, 1, 9. *D.* 38, 6, 4 (*Paul.* 1627). 37, 1, 6, 1 (*Paul.*
575) 38, 15, 1, 2 (*Mod.* 120). *Cic. Verr.* 2, 1, 44, 114.

gives **emancipated children no claim** to their parents' inheritance, because they are no longer **immediate heirs**. 20. It is the same if children are not in their father's power because they were granted Roman citizenship along with him but the emperor's grant did not bring them into his power. 21. Again, that law does not admit to the inheritance agnates who have suffered status-loss* because status-loss destroys the title of agnate. 22. Again, even if the nearest agnate does not accept the inheritance the next one has no claim by statutory right. 23. Again, female agnates beyond the degree of sisters have no right by statute. 24. Similarly, **cognates*, who are connected through females**, are not admitted; so much so, **in fact, that no right of succession is recognised in either direction even between a mother and her children**, unless where a relationship of consanguinity has been created between them through the mother's marital subordination to the father.

25. But these injustices have been corrected by the praetor's* Edict*. 26. It gives rights of succession to all descendants who have no statutory right, **just as if they were still in power at the time of the death, not only when they are the sole survivors but even when immediate heirs**, that is, descendants still in the father's power, **are in competition** with them. 27.

patris fuerunt, concurrant. 27. Ad*g*natos autem capite
deminutos non secundo gradu post suos heredes uocat,
id est, non eo gradu uocat, quo per legem uocaren-
tur, si kapite minuti non essent, sed tertio proximi-
tatis nomine. licet enim capitis deminutione ius legitimum perdiderint, certe cognationis iura retinent.
itaque si quis alius sit, qui integrum ius agnationis
habebit, is potior erit, etiamsi longiore gradu fuerit.
28. Idem iuris est, ut quidam putant, in eius agnati
persona, qui proximo agnato omittente hereditatem
nihilo magis iure legitimo admittitur; sed sunt, qui
putant hunc eodem gradu a praetore uocari, quo etiam
per legem agnatis hereditas datur. 29. Feminae certe
agnatae, quae consanguineorum gradum excedunt, tertio
gradu uocantur, id est, si neque suus heres neque
agnatus *u*llus erit. 30. Eodem gradu uocantur etiam[1]
eae[2] personae, quae per feminini sexus personas copu-
latae sunt. 31. Liberi quoque, qui in adoptiua familia
sunt, ad naturalium parentum hereditatem hoc eodem
gradu uocantur.[3]

32. Quos autem | praetor uocat ad hereditatem, hi 132

---

1) etiamsi V.   2) heae V.   3) uocatur V.

---

§ 27. *cf. supra* 3, 21. *Gai epit.* 2, 8, 7. *Ulp.* 28, 9. *I.* 3,
5, 1. *supra* 1, 158. *D.* 38, 7, 1 (*Iul.* 409). 38, 8, 5 (*Pomp.* 430).
licet enim] *cf. supra* 3, 21. 1, 158. *I.* 3, 4, 2. *D.* 38, 16, 11
(*Pomp.* 264). 38, 17, 1, 8 (*Ulp.* 2514).

§ 28. *cf. supra* 3, 12; 22. *I.* 3, 2, 7.

§ 29. *cf. supra* 3, 23. *Paul.* 4, 8, 22 a. *D.* 38, 7, 2, 2
(*Ulp.* 1198).

§ 30. *cf. supra* 3, 24. *Ulp.* 28, 9. *Gai epit.* 2, 8, 7. *I.* 3,
5, 2. *D.* 38, 8, 2 (*Gai.* 295). 38, 8, 4 (*Ulp.* 2380). 38, 10, 10, 6
(*Paul.* 876). *B G U* 140 (*Bruns* 1[7], 421). *Pap. Oxy.* 8, 1114.
9, 1201. *ZS* 32, 378 *sq.* (*Meyer, Iur. Pap. nr.* 27).

§ 31. = *I.* 3, 5, 3. *cf. I.* 3, 1, 13. *D.* 38, 8, 1, 4 (*Ulp.* 1201).

§ 32. = *I.* 3, 9, 2 *in.* *cf. Ulp.* 28, 12. *infra* 3, 80. 4, 34;
111. *I.* 4, 12 *pr.* *D.* 5, 5, 2 (*Gai.* 149). 5, 5, 1 (*Ulp* 539). 37,
1, 1 (*Ulp.* 1015). 37, 1, 2 (*Ulp.* 486). 50, 16, 138 (*Paul.* 946).
50, 17, 117 (*Paul.* 202).

However, **agnates who have suffered status-loss qualify**, not in the second class after immediate heirs, that is, not in the class in which they would have qualified by statute if they had not suffered status-loss, but under the **third** category of relationship. Although they have lost their statutory rights through status-loss they certainly retain their cognatic rights. And so anyone with subsisting rights as agnate will be preferred, even if he is more distantly related. 28. Some people think that the same applies to agnates who still get no statutory right even if the nearest agnate fails to accept the inheritance. But others think that the praetor calls them in the same class as agnates who are given statutory rights of succession. 29. Female agnates beyond the degree of sisters certainly qualify in the **third class**, that is, if there is neither an immediate heir nor any male agnate. 30. **Persons related through females** also qualify in this class. 31. **Descendants in adoptive families are also qualified in this class to claim the estates of their real ascendants.**

32. **Note that a person entitled to the estate by the praetor does not become heir by operation of**

heredes ipso¹ quidem iure non fiunt: nam praetor
heredes facere non *potest; per legem enim tantum uel
similem iuris constitutionem* heredes *fiunt*, uelut per
senatus consultum et constitutionem principalem: sed
cum eis praetor dat bonorum possessionem, loco heredum *constituuntur.*²

33. *Adhuc autem etia*m alios conplures gradus *praetor facit in bonorum possessionibus dandis, dum id
agit, ne quis sine successore moriatur.* de quibus in
his commentariis consul*to non agimus, quia* hoc ius
totum³ propriis commentariis *exsecuti sumus.* 33ª. *Hoc*
solum admonuisse sufficit, | ———————— *vv. 3 exceptis fru-
stulis legi nequeunt* ——————— *per* | in man*um conuentio-*
nem iura consanguin*itatis* na|cta⁴ ————————
———————————————— *vv. 10* ————————

133
t. s.
————————————————————————— |⁵ ———————
————————————— *vv. 19* ————————

34. ⁶*Aliquando tamen neque emendandi neque impugnandi ueteris iuris, sed magis confirmandi gratia
pollicetur bonorum possessionem. nam illis quoque*, qui
recte *facto testamento heredes instituti sunt*, dat secun-
134 *dum tabulas bonorum possessionem: item ab in*|testato
heredes suos et agnato*s* ad bonorum possessionem

1) ipse V.   2) *lacunae huius paragraphi suppl. ex Inst.*
3) tutum V.   4) *inde apparet de iure matris hic Gaium
egisse; recte igitur Hu. de SCto Tertulliano cogitavit.*
5) '*initio huius paginae vel paulo post probabile est Gaium
dixisse ex SCto Tertulliano matri non modo b. possessionem, sed
etiam hereditatem competere, eamque b. possessionem adversus
agnatos semper cum re praetorem dare. proinde hanc b. possessionem non modo supplendi, sed etiam impugnandi iuris civilis
causa dari: quod etiam in aliis causis fieri*'. *Hu. cf. Ferrini,
Opere* 1, 98.   6) *suppl. Goeschen ex Inst.*

§ 33. = *I.* 3, 9, 2 *mcd.*
§ 33a. *cf. supra* 3, 24.   *Ulp.* 26, 8.   *I. tit.* 8, 3.   *D.* 34, 5,
θ (10), 1 (*Tryph.* 72).
§ 34. = *I.* 3, 9, 1. *cf. Coll.* 16, 8, 5 *fin.* (*Paul. Sent.* 4, 8, 5). *Pap. Oxy.*
9, 1201.   *Pap. Amh.* 2, 72 (*Bruns* I⁷, 320).   *Meyer, Iur. Pap.
nr.* 27.   suo loco] *cf. infra* 4, 144.

law. The praetor cannot make heirs. That has to be done under statute* or an equivalent source – a resolution of the Senate* or an imperial pronouncement*. But such a person, with estate-possession* from the praetor, is in as good a position as an heir.

33. In pursuit of his policy that the deceased should not be left without a successor, the praetor also enlarges the number of classes qualified to claim. We deliberately do not deal with them in these commentaries because we have covered all this law in those devoted specifically to the subject. 33a. We need to know only one point ... [in the following passage, which is illegible, Gaius probably dealt with a mother's right of succession to her children under the Tertullian Resolution. He may have explained that she not only became successor by state law* but could obtain from the praetor estate-possession which effectively excluded the agnates. This estate-possession would then both improve upon and oppose state law, leading in to what is said in the next paragraph].

34. Some cases of estate-possession are designed to reinforce the old law, not to improve or oppose it. For instance, it is available to heirs validly appointed in the will*. This is estate-possession in support of the will. Again, on intestacy the praetor entitles immediate heirs and agnates to estate-possession. In these cases the sole benefit derived by

uocat. quibus casibus beneficium eius in eo solo uidetur aliquam utilitatem habere, ut is, qui ita bonorum possessionem petit, interdicto, cuius principium est QVORVM BONORVM, uti possit, cuius interdicti quae sit utilitas, suo loco proponemus; alioquin remota quoque bonorum possessione ad eos hereditas pertinet iure ciuili.

35. Ceterum saepe quibusdam ita datur bonorum possessio, ut is, cui data sit, *non* optineat hereditatem; quae bonorum possessio dicitur sine re. 36. Nam si uerbi gratia iure facto testamento heres *institutus* creuerit hereditatem, sed bonorum possessionem secundum tabulas testamenti petere noluerit, contentus eo, quod iure ciuili heres sit, nihilo minus ii, qui nullo facto testamento ad intestati bona uocantur, possunt petere bonorum possessionem; sed sine re ad eos [hereditas][1] pertinet, cum testamento scriptus heres euincere hereditatem possit. 37. Idem iuris est, si intestato aliquo mortuo suus heres nolu*erit* petere *bonorum* possessionem, *contentus legitimo iure*. *nam*[2] et agnato competit quidem bonorum possessio, sed sine re, quia euinci hereditas a[3] suo herede potest. et illud conuenien*ter dice*tur[4]: si ad agnatum iure ciuili pertinet hereditas et is adierit hereditatem, sed[5] bonorum possessionem petere noluerit, et si quis ex proximis cognatis[6] petierit, sine re habebit bonorum possessionem propter eandem rationem. 38. Sunt et alii quidam similes casus, quorum aliquos | superiore commentario tradidimus.[7] 135

---

1) *ut glossema del. Polenaar.*   2) nam *suppl. Hollweg.*
3) ap V.   4) conuenienter dicetur *Goeschen.* conuenientur V.
5) sed si V.   6) cognatus V.   7) *sequitur linea vacua.*

---

§§ 35—37. cf. *Ulp.* 28, 13. 23, 6. 26, 8. *supra* 2, 148; 151a.
§ 38. sup. comm.] 2, 119; 148; 149.

anyone claiming estate-possession in this way is that he has the advantage of using the interdict* beginning 'of whose estate', in Latin 'quorum bonorum'. We shall explain this advantage at the proper place. **Yet if this estate-possession were out of the question, the inheritance would go to the same people by state law.**

35. But often estate-possession is granted in such a way that the person to whom it is given does not keep the inheritance; this estate-possession is said to be provisional. 36. Suppose, for example, that the heir appointed in a properly made will makes formal acceptance* of the estate but prefers not to claim estate-possession in support of the will, being content with the fact that he is heir by state law. Those entitled to the estate on intestacy in the absence of a will can claim estate-possession; but the estate goes to them only provisionally, as the heir appointed in the will can evict them. 37. The same applies if someone dies intestate and his immediate heir prefers not to claim estate-possession, being content with his statutory right. An agnate can certainly claim estate-possession, but provisionally, because he can be evicted from the estate by the immediate heir. And on the same pattern, if an agnate is entitled to the inheritance by state law and accepts it but prefers not to claim estate-possession, if one of the nearest cognates does claim, following the same reasoning he will get provisional estate-possession. 38. There are other similar cases, some of which we explained in the previous commentary.

39. Nunc de libertorum bonis uideamus. **40.** Olim itaque licebat liberto patronum suum *im*pune testamento praeterire. nam ita demum lex XII tabularum ad hereditatem liberti uocabat patro*n*um, si intestatus[1] mortuus esset libertus nullo suo herede *re*licto. itaque intestato quoque mortuo liberto, si is suum heredem reliquerat, nihil in bonis eius patrono iuris erat; et si quidem ex naturalibus liberis aliquem suum heredem reliquisset, nulla uidebatur esse querella; si uero uel adoptiuus filius filiaue uel uxor, quae in manu esset, *suus uel*[2] sua heres esse*t*, aperte ini*qu*um erat nihil iuris patrono superesse. **41.** Qua de causa postea praetoris edicto haec iuris iniquitas emendata[3] est. siue enim faciat testamentum libertus, iubetur ita testari, ut patrono suo partem dimidiam bonorum suorum relinquat[4], et si aut nihil aut minus quam partem dimidiam reliquerit, datur patrono coutra tabulas testamenti partis dimidiae bonorum possessio; si uero intestatus moriatur suo herede relicto adoptiuo filio *uel* uxore, quae in manu ipsius esset, uel nuru[5], quae in manu filii eius fuerit, datur[6] aeque patrono aduersus hos suos heredes partis dimidiae bonorum possessio. 13 prosunt autem liberto ad ex|cludendum patronum naturales liberi, non solum quos in potestate mortis tempore habet, sed etiam emancipati et in adoptionem dati, si modo aliqua ex parte heredes scripti *sint aut praeteriti con*tra tabulas testamenti bonorum possessio-

---

1) intestatis V.   2) suuꞓ uel *suppl. Hu.*   3) emandata V.   4) relinquatur V.   5) nurus V.   6) dat V.

---

§§ 39. 40.˙ = *I.* 3, 7 *pr. cf. Ulp.* 27, 1. 29, 1. *D.* 38, 16, 3 *pr.* (*Ulp.* 2525). lex XII tab.] 5, 8. *cf. Coll.* 16, 8, 2 (*Ulp.* 1928). *D.* 37, 14, 11 (*Ulp.* 2022). *infra* 3, 46; 49; 51. *supra* 1, 165.

§ 41. = *I.* 3, 7, 1. *cf. Ulp.* 29, 1. *D.* 38, 2, 1, 2 (*Ulp.* 1149). 38, 2, 6 *pr.* (*Ulp.* 1153). *Cass. Dio* 51, 15, 7. *Suet. Nero* 32.

39. The next subject is the estates of freedmen*.
40. A patron* could at one time be ignored without penalty in his freedman's will. The Twelve Tables only gave him a claim if the freedman died intestate and without immediate heirs. If a freedman died intestate but with an immediate heir the patron got nothing. There was no cause for complaint if the heir was really the freedman's son or daughter, but it was wrong that an adoptive child or his wife in marital subordination taking as immediate heir should displace the patron's claims.
41. The praetor's Edict later cured this injustice. If the freedman makes a will, he has to leave his patron half his estate. If he leaves nothing or less than half, the patron is entitled to estate-possession counter to the will for his half. If the freedman dies intestate leaving as his immediate heir an adoptive son or a wife who is in subordination to him or a daughter-in-law who is in subordination to his son, the patron is again entitled to estate-possession for a half. Real children suffice to exclude the patron. This is so even if they are emancipated or given in adoption so long as the will makes them heirs or if they obtain estate-possession counter to the will because of their

nem ex edicto petierint; nam exheredati nullo modo
repellunt patronum. 42. Postea lege Papia aucta sunt
iura patronorum, quod ad locupletiores libertos pertinet. cautum est enim ea lege, ut ex bonis eius, qui
sestertium[1] *centum* milibus *amplius* patrimonium reli-
querit et pauciores quam tres liberos habebit, siue is
testamento facto siue intestato mortuus erit, uirilis
pars patrono debeatur; itaque cum unum filium unamue
filiam heredem reliquerit[2] libertus, proinde pars dimidia patrono debetur, ac si sine ullo filio filiaue moreretur; cum uero duos duasue heredes reliquerit, tertia
pars debetur[3]; si tres relinquat, repellitur patronus.
43. In bonis libertinarum nullam iniuriam antiquo iure
patiebantur patroni. cum enim hae in patronorum
legitima tutela essent, non aliter scilicet testamentum
facere poterant quam patrono auctore; itaque siue
auctor ad testamentum faciendum | factus e*rat, aut de*
se queri debebat, quod heres a liberta | relictus *non erat,*
aut ipsum ex testamento, si heres ab ea reli|ctus erat,
sequebatur[4] hereditas. si uero auctor | ei fa*ctus* non
erat et intestata liberta moriebat*ur,* | ad *eundem, quia*
suos heredes femina habere non potest, hereditas per|ti-
nebat[5]: nec enim ullus olim *alius iure ciuili heres erat,*
qui | posset[6] patronum a bonis libe*rtae intestatae*[7] re|pel-
lere. 44. Sed postea lex Papia cum quattuor libero-
rum iure libertinas tutela patronorum liberaret et eo

137
t. s.

---

1) sestertiorum *Inst.* sestertiorum | | | | V?   2) relinque-
rit V.   3) debet V.   4) erat—sequebatur *suppl. Krueger et*
Hu.   5) eundem—pertinebat *suppl. Hu.; cf. infra* 3, 51.
6) posset *Lachmann.* possit V.   7) *suppl. Hu.*

---

§ 42. = *I.* 3, 7, 2. *cf. D.* 37, 14, 16 (*Ulp.* 2020). 35, 3,
1, 14 (*Ulp.* 1711). 50, 16, 145 (*Ulp.* 2021).
§ 43. *cf. Ulp.* 29, 2. *Fr. de iure fisci* 12. *supra* 1, 192.
2, 118; 122.
§ 44. *cf. Ulp.* 29, 3. *supra* 1, 194. *D.* 50, 16, 153 (*Ter.*
Clem. 26). 50, 16, 145 (*Ulp.* 2021). *C. I. L.* VI 1877 (*Dessau*
1910).

omission. But disinherited issue never displace the patron. 42. Since then the Papian Act has enlarged the patron's rights in relation to rich freedmen. It gives **the patron a proportional share in the estate of one who** dies, **testate or intestate, with an estate of 100,000 sesterces* or more, and less than three children. If he** leaves **one son or daughter, the patron thus** takes **his half just as if there had been none; if two, a third; if three, nothing.** 43. Under the old law patrons suffered no injustice where the estates of freedwomen were concerned. As freedwomen were under their patron's statutory guardianship*, they could not make a will except with their patron's authorisation*. And so if a patron was asked to authorise his freedwoman's will it was his own fault if she did not appoint him heir, and if she did appoint him the inheritance followed; if, on the other hand, he did not give his authorisation and the freedwoman died intestate he got the inheritance because a woman cannot have immediate heirs; formerly there was no other heir or estate-possessor who could exclude a patron from the estate of an intestate freedwoman. 44. But later, when the Papian Act released freedwomen with the privilege of four children* from their patron's guardianship and so

modo concederet eis etiam sine tu|toris auctoritate *testa-*
mentum facere, prospexit, | ut pro numero liberor*um,*
quos liberta mortis tempo|re habuerit, uirilis pars patrono
debeatur; ergo ex bonis eius, quae | —————— *vv. 2½ legi*
nequeunt —————— | [1] *heredit*as ad patronum pertinet.

45. Quae diximus de patrono, eadem intellegemus
et de filio patroni, item de ne*pote* ex filio *et de* pro-
nepo*te ex nepote fili*o nato progn*a*to. 46. Filia uero
patroni et *neptis* ex filio et pronep*tis ex* nepote filio
nat*o* progna*ta* olim quide*m habebant idem ius, quod*
lege XII tabularum patrono datum est; praetor *autem*

138   *non nisi uirilis* sexus patronorum libero*s uocat; filia*
t. s.   *uero ut contra tabulas*[2] testa|menti liberti *aut*[3] ab in-
testato contra filium adoptiuum uel uxorem nurumue,
quae in manu fuerit, bonorum possessionem petat,
trium liberorum iure lege Papia consequitur; aliter hoc
ius non habet. 47. Sed ut ex bonis libertae testatae
quattuor liberos habentis uirilis pars ei debeatur, ne
liberorum quidem iure consequitur, ut quidam putant;
sed tamen intestata liberta mortua uerba legis Papiae
faciunt, ut ei uirilis pars debeatur; si uero testamento
facto mortua sit liberta, tale ius ei datur, quale datum
est contra tabulas testamenti liberti, id est, quale et
uirili*s* sexus patronorum liberi contra tabulas testamenti liberti habent, quamuis parum diligenter ea pars
legis scripta sit. 48. Ex *h*is apparet *e*xtraneos heredes patronorum longe remotos *esse* ab om*n*i eo iure,
quod uel in *in*testatorum bonis uel *con*tra tabulas
testamenti patrono competit.

---

1) *cf. apographi supplementum.*   2) praetor — tabulas
suppl. Krueger.   3) *suppl. Hu.*

---

§ 45. *cf. infra* 3, 58. *Ulp.* 29, 4. 27, 1. *I.* 3, 8 *pr. D.* 38,
2, 5 (*Gai.* 288).
§ 46. *cf. Ulp.* 29, 5. 27, 1. *D.* 38, 2, 39 (*Tcr. Clem.* 25).
§ 47. *cf. supra* 3, 44. *C.* 6, 4, 4, 21 (*a.* 531).
§ 48. *cf. infra* 3, 58; 64.

allowed them to make a will even without their guardian's authorisation, it provided that the patron should have a share proportional to the number of children whom the freedwoman had at the time of her death. And so in the case of a freedwoman's estate ... [in the illegible passage which follows, ending with the words 'the inheritance goes to the patron', Gaius evidently gave an example, such as that if a freedwoman left four children the patron got a fifth; if she survived all her children the whole would go to him.]

45. What we have said about patrons, we are to understand as applying to a patron's son as well, and to a grandson by the son and to a great-grandson by a grandson through the son. 46. On the other hand, note that while the daughter of a patron and a granddaughter by a son and a great-granddaughter by a grandson through a son used to have the same rights as a patron has under the Twelve Tables, the praetor admits only male children of the patron; but the right which a daughter with the privilege of three children has to claim estate-possession counter to the will of a freedman or estate-possession on intestacy against an adoptive son or a wife or daughter-in-law who was in marital subordination is given to her under the Papian Act. She has no right otherwise. 47. But some people think that even if she has the privilege of children she does not get a right to a proportional share of the estate of a freedwoman with four children who leaves a will; but if the freedwoman dies intestate the wording of the Papian Act gives her a proportional share. On the other hand, if the freedwoman dies testate the daughter of a patron gets the same right as is available counter to the will of a freedman, that is, the same right as a patron's male children have counter to the will of a freedman; although that part

49. Patronae olim ante legem Papiam hoc solum ius habebant in bonis libertorum, quod etiam patronis *ex* lege XII tabularum datum est. nec enim ut contra tabulas te*sta*menti ingrati liberti uel ab intestato contra filium adoptiuum uel uxorem nurumue bonorum possessionem partis dimidiae peterent, praetor similiter ut de patrono liberisque eius curabat. 50. Sed lex Papia duobus liberis honor*at*ae ingenuae patronae, | libertinae tribus eadem fere iura dedit, quae ex edicto 139 praetoris patroni habent; trium uero liberorum iure honoratae ingenuae patronae ea iura dedit, quae per eandem legem patrono data sunt; libertinae autem patronae non idem iuris praestitit. 51. Quod autem ad libertinarum bona pertinet, si quidem intestatae decesserint, nihil noui patronae liberis honoratae lex Papia praestat; itaque si neque ipsa patrona neque liberta kapite deminuta sit, ex lege XII tabularum ad eam hereditas pertinet, et excluduntur libertae liberi; quod iuris est, etiam si liberis honorata non sit patrona; numquam enim, sicut supra diximus, feminae suum heredem habere possunt. si uero uel huius uel illius kapitis deminutio interueniat, rursus liberi libertae excludunt patronam, quia legitimo iure kapitis deminutione *p*erempto euenit, ut liberi libertae cognationis iure potiores habeantur.[1] 52. Cum autem testamento facto moritur liberta, ea quidem patrona, quae liberis *h*onorata non est, nihil iuris habet contra libertae testamentum; ei[2] uero, quae liberis honorata sit, hoc ius tribuitur per legem Papiam, quod habet ex edicto patronus contra tabulas liberti.

---

1) habeant V.   2) ea V.

§§ 49. 50. *cf. Ulp.* 29, 5; 6. 27, 1. *D.* 38, 2, 17 (*Ulp.* 1205). *Coll.* 16, 8, 2 (*Ulp.* 1928).

§ 51. *cf. Ulp.* 27, 5. *I.* 3, 4, 2. *supra* 1, 158. sicut supra dix.] *supra* 3, 43. *cf.* 2, 161. 1, 104. *Ulp.* 26, 7. *D.* 38, 16, 13 (*Gai.* 460). 37, 4, 4, 2 (*Paul.* 578).

§ 52. *cf. supra* 3, 47. *Ulp.* 29, 7.

of the Act has not been drafted with sufficient care.
48. From what has been said it is apparent that a
patron's outside heirs* are far from having any of the
rights which a patron has either in the estate of an
intestate freedman or counter to his will.

49. At one time, before the Papian Act, the rights of
a patroness in the estates of her freedmen were
restricted to the rights given to patrons by the Twelve
Tables. The praetor did not make the same provision
for her as he did for a patron and his children, in
allowing them to claim estate-possession for a
half-share counter to the will of an ungrateful
freedman or on intestacy against an adoptive son or a
wife or a daughter-in-law. 50. But the Papian Act gave
a freeborn patroness with the distinction of having
two children, and a freed patroness with three
children, almost the same rights as patrons have
under the praetor's Edict. But while it gave a freeborn
patroness with the privilege of three children the same
rights as a patron is given by that Act it did not do the
same for a freed patroness. 51. Where the estates of
freedwomen are concerned, however, note that the
Papian Act gives no new rights to a patroness with
children if the freedwoman dies intestate. And so if
neither the patroness herself nor the freedwoman has
suffered status-loss, the inheritance goes to the
patroness under the Twelve Tables and the
freedwoman's children are excluded. This is the law
even if the patroness has no children; for, as we have
said above, women can never have immediate heirs.
But if one or other has suffered status-loss the
children of the freedwoman now exclude the patroness
because when her statutory right is taken away by her
status-loss the result is that the freedwoman's
children are preferred, as being cognates. 52.
However, when a freedwoman dies testate, note that a

53. Eadem lex patronae filio liberis honorato ∗ ∗ ∗[1]
patroni[2] iura dedit; sed in huius persona etiam unius |
140 filii filiaeue ius sufficit.

54. Hactenus omnia iura quasi per indicem tetigisse satis est. alioquin diligentior interpretatio propriis commentariis exposita est.[3]

55. Sequitur, ut de bonis Latinorum libertinorum
dispiciamus. 56. Quae pars iuris ut manifestior fiat,
admonendi sumus, id quod alio loco diximus, eos, qui
nunc Latini Iuniani dicuntur, olim ex iure Quiritium
seruos fuisse, sed auxilio praetoris in libertatis forma[4]
seruari solitos; unde etiam res eorum peculii iure ad
patronos pertinere solita est.[5] postea uero per legem
Iuniam eos omnes, quos praetor in libertate[6] tuebatur,
liberos esse coepisse et appellatos esse Latinos Iunianos: Latinos ideo, quia lex eos liberos proinde[7] esse
uoluit, atque si essent ciues Romani ingenui, qui ex
urbe Roma in Latinas colonias deducti Latini colo-
niarii esse coeperunt; Iunianos ideo, quia per legem
Iuniam liberi facti sunt, etiamsi non essent ciues Romani. legis itaque Iuniae lator cum intellegeret futurum, ut ea fictione res Latinorum defunctorum ad patronos pertinere desinerent, quia scilicet neque ut serui
decederent, ut possent iure peculii res eorum ad pa-
141 tronos pertinere, neque | liberti Latini hominis bona[8]
possent manumissionis iure ad patronos pertinere,

---

1) cre? V. fere *Krueger.* fere omnia *Polenaar.*   2) patronae *Goudsmit.*   3) *in* V *sequitur linea vacua.*   4) formam V.
5) solita est] solitae sunt *Hu.*   6) libertatem V.   7) perinde V.   8) b p (*i. e.* bonorum possessio) V

---

§ 53. *cf. D.* 50, 16, 148; 149 (*Gai.* 459. 461). 38, 2, 42 *pr.*
(*Pap.* 223). 38, 2, 18 (*Paul.* 601).

§ 54. propriis commentariis] *libris ad legem Iuliam et
Papiam?*

§ 56. *cf. I.* 3, 7, 4. *Dosith.* 5. 6. *Ulp.* 1, 10. *C.* 7, 6, 1 *pr.*
(*a.* 531). *cf. lex Salp. c.* 23 (*Bruns* I⁷, 144). *Gnom. Id. Log.* § 22.
alio loco] *supra* 1, 22.

patroness with no children has no right counter to the freedwoman's will; by the Papian Act, on the other hand, one who has children is granted the right which a patron has under the Edict counter to the will of a freedman.

53. The same Act gave to a patroness's son with children [almost] the same rights as a patron; but in this case even one son or one daughter is sufficient.

54. So far it has been enough to touch on all the various rights, drawing attention to them as it were; besides, there is a more careful discussion in the commentaries specifically dealing with them.

55. Next, we must look at the estates of Latin* freedmen. 56. And to make this area of the law easier to grasp, we must remember what was said elsewhere, that the people who are now called Junian Latins at one time were slaves by quiritary law*, although they were normally kept in a state of liberty with the praetor's assistance; and so their property also normally went to their patrons as being a slave's personal fund*. Subsequently, however, as a result of the Junian Act, all those whose liberty the praetor protected came to be free and were called Junian Latins: Latins, because the Act intended them to have their freedom exactly as if they were freeborn Roman citizens who came to be colonial Latins through emigration from the City of Rome to Latin colonies; Junian, because they were made free by the Junian Act, even though they were not to be Roman citizens. That being so, the draftsman of the Junian Act realised that the result of this fiction would be that the property of deceased Latins would cease to go to their patrons. They did not die as slaves and so their property could not go to their patrons by virtue of being a slave's personal fund; and the estate of a freed Latin could not go to his patron by virtue of his manumission. So that the benefit given to Latins

necessarium existimauit, ne beneficium istis datum in
iniuriam patronorum conuerteretur, cauere [uoluit][1],
ut bona eorum proinde ad manumissores pertinerent,
ac si lex lata non esset. itaque iure quodam modo
peculii bona Latinorum ad manumissores ea lege pertinent. 57. Unde accidit, ut longe differant ea iura,
quae in bonis Latinorum ex lege Iunia constituta sunt,
ab his, quae in hereditate[2] ciuium Romanorum libertorum obseruantur. 58. Nam ciuis Romani liberti
hereditas ad extraneos heredes patroni nullo modo
pertinet; ad filium autem patroni nepotesque ex filio
et pronepotes ex nepote *filio nato*[3] prognatos omni
modo pertinet, etiamsi·a parente fuerint exheredati;
Latinorum autem bona tamquam peculia seruorum
etiam ad extraneos heredes pertinent et ad liberos
manumissoris exheredatos non pertinent. 59. Item
ciuis Romani liberti[4] hereditas ad duos pluresue patronos aequaliter pertinet, licet dispar in eo seruo dominium habuerint; bona uero Latinorum pro ea parte
pertinent, pro qua parte quisque eorum dominus fueri*t*.
60. Item in hereditate ciuis Romani liberti patronus
alterius patroni filium excludit[5], et filius patroni alte-
rius patroni nepotem repellit; bona autem La|tinorum 142
et ad ipsum patronum et ad *a*lterius patroni heredem
simul pertinent, pro qua parte ad ipsum manumissorem pertinerent. 61. Item si unius patroni tres forte
liberi sunt et alterius unus, hereditas ciuis Romani

---

1) uoluit *del. Lachmann.*   2) hereditatem V.   3) filio
nato *add. Lachmann.*   4) ciuis Romani liberti *Goeschen.*
scrib. V.   5) excluditur V.

---

§ 58. *cf. supra* 3, 45—48. 2, 155. *D.* 37, 14, 9 *pr.* (*Mod.*
261). *Plin. ad Trai.* 104 (105).
    § 59. *cf. C.* 6, 4, 4, 19 (*a.* 531). *D.* 38, 2, 34 (*Iav.* 16).
    § 60. *cf. Ulp.* 27, 2; 3. *Paul.* 3, 2, 1. *D.* 38, 2, 23, 1 (*Iul.*
414). *C.* 6, 4, 4, 19 a (*a.* 531). *I.* 3, 7, 3.
    § 61. *cf. Ulp.* 27, 4. *Paul.* 3, 2, 3. *D.* 38, 2, 23, 2 (*Iul.*
414). *C.* 6, 4, 4, 19 b (*a.* 531). *I.* 3, 7, 3.

should not rebound to the prejudice of their patrons, therefore, he considered it necessary to provide that their estates should go to the persons who manumitted them as if the Act had not been passed; and so by this Act the estates of Latins go to those who manumit them, in a certain sense as being a slave's personal fund. 57. And this is why the rights created in the estates of Latins by the Junian Act are far different from those which are recognised in the inheritances of freed Roman citizens. 58. The inheritance of a freed Roman citizen never goes to his patron's outside heirs; it always goes to the patron's son and grandsons by a son and great-grandsons by a grandson through a son, even though they have been disinherited by their father. But the estates of Latins, like the personal funds of slaves, go even to outside heirs and do not go to the disinherited children of the person who manumitted them. 59. Again, the inheritance of a freed Roman citizen goes to two or more patrons in equal shares, although they did not share ownership of the slave equally; estates of Latins, on the other hand, go to the patrons in proportion to their shares of ownership. 60. Again, in the case of the inheritance of a freed Roman citizen, a patron excludes the son of another patron and the son of one patron keeps out the grandson of another patron; the estates of Latins, however, go at the same time to the one patron and to the heir of the other in proportion to the share held by the person who manumitted them. 61. Again, suppose that one patron has, say, three children and the other has one, the inheritance of a freed Roman citizen is divided by heads, that is, the

liberti in capita diuiditur, id est tres fratres tres portiones ferunt et unus quartam[1]; bona uero Latinorum
pro ea parte ad successores pertinent, pro qua parte
ad ipsum manumissorem pertinerent. 62. Item si
alter ex [is] patronis suam partem in hereditate[2] ciuis
Romani liberti spernat uel ante moriatur, quam cernat,
tota hereditas ad alterum pertinet; bona autem Latini
pro parte deficientis[3] patroni caduca fiunt et ad populum pertinent.

63. Postea Lupo et Largo consulibus senatus censuit, ut bona Latinorum primum ad eum pertinerent,
qui eos liberasset; deinde ad liberos eorum non nominatim exheredatos, uti quisque proximus esset; tunc
antiquo iure ad heredes eorum, qui liberassent, pertinerent. 64. Quo senatus consulto[4] quidam *id*[5] actum
esse putant, ut in bonis Latinorum eodem iure utamur, quo utimur in hereditate ciuium Romanorum
libertinorum. idque[6] maxime Pegaso placuit; quae
sententia aperte falsa est. nam ciuis Romani liberti
143 hereditas numquam ad extraneos patroni heredes | pertinet; bona autem Latinorum etiam[7] ex hoc ipso senatus consulto non obstantibus liberis manumissoris
etiam[8] ad extraneos heredes pertinent. item in hereditate[2] ciuis Romani liberti liberis manumissoris nulla
exheredatio nocet, in bonis Latinorum nocere nominatim factam exheredationem ipso senatus consulto

---

1) quarta V.   2) hereditatem V.   3) deficientis
Goeschen. decedentis V.   4) quo senatus consulto *Goeschen.*
quod sc. V.   5) *add. Goeschen.*   6) idque *Goeschen.* idemque V.   7) '*h. e. non tantum antiquo iure, sed etiam*'. Hu.
8) '*h. e. non tantum ad liberos, sed etiam*'. Hu.

---

§ 62. *cf. C.* 6, 4, 4, 19 c (*a.* 531). *Paul.* 3, 2, 2. *supra* 2,
150; 189.
   § 63. *cf. I.* 3, 7, 4. *C.* 7, 6, 1, 1 a; 12 a (*a.* 531). *Nov.* 78
praef.   Lupo et Largo] *a.* 42 *p. Chr.*
   § 64. *cf. supra* 3, 48; 58. *D.* 38, 2, 40 (*Ter. Clem.* 27).
I. 3, 7, 4.

three brothers take three shares and the one child takes the fourth; the estates of Latins, on the other hand, go to their successors in proportion to the share held by the person who manumitted them. 62. Again, if one patron rejects his share of the inheritance of a freed Roman citizen or dies before he can solemnly declare his acceptance, the whole inheritance goes to the other; the estate of a Latin, however, is forfeited in respect of the share of the patron who does not come in, and it goes to the Roman people.

63. Later, when Lupus and Largus were consuls, the Senate resolved that the estates of Latins should go in the first place to the person who freed them; then to his descendants not specifically disinherited, starting with the nearest; then, under the old law, to the heirs of the persons who freed them. 64. Some people think that the effect of this resolution is that we apply the same law to the estates of Latins as we apply to the inheritances of freed Roman citizens; Pegasus in particular took this view. This opinion is clearly wrong. The inheritance of a freed Roman citizen never goes to his patron's outside heirs, while by this Senate resolution the estates of Latins do go to outside heirs in the absence of descendants of the person who manumitted them. Again, where the inheritance of a freed Roman citizen is concerned, disinheriting the descendants of the person who manumitted him never deprives them of their rights; the resolution of the Senate states that if they are specifically disinherited they do lose their rights in the estates of Latins. And

significatur. uerius est ergo hoc solum eo senatus
consulto actum esse, ut manumissoris liberi, qui nominatim exheredati non sint, praeferantur extraneis heredibus. 65. Itaque emancipatus filius patroni praeteritus, quamuis contra tabulas testamenti parentis sui
bonorum possessionem non petierit, tam*en* extraneis
heredibus in bonis Latinorum poti*or* habetur. 66. Item
filia ceterique sui heredes licet iure ciuili inter ceteros
exheredati sint et[1] ab omni hereditate patris sui sum-
moueantur, tamen in bonis Latinorum, nisi nominatim
a parente fuerint exheredati[2], potiores erunt extraneis
heredibus. 67. Item ad liberos, qui ab hereditate parentis se abstinuerunt, *nihilo minus tamen*[3] *bona* Latinorum pertinent; *scilicet quia* exheredati nullo modo
dici possunt, non magis quam qui testamento silentio
praeteriti sunt. 68. Ex *h*is omnibus satis illud apparet, si is, qui Latinum fecerit, ——————————————
—————— | —————— *vv. 21 exceptis frustulis legi nequeunt* 144
—————— | 69. Item illud quoque constare uidetur, si
solos liberos ex disparibus partibus patron*us* | ———
vv. 1⅓ legi nequeunt —————— |[4] tant, ad eos pertinere, quia 145
nullo interueniente extraneo herede senatus consulto
locus non est. 70. Sed[5] si cum liberis suis etiam ex-
traneum heredem patronus reliquerit, Caelius[6] Sabinus
ait tota bona pro uirilibus partibus ad liberos defuncti pertinere, quia cum extraneus heres[7] interuenit,
non habet lex Iunia locum, sed senatus consultum;
Iauolenus autem ait tantum eam partem ex senatus
consulto liberos patroni pro uirilibus partibus habitu-

---

1) sint et *del. Polenaar.*   2) exhereditati V.   3) nihilo minus *add. Lachmann.* tamen *add. Hu.*   4) *Krueger
exempli causa supplet:* heredes instituerit, ex isdem partibus
bona Latini, si patri heredes exis|tant.   5) ei V.   6) se-
lius V.   7) extraneos *heres correctum ex* extraneos heredes V.

---

§ 66. *cf. supra* 2, 132.
§ 67. *cf. supra* 2, 158.

so the better view is that the only effect of this resolution is to prefer the descendants of the person who manumitted the Latin to the outside heirs if they have not been specifically disinherited. 65. And so, if an emancipated son of a patron is passed over, even if he does not claim estate-possession counter to his parent's will, he still has a stronger claim to the estates of Latins than have outside heirs. 66. Again, even if daughters or other immediate heirs are disinherited by a general clause under the state law and are wholly excluded from the father's inheritance, they still have a stronger claim to the estates of Latins than outside heirs, unless they are specifically disinherited. 67. Again, the estates of Latins go to descendants who have not taken up their parent's inheritance; they can no more be said to have been disinherited than anyone passed over in silence in the will.

68. From all of this it is clear enough that a person who has made someone a Latin ... [in the following lines only a few words here and there can be read. Gaius seems to have continued his discussion and dealt with points which were settled or open to question, as in the following paragraphs.] 69. Again, it also seems to be settled that, if a patron appoints as heirs, in unequal shares, descendants only and they become their father's heirs, [the estates of Latins go to them in those same shares,] because there is no room for the Senate resolution where no outside heir is involved. 70. But if a patron appoints an outside heir along with his descendants, Caelius Sabinus says that the whole estate goes to the descendants of the deceased in proportional shares; as an outside heir is involved it is not the Junian Act which applies but the Senate resolution. Javolenus, however, says that the Senate resolution will give the patron's descendants proportional shares only of the share which the

ros esse, quam extranei heredes ante senatus consultum lege Iunia habituri essent, reliquas uero partes
pro hereditariis partibus ad eos pertinere. 71. Item
quaeritur, an hoc senatus consultum ad eos patroni
liberos pertineat, qui ex filia nepteue procreantur, id
est, ut nepos meus ex filia potior sit in bonis Latini
mei quam extraneus heres; item *an* ad maternos Latinos hoc senatus consultum pertineat, quaeritur, id
est, ut in bonis Latini materni potior sit patronae
filius quam heres extraneus matris. Cassio placuit
utroque casu locum esse senatus consulto; sed huius
sententiam plerique inprobant, quia senatus de his
liberis patronorum[1] nihil sentiat, qui aliam familiam
sequerentur; idque ex eo adparere[2], quod nominatim
exheredatos summoueat; nam uidetur de his sentire,
qui exheredari a parente solent, si heredes non instituantur; neque autem matri filium filiamue neque
146 auo | materno nepotem neptemue, si eum eamue here-
dem non instituat, exheredare necesse est, siue de iure
ciuili quaeramus siue de[3] edicto praetoris, quo prae-
teritis liberis contra tabulas testamenti bonorum possessio promittitur.

72. Aliquando tamen ciuis Romanus libertus tamquam Latinus moritur, uelut si Latinus saluo iure
patroni ab imperatore ius Quiritium consecutus fuerit.
nam, ut diuus Traianus constituit, si Latinus inuito uel
ignorante patrono ius Quiritium ab imperatore consecutus sit, [quibus casibus][4], dum uiuit iste libertus,
ceteris ciuibus Romanis libertis similis est et iustos
liberos procreat, moritur autem Latini iure, nec ei

---

1) patronorum *Hu. ed. 4.* patronarum V.   2) adparere
Polenaar. adparet V.   3) de ex V.   4) quibus casibus
del. Mommsen; cf. supra 2, 144.

---

§ 72. *cf. I.* 3, 7, 4. *C.* 7, 6, 1, 1 a; 12 a (*a.* 531). *Plin. ad
Trai.* 5, 2. 11, 2. 104 (105).

outside heirs would have had under the Junian Act before the Senate resolution was passed; they will get the remaining shares in proportion to their shares of the inheritance. 71. There are other questions: does the Senate resolution relate to descendants of a patron by a daughter or a granddaughter? That is, does my grandson by my daughter have a stronger claim on my Latin's estate than an outside heir? Does this resolution relate to maternal Latins? That is, does the son of a patroness have a stronger claim on his maternal Latin's estate than his mother's outside heir? Cassius held that the resolution applied in both cases. But most people reject his opinion because the Senate is not thinking of descendants of patrons who are in another family. This appears from the fact that it excludes those specifically disinherited; it appears to be thinking of those who normally are disinherited by a parent if they are not appointed as heirs. But whether we think of state law or the praetor's Edict promising estate-possession counter to the will to children who are passed over, there is no necessity for a mother to disinherit her son or daughter nor for a maternal grandfather to disinherit his grandson or granddaughter if either fails to appoint the child as heir.

72. All the same, sometimes a freed Roman citizen at death is treated as if he were a Latin, for instance, if a Latin obtains quiritary right from the Emperor without prejudice to the right of his patron. There is a pronouncement of the Emperor* Trajan to the effect that, if a Latin obtains quiritary right from the emperor against the wishes or without the knowledge of his patron, he is in the same position as other freed Roman citizens during his lifetime and his children are legitimate, but he dies as a Latin and his children

liberi eius heredes *esse* possunt; et in hoc tantum habet testamenti factionem, ut[1] patronum heredem instituat eique[2], si heres esse noluerit, alium substituere possit. 73. Et quia hac constitutione uidebatur effectum, ut ne umquam isti homines tamquam ciues Romani morerentur, quamuis eo iure postea usi[3] essent, quo uel ex lege Aelia Sentia[4] uel ex senatus consulto ciues Romani essent, diuus Hadrianus iniquitate rei motus auctor fuit senatus consulti faciundi[5], ut qui ignorante uel recusante patrono ab imperatore ius Quiritium consecuti essent, si eo iure postea usi essent, quo ex lege Aelia Sentia uel ex senatus consulto, si Latini mansissent[6], ciuitatem Romanam consequerentur, proinde ipsi haberentur, ac si lege Aelia Sentia uel senatus consulto ad ciuitatem Romanam peruenissent. |

74. Eorum autem, quos lex Aelia Sentia dediti- 147 ciorum numero facit, bona modo quasi ciuium Romanorum libertorum[7] modo quasi Latinorum ad patronos pertinent. 75. Nam eorum bona, qui si *in* aliquo uitio non essent, manumissi ciues Romani futuri essent, quasi ciuium Romanorum patronis eadem lege tribuuntur. non tamen hi habent etiam testamenti factionem. nam id plerisque placuit, nec inmerito. nam incredibile uidebatur pessimae condicionis hominibus uoluisse legis latorem testamenti faciundi ius concedere.[8] 76. Eorum uero bona, qui si non in aliquo uitio essent, manumissi futuri Latini essent, proinde

---

1) aut V.   2) ei qui V.   3) ut si V.   4) Aelia Sentia *Goeschen.* x̄ s̄ V.   5) senatus consulti paciundi V. senatui censendi *Solazzi.*   6) mansissent *Goeschen.* manumissi essent V. 7) ciuium Romanorum libertorum *Goeschen.* s̄c̄. libustorum V 8) §§ 74—76 *del. Beseler Z. S.* 47, 356, *immemor Gnomonis Id. Log.* § 20.

---

§ 73. *cf. supra* 1, 29 *sq.*; 66 *sq.*; 69 *sq.*
§ 74. *cf. supra* 1, 13 *sq. Gnom. Id. Log.* § 20
§ 75. *cf. supra* 1, 25; 26. *Ulp.* 20, 14; 15.
§ 76. *cf. Ulp.* 1, 16.

cannot be his heirs; his testamentary capacity is limited to appointing his patron as heir and substituting someone else to his patron if he rejects the inheritance. 73. This pronouncement seemed to mean that such men would never have the rights of Roman citizens at death, even though they later took advantage of the Aelian-Sentian Act or a Senate resolution in order to become citizens. The Emperor Hadrian, moved by the inequity of the situation, proposed a Senate resolution to the effect that anyone obtaining quiritary right from the Emperor unknown to or against the objection of his patron, and later taking advantage of the Aelian-Sentian Act or a Senate resolution which would have allowed him to become a citizen if he had remained a Latin, should be treated as if he had attained Roman citizenship under the Aelian-Sentian Act or the resolution.

74. Now, the estates of those whom the Aelian-Sentian Act counts among capitulated aliens* sometimes go to their patrons as if they were freed Roman citizens and sometimes as if they were Latins. 75. That law gives to their patrons the estates of those who would have been citizens on manumission if there were not some blot on their characters, just as if they were Roman citizens. But even these do not have the capacity to make a will. That is what most people accept, with some justice; it seemed incredible that the legislator intended men of the lowest condition to be conceded the right to make a will. 76. On the other hand, the estates of those who would have been Latins if there were not some blot on their character, are

tribuuntur patronis, ac si Latini[1] decessissent. nec me
praeterit non satis in ea re legis latorem[2] uoluntatem
suam uerbis expres*sisse*.

77. Videamus autem et de *ea* successione, quae
nobis ex emptione bonorum[3] competit. 78. Bona autem
ueneunt aut uiuorum aut mortuorum: uiuorum, uelut
eorum, qui fraudationis causa latitant nec absentes[4]
defenduntur; item eorum, qui ex lege Iulia bonis ce-
dunt; item iudicatorum post tempus, quod eis partim[5]
lege XII tabularum, partim edicto praetoris ad expe-
diendam pecuniam tribuitur. mortuorum bona ueneunt
uelut eorum, quibus certum est neque heredes neque
148 bonorum possessores neque ullum alium | iustum suc-
cessorem existere. 79. *Et* si quidem uiui bona ueneant, iubet ea praetor per dies continuos XXX possideri

---

1) Latinis V.   2) legatorem V.   3) bonarum V.
4) nec absentes] *desideratur* aut absentes non; *fortasse quaedam exciderunt, ut Gaius sic fere scripserit:* nec defenduntur;
item eorum qui absentes non.   5) eis partim *Goeschen.*
eius parti V.

---

§ 77. *cf. supra* 2, 98. *I.* 3, 12 *pr. cum Theoph.* (*p.* 314 *sq.
Ferr.*).
§ 78. uiuorum] *cf. infra* 3, 154. qui fraud. c. lat.] *cf. Cic.
pro Quinct.* 19, 60. 23, 74. *Prob. Einsidl.* 66 (*Iurispr.* I, 91). *D.* 15,
1, 50 *pr.* (*Pap.* 158). 4, 6, 21, 2 (*Ulp.* 434) 42, 4, 7, 1 (*Ulp.* 1390).
42, 5, 36 (*Ulp.* 2922). 2, 4, 19 (*Paul.* 89). *C.* 7, 72, 9 (*a.* 299).
nec abs. defend.] *cf. Cic. pro Quinct.* 19, 60. 23, 74. *D.* 42, 5, 5
(*Ulp.* 1394). 3, 5, 1 (*Ulp.* 346). 4, 6, 21, 2 (*Ulp.* 434). *cf. etiam
D.* 3, 4, 1, 2 (*Gai.* 87). ex l. Iulia] *cf. D. tit.* 42, 3. *C. Theod.
tit.* 4, 20. *C. Iust. tit.* 7, 71. *C.* 2, 11 (12), 11 (*a.* 223). iudica-
torum] *cf. D.* 15, 1, 51 (*Scaev.* 142). *C.* 8, 17 (18), 4 (3) (*a.* 215).
lege XII tab.] 3, 1. edicto praetoris] '*puta in iudiciis imperio
continentibus*'. *Hu.* mortuorum etc.] *cf. supra* 2, 154; 158. certum est] *cf. D.* 42, 4, 8 (*Ulp.* 1398). neque heredes] *cf. Cic.
pro Quinct.* 19, 60. *D.* 29, 2, 91 (*Paul.* 1576). neque ullum
alium etc.] *cf. supra* 2, 150. *Ulp.* 28, 7. *D.* 38, 9, 1 *pr.* (*Ulp.*
1212). 49, 14, 1, 1 (*Call.* 79). *C.* 7, 72, 5 (*a.* 293). *Cic. de leg.*
2, 19, 48.
§ 79. *cf. infra* 4, 35; 65 *sq.*; 102; 145. *Theoph.* 3, 12 *pr.*
(*p.* 314 *sq. Ferr.*). *lex Iul. munic. lin.* 116 *sq.* (*Bruns* [7. 108]).

given to their patrons as if they had died as Latins. And I have not forgotten the fact that the legislator did not express his intention on this matter clearly enough.

77. Now, we look at the succession competent to us on **sale of a bankrupt* estate**. 78. The assets sold may belong either to living debtors or to dead ones: living ones, where, for instance, they are in hiding with a fraudulent purpose and [perhaps 'or'] are not defended in their absence; or where they surrender their estate under the Julian Act; or where they are judgment debtors and the time granted to them for producing the money, partly by the Twelve Tables, partly by the praetor's Edict, has passed. Estates of dead debtors are sold, where, for instance, it is certain that they have neither heirs nor estate-possessors nor any other lawful successors. 79. And note that if the estate of a living person is sold, the praetor orders possession of it to be held for thirty successive days

et[1] proscribi, si uero mortui, per[2] dies xv; postea
iubet[3] conuenire creditores et ex eo[4] numero magistrum
creari, id est eum, per quem bona ueneant. itaque
si uiui bona ueneant, in diebus x[5] *legem bonorum uendundorum* fieri[6] iubet, si mortui, in dimidio. *d*iebus
tandem[7] uiui bona xxx, mortui uero xx emptori ad-
dici iubet. quare autem tardius uiuentium bonorum
uenditionem compleri[8] iubet[9], illa ratio est, quia de
uiuis curandum erat, ne facile bonorum uenditiones
paterentur. 80. Neque autem bonorum possessorum
neque bonorum emptorum *res*[10] pleno iure fiunt, sed
in bonis efficiun*tur*; *ex iure Quiritium* autem ita
demum adquiruntur, si usuceperunt.[11] interdum quidem bonorum emptoribus *ne* *u*sus quidem capio con-
tingit, uelut si pereos ＊＊＊＊＊＊＊ | bonorum emptor[12]
———————— *vv. 2½ legi nequeunt* ———— |———

1) possideri et *Goeschen.* possederit V.   2) post V.
3) iubent V.   4) eorum *Berger.*   5) *de numero nil constat;
hoc tantum requiritur, ne impar sit numerus dierum.*   6) X legem bonorum uendundorum fieri *coni. Hu. ('Nexum' p. 153)
ex Theoph.*   7) tandem *Hu.* ita ＊＊ V.   8) compleri
Lachmann. complere V.   9) iubeat *Polenaar.*   10) bonorum possessorum neque bonorum emptorum res *Goeschen.*
bonorum possessio neque uerii? V.   11) usuceperunt *Lachmann.* ususceperiunt? V.   12) *Hu. supplementa proposuit
haec:* uelut si peregrinus sit bonorum emptor nec senatus consultum concesserit eius ciuitati ius, quo, quae
ciuibus eius populi a ciuibus Romanis alienantur, usucapere

Cic. pro Quinct. 6, 25; 27. *Senec. de benef.* 4, 12, 3. dies continuos xxx] *cf. Cic. pro Quinct.* 8, 30. *C.* 7, 72, 9 *i. f. (a.* 299).
poss. et proscr.] *cf. Prob.* 5, 24 (*Iurispr.* I, 88). *infra* 3, 220.
Charis. Gramm. lat. ed. Keil I, 235, 19. *l. Rubr. c.* 22 *i. f.*
(*Bruns* I[7], 100). creditores] *cf. D.* 50, 16, 54 (*Ulp.* 1420); 55
(*Paul.* 38). magistrum] *cf. D.* 50, 16, 57 (*Paul.* 719). *Cic. pro
Quinct.* 15, 50. *ad Attic.* 1, 1, 3. 6, 1, 15. *Quint. inst. or.*
6, 3, 51.
   §§ 80. 81. *cf. infra* 4, 34; 35; 65; 68; 145. *Theoph.*
3, 12 *pr.* (*p.* 314 *sq. Ferr.*). *D.* 41, 4, 2, 19 (*Paul* 664). *Varro
r. r.* 2, 10, 4 (*Bruns* II[7], 63).

and public notice to be given; where the person is dead, on the other hand, the period is fifteen days. Then he orders the creditors to meet and appoint one of their number as manager, that is, as seller of the estate. And then if a living person's estate is being sold he orders the sale to take place in ten days' time; if the person is dead, the time is halved. Finally, he orders the estate of a living person to be decreed to the purchaser after thirty days, and the estate of a dead one after twenty. And the reason why he orders more time to be taken over the sale of the estates of the living is that care must be taken that living debtors do not easily find their estates being sold in execution. 80. But neither estate-possessors nor purchasers of estates acquire full ownership. The things they acquire merely become part of their own estates*; quiritary right to these things is acquired only by usucapion*. And note that sometimes even usucapion does not run in favour of the purchasers of estates, for instance, ... [there are different suggestions for completion of the illegible passage which follows. Gaius may have referred to a foreigner incapable of usucapting or to cases where the sale was invalid, because, for example, no debts were due to the purported creditors who brought about the sale.] 81.

81. Item quae debi*ta sunt ei, cuius fuerunt bona*[1], aut
ipse debuit, neque bonorum possessor ne*que* bonorum
emptor ipso iure debet[2] *aut ipsis debentur, et ideo* de
omnibus rebus *utilibus actionibus et agunt et conueniun-
tur, quas*[3] in sequenti commentario proponemus. |

149   82. Sunt autem etiam alterius generis successiones,
quae neque lege XII tabularum neque praetoris edicto,
sed eo iure, *quod tacito* consensu[4] receptum est, introductae sunt. 83. Etenim cum pater familias se in adoptionem de*dit* mulierue[5] in manum conuenit, omnes eius
res incorporales et corporales, quaeque ei debitae[6] sunt,
patri adoptiuo coemptionatoriue adquiruntur exceptis
his, quae per capitis deminutionem pereunt, quales
sunt ususfructus, operarum obligatio *libertorum*, quae
per iusiurandum contracta est, et *lites contestatae*[7] legitimo iudicio. 84. Ex diuerso quod is debu*it, qui se
in* adoptionem dedit quaeue[8] in manum conue*nit, non*
transit ad coemptionatorem aut ad patrem adoptiuum,

---

possunt. *Kruegero videtur Gaius egisse de usucapione, quae
non contingit, si per eos bona venierunt, quibus nihil debitum
erat, vel de bonorum venditione aliam ob causam irrita facta
(cf. Dig. 42, 4, 7, 3 et 42, 5, 30).*

   1) debita—bona *suppl. Lachmann.*   2) debeat(?) V.
3) utilibus—quas *suppl. fere Hu.*   4) concessu V.   5) mulierue *Boecking.* mulierque V.   6) *num* debita?   7) lites
contestatae *suppl. Rudorff.*   8) quaeque V.

---

   § 82. = *I.* 3, 10 *pr.*
   § 83. = *I.* 3, 10, 1. *cf. infra* 4, 80. in adoptionem] *cf.*
D. 43, 26, 16 (*Pomp.* 771). 37, 11, 11, 2 (*Pap.* 221). 1, 7, 15 *pr.*
(*Ulp.* 2689). *Suet. Tib.* 15. *Gell.* 5, 19, 6. in manum] *Cic. top.*
4, 23. per cap. dem. pereunt] *cf. D.* 46, 3, 38 *pr.* (*Afr.* 79).
infra 3, 114. ususfructus] *cf. D.* 7, 1, 35, 1 (*Iul.* 887). 7, 1, 56
(*Gai.* 297). 7, 4, 1; 3 = *Vat.* 61—64 (*Ulp.* 2550 *sq.*). *Paul.* 3, 6,
28; 29. *I.* 2, 4, 3. *C.* 3, 33, 16 (*a.* 530). operar. obl.] *cf. D.*
33, 2, 2 (*Pap.* 259). 38, 1, 7 (*Ulp.* 2702). *infra ad* 3, 96. legit.
iud.] *cf. infra* 3, 181. 4, 104.
   § 84. *cf. I.* 3, 10, 3. *infra* 4, 38; 80. *D.* 4, 5, 2 (*Ulp.*
413 *sq.*). 15, 1, 42 (*Ulp.* 418). hereditarium aes alienum] *cf.*
D. 42, 5, 7 (*Gai.* 344). 44, 7, 40 (*Paul.* 225).

Again, where an estate-possessor or the purchaser of an estate is concerned, neither debts due to the person whose estate it was nor debts due by him pass by operation of law, and so in all these cases policy actions* are granted to and brought against them, as we explain in the following commentary.

82. Now, **there** are **still other ways in which an** entire **estate can be acquired**. These **did not originate in the Twelve Tables or the praetor's Edict but in the law accepted by convention**. 83. On the adoption **of the head of a family** or on a woman's falling into marital subordination the adoptive father and the person to whom she becomes subordinate by the contrived sale* **become entitled to all** their respective **corporeal and incorporeal assets and claims, except those destroyed by status-loss, such as usufruct, claims to services** of freedmen created by oath and obligations arising from joinder of issue* in a statutory court*. 84. **On the other side**, neither the adoptive father nor the person to whom she becomes subordinate by the contrived sale succeeds automatically to **the liabilities of the adoptee** or the woman, unless these arise from an inherited debt;

nisi si hereditarium aes alienum fuerit; de eo enim,
quia ipse pater adoptiuus aut coemptionator heres fit,
directo tenetur iure, is uero, qui se adoptandum dedit,
quaeue[1] in manum conuenit, desinit esse heres[2]; de
eo uero, quod proprio nomine eae[3] personae debuerint,
licet neque pater adoptiuus teneatur neque coemptionator et ne[4] ipse quidem, qui se in adoptionem[5] dedit,
uel ipsa[6], quae in manum conuenit, maneat obligatus obligataue, quia scilicet[7] per capitis diminutionem libere-
tur, tamen in eum eamue utilis actio datur rescissa |
capitis deminutione, et, si aduersus hanc actionem non 150
defendantur[8], quae bona eorum futura fuissent, si se
alieno iuri non subiecissent, uniuersa uendere creditoribus praetor permittit.[9]

85. *Item si* legitimam hereditatem heres, *antequam*
cernat aut pro herede gerat, alii in iure cedat, pleno
iure fit ille heres, cui cessa est hereditas, *proinde ac*
si ipse per legem ad hereditatem uocaretur; quod si
postea quam heres extiterit, cesserit, adhuc heres manet
et ob id creditoribus[10] ipse tenebitur; sed res corporales transferet, proinde ac si singulas in iure cessisset,
debita uero pereunt, eoque modo debitores hereditarii
lucrum faciunt. 86. Idem iuris est, si testamento
scriptus heres, postea quam heres extiterit, in iure
cesserit hereditatem; ante aditam uero hereditatem cedendo nihil agit. 87. Suus autem et[11] necessarius heres
an aliquid agant[12] in iure cedendo, quaeritur. nostri
praeceptores nihil eos agere existimant; diuersae scho-

---

1) quaeue *Lachmann.* queque V. 2) heredes V.
3) ea V. 4) et ne *suppl. Krueger.* 5) in adoptionem
Goeschen. adem in optionem V. 6) uel ipsa *supplevimus.*
7) scilicet *Goeschen.* scetsi? V. 8) defendatur V. 9) permittitur V. *deinde versus unus in* V *vacuus relictus.*
10) a creditoribus V. 11) seruus *add. Solazzi.* 12) agant
Lachmann. agat V.

---

§§ 85—87. *cf. supra* 2, 35—37.
§ 87. cernendo aut pro herede gerendo] *cf. supra* 2, 116.
Consult. 6, 19 (*Cod. Hermog. a.* 294).

then, because the adoptive father or the person taking the woman into subordination becomes heir, he is liable directly; the adoptee or the woman ceases to be heir. On the other hand, although neither the adoptive father nor the person taking the woman into subordination is liable for debts owed by the adoptee or the woman in their own names, and not even they themselves remain bound because of course they are released by their status-loss, policy actions are given against them. If they are not **defended** against these actions the praetor **allows the creditors** to sell off all the **assets which** they **would have had if** they **had stayed independent**.

85. Again, if an heir assigns his statutory inheritance in court* to someone else before he makes a solemn declaration of acceptance or acts as heir, the person to whom he has assigned it gets the full rights of heir as if he himself were entitled to the inheritance by statute; but if he makes the assignment after becoming heir he remains heir and so is himself liable to the creditors. But he transfers the physical things as if he had assigned them in court individually; on the other hand, debts owed are extinguished and so the debtors to the inheritance gain. 86. The same applies if the heir appointed by will assigns the inheritance in court after becoming heir; but if he makes the assignment before accepting the inheritance he achieves nothing at all. 87. But does an immediate or compulsory heir achieve anything by an assignment in court? Our teachers consider that they achieve nothing at all. The authorities of the other

lae auctores idem eos agere putant, quod ceteri post
aditam[1] hereditatem; nihil enim interest, utrum aliquis cernendo aut pro herede gerendo heres fiat an
iuris necessitate hereditati adstringatur.[2] |

151   88. *Nunc transeamus*[3] ad obligationes, quarum summa
diuisio in duas species diducitur: omnis enim obligatio
uel ex contractu nascitur uel ex delicto.

89. Et prius uideamus de his, quae ex contractu
nascuntur. harum autem quattuor genera sunt: aut
enim re *contrahitur* obligatio aut uerbis aut litteris
aut consensu.

90. Re contrahitur obligatio uelut mutui datione;
mutui autem datio proprie in his fere[4] rebus contingit,
quae[5] res pondere, numero, mensura constan*t*, qualis
est pecunia numerata, uinum, oleum, frumentum, aes,
argentum, aurum; quas res aut numerando aut me-
tiendo aut pendendo in hoc damus, ut accipientium
fiant et quandoque nobis non eaedem[6], sed aliae[7] eiusdem naturae reddantur. unde etiam mutuum appella-
tum est, quia quod ita *ti*bi a me datum est, ex meo
tuum fit.[8] 91. Is quoque, qui non debitum accepit ab

---

1) aditatam V.   2) §§ 85—87 *Polenaar a. Gaio abiudicat.
ultima linea p.* 150 *(rubricae destinata) et initium primae lineae
p.* 151 *litteris vacant in* V.   3) nunc transeamus *suppl. ex Inst.*
4) *del. Hu.; om. Inst.*   5) qua V.   6) eaedem *Inst.* eadem V.
7) aliae *Inst.* alia V.   8) fiat V. '*non inprobabiliter hic excidit ex
Inst. supplendum:* (at) ex eo contractu nascitur actio, quae
uocatur condictio. *etiam Theophilus:* ἐκ δὲ τούτου κτλ.' *Hu.*

---

§§ 88. 89. *cf. I.* 3, 13 *pr.*; 2. *Gai epit.* 2, 9 *pr. D.* 44,
7, 1 *pr.*; 1 (*Gai.* 498). *infra* 3, 182. 4, 2. *D.* 44, 7, 52 *pr.* (*Mod.*
192). re] *infra* 3, 90; 91. uerbis] *infra* 3, 92—127. litteris]
infra 3, 128—134. consensu] *infra* 3, 135—162.
§ 90. *inde a verbis* quas res = *I.* 3, 14 *pr. cf. Gai epit.*
2, 9, 1. *D.* 44, 7, 1, 2 (*Gai.* 498). *supra* 2, 81. *Ulp. Inst.
fragm.* 2, 1. *D.* 12, 1, 2 *pr.*—2 (*Paul.* 430). 44, 7, 52, 1 (*Mod.*
192). *Varro de l. l.* 5, 179 (*Bruns* II[7], 54). *Non. p.* 439, 15 *Merc.
Boeth. ad Cic. top. p.* 300 *Bait. Isid. orig.* 5, 25, 18.
§ 91. = *I.* 3, 14, 1. *cf. D.* 44, 7, 5, 3 (*Gai.* 506). *I.* 3,

school* think that they achieve the same as others do after accepting the inheritance; for it does not matter whether someone becomes heir by making a formal declaration of acceptance or by acting as heir or is bound to the inheritance by necessity of law.

88. **We turn to obligations. They divide first into two: all obligations** arise **from a contract** or from a delict.

89. **Those from contract are our first concern.** Now, they fall into **four classes: they are contracted by conduct*, by words, by writing, or by agreement.**

90. **One case where an obligation is contracted by conduct is when a loan* is made, of the kind called in Latin 'mutuum'. This applies only to things identified by weight, number or measure, such as money, wine, oil, corn, bronze, silver, and gold. When we lend such things by number, measure, or weight we intend that they should become the property of the recipient and that when the time comes for getting them back we should receive not the very things we gave but others of the same kind and quality. This is the origin of the term 'mutuum': I give so as to make my property your property, in Latin 'ex meo tuum'. 91. A person also incurs an obligation by conduct if he receives**

eo, qui per errorem soluit, re obligatur; nam proinde
ei condici potest SI PARET EVM DARE OPORTERE, ac
si mutuum accepisset. unde quidam putant pupillum
aut mulierem, cui sine tutoris auctoritate[1] non debitum per errorem datum est, non teneri condictione,
non magis quam mutui datione. sed haec species
obligationis non uidetur ex contractu consistere, quia
is, qui soluendi animo dat, magis distrahere uult negotium quam contrahere.[2]

92. Verbis | obligatio fit ex interrogatione et re- 152
sponsione, uelut DARI SPONDES? SPONDEO, DABIS?
DABO, PROMITTIS? PROMITTO, FIDEPROMITTIS? FIDE-
PROMITTO, FIDEIVBES? FIDEIVBEO, FACIES? FACIAM.
93. Sed haec quidem uerborum obligatio DARI SPON-
DES? SPONDEO propria ciuium Romanorum est; ceterae[3] uero iuris gentium sunt, itaque inter omnes homines, siue ciues Romanos siue peregrinos, ualent. et
quamuis ad Graecam uocem expressae fuerint, uelut
hoc modo δώσεις; δώσω· ὁμολογεῖς; ὁμολογῶ· πίστει
κελεύεις; πίστει κελεύω· ποιήσεις; ποιήσω[4], etiam hae[5]
tamen inter ciues Romanos ualent[6], si modo Graeci

---

1) tutoris auctoritate *Inst.* totae V. 2) sed — contrahere
del. Albertario, quod improbat Segré. 3) cetera V. 4) *Graeca
ex Theophilo suppleta sunt.* 5) haec V. 6) ua lent t͞m V.

27, 6. *D.* 26, 8, 5 *pr.* (*Ulp.* 2854). 44, 4, 4, 4 (*Ulp.* 1678). SI
PARET] *cf. infra* 4, 4; 5; 41. quidam putant] *cf. D.* 26, 8, 13
(*Iul.* 322). 46, 3, 66 (*Pomp.* 354).

§ 92. *cf. Gai epit.* 2, 9, 2. *Paul.* 2, 3. 5, 7. 1. *I.* 3, 15 *pr.*
D. 45, 1, 5, 1 (*Pomp.* 722). 44, 7, 1, 7 (*Gai.* 498). 44, 7, 52, 2
(*Mod.* 192). *C.* 8, 37(38), 10 (*a.* 472). *Plaut. Aul.* 2, 2, 78 = 256.
Pseud. 1, 1, 112 *sq.* = 114 *sq.*; 1, 5, 121 *sq.* = 535 *sq.*; 4, 6, 6 *sq.*
= 1068 *sq. Menaechm.* 5, 4, 6 = 894. *Bacch.* 4, 8, 43 = 883.
Cic. pro Caec. 3, 7. *Fest. v. spondere p.* 329; 343 (*Bruns* II[7], 40).
Varro de l. l. 6, 69 *sq.* (*Bruns* II[7], 56). *Seneca ep.* 7, 1. *Isid.*
orig. 5, 24, 30 (*Bruns* II[7], 81).

§ 93. *cf. infra* 3, 119; 179 *i. f. I.* 3, 15, 1 *cum Theoph.*
(*p.* 322 *sq. Ferr.*). *D.* 45, 1, 1, 6 (*Ulp.* 2949). 46, 4, 8, 4 *i. f.*
(*Ulp.* 2957). *C.* 8, 40 (41), 12 (*a.* 230). 2, 55 (56), 4, 6 (*a.* 529).
Gell. 4, 4 (*Serv.* 2, *Iurispr.* I, 33).

something not due to him from a person who pays him by mistake. This recipient is just as much caught by the words of that action – 'if it appears that he has a duty to give' – as if he had been given a loan. And so some people think that if a child or a woman **receives a mistaken payment not due to them without getting their guardian's authorisation, they are no more liable to the action of debt*** for something not due **than** they are **when the same action is brought on a loan. But here the obligation cannot be said to arise from contract. Someone who gives intending to discharge a debt means, not to tie up a deal, but to untie one, 'distrahere' not 'contrahere'.**

92. **An obligation by words** is created by **question and answer**, such as: **'Do you solemnly promise to give? I solemnly promise. Will you give? I will give. Do you promise? I promise. Do you faithfully promise? I faithfully promise. Do you faithfully authorise? I faithfully authorise. Will you perform? I will perform'.** 93. But note that the form using the term 'solemnly promise', in Latin 'spondere', is confined to Roman citizens; the others are part of the law of all peoples* and so are valid between any parties, whether Roman citizens or foreigners*. Even if they are put into Greek, like this, for instance: 'Will you give? I will give. Do you promise? I promise. Do you faithfully authorise. I faithfully authorise. Will you perform? I will perform' they are valid between Roman citizens, provided that they **under-**

sermonis intellectum habeant; et e contrario quamuis
Latine enuntientur, tamen etiam inter peregrinos ualent,
si modo Latini sermonis intellectum habeant.[1] at illa
uerborum obligatio DARI SPONDES? SPONDEO adeo
propria ciuium Romanorum est, ut ne quidem in Grae-
cum sermonem per interpretationem proprie transferri[2]
possit, quamuis dicatur a Graeca uoce figurata esse.
94. Unde dicitur uno casu hoc uerbo peregrinum quoque obligari posse, uelut si imperator noster principem
alicuius peregrini populi de pace ita interroget: PACEM
FVTVRAM SPONDES? uel ipse eodem modo interrogetur.
quod nimium subtiliter dictum est, quia si quid aduersus pactionem fiat, non ex stipulatu[3] agitur, sed iure
belli res uindicatur. 95. Illud dubitari potest, si quis[4]

153 | ———————————— *vv. 13* ————————————
t. s. 95ᵃ. — | si debitor mulieris iussu eius, dum ———— [5] |
doti dicat quod debet. alius autem obliga*ri eo*
modo | non potest. | et ideo si quis ali*us pro mu-*
liere dotem uiro promittat, com|muni iure obliga ————.[6]

---

1) habeantur V.   2) transferri *Goeschen.* transfieri V.
3) stipulat V.   4) *cf. apographum; de supplementis vid. epit.*
2, 9, 3; 4.   5) *Hu. supplevit*: modo auctore tutore eidem.
6) *Hu. suppl.:* obligari debebit, scilicet ut ante stipuletur
maritus.

---

§ 94. *cf. Liv.* 9, 5, 2*sq.* 9, 8, 4*sq.* 9, 11, 3*sq.* 9, 41, 20. *Cic.*
pro Balbo 12, 29. *cf. etiam D.* 2, 14, 5 (*Ulp.* 241).
§ 95ᵃ. *cf. Gai epit.* 2, 9, 3. *Ulp.* 6, 1; 2. 11, 20. *Fr. Vat.*
99 *sq.* (*Paul.* 1506 *sq.*). *D.* 23, 3, 79, 1 (*Lab. ap. Iav.* 221). 23, 3, 80
et 83 (*Lab. ap. Iav.* 222). 23, 4, 32, 1 (*Lab. ap. Iav.* 223). 50,
16, 125 (*Proc.* 20). 23, 3, 57 (*Iav.* 147). 23, 3, 44 (*Iul.* 268). 23, 3,
46 (*Iul.* 269). 23, 3, 61 *pr.* (*Ter Clem.* 5). 23, 3, 59 *pr.*; 1 (*Mar-*
cell. 82). 23, 3, 45 (*Tryph.* 29). 23, 3, 77 (*Tryph.* 36). 23, 3, 25
(*Paul.* 1758). *C. I.* 5, 12, 1 (*a.* 201). *C. Th.* 3, 12, 3 (= *C. I.* 5, 5,
6; *a.* 396). 3, 13, 4 (= *C. I.* 5, 12, 6; *a.* 428). *Plaut. Aul.* 2, 2,
78 = 256. *Amphitr.* 2, 2, 209 = 839. *Ter. Heaut.* 5, 1, 64 = 937.
5, 5, 4 = 1048. *Cic. pro Caec.* 25, 73. *pro Flacc.* 35, 86. *Ov. Fast.*
6, 594. *Senec. controv.* 1, 6, 5 (*p.* 66, 7 ed. *Mueller*). *Plin. ep.*
2, 4, 2. *Apul. apol.* 102. *Non. Marcell.* p. 280, 22 *sq.* (*dicere*
etiam promittere). *Mart. Cap.* 9, 898. *Schol. ad. Pers. sat.* 2, 14.

stand Greek; conversely, even if Latin is used the obligations are valid between foreigners, provided that they understand Latin. But the obligation using the form, 'Do you solemnly promise to give? I solemnly promise' is so much confined to Roman citizens that it cannot properly be translated – not even into Greek, although the verb 'spondere' is said to be derived from the Greek. 94. And so it is said that there is only one case in which a foreigner can come under an obligation by using this word, and that is where our emperor puts the question of peace to the leader of a foreign people: 'Do you solemnly promise that there will be peace?' or where the question is put to him in the same form. But this example is just too clever because if the peace treaty is broken there is no action on stipulation; the matter is pursued by the law of war.

95. There is a doubtful question whether, if someone ... [most of the following passage is illegible but in it Gaius seems to have dealt with the unilateral obligation to create a dowry known as 'dotis dictio', declaration of a dowry. Only a woman or her father or her debtor could bind themselves by such a declaration]. 95a. ... If the debtor of a woman on her orders [?and with her guardian's authorisation] declares as dowry the debt he owes to her [he is bound]. But no one else can incur an obligation in this way. And so, if anyone else wants to promise a dowry for a woman to her husband he must enter into an obligation according to the ordinary law, [that is he must promise in response to a stipulation by the husband]. 96. Again, an obligation is contracted by a

96. Item uno loquente *et sine interrogatione alii promittente contrahitur obligatio, si libertus patrono aut donum aut munus aut operas se daturum esse iurauit*[1], *et*si haec sola[2] causa est[3], ex qua iureiurando contrahitur obligatio. sane ex alia nulla causa iureiurando homines | obligantur, utique cum quaeritur de iure Romanorum. nam apud peregrinos quid iuris sit, singularum ciuitatium iura requirentes aliud intellegere poterimus ———.[4]

154
t. s.

97. Si id, quod dari stipulamur, tale sit, ut dari non possit, inutilis est stipulatio, uelut si quis hominem liberum, quem seruum esse credebat, aut mortuum, quem uiuum esse credebat, aut locum sacrum uel religiosum, quem putabat[5] humani iuris esse, dari *stipuletur.* 97ª. *Item si quis rem, quae in rerum natura esse non potest, uelut hippocentaurum*[6], stipuletur, aeque inutilis est stipulatio. 98. Item si quis sub ea condicione stipuletur, quae existere non potest, uelut 'si digito caelum tetigerit', inutilis est stipulatio. sed legatum sub inpossibili condicione[7] relictum nostri praeceptores proinde deberi putant, ac si sine condi-

---

1) et—iurauit *suppl. ex epitoma.* 2) solo(?) V. 3) s. V. 4) *fortasse sequitur in* V: in aliis ualere. *deinde sequitur linea uacua.* 5) putabatat V. 6) stipuletur—hippocentaurum *suppl. Lachmann ex Inst.* 3, 19, 1. 7) cocondicione V.

---

§ 96. *cf. Gai epit.* 2, 9, 4. *supra* 3, 83. *Paul.* 2, 32. *D.* 38, 1, 7 (*Ulp.* 2702). 38, 1, 8 (*Pomp.* 528). 40, 12, 44 *pr.* (*Ven.* 3). 46, 4, 13 *pr.* (*Ulp.* 2980). *Cic. ad Att.* 7, 2, 8.
§ 97. *cf. Gai epit.* 2, 9, 5. *I.* 3, 19, 1; 2. *D.* 44, 7, 1, 9 (*Gai.* 498). 45, 1, 103 (*Mod.* 115).
§ 97ª. *cf. I.* 3, 19, 1. *D.* 45, 1, 97 *pr.* (*Cels.* 222). *Lucret.* 5, 878 *sq. Cic. de nat. deor.* 2, 2, 5. *Ovid. Trist.* 4, 7, 15. *Senec. ep.* 58, 15. *Plin. n. h.* 7, 35. *Isid. orig.* 1, 39, 5. 11, 3, 37; 39.
§ 98. *cf. Gai epit.* 2, 9, 6. *Paul.* 3, 4ᵇ, 1. *I.* 3, 19, 11. *D.* 44, 7, 1, 11 (*Gai.* 498). 45, 1, 137, 6 (*Ven.* 53). 44, 7, 31 (*Maecian.* 16). 45, 1, 7 (*Ulp.* 2474). sed legatum *etc.*] *cf. I.* 2, 14, 10. *D.* 28, 5, 46 (45) (*Alf.* 34). 33, 4, 12 (*Scaev.* 264). 35, 1, 3 (*Ulp.* 2474). diuersitatis] *cf. supra* 2, 78.

single person's speaking and making a promise to
another without interrogation if a freedman swears
that he will render his patron a gift or service or
labour; although this is the only case in which an
obligation is contracted by means of an oath.
Certainly there is no other situation in which men
incur obligations by taking an oath, at least if the
question is confined to Roman law. If we extend the
question to the individual laws of foreign states, we
may find that a different rule [prevails in some].

97. If we stipulate for something to be given which
cannot be given, the stipulation has no effect; if, for
instance, someone stipulates for a free man whom he
believes to be a slave **or for a dead slave believed to
be alive or for sacred* or religious*** land, believing
it to be governed by human law. 97a. **Again, if
someone stipulates for a thing which cannot exist
in nature, such as a centaur, the stipulation** equally
has no effect. 98. Again if someone stipulates subject
to a condition which cannot be fulfilled, **for instance
'if he touches the sky',** the stipulation is ineffective.
But where a legacy is left under an impossible
condition our teachers hold it to be due, as if it had
been left unconditionally; the authorities of the other

cione relictum esset; diuersae[1] scholae auctores nihilo[2] minus legatum inutile existimant quam stipulationem. et sane uix idonea diuersitatis ratio reddi potest. 99. Praeterea inutilis est stipulatio, si quis ignorans rem suam esse dari sibi eam stipuletur; quip*pe* quod alicuius est, id ei dari non potest. 100. Denique inutilis est talis stipulatio, si quis ita dari stipuletur: POST MORTEM MEAM DARI SPONDES? uel ita: POST MORTEM TVAM DARI SPONDES? *ualet autem, si quis ita dari stipuletur: CVM MORIAR, DARI SPONDES? uel ita*[3]: CVM MORIERIS, DARI | SPONDES? id est, ut in nouissimum uitae tempus stipulatoris aut promissoris obligatio conferatur: nam inelegans esse uisum est ab heredis persona incipere obligationem. rursum ita stipulari non possumus: PRIDIE QVAM MORIAR, aut PRIDIE QVAM MORIERIS, DARI SPONDES? quia non potest aliter intellegi 'pridie quam aliquis morietur', quam si mors secuta sit; rursus morte secuta in praeteritum reducitur[4] stipulatio et quodam modo talis est: HEREDI MEO DARI SPONDES? quae sane inutilis est.[5] 101. Quaecumque de morte diximus, eadem et de capitis diminutione dicta intellegemus.[6] 102. Adhuc inutilis est stipu-

155

---

1) diuersi V.   2) no V.   3) post—ita *suppl. Hu.*
4) redducitur V.   5) quia — inutilis est *del. Vassalli. cf. Beseler*
ZS 46, 268.   6) intellegemus *Lachmann.* intellegimus V.

§ 99. *cf. infra* 4, 4. *I.* 3, 19, 2; 22. *D.* 44, 7, 1, 10 (*Gai.* 498). 45, 1, 31 (*Pomp.* 713). 45, 1, 98 *pr.* (*Marcell.* 218). 45, 1, 29, 1 (*Ulp.* 2928). 45, 1, 82 *pr.* (*Ulp.* 1709). 7, 9, 1, 7 (*Ulp.* 1721). 45, 1, 87 (*Paul.* 821). 45, 1, 128 (*Paul.* 1366).

§ 100. *cf. Gai epit.* 2, 9, 7; 8. *supra* 2, 232; 277. *infra* 3, 117; 119; 158; 176. *I.* 3, 19, 13; 15. *Fr. Vat.* 57 (*Paul.* 996). 98 (*Paul.* 1505). *D.* 35, 2, 32 *pr.* (*Maecian.* 42). 31, 67, 6 (*Pap.* 281). 45, 1, 121, 2 (*Pap.* 664). 23, 3, 76 (*Tryph.* 35). 23, 3, 20 (*Paul.* 1756). 45, 1, 46, 1 (*Paul.* 1850). 45, 1, 45, 1; 3 (*Ulp.* 2976). *C.* 8, 37 (38), 4 (*a.* 222); 11 (*a.* 528); 15 (*a.* 532). 4, 11, 1 (*a.* 531).

§ 101. *cf. infra* 3, 153. *D.* 46, 3, 38 *pr.* (*Afr.* 79).

§ 102. = *I.* 3, 19, 5. *cf. Gai epit.* 2, 9, 9; 10. *D.* 45, 1, 1, 3; 4 (*Ulp.* 2949). 45, 1, 83, 2; 3 (*Paul.* 798). 45, 1, 35, 2 (*Paul.* 1844). *Varro de l. l.* 6, 72 (*Bruns* II[7], 57).

school think that the legacy is as ineffective as a stipulation. And certainly it is hardly possible to give a satisfactory reason for the distinction. 99. Moreover, a stipulation is ineffective where **someone stipulates for a thing which**, unknown to him, **is already his**; obviously what belongs to someone cannot be conveyed to him. 100. Next, a stipulation is ineffective if someone makes a stipulation of this kind: 'Do you solemnly promise **to give after** my **death?**' or this: 'Do you solemnly promise to give after your **death?**' **But a stipulation** framed **like this: 'Do you solemnly promise to give as I lie dying?'** or like this: 'Do you solemnly promise to give **as you lie dying?**', that is, one so framed that the obligation is postponed to the last moment of the stipulator's or promissor's life, **is valid**. It was perceived as awkward that an obligation should first come into being with the person of the heir. Then again, we cannot stipulate like this: 'Do you solemnly promise **to give on the day before I die?'** or **'on the day before you die?'**. There is no way of discovering 'the day before someone dies' other than by waiting for him to be dead; and then, once the death has happened, the stipulation is pushed back into the past and this is tantamount to saying: 'Do you promise to give to my heir?' and this, of course, is ineffective. 101. Whatever we have said of death we mean to apply to status-loss as well.

102. Besides, **a stipulation is ineffective if the**

latio, si quis ad id, quod interrogatus erit, non
responderit, uelut si sestertia x a te dari stipuler, et
tu nummum sestert*ium* v milia[1] promittas, aut si ego
pure[2] stipuler, tu sub condicione promittas. 103. Praeterea inutilis est stipulatio, si ei dari stipulemur, cuius
iuri[3] subiecti non sumus. unde illud quaesitum est, si
quis sibi et ei, cuius iuri subiectus non est, dari stipuletur, in quantum ualeat stipulatio. nostri praeceptores putant in uniuersum ualere et proinde ei soli, qui
stipulatus sit, solidum deberi, atque si extranei nomen
non adiecisset. sed diuersae scholae auctores | dimi- 156
dium ei deberi existimant; pro altera uero parte in-
utilem esse stipulatiohem. 103ª. Alia causa est, |
————————— DARI SPONDES | ——————— solidum de-
beri et me | sol ——————— etiam —— | ——————— [4]
104. *Praeterea*[5] inutilis est stipulatio, si ab eo stipuler,
qui iuri meo subiectus est, item si is a me stipuletur.
seruus quidem et qui in mancipio est et *filia familias*[6]
et quae in manu est, non solum ipsi, cuius iuri subiecti subiectaeue sunt, obligari non possunt, sed ne

---

1) nummum — milia *Hu.* nsestertia ū. milia V. sestertia v
Krueger. 2) pute V. 3) iuris V. 4) *supplementa Hu.*:
Alia causa est, si ueluti SERVO uel FILIO FAMILIAS MEO ET
MIHI DARI SPONDES stipulatus sim. tunc enim constat solidum
deberi et me solidum a promissore petere posse: quod
etiam fit, cum tantum uelut FILIO FAMILIAS stipulor; —
supplementa Kruegeri: Alia causa est, si ita stipulatus sim
MIHI AVT TITIO DARI SPONDES? quo casu constat mihi solidum deberi et me solum ex ea stipulatione agere posse,
quamquam etiam Titio soluendo liberaris. 5) item *Inst.*
6) filia familias *suppl. Krueger.*

---

§ 103. *cf. I.* 3, 19, 4; 19. *supra* 2, 86. *infra* 3, 114; 163.
D. 50, 17, 73, 4 (*Q. Muc.* 50). 18, 1, 64 (*Iav.* 78). 45, 1, 110 pr.
(*Pomp.* 237). 45, 3, 18, 2 (*Pap.* 328). 45, 3, 4 (*Ulp.* 2616). 45, 1,
38, 17 (*Ulp.* 2971). 45, 1, 126, 2 (*Paul.* 1296). *C.* 8, 37 (38), 3
(*a.* 217). 8, 38 (39), 3 (*a.* 290); 6 (*a.* 294). *Nov.* 115, 6 (*a.* 542).
§ 104. *cf. I.* 3, 19, 6. *Fr. Vat.* 99 (*Paul.* 1506). *D.* 45, 1,
141, 2 (*Gai.* 513). 44, 7, 14 (*Ulp.* 128). 13, 6, 3, 4 (*Ulp.* 801).
50, 17, 22 pr. (*Ulp.* 2702). 46, 1, 56, 1 (*Paul.* 1397).

answer fails to match the question, as where I ask whether you promise to give 10,000 and you answer 5,000, or where I put the question absolutely, and you promise conditionally. 103. Moreover, a stipulation is ineffective if we take a stipulation that something is to be given to someone other than the head of our family and so, if a person takes a stipulation for something to be given to himself and to a third party other than the head of his family, how far is the stipulation valid? Our teachers think that it is wholly valid and that the full amount has to be paid to the stipulator alone, as if the outsider's name had not been mentioned. But the authorities of the other school consider that only half has to be paid to him, and that the stipulation is ineffective in respect of the other half. 103a. The case is different ... [in the following passage practically all that can be read is 'Do you solemnly promise to give?' and 'that the full sum is payable and I...'. Gaius may have said that if the promise was to me and to a third party I can claim the whole amount but the debtor can be discharged by payment to the third party, or he may have said that if the promise was to me and a person in my power I can claim the whole amount]. 104. Moreover, **a stipulation is ineffective if I stipulate from someone in** my **paternal power and again if he stipulates from** me. But **note that a slave**, a person in bondage*, a daughter in paternal power, and a woman in marital subordination **not only cannot incur an obligation to** the person in whose power they are; **they cannot incur one to any other person**

alii quidem ulli. 105. Mutum neque stipulari neque
promittere posse palam est. idem etiam in surdo receptum est; quia et is, qui stipulatur, uerba promit-
tentis, et qui promittit, uerba stipulantis exaudire
debet. 106. Furiosus nullum negotium ger*e*re potest,
quia non intellegit, quid agat. 107. Pupillus omne
negotium recte gerit, ut tamen[1], sicubi tutoris
auctoritas necessaria sit, adhibeatur[2], uelut si ipse obligetur; nam alium sibi obligare etiam sine tutoris
auctoritate potest. 108. Idem iuris est in feminis, quae
in tutela sunt. 109. Sed quod diximus de pupillo,
utique de eo uerum est, qui iam aliquem intellectum
habet; nam infans et qui infanti proximus est[3] non
157 multum a furioso | differt, quia huius aetatis pupilli
nullum intellectum habent. sed in his pupillis[4] propter[5] utilitatem benignior iuris interpretatio facta est.[6]
110. [7]Possumus tamen ad id, quod stipulamur,

---

1) *cf. infra* 3, 175.   2) *nihil mutandum; cf. D.* 26, 8, 2.
3) et qui — est *del. Albertario.*   4) qui infanti proximi
sunt *ins. Hu.*   5) per V.   6) *sequitur in* V *linea vacua.*
quia — est *del. Albertario.*   7) *Hu. librarium ea, quae omisit,
pro rubrica habuisse ratus supplevit haec:* Quamquam uero, ut
diximus, alius, qui iuri nostro subiectus non est, inutiliter
nobis stipulatur.

§ 105. == *I.* 3, 19, 7. *cf. D.* 44, 7, 1, 14; 15 (*Gai.* 498). 45,
1, 1 *pr.* (*Ulp.* 2949).
§ 106. == *I.* 3, 19, 8. *cf. D.* 44, 7, 1, 12 (*Gai.* 498). 46, 1,
70, 4 (*Gai.* 510).
107. == *I.* 3, 19, 9. *cf. supra* 2, 83. 3, 91. *infra* 3, 119:
176. *Ulp.* 11, 27. *I.* 1, 21 *pr. D.* 26, 8, 9 *pr.* (*Gai.* 267). 50, 17, 5
(*Paul.* 1614). *C.* 8, 38 (39). 1 (*a.* 215).
108. *cf. supra* 1, 144; 192. 2, 80 *sq.* 3, 91. *infra* 3, 119;
176.
§ 109. == *I.* 3, 19, 10. *cf. infra* 3, 208. *D.* 44, 7, 1, 13
(*Gai.* 498). 46, 6, 6 (*Gai.* 366). 26, 7, 1, 2 (*Ulp.* 992). 29, 2, 9
(*Paul.* 1614).
§ 110. *cf. Fest. v. reus p.* 273 (*Bruns* II[7], 32). *D.* 17, 1,
59 *pr.* (*Paul.* 1480). *Cic. pro Quinct.* 18, 58. *in Pison.* 9, 18.
Epist. ad Octav. (*inter Cic. epp. ad Brut.* 2, 8) § 9.

at all. 105. It is obvious that a person who is dumb cannot stipulate or promise. The same has been accepted of the deaf as well. The stipulator must hear the words of the promissor, and the promissor must hear the words of the stipulator. 106. An insane person cannot perform any transaction because he does not know what he is doing. 107. A child* under guardianship has capacity to perform any act so long as he gets his guardian's authorisation when that is required, as when he puts himself under an obligation. He can put another under an obligation towards himself even without his guardian's authorisation. 108. The same applies to women under guardianship. 109. But what we have said of a child is only true of one who has attained some understanding. A baby and a child barely past infancy hardly differ from the insane, in that they are too young to understand anything. With the latter group of children, convenience has encouraged a generous interpretation of the law.

110. [Although, as we have said, someone not in our paternal power cannot effectively stipulate for us] we can join in our stipulation a person who stipulates for

alium adhibere, qui idem stipuletur[1], quem uulgo adstipulatorem uocamus. 111. Et[2] huic proinde actio
conpetit proindeque ei recte soluitur ac nobis; sed
quidquid consecutus erit, mandati iudicio[3] nobis restituere cogetur. 112. Ceterum potest etiam aliis uerbis
uti adstipulator, quam quibus nos usi sumus. itaque
si uerbi gratia ego ita stipulatus sim: DARI SPONDES?
ille sic adstipulari potest: IDEM FIDE TVA PROMITTIS?
uel: IDEM FIDE IVBES? uel contra. 113. Item minus[4]
adstipulari potest, plus non potest. itaque si ego sestertia X stipulatus sim[5], ille sestertia V stipulari potest;
contra uero plus non potest. item si ego pure stipulatus sim, ille sub condicione stipulari potest; contra
uero non potest. non solum autem in quantitate, sed
etiam in tempore minus et plus intellegitur; plus est
enim statim aliquid dare, minus est post tempus dare.
114. In hoc autem iure quaedam singulari iure obseruantur. nam adstipulatoris heres non habet actionem.
item | seruus adstipulando nihil agit, qui[6] ex ceteris 158
omnibus causis stipulatione domino adquirit. idem de
eo, qui in mancipio est, magis placuit; nam et is
serui loco est. is autem, qui in potestate patris est,
agit aliquid, sed parenti non adquirit, quamuis ex
omnibus ceteris causis stipulando ei adquirat; ac ne
ipsi quidem aliter *actio* conpetit, quam si sine kapitis[7]
diminutione exierit de potestate parentis, ueluti morte

---

1) stipuletur *Goeschen.* stipulatur V.   2) sed V.
3) indicio V.   4) item minus *Goeschen.* idem rginus **V.**
5) sum V.   6) quia V.   7) R V.

§ 111. *cf. infra* 3, 117; 215.
§ 112. *cf. infra* 3, 116.
§ 113. *cf. I.* 3, 20, 5. *infra* 3, 126. non solum autem]
cf. infra 4, 53. *D.* 46, 3, 85 (*Call.* 56). 50, 16, 12, 1 (*Ulp.* 286).
§ 114. adstipulatoris heres] *cf. infra* 4, 113. seruus] *cf.*
supra 2, 87. *infra* 3, 163. *I.* 3, 17, 1. nam et is] *cf. supra*
1, 123; 138. 2, 160. si sine kapitis diminutione] *cf. supra* 1,
127; 130. *D.* 46, 3, 38 *pr.* (*Afr.* 79).

the same performance, commonly called an 'adstipulator', an additional stipulator. 111. He can sue just as we can and the payment can be made as well to him as to us; but he is compelled to make over to us anything he gets by the action on mandate. 112. But an additional stipulator can even use different words from us. And so, for example, if I put the question: 'Do you solemnly promise to give?' the additional stipulator can say: 'Do you faithfully promise the same?' or: 'Do you faithfully authorise the same?' or vice versa. 113. Again, the additional stipulator can stipulate for **less**, but **not** for **more**. And so if I stipulate for 10,000 he can stipulate for 5,000, but not the other way round, stipulating for more. Again, if I make **an absolute** stipulation, he can stipulate **conditionally, but not the other way round**. However, **the notions of more and less are applied not only to amount but also to time; and so it is more to give something at once, less to give it after an allowance of time**. 114. Note that in this area of the law some special rules apply. The additional stipulator's heir has no action. Again, a slave who makes an additional stipulation achieves nothing, although in all other cases he acquires for his owner by a stipulation. It is the received opinion that the same applies to a person in bondage; his position is that of a slave. An additional stipulation by a person in his father's power does have some effect, but not that of acquisition for his parent, although in all other cases he acquires for his father by making a stipulation. Indeed, he himself can sue only if he leaves his father's power without suffering status-loss, for instance, by his father's death or by himself being

eius aut quod ipse flamen Dialis inauguratus est.
eadem de filia[1] familias et quae in manu est, dicta
intellegemus.[2]

115. Pro eo quoque, qui promittit, solent alii obligari, quorum alios sponsores, alios fidepromissores,
alios fideiussores appellamus. 116. Sponsor ita interrogatur: IDEM DARI SPONDES? fidepromissor *ita*: IDEM
FIDEPROMITTIS? fideiussor ita: IDEM[3] FIDE TVA ESSE
IVBES? uidebimus de his autem[4], quo nomine possint
proprie adpellari, qui ita interrogantur: IDEM DABIS?
IDEM PROMITTIS? IDEM FACIES? 117. Sponsores quidem et fidepromissores et fideiussores saepe solemus
accipere, dum curamus, ut diligentius nobis cautum
sit; adstipulatorem uero fere tunc solum adhibemus,
cum ita stipulamur, ut aliquid post mortem nostram
detur; *quia enim ut ita nobis detur*[5] stipulando nihil
agimus, adhibetur adstipulator[6], ut is post mortem
nostram agat; qui si quid fuerit consecutus, | de *resti-
tue*ndo eo mandati iudicio heredi meo tenetur.

159
t. 8.

118. Sponsoris u*ero* et fidepromissoris similis condicio *est*, fideiussoris ualde dissimilis. 119. Nam illi
quidem nullis obligationibus accedere possunt nisi uer-

---

1) filiae V.   2) intellegemus pro eo V. *deinde sequitur
linea vacua.*   3) iδ (*quod ter scribit V pro* idem, *cf. Apogr.
p.* 262 *i. f.*) V. id *A. Pernice.*   4) an *Hu.; sed hac emen-
datione locus corruptus non magis sanatur, quam ceterorum
conatibus. videtur Gaius egisse de differentia, quae est inter
adpromissores et duos reos promittendi.*   5) quia—detur *suppl.
Hu. Mommsenum secutus.*   6) autem stipulato⁻ V.

§ 115. *cf. I.* 3, 20 *pr. Paul.* 1, 9, 5. 1, 20. *Fest. v. adpro-
missor* (*Bruns* II⁷, 2).

§ 116. *cf. supra* 3, 92. *infra* 4, 137. *Gai epit.* 2, 9, 2.
C. Greg. tit. de sponsoribus et fideiussoribus (*lib.* XII). *I.* 3, 20, 7.
D. 45, 1, 5, 2 (*Pomp.* 722). 45, 1, 75, 6 (*Ulp.* 675). 46, 1, 8 *pr.*
(*Ulp.* 2938). *C.* 8, 40 (41), 12 (*a.* 230). *Corn. Nep. Att.* 9, 4.
Cic. ad Att. 1, 8, 3; 10, 6.

§ 117. *cf. I.* 3, 20 *pr. supra* 3, 100; 110. *infra* 3, 216.
D. 44, 7. 1, 8 (*Gai.* 498). 17, 1, 59 *pr.* (*Paul.* 1480).

§ 119. *cf. I.* 3, 20, 1. si mulier] *cf. supra* 3, 108. aut

inaugurated as a priest of Jupiter. We are to understand what we have said as applying to a daughter in power or to a woman in marital subordination as well.

115. **It is common for others to bind themselves on behalf of the promissor**; we **call** them either personal sureties* or sureties* or **guarantors***, according to the promise which they give. 116. The question put to a personal surety is: 'Do you solemnly promise to give the same?'; to a surety: 'Do you faithfully promise the same?'; to a guarantor: 'Do you faithfully authorise the same?' However, we must consider the proper name for people to whom the question put is: 'Will you give the same?', 'Do you promise the same?' or 'Will you do the same?' 117. Note that a frequent **reason for invoking** these various kinds of **guarantee is that** we **are anxious to have greater security**; almost the only case for bringing in an additional stipulator, on the other hand, is that we are stipulating for something to be given after our death. As we ourselves achieve nothing by making such a stipulation, an additional stipulator is brought in so that he can sue after our death. And if he gets anything, he is liable to my heir by an action on mandate to make it over.

118. While the legal position of a personal surety and a surety is similar, that of a guarantor is markedly different. 119. For note that the first two cannot accede to any obligation except one by words, and

borum, quamuis interdum ipse, qui[1] promiserit, non
fuerit obligatus, uelut si *mulier* aut pupillus sine tutoris auctoritate aut quilibet post mortem suam dari
promiserit. at illud quaeritur, si seruus aut peregrinus spoponderit, an pro eo sponsor aut fidepromissor
obligetur. 119ᵃ. Fideiussor uero omnibus obligationibus, id est siue re siue uerbis siue litteris siue consensu contractae fuerint obligationes, adici potest. at
ne illud quidem interest, utrum ciuilis an naturalis
obligatio sit, cui adiciatur; adeo quidem, ut pro seruo
quoque obligetur, siue extraneus sit, qui a seruo fide-
iussorem accipiat, siue ipse dominus in id, quod sibi
debeatur. 120. Praeterea sponsoris et fidepromissoris
heres non tenetur, nisi si de peregrino fidepromissore
quaeramus et alio iure ciuitas eius utatur; fideiussoris
autem etiam heres tenetur. 121. Item sponsor et fide-

---

1) quid V.

---

pupillus] *cf. supra* 3, 107. *D.* 46, 1, 25 (*Ulp.* 404). post mor-
tem] *cf. supra* 3, 100. si seruus] *cf. supra* 3, 93. *Pers. sat.* 5, 78.
§ 119ᵃ. *cf. D.* 46, 1, 70, 3 (*Gai.* 510). 46, 1, 8, 1 (*Ulp.* 2939).
46, 1, 56, 1 (*Paul.* 1397). *C. I. L.* VIII 2553. Ill 940 (*Bruns* I⁷,
329). *BGU* 887 (*Chrest.* 272). *Pap. Lips.* 4, 6. 5 II 2 (*Chrest.* 171).
§ 120. *cf. I.* 3, 20, 2. *Gai epit.* 2, 9, 2. *infra* 4, 113. *Paul.*
2, 17, 16. *D.* 46, 1, 69 (*Tryph.* 32). 17, 1, 14 *pr.* (*Ulp.* 913). 46,
1, 4, 1 (*Ulp.* 2919). 46, 1, 27, 3 (*Ulp.* 656). *C.* 8, 40 (41), 24
(*a.* 294).
§ 121. per legem Furiam] *cf. infra* 4, 22. biennio liberan-
tur] *cf. Ulp. fr. disp.* 3 (*Iurispr.* I 498). *D.* 46, 3, 71, 1 (*Cels.*
229). 44, 3, 4 (*Iav.* 107). 45, 3, 25 (*Ven.* 69). 46, 1, 69 (*Tryph.* 32).
17, 1, 29, 6 (*Ulp.* 130). *C.* 8, 40 (41), 29 = *Bas.* 26, 1, 93. *Cic.
ad Att.* 12, 14, 2. 12, 17. 12, 19, 2. tempore quo] *D.* 46, 1, 57
(*Scaev.* 184). 45, 1, 60 (*Ulp.* 644). 45, 1, 72, 1; 2 (*Ulp.* 645). 46,
6, 4, 4; 7 (*Ulp.* 1734). 45, 1, 73 *pr.* (*Paul.* 400). 46, 6, 1 (*Paul.*
401). 46, 7, 1 (*Paul.* 402). tot partes] *cf. D.* 46, 3, 34, 1; 10 (*Iul.*
717). 46, 3, 37 (*Iul.* 906). 46, 3, 5, 1 (*Ulp.* 2908). 45, 1, 72 *pr.*
(*Ulp.* 643). fideiussores uero] *cf. I.* 3, 20, 4. *Paul.* 1, 20. *D.* 46,
1, 17 (*Iul.* 839). 46, 1, 26 (*Gai.* 199). 46, 6, 12 (*Pap.* 205). 27,
7, 7 (*Pap.* 440). 46, 1, 51, 1; 2; 4; 5 (*Pap.* 441). 46, 1, 27, 1
(*Ulp.* 656). 46, 1, 28 (*Paul.* 409). *C.* 8, 40 (41), 10, 1 (*Alex.*).
8, 40 (41), 16 (*a.* 241). 4, 18, 3 (*a.* 531).

sometimes are bound when the actual promissor is not, for instance, where a woman or child under guardianship promises something without a guardian's authorisation or where someone promises to give after his own death. But there is a question whether a personal surety or surety is bound if a slave or foreigner has promised using the verb 'spondere'. 119a. **A guarantor**, on the other hand, **can be** taken **for all sorts of obligations, by conduct, by words, by writing, or by agreement. It does not even matter whether the obligation is legal or natural. The use of a guarantor for natural obligations allows even a slave's obligation to be guaranteed. The party requiring the slave to provide a guarantor can be an outsider or the slave's owner securing a debt owed to himself.** 120. Moreover, the heir of a personal surety or surety is not bound, unless a foreign surety is in question and his state applies a different rule; **the heir of a guarantor**, however, **is also** liable. 121. Then, the personal surety and surety

promissor *per* legem Furiam biennio liberantur, et
quotquot erunt numero eo tempore, quo pecunia peti
potest, in tot partes diducetur¹ inter eos obligatio, et
singuli *in* uiriles partes uocabuntur²; fideiussores uero
perpetuo tenentur, et quotquot erunt numero, singuli
160 in solidum | obligantur. itaque liberum est creditori,
t. 8. a quo ue*lit*, *so*lidum petere. sed nunc ex epistula
diui Hadri*ani compellitur* creditor a singulis, qui modo
soluendo sint, par*tes* pete*re.* eo igitur distat haec
epistula a lege Furia, quod si quis ex sponsoribus
aut fidepromissoribus soluendo non sit, hoc onus *ad
ceteros non pertinet, si uero ex fideiussoribus*³, ad cete-
ros⁴ quoque pertinet. 121ᵃ. Sed cum lex Furia tantum in Italia locum habeat, euenit, ut in cete*ris*⁵ prouinciis sponsores quoque et fidepromissores proinde
ac fideiussores in perpetuum⁶ teneantur et singuli in
solid*um* obligentur, nisi ex epistula diui Hadriani hi
quoque⁷ adiuuen*tur* in parte.⁸ 122. Praeterea inter
sponsores et fidepromissores lex Apuleia quandam
societatem introduxit. nam si quis horum plus sua
portione soluerit, de eo, quod amplius dederit, aduersus
ceteros actiones constituit. quae lex ante legem Furiam lata est, quo tempore in solidum obligabantur.
unde quaeritur, an post legem Furiam adhuc legis
Apuleiae beneficium supersit; et utique extra Italiam
superest. nam lex quidem Furia tantum in Italia
ualet, Apuleia uero etiam in ceteris prouinciis.⁹ sed

---

1) deducitur V. diducitur *edd.*   2) uocabuntur *Poeschmann.* hocabentur V.   3) ad—fideiussoribus *suppl. Hu.;*
Mommsen ita: hoc onus ad ceteros non pertinet; sed ex
fideiussoribus etsi unus tantum soluendo sit, ad hunc onus ceterorum quoque pertinet.   4) ceterorum V.   5) *del.*
Albertario.   6) perpetuo V. *cf. infra* § 145.   7) qc. V
8) nisi—in parte *del. Beseler.*   9) nam—prouinciis *del. Albertario.*

---

§ 121ᵃ. *cf. Ulp. disp. fr.* 8 (*Iurispr.* 1, 498).
§ 122. *cf. I.* 3, 20, 4. *D.* 50, 16, 32 (*Paul.* 403). 46, 1, 39
(*Mod.* 194).

are discharged after two years by the Furian Act; and, when it becomes possible to sue for the money, the obligation will be divided into as many shares as there are then sureties and each will be liable for his proportional share only. On the other hand, guarantors are liable without limit of time and, **however many there are, each is liable for the whole amount. And so the creditor can sue whichever he pleases for the whole. But now under a letter of the Emperor Hadrian the creditor is compelled to divide the burden of his demand between all the solvent guarantors.** And so the regime in this letter differs from that of the Furian Act in that if any personal surety or surety **is insolvent** this **burden** does not fall on **the others**; with **a guarantor**, on the other hand, it does. 121a. But as the Furian Act applies only in Italy the effect is that in the other provinces* personal sureties and sureties are bound without limit of time and are each under an obligation for the whole amount, as in the case of guarantors, unless they too are helped in part by the letter of the Emperor Hadrian. 122. Moreover, the Apuleian Act introduced a kind of partnership between personal sureties and sureties. If one of them paid more than his share, this law established actions for him against the others in respect of the overpayment. This Act was passed before the Furian Act, when they were each liable for the full amount. And so the question arises whether the benefit of the Apuleian Act survives the Furian Act. It certainly survives outside Italy; for the Furian Act only applies in Italy, while the Apuleian Act applies in the other provinces as well. But there

an etiam in Italia[1] beneficium legis Apuleiae supersit, ualde quaeritur. ad *fideiussores autem lex* Apuleia non pertinet. itaque si creditor ab uno totum *con*secutus fuerit, huius sol*i*us detrimentum er*it*, scilicet si is, pro quo fideiussit, soluendo non sit. sed *ut ex* | supra 161 dictis[2] apparet, is, a quo creditor totum petit, poterit ex epistula diui Hadriani desiderare, ut pro parte in se detur actio. **123.** Praeterea lege Cicereia cautum est, ut is, qui sponsores aut fidepromissores accipiat, praedicat[3] palam et declaret, et de qua re satis accipiat et quot sponsores a*ut* fidepromissores in eam obligationem accepturus sit; et nisi praedixerit, permittitur[4] sponsoribus et fidepromissoribus intra diem XXX. praeiudicium postulare, quo quaeratur, an ex ea lege praedictum sit; et si iudicatum fuerit praedictum non[5] esse, liberantur. qua lege fideiussorum mentio[6] nulla fit; sed in usu[7] est, etiam si fideiussores accipiamus, praedicere.

124. Sed beneficium legis[8] Corneliae omnibus commune est. qua lege idem[9] pro eodem apud eundem eodem anno uetatur in ampliorem summam obligari creditae pecuniae quam in XX milia[10]; et quamuis sponsores uel fidepromissores in amplam pecuniam, uelut in[11] sestertium C milia *se obligauerint, tamen dumtaxat*

---

1) in Italia *Krueger*. alis V.   2) dicti V.   3) praedicatur V.   4) promittit V.   5) nam V.   6) menti V. 7) usum V. 8) legum V. 9) id V. 10) milib. V.   11) si V.

---

§ 123. *cf. D.* 50, 16, 33 (*Ulp.* 647). *Schol. Bobiens. in Cic. orat. in Clod. et Cur.* 5 (*p.* 333 *Orell.*). *Liv.* 42, 7, 1; 21, 7. § 124. *cf. D.* 39, 5, 24 (*Iav.* 59). 45, 1, 59 (*Iul.* 838). 12, 1. 22 (*Iul.* 867). 46, 1, 49, 1 (*Pap.* 336). 44, 7, 22 (*Afr.* 17). 46, 1, 63 (*Scaev.* 313). *Plutarch. Caes.* 11. *Anton.* 2. idem pro eodem] *cf. D.* 50, 17, 193 (*Cels.* 270). pecuniam creditam] *cf. D.* 44, 7, 42 (*Ulp.* 649). sine ulla condicione] *cf. D.* 12, 1, 37; 39 (*Pap.* 32). 45, 1, 120 (*Pap.* 383). 45, 1, 73, 1 (*Paul.* 405). appellatione pecuniae] *cf. D.* 50, 16, 178 *pr.* (*Ulp.* 296). 50, 16. 222 (*Herm.* 41). *C.* 4, 18, 2, 1[b] (*a.* 531).

really is room for debate whether the benefit of the Apuleian Act also survives in Italy. But the Apuleian Act does not apply to guarantors. And so **if the creditor gets the whole amount from one** guarantor, **he alone must bear the loss if the principal debtor is insolvent**. But as appears from what has been said above, **the one from whom the creditor claims the whole can,** in terms of **the Emperor Hadrian's letter, ask for the action against him to be limited to his share**. 123. Moreover, the Cicereian Act provides that anyone taking personal sureties or sureties should openly state in advance and declare both the matter in respect of which he is taking security and how many personal sureties and sureties he proposes to take; and if he does not make this statement in advance the personal sureties and sureties are allowed to ask for a preliminary declaratory judgment within thirty days on the question whether the statutory statement was made. If it is found that the statement was not made they are released. Under this Act no mention is made of guarantors; but the practice is to make a statement in advance even when we take guarantors.

124. But all of them have the benefit of the Cornelian Act. This Act prohibits anyone from binding himself on behalf of any one debtor to any one creditor in any one year for a sum of money lent greater than 20,000 sesterces. Even if personal sureties or sureties bind themselves in a large sum, 100,000 sesterces for instance, their liability is still limited to a

in xx milia tenentur.[1] pecuniam autem creditam dicimus non solum eam, quam credendi causa damus, sed
omnem, quam tum, cum[2] contrahitur[3] obligatio, certum est[4] debitum iri, id est, *quae* sine ulla condicione
deducitur in obligationem[5]; itaque et ea pecunia, quam
in diem certum dari stipulamur, eodem numero est, quia
certum est eam debitum iri[6], licet post tempus petatur. appellatione autem pecuniae omnes res in ea
lege significantur; itaque *et*[7] si uinum uel frumentum
162 aut[8] si fundum | uel hominem stipulemur, haec lex
obseruanda est. **125.** Ex quibusdam tamen causis permittit ea lex in infinitum satis accipere, ueluti si
dotis nomine uel eius, quod ex testamento tibi debeatur, aut iussu iudicis satis accipiatur. et adhuc lege
uicesima hereditatium cauetur, ut ad eas satisdationes,
quae ex ea lege proponuntur, lex Cornelia non pertineat. **126.** In eo[9] quoque iure par condicio est
omnium, sponsorum, fidepromissorum, fideiussorum,
quod ita obligari non possunt, ut[10] plus debeant, quam
debet[11] is, pro quo obligantur.[12] at ex diuerso, ut
minus debeant, obligari possunt, sicut in adstipulatoris persona diximus; nam ut adstipulatoris, ita et
horum obligatio accessio est principalis obligationis,
nec plus in accessione esse potest quam in principali

---

1) se—tenentur *suppl. Hu.*   2) tum cum *Krueger.*
tunc V.   3) contrahit V.   4) esset V.   5) obligatione V.
6) debitum iri] debitiuri V.   7) *add. Hu.*   8) et V.
9) iure *ins.* V. *del. Hu.*   10) possunt ut *Inst.* possit ut regula V.   11) deberet V.   12) obligaretur V.

§ 125. dotis nomine] *cf. D.* 24, 3, 41 (*Pap.* 382). lege
uicesima hereditatium] *cf. D.* 1, 2, 2, 44 (*Pomp.* 178). 2, 15, 13.
11, 7, 37. 28, 1, 7. 35, 2, 68. 50, 16, 154 (*Macer* 45—49). *Paul.*
4, 6. *Plin. panegyr.* 37—39. *Dio Cass.* 55, 25, 5. *C. I. L.*
VI 10229 *l.* 116—119 (*Bruns* I⁷, 308). *B. G. U.* 326 *col.* II 10
(*Bruns* I⁷, 314). *Pap. Amh.* II, 72 (*Bruns* I⁷, 320). *Pap. Oxy.*
8, 1114, 15. 10, 1274, 14.
§ 126 *cf. I.* 3, 20, 5. *supra* 3, 113. *D.* 46, 1, 9 (*Pomp.*
727). 46, 1, 8, 7—11 (*Ulp.* 2940. 2941).

maximum of 20,000. We define money lent, however, as including not only money which we give on loan but also all money which is certain to be owed at the time when an obligation is contracted – that is, money which there is an obligation to pay with no conditions attached; and so even if we stipulate for money to be paid on a specific day, it is counted, because it is certain that the money is payable, although action for it is postponed for a time. Note that the term 'money' in this Act means everything; and so if we stipulate for wine or corn or a farm or a slave, this Act must be adhered to. 125. All the same, the Act does allow unlimited guarantees in some cases, for instance, guarantees for dowry or for what is owed you under a will or those given by judicial orders. And, in addition, the Act on the 5% estate duty provides that the Cornelian Act does not apply to the guarantees required under its provisions. 126. Another respect in which all of them, personal sureties, sureties and guarantors, are in the same legal situation is this: **their obligation cannot be greater than the principal debtor's. But, conversely, they can have a lesser obligation**, as we said in the case of an additional stipulator; for like the additional stipulator's, **their obligation is accessory to the principal obligation, and an accessory cannot be greater than the principal.** 127. They are all in the

reo.[1] 127. In eo quoque par omnium causa est[2], quod si qui*d* pro reo[3] soluer*int*, eius reciperandi causa hab*ent* cum eo mandati iudicium; et ho*c* amplius sponsores ex lege Publilia propriam habent actionem in duplum, quae appellatur depensi.
128. Litteris obligatio fit ueluti in[4] nominibus[5] transscripticiis. fit autem[6] nomen transscripticium duplici modo, uel a re in personam uel a persona in personam. 129. *A re in personam trans*scriptio fit, ueluti si id, quod *tu* ex emptionis causa aut conductionis aut societatis mihi debeas, id expensum tibi tulero. 130. A persona in personam transscriptio fit, ueluti si id, quod mihi Titius debet, tibi id ex¦pen- 163 sum tulero, id est si Titius te *pro*[7] se delegauerit mihi. 131. Alia causa est eorum nominum, quae arcaria uocantur. in his enim rei[8], non litterarum obligatio consistit, quippe non aliter ualent[9], quam si numerata

---

1) re *Inst.* 2) esse V. 3) eo V. 4) *del. Hu. sine ratione probabili. cf. infra* 3, 135. 5) nominibus *Hu.* nobis V. 6) an V. 7) *add. Hu.* 8) rebus V. 9) ualet V.

---

§ 127. *cf. I.* 3, 20, 6. *D.* 46, 1, 15 *pr.* (*Iul.* 693). 46, 1, 18 (*Iul.* 841). 46, 1, 21, 5 (*Afr.* 82). 17, 1, 6, 2 (*Ulp.* 907). 17, 1, 10, 11 (*Ulp.* 910). 46, 1, 4 *pr.* (*Ulp.* 2919). 16, 1, 31 (*Paul.* 1024). 46, 1, 66 (*Paul.* 1025). 46, 1, 67 (*Paul.* 1047). 17, 1, 20, 1 (*Paul.* 1836). 17, 1, 40 (*Paul.* 192). *C.* 4, 35, 6 (*a.* 238). 8, 40 (41), 14 *pr.* (*a.* 239). lege Publilia] *cf. infra* 4, 22. depensi] *cf. infra* 3, 216. 4, 9; 25; 102; 171; 186. *Paul.* 1, 19, 1. *D.* 17, 1, 52 (*Iav.* 71). 17, 1, 50 (*Cels.* 266). 46, 3, 71, 1 (*Cels.* 229). *lex Rom. Burg.* 14, 8. *lex Iul. munic.* 114 (*Bruns* I[7], 108). *Cic. ad fam.* 1, 9, 9. *ad Att.* 1, 8, 3.
§§ 128. 129. *cf. Gai epit.* 2, 9, 12. *Theoph.* 3, 21 *pr.* (*p.* 348 *Ferr.*). *infra* 3, 137 *sq. I.* 3, 21. *Plaut. Truc.* 1, 1, 51 = 70 *sq. Cic. de offic.* 3, 14, 59. *ad Att.* 4, 18, 2. *pro Rosc. Com.* 1, 4. 2, 5 *sq. in Verr.* 2, 1, 23, 60; 36, 92; 39, 100. *orat.* 46, 158. *Velius Longus* (*Grammat. Latin. ed. Keil, vol. VII*) 60, 10. *Gell.* 14, 2, 7.
§ 130. *cf. D.* 16, 1, 13 *pr.* (*Gai.* 229). *Liv.* 35, 7, 2. *C. I. L.* XIV 3471 (*Bruns* I[7], 353).
§ 131. *cf. Cic. top.* 3, 16.

13*

same case in this respect also, that **if** they **pay anything on behalf of the principal** they **can recoup** themselves **by bringing an action on mandate against him**; beyond this, personal sureties have an action of their own for double under the Publilian Act, called the action on expenditure*.

128. An **obligation** is created by writing **in account-entries**, for instance. Now, an account-entry creates a debt in two ways, either by transfer from a transaction to a person or by transfer from one person to another. 129. An account-entry is made by transfer from a transaction to a person when, for instance, I enter as paid out to you what you owe me as a result of a purchase, a hire or a partnership. 130. An account-entry is made by transfer from one person to another when, for instance, I enter as paid out to you what Titius owes to me, that is to say, if Titius has offered me you as a substitute debtor in place of himself. 131. It is a different case with debts called 'cash-entries'. With them the obligation arises by conduct, not by writing, because, of course, they are effective only if the money is actually paid out; the

sit pecunia; numeratio autem pecuniae rei[1] facit obligationem. qua de causa recte dicemus arcaria nomina
nullam facere obligationem, sed obligationis factae
testimonium praebere. 132. Unde *non*[2] proprie dicitur[3]
arcariis nominibus etiam peregrinos obligari, quia non
ipso nomine, sed numeratione pecuniae[4] obligantur;
quod genus obligationis iuris gentium est. 133. Transscripticiis uero nominibus an obligentur peregrini,
merito quaeritur[5], quia quodam modo iuris ciuilis est
talis obligatio; quod Neruae placuit. Sabino autem
et Cassio uisum est, si a re in personam fiat nomen
transscripticium, etiam peregrinos obligari; si uero a
persona in personam, non obligari. 134. Praeterea
litterarum obligatio fieri uidetur chirografis et syn-
grafis, id est, si quis debere se aut daturum se scri-
bat, ita scilicet[6], si eo nomine stipulatio non fiat.
quod genus obligationis proprium peregrinorum est.

135. Consensu fiunt obligationes in emptionibus et
uenditionibus, locationibus conductionibus, societatibus,
mandatis. 136. Ideo autem *istis* modis consensu dici-
mus obligationes contrahi, quod[7] neque uerborum |

---

1) rein V.   2) *add. Hu.*   3) dicit V.   4) ipso nomine
sed numeratione pecuniae *Goeschen.* ipse nome s nomen ratione
pēcae V.   5) quaerit V.   6) scilic. ut V.   7) quod] quo V.
quia *Dig. Inst.*

---

§ 132. *cf. Ascon. in Cornelian. p.* 57 *ed. Orelli.*

§ 133. *cf. Liv.* 35, 7, 2. *Cic. pro Fonteio* 5, 11.

§ 134. *cf. Ps.-Ascon. in Verr.* 2, 1, 60; 91 *p.* 175; 184 *ed.*
Baiter (Bruns II[7], 72). *Cic. in Verr.* 2, 1, 36, 91. *de dom.* 50,
129. *de haruspic. resp.* 13, 29. 16, 34. *pro Rabir. Postum.* 3, 6.
Philippic. 2, 37, 95. *ad Attic.* 5, 21, 10. 6, 2, 7. 6, 1, 15. *Am-*
mian. 18, 5, 2.

§§ 135—137. = *I.* 3, 22. *D.* 44, 7, 2. *cf. Gai epit.* 2, 9, 13.

§ 135. *cf. D.* 19, 4, 1, 2 *(Paul.* 502). 44, 7, 48 *(Paul.* 1224).
45, 1, 35, 2 *(Paul.* 1845).

§ 136. *cf. D.* 19, 2, 14 *(Ulp.* 1607). 17, 1, 1 *pr.*; 1 *(Paul.*
484). 18, 1, 1, 2 *(Paul.* 503). 45, 1, 35, 2 *(Paul.* 1845). 17, 2,
4 *pr. (Mod.* 199).

paying out of the money creates an obligation by conduct. And for this reason we can properly say that cash-entries do not create any obligation but provide evidence of an obligation already created. 132. And so it is not correct to say that even foreigners come under an obligation by cash-entries, as their obligation arises not from the entry itself but from payment of the money; and this kind of obligation belongs to the law of all peoples. 133. It is a good question, on the other hand, whether foreigners incur obligations by account-entries, because this kind of obligation is in a sense part of state law. Nerva so held, but Sabinus and Cassius took the view that if the account-entry is by transfer from a transaction to a person even foreigners are bound; they are not bound if the account-entry is from one person to another. 134. Moreover, an obligation by writing appears to arise through the documents called in Greek 'chirographs' and 'syngraphs', that is to say, where a person writes that he owes or that he will give something, but, of course, only where no stipulation is involved. This kind of obligation is peculiar to foreigners.

135. **Obligations are created by agreement in sale, hire, partnership, and mandate. 136. They are said to arise by agreement in these cases because for the obligation to come into being there is absolutely no need for** any special form of words **or of**

neque scripturae ulla proprietas desideratur[1], sed suffi- 164
cit eos, qui negotium gerunt, consensisse. unde inter
absentes quoque talia negotia contrahuntur, ueluti per
epistulam aut per internuntium, cum alioquin uerborum obligatio inter absentes fieri non possit. 137. Item
in his contractibus alter alteri obligatur de eo, quod
alterum alteri ex bono et aequo praestare oportet[2],
cum alioquin in uerborum obligationibus alius stipuletur alius promittat et in nominibus alius expensum
ferendo obliget alius obligetur. 138. [sed absenti expensum ferri potest, etsi uerbis obligatio cum absente
contrahi non possit.][3]

[De emptione et uenditione.]

139. Emptio et uenditio contrahitur, cum de pretio
conuenerit, quamuis nondum pretium numeratum sit
ac ne arra quidem data fuerit. nam quod arrae nomine datur, argumentum est emptionis et uenditiouis

---

1) desiderat V.   2) de — oportet *suspecta habet Pringsheim*
Z. S. 52, 123.   3) *§ 138 ut glossema damnavit Krueger.*

---

§ 137. *cf. infra* 4, 61. ex bono et aequo] *cf. D.* 17, 1,
12, 9 *i. f.* (*Ulp.* 911). praestare] *cf. Non. s. h. verb.* p. 371 *ed.*
Mercier. infra 4, 2. in uerborum obligationibus] *cf. supra*
3, 92. in nominibus] *cf. supra* 3, 128 *sq.*
    § 139. = *I.* 3, 23 *pr. cf. Gai epit.* 2, 9, 14. de pretio
conuenerit] *cf. D.* 18, 1, 72 *pr.* (*Pap.* 173). 18, 1, 2, 1 (*Ulp.* 2427).
18, 1, 36 (*Ulp.* 1156). 18, 1, 38 (*Ulp.* 127). *C.* 4, 48, 4 (*a.* 239).
4, 38, 9 (*a.* 294). arra] *cf. D.* 18, 1, 35 *pr.* (*Gai.* 238). 18, 3,
6 *pr.* (*Scaev.* 237). 18, 3, 8 (*Scaev.* 28). 14, 3, 5, 15 (*Ulp.* 825).
19, 1, 11, 6 (*Ulp.* 931). *C.* 4, 45, 2, 1 (*a.* 293). 4, 49, 3 (*a.* 290).
4, 21, 17 (*a.* 528). *Liber iuris Syro-Roman. ed. Bruns-Sachau*
L. 38 (*p.* 13). 51 (*p.* 17). *P.* 21 (*p.* 52). *Ar.* 20 (*p.* 84). 32 (*p.* 87).
98 (*p.* 108). *Arm.* 14 (*p.* 120). 27 (*p.* 123). 97 (*p.* 139). *Plaut.*
Most. 3, 1, 115 = 649. 3, 3, 15 = 918. 4, 3, 21 = 1013. *Poenul.*
5, 6, 22 = 1359. *Rud. prol.* 46. 2, 6, 71 = 555. 3, 6, 23 = 861.
Mil. Glor. 4, 1, 11 = 957. *Trucul.* 3, 2, 20 = 688. *Varro de*
l. l. 5, 175 (*Bruns* II[7], 53). *Gell.* 17, 2, 21. *Isid. orig.* 5, 25,
20; 21 (*Bruns* II[7], 82). 9, 7, 6. *Hieron. epistol. ad Ephes.* 1, 13.
Suidas v. Ἀρραβών.

writing. It is enough if the parties to the transaction merely come to an agreement. Consequently, contracts of this kind can be made by people at a distance, by letter or messenger for example; by contrast an obligation by words cannot be entered into between parties who are at a distance. 137. Another feature of these contracts is that both parties come under reciprocal obligations to conform to the standard of what is fair and reasonable. By contrast, in obligations by words, only one party promises in response to the other's question and in account-entries one party binds and the other is bound by the entry of a payment out. 138. [But the entry of a payment out can be made when the party bound is at a distance – although an obligation by words cannot be contracted with a person who is at a distance.]

[Sale]

139. The contract of sale is concluded when the parties agree on the price. It makes no difference if it is not then paid, or if no token* of agreement is given. A token of agreement only goes towards proving that a contract of sale has been made. 140.

contractae. 140. Pretium autem certum esse debet.
nam alioquin si ita inter nos conuenerit, ut quanti
Titius rem aestimauerit, tanti sit empta, Labeo negauit
ullam uim hoc negotium habere; cuius opinionem
Cassius probat. Ofilius et eam emptionem et uenditionem *esse putauit*[1]; cuius opinionem Proculus secu-
tus est. 141. Item pretium in numerata pecunia con|-
165 sistere debet. *nam* in ceteris rebus an pretium esse
possit, ueluti homo[2] aut toga aut fundus alterius rei
pretium esse possit, ualde quaeritur.[3] nostri praeceptores putant etiam in alia re posse consistere pretium;
unde illud est, quod uulgo putant per permutationem
rerum emptionem et uenditionem contrahi, eamque
speciem emptionis[4] uenditionisque uetustissimam esse;
argumentoque utuntur Graeco poeta Homero, qui aliqua parte sic ait:

ἔνθεν ἄρ' οἰνίζοντο καρηκομόωντες Ἀχαιοί,
ἄλλοι μὲν χαλκῷ, ἄλλοι δ' αἴθωνι σιδήρῳ,
ἄλλοι δὲ ῥινοῖς, ἄλλοι δ' αὐτῇσι βόεσσιν,
ἄλλοι δ' ἀνδραπόδεσσι,[5]

et reliqua. diuersae scholae auctores dissentiunt aliud-
que esse existimant permutationem rerum, aliud emptionem et uenditionem; alioqu*in* *non posse* rem ex-
pediri permutatis rebus, quae uideatur res uenisse et
quae pretii nomine data esse, sed rursus utramque

---

1) esse putavit *suppl. Hu.*   2) hoc modo V.   3) quaerit V.   4) emptionisque V.   5) *Graeca om.* V.

---

§ 140. *cf. I.* 3, 23, 1. *D.* 18, 1, 35, 1 (*Gai.* 238). 18, 1, 7,
1; 2 (*Ulp.* 2713). 18, 1, 37 (*Ulp.* 54). *C.* 4, 38, 15 (*a.* 530). *infra*
3, 142; 143.
§ 141. = *I.* 3, 23, 2. *cf. Serv. ad Verg. Georg.* 3, 306.
Maecian. assis distrib. 45. *D.* 18, 1, 1, 1 *et* 19, 4, 1 *pr.* (*Paul.*
502). 19, 5, 5, 1 (*Paul.* 1322). *C.* 4, 64, 1 (*a.* 238). 4, 64, 8
(*a.* 294). *Plin. nat. hist.* 33, 6; 7; 46. *Isid. orig.* 5, 24, 23. *Arist.*
Pol. 1, 9 (12 *sq.*) *p.* 1357ᵃ. *C. I. L.* IX 3513 (*Bruns* I⁷, 284). *l.* 12
(*quod emptum erit aere aut argento etc.*). Homero] *Il.* 7, 472—475.

The price must be certain. Otherwise, if we come to an agreement that the buyer can have the thing at a price to be fixed by the valuation of Titius, Labeo denied that the arrangement had any effect whatever; Cassius approves his opinion. Ofilius thought that even this was a sale, and Proculus has followed the latter's opinion. 141. The price must be in money. There is a considerable dispute whether the price of something can consist in other things, a slave, a toga or a piece of land. Our teachers think that it can. That is their inference from the common belief that an exchange of things is a sale, actually the oldest type. They appeal for support to Homer, who at one place says: 'Then the long haired Achaeans bought wine, some with bronze and others with shining steel, some with hides and some with live oxen, others with slaves' and so on. The authorities of the other school take a different position and hold that exchange and sale are different contracts. In particular, they think it impossible in an exchange of goods to settle which thing has been sold and which given as price; they hold it absurd, again,

rem uideri et uenisse et utramque pretii nomine datam
esse absurdum uideri. sed ait Caelius Sabinus, si rem
tibi uenalem habenti, ueluti fundum, [acceperim et][1]
pretii nomine hominem forte dederim, fundum quidem
uideri uenisse, hominem autem pretii nomine datum
esse, ut fundus[2] acciperetur.[3]

142. Locatio autem et conductio similibus regulis
constituitur[4]; nisi enim merces certa statuta sit, non
uidetur locatio et conductio contrahi. 143. Unde si
alieno arbitrio merces permissa sit, uelut quanti[5] Titius
aestimauerit, | quaeritur, an locatio et conductio con- **166**
trahatur. qua de causa si fulloni polienda curandaue,
sarcinatori sarcienda uestimenta dederim[6] nulla statim
mercede constituta, postea tantum daturus, quanti inter
nos conuenerit, quaeritur, an locatio et conductio contrahatur. 144. Item[7] si rem tibi utendam dederim et
inuicem aliam rem utendam acceperim, quaeritur, an
locatio et conductio contrahatur. 145. Adeo autem
emptio et uenditio et locatio et conductio familiarita-
tem aliquam inter se habere uidentur, ut in quibusdam causis quaeri soleat, utrum emptio et uenditio
contrahatur an locatio et conductio, ueluti si qua res

---

1) acceperim et *del. Mommsen.* accesserim et *Hu.* 2) fundum V. 3) *sequitur linea vacua in* V. 4) constituuntur V.
5) qua V. 6) dederimus V. 7) item *Polenaar.* uel V.

§ 142. *cf. I.* 3, 24 *pr. D.* 19, 2, 2 *pr.* (*Gai.* 501). *Gai epit.*
2, 9, 15. *infra* 3, 162. *D.* 24, 1, 52 *pr.* (*Pap.* 184). 41, 2, 10, 2
= 19, 2, 46 (*Ulp.* 1525). *Isid. orig.* 5, 25, 12.
§ 143. *cf. I.* 3, 24, 1. 3, 23, 1 *i. f. D.* 19, 2, 25 *pr.* (*Gai.*
245). 19, 5, 22 (*Gai.* 244). *C.* 4, 38, 15, 3 (*a.* 530). *infra* 3, 205.
§ 144. *cf. I.* 3, 24, 2. *D.* 19, 5, 17, 3 (*Ulp.* 806).
§ 145. *cf. I.* 3, 24, 3. *D.* 19, 2, 2, 1 (*Gai.* 501). in praediis municipum] *cf. D.* 30, 71, 5 (*Ulp.* 1246). 39, 2, 15, 27 (*Ulp.*
1278). 6, 3, 1; 3 (*Paul.* 345). 39, 4, 11, 1 (*Paul.* 2027). *Gro-
matici Latin. ed. Lachm. p.* 116. *Cic. ad fam.* 13, 7; 11. 8, 9, 4.
Plin. epist. 7, 18 (*Bruns* I[7], 349). *Tabul. Veleias* (*C. I. L.*. XI
1147. *Bruns* I[7], 348) *n.* 43. *C. I. L.* IX 136 (*Bruns* I[7], 378
n. 10). *C. I. L.* X 5853 (*Bruns* I[7], 351). *C. I. L.* IV *Suppl.* 1,
3340 *nr.* 125 [138] (*Bruns* I[7], 360).

that each thing be regarded as both sold and paid
as the price. But Caelius Sabinus says that if you
have something on offer for sale, a farm, for instance,
and I give, say, a slave as its price, it is the farm which
is to be regarded as sold and the slave as given by way
of price, for the purpose of acquiring the farm.

142. **Hire is formed under** similar **rules**; unless a
definite **charge is settled** there is considered to be no
hire. 143. And so the question arises whether hire is
formed **when the hire charge is left to be decided by
another party,** for instance, where it is the valuation
made by Titius. **For this reason if** I **give clothes to a
cleaner to be cleaned or to have some other
treatment, or to a tailor to be mended, and the
charge is not fixed then and there but left to** our
later agreement, there is a question whether **hire** is
contracted. 144. Again, **there** is a **question whether
hire** is **contracted if you and** I **exchange things for
temporary use.** 145. **The relationship between hire
and sale is so close that on some facts it has been
difficult to say which of the two contracts is made,**
for instance, where something is leased in **perpetuity.**

in perpetuum locata sit. quod euenit in praediis muni-
cipum, quae ea lege locantur, ut, quamdiu [id][1] uecti-
gal praestetur, neque ipsi conductori neque heredi
eius praedium auferatur; sed magis placuit locationem
conductionemque esse. 146. Item[2] si gladiatores ea
lege tibi tradiderim, ut in singulos, qui integri exierint, pro sudore denarii XX mihi darentur, in eos uero
singulos, qui occisi aut debilitati fuerint, denarii[3] mille,
quaeritur, utrum emptio et uenditio an locatio et conductio contrahatur. et magis placuit eorum, qui integri exierint, locationem et conductionem contractam
uideri, at eorum, qui occisi aut debilitati sunt, emptionem et uenditionem esse; idque ex accidentibus
167 apparet[4], tamquam sub condicione | facta cuiusque
uenditione aut locatione.[5] iam enim non dubitatur,
quin sub condicione res uenire[6] aut locari possint.
147. Item quaeritur, si cum aurifice mihi conuenerit,
ut is ex auro suo certi ponderis certaeque formae
anulos mihi faceret[7] et acciperet uerbi gratia denarios CC, utrum emptio et uenditio an locatio et conductio contrahatur. Cassius ait materiae quidem emptionem uenditionemque contrahi, operarum autem
locationem et conductionem; sed plerisque placuit
emptionem et uenditionem contrahi. atqui si meum
aurum ei dedero mercede pro opera constituta, conuenit locationem conductionem contrahi.[8]

---

1) id *del. Puchta.* inde *Hu.*   2) item quaeritur V.
3) denarios V.   4) apparere *Hu.*   5) uenditione aut loca-
tione] uenditionem an locationem V.   6) ueniri V.
7) facere V   8) *sequitur linea vacua in* V.

---

§ 146. *cf. C. I. L.* II *suppl.* 6278 (*Bruns* I[7], 209) *l.* 36 *sq.*
56 *sq.* 63. non dubitatur] *cf. D.* 19, 2, 20 *pr.* (*Paul.* 518).
§ 147. = *I.* 3, 24, 4. *cf. D.* 19, 2, 2, 1 (*Gai.* 501). 19, 2,
31 (*Alf.* 71). 18, 1, 80, 3 (*Lab. ap. Iav.* 208). 18, 1, 65 (*Iav.*
123). 18, 1, 20 (*Pomp.* 548). 34, 2, 34 *pr.* (*Pomp.* 261). 19, 2,
22, 2 (*Paul.* 519).

This happens in relation to municipal **land**, which is leased on the express terms that, **so long as** the ground rent **is paid, it will not be taken away either from the lessee himself or from his heir**; but the received opinion does make this a hire. 146. Again, suppose I deliver gladiators to you on the express terms that I will get 20 for the efforts of each one who comes off unharmed but 1,000 for each one killed or maimed, is this sale or hire? The received opinion is that there is hire of the ones who come off unharmed but sale of those killed or maimed, and events determine the classification, as if there were a conditional sale or hire of each one. For there is no longer any doubt that things can be sold and hired subject to conditions. 147. **Another borderline case: a goldsmith agrees with** me **to make** me **rings of a given weight and design. The goldsmith is to use his own gold, and the charge is to be, say,** 200; **Cassius holds that this is sale of the material and hire of the work. But the** majority **decision has been to treat the whole transaction as sale. But suppose I bring my own gold and a charge is fixed for the work?** It is agreed **that the contract is hire.**

148. Societatem coire solemus aut totorum[1] bonorum aut unius alicuius negotii, ueluti mancipiorum emendorum aut uendendorum. 149. Magna autem quaestio fuit, an ita coiri possit societas, ut quis maiorem partem lucretur, minorem damni praestet. quod Quintus Mucius *contra naturam societatis esse censuit. sed Seruius Sulpicius, cuius*[2] etiam praeualuit sententia, adeo ita coiri posse societatem existimauit, ut dixerit illo quoque modo coiri posse, ut quis nihil omnino damni praestet, sed lucri partem capiat, si modo opera eius tam pretiosa uideatur, ut aequum sit eum cum hac pactione in societatem admitti. nam et ita posse coiri[3] societatem constat, ut unus pecuniam conferat, alter non conferat | et tamen lucrum inter 168 eos commune sit; saepe enim opera alicuius pro pecunia ualet. 150. Et illud certum est, si de partibus lucri et damni nihil inter eos conuenerit, tamen aequis ex partibus commodum ut incommodum inter eos commune esse; sed si in altero partes expressae fuerint, uelut in lucro, in altero uero omissae, in eo[4] quoque, quod omissum est, similes partes erunt. 151. Manet autem societas eo usque, donec in eodem sensu[5] per-

---

1) tutorum V.   2) contra—cuius *suppl. ex Inst.; sed cf. Rotondi Bull.* 24, 13.   3) coire V.   4) eodem V.   5) consensu *Inst.*

---

§ 148. = *I.* 3, 25 *pr. cf. Gai epit.* 2, 9, 16. *D.* 17, 2, 5 *pr.* (*Ulp.* 917). 17, 2, 63 *pr.* (*Ulp.* 923).

§ 149. *cf. I.* 3, 25, 2. *Gai epit.* 2, 9, 16. *D.* 17, 2, 6 (*Pomp.* 532). 17, 2, 5, 1 (*Ulp.* 917). 17, 2, 29, 1; 2 (*Ulp.* 2742). 17, 2, 52, 2 (*Ulp.* 922). 17, 2, 30 (*Paul.* 1732). *C.* 4, 37, 1 (*a.* 293). *Cic. pro Rosc. Com.* 10, 29. *Quintil. Declam.* 320.

§ 150. *cf. I.* 3, 25, 1; 3. *Paul.* 2, 16. *D.* 17, 2, 29 *pr.* (*Ulp.* 2742). *C. I. L.* III 950 (*Bruns* I[7], 376 *n.* 171).

§ 151. = *I.* 3, 25, 4. *cf. Gai epit.* 2, 9, 17. *D.* 17, 2, 63, 10 *i. f.* (*Ulp.* 925). 17, 2, 73 (*Ulp.* 2388). 17, 2, 65 *pr.*; 3—8 (*Paul.* 495). 17, 2, 3, 1 (*Paul.* 493). 17, 2, 4, 1 (*Mod.* 199). *C.* 4, 37, 5 (*a.* 294). 3, 37, 5 (*a.* 294); 7 (*a.* 531). *Petron. Satir.* 10. *Apul. Metam.* 10, 14.

148. **Partnerships usually cover either all the partners' worldly wealth or else a single business, for instance, buying and selling slaves.** 149. However, there was a great question whether a partnership could be formed on such terms that one party would take a larger share of the profit but a smaller share of loss. And **Quintus Mucius thought** not, because **it was contrary to the nature of partnership.** But **Servius Sulpicius, whose view has prevailed**, considered that such a partnership could be made; indeed, he went so far as to say that the contract can be entered on the terms that one party makes no contribution at all to the loss, but takes a share in any profit, so long as his **services** are regarded as **so valuable** that it is fair for him **to be brought in to the partnership** on those terms. **For** it is now accepted that **a partnership agreement can validly require one party to put up money but not the other, while still giving both parties equal shares of profit. Some people's services are often as valuable as a money contribution.** 150. And this is certain, that **if nothing is agreed** among them **about the shares of profit and loss**, then both advantage and disadvantage must be shared **equally**. But if **shares** are **stated** for the one, **the profit for instance, but not stated for the other, then the shares for the one not** stated will be the same. 151. **A partnership lasts as long as the partners remain of the same mind but ends when one party renounces. Clearly**

seuerant; at cum aliquis renuntiauerit societati, societas soluitur. sed plane si quis in hoc renuntiauerit
societati, ut obueniens aliquod lucrum solus habeat,
ueluti si mihi totorum bonorum socius, cum ab aliquo
heres esset relictus, in hoc renuntiauerit societati, ut
hereditatem solus lucri faciat, cogetur[1] hoc lucrum
communicare; si quid uero aliud lucri fecerit, quod
non captauerit, ad ipsum solum pertinet. mihi uero,
quidquid omnino post renuntiatam societatem adquiritur, soli conceditur. 152. Soluitur adhuc societas etiam
morte socii, quia qui societatem contrahit, certam personam sibi eligit. 153. Dicitur etiam kapitis deminutione solui societatem, quia ciuili ratione kapitis deminutio[2] morti coaequatur; sed utique si adhuc consen-
tiant in societatem[3], noua uidetur incipere societas.
154. Item si cuius ex sociis bona publice aut pri-
uatim uenierint, soluitur societas. sed ea quidem[4]
societas, de qua loquimur, id est, quae nudo consensu
contrahitur[5], iuris gentium[6] est; itaque inter omnes
homines naturali ratione consistit. 154.[a][7] Est autem

---

1) coget V.　　2) *hinc incipit* F *inde a* tio.　　3) societatem F.
societate V.　　4) ea quidem F.　haec quoque V.　　5) nudo
consensu contrahitur F. consensu contrahitur nudo V.　6) gentium F.　cogentium V.　　7) §§ 154[a]. 154[b] *desunt in* V.

---

§ 152. = *I.* 3, 25, 5. *init. cf. Gai. epit.* 2, 9, 17. *D.* 17,
2, 59 *pr.* (*Pomp.* 577). 17, 2, 35 (*Ulp.* 2744). 17, 2, 52, 9 (*Ulp.*
992). 17, 2, 63, 10 (*Ulp.* 925). 17, 2, 65, 9; 10 (*Paul.* 495). 17,
2, 4, 1 (*Mod.* 199).　3, 5, 20 (21), 2 (*Paul.* 191).
　　§ 153. *cf. Gai. epit.* 2, 9, 17. *supra* 3, 101. 1, 159 *sq. D.* 17,
2, 58, 2 (*Utp.* 927). 17, 2, 63, 10 (*Ulp.* 925). 17, 2, 65, 11 (*Paul.*
495). 17, 2, 4, 1 (*Mod.* 199).
　　§ 154. *cf. I.* 3, 25, 7; 8. *supra* 3, 78 *sq. cf. D.* 17, 2, 63,
10 (*Ulp.* 925). 17, 2, 65, 1; 12 (*Paul.* 495). 17, 2, 4, 1 (*Mod.*
199). priuatim] *cf. D.* 12, 6, 67, 2 (*Scaev.* 14). 21, 2, 57 *pr.*
(*Gai.* 388). iuris gentium] *cf. D.* 2, 14, 7 *pr.*; 1 (*Ulp.* 242).
　　§ 154[a]. *cf. supra* 2, 219. 3, 148. *D.* 10, 2, 39, 3 (*Scaev.* 223).
27, 1, 31, 4 (*Paul.* 1340). *Varro de re rust.* 3, 16, 2. *Val. Max.*

though, if someone withdraws with an eye to a profit for himself alone, for example, where a partner with me in all worldly wealth is left heir to somebody's estate and renounces the partnership in order to take the inheritance himself, he will be compelled to share his profit. But if he makes some gain without having snatched at it, it does go to him alone. I, on the other hand, keep for myself anything at all which I receive after the renunciation. 152. **Partnership is also dissolved by the death of a partner, because when one enters a partnership one does so with a specifically chosen person.** 153. It is said that partnership is also dissolved by status-loss because, according to the principles of state law, status-loss is equivalent to death; but the truth is that, if the people still want to be partners, a new partnership is held to come into being. 154. Again, if **the estate of any of the partners**

aliud genus societatis proprium ciuium Romanor*um*.
olim enim mortuo patre familias inter suos heredes
quaedam erat legitima simul et naturalis societas quae
appell*abatur ercto non cito, id est dominio non di-
uiso: erct*um[1] enim do*minium est, unde*[2] erus dominus dicitur: ciere a*utem* diuidere est: unde caedere[3]
et secare [et diuidere][4] dicimus. 154ᵇ. Alii quoque
qui uolebant eandem habere societatem, poterant id
consequi apud praetorem certa[5] legis actione. in hac
autem societate fratrum ceterorumue, qui ad exemplum
fratrum suorum societatem coierint, illud proprium
erat, [unus] quod uel unus ex sociis communem seruum
manumittendo liberum faciebat et omnibus libertum
adquirebat: item unus *rem c*ommunem man*cipando eius
faciebat, qui mancipio accipiebat.*[6]

155. Mandatum consistit, siue nostra gratia mandemus siue aliena; itaque siue ut mea negotia geras
siue ut alterius, mandauerim, contrahitur mandati ob-

---

1) ercto — erctum *suppl. Arangio-Ruiz, qui tamen scribit*
erctum, citum, dominium, diuisum; *in F legi iam non possunt
nisi duae ultimae litterae vocis* erctum.   2) dominium est
unde *suppl. Arangio-Ruiz.*   3) cedere F.   4) et diuidere
del. Arang.   5) cepta F?   6) *suppl. Arangio-Ruiz.*

4, 4, 8. *Plut. Aem. Paul.* 5. 28. *Liv.* 41, 27, 2. *Vell.* 1, 10, 6.
Val. Max. 2, 7, 5. *Frontin. Strat.* 4, 1, 31. ercto non
cito] *cf. Cic. de orat.* 1, 237. *Quintil. inst. or.* 7, 3, 13. *Gell.*
1, 9, 12. *Fest. p.* 82 *s. v.* erctum citumque. *p.* 72 *s. v.* diser-
tiones. *p.* 110 *s. v.* inercta. *Serv. ad Aen.* 8, 642. *Stephan.
ad Dig.* 17, 2, 52, 6 (*Schol. Basil.* I *p.* 753 *ed. Heimb.*); *cf.
Pringsheim Z. S.* 45, 491 *sq. Lawson ibid.* 49, 208. *Plaut.
Trucul.* 21?

§ 154ᵇ. ad exemplum fratrum] *cf. D.* 17, 2, 5 *pr.* (*Ulp.*
917). 17, 2, 52, 8 (*Ulp.* 922). 17, 2, 63 *pr.* (*Ulp.* 922). 17, 2, 1, 1
(*Paul.* 493). 17, 2, 2 (*Gai.* 233, *interpol.*).

§ 155. *cf. Gai epit.* 2, 9, 18. *I.* 3, 26 *pr.* = *D.* 17, 1, 2 *pr.*
(*Gai* 503). *D.* 44, 7, 5 *pr.* (*Gai.* 506). 3, 3, 46, 4—6 (*Gai.* 85).
17, 1, 10 *pr.* (*Ulp.* 909).

is **sold** up by **public or private** creditors **the partnership is dissolved**. But note that the partnership of which we are speaking, that is, one contracted by mere agreement, is part of the law of all peoples and so as a matter of natural reason it can subsist among all men.

154a. There is, however, another kind of partnership peculiar to Roman citizens. For in former times on the death of the head of a family there arose among his immediate heirs a kind of partnership which was at the same time statutory and natural; it was called 'ercto non cito', that is 'ownership undivided'; for 'erctum' means ownership and hence 'erus' is a word for 'owner'; and 'ciere' means 'to divide' so that 'caedere', to strike, and 'secare' to cut, are related words for division. 154b. Other people also, if they wanted to have this kind of partnership, could achieve that before the praetor using a set action in the law*. However, in this partnership between brothers and between other people entering a partnership in imitation of brothers, a special feature was that even one of the partners by manumitting a slave held in co-ownership made him free and the freedman of all of them; again, one partner by mancipating a thing held in co-ownership made it the property of the recipient.

155. **Mandate** exists **whether** we **give a commission in** our **interest or in the interest of a third party**. And so whether I commission you **to do** my **business** or someone else's the obligation of mandate

ligatio, et inuicem alter alteri tenebimur in id[1], quod
uel me tibi uel te mihi bona fide praestare oportet.[2]
156. Nam si tua gratia tibi mandem, superuacuum est
mandatum; quod enim tu tua gratia facturus sis, id
de tua sententia, non ex meo mandatu facere debes;
itaque si otiosam pecuniam domi tuae *te* habentem
hortatus fuerim, ut eam faenerares, quamuis iam ei
mutuam dederis, a quo seruare non potueris, non tamen
habebis mecum man*dati* actionem. item si hortatus
sim, ut rem aliquam emer*es*, quam*uis* non expedierit
tibi eam emisse, non tamen tibi mandati tenebor.[3] et
adeo haec ita sunt, ut quaeratur, an mandati teneatur[4],
qui mandauit tibi, ut Titio pecuniam faenerares. Seruius[5] negauit: non magis hoc casu obligationem[6] consistere putauit, quam si generaliter alicui mandetur,
uti pecuniam suam faeneraret. *sed* sequimur Sabini
opinionem contra sentientis[7], q*uia* non aliter Titio
credidisses, quam si tibi mandatum esset. 157. Illud
constat, si quis de ea re mandet, quae contra bonos
170 mores | est, non contrahi obligationem, ueluti si tibi[8]
mandem[9], ut Titio furtum aut[10] iniuriam facias.
158. Item si quis *quid* post mortem meam faciendum

---

1) in id *Hu.* id in V.   2) oportere V.   3) teneri V.
4) teneantur V.   5) sed seruius V.   6) obligatum V.
7) contra sentientis *Mommsen.* consentientis V.   8) si tibi
Goeschen. ti sibi V.   9) mandem *Goeschen.* mandemus V.
10) autem V.

---

§ 156. *cf. I.* 3, 26 *pr.*; 6 = *D.* 17, 1, 2 *pr.*; 6 (*Gai.* 503).
Plaut. Epid. 263. *D.* 17, 1, 32 (*Iul.* 919). 17, 1, 6, 5 (*Ulp.* 907).
17, 1, 16 (*Ulp.* 914). 50, 17, 47 *pr.* (*Ulp.* 909). et adeo haec ita
sunt] *cf. D.* 46, 1, 13 (*Iul.* 232). 46, 3, 95, 10 (*Pap.* 340). 17, 1, 6, 4
(*Ulp.* 907). 17, 1, 10, 11 (*Ulp.* 910). 4, 4, 13 *pr.* (*Ulp.* 404).
§ 157. *cf. Gai epit.* 2, 9, 18. *I.* 3, 26, 7. *D.* 18, 1, 35, 2
(*Gai.* 238). 17, 1, 6, 3 (*Ulp.* 907). 17, 1, 12, 11 (*Ulp.* 911). 17,
1, 22, 6 (*Paul.* 487). *C.* 1, 14, 5, 2 (*a.* 439).
§ 158. *cf. supra* 3, 100. *D.* 17, 1, 13 (*Gai.* 232). 17, 1, 12,
17 (*Ulp.* 912).

is contracted, and we will be bound one to another for what I must do for you or you do for me in good faith. 156. For if I give you **a commission in your own interest it is superfluous**; in respect of anything you propose to do in your interest you should rely on your own decision and not on my mandate. **And so if you have money lying idle at home and I encourage you** to lend it out at interest, you will not have an action of mandate against me, even if you lend it out to someone from whom you cannot get it back. Again, if I have encouraged you **to buy something I will not be liable in an action on mandate even if it turns out that the purchase was not to your advantage. This has been carried so far as to raise a question whether the action of mandate can lie against someone who asks you to lend to Titius at interest.** Servius said not; he thought that no obligation could arise in this case any more than in the case of a general mandate to lend out money at interest. But we follow **Sabinus's** contrary opinion **based on the argument that, but for the mandate, you would not have chosen to lend to Titius.** 157. It is settled that if someone gives a mandate **for an immoral act**, no obligation is contracted, **as where I give you a mandate to commit a theft or contempt* against Titius.** 158. Again, if someone gives me a commission to be executed after my death the mandate is

mihi[1] mandet, inutile mandatum est, quia generaliter placuit ab heredis persona obligationem incipere non posse. 159. Sed recte quoque *contractum*[2] mandatum, si dum adhuc integra res sit, reuocatum fuerit, euanescit. 160. Item si adhuc integro mandato[3] mors alterutrius alicuius[4] interueniat, id est uel eius, qui mandarit, uel eius, qui[5] mandatum susceperit, soluitur mandatum; sed utilitatis causa receptum est, ut si mortuo eo, qui mihi mandauerit, ignorans eum decessisse exsecutus fuero mandatum, posse me[6] agere mandati actione; alioquin iusta et probabilis ignorantia damnum mihi [non] adferet.[7] et huic simile est, quod plerisque placuit, si debitor meus manumisso dispensatori meo per ignorantiam soluerit, liberari eum, cum alioquin stricta iuris ratione non posset[8] liberari eo, quod alii soluisset, quam cui soluere deberet. 161. Cum autem is, cui recte mandauerim, egressus fuerit mandatum, ego quidem[9] eatenus cum eo habeo mandati actionem, quatenus mea interest inplesse eum mandatum, si modo

---

1) *suppl. Hu.*   2) contractum *Inst.* consummatur V; *del. Hu.* 3) mandatum V.   4) alicuius *om. Inst.; del. Goeschen.*   5) cui V. 6) posse me V. *Inst.* possem *Gradenwitz.*   7) alioquin—adferet *del. Beseler Beitr.* 4, 111.   8) possent V.   9) quid V.

---

§ 159. = *I.* 3, 26, 9. *cf. Gai epit.* 2, 9, 19. *Vat.* 333. *D.* 17, 1, 12, 16 (*Ulp.* 912). 46, 3, 12, 2 (*Ulp.* 2736). 17, 1, 15 (*Paul.* 1609).

§ 160. = *I.* 3, 26, 10. *cf. Gai epit.* 2, 9, 19. *Vat.* 333. *D.* 17, 1, 34, 1 (*Afr.* 92). 17, 1, 27, 3 (*Gai.* 232). 17, 1, 57 (*Pap.* 639). 39, 5, 19, 3 (*Ulp.* 1689). 17, 1, 26 *pr.*; 1 (*Paul.* 488). 17, 1, 58 *pr.* (*Paul.* 1316). 2, 1, 6 (*Paul.* 96). 17, 2, 65, 10 (*Paul.* 495). 46, 3, 108 (*Paul.* 1016). *C.* 4, 35, 15 (*a.* 294). et huic simile est *etc.*] *cf. D.* 12, 1, 41 (*Afr.* 85). 46, 3, 18 *et* 16, 3, 11 (*Ulp.* 2869). 46, 3, 51 (*Paul.* 178). *C.* 8, 42 (43), 3 (*a.* 238). dispensatori] *cf. supra* 1, 122 *i. f.*

§ 161. *cf. I.* 3, 26, 8. *Gai epit.* 2, 9, 20. *Paul.* 2, 15, 3. *D.* 17, 1, 33 (*Iul.* 868). 17, 1, 4 (*Gai.* 504). 17, 1, 41 (*Gai.* 89). 17, 1, 3, 2 (*Paul.* 485). 17, 1, 5 *pr.* — 3; 5 (*Paul.* 485). 17, 1, 22 *pr.*; 1 (*Paul.* 487). *Gell.* 1, 13.

ineffective, because it is generally accepted that an obligation cannot begin in the person of one's heir. 159. **But a contract of mandate, although properly made, is dissolved by a revocation before any change of position. 160. It is similarly discharged by the death of either party – that is, of either the mandator or the person who accepted the mandate – before the task is performed. But convenience has required that if** my **mandator dies and I carry through his commission in ignorance of his death I should nonetheless have the action on mandate. Otherwise I would suffer loss through a reasonable and demonstrable mistake. As** most people **accept, this is a similar case to that in which** my **debtor makes payment to** my **cashier without knowing that the cashier has been freed. He is discharged by his payment despite the fact that in the strict sense of the law he could not be released, in that he paid to the wrong person.** 161. However, if I give someone an effective mandate and he exceeds its terms, note that I have an action of mandate against him to the extent of my interest in his performance of the mandate, provided that he could perform it; but

implere potuerit; at ille mecum agere non potest. itaque si mandauerim tibi, ut uerbi gratia fundum mihi
sestertiis C emeres, tu sestertiis CL emeris, non habe-
171 bis mecum | mandati actionem, etiamsi tanti uelis
mihi dare[1] fundum, quanti emendum tibi mandassem;
idque maxime Sabino et Cassio placuit. quod si minoris emeris, habebis mecum scilicet actionem, quia qui
mandat, ut C milibus emeretur, is utique mandare[2]
intellegitur, uti minoris, si posset, emeretur.[3] 162. In
summa sciendum *est, quotiens faciendum* aliquid gratis
dederim, quo nomine si mercedem statuissem, locatio
et conductio contraheretur, mandati esse actionem,
ueluti si fulloni polienda curandaue uestimenta *dede-*
rim aut sarcinatori sarcienda.

163. Expositis generibus obligationum, quae ex
contractu nascuntur, admonendi sumus adquiri nobis
non solum per nosmet ipsos, sed etiam per eas personas, quae in nostra potestate, manu mancipioue sunt.
164. Per liberos quoque homines et alienos seruos,
quos bona fide possidemus, adquiritur nobis; sed tantum ex duabus causis, id est, si quid ex operis suis
uel ex re nostra adquirant. 165. Per eum quoque seruum, in quo usumfructum habemus, similiter ex duabus istis causis nobis adquiritur. 166. Sed qui nudum
ius Quiritium in seruo habet, licet dominus sit, minus

---

1) dari V.　　2) mandari V.　　3) emeret V.

---

§ 162. *cf. I.* 3, 26, 13. *D.* 17, 1, 36, 1 (*Iav.* 28). 19, 5, 22
(*Gai.* 244). 19, 5, 13 *pr.* (*Ulp.* 2747). 14, 1, 1, 18 (*Ulp.* 817)
17, 1, 1, 4 (*Paul.* 484). *C.* 4, 35, 1 (*Sever. et Anton.*). 4, 35, 20
(*Diocl. et Maxim.*).
　　§ 163. = *I.* 3, 28 *pr. cf. supra* 2, 86. *Paul.* 5, 8. *Plaut.*
Rud. 5, 3, 28 *sq.* = 1384.
　　§ 164. = *I.* 3, 28, 1. *cf. supra* 2, 86; 92. *cf. D.* 17, 1, 8, 5
(*Ulp.* 908).
　　§ 165. = *I.* 3, 28, 2. *cf. supra.* 2, 86; 91.
　　§ 166. *cf. supra* 2, 88. *D.* 45, 3, 36 (*Iav* 141).

he cannot bring an action against me. And so, if I **commission** you, say, to **buy a farm** for me **for 100,**000 and you buy it for 150,000 you will have no action of mandate against me, even though you are willing to let me have the farm for the sum at which I commissioned you to buy; and **Sabinus and Cassius** especially **were of that view. But if you buy below the limit you will of course have your action** against me, **because a person who gives a mandate for a purchase at 100,000 indisputably asks for it to be got for less if possible.** 162. **Lastly, it is important to notice** that wherever I give something to be done for nothing in circumstances in which, had I fixed a charge, there would have been **a contract of hire**, the action of mandate lies, for instance, **if I give clothes to a cleaner for cleaning or for some other treatment or to a tailor for repair.**

163. **So much for obligations from a contract. Now we must note that we can acquire rights not only through our own acts but also through the agency of persons within our paternal power,** or held in marital subordination or bondage by us. 164. **We acquire also through persons whom we hold in good faith as our slaves, whether they are in fact free or slaves of third parties. But we acquire only in two circumstances, namely, where they obtain something by their labour or from our capital.** 165. **We also acquire in the same two circumstances through a slave in whom we have a usufruct.** 166. But although a person who has the bare quiritary title in a slave is owner, nevertheless his rights in this matter are taken to be less than those of a

tamen iuris in ea[1] re habere intellegitur **quam** usufructuarius et bonae fidei possessor. nam placet ex
nulla causa[2] ei adquiri posse, adeo ut, etsi nominatim
ei dari stipulatus fuerit seruus mancipioue nomine[3]
eius acceperit, | quidam existiment[4] nihil ei adquiri. 172
167. Communem seruum pro dominica parte dominis
adquirere certum est, excepto eo, quod uni nominatim
stipulando[5] aut mancipio accipiendo illi soli adquirit[6],
uelut cum ita stipuletur: TITIO DOMINO MEO DARI
SPONDES? aut cum ita mancipio accipiat: HANC REM
EX IVRE QVIRITIVM LVCII TITII DOMINI MEI ESSE AIO,
EAQVE EI EMPTA ESTO HOC AERE AENEAQVE LIBRA.
167ᵃ. Illud quaeritur, an. quod[7] nomen domini[8] adiectum
efficit[9], idem faciat unius ex dominis iussum inter-
cedens. nostri praeceptores proinde[10] ei, qui iusserit,
soli adquiri existimant, atque si nominatim ei soli[11]
stipulatus esset seruus mancipioue quid[12] accepisset;
diuersae scholae auctores proinde utrisque adquiri
putant, ac si nullius[13] iussum interuenisset.
168.[14] Tollitur autem obligatio praecipue solutione
eius, quod debeatur.[15] unde quaeritur, si quis consen-
tiente creditore aliud pro alio soluerit, utrum ipso

---

1) ea V. adquisita ab eo *Hu.*   2) causa alia V.   3) nomen V.
4) existimant V.   5) stipuland∗ F. stipulando uel mancipiando V.
6) adquirit F. adquiritur V.   7) an quod F; *Goeschen.* tamquam V.
8) nomen domini F. domini nomen V.   9) efficit F; *Goeschen.* domini
et fecit V.   10) proinde F. perinde (?) V.   11) *om.* F.   12) *om.* V.
13) nullis V. *in* F *iam non legitur.*   14) [QVIBVS MO]DIS SOLVVNTVR
[OBLI]GATIONES R(ubrica) F.   15) debeatur F. V. debetur. *Inst.*

§ 167. = *I.* 3, 28, 3 *cum Theoph.* (*p.* 376 *Ferr.*). cf. *I.* 3,
17, 3. *D.* 41, 1, 37, 3 (*Iul.* 608). mancipio accipiendo] *cf. supra*
1, 119. 2, 87.
§ 167ᵃ. cf. *D.* 45, 3, 6 (*Pomp.* 726). 41, 1, 63, 2 (*Tryph.*
19). 45, 3, 5; 7 (*Ulp.* 2952). 7, 1, 25, 6 (*Ulp.* 2587). 45, 3, 33, 1
(*Paul.* 1199). *C.* 4, 27, 2 (3) (*a.* 530).
§ 168. cf. *I.* 3, 29 *pr.* *Gai epit.* 2, 10 *pr.* *D.* 50, 16, 176
(*Ulp.* 2924). aliud pro alio] *cf. D.* 23, 3, 25 (*Paul.* 1758). 12,
1, 2, 1 (*Paul.* 430). 46, 3, 46 *pr.* (*Marcian.* 255). *C.* 8, 42 (43), 17
(*a.* 293); 24 (*a.* 294). *Senec. de ben.* 6, 5, 2.

usufructuary or possessor in good faith. For it is accepted that he has no basis for acquisition and this is carried so far that some people consider that even if a slave stipulates that something be given to the person with bare quiritary title by name or receives something by mancipation in his name nothing is acquired for him. 167. **A slave held in co-ownership certainly acquires for his owners in proportion to their shares. That does not apply where he acquires for one of the owners by taking a stipulation in his name alone or by receiving** a mancipation **in his name, as where, for instance, he takes a stipulation in these words: 'Do you solemnly promise to give to my owner Titius?'** or when the mancipation takes the form: 'I say that this thing belongs by quiritary right to Lucius Titius my owner and let it be bought for him with this bronze and these bronze scales*'. 167a. But does **an order** to act **given by one of the owners** have the same effect as inserting his name? Our teachers consider that where an owner has given an order, the acquisition is to him alone, in exactly the same way as where a slave has taken a stipulation or received by mancipation in his name alone. The authorities of the other school think that there is acquisition to each of them, exactly as if no order had been given by any of them.

168. **Now, an obligation is discharged** primarily **by performance**. And so, **where someone makes a substituted performance with the consent of the creditor** is he freed by operation of law as our teachers

iure liberetur, quod nostris praeceptoribus placuit[1], an
ipso iure maneat obligatus, sed aduersus petentem per
exceptionem[2] doli mali defendi debeat, quod diuersae
scholae auctoribus uisum est.

169.[3] Item[4] per acceptilationem tollitur obligatio.
acceptilatio autem est ueluti imaginaria solutio. nam
quod[5] ex uerborum obligatione tibi debeam, id si uelis mihi
173 remittere, poterit sic fieri, ut patiaris haec uerba m|e
dicere: QVOD TIBI EGO[6] PROMISI, HABESNE ACCEPTVM? et
tu respondeas: HABEO. 170. Quo[7] genere, ut diximus,
tolluntur illae obligationes, quae in[8] *uerbis consistunt*[9],
non etiam ceterae; consentaneum enim est uisum[10] uerbis
factam obligationem posse aliis uerbis dissolui. sed id,
quod ex alia causa debeatur, potest in stipulationem
deduci et per acceptilationem dissolui. 171. Quamuis autem
acceptilatio ueluti[11] imaginaria solutio sit[12], tamen mulier
sine tutore auctore[13] acceptilationem[14] facere non potest,
cum alioquin solui ei sine tutore auctore[15] possit. 172. Item
quod debetur[16], pro parte recte soluitur[17]; an autem
in partem acceptilatio[18] fieri possit, quaesitum *est*.

---

1) placuit F. *Lachmann.* placet V.   2) per exceptionem F.
exceptione V.   3) R(ubrica) de acceptilatione R(ubrica) F. *om.* V.
4) item F.   fit V.   5) nam quod F.   quod enim V.   6) tibi ego F.
ego tibi V.   7) q**o F.   quod V.   8) tolluntur illae obligationes,
quae in F. *om.* V.   9) *rest. ex Inst.; om.* V.   *in* F *legi iam non
possunt.*   10) est uisum F.   uisum est V.   11) dissolui — ueluti F.
om. V.   12) solutio sit F.   solutione V.   13) tutore auctore
Arangio. t. a V.   *in* F *legi non potest.* 14) acceptum V.   15) **tore
aucto*e F.   t. ā V.   16) deb***r F.   debet V.   17) **cte sol****-
tur F.   debet recte solui recte soluit V.   18) acceptum V.

§§ 169. 170. = *I.* 3, 29, 1.
§ 169. *cf. D.* 46, 4, 15 (*Pomp.* 737). 46, 4, 18, 1 (*Flor.* 21).
46, 4, 6 (*Ulp.* 2946). 46, 4, 8, 4 (*Ulp.* 2957). 46, 4, 9 (*Paul.*
1851). 34, 3, 7, 1 (*Ulp.* 2656). 46, 4, 1 (*Mod.* 195). *cf. etiam
apochas Pompeianas C. I. L.* IV (*Bruns* I⁷, 355 *sq.*).
§ 170. *cf. I.* 3, 29, 2. *D.* 46, 4, 18, 1 (*Flor.* 21). 46, 3, 80
(*Pomp.* 239). 46, 4, 8, 3 *et* 50, 17, 35 (*Ulp.* 2955).
§ 171. *cf. supra* 2, 85.
§ 172. *cf. I.* 3, 29, 1. pro parte| *cf. D.* 12, 1, 21 (*Iul.* 652).
46, 3, 9, 1 (*Ulp.* 2669). 12, 6, 26, 13 (*Ulp.* 774). 45, 1, 2, 1
(*Paul.* 1841). 45, 1, 85 (*Paul.* 810). 22, 1, 41, 1 (*Mod.* 293). an

have accepted? Or is he still bound as a matter of law but protected by the defence* of deceit against the creditor suing him – the view taken by the authorities of the other school?

169. **Next, obligations are discharged by verbal release, which involves a** sort of **pretence of performance. Suppose** you **have me as debtor under a stipulation and want to release me from my obligation. It can be done in this way:** you **should get** me **to say: 'What I have promised, have you received?' and then** you **should answer: 'I have'.** 170. **This type of discharge, as we have indicated, is applicable to verbal obligations, not to the others. It is appropriate that an obligation created by words should be dissoluble by other words. But obligations with another basis can be converted into a stipulation and then released verbally.** 171. But note that although a verbal release may be a sort of pretence of performance, a woman cannot give a verbal release without her guardian's authorisation, whereas otherwise performance can be made to her without her guardian's authorisation. 172. Again, while **there can be genuine performance of part of what is due**, it has been questioned whether **there can be a verbal release of part of a debt.**

173. Est et[1] alia species imaginariae solutionis, per aes et[2] libram; quod et ipsum genus certis ex[3] causis receptum[4] est, ueluti si quid eo nomine debeatur[5], quod per aes et libram gestum sit[6], siue quid[7] ex iudicati causa debeatur.[8] **174.** Adhibentur[9] non minus quam quinque testes et libripens; deinde is, qui liberatur[10], ita oportet loquatur[11]: QVOD EGO TIBI TOT MILIBVS[12] SESTERTIORVM[13] IVDIC*ATVS uel* DAMNATVS SVM[14] EO NOMINE ME A TE[15] SOLVO LIBEROQVE HOC AERE AENEAQVE LIBRA. HANC TIBI[16] LIBRAM PRIMAM POSTREMAMQVE EXPENDO[17] *SECVNDVM* LEGEM PVBLICAM. deinde asse percutit libram eumque dat ei[18], a quo[19] liberatur[20], ueluti soluendi causa. **175.** Similiter legatarius heredem eodem modo liberat de legato, quod per damnationem relictum est, ut tamen scilicet, sicut iudicatus condemnatum[21] se esse significat, ita heres *testamento* se dare damnatum esse dicat. de eo tamen tantum potest heres eo modo liberari, quod pondere numero constet, et ita, si certum sit. quidam et de eo, | quod mensura constat, idem[22] existimant.

174

1) et F. etiam V.   2) et F. etiam V.   3) *×* x F. in V.   4) receptisum V. 5) debeat V.   6) et V. *in* F *legi non potest*.   7) quod t V. *in* F *legi non potest*.   8) debeatur *Krueger*. debit V. *in* F *nihil legitur; sed quae Krueger addidit:* eaque res ita agitur, *haec spatium codicis* F *non admittit.*   9) athibemur(?) V. *in* F *nihil legi potest*.   10) liberat V. *in* F *nihil legi potest*.   11) oportet loquatur V. dicit *Arangio ratione habita spatii codicis* F, *cuius lineae nihil legitur nisi* de.   12) milibus V. ***us F.   13) sestertiorum *om.* V. 14) iudicatus uel damnatus sum *Levy sec.* F. condemnat****V.   15) EO NOMINE ME A TE] conmen*cte V. eo *nomine me a te* F.   16) *hic finit* F.   17) expende V.   18) dat ei *Bluhme*. dct el V.   19) quod V.   20) liberatum V.   21) condemnati V.   22) ind V.

autem *etc.*] *cf. D.* 46, 4, 10 (*Pomp.* 728). 46, 4, 17 (*Inl.* 721). 46, 4, 13, 1—3; 5 (*Ulp.* 298). 46, 4, 9 (*Paul.* 1851).

§ 173. *cf. Fest. v. nexum p.* 165 (*Bruns* II[7], 17). *Liv.* 6, 14, 5. *Cic. de leg.* 2, 21, 53 (*Iurispr.* I, 8). *cf.* 2, 19, 49. *de or.* 3, 40, 159. *Varro de l. l.* 7, 105 (*Bruns* II[7], 60). *Symm. ep.* 9, 114, 2.

§ 174. *cf. supra* 1, 119. 2, 104. *D.* 34, 3, 20 *pr.* (*Mod.* 322). soluo liberoque] *cf. Liv.* 22, 10, 6.   primam postremamque] *cf. Liv.* 1, 24, 7.

§ 175. *cf. supra* 2, 201 *sq. Cic. de leg.* 2, 19, 49; 21, 53.

173. There is also another kind of pretended performance, by bronze and scales. And this kind, too, has been recognised only for certain cases, for instance, where something is owed as a result of a transaction by bronze and scales or under a judgment. 174. No less than five witnesses and a scale-holder are assembled. Then the person being released should say: 'Whereas I have been judged liable or become bound to pay you so many thousands I release and free myself from you on that account by this bronze and these bronze scales. I weigh out this pound for you as first and last in accordance with the public statute'. Then he strikes the scales with the bronze and gives it to the person from whom he is obtaining his release, as if to make payment. 175. Similarly, a legatee can release an heir from payment of an obligatory legacy* by this method, but of course, just as a judgment-debtor states that he has been condemned the heir declares that he has had an obligation to give imposed on him by will. But all the same the heir can be freed in this way only in respect of things reckoned by weight or number and then only when the amount is fixed. Some people consider that the procedure also applies to things dealt with by measure.

176. Praeterea nouatione tollitur obligatio ueluti si
quod tu mihi debeas, a Titio dari stipulatus sim; nam
interuentu nouae personae noua nascitur obligatio et
prima tollitur translata in posteriorem, adeo ut *inter*dum, licet posterior stipulatio inutilis sit, tamen prima
nouationis iure tollatur, ueluti si quod mihi debes, a
Titio post mortem eius uel a muliere pupilloue sine
tutoris auctoritate stipulatus fuero; quo[1] casu rem
amitto; nam et prior debitor liberatur, et posterior
obligatio nulla est. non idem[2] iuris est, si a seruo
stipulatus fuero; nam tunc *prior* proinde adhuc obligatus tenetur, ac si postea a nullo stipulatus fuissem.
177. Sed si eadem persona sit, a qua postea stipuler,
ita demum nouatio fit, si quid in posteriore stipulatione noui sit, forte si condicio uel dies aut sponsor[3]
adiciatur aut detrahatur.[4] **178.** Sed quod[5] de sponsore
dixi*mus*, non constat. nam diuersae scholae auctoribus placuit nihil ad nouationem proficere sponsoris
adiectionem aut detractionem.[6] **179.** Quod autem diximus, si condicio adiciatur, nouationem fieri, sic intellegi oportet[7], ut ita dicamus factam nouationem, si
condicio extiterit; alioquin si defecerit, durat prior obligatio. sed uideamus, num is, qui eo nomine agat,
doli mali aut[8] pacti conuenti exceptione possit summoueri, quia uidetur inter eos id actum, ut ita ea res
peteretur, si posterioris | stipulationis exstiterit condicio. Seruius tamen Sulpicius existimauit statim et

175

---

1) quod V.   2) id V.   3) dies aut sponsor] sponsor
aut dies V.   4) trahatur V.   5) quae V.   6) detracta-
tionem V. 7) oportet *Inst.* c̄ V.   8) doli m. aut *del. Koschaker.*

§ 176. = *I.* 3, 29, 3. *cf. Theophil. ad h. l.* (*p.* 379 *Ferr.*).
Gai epit. 2, 9, 11. *supra* 2, 38. 3, 100; 107; 108; 119. *D.* 2, 14,
30, 1 (*Gai.* 62). 46, 2, 1 (*Ulp.* 2925).
§ 177. = *I.* 3, 29, 3. *cf. C.* 8, 41 (42), 8 (*a.* 530).
§ 179. = *I.* 3, 29, 3. *cf. D.* 46, 2, 24 (*Pomp.* 348). 46, 2,
31 *pr.* (*Ven.* 59). 2, 14, 30, 1; 2 (*Gai.* 62). 46, 3, 72, 1 (*Marcell.* 227). 46, 2, 8, 1 (*Ulp.* 2929). 46, 2, 14 (*Ulp.* 133). diximus]
supra § 177. a peregrino] *cf. supra* 3, 93; 119; 176.

176. **Obligations are also discharged by novation, where, for example, a stipulation is taken from Titius for what you owe to me. With the intervention of a new person, a new obligation is created; the earlier obligation is converted into the later and extinguished. Sometimes although the later stipulation is unenforceable the earlier is still extinguished by the novation. Suppose I stipulate for what you owe me from Titius after his death or from** a woman or **a child acting without a guardian's authorisation. I lose my right. The first debtor is released; the subsequent obligation is void. It is different where I take the stipulation from a slave. There the first debtor remains bound as if I had taken the later stipulation from no one at all.** 177. **If it is from the same person that I take the later stipulation, novation only happens if the second stipulation has some new feature, as, for instance, the addition or subtraction of a condition, a postponement, or a** personal surety. 178. But what we say about a personal surety is not settled; for the authorities of the other school have taken the view that the addition or subtraction of a personal surety does nothing to effect a novation. 179. **But when we say that adding a condition achieves a novation, we mean only that the novation happens if and when the condition is fulfilled. The old obligation survives if it fails.** But should not anyone suing on it be met by the defence of deceit or of agreement because the parties' arrangement would seem to have been that the object should be sued for only if the condition in the later stipulation were fulfilled? Yet Servius Sulpicius considered that there was an immediate novation even while the condition was

pendente condicione nouationem fieri, et si defecerit condicio, ex neutra causa agi posse *et* eo modo rem perire; qui consequenter et illud respondit, si quis id, quod sibi L. Titius deberet, a seruo fuerit stipulatus, nouationem fieri et rem perire, quia cum seruo agi non posset. *sed* in utroque casu alio iure utimur. nec magis his casibus nouatio fit, quam si id, quod tu mihi debeas, a peregrino, cum quo sponsus[1] communio non est, SPONDES uerbo stipulatus sim.

180. Tollitur adhuc obligatio litis contestatione, si modo legitimo iudicio fuerit actum. nam tunc obligatio quidem principalis dissoluitur[2], incipit[3] autem teneri reus litis contestatione. sed si[4] condemnatus sit, sublata litis contestatione incipit ex causa iudicati teneri. et hoc *est*, quod apud ueteres scriptum est ante litem contestatam dare debitorem oportere, post litem contestatam condemnari oportere, post condemnationem iudicatum facere oportere. 181. Unde fit, ut si legitimo iudicio debitum petiero, postea de eo ipso iure agere non possim, quia inutiliter intendo[5] DARI MIHI OPORTERE, quia litis contestatione dari oportere desiit, aliter atque si imperio continenti iudicio egerim; tunc enim nihilo minus obligatio durat, et ideo ipso iure postea agere possum[6], sed debeo per[7] exceptionem rei iudicatae uel in iudicium deductae summoueri. quae autem legitima *sint* | iudicia et quae 176 imperio continentia[8], sequenti commentario referemus.

---

1) sponsus *Savigny.* sponsio V.   2) dissoluit V.   3) incipiat V.   4) s' V.   5) indo V.   6) possumus V.
7) prae V.   8) *lectio incerta.* continentia *Mommsen.* contineantur *Hu.*

---

§§ 180. 181. cf. *infra* 4, 103 *sq.*; 114; 121; 123. *supra* 3, 83. *Fr. Vat.* 263 (*Pap.* 697). *I.* 4, 13, 10. *D.* 16, 2, 8 (*Gai.* 214). 15, 1, 50, 2 (*Pap.* 158). 46, 2, 11, 1 (*Ulp.* 797). 15, 1, 3, 11 (*Ulp.* 851). 12, 6, 60 *pr.* (*Paul.* 1301). 46, 2, 29 (*Paul.* 1420). *C.* 7, 54, 3 *pr.* (*a.* 531). sequenti commentario] 4, 103 *sq.*

outstanding and that if the condition had failed there could be no action on either basis, so that there was then an end to the matter. Following the logic of this he also gave an answer* that if someone stipulated from a slave for what was owed to him by L. Titius, a novation occurred and that was an end of the matter because no action could be brought against a slave. But in both cases we follow a different rule. There is no more a novation in these cases than there is if, in stipulating for what you owe me from a foreigner who does not share the use of the word 'spondere', I use the words: 'Do you solemnly promise?'

180. Next, an obligation is discharged by joinder of issue, so long as the case was taken in a statutory court. While the original obligation is then discharged, the defender now comes under an obligation through the joinder of issue. But if he is found liable, the joinder of issue is displaced and he comes under an obligation through the judgment. This is what the old lawyers* meant when they wrote that before joinder of issue a debtor has a duty to give; after joinder of issue he ought to be found liable; after being found liable he has a duty to satisfy the judgment. 181. And it follows from this that, if I sue for what is owed to me in a statutory court, I cannot as a matter of law sue for the same thing again thereafter, because I cannot effectively put in my principal pleading* 'that the thing ought to be given to me' because with joinder of issue the obligation to give ceased. It is different if I sue in a court dependent on magistral authority*; for then the obligation still survives, and so I can as a matter of law maintain another action later, but then I should be met by the defence of matter decided or carried to trial. Which courts are statutory and which are dependent on magistral authority will be dealt with in the next commentary.

182. Transeamus nunc ad obligationes, quae ex delicto nascuntur, ueluti si quis furtum fecerit, bona rapuerit, damnum dederit, iniuriam commiserit. quarum omnium rerum uno genere consistit[1] obligatio, cum ex contractu obligationes in IIII genera diducantur[2], sicut supra exposuimus. **183.** Furtorum autem genera Ser. Sulpicius et Masurius Sabinus IIII esse dixerunt, manifestum et nec manifestum, conceptum et oblatum[3]; Labeo duo, manifestum *et* nec manifestum; nam conceptum et oblatum species potius actionis esse furto cohaerentes quam genera furtorum; quod sane uerius uidetur, sicut inferius apparebit. **184.** Manifestum furtum[4] quidam id esse dixerunt, quod[5] dum fit, deprehenditur. alii uero ulterius, quod eo loco deprehenditur[6], ubi fit, uelut si in oliueto[7] oliuarum, in uineto uuarum furtum factum est[8], quamdiu in eo oliueto aut uineto fur[9] sit; aut si in domo furtum factum sit, quamdiu in ea domo fur sit. alii adhuc ulterius eo usque **** manifestum furtum esse dixerunt, donec perferret eo, quo perferre fur destinasset. alii adhuc ulterius, quandoque eam rem fur tenens uisus fuerit; quae sententia non optinuit. sed et illorum sententia, qui existimauerunt, donec perferret eo, quo fur destinasset, deprehensum furtum manifestum esse, ideo non uidetur probari, quia magnam recipit dubitationem, utrum |
177 unius diei an etiam plurium dierum spatio id terminandum sit; quod eo pertinet, quia[10] saepe in aliis

---

1) constitit V   2) diducantur *Krueger*. deducantur V. 3) obligatum V.   4) fructum V   5) quo V.   6) deprehendit V.   7) solibeto V.   8) sit *Polenaar*   9) fuerita V. 10) quod *Polenaar*.

---

§ 182. *cf. Gai epit.* 2, 10, 1. *I.* 4, 1 *pr. D.* 44, 7, 4 (*Gai.* 505). 44, 7, 25, 1 (*Ulp.* 2583). 44, 7, 52, 8 (*Mod.* 192). supra] § 89.

§ 183. *cf. Gai epit.* 2, 10, 2. *Paul.* 2, 31, 2 = *Coll.* 7, 5, 3. *I.* 4, 1, 3. *D.* 47, 2, 2 (*Gai.* 269). *Gell.* 11, 18, 10 *sq.* inferius] § 186 *sq.*

§§ 184. 185. *cf Gai epit. Paul. Inst. Gell. loc. cit. D.* 47, 2, 3—8 (*Gai.* 270. *Ulp.* 2375. *Paul.* 1790).

182. We now pass on to obligations which arise from delict, where, for instance, someone has committed a theft, has taken things by force, has caused loss wrongfully, or has committed a contempt. All these types of conduct fall into **one class** of obligation, whereas obligations arising from contract **resolve into four classes**, as we have explained above.

183. Now, Servius Sulpicius and Masurius Sabinus said that there are four **kinds of theft**, manifest theft, non-manifest theft, theft by receiving and theft by planting; Labeo said there are **two, manifest and non-manifest, for receiving and planting are not really kinds of theft so much as ancillary actions**. That certainly seems nearer the truth, **as will appear from the discussion below**. 184. Some people have said that theft is **manifest** when **the thief is caught** in the act; on the other hand, others have gone further, saying that it is enough if **he is caught in the place, for instance, if the theft is of olives in a grove or of grapes in a vineyard, while he is in the grove or the vineyard, or, if the theft is in a house**, so long as he is in the house. Others have gone even **further** and said that it remains manifest **so long as the thief is carrying the thing to the place to which he planned to take it**. Yet others have gone even **beyond this** and said that it is manifest **whenever the thief is seen with the thing**; and this opinion has not prevailed. But even the opinion of those who considered the theft manifest if the **thief was caught while carrying the thing to the place to which he planned to take it**, is not to be regarded with approval, because it admits of great doubt whether the test applies for a period of one day or also for several; the relevance of this is that thieves often plan to carry goods stolen in one city to

ciuitatibus surreptas[1] res in alias ciuitates uel in alias
prouincias destinant fures perferre.[2] ex duabus itaque
superioribus opinionibus alterutra adprobatur[3]; magis
tamen plerique posteriorem probant. 185. Nec[4] manifestum furtum quid[5] sit, ex iis, quae diximus, intellegitur. nam quod[6] manifestum non est, id nec manifestum est. 186. Conceptum furtum dicitur, cum apud
aliquem testibus praesentibus furtiua[7] res quaesita et
inuenta est. nam in eum propria actio constituta
est, quamuis fur non sit, quae appellatur concepti.
187. Oblatum furtum dicitur, cum res furtiua tibi ab
aliquo oblata sit eaque apud te concepta sit, utique[8]
si ea mente data tibi fuerit, ut apud te potius quam
apud eum, qui dederit, conciperetur. nam tibi, apud
quem concepta est, propria aduersus eum, qui optulit,
quamuis fur non sit, constituta est actio, *quae* appellatur oblati.[9] 188. Est et*iam* prohibiti furti *actio* aduersus eum, qui furtum quaerere uolentem prohibuerit.

189. Poena manifesti furti ex lege XII tabularum
capitalis erat. nam liber uerberatus addicebatur ei,
cui furtum fecerat; utrum autem seruus efficeretur ex
addictione an adiudicati[10] loco constitueretur, ueteres

---

1) surrepte V.   2) proferre V.   3) adprobat V.
4) ni V.   5) quod V.   6) q̄˙ (*i. e.* quae) V.   7) furti-
busa V.   8) uel utique V.   9) obliti V.   10) *num* iudicati?

§§ 186—188. = *I.* 4, 1, 4. *cf. Gai epit.* 2, 10, 2.
§ 186. *cf. Paul.* 2, 31, 3; 5 = *Coll.* 7, 5, 4; 6. *D.* 22, 5, 12
(*Ulp.* 1053). testibus praesentibus] *cf. Plaut. Poenul.* 3, 5, 16
—50 = 761—795.
§ 187. *cf. Paul.* 2, 31, 3; 5 = *Coll.* 7, 5, 4; 6.
§ 189. *cf. leg.* XII *tab.* 8, 14 (*Bruns* I[7], 32). *infra* 4, 111.
Gell. 11, 18, 9. 20, 1, 7. 6 (7), 15. *Plaut. Poen.* 4, 2, 11 = 833.
Serv. ad Aen. 8, 205 *unde Isidor. orig.* 5, 26, 18. *Ovid. Fast.*
3, 845. quadrupli actio] *cf. infra* 4, 111; 173. *Paul.* 2, 31, 13.
I. 4, 1, 5. 4, 2 *pr.* 4, 12 *pr. cum Theoph.* (*p. 463 Ferr.*). *D.* 39,
4, 1, 3 (*Ulp.* 1304). 47, 2, 46, 2 (*Ulp.* 2878). 47, 2, 50 *pr.* (*Ulp.*
1040). *Plaut. Asin.* 3, 2, 23 = 569. *Curc.* 5, 2, 21 = 619.
Quintil. Inst. or. 7, 4, 44. 7, 6, 2.

other cities or provinces. And so, of the two other opinions reported above each has its supporters, but most people prefer the second. 185. **The definition of non-manifest theft must now be clear: any theft which is not manifest is non-manifest. 186. 'Theft by receiving' is where a stolen thing is found in someone's premises after a search before witnesses. A special action, the action for theft by receiving, is given against such a person, even if not the thief. 187. 'Theft by planting' is where a stolen thing is planted on you and found on your premises. The liability arises when the planter intended that it be found with you rather than him. Again the name comes from the special action available to you with whom the thing was found against him who planted it even where he was not the thief, the action for theft by planting. 188. Another action for theft by prohibition lies for preventing someone from making a search.**

189. **For manifest theft the penalty** under the Twelve Tables was capital. A free man after flogging was assigned to the person against whom he had committed the theft; but the old lawyers debated whether he was made a slave by this assignment or was put in the position of a judgment-debtor. A slave

quaerebant. in seruum aeque[1] uerberatum animaduertebatur. sed[2] postea inprobata est asperitas poenae,
et tam ex serui persona quam ex liberi quadrupli
178 actio praetoris edicto constituta est. | 190. Nec mani-
festi furti poena per legem *xii* tabularum dupli inro-
gatur, eamque etiam praetor conseruat. 191. Concepti
et oblati poena ex lege xii tabularum tripli est, eaque[3] similiter a praetore seruatur. 192. Prohibiti actio
quadrupli est ex edicto praetoris introducta. lex autem
eo nomine nullam poenam constituit; hoc solum praecipit[4], ut qui quaerere uelit, nudus quaerat, licio[5]
cinctus, lancem habens; qui si quid inuenerit, iubet
id lex furtum manifestum esse.[6]   193. Quid sit autem
licium[7], quaesitum est; sed uerius est[8] consuti genus
esse, quo necessariae partes tegerentur.[9]   193ᵃ. Quae
[res][10] lex tota ridicula est; nam qui uestitum quaerere prohibet[11], is et nudum quaerere prohibiturus[12]
est, eo magis quod ita quaesita re et[13] inuenta maiori
poenae subiciatur.   deinde quod lancem siue ideo

---

1) seruum aeque *Hu.* eum atque V (?).   2) uerberatum
animaduertebatur sed *Hu.* uerbera(ta?) *deinde lacuna* V.
3) est eaque *Lachmann.* esse qua V.   4) praecepit V.
5) licio *v. d. Hoeven.* linteo V.   6) esset V.   7) linteum V.
8) est] seam V, s *littera lineola inducta.*   9) tegerent V.
10) res *delevimus.*   11) perhibet V.   12) prohibiturus
Sander. prohibitus V.   13) re et *Hu.* res V. *cf. supra* § 186.

---

§ 190. *cf. I.* 4, 1, 5. *lex xii tab.* 8, 16 (*Bruns* I⁷, 33). *infra*
4, 173. *D.* 47, 2, 75 (*Iav.* 93). 47, 2, 68, 2 (*Cels.* 106). 47, 2,
50 *pr.* (*Ulp.* 1040). *Plaut. Poen.* 3, 1, 61 = 564. 5, 6, 14 = 1351.
Cato de agricult. praef. § 1. *Gell.* 11, 18, 15.
    § 191. *cf. I.* 4, 1, 4. *lex xii tab.* 8, 15ᵃ (*Bruns* I⁷, 32).
infra 4, 173. *Paul.* 2, 31, 14. *Gell.* 11, 18, 11. *Plaut. Poen.*
3, 4, 27 = 737.
    § 192. *cf. supra* 3, 188. *lex xii tab.* 8, 15ᵇ (*Bruns* I⁷, 32).
Lex Rom. Burgund. 12. *Fest. p.* 117 *v. lance et licio* (*Bruns*
II⁷, 11). *Gell.* 11, 18, 9. 16, 10, 8. *Inst. gl. Taur.* § 936 *ed.*
Alberti. Petron. Satir. 97. *Aristoph. Nub.* 497 *sq. cum scholiis.*
Plato de legib. 12 *p.* 594 a.

was put to death, likewise after flogging. But later the severity of this penalty was disapproved and **an action for fourfold damages** was created in the praetor's Edict, **whether the culprit is slave or free.** 190. **For non-manifest theft** the Twelve Tables appointed **a penalty of double damages**, and this the praetor still retains. 191. Under the Twelve Tables the penalty for theft by receiving and planting is threefold damages and this too is kept by the praetor. 192. The action for theft by prohibition, with a fourfold penalty, was introduced by the praetor. The Twelve Tables lay down no penalty under this head; their only provision is that anyone wishing to conduct a search should do so naked, girt with a 'licium' and holding a dish; and if he should find anything the Twelve Tables provide that this is manifest theft. 193. Now, there has been a question what a 'licium' is. But the sounder view is that it is a kind of loin-cloth to cover the private parts. 193a. And this whole provision is ridiculous. For anyone who prohibits a person with clothes on from searching is going to prohibit him from searching naked, all the more so when he is to be subject to a higher penalty when a thing is searched for in this way and found. Next, on the explanation of the dish – is he instructed to have it in order to keep

haberi iubeat, ut manibus occupatis[1] nihil subiciat,
siue ideo, ut quod inuenerit, ibi imponat, neutrum
eorum procedit, si id, quod quaeratur, eius magnitu-
dinis aut naturae sit, ut neque subici neque ibi inponi
possit. certe non dubitatur, cuiuscumque materiae sit
ea lanx, satis legi fieri. 194. Propter hoc tamen, quod
lex ex ea causa manifestum furtum esse iubet, sunt,
qui scribunt furtum manifestum aut lege intellegi aut
natura: lege id ipsum, de quo loquimur, natura illud,
de quo superius exposuimus. sed uerius est natura
tantum manifestum furtum intellegi; neque enim lex
facere potest, ut qui manifestus fur non sit, manifestus sit, non magis quam qui omnino fur non sit,
fur sit, et qui adulter aut homicida non sit, adulter
uel | homicida sit; at illud sane lex facere potest, 179
ut proinde aliquis poena teneatur[2], atque si[3] furtum
uel adulterium uel homicidium admisisset, quamuis
nihil eorum admiserit.

195. Furtum autem fit non solum, cum quis inter-
cipiendi causa[4] rem alienam amouet[5], sed[6] generaliter,
cum quis[7] rem alienam inuito domino contrectat.
196. Itaque si quis re[8], quae apud eum deposita sit,
utatur, furtum committit; et si quis utendam rem
acceperit eamque in alium usum transtulerit, furti obligatur, ueluti si quis argentum utendum acceperit,
quasi amicos ad cenam inuitaturus[9], et id peregre

1) occupatis Vangerow. occupantis V. 2) teneat V. 3) atque si Goeschen. at quasi V. 4) causam V. 5) admouet V.
6) et V. 7) qui V. 8) rem V. 9) inutaturus rogauerit V.

§ 194. cf. D. 7, 5, 2, 1 (Gai. 168). superius] § 184.
§ 195. = I. 4, 1, 6. cf. Gai epit. 2, 10, 3. Paul. 2, 31, 1
= Coll. 7, 5, 2. Gell. 11, 18, 20 (Sabin. 2, Iurispr. I, 73).
§ 196. cf. I. 4, 1, 6. Gai epit. 2, 10, 4; 5. Paul. 2, 12,
5 = Coll. 10, 7, 5 = D. 16, 3, 29 pr. (Paul. 1962). 2, 31, 29 = D.
42, 2, 83 pr. (Paul. 1980). 13, 1, 16 et 47, 2, 77 pr. (Pomp. 321).
13, 6, 5, 8 (Ulp. 802). 47, 2, 40 (Paul. 1798). Gell. 6 (7), 15, 2
(Q. Muc. 2, Iurispr. I, 17). Val. Max. 8, 2, 4. Symmach. epist. 7, 69, 1.

his hands occupied so that he smuggles nothing in, or is it so that he can put on it anything which he may find? Neither suggestion fits the case, if the thing searched for is of such a size or kind that it can neither be smuggled in nor put on it. At least there is no doubt that the dish meets the statutory requirement whatever it is made of. 194. Nevertheless, because the Twelve Tables provide that the theft is manifest in this case, some writers hold that a theft can be manifest either by statute or by its nature: by statute in the case of which we are speaking, by nature in the cases which we explained above. But the sounder view is that theft can be manifest only by its nature; for statute cannot make a person into a manifest thief when he is not a thief, any more than it can make him into a thief when he is not a thief at all or can make an adulterer, or a murderer, of a person who is not an adulterer or a murderer. But what, of course, statute can do is to make someone liable to the same penalty as if he had committed theft, adultery or murder even although he has committed none of them.

195. **Theft is committed not only when someone removes something belonging to another to have it for himself but, more comprehensively, whenever someone handles something belonging to another without the owner's consent. 196. And so a depositee commits theft if he uses a thing deposited. A borrower of a thing for use commits theft if he puts it to another use. And so, it is theft if a person borrows silver saying that he wants it for a dinner for his friends and takes it off with him**

secum tulerit, aut si quis equum[1] gestandi gratia commodatum longius aliquo[2] duxerit, quod ueteres scripserunt de eo, qui in aciem[3] perduxisset. 197. Placuit
tamen eos, qui *re*bus commodatis aliter uterentur
quam utendas accepissent, ita furtum committere, si
intellegant id se inuito domino facere eumque, si
intellexisset[4], non permissurum; at[5] si permissurum
credant[6], extra furti crimen uideri, optima sane di-
stinctione, quod furtum sine dolo malo non committitur. 198. Sed et si credat aliquis inuito domino se
rem *con*trectare, domino autem uolente id fiat, dicitur
furtum non fieri. unde illud quaesitum [et probatum]
est: cum Titius seruum meum sollicitauerit[7], ut quasdam res mihi subriperet et ad eum perferret[8], *et ser-*
180 *uus* | id ad me pertulerit[9], ego, dum uolo Titium in
ipso delicto deprehendere, permiserim seruo[10] quasdam
res ad eum perferre, utrum[11] furti an serui corrupti
iudicio teneatur[12] Titius mihi, an neutro? responsum
neutro eum teneri, furti ideo, quod non inuito me res
contrectarit[13], serui corrupti ideo, quod deterior seruus
factus non sit.[14] 199. Interdum autem etiam[15] liberorum hominum furtum fit, uelut si quis liberorum

---

1) aecum V.   2) cum aliquo V. quam quo rogauerit
(*cf. p.* 181 *not.* 9) aliquo *Hu.*   3) in aciem V. uls Ariciam *Polenaar; cf. Val. Max.* 8, 2, 4.   4) intellexissent V.   5) ut V.
6) credent V.   7) sollicitauerit *Inst.* colligitaret V.   8) per-
feret V.   9) pertulerit *Inst.* pertulit V.   10) permiserim
seruo *Goeschen.* permiserumuo V.   . 11) q̄eumtrum V.
12) corrupti iudicio teneatur *Inst.* corruptio iudicium teneat V.
13) contrectaret V.   14) sit *Hu.* est V.   15) etiam *Inst.* et V.

---

§ 197. = *I.* 4, 1, 7.   *cf. supra* 2, 50.   *infra* 3, 208. 4, 178.
Paul. 2, 31, 1 = *Coll.* 7, 5, 1.   *D.* 9, 2, 41, 1 (*Ulp.* 2863). 17, 2,
51 *pr.* (*Ulp.* 2745).
§ 198.   *cf. I.* 4, 1, 8.   *D.* 47, 2, 46, 8 (*Ulp.* 2879).   11. 3,
1, 5 (*Ulp.* 698).   *C.* 6, 2, 20 (*a.* 530).
§ 199. = *I.* 4, 1, 9.   *D.* 47, 2, 14, 13 (*Ulp.* 2734).   47, 2, 38
(*Paul* 1797).   in potestate — et manu] *cf. supra* 2, 87; 90.

on a journey, or borrows a horse for a ride and uses it to go somewhere far away, as in the case in the old books of the horse borrowed and taken into battle. 197. But it was accepted that borrowers who put the thing to an extra use only commit theft if they know the owner does not consent and would not consent if he knew; if they believe he would allow it, they are not liable. This is an excellent distinction. Theft cannot be committed without wrongful intent. 198. There is no theft if a person believes that he is handling a thing without the owner's consent but in fact the owner does consent. That gives rise to the following problem [and solution]. Titius approaches a slave of mine and urges him to take some things from me and bring them out to him. The slave reveals the plan to me. I want to catch Titius in the act of committing the delict. I therefore allow the slave to take some things to him. Is Titius liable to me for theft? Or for corruption of a slave? Or for neither? The authoritative answer given has been that he is liable for neither, not for theft, because the things were not handled without my consent, and not for corruption of the slave, because the slave was not made worse. 199. There can even be theft of free people, as where one of our children still under paternal power is

nostrorum, qui in potestate nostra sint[1], siue etiam
uxor, quae in manu nostra sit, siue etiam iudicatus
uel auctoratus meus subreptus fuerit.[2] 200. Aliquando
etiam *suae* rei quisque furtum committit, ueluti si
debitor rem, quam creditori[3] pignori dedit, subtraxerit,
uel si[4] bonae fidei possessori rem meam possidenti
subripuerim. unde placuit eum, qui seruum suum,
quem alius bona fide possidebat, ad se reuersum cela-
uerit, furtum committere. 201. Rursus ex diuerso
interdum[5] alienas res occupare et usucapere concessum
est nec creditur furtum fieri, uelut res hereditarias,
quarum heres non est nactus possessionem, nisi necessarius heres extet; nam necessario herede extante
placuit nihil pro herede usucapi posse.[6] item[7] debitor
rem, quam fiduciae causa creditori mancipauerit aut
in iure cesserit, *secun*dum ea, quae in superiore commentario rettulimus, sine furto possidere et usucapere

---

1) s (*id est* sunt) V. sit *Inst.*   2) queri(?) V.   3) quam
creditori *Inst.* quae creditor V.   4) si *Goeschen. incerta*
vestigia in V.   5) inestdum V.   6) nisi — posse *del. Solazzi.*
7) posse. item] possit V.

---

iudicatus] *cf. supra* 3, 78. 175. 189. *infra* 4, 21. *Gell.* 20, 1, 42
(*Iurispr.* I, **105**). auctoratus] *cf. Coll.* 4, 3, 2 (*Paul.* 19). 9, 2, 2
(*Ulp.* 2203). *Asin. Pollio ap. Cic. ad fam.* 10, 32, 3. *Sen. ep.*
37, 1. *Petr. Sat.* 117. *Quint. Decl.* 302. *Hor. Sat.* 2, 7, 59.
Manil. Astron. 4, 225. *Tert. ad martyr.* 5. *ad nation.* 1, 18.
lex Iul. munic. 113 (*Bruns* I[7], 108). *C. I. L.* I 1418 (*Bruns* I[7], 381
n. 35). II *suppl.* 6278 l. 60 (*Bruns* I[7], 210).
   § 200. = *I.* 4, 1, 10. *cf. infra* 3, 204. *Paul.* 2, 31, 21; 36.
I. 4, 2, 1; 2. *D.* 41, 3, 49 (*Lab.* 217). 47, 2, 60 (59) (*Iul.* 860).
47, 2, 80 (79) (*Pap.* 168). 13, 7, 22 *pr.* (*Ulp.* 902). 47, 2, 12, 2
(*Ulp.* 2733). 47, 2, 19, 5; 6 (*Ulp.* 2857). 47, 2, 15, 2 (*Paul.* 1726).
47, 2, 20 (*Paul.* 1787. 1788). 47, 2, 54 (53), 4 (*Paul.* 564). 47,
2, 67 (66) *pr.* (*Paul.* 1141). 47, 2, 88 (87) (*Paul.* 61). 41, 3, 4, 21
(*Paul.* 673). *C.* 7, 26, 6 (*Philipp.*).
   § 201. *cf. supra* 2, 9; 52; 56—60. *Paul.* 2, 31, 11. *D.* 9,
4, 40 (*Iul.* 353). 47, 2, 69; 71 (*Marcell.* 115). 47, 4, 1, 15 (*Ulp.*
1066). 47, 19, 2 (*Ulp.* 2228). 47, 19, 6 (*Ner.* 98. *Paul.* 1030).
C. 7, 29, 2 (*a.* 293).

kidnapped; as also a wife in marital subordination to us, a judgment debtor, or my bonded gladiator. 200. **Sometimes an owner can commit theft of his own property, as where a debtor takes back something which he has given his creditor as a pledge***, or I carry off from a possessor in good faith a thing of mine of which he has possession. And so it has been accepted that a person commits theft if he hides away his own slave who has come back to him from someone who was possessing him in good faith. 201. Then, conversely, sometimes one is allowed to take and usucapt someone else's property and it is not regarded as theft, for instance, where one takes things belonging to an inheritance of which the heir has not yet got possession, except where there is a compulsory heir; if there is a compulsory heir it has been accepted that nothing can be usucapted as heir. Again, a debtor who has mancipated a thing or assigned it in court to his creditor under a trust*, can possess and usucapt it without committing theft in the circumstances which we discussed in the previous commentary. 202.

potest. 202. Interdum furti tenetur, qui[1] ipse furtum
181 non fecerit, qualis | est, cuius ope consilio furtum
factum est. in quo numero est, qui nummos tibi ex-
cussit, ut eos alius surriperet, uel opstitit tibi, ut
alius surriperet, aut oues aut boues tuas fugauit, ut
alius eas exciperet. et hoc ueteres scripserunt de eo,
qui panno[2] rubro fugauit armentum; sed si quid[3] per
lasciuiam et non data opera, ut furtum committeretur,
factum sit, uidebimus, an[4] utilis actio dari[5] debeat,
cum per legem Aquiliam[6], quae de damno lata *est*,
etiam culpa puniatur.

 203. Furti autem actio[7] ei conpetit, cuius interest
rem saluam esse, licet dominus non sit. itaque nec
domino aliter conpetit, quam si eius intersit[8] rem non
perire. 204. Unde constat creditorem de pignore sub-

---

1) cum V. 2) eo panno V. 3) quis V. 4) ā· V.
5) actio dari *Inst.* atque deari V. 6) aliquiliam V.
7) aoue V. 8) eius intersit *Inst.* eum insit V.

---

 § 202. = *I.* 4, 1, 11. *cf. Gai epit.* 2, 10, 6. *infra* 4, 37.
3, 219; 211. *Paul.* 2, 31, 10. *D.* 47, 2, 91 (90), 1 (*Iav.* 230).
47, 2, 55 (54), 4 (*Gai.* 272). 47, 2, 36 *pr.* (*Ulp.* 2865). 47, 2,
50, 1—3 *et* 47, 2, 52 *pr.* (*Ulp.* 1041). 47, 2, 52, 19; 21 (*Ulp.*
1042). 11, 3, 11, 2 (*Ulp.* 703). 13, 1, 6 (*Ulp.* 1057). 47, 5,
1 *pr.* (*Ulp.* 1068). 47, 2, 34 (*Paul.* 1796). 50, 16, 53, 2 (*Paul.*
721). *C.* 3, 41, 5 (*a.* 294). *Cic. de nat. deor.* 3, 30, 74. *Gell.*
11, 18, 23. nummos tibi excussit] *cf. D.* 47, 2, 52, 13 (*Ulp.*
1042). 9, 2, 27, 21 (*Ulp.* 624). panno rubro] *cf. D.* 47, 2, 50, 4
(*Ulp.* 1041). *Lex Rom. Burg.* 29.
 § 203. = *I.* 4, 1, 13. *cf. Paul.* 2, 31, 4 = *Coll.* 7, 5, 5.
Coll. 10, 2, 6 (*Mod.* 9). *D.* 47, 2, 77 (76), 1 (*Pomp.* 322). 47,
2, 49 *pr.* (*Gai.* 238). 47, 2, 81 (80) *pr.*; 1 (*Pap.* 210). 47, 2, 10
(*Ulp.* 2733). 47, 2, 14 *pr.*—4; 10 *sq.* (*Ulp.* 2734). 47, 2, 83 (82), 1
(*Paul.* 1980). 47, 2, 86 (85) (*Paul.* 1005). 47, 2, 11 (*Paul.* 1791).
C. 6, 2, 22 *pr.* (*a.* 530).
 § 204. = *I.* 4, 1, 14. *cf. Paul.* 2, 31, 19. *D.* 47, 2, 49 *pr.*
(*Gai.* 238). 47, 2, 80 (79) (*Pap.* 168). 13, 7, 22 *pr.* (*Ulp.* 902).
47, 2, 12, 2 (*Ulp.* 2733). 47, 2, 46, 4 (*Ulp.* 2878). 47, 2, 15 *pr.*
(*Paul.* 1726). 47, 2, 88 (87) (*Paul.* 61).

Sometimes a man is liable to the action for theft who has not himself committed theft, for example, where a theft has been committed by his help and advice: someone knocks coins from your hand so that another can relieve you of them, or obstructs you for the same purpose, **or drives off your sheep or cattle so that another can take them. The case in the old books is the herd stampeded with a red rag. Where this is mindless hooliganism, not aimed at theft**, we shall see whether a policy action **should be given**, since under the Aquilian Act which was passed to deal with loss wrongfully caused even unintentional fault is punished.

203. **The action for theft can be brought by anyone with an interest in the safety of the thing, even if he is not the owner; and so it cannot be brought by the owner if he does not have such an interest. 204. And so it is settled that a creditor can sue for theft if a pledge is taken from him, and this**

repto furti agere posse; adeo quidem, ut quamuis[1] ipse dominus [id est ipse debitor][2] eam rem subripuerit, nihilo minus creditori conpetat actio furti. 205. Item si fullo polienda[3] curandaue aut sarcinator sarcienda uestimenta mercede certa acceperit eaque furto amiserit, ipse furti habet actionem, non dominus, quia domini nihil interest[4] ea non periisse, cum iudicio locati a fullone aut sarcinatore suum *consequi* possit[5], si modo is fullo aut sarcinator[6] rei[7] praestandae[8] sufficiat; nam si soluendo non est, tunc quia ab eo dominus suum[9] consequi non potest, ipsi furti actio conpetit, quia hoc casu ipsius interest rem saluam esse. 206. Quae de[10] fullone | aut sarcinatore[11] 182 diximus, eadem transferemus et ad eum, cui rem commodauimus. nam ut illi mercedem capiendo custodiam praestant, ita hic[12] quoque utendi[13] commodum percipiendo similiter necesse habet[14] custodiam praestare. 207. Sed is, apud quem res deposita est, custodiam non praestat[15] tantumque in eo obnoxius est, si quid ipse dolo *malo*[16] fecerit; qua de *causa si*[17] res ei subrepta fuerit, quia[18] restituendae[19] eius nomine[20] depositi

---

1) que ū V.   2) *eiecimus glossema, quamvis iam Institutionibus subsit.*   3) pullienda V.   4) idē V.   5) posset V. 6) sarcitor V.   7) rem V.   8) *in* V *sequuntur tres litterae evanidae* (pic?) *plene* coni. *Hu.*   9) sim V.   10) quae de *Inst.* de que V.   11) sarcitore V.   12) hi V.   13) utendo V.   14) sehabent V.   15) praestatum V.   16) dolo V. dolo malo *Inst.*   17) qua de causa si *Inst.* qua de ḡ V. 18) quia *Inst.* quae V.   19) restituendae *Inst.* restituenda est V.   20) nomine *Inst.* non omninoe V.

§ 205. = *I.* 4, 1, 15. *cf. Paul.* 2, 31, 29. *D.* 19, 2, 60, 2 (*Iav.* 212). 47, 2, 12 *pr.* (*Ulp.* 2733). 47, 2, 48, 4 (*Ulp.* 2884).

§ 206. = *I.* 4, 1, 16. *cf. Paul.* 2, 4, 3. *Coll.* 10, 2, 1; 6 (*Mod.* 9). *D.* 47, 2, 60 (59) (*Iul.* 860). 13, 6, 18 *pr.* (*Gai.* 208). 44, 7, 1, 4 (*Gai.* 498). 13, 6, 5, 3; 5 (*Ulp.* 802). 47, 2, 14, 16 (*Ulp.* 2734). 47, 2, 48, 4 (*Ulp.* 2884). 47, 2, 15, 2 (*Paul.* 1726). *C.* 6, 2, 22 (*a.* 530).

§ 207. = *I.* 4, 1, 17. *cf. Coll.* 10, 2, 6 (*Mod.* 9). *D.* 44, 7, 1, 5 (*Gai.* 498). 13, 6, 5, 2 (*Ulp.* 802). 19, 5, 17, 2 (*Ulp.* 806). 16, 3, 1, 10 (*Ulp.* 890). 16, 3, 1, 43 (*Ulp.* 896). 50, 17, 23 (*Ulp.* 2731). 47, 2, 14, 3; 4 (*Ulp.* 2734). 47, 8, 2, 23 (*Ulp.* 1321).

is carried so far that even if it is the owner himself [that is, the debtor himself] who takes it, the creditor can bring the action for theft. 205. Again, suppose a cleaner charges a given sum for cleaning clothes or giving them some other treatment or a tailor for repairing them. If he loses the clothes to a thief, he, not the owner, has the action. The owner has no interest in the safety of the clothes since he can recover from the cleaner or the tailor in the action on hire, so long as that cleaner or tailor has sufficient means to make good the value of the property. If he is insolvent, the owner cannot recover from him, and so the action for theft reverts to him, since now he has an interest in the safety of the thing. 206. What we have said of cleaners or tailors applies equally to the borrower for use. The cleaner incurs insurance liability because he receives a reward. Similarly, the borrower attracts the same liability, because he gets the advantage of using the thing. 207. By contrast, the depositee has no insurance liability but is answerable only for his own wilful defaults. Suppose the thing is taken from him. He has no interest in its safety; his obligation to restore the

non tenetur nec ob id eius interest rem saluam esse,
furti [itaque] agere non potest, sed[1] ea actio domino
conpetit.

208. In summa sciendum est quaesitum esse, an
impubes rem alienam amouendo[2] furtum faciat. plerisque placet, quia furtum ex adfectu[3] consistit, ita demum obligari eo crimine impuberem, si proximus[4]
pubertati sit et ob id intellegat se delinquere.

209. Qui res alienas rapit, tenetur etiam[5] furti.
quis enim magis alienam rem inuito domino contrectat[6] quam qui *ui*[7] rápit? itaque recte *dict*um est
eum improbum furem esse; sed propriam actionem[8]
eius delicti nomine[9] praetor introduxit, quae appellatur ui bonorum raptorum, et est intra annum quadrupli [actio], post annum simpli. quae actio utilis
est, etsi[10] quis unam rem licet minimam rapuerit.

210. Damni iniuriae actio constituitur[11] per legem
Aquiliam, cuius primo capite cautum est, *ut* si quis
183 hominem alienum | alienamue[12] quadrupedem, quae

---

1) et V.   2) alienam amouendo *Inst.* alienouendo V.
3) adiectum V.   4) proximus m V.   5) et V.   6) tretat V.
7) ui *Inst.*; *om.* V.   8) actione V.   9) delicti nomine *Inst.* lecti
nomen V.   10) set si V.   11) constituit V.   12) alienamue
Inst. Dig. eamue V.

§ 208. = *I.* 4, 1, 18. *cf. D.* 50, 17, 111 *pr.* (*Gai.* 73). 9, 2,
5, 2 (*Ulp.* 613). 47, 2, 23 (*Ulp.* 2861). *lex* xii *tab.* 8, 14 (*Bruns*
I[7], 32). *Gell.* 11, 18, 8. *Serv. ad Verg. Buc.* 8, 39. *cf. etiam*
D. 29, 5, 14 (*Maecian.* 56). 4, 3, 13, 1 (*Ulp.* 390). 44, 4, 4, 26
(*Ulp.* 1681). 47, 12, 3, 1 (*Ulp.* 739). ex adfectu] *cf. supra* 3,
197 *et ibi citat.*

§ 209. = *I.* 4, 2 *pr. cf. infra* 4, 8. *I.* 4, 6, 19. *D.* 47, 8,
2, 10; 12; 17 (*Ulp.* 1313. 1315. 1318). 47, 2, 53 (*Ulp.* 1055).
C. 3, 41, 4 (*a.* 294). *Lex Rom. Burg.* 8, 5. *Ed. Theoder.*
109. 124.

§ 210. = *I.* 4, 3 *pr. cf. Bruns* I[7], 45. *D.* 9, 2, 2 *pr.* (*Gai.*
183). 9, 2, 21 *pr.* (*Ulp.* 616). *Cic. pro Tull.* 4, 9. 5, 11. 17, 41.
Brut. 34, 131. *Anon. ad Bas.* 60, 3, 1. *Theoph.* 4, 3 (*p.* 398 *sq.*
Ferr.). eamue quadrupedem] *cf. D.* 9, 2, 2, 2 (*Gai.* 183). domino]
cf. D. 9, 2, 11, 6 (*Ulp.* 615).

thing in the action on deposit is discharged, and so he cannot sue for the theft. The owner consequently has that action.

208. Finally, does a child commit theft if he removes something belonging to another? The majority view accepts that since theft depends on intent, a child only incurs the liability if he is near puberty. He can then understand that he is doing wrong.

209. A robber is also liable to the action for theft. Who can more truly be said to handle the property of another without his consent than one who takes it by force? And so it is a good description of a robber to say that he is disgraceful even among thieves. But the praetor introduced a special action to deal with this wrong, the action for things taken by force. It lies for fourfold damages within one year, for single damages after the year is up. It can be used where even a single thing is taken, however small.

210. The action for wrongful loss is founded on the Aquilian Act. Its first section provides that if anyone wrongfully kills another's slave, male or female, or another's four-footed stock he must pay

pecudum[1] numero sit, iniuria occiderit, quanti ea res
in eo anno plurimi fuerit[2], tantum[3] domino dare
damnetur. 211. Iniuria[4] autem occidere intellegitur,
cuius dolo aut culpa id acciderit, nec ulla alia lege
damnum, quod sine iniuria datur, reprehenditur[5]; itaque inpunitus est, qui sine culpa et dolo malo casu
quodam damnum committit.[6] 212. Nec solum corpus
in actione huius legis aestimatur; sed sane si[7] seruo
occiso plus dominus capiat damni, quam pretium serui
sit[8], id quoque aestimatur, uelut si seruus meus ab
aliquo heres institutus, antequam iussu meo hereditatem cerneret, occisus fuerit; non enim tantum ipsius
pretium aestimatur, sed et hereditatis amissae quan-
titas. item si ex gemellis uel ex comoedis uel ex
symphoniacis unus occisus fuerit, non solum occisi
fit aestimatio, sed eo amplius id quoque[9] conputatur[10],
quod ceteri, qui supersunt, depretiati sunt. idem iuris
est etiam, si ex pari mularum unam uel etiam ex
quadrigis equorum unum occiderit. 213. Cuius autem
seruus occisus est, is liberum arbitrium habet uel
capitali crimine reum facere eum, qui occiderit, uel
hac lege damnum persequi. 214. Quod autem adiectum[11] est in hac lege 'quanti in eo anno plurimi ea

---

1) quae pecudum *Inst.* quarecudum V.   2) fuit V. *Inst.*
3) tantum aes *Hu. ex Dig.*   4) is iniuria V.   5) datur
reprehenditur] dat repraehendic V.   6) § 211 *Beseler et Kunkel*
(*Z. S.* 49, 182) *a Gaio abiudicant.*   7) si *Goeschen.* i V.   8) s V.
9) id quoque *Inst.* qui V.   10) conputat V.   11) adistum V.

---

§ 211. *cf. I.* 4, 3, 2; 3; 14. *Coll.* 7, 3, 1; 4 = *D.* 9, 2, 3
et 9, 2, 5, 1 (*Ulp.* 613). 40, 12, 13 *pr.* (*Gai.* 43). 50, 17, 23 (*Ulp.*
2731). *Cic. pro Tull.* 5, 11.
§ 212. *cf. I.* 4, 3, 10. *D.* 9, 2, 22, 1 (*Paul.* 362). 9, 2, 21,
2 *et* 23 *pr.*—2 (*Ulp.* 616).
§ 213. *cf. I.* 4, 3, 11. *D.* 9, 2, 23, 9 (*Ulp.* 617). *C.* 3, 35, 3
(*a.* 241).
§ 214. *cf. I.* 4, 3, 9. 4, 6, 19. *supra* 3, 210. *infra* 3, 218.
D. 47, 1, 2, 3 (*Ulp.* 2905). 9, 2, 23, 3; 5—7 (*Ulp.* 616).

the owner the highest value which the thing had in that year. 211. **Now, a person kills wrongfully** when the death happens by his malicious intent or by his fault, and there is no other statute which sanctions loss caused without wrongfulness; and so no liability is imposed on someone who inflicts loss without either fault or malicious intent, but by some accident. 212. And in the action under this Act, it is **not only the** dead **body** which is valued but, if the owner in fact suffers any extra loss by the death of his slave over and above his price, this comes into **the valuation. To take an example, when** my **slave has been appointed heir by someone, if he is killed before he can obey** my **order to** declare his formal **accept**ance of **the inheritance, the valuation** includes not only his price but **also** the amount of **the lost inheritance.** Again, if one of twins or **one member of a company of actors** or musicians is killed, **the valuation must cover not only the one who has been killed but also the depreciation in the value of the survivors.** The same rule applies **where one of a pair of mules or one of a four-horse team is killed.** 213. **One whose slave has been killed, however, has a free** choice **whether to prosecute** the killer **criminally on a capital charge or to sue for his loss under** this **Act.** 214. When this statute says **'the highest value which the thing had in that year'**, the fact is that **if**

res fuerit', illud efficit, si clodum puta aut luscum
seruum occiderit, qui in eo anno integer fuerit[1], *ut
non quanti clodus aut luscus, sed quanti integer fuerit*[2],
aestimatio fiat; quo fit, ut quis plus in*ter*dum *conse*-
184 quatur, quam ei damnum | datum est.

215. Capite secundo *aduersus*[3] adstipulatorem, qui
pecuniam in fraudem stipulatoris acceptam fecerit,
quanti ea res est[4], tanti actio constituitur. 216. Qua[5]
et ipsa parte legis damni nomine actionem introduci
manifestum est; sed id caueri non fuit necessarium,
cum actio mandati ad eam rem sufficeret; nisi quod
ea lege aduersus infitiantem in duplum agitur.

217. Capite tertio de omni cetero damno cauetur.[6]
itaque si quis seruum uel eam quadrupedem, quae
pecudum numero est, uulnerauerit siue · eam quadru-
pedem, quae pecudum numero non est[7], uelut canem,
aut feram bestiam, uelut[8] ursum, leonem, uulnerauerit
uel occiderit, hoc[9] capite actio constituitur.[10] in ceteris quoque animalibus, item in omnibus rebus, quae
anima carent, damnum iniuria datum hac parte uindicatur. si quid enim ustum aut ruptum aut fractum
fuerit, actio hoc capite constituitur[10], quamquam[11]
potuerit sola rupti appellatio in omnes istas causas
sufficere; ruptum *enim intellegitur, quod quoquo modo*
corruptum est; unde non solum usta aut rupta aut

---

1) fuit V.   2) ut non—fuerit] ut non quanti mortis tempore, sed quanti in eo anno plurimi fuerit *Boecking; similiter*
Studemund.   3) *add. Poeschmann.*   4) ēe V.   5) quam V.
6) cauet V.   7) non est *Inst.* de V.   8) ū V.   9) eahoc
vel cahoc V.   10) constituit V.   11) quoque V.

---

§ 215. *cf. supra* 3, 110 *sq.*   *I.* 4, 3, 12.   *D.* 9, 2, 27, 4
(*Ulp.* 622).

§ 216. *cf. supra* 3, 111. *infra* 4, 9; 171. *Lex Rom. Burg.*
14, 8.

§ 217. = *I.* 4, 3, 13. *cf. Coll.* 2, 4 = *D.* 9, 2, 27, 17 (*Ulp.*
624). *Coll.* 12, 7 = *D.* 9, 2, 27, 7—12 (*Ulp.* 623). *D.* 9, 2, 27,
5—35 (*Ulp.* 623—625). 9, 2, 29, 6 (*Ulp.* 626).

someone kills, say, **a lame** or **one-eyed** slave **who within the year was whole,** the valuation is made not on the basis of his value as lame or one-eyed but on the basis of his value when whole, and so it sometimes happens that a person recovers more than the loss inflicted on him.

215. The second section of the Act provides an action against an additional stipulator who grants a verbal release of a debt in fraud of the stipulator, and it gives an action for the value in money of what is involved. 216. Obviously an action in respect of loss was introduced by this section of the Act as well. But the provision was unnecessary because the action on mandate would cover the case; except that under the Act an action lies for double damages against anyone who denies liability.

217. **The third section provides for all other loss. If someone wounds a slave or four-footed stock, or if he wounds or kills a quadruped not classed as stock, such as a dog or a wild beast,** for instance a bear or a lion, **an action lies under this section. This section gives a remedy for loss wrongfully caused to other animals and to all inanimate things. For if anything is burned or damaged or broken, an action is established under this section. The word 'damaged'** – the Latin verb 'rumpere' – **could have covered all these cases, since it is construed to include every kind of spoiling,** in Latin 'cor-rumpere'. **That word covers not only burning,** damaging **or breaking but also tearing, squashing,**

fracta, sed etiam[1] scissa et collisa et effusa et quoquo
modo uitiata aut perempta atque deteriora facta hoc
uerbo continentur. **218.** Hoc tamen capite non quanti
in eo anno, sed quanti in diebus XXX proxumis[2] ea
res fuerit, damnatur[3] is, qui damnum dederit. ac ne
'plurimi' quidem uerbum adicitur; et ideo quidam
putauerunt liberum esse iudici[4] ad id tempus ex die-
bus XXX aestimationem redigere, quo plurimi | res 185
fuit, uel ad id, quo[5] minoris fuit. sed Sabino placuit
proinde habendum ac si etiam[6] hac parte 'plurimi'
uerbum adiectum esset; nam legis[7] latorem conten-
tum fuisse, *quod prima parte eo uerbo usus esset.*
219. *Ceterum* etiam[8] placuit ita demum ex ista lege
actionem esse, si quis corpore suo damnum dederit,
ideoque[9] alio modo damno dato utiles actiones dantur[10],
uelut si quis alienum hominem aut[11] pecudem inclu-
serit et fame necauerit, aut iumentum tam uehementer
egerit, ut rumperetur[12]; item si quis alieno seruo per-
suaserit, ut in arborem ascenderet uel in puteum
descenderet, et is[13] ascendendo aut descendendo ceciderit et[14] aut mortuus fuerit aut aliqua parte corporis laesus sit. item contra[15] si quis alienum seruum
de ponte aut[16] ripa in flumen proiecerit et is suffo-
catus fuerit, hic quoque[17] corpore suo damnum

---

1) et V.   2) proxumus V.   3) damnat V.   4) iudicium V.   5) quod V.   6) si etiam *Inst.* set V.   7) legibus V.   8) et V.   9) ideoque *Inst.* quo V.   10) dant V.
11) an V.   12) rumpet V.   13) si V.   14) ceciderit et]
cecideri V.   15) p V. *cf. supra* 1, 81.   16) an V.
17) hic quoque] quoque hic V.

---

§ 218. *cf. I.* 4, 3, 14; 15. *D.* 9, 2, 29, 8 (*Ulp.* 628).
§ 219. *cf. I.* 4, 3, 16. *Coll.* 12, 7, 4—8 = *Dig.* 9, 2, 27,
8—10 (*Ulp.* 623). *D.* 9, 2, 7; 9; 11 *pr.*—5 (*Ulp.* 614). 9, 2, 53
(*Ner.* 3). 19, 5, 11 (*Pomp.* 325). 47, 2, 51 (*Gai.* 271). 9, 1, 1, 7
(*Ulp.* 607). 47, 8, 2, 20 (*Ulp.* 1319). 11, 3, 3, 1 (*Ulp.* 699). *cf.*
11, 3, 4 (*Paul.* 302). 9, 2, 33, 1 (*Paul.* 1084). *C.* 3, 35, 5 (*a.* 293).
Lex Rom. Burg. 29.

spilling, and every sort of corruption or ruining or
making worse. 218. Under this section the person
causing loss is obliged to pay the value of the thing
in the nearest thirty days, not the year. It is true
that the word 'highest' is not inserted; and so some
people thought that the judge was free to make his
valuation as at the time in the thirty days when the
thing was at its highest or when it stood lower. But
Sabinus held that the valuation was to be made
just as though the word 'highest' had been
included. In his view the legislator was content to
use the word just in the first section. 219. The
conclusion was also reached that the statutory
action lies only where someone causes loss by his
bodily force. Where people cause loss in other ways
actions are given based on the policy of the statute.
These policy actions are given against one who
shuts up another's slave or animal and it dies of
starvation, or drives a draught animal so hard that
it is injured, or induces another's slave to climb up
a tree or go down a well so that in climbing up or
down he falls and is killed or injured. But against
this, suppose someone pushes another's slave from
a bridge or river-bank into the river and the slave
drowns. Here also it is easy to conclude from the
fact that he pushed him in, that he has caused the

dedisse¹ eo, quod proiecerit, non difficiliter intellegi
potest.

220. ²Iniuria autem committitur³ non solum, cum
quis pugno puta aut fuste percussus uel etiam uerberatus erit, sed etiam⁴ si cui conuicium factum fuerit,
siue quis bona alicuius quasi debitoris sciens eum
nihil sibi debere⁵ proscripserit siue quis ad infamiam
alicuius libellum aut carmen scripserit siue quis matrem familias aut praetextatum adsectatus fuerit et
denique aliis pluribus modis.   221. Pati autem⁶ iniuriam uidemur non solum per nosmet ipsos, sed
etiam⁷ per liberos nostros, quos in potestate habe-
186 mus, | item per uxores nostras, quamuis⁸ in manu
nostra non⁹ sint; itaque si ueluti¹⁰ filiae meae, quae
Titio nupta est, iniuriam feceris, non solum filiae nomine tecum agi iniuriarum potest, uerum etiam meo
quoque et Titii nomine.¹¹   222. Seruo autem ipsi

---

1) dedisset V.   2) 'excidisse aliquid videtur, cui respon-
det pr. I. h. t. = Coll. 2, 5, 1'. Hu.   3) committit V.
4) etiam Inst. et V.   5) debere] debere sibi V.   6) pati
autem Goeschen. spatia V.   7) etiam Inst. et V.   8) quamuis Lachmann. c. (id est cum) V.   9) add. Boecking.
10) ueluti Hu. ueltiae V.   11) nomen V. 'an quae in Instit.
4, 4, 2 sequuntur, Gaiana sint, ut videntur, et a librario omissa,

---

§ 220. = I. 4, 4, 1. cf. Paul. 5, 4, 1; 4; 14 sq. Coll. 2, 5, 4
(Paul. 881). D. 47, 10, 1, 2 (Ulp. 1335). 47, 10, 9, 4 (Ulp. 1340).
47, 10, 15, 2—33 (Ulp. 1350—1353). C. 9, 35, 5 (a. 290). Plaut.
Asin. 2, 2, 104 = 371. Auct. ad Her. 2, 13, 19. 2, 26, 41. 4,
25, 35. Cic. in Verr. 2, 2, 27, 66. Senec. de benef. 2, 35, 2.
bona alicuius] cf. supra 3, 78. infra 4, 102. D. 47, 10, 15,
31—33 (Ulp. 1353). 47, 10, 20 (Mod. 335). Cic. pro Quinct.
15, 48 sq. ad infamiam alicuius libellum] cf. C. Th. tit. 9, 34.
C. Iust. tit. 9, 36.
    § 221. = I. 4, 4, 2. cf. Paul. 5, 4, 3. D. 47, 10, 41 (Ner.
40). 47, 10, 1, 3 (Ulp. 1335). 47, 10, 5, 6 (Ulp. 1337). 47, 10,
11, 7 (Ulp. 1345). 47, 10, 15, 24 (Ulp. 1352). 47, 10, 2 (Paul.
679). 47, 10, 18, 2; 5 (Paul. 689). C. 9, 35, 2 (a. 230).
    § 222. = I. 4, 4, 3. D. 47, 10, 15, 34—49; 17 pr.—2 (Ulp.
1354—1359). 47, 10, 16 (Paul. 685). 48, 7, 4, 1 (Paul. 687). 47,

loss by his bodily force.

220. Now, contempt is committed not only when someone is struck with a fist or with clubs, or even flogged, but also when a vocal attack is made on him, when his goods are advertised for sale as a debtor's by someone who knows he owes him nothing, when someone writes a defamatory book or poem about someone, or when someone harasses a lady or a youth; and finally in many other ways. 221. Now, we can be the victim of contempt not only in our own person but also through our children, if they are still within paternal power, and also through our wives, even if they are not in marital subordination to us. And so, for instance, if you commit a contempt against my daughter, who is married to Titius, an action can be brought against you not only for my daughter herself but also for both myself and Titius. 222. The law holds that no

quidem[1] nulla iniuria intellegitur[2] fieri, sed domino
per eum fieri uidetur; non tamen iisdem modis, quibus etiam per liberos nostros uel uxores iniuriam pati
uidemur, sed ita, cum quid atrocius commissum fuerit,
quod aperte[3] in *contumeliam* domini fieri uidetur,
ueluti si quis alienum seruum uerberauerit, et in hunc
casum formula proponitur; at si quis seruo conuicium
fecerit uel pugno eum percusserit, non proponitur[4]
ulla formula nec temere petenti[5] datur.

223. Poena autem iniuriarum ex lege[6] XII tabularum[7] propter membrum quidem ruptum talio erat;
propter os uero fractum aut conlisum trecentorum
assium poena erat[8], si libero os fractum erat; at si
seruo, CL; propter ceteras uero iniurias XXV assium
poena erat[9] constituta. et uidebantur illis temporibus
in magna paupertate satis idoneae istae pecuniae[10]
poenae esse.[11] 224. Sed nunc alio iure utimur. permittitur[12] enim nobis a praetore ipsis[13] iniuriam aestimare, et iudex uel tanti condemnat, quanti nos aesti-

---

statui iam non potest'. Hu. Paulo adscribit Ferrini coll. D.
47, 10, 2. 1) quidem *Inst.* quod V. 2) intellegit V.
3) aperte *Inst.* aptem V. 4) proponit V. 5) potenti V.
6) legum V. 7) tabulas V. 8) erat ūū V. 9) erit V.
10) pecuniariae *Boecking. ed. 5.* nummariae *Inst.* 11) ne V.
12) promittit V. 13) siis V.

10, 1, 3; 7 (*Ulp.* 1335). 47, 10, 9, 4 (*Ulp.* 1340). 47, 10, 18, 1
(*Paul* 688). 47, 10, 26 (*Paul.* 308). 47, 10, 29 (*Paul.* 1814).
21, 1, 43, 5 (*Paul.* 835). 44, 7, 34 *pr.* (*Paul.* 54). *C.* 9, 35, 1
(*a.* 222). 9, 35, 8 (*a.* 294). *Salvian. de gub. dei* 8, 3, 15. *Ioh.*
Chrysost. ad pop. Antioch. 20, 4 (*Migne Tom.* 49 *p.* 202).

§ 223. = *I.* 4, 4, 7. *cf. lex* XII *tab.* 8, 2—4 (*Bruns* I⁷, 29).
Paul. 5, 4, 6. *Coll.* 2, 5, 5 (*Paul.* 881). *Gell.* 20, 1, 12; 14; 32.
16, 10, 8. *Fest. v. talionis p.* 363 (*Bruns* II⁷, 42). *v. viginti quin-*
que p. 371 (*Bruns* II⁷, 46). *Cato ap. Priscian.* 6, 13, 69 *p.* 254
ed. Hertz. Isid. orig. 5, 27, 24 (*Bruns* II⁷, 83).

§ 224. *cf. I.* 4, 4, 7. *Paul.* 5, 4, 7. *Coll.* 2, 6 (*Paul.* 882).
2, 2, 1 (*Ulp.* 2384). *D.* 2, 12, 2 *fin.* (*Ulp.* 255). 2, 12, 3 (*Ulp.*
206). 47, 10, 7, 6 (*Ulp.* 1340). *Gell.* 20, 1, 37 *sq.* (*Iurispr.* I, 104).
Sueton. Vitell. 7. uadimonium] *cf. infra* 4, 186.

contempt can be committed against a slave, but that the delict is committed against the owner through the slave. But we do not suffer contempt in quite the same way as through our wives and children but only where something more gross occurs, manifestly done in contempt of the owner, for example, where one person flogs another's slave. There is a pattern **formula*** in the Edict for that. There is **no** pattern formula **for the case where someone abuses a slave vocally or strikes him with a fist**, nor is one readily given on application to the praetor.

223. **Under the Twelve Tables the penalty for this delict was, for a damaged limb, retaliation; for a broken** or bruised bone, **on the other hand**, it was 300 'asses' if a free man's bone had been broken but 150 if it was a slave's; for all other contempts, on the other hand, the penalty **established** was twenty-five 'asses'. And in those times **of great poverty** it seemed that these pecuniary **penalties** were satisfactory enough. 224. But now the law is different. The **praetor** allows us **to put our own value on the contempt and the judge*** condemns either for our **valuation or for**

mauerimus, uel minoris, pro*ut* illi uisum fuerit; sed
187 cum atrocem iniuriam praetor | aestimare soleat, si
simul constituerit, quantae pecuniae eo nomine fieri
debeat uadimonium, hac ipsa quantitate taxamus[1] formulam, et iudex, qui possit uel minoris damnare, plerumque tamen propter ipsius praetoris auctoritatem
non audet minuere condemnationem. 225. Atrox autem
iniuria aestimatur uel ex facto, uelut si quis ab aliquo
uulneratus aut uerberatus fustibusue caesus fuerit; uel
ex loco, uelut si cui in theatro aut in foro iniuria
facta sit; uel ex persona, uelut si magistratus iniuriam
passus fuerit, uel senatori[2] ab humili persona facta
sit iniuria.

LIB. III. EXPLIC. |

188   [3]_____

---

1) taxamur V.   2) senatori *Inst.* senatoribus V.
3) *pagina vacua in* V.

---

§ 225. = *I.* 4, 4, 9.   cf. *Paul.* 5, 4, 10.   *Coll.* 2, 2, 1 (*Ulp.*
2384).   *D.* 47, 10, 7, 7; 8 (*Ulp.* 1340).   47, 10, 9 *pr.* — 3 (*Ulp.*
1340).   47, 10, 17, 3 (*Ulp.* 1360).   47, 10, 35 (*Ulp.* 2269).   48, 5,
39, 9 (*Pap.* 378).   47, 10, 8 (*Paul.* 681).   47, 10, 40 (*Macer* 31).
C. 9, 35, 4 (a. 259).   *Lex Rom. Burg.* 5, 1.   *Cic. de invent.* 2,
20, 60.   *Quintil. Inst. or.* 6, 1, 15.   *Salvian. de gubern. dei* 6,
10, 53.

such lesser sum as seems **right to him**. But as the practice is for the praetor to set the value of an aggravated contempt himself, if he at the same time settles the amount of the defender's special undertaking* for his appearance in court, we put that same sum as the upper limit in our formula. Although the judge can go lower, out of respect for the praetor's authority he will generally not be so bold as to reduce the judgment below that figure. 225. **Contempt, however, can be aggravated: in conduct, as where someone is wounded by another** or flogged **or struck with clubs; in place, as where he is subjected to a contempt in the theatre or a city square; in person, as where a magistrate suffers a contempt, or a senator at the hands of a common person.**

COMMENTARIVS QVARTVS.

1. *Superest, ut de actionibus loquamur. et si quae-* 189
ramus[1], quot genera actionum sint, uerius uidetur
duo esse, in rem et in personam. nam qui IIII esse
dixerunt ex sponsionum generibus, non animaduerte-
runt quasdam species actionum inter genera se rettu-
lisse. 2. In personam actio est, qua agimus, quotiens
litigamus cum aliquo, qui nobis uel ex contractu uel
ex delicto obligatus est, id est, cum intendimus DARE
FACERE PRAESTARE[2] OPORTERE. 3. In rem actio est,
cum aut corporalem rem intendimus nostram esse aut
ius aliquod nobis conpetere, uelut utendi aut utendi
fruendi, eundi, agendi aquamue ducendi uel altius tol-
lendi prospiciendiue, *aut cum*[3] actio ex diuerso aduersario est negatiua. 4. Sic itaque discretis actionibus
certum est non posse nos rem nostram ab alio ita
petere: SI PARET EVM DARE OPORTERE; nec enim

---

1) *fere ex Goesch. coni. restituit Hu.; in* V *primus versus et
initium secundi litteris vacant.*   2) praestarie V.   3) aut cum
add. Hu.

§ 1. cf. *I.* 4, 6 *pr.*; 1. *D.* 44, 7, 25 *pr.*; 1 (*Ulp.* 2383).
50, 16, 178, 2 (*Ulp.* 2964). 44, 2, 14, 2 (*Paul.* 783). *infra* 4, 41.
Iuven. 16, 36—41.   quattuor] ʽ1) *personalis actio*; 2) *petitoria
formula*; 3) *in rem actio per sponsionem, cuius summa per formulam, et* 4) *per sponsionem, cuius summa sacramenti actione
petitur. cf. infra* 4, 91; 94; 95ʼ. *Hu.*
§ 2. cf. *I.* 4, 6, 1. *supra* 3, 88. *infra* 4, 5; 41.
§ 3. cf. *I.* 4, 6, 1; 2. *D.* 8, 5, 2 *pr.* (*Ulp.* 593).
§ 4. = *I.* 4, 6, 14. cf. *supra* 2, 79. 3, 91; 99; 189; 190.
I. 4, 1, 19 (21). *D.* 13, 1, 7, 1 (*Ulp.* 2876). 7, 9, 12 *i. f. et* 13, 3,
2 (*Ulp.* 2591). 13, 3, 1, 1 (*Ulp.* 779).

15*

BOOK FOUR

1. It remains to speak of actions. If we should ask how many classes of actions there are, the better view is that there are two, real and personal. For those who say that there are four, following the classes of legal wagers*, fail to notice that certain kinds have been counted among the classes of actions. 2. A **personal action*** is one which we raise when we sue someone **who is under an obligation to us, either contractual or delictual.** That is when we **claim** in our principal pleading* that: **'there is a duty to give, to do, to fulfil'.** 3. A **real action*** is when we claim either that some corporeal thing is ours, or that some right is available to us, for instance a right of use or of usufruct, **a right of way for man or beast, a right to lead water or a right of building higher or of prospect.** Conversely, we use real actions **to deny** such a right to an opponent. 4. **This distinction between real and personal actions means that** we **definitely cannot seek something of** our **own from another by a pleading: 'if it appears that he has a duty to give'. For what** we **own cannot be given to**

quod nostrum est, nobis dari potest, cum scilicet id
dari nobis intellegatur, quod *ita datur*, *ut* nostrum
fiat; nec res, quae *nostra iam est*, nostra amplius fieri
potest. plane odio furum, quo magis pluribus actionibus teneantur[1], receptum est, ut extra poenam dupli
aut quadrupli rei recipiendae nomine fures etiam[2] hac
actione teneantur: SI PARET EOS DARE OPORTERE,
quamuis sit etiam aduersus eos haec actio, qua rem
nostram esse petimus. 5. Appellantur autem in rem
quidem actiones uindicationes, in personam uero actiones, quibus dari[3] fieriue[4] oportere intendimus, condictiones.

6. Agimus autem interdum, ut rem tantum con|
190 sequamur, interdum ut poenam tantum, alias ut rem
et poenam. 7. Rem tantum persequimur uelut actionibus, *quibus*[5] ex contractu agimus. 8. Poenam tantum persequimur[6] uelut actione furti et iniuriarum et
secundum quorundam opinionem actione ui bonorum
raptorum; nam ipsius rei et uindicatio et condictio
nobis conpetit. 9. Rem uero et poenam persequimur
uelut ex his causis, ex quibus aduersus infitiantem in

---

1) teneant V.   2) etiam *Inst.* ex V.   3) dare V.
4) *del. Pflueger.*   5) *add. Lachmann.*   6) consequimur V.

---

§ 5. = *I.* 4, 6, 15. *cf. supra* 3, 91. *D.* 44, 7, 25 *pr.* (*Ulp.*
2383). *C.* 8, 54 (55). 1 (*a.* 258).

§ 6. *cf. I.* 4, 6, 16.

§ 7. *cf. I.* 4, 6, 17. *D.* 44, 7, 35 *pr.* (*Paul.* 84).

§ 8. *cf. I.* 4, 6, 18; 19. 4, 2 *pr. supra* 3, 209. *D.* 4, 2, 14,
10 (*Ulp.* 378). 47, 8, 2, 26 (*Ulp.* 1322). 39, 4, 9, 5 (*Paul.* 2026).
C. 9, 33, 1 (*a.* 242).

§ 9. *cf. infra* 4, 171. *Paul.* 1, 19, 1. *I.* 4, 6, 19. *Cic. de
off.* 3, 16, 65. actionem iudicati] *cf. D.* 42, 1, 6, 3 (*Ulp.* 1456).
Cic. p. Flacc. 21, 49. depensi] *cf. supra* 3, 127. damni in-
iuriae] *cf: supra* 3, 210. *D.* 9, 2, 2, 1 (*Gai.* 183). 9, 2, 23, 10
(*Ulp.* 617). 9, 3, 1, 4 (*Ulp.* 685). *C.* 3, 35, 4. 5 (*a.* 293). *I.* 4,
6, 23; 26. *Nov.* 18, 8. *Lex Rom. Burg.* 14, 8. 29. legatorum
nomine] *cf. supra* 2, 282.

us, **because 'give' is to be understood as meaning giving so that it may become** ours. **What is already** ours **cannot be made more so. No doubt it was from hatred of thieves, to multiply their liabilities, that the law came to allow against them not only the claims for twofold or fourfold penal damages but also the pleading: 'if it appears that they have a duty to give', even though the real action, by which** we **claim what is** ours, **is also competent against them. 5. Real actions are called 'vindications'*; the personal actions, on the other hand, in which** we **claim that there is a duty to give or to do, are actions of debt*, in Latin 'condictiones'.**

6. Sometimes we raise an action solely for restoration, sometimes solely for a penalty, at other times for both a thing and a penalty. 7. We seek only restoration when, for instance, we raise a contractual action. 8. We seek only a penalty by the actions for theft and contempt*, for instance, and in the opinion of some, by an action for things taken by force, for in this matter both vindication and action of debt are available to us. 9. We seek both property and penalty, on the other hand, in those cases where, for instance, we raise an action for double damages against

duplum agimus; quod accidit per actionem iudicati,
depensi, damni in*iuriae* *legis* Aqu*iliae*, aut legatorum
nomine, quae per damnationem certa relicta[1] sunt.

10. Quaedam praeterea sunt actiones, quae ad legis
actionem[2] exprimuntur, quaedam sua ui ac potestate
constant. quod ut manifestum fiat, opus est, ut prius
de legis actionibus loquamur.

11. Actiones, quas in usu ueteres habuerunt, legis
actiones appellabantur[3] uel ideo, quod legibus proditae
erant, quippe tunc edicta praetoris, quibus conplures[4]
actiones introductae sunt, nondum in usu habebantur,
uel ideo, quia ipsarum legum uerbis accommodatae
erant et ideo immutabiles proinde atque leges obser-
ua*b*antur[5]. unde eum, qui de uitibus succisis ita egisset,
ut in actione uites nominaret, responsum est[6] rem
perdidisse, quia[7] debuisset arbores nominare, eo quod
lex XII tabularum, ex qua de uitibus succisis actio
conpeteret, generaliter de arboribus succisis loquere-
tur. 12. Lege autem agebatur modis | quinque: sacra- 191
mento, per iudicis[8] postulationem, per condictionem[9],
per manus iniectionem, per pignoris capionem.[10]

13. Sacramenti actio generalis erat. de[11] quibus
enim rebus ut aliter ageretur, lege cautum non erat,

---

1) certa relicta *Goeschen.* certe relictae V.   2) actio(nis
fictio)nem *Ablaing.*   3) appellabatur V.   4) conpluris V.
5) et ideo — observabantur *del. Beseler.*   6) eum V.   7) cun
quia V.   8) iudices V.   9) conductionem V.   10) captio-
nem V.   11) de *Savigny.* ad V.

---

§ 10. *cf. infra* 4, 32; 33.
§ 11. *cf. D.* 1, 2, 2, 6 (*Pomp.* 178). *Cic. partit. orat.* 28, 99.
de uitibus succisis] *cf. leg.* XII *tab.* 8, 11 (*Bruns* I⁷, 31). *Plin.
nat. hist.* 17, 1, 7.   *D.* 12, 2, 28, 6 (*Paul.* 281). 47, 7, 1 (*Paul.*
1803). 47, 7, 5 (*Paul.* 1804).
§ 12. sacramento] §§ 13—17. per iudicis postulationem]
§ 17ᵃ. per condictionem] §§ 17ᵇ—20. per manus iniectionem]
§§ 21—25. per pignoris capionem] §§ 26—29.
§ 13. *cf. infra* 4, 171; 180. *Varro de l. l.* 5, 36, 180
(*Bruns* II⁷, 54). 6, 7, 74 (*Bruns* II⁷, 57). *Fest. v. sacramentum,*

someone who denies a claim, as happens with an action on a judgment debt, on expenditure*, for wrongful loss under the Aquilian Act, or for definite things left by obligatory legacy*.

10. There are, moreover, certain actions which are expressed in terms of actions in the law*, while others are valid by their own force and effect. To make this clear, we must first speak of actions in the law.

11. The actions used by the old lawyers* were described as actions in the law, either because they were set out in statutes*, since at that time the praetor's* edicts*, which introduced numerous actions, were not yet in use – or because they were precisely adjusted to the words of statutes, and were accordingly observed as immutably as if they had been statutes. This was why the opinion was given that a man who raised an action over the cutting down of vines in a way that used the word 'vines' in the action had lost his case. He ought to have used the word 'trees', because the Twelve Tables*, under which the action for cutting down vines was available, spoke in general terms about cutting down trees. 12. Actions in the law were raised in five forms: by oath, by application for a judge, by action of debt, by the laying on of a hand, and by the taking of a pledge.

13. The action by oath was of a general nature. It was the mode of action employed in those matters for which statute did not otherwise provide. This action

de his sacramento agebatur: eaque actio proinde peri-
culosa erat falsi*********[1] atque hoc tempore peri-
culosa est actio certae creditae pecuniae propter sponsionem, qua periclitatur[2] reus, si temere neget, *et*
restipulationem, qua periclitatur actor, si non debitum
petat. nam qui uictus erat, summam sacramenti prae-
stabat poenae nomine; eaque in publicum cedebat
praedesque eo nomine praeto*ri* dabantur[3], non ut nunc
sponsionis et restipulationis poena lucro cedit aduersarii[4], qui uicerit.[5]   14. Poena autem sacramenti aut
quingenaria erat aut quinquagenaria. nam de rebus
mille aeris plurisue quingentis assibus, de minoris uero
quinquaginta assibus sacramento contendebatur; nam
ita lege XII tabularum cautum erat. *at* si de libertate
hominis controuersia erat, etiamsi pretiosissimus homo
esset, tamen ut L assibus sacramento contenderetur[6],
eadem lege cautum est fauore[7] scilicet libertatis,[8] ne
*on*erarentur adsertor*es*. |[9] ————————————

**192
t. s.**   ————————— *vv. 11* ———————— |

———

1) *verba inde a* falsi *usque ad* uictus erat *in* V *per erro-*
rem bis scripta sunt, nisi quod verba periclitaretur reus si
temere neget restipulationem qua *priore loco omissa sunt.*
falsi *priore loco evanuit; quae secuntur fere 8 litterae, utroque*
loco certo legi nequeunt. falsiloquo propter iusiurandum *suppl.*
Hu.   2) periclitaretur V.   3) dabatur V.   4) aduersario
Goeschen. adueteari V. *cf. V. I. R. s. v.* cedo *p. 706, 1.*   5) uice-
ritut V.   6) contenderet V.   7) fabori V.   8) favore —
libertatis *del. Albertario.*   9) *pag. 192, cuius pauca tantum*
verba legi possunt, Gaius tractavit de actione sacramenti, qua
in personam agebatur.

sacramento *p.* 344 *sq. Bruns* II[7], 34). *Cic. in Verr.* 2, 1, 45, 115.
pro Caec. 33, 97. *pro dom.* 29, 78. *pro Mil.* 27, 74. *de orat.*
1, 10, 42. *de rep.* 2, 35, 60. *ad. fam.* 7, 32, 2. *Val. Max.* 7,
8, 2. *Arnob. adv. gent.* 4, 16 (*p.* 155 *ed. Reiffersch.*). *Isid.*
orig. 5, 24, 31 (*Bruns* II[7], 81). *lex Acil. repet. v.* 23 (*Bruns*
I[7], 63).
    § 14. *cf. Varr. Fest. ll. cc. Val. Prob.* 4, 2 (Q. N. T. S.
Q. P. quando negas, te sacramento quingenario prouoco). lege
XII tab.] 2, 1 (*Bruns* I[7], 20). si de libertate] *cf. Liv.* 3, 44 *sq.*

was as hazardous in the case of fraud as is our present-day action on a fixed loan because of the wager by stipulation which puts the defender at risk if he rashly denies his obligation and the counter-stipulation which puts the pursuer at risk if he claims what is not owing to him. For whoever lost the action by oath would hand over as penalty the amount sworn to, and this went to the public purse, with special sureties* for it given to the praetor, not as now, when the penalty resulting from the stipulation and the counter-stipulation profits the successful party. 14. The sworn penalty was either five hundred or fifty 'asses'*. For property worth a thousand asses or more the action on oath was for a fine of five hundred, but for that of less value for fifty, as was provided in the Twelve Tables. But if the subject in dispute was a man's freedom then, even if he was a highly valuable slave, the same law provided that the action on oath was for a fine of fifty. This showed a disposition to favour freedom, so that those who claimed him to be free should not be burdened. [In the next, largely illegible, page, Gaius must have dealt with the personal action by oath.] 15. .... they should come in

15. ——————————— i|stae omnes actiones ——————— ı
| ——————— | ——————— vv. 5 ——————— |
| ——————————— captus ——————————— |
| ——————————— vv. 5 ——————————— | 193
| ——————————— ad iudicem accipiundum | ueni-
rent. postea uero[1] reuersis dabatur. ut autem *die*
xxx. iudex detur[2], per legem Pinariam factum est;
ante eam autem legem *statim*[3] dabatur iudex.
illud ex superioribus intellegimus, si de re minoris quam[4]
м aeris agebatur, quinquagenario sacramento, non quingenario eos contendere solitos fuisse.[5] postea tamen
quam iudex ᵈdatus[6] esset, comperendinum diem, ut ad
iudicem uenirent, denuntiabant; deinde cum ad iudicem
uenerant, antequam apud eum causam perorarent, solebant breuiter ei et quasi per indicem rem exponere;
quae dicebatur causae coniectio[7] quasi causae suae[8] in
breue coactio.

16. Si in rem agebatur, mobilia quidem et mouen-

---

1) ū. (*id est* uel?) V.   2) daretur *Wieding*.   3) statim *Hollweg.* nondum *Heffter. lectio codicis* V *incertissima est.*   4) q̄. (*id.
est* quae) V.   5) illud—fuisse *del. Iuncker.*   6) datum V.
7) coniectio *Ps.-Ascon.* collectio V.   8) suae *del. Beseler.*

§ 15. *cf. Val. Prob.* 4, 8 (T. PR. I. A. V. P. V. D. te
praetor iudicem arbitrumue postulo uti des). ad iudicem] *cf.
infra* 4, 18. die xxx.] *cf. Ps.-Ascon. ad Cic. Verr.* 2, 1, 9, 26
p. 164 *ed. Bait.* (*Bruns* II⁷, 71). per legem Pinariam] *cf. Macrob. Sat.* 1, 13, 21 (hoc arguit Varro scribendo antiquissimam
legem fuisse incisam in columna aerea a L. Pinario et Furio
consulibus (*a.* 472 *a. Chr.*), cui mensis intercalaris adscribitur).
ex superioribus] § 14. comperendinum] *cf. Val. Prob.* 4, 9
(*I. D. T. S. P.* in diem tertium siue perendinum). *Cic. pro
Mur.* 12, 27. *Plin. ep.* 5, 9 (21), 1. *Gell.* 6 (7), 1, 10. 10, 24, 9.
Fest. v. res comperendinata p. 282 *M.* (*Bruns* II⁷, 32). *Macrob.
Sat.* 1, 16, 13; 14, *Pseudo-Ascon. l. c.* causae coniectio] *cf. D.*
50, 17, 1 (*Paul.* 1230). *Auct. ad Her.* 2, 21, 33. *Gell.* 5, 10, 9.
Non. Marc. 4, 89 *v. conicere p.* 183 *Merc.* (*Bruns* II⁷, 64). *Ps.-
Ascon. l. c. cf. etiam Auct. ad Her.* 2, 13, 20. *Gell.* 17, 2, 10.
§ 16. *cf. Plaut. Rud.* 4, 3, 86 = 1025. *Mil. glor.* 4, 1,
15 = 961. *Cic. pro Mur.* 12, 26. *pro Mil.* 27, 74. *de orat.*

order to receive a judge*. Subsequently, however, he was appointed on their return. The provision that the judge should be appointed on the thirtieth day was made by the Pinarian Act; before that the judge was appointed forthwith. We learn from what is said above that, if an action was raised about property worth less than a thousand 'asses' they customarily took an action on oath for fifty, not five hundred. Once the judge had been appointed, they would announce that they would go before him on the third day following. When they had come before the judge, they used to set out the matter to him briefly, by way of summary, before they pleaded the case in front of him. This was called 'putting the arguments together', the bringing together of the grounds of action in brief, as it were.

16. If it was a real action, they vindicated before the court moveable and living property, which could be

tia, quae modo in ius adferri adduciue possent, in iure
uindicabantur ad hunc modum: qui uindicabat, festucam tenebat; deinde ipsam rem adprehendebat, uelut
hominem, et ita dicebat: HVNC EGO HOMINEM EX IVRE·
QVIRITIVM MEVM ESSE AIO SECVNDVM SVAM CAVSAM;
SICVT DIXI, ECCE TIBI, VINDICTAM INPOSVI, et simul
homini festucam inponebat. aduersarius eadem similiter dicebat et faciebat. cum uterque uindicasset,
praetor dicebat: MITTITE AMBO HOMINEM, illi mitte-
bant. qui prior uindicauerat, ita alterum interrogabat[1]:
POSTVLO, ANNE DICAS, QVA EX CAVSA VINDICAVERIS?
ille respondebat: IVS FECI[2], SICVT VINDICTAM IN-
POSVI. deinde qui prior uindicauerat, dicebat: QVANDO
194 TV INIVRIA VINDICAVISTI, | QVINGENTIS ASSIBVS[3] SACRA-
MENTO TE PROVOCO; aduersarius quoque dicebat similiter: ET EGO TE[4]; aut si res infra mille asses erat, quin-
quagenarium scilicet sacramentum[5] nominabant. deinde
eadem[6] sequebantur, quae cum[7] in personam ageretur.
postea praetor secundum alterum eorum uindicias dice-

---

1) vindicaverat—interrogabat *suppl. Goeschen.*   2) fecii V.
3) quingentis assibus F, *qui hinc denuo incipit.* D AERIS V.   4) aduersarius — EGO TE *om.* F.   5) aut si res — sacramentum F.
scilicet L asses sacramenti V.   6) eadem F. at V.   7) quae
cum] quaecumque V. quae si F.

1, 10, 41. *Gell.* 20, 10. *Boeth. in Cic. top.* 2, 10 *p.* 288 *Bait.*
(*Bruns* II[7], 73). SEC. SVAM CAVSAM] *cf. Val. Prob.* 4, 6 (S. S. C.
S. D. E. T. V. secundum suam causam sicut dixi ecce tibi
uindicta). eadem sequebantur] *cf. supra* 4, 15. uindicias] *cf.*
D. 1, 2, 2, 24 (*Pomp.* 178). *Liv.* 3, 44; 47; 56 *sq. Cic. pro Mil.*
27, 74. *Arnob.* 4, 16 (*p.* 155 *ed. Reiffersch.*). *Fest. v. vindiciae*
p. 376 (*Bruns* II[7], 46). *Gloss. Philox. v. vindiciae.* praedes
aduersario] *cf. infra* 4, 94. *Plaut. Menaechm.* 4, 2, 25. 26
= 592. 593. festuca] *cf. Plaut. Mil.* 4, 1, 75 = 961. *Pers. Sat.*
5, 175. quod maxime] *cf. supra* 2, 69. *Dionys.* 6, 32; 36. 8, 10.
in centumuiralibus iudiciis] *cf. Suet. Aug.* 36. *Laus Pison.*
41 (*Poet. lat. min. ed. Baehr.* I, 227). *Quint. Inst. orat.* 5, 2, 1.
Martial. 7, 63, 7. *Stat. Silv.* 4, 4, 43. *Val. Max.* 7, 8, 1.

carried or led into the court, in this way. The claimant
would hold a rod*; then he would take hold of the
actual property, for instance a slave, and say: 'I
declare that this slave is mine by quiritary right* in
accordance with my case*. As I have spoken, see, I
have imposed the claim', and at the same time he laid
the rod on the slave. His opponent likewise said and
did the same. When each of them had made his claim
the praetor would say: 'Both of you, let go the slave.'
They then let go of him. The first claimant would then
put a question to the other in these words: 'I demand
that you tell me the grounds of your claim.' The other
replied: 'I have exercised my right in imposing the
claim.' The first claimant would then say: 'Inasmuch
as you have claimed wrongfully, I challenge you on
oath for five hundred "asses".' His opponent then said
likewise: 'And I you.' If the property was worth less
than a thousand 'asses', the sworn penalty that they
named would be for fifty. The following stages were
the same as for a personal action. Then the praetor
would pronounce on the claim* in favour of one of the
parties; that is to say, he made one of them interim

bat, id est interim aliquem possessorem constituebat, eumque iubebat praedes[1] aduersario dare litis et uindiciarum, id est rei et fructuum; alios autem praedes ipse praetor ab utroque accipiebat sacramenti causa, quia[2] id in publicum cedebat. festuca autem utebantur quasi hastae loco, signo quodam iusti dominii, quando iusto dominio ea maxime[3] sua esse credebant, quae ex hostibus cepissent; unde in centumuiralibus iudiciis hasta proponitur.[4] 17. Si qua res talis erat, ut sine incommodo non posset[5] in ius adferri uel adduci, uerbigratia[6] si columna aut nauis[7] aut grex alicuius pecoris esset, pars aliqua inde sumebatur eaque in ius adferebatur[8], deinde in eam partem quasi in totam rem praesentem fiebat uindicatio; itaque ex[9] grege uel una ouis siue[10] capra in ius adducebatur, uel etiam pilus inde[11] sumebatur et[12] in ius adferebatur; ex naue uero et columna aliqua pars defringebatur; similiter si de fundo uel de aedibus siue de hereditate controuersia erat, pars aliqua inde sumebatur et in ius adferebatur, et in eam partem proinde[13] atque in totam rem praesentem fiebat uindicatio, uelut ex fundo gleba sumebatur et ex aedibus tegula, et si de hereditate controuersia erat, aeque | *res uel rei pars aliqua inde sumebatur.*[14]

[*Fol. deperditum in codice Veronensi, cuius pagina posterior suppletur codice Antinoensi.*][15]

---

1) praedes F. praesides V. 2) causa quia] c(ausa) quia F. quod V. eo quia *Arangio.* 3) dominii quando — maxime F. dominio xxi. me V. dominii quod maxime *Hu.* 4) proponitur F. praeponitur V. 5) possit F. 6) uerbigratia F. uelut V. 7) aut nauis *om.* V. 8) eaque — adferebatur *om.* V. 9) uel ex V. 10) aut V. 11) *om.* F. 12) *hic finit* F. 13) pinde V. 14) res — sumebatur *suppl. Hu.* 15) *in his duabus paginis Gaius primum videtur solemnes ritus ac verba, quae ad rerum*

---

§ 17. *cf. Fest. v. vindiciae p.* 326 (*Bruns* II[7], 46). *v. membrum abscidi p.* 148. *Cic. pro Mur.* 12, 26. *Gell.* 20, 10.

possessor and ordered him to give his opponent special sureties for the action and the claim, that is, for the property and its fruits. The praetor himself took other special sureties from both parties in the matter of the oath, because that went to the public purse. They made use of a rod, as it were in place of a spear, as a sign of lawful ownership, because they believed that property to which there was the strongest claim of lawful ownership was that which they had captured from the enemy. Therefore a spear is on display before the judges of the centumviral court*. 17. If property was of such a kind that it could not be carried or led into the court without inconvenience, for example, a pillar, a ship, or a flock of some herding beast, they used to take some part of it and carry that into the court; then the vindication was made on that part as if the whole had been present. So from a flock a single ewe or she-goat would be led into the court, or even a hair would be taken from them and brought into the court, while a piece would be broken off a ship or a pillar. Likewise, if there was a dispute over land or buildings or an inheritance, a part of it would be taken and brought into the court and a vindication would be made on that part, just as if the whole had been present. For instance, a clod of earth was taken from a farm, a roof tile from a house, while if the dispute was about an inheritance some item or part of some thing would likewise be brought. [A folio is missing from the Verona MS, but its second side is supplied from Egyptian finds. Gaius seems to have dealt next with the formalities for claiming things in their absence.]

Que leg*is* act*ione* restitut*um* est.[1]

17.ᵃ Per iudic*is* *p*ostulationem ageba*tur*, *si* q*u*a de re
ut ita age*re*tur lex iuss*is*set sicu*ti* lex XII *t*abularum de *co*
quod ex stipul*atio*ne petitur. eaque res talis fere erat.
qui agebat sic dicebat: EX SPONSIONE TE MI*H*I X MILIA
SESTERTIORVM DARE OPORTERE AIO: ID POSTVLO AIAS[2]
AN NEGES.[3] aduersarius dicebat non oportere. actor[4]
dicebat: QVANDO TV NEGAS, TE PRAETOR IVDICEM SIVE
ARBITRVM POSTVLO VTI DES.[5] itaque in eo genere
actionis sine poena quisque negabat. item de hereditate diuidenda inter coheredes eadem lex per iudicis
postulationem agi ins*sit.* idem fecit lex Licinn*ia,* si
de al*i*qua re comm*u*ni diuidenda ageretur. itaque no-
*mi*nata causa ex qua ageba*tur* statim arb*i*ter pete-
batu*r.*

17ᵇ. Per condi*c*tionem ita agebatur: AIO TE MIHI
SESTERTIORVM X MILIA DARE OPORTERE: ID POSTVLO,
AIAS[2] AVT NEGES. aduersarius dicebat non oportere.
actor dicebat: QVANDO TV NEGAS, IN DIEM TRIGENSI-
MVM TIBI IVDICIS CAPIENDI CAUSA CONDICO. deinde
die[6] tricensimo ad iudicem capiendum praesto esse
debebant. condice̅re autem denuntiare est prisca[7] lingua.

---

absentium vindicationem pertinebant (Gell. 20. 10. Cic. pro Mur.
12) addidisse (cf. infra 4, 48), deinde ad legis actionem, quae
per iudicis postulationem fiebat, transiit.

1) *hæc et quae sequuntur* servavit F.   2) AIES F.
3) NEGAS F.   4) auctor F.   5) dest F.   6) *hic iterum*
incipit cod. V.   7) prisca V. pristina F.

---

§ 17ᵃ. AIAS AN NEGES] *cf. Plaut. Rud.* 430. 1331. TE PRAETOR
IVDICEM ARBITRVMVE POSTVLO VTI DES] *cf. Val. Prob. de not.* 4, 8.
Plaut. Rud. 1380. sine poena] *vide supra* 4, 13. de hereditate
diuidenda] *cf. infra* 4, 42. lex Licinia] *cf. D.* 4, 7, 12 (*Mar-*
cian. 159). de aliqua re communi diuidenda] *cf. infra* 4, 42.

§ 17ᵇ. condicere autem *etc.* = *I.* 4, 6, 15. *cf. Corp. gloss.*
Lat. II, 394.

What is restored by an action in the law.

17a. An action by application for a judge was raised in those cases where this was required by statute, for example, by the Twelve Tables for what is claimed under a stipulation. Now that procedure was generally as follows. The pursuer* would say: 'I declare that you have a duty to give me ten thousand under your solemn promise. I demand that you affirm or deny this.' His opponent said that he had no such duty. The pursuer would then say: 'In that you deny it, I demand that you, praetor, appoint a judge or arbiter for me.' In this kind of action, therefore, both parties could deny liability without penalty. The same statute required that an action in the law by application for a judge be brought for the dividing of an inheritance among the co-heirs. The Licinnian Act made the same provision where an action was raised for dividing common property. And so, once the grounds on which the action was raised had been named, an arbiter would immediately be sought.

17b. The action in the law by action of debt was brought as follows: 'I declare that you have a duty to give me ten thousand. I demand that you affirm or deny this.' His opponent declared that he had no such duty. The pursuer would then say: 'In that you deny it, I serve notice on you to be present in thirty days' time to receive a judge.' Then they were required to be present on the thirtieth day to receive a judge. **In archaic speech the word 'condicere' means 'to serve notice'.** 18. This action was therefore properly

18. Itaque haec quidem actio proprie condictio uocabatur. nam actor[1] aduersario denuntiabat, ut ad iudicem capiendum[2] die XXX. adesset; nunc uero non proprie condictionem dicimus actionem in personam *esse, qua*[3] intendimus dari[4] nobis oportere. nulla[5] enim hoc tempore eo nomine denuntiatio fit. 19. Haec autem legis actio constituta est per legem Siliam et Calpurniam, lege quidem Silia certae pecuniae, lege uero Calpurnia de omni certa re. 20. Quare autem haec actio desiderata sit, cum de eo, quod nobis dari oportet, potuerit aut sacramento aut per iudicis postulationem agi[6], ualde quaeritur.

21. Per manus iniectionem aeque *de* his rebus agebatur, de quibus ut ita ageretur, lege aliqua[7] cautum est, uelut iudicati lege XII tabularum. quae actio talis erat: qui agebat, sic dicebat: QVOD TV MIHI IVDI-

---

1) auctor V. 2) iudicem capiendum V. accipiendum F, *qui hoc verbo finit.* 3) esse qua *add. Lachmann ex Inst.* 4) id V. 5) nullam V. 6) agere V. 7) aquilia V.

---

§ 18. *cf. supra* 4, 5. *infra* 4, 33. *I.* 4, 6, 15. *Fest. ep. v.* condictio, condicere p. 64. 66 (*Bruns* II[7], 5). *Donat. ad Terent.* Phorm. 1, 2, 77. *Serv. ad Aen.* 3, 117 (*Bruns* II[7], 76). *Gell.* 10, 24, 9. 16, 4, 4 (status condictusque dies cum hoste). *Tac. Germ.* 11. *Corp. gloss. Lat.* II, 394.

§ 19. Lex Calpurnia] *cf. C. I. L.* I 198 (*Bruns* I[7], 71) *l.* 74. *Cic. Brut.* 27, 106. *de offic.* 2, 21, 75. *in Verr.* 3, 84, 195. 4, 25, 56. *Schol. Bob. ad Cic. p. Flacc. p.* 233 *Bait.* (*p.* 37 *ed. Hildebrandt*). *Tacit. ann.* 15, 20.

§ 21. *cf. Serv. ad Aen.* 10, 419 (*Bruns* II[7], 78). *lex* XII *tab.* 1, 2 (*Bruns* I[7], 18). *Fest. v. struere p.* 310. *Non. p.* 4 (*Bruns* II[7], 64). *lex col. Iul. Genet. c.* 61 (*Bruns* I[7], 123). *cf. Fr. Vat.* 6 (*Pap.* 471). *D.* 2, 4, 10, 1 (*Ulp* 261). 18, 7, 9 (*Paul.* 1325). 40, 8, 7 (*Paul.* 979). *C.* 4, 55, 1; 2 (*a.* 200). 7, 6, 1, 4 (*a.* 531). *Senec. Controv.* 1 *praef.* § 14 (*p.* 8 *ed. Mueller*). *Macr. Sat.* 3, 7, 4. iudicati] *cf. Gell.* 20, 1, 45 *sq.* (*Iurispr.* I, 105). lege XII tab.] 3, 3 (*Bruns* I[7], 21). uindicem] *cf. infra* 4, 25; 46 *fin. Fest. v. vindex p.* 376 (*Bruns* II[7], 46). *Boeth. ad Cic. top.* 2, 10 *p.* 291 *Bait. Gell.* 16, 10, 5. *Liv.* 3, 44 *sq. Dionys.* 11, 28 *sq. lex col. Iul. Genet. c.* 61 (*Bruns* I[7], 123).

called 'condictio'; for the pursuer would serve notice on his opponent to attend on the thirtieth day to receive a judge. **Now, however**, we improperly **keep the name for the personal action in which** we **claim that something ought to be given to** us; **nowadays there is no serving of notice in this context**. 19. This action in the law was introduced by the Silian and Calpurnian Acts: by the Silian Act for a fixed sum of money and by the Calpurnian Act for all other definite objects. 20. But why this action should have been required, since one can raise an action for what ought to be given to us either by oath or by application for a judge, is a very fair question.

21. An action by the laying on of a hand was likewise brought in those matters where such procedure had been provided by a statute, for instance, by the Twelve Tables for a judgment debt. This action was as follows. The pursuer would say: 'Because the court has awarded that you' or 'because

CATVS siue DAMNATVS ES SESTERTIVM X MILIA, QVAN
DOC[1] NON SOLVISTI, OB EAM REM EGO TIBI SESTER
TIVM X MILIVM IVDICATI MANVM[2] INICIO, et simul
aliquam[3] partem corporis eius prendebat; nec licebat
iudicato manum sibi depellere et pro se lege agere,
sed uindicem dabat, qui pro se causam agere solebat.[4]
qui uindicem non dabat, domum[5] ducebatur ab actore et uinciebatur.[6] 22. Postea quaedam leges ex
196 aliis quibusdam causis | pro iudicato manus iniectionem in quosdam dederunt, sicut lex Publilia in eum,
pro[7] quo sponsor dependisset, si[8] in sex mensibus
proximis, quam pro eo depensum esset, non soluisset
sponsori pecuniam; item lex Furia de sponsu aduersus
eum, qui a sponsore plus quam uirilem partem exegisset, et denique conplures aliae leges in multis causis
talem actionem dederunt. 23. Sed aliae leges ex quibusdam causis[9] constituerunt quasdam actiones per[10]
manus iniectionem, sed puram, id est non pro iudicato, uelut lex[11] *Furia* testamentaria aduersus eum, qui
legatorum nomine mortisue causa plus M[12] assibus cepisset, cum ea lege non esset exceptus, ut ei plus
capere liceret; item lex Marcia aduersus faeneratores,
ut si usuras exegissent, de his reddendis per manus
iniectionem cum eis ageretur. 24. Ex quibus legibus

---

1) quando te *Eisele*.   2) manum *Heffter*. manus V.
3) aliquae V.   4) agere solebat] ageret *postulat Krueger*.
5) dominum V.   6) uindiciebatur V.   7) per V.   8) i V
per notam.   9) ex quibusdam causis *Savigny*. in multis causis
ex quibusdam si V.   10) pro V.   11) lege V.   12) C V.

---

§ 22. cf. *lex luci Luccrini C. I. L.* IX 782 (*Bruns* I⁷, 283).
pro iudicato] cf. D. 2, 14, 7, 13 (*Ulp.* 247). lex Publilia] cf.
supra 3, 127. lex Furia] cf. supra 3, 121 sq.
§ 23. cf. *Plaut. Pers.* 1, 2, 19—21 = 70—72. lex Furia]
cf. supra 2, 225. lex Marcia] a. 352 a. *Chr.?* cf. *Liv.* 7, 21.
cf. etiam *Liv.* 7, 42, 1. *Appian. Bell. civ.* 1, 54. *Tac. ann.*
6, 16.

you are condemned to give me ten thousand, in that you have not paid, I accordingly lay my hand on you for the ten thousand of the judgment', at the same time taking hold of some part of his body. The judgment debtor could not lawfully shake off the hand from himself and conduct his own action but would appoint a champion*, who used to conduct the case on his behalf. A defender who failed to appoint a champion would be led by the pursuer to his house and put in chains. 22. Subsequently certain statutes dealing with various other cases appointed the action by the laying on of a hand against others, as if they were judgment debtors. For example, by the Publilian Act against a person on whose behalf a personal surety* had expended money, if he had not repaid the money to the personal surety in the six months following the time at which the expenditure was made; again, by the Furian Act on personal suretyship against one who exacted more than his share from a personal surety; and finally a large number of other statutes appointed an action of this kind in many cases. 23. There were, however, other statutes which for various reasons laid down certain actions by 'pure' laying on of a hand, that is, not as if arising from a judgment debt. An example is the Furian Act on wills against someone who had taken, by way of legacies or from gifts in contemplation of death, more than one thousand 'asses', when under that Act he was not privileged to take more; again, the Marcian Act against moneylenders provided that, if they exacted usurious interest, an action by the laying on of a hand might be brought against them for repayment. 24. Under these Acts and those analogous

et si quae aliae similes essent cum agebatur, manum
sibi depellere et pro se lege agere *reo licebat*.[1] nam
et actor in ipsa legis actione non adiciebat hoc uerbum PRO IVDICATO, sed nominata causa, ex qua agebat, ita dicebat: OB EAM REM EGO TIBI MANVM INICIO;
cum hi, quibus pro iudicato actio data erat, nominata
causa, ex qua agebant[2], ita inferebant[3]: OB EAM REM
EGO TIBI PRO IVDICATO MANVM INICIO. nec me praeterit in forma legis Furiae testamentariae PRO IVDI-
CATO uerbum inseri, cum[4] in ipsa lege non sit; quod
uidetur | nulla ratione factum. 25. Sed postea lege 197
Vallia[5], excepto iudicato et eo, pro quo depensum est,
ceteris omnibus, cum quibus per manus iniectionem
agebatur, permissum est sibi manum depellere et pro
se agere. itaque iudicatus et is, pro quo depensum est,
etiam post hanc legem uindicem dare debebant[6] et,
nisi darent, domum ducebantur. istaque[7], quamdiu legis
actiones in usu erant, semper ita obseruabantur; unde
nostris temporibus is, cum quo iudicati depensiue agitur, iudicatum[8] solui satisdare cogitur.

26. Per pignoris capionem lege agebatur de quibusdam rebus moribus, *de quibusdam rebus*[9] lege.
27. Introducta est moribus rei militaris. nam [et]

---

1) reo licebat *suppl. Hu.*　　2) agebat V.　　3) infere-
bat V.　　4) cumr V.　　5) *nomen num recte traditum sit,
dubitat Hu.; olim* Valeria *scripserat, Recht des Nexum p.* 141.
6) debebat V.　　7) istaque *Hu.* itaque V　　8) iudicati V.
9) de quibusdam rebus *suppl. Boecking.*

---

§ 25. uindicem] *cf. supra* 4, 21. *lex col. Genet. Iul. c.* 61
(*Bruns* I[7], 123). iudicatum solui] *cf. infra* 4, 102.
§ 26. *cf. Gell.* 6 (7), 10. *Dionys.* 6, 29.
§ 27. *cf. Plaut. Aulul.* 3, 5, 53 = 526 *sq. Poen.* 5, 5, 6; 7
= 1285. *Varr. de l. l.* 5, 36, 181 (*Bruns* II[7], 54). *Cic. de
rep.* 2, 20, 36. *Liv.* 1, 43, 9. *Gell.* 6 (7), 10. *Fest. v. aerarii
tribuni p.* 2 (*Bruns* II[7], 3); *equestre aes p.* 81 (*Bruns* II[7], 8);
hordiarium aes p. 102 (*Bruns* II[7], 10); *pararium aes p.* 221
(*Bruns* II[7], 21); *vectigal p.* 371 (*Bruns* II[7], 44). *Non. Marc. v.*

to them it was lawful when the action was brought for the defender to shake off the hand and conduct his own action. For the pursuer in that action did not add the words: 'as if for a judgment debt' but, after specifying the grounds of the action, he would say: 'I accordingly lay my hand on you'; while those who had been granted the action as if for a judgment would introduce it thus: 'I accordingly lay my hand on you as if for a judgment debt'. I have not forgotten that in the formula under the Furian Act on wills the phrase 'as if for a judgment debt' is inserted, although it is not in the Act itself. There seems to be no reason why this was done. 25. Subsequently, however, under the Vallian Act, all persons against whom an action was brought by the laying on of a hand were permitted to shake off the hand laid on them and conduct their own case, with the exception of the judgment debtor and the man for whom a personal surety had expended money. And so, even after the passing of this Act, the judgment debtor and the man for whom a personal surety had expended money were required to appoint a champion, failing which they were led to the creditor's house. This practice was always observed as long as actions in the law continued in use. This is why in our own time a person against whom an action is raised on a judgment debt or on expenditure is compelled to give security for the payment of the sum in the judgment.

26. An action in the law by the taking of a pledge was brought in some circumstances by custom, in others by statute. 27. Its origin in custom was in

propter stipendium licebat militi ab eo, qui aes tribuebat[1], nisi daret, pignus capere; dicebatur autem ea
pecunia, quae stipendii nomine dabatur, aes militare.
item propter eam pecuniam licebat pignus capere, ex
qua equus[2] emendus erat; quae pecunia dicebatur aes
equestre. item propter eam pecuniam, ex qua[3] hor-
deum equis erat conparandum; quae pecunia dicebatur
aes hordiarium. 28. Lege autem introducta est pignoris capio uelut lege XII tabularum aduersus eum, qui
hostiam emisset nec pretium redderet; item[4] aduersus
eum, qui mercedem non redderet pro eo iumento, quod
quis ideo locasset, ut inde pecuniam acceptam[5] in
198 dapem[6], id est in sacrificium, inpenderet; | item lege
censoria data est pignoris capio[7] publicanis uectigalium
publicorum populi Romani aduersus eos, qui aliqua
lege[8] uectigalia deberent. 29. Ex omnibus autem istis
causis certis uerbis pignus capiebatur, et ob id plerisque placebat hanc quoque actionem legis actionem
esse; quibusdam autem placebat *legis actionem non
esse*, primum quod pignoris capio[7] extra ius perage-
batur, id est non apud praetorem[9], plerumque etiam
absente[10] aduersario, cum alioquin ceteris actionibus

---

1) aes tribuebat *Niebuhr*. distruebat V. *cf. Fest. v.* aerarii
tribuni *p.* 2.   2) qua equus *Savigny*. quae ciuis V.
3) q̄ (*i. e.* quae) V.   4) it V.   5) accepta V.   6) darem V.
7) captio V.   8) leges V.   9) p. r. (*id est* populum Romanum) V.   10) absentem V.

---

aere diruti p. 532 *Merc. Ps.-Ascon. ad Cic. Verr.* 2, 1, 13, 34
p. 167 *Bait. Cato ap. Priscian.* 7, 38 *p.* 318 *Hertz. Dionys.*
9, 25. *Plut. Camill.* 2.

§ 28. lege XII tabularum] 12, 1 (*Bruns* I[7], 39). in dapem]
cf. Cato de agricult. 131. 132. *Fest. v. daps p.* 68. *Tibull.*
1, 5, 28. *Serv. ad Aen.* 3, 224. publicanis] *cf. D.* 47, 8, 2, 20
(*Ulp.* 1319). *Cic. in Verr.* 2, 3, 11, 27.   *lex agr.* 19, 20
(*Bruns* I[7], 77).

§ 29. *cf. Varro de l. l.* 6, 29 *sq.*; 53.   *Ovid. Fast.* 1, 47.
Macrob. Sat. 1, 16, 14.

military affairs. For it was lawful for a soldier to take a pledge from the person required to contribute the money for his pay if that person failed to make the payment. This money, which was given in the name of pay, was called 'military dues'. Again, he might lawfully take a pledge for money to buy a horse; this was called 'cavalryman's dues', or for money with which to procure barley for the horses, which was called 'barley dues'. 28. The origin in statute of the taking of a pledge was in the Twelve Tables, against a person who had bought a victim for sacrifice and failed to pay for it; also, against someone who failed to pay the charge for a beast of burden which the hirer had let out so that he could use the money received for a feast, that is, a sacrifice. Again, by censorian law tax gatherers collecting the public taxes of the Roman people were given the right to take a pledge from those owing taxes under any statute. 29. In all these cases the pledge was taken with certain set words, and for this reason most people have agreed that this action also is an action in the law. Others, however, disagreed, in the first place because the taking of the pledge was enacted outside the court, that is, not before the praetor and generally also in the absence of the opponent, while other actions could not be

non aliter uti *quis* posset quam apud praetorem prae-
sente aduersario; praeterea quod nefasto[1] quoque die[2],
id est, quo non licebat lege agere, pignus capi poterat.
30. Sed istae omnes legis actiones paulatim in
odium uenerunt. namque[3] ex nimia subtilitate uete-
rum, qui tunc iura condiderunt, eo res perducta est,
ut uel qui minimum errasset, litem[4] perderet; itaque
per legem Aebutiam et duas Iulias sublatae sunt istae[5]
legis actiones, effectumque est, ut per concepta uerba,
id est[6] per formulas, litigaremus. 31. Tantum ex duabus causis permissum est [id legis actionem facere]
lege agere, damni infecti et si centumuirale iudicium
futurum[7] *est*; sane[8] cum ad centumuiros itur[9], ante
lege agitur sacramento apud praetorem urbanum uel
peregrinum[10]; damni uero infecti nemo uult lege agere,
sed potius stipulatione, quae in edicto proposita est,
obligat aduersarium suum, idque[11] et commodius ius
et plenius est. per pignoris | *capionem*[12]————————

199
t. s.

apparet. 32. Contra[13] in ea forma, quae publicano
proponitur[14], talis fictio est, ut quanta pecunia olim,
si pignus captum esset, id pignus is, a quo captum
erat, luere deberet, tantam pecuniam condemnetur.

200
t. s.

---

1) nefacto V. 2) de V. 3) namqui V. 4) litem *Goeschen.*
it V. 5) *del. Beseler.* 6) per—est *del. idem.* 7) furum(?) V.
8) saneq. V. 9) it V. 10) peregrinum pr. V. 11) itaque V.
12) *in pagina* 199 *Gaius de pignoris capione peregit et rever-
titur ad actiones* quae ad legis actionem exprimuntur. *cf. supra*
§ 10. 13) cont V. 14) proponit V.

---

§ 30. *cf. supra* 1, 184. 4, 11. *Gell.* 16, 10, 8. duas Iulias]
cf. D. 4, 8, 41 (*Call.* 60). *Fr. Vat.* 197; 198 (*Ulp.* 2111. 2112).
Gell. 14, 2, 1. *Macrob. Sat.* 1, 10, 4.
§ 31. centumuirale iudicium] *cf. supra* 4, 16. *infra* 4, 95.
D. 34, 3, 30 (*Paul.* 1365). 50, 17, 124 (*Paul.* 262). *C.* 3, 31,
12 *pr.* (a. 531). *Gell.* 16, 10, 8. *Cic. p. Caec.* 33, 97. stipu-
latione] *cf. D.* 39, 2, 7 *pr.* (*Ulp.* 1271).
§ 32. *cf. supra* 4, 18; 28.

employed except before the praetor and with the opponent present; moreover, because a pledge could be taken even on a non-business day, that is, one on which actions in the law could not lawfully take place.

30. But gradually all these actions in the law fell into disfavour. For, as a result of the excessive subtlety of the old lawyers who built up the legal institutions of those times, matters reached such a pitch that a person who made even the slightest error lost his case. Therefore, by the Aebutian Act and the two Julian Acts these actions in the law were swept away and the system of litigating by means of specially drafted phrases, that is, by formulas*, was introduced. 31. It remains permissible [to bring an action in the law] on two grounds only, for threatened loss, and if the court will be the centumviral court. Indeed, when recourse is had to the centumviral court, there is an action in the law by oath before the Urban or the Peregrine Praetor. No one, however, wants to bring an action in the law for threatened loss but rather, he binds his opponent by a stipulation, as set out in the Edict*; that gives him a more convenient and comprehensive right. By taking a pledge ... [a page in the MS illegible] ... appears. 32. On the other hand, in the formula which is issued to a tax gatherer the fiction is that the debtor is condemned to pay as much as he would have had to pay to ransom it from its taker, had the pledge been seized in times past. 33. There is, however, no formula

33. Nulla autem formula ad condictionis fictionem exprimitur. siue enim pecuniam[1] siue rem aliquam certam debitam nobis petamus, eam ipsam dari nobis oportere intendimus nec ullam adiungimus condictionis fictionem; itaque simul intellegimus eas formulas, quibus pecuniam aut rem aliquam nobis dari[2] oportere intendimus, sua ui ac potestate ualere. eiusdem naturae sunt actiones commodati, fiduciae, negotiorum gestorum et aliae innumerabiles.

34. Habemus adhuc alterius[3] generis fictiones *in* quibusdam formulis, uelut cum is, qui ex edicto bonorum possessionem petiit[4], ficto se herede agit. cum enim praetorio iure is[5], non legitimo, succedat in locum defuncti, non habet[6] directas actiones et neque id, quod defuncti fuit, potest intendere suum *esse neque id, quod ei* debebatur, potest intendere *dari* sibi oportere; itaque ficto se herede intendit, uelut hoc modo: IVDEX ESTO. SI AVLVS AGERIVS, id es*t* si ipse actor, *LVCIO TITIO* HERES *ESSET, TVM SI* FVND*VM*, DE QVO AGITVR, EX IVRE QVIRITIVM *EIVS* ESSE[7] *OPORTERET*; et si ——[8] praeposita simili *fictione* heredis[9] ita subicitur: TVM SI[10] NVMERIVM NEGIDIVM AVLO *AGERIO* SESTERTIVM X MILIA DARE OPORTERET[11]. **35.** Similiter et bonorum emptor ficto se herede agit. sed 201 interdum et alio modo agere solet. | nam ex persona

---

1) pecunia V.   2) dare V.   3) alterius a V.
4) petit V.   5) is *Polenaar.* es V.   6) havent V.   7) eius esse *Bluhme.* fuisse(?) V.   8) ✳✳✳deueat'✳✳✳ V? de debito agatur *Hu.; an* нs x̄ debeantur, tum?   9) heredis *Krueger.* intentio *Hu.* V *legi nequit.*   10) si paret V.   11) oportere V.

---

§ 33. *cf. supra* 4, 18; 19.
§ 34. *cf. supra* 3, 32; 81. *infra* 4, 111. IVDEX ESTO] *cf. infra* 4, 36; 37; 47; 136. (recuperatores sunto **4,** 46). *Cic. in Verr.* 2, 2, 12, 31. *lex Rubr. c.* 20 (*Bruns* I⁷, 97).
§ 35. *cf. supra* 3, 80. *D.* 40, 5, 4, 21 (*Ulp.* 1395). praetor Rutilius] *cf. D.* 38, 2, 1, 1 (*Ulp.* 1149). Seruiana] *cf. D.* 31, 69, 1 (*Pap.* 282).

expressing the fiction of an action of debt. For whether we are seeking money or some other definite thing owing to us, we claim in our principal pleading that there is a duty to give to us; we do not add any fiction of service of notice. And so we may at once understand that those formulas in which we claim that money or some particular thing should be given to us are valid by their own force and effect. Of the same nature are actions on loan* for use, on trust conveyance*, on unsolicited administration, and countless others.

34. We have fictions of still another kind in certain formulas, for instance, when a person seeking estate-possession* under the Edict raises an action with the fiction that he is heir. For since he succeeds to the place of the deceased by praetorian not statutory right, he does not have the direct actions. He cannot claim that the property of the deceased is his, nor can he claim that what was due to the dead man ought to be given to himself. And so he makes his claim with the fiction that he is heir, as thus: 'Let X be the judge. If Aulus Agerius*, i.e. the pursuer, were heir to Lucius Titius, then if the farm which is the subject of the action ought to be his by quiritary right', and if [the action concerned a debt], having begun with a similar fiction of being heir, he adds: 'then if Numerius Negidius* [i.e. the defender] has a duty to give ten thousand to Aulus Agerius'. 35. Similarly, the **buyer of a bankrupt estate*** raises actions as a fictitious heir; but sometimes he prefers to raise an action in another manner. For, having raised the

eius, cuius bona emerit, sumpta intentione conuertit
condemnationem in suam personam, id est, ut quod
illius esset uel illi dari[1] oporteret, eo nomine aduersarius huic condemnetur. quae species actionis appellatur Rutiliana, quia a praetore Publio Rutilio, qui et
bonorum uenditionem introduxisse dicitur, conparata
est.[2] superior autem species actionis, qua ficto se herede
bonorum emptor agit[3], Seruiana uocatur. 36. *Item
usucapio fingitur in ea actione, quae Publiciana uocatur.*[4] datur autem haec actio ei, qui ex iusta causa
traditam sibi rem nondum usu cepit eamque amissa[5]
possessione petit; nam quia non potest eam ex iure
Quiritium suam esse intendere, fingitur rem usu cepisse,
et ita, quasi ex iure Quiritium dominus factus esset,
intendit ue*l*ut hoc modo: IVDEX ESTO. SI QVEM HO-
MINEM AVLVS AGERIVS EMIT *ET* IS EI TRADITVS EST,
ANNO POSSEDISSET, TVM SI EVM HOMINEM, DE QVO
AGITVR[6], EIVS EX IVRE QVIRITIVM[7] ESSE OPORTERET
et reliqua. 37. Item ciuitas Romana peregrino fingitur, si eo nomine agat aut cum eo agatur, quo nomine
nostris legibus actio constituta est, si modo iustum sit
eam actionem etiam ad peregrinum extendi. uelut si furti[8]
agat peregrinus aut cum eo agatur[9], formula ita concipitur: IVDEX ESTO. SI PARET *LVCIO TITIO A DIONE HERMAEI
FILIO OPEVE* CONSILIO[10] DIONIS HERM*A*EI[11] FILII[12] FVRTVM
FACTVM ESSE PATERAE AVREAE, QVAM OB REM EVM, SI
CIVIS ROMANVS ESSET, PRO[13] FVRE DAMNVM DECIDERE
OPORTERET et reliqua; item si peregrinus furti agat,

---

1) dare V.   2) esse V.   3) *gis V.   4) item—uocatur *suppl. Krueger.*   5) admissat V.   6) agit V.   7) eius
ex iure Quiritium] ex iure Quiritium eius *Hu.*   8) furtum V.
9) agat in V.   10) opeue consilio] consilioue V. *cf. Lenel Edict.*[3]
p. 324 *sq.*   11) Dionis Hermaei] dihoniser. mei V.   12) filio V.
13) p (*id est* per) V.

§ 36. *cf.* I. 4, 6, 3; 4.   D. 6, 2, 1 *pr.* (*Ulp.* 561).
§ 37. *cf. Cic. in Verr.* 2, 2, 12, 31 *fin. de nat. deor.* 3,
30, 74. — *Ascon. p.* 75 *Kiessl.* (*p.* 84 *Bait.*). *Plut. Caes.* 4.

claim in the person of the one whose bankrupt goods he bought, he converts it to his own person in the condemnation*, that is, the other party is condemned, for what was the bankrupt's or what was owed to him, in the name of the estate buyer. This kind of action is described as Rutilian because it was established by the praetor P. Rutilius, who is said also to have introduced this forced sale of property. The earlier kind of action, in which the buyer of the estate raises an action with the fiction that he is heir, is called Servian. 36. Again, a fiction of usucapion* is established in what is called the Publician action. This action is granted to someone who has not yet usucapted property which was delivered to him on a legally sufficient ground and who, having lost possession of it, seeks it back. Because he cannot claim it as his by quiritary right, there is a fiction that he has usucapted it. And so he claims as if he had become owner by quiritary right, as thus: 'Let X be the judge. If Aulus Agerius bought a slave and the same had been delivered to him and he had had a year's possession, then, if the slave who is the subject of the action ought to be his by quiritary right' and so forth. 37. Again, there is a fiction of Roman citizenship for a foreigner* who is raising or defending an action established by our statutes, provided that it is equitable for that action to be extended to a foreigner. For example, if a foreigner is raising or defending an action for theft, the formula runs as follows: 'Let X be the judge. If it appears that the theft of a gold dish from Lucius Titius was carried out by Dio, son of Hermaeus, or with the aid or counsel of Dio, son of Hermaeus, for whatever, if he were a Roman citizen, he ought as a thief to pay as damages' and so forth. Again, if a foreigner raises an action for theft there is a fiction of Roman citizenship for him.

ciuitas ei Romana fingitur. similiter si ex lege Aquilia
202 peregrinus damni | iniuriae agat aut cum eo agatur[1],
ficta ciuitate Romana iudicium datur. 38. Praeterea
aliquando fingimus aduersarium[2] nostrum kapite demi-
nutum non esse. nam si ex contractu nobis obligatus
obligataue sit et kapite deminutus deminutaue fuerit[3],
uelut mulier per coemptionem, masculus per adrogationem[4], desinit iure ciuili debere nobis, nec directo
intendi potest sibi dare eum eamue oportere; sed ne
in potestate eius sit ius nostrum corrumpere, introducta est[5] contra eum eamue actio utilis rescissa kapitis deminutione, id est, in qua fingitur kapite deminutus deminutaue non esse.

39. Partes autem formularum hae sunt: demonstratio, intentio, adiudicatio, condemnatio. 40. Demon-
stratio est ea pars formulae, quae principio[6] ideo in-
seritur, ut demonstretur[7] res, de qua agitur, uelut
haec pars formulae: QVOD AVLVS AGERIVS NVMERIO
NEGIDIO HOMINEM VENDIDIT, item haec: QVOD AVLVS
AGERIVS *APVD* NVMERIVM NEGIDIVM HOMINEM DEPO-
SVIT. 41. Intentio est ea pars formulae, qua actor
desiderium suum concludit, uelut haec pars formulae:
SI PARET NVMERIVM NEGIDIVM AVLO AGERIO SESTER-
TIVM X MILIA DARE OPORTERE; item haec: QVIDQVID
PARET NVMERIVM NEGIDIVM AVLO AGERIO DARE FA-

---

1) agat V.   2) adcontrarium V.   3) fuerint V.
4) uelut — adrogationem *del. Solazzi*.   5) estao V.   6) principio *Krueger*. praecipue V.   7) demostraretur V.

---

§ 38. *cf. supra* 1, 162. 3, 84. *D.* 4, 5, 2, 1 (*Ulp.* 413).
§ 39. *de demonstratione et intentione cf. Schol. Bas.* 11,
1, 7 (*p.* 560. 566 *ed. Heimb.*).
§ 40. *cf. Coll.* 2, 6, 2 (*Paul.* 882).
§ 41. *cf. Cic. pro Rosc. Com.* 4, 11. *Divin.* 17, 56. *in
Verr.* 2, 2, 12, 31. 3, 22, 55. 3, 28, 69. *Fest. v. parret p.* 233.
paret p. 221 (*Bruns* II[7], 21). *Petron. Satir.* 137. *Theoph.* 4, 6, 6
(*p.* 420 *Ferr.*). *lex Rubr. c.* 20 (*Bruns* I[7], 97). QVIDQVID PARET]
cf. infra 4, 131.

Likewise, if a foreigner raises or defends an action for wrongful loss under the Aquilian Act, the court grants him a hearing on the fiction of Roman citizenship. 38. Moreover, we sometimes use the fiction that our opponent has not undergone status-loss*. For if some man or woman is under a contractual obligation to us and undergoes status-loss, for example, a woman through a contrived sale* of herself or a man through adrogation*, he or she ceases to be our debtor by state law*; it is not possible to claim directly that he or she is under an obligation. However, to make it impossible to prejudice our right, a policy action* has been introduced against him or her which assumes that the status-loss has been annulled, that is to say, in which the fiction is observed that he or she has not undergone status-loss.

39. The parts of the formula are these: statement of facts alleged*, principal pleading, adjudication*, condemnation. 40. The statement of facts alleged is that part of the formula which is put at the beginning so that the facts may be stated on which the action is grounded, for instance: 'Insofar as Aulus Agerius sold a slave to Numerius Negidius' and: 'Insofar as Aulus Agerius deposited a slave with Numerius Negidius'. 41. The principal pleading is that part of the formula in which the pursuer summarizes what he claims, for instance: 'If it appears that Numerius Negidius is under a duty to pay Aulus Agerius ten thousand' or 'Whatever it appears that Numerius Negidius is under a duty to give to or do for Aulus Agerius' or 'If it

CERE *OPORTERE*; item haec: SI PARET HOMINEM EX
IVRE QVIRITIVM AVLI AGERII ESSE. 42. Adiudicatio
est ea pars formulae, qua permittitur iudici rem alicui ex litigatoribus adiudicare, uelut si inter coheredes
familiae erciscundae agatur aut inter socios communi
diuidundo aut inter uicinos finium regundorum. nam
illic ita est: QVANTVM[1] ADIVDICARI OPORTET, IVDEX,
Titio[2] ADIVDICATO. 43. Condemnatio est ea pars for-
mulae, qua iudici condemnandi | absoluendiue potestas 203
permittitur[3], uelut haec pars formulae: IVDEX, NVME-
RIVM NEGIDIVM AVLO AGERIO SESTERTIVM X MILIA
CONDEMNA[5]. SI NON PARET, ABSOLVE; item haec:
IVDEX, NVMERIVM NEGIDIVM AVLO AGERIO DVMTAXAT
X MILIA[4] CONDEMNA[5], SI NON PARET[6], ABSOLVITO;
item haec: IVDEX, NVMERIVM NEGIDIVM AVLO AGERIO[7]
CONDEMNATO et reliqua, ut non adiciatur DVMTAXAT
X MILIA.[4] 44. Non tamen istae omnes partes simul[8]
inueniuntur; sed[9] quaedam inueniuntur, quaedam non
inueniuntur.[10] certe intentio aliquando sola inuenitur[11],
sicut in praeiudicialibus formulis, qualis est, qua quaeritur, aliquis[12] libertus sit, uel quanta dos sit, et aliae
complures; demonstratio autem et adiudicatio et condemnatio numquam solae inueniuntur; nihil enim
omnino *demonstratio*[13] sine intentione uel condemna-

---

1) quantam(?) V.   2) *vix sanum*. tantum *olim proposuit*,
postea reiecit Krueger. cui oportet *Hu.; an* TITIO SEIOVE?
3) promittitur V.   4) x milia *suppl. Hu.*   5) condemnato
Wlassak; sed cf. Theoph. 4, 6, 1; 13. 4, 10, 2.   6) parret V.
7) x milia *ins.* V.   8) in omnibus formulis *add. Hu. propter
iudicia divisoria.*   9) *add. Mommsen:* abesse potest una aliaue;
item solae.   10) inueniunt V.   11) inuenit V.   12) *num* an
quis?   13) *add. Boecking.*

---

§ 42. c͞f. *Ulp.* 19, 16. *I.* 4, 6, 20. 4, 17, 4—6. *Apul.
Metam.* 9, 27.
§ 43. *cf. infra* 4, 47—52; 57; 68; 73. *lex Rubr. c.* 20
(*Bruns* I[7], 97).
§ 44. *cf. supra* 3, 123. *Paul.* 5, 9, 1. *Schol. Basil.* 8, 2, 35
(*p.* 372 ed. *Heimb.*). aliquis libertus] *cf. I.* 4, 6, 13 *cum Theoph.*
(*p.* 424 *Ferr.*).

appears that the slave belongs to Aulus Agerius by quiritary right'. 42. The adjudication is that part of the formula which allows the judge to adjudge an item to one of the litigants, for instance, if an action is raised among co-heirs for the splitting of an inheritance, or among partners for the division of common property, or among neighbours for the regulation of their boundaries. This runs as follows: 'Let the judge adjudge to Titius as much as ought to be adjudged'. 43. The condemnation is that part of the formula which allows the judge the power of condemning or exonerating*, for instance: 'Judge, condemn Numerius Negidius to pay ten thousand to Aulus Agerius. If it does not so appear, exonerate him' or 'Judge, condemn Numerius Negidius to pay not more than ten thousand to Aulus Agerius. If it does not so appear, exonerate him' or 'Judge, condemn Numerius Negidius to Aulus Agerius' and so forth, not adding 'not more than ten thousand'. 44. Not all of these parts of the formula are found together; some are and some are not. Indeed, the principal pleading is sometimes found on its own, for example, in formulas establishing the facts prior to the issue, such as whether someone is a freedman*, or the extent of a dowry, and numerous others. However, a statement of facts alleged, an adjudication, and a condemnation are never found on their own; for a statement of facts alleged is meaningless without a claim or a

tione ualet; item condemnatio sine intentione uel adiudicatio sine demonstratione nullas[1] uires habet *et*
ob id numquam solae inueniuntur.

45. Sed eas quidem formulas, in quibus de iure
quaeritur, in ius conceptas uocamus, quales sunt, quibus intendimus nostrum esse aliquid ex iure Quiritium
au*t* nobis dari oportere aut pro fure damnum *decidi
oportere; sunt et* aliae, in[2] quibus iuris ciuilis intentio
est. 46. Ceteras uero in factum conceptas uocamus,
id est, in quibus nulla talis intentio concepta[3] est, *sed*
initio formulae nominato eo, quod factum est, adiciuntur[4] ea uerba, per quae iudici damnandi absoluendiue
potestas datur; qualis est formula, qua utitur patronus[5]
contra libertum, qui eum contra edictum praetoris in
204 ius uocauit.[6] | nam in ea ita est: RECVPERATORE*s*
SVNT*o*. SI PARET ILLVM PATRONVM AB ILLO [PATRONO]
LIBERTO CONTRA EDICTVM ILLIVS PRAETORIS IN IVS
VOCATVM ESSE, RECVPERATORES, ILLVM LIBERTVM ILLI

---

1) item condemnatio sine intentione uel adiudicatio sine
demonstratione nullas *nos*; item condomnatio sine demonstratione uel intentione uel adiudicatione nullas V. *in vindicatio-
nibus et condictionibus, utique certi, condemnatio sine demonstratione valet. de adiudicatione confer, quae Lenel dicit in
Edicto*[3] *p.* 206 *sq. de iudiciis divisoriis.*   2) aliae in *cod. Au-
gustod.; om.* V. sunt et *suppl. Krueger.*   3) intentio concepta
Goeschen. intentionis concepta V. intentionis conceptio *Lenel.*
4) adiqutur V.   5) patronos V.   6) euocauit V.

---

§ 45. *cf. supra* 4, 41. pro fure damnum decidere] *cf. D.*
4, 4, 9, 2 (*Ulp.* 401). 13, 1, 7 *pr.* (*Ulp.* 2876). 47, 2, 46, 5 (*Ulp.*
2878).
§ 46. *cf. infra* 4, 60. *I.* 4, 6, 12. patronus contra liber-
tum] *cf. infra* 4, 183; 187. *I.* 4, 16, 3. *D.* 2, 4, 4, 1 (*Ulp.* 259).
44, 7, 25, 1 (*Ulp.* 2383). x milia] *cf. D.* 2, 6, 2 (*Call.* 55).
2, 4, 12 (*Ulp.* 1366). 2, 4, 24 (*Ulp.* 264). de in ius uocando]
cf. D. tit. 2, 5 (*si quis in ius vocatus non ierit*). 2, 6 (*in ius
vocati ut eant*). 2, 7 (*ne quis eum qui in ius vocabitur vi exi-
mat*). *C.* 2, 2 (*de in ius voc.*). uindicem] *cf. supra* 4, 21. *lex
Rubr. c.* 21 (*Bruns* I[7], 99). innumerabiles] *cf. Cic. divin.* 17,
56. *in Verr.* 2, 3, 22, 55; 28, 69.

condemnation. Similarly a condemnation without a claim, or an adjudication without a statement of facts alleged has no force; therefore they are never found alone.

45. Now, we call those formulas which are based on state law 'framed in law', such as those in which we claim that something is ours by quiritary right or that there is a duty to give us something or that damages ought to be awarded for theft, and there are others in which the claim is founded on state law. 46. The remainder, however, we call actions 'framed on the facts'. In these no such principal pleading as above is drafted, but the formula begins by naming what has been done, to which are added the words by which the judge is given power to condemn or exonerate. An example of this kind is the formula used by a patron* against a freedman who has summoned him to court contrary to the praetor's Edict. This runs as follows: 'Let assessors* be appointed. If it appears that this patron has been summoned to court by this [patron] freedman contrary to the Edict of this praetor, assessors, condemn this freedman to pay ten thousand

PATRONO SESTERTIVM X MILIA[1] CONDEMNATE.[2] SI NON
PARET, ABSOLVITE.[3] ceterae quoque formulae, quae sub
titulo DE IN IVS VOCANDO propositae sunt, in factum
conceptae sunt, uelut aduersus eum, qui in ius uoca-
tus neque uenerit[4] neque uindicem dederit; item contra
eum, qui ui exemerit eum, qui in ius uocaretur; et
denique innumerabiles eius modi aliae formulae in
albo proponuntur. 47. Sed ex quibusdam causis praetor et in ius et in factum conceptas formulas proponit, ueluti depositi et commodati. illa enim formula,
quae ita concepta est: IVDEX ESTO. QVOD AVLVS
AGERIVS APVD NVMERIVM NEGIDIVM MENSAM ARGEN-
TEAM DEPOSVIT[5], QVA DE RE AGITVR[6], QVIDQVID OB
EAM REM NVMERIVM NEGIDIVM AVLO AGERIO DARE
FACERE OPORTET EX FIDE BONA, EIVS, IVDEX[7],
NVMERIVM NEGIDIVM AVLO AGERIO CONDEMNATO.[8]
SI NON PARET, ABSOLVITO, in ius concepta est.
at illa formula, quae ita concepta est: IVDEX ESTO.
SI PARET AVLVM AGERIVM APVD NVMERIVM NEGIDIVM
MENSAM ARGENTEAM DEPOSVISSE EAMQVE DOLO MALO
NVMERII NEGIDII AVLO AGERIO REDDITAM[9] NON ESSE,
QVANTI EA RES ERIT, TANTAM PECVNIAM, IVDEX,
NVMERIVM NEGIDIVM AVLO AGERIO CONDEMNATO.
SI NON PARET, ABSOLVITO, in factum concepta est.
similes etiam commodati formulae sunt.
48. Omnium autem formularum, quae condem-

---

1) X milia V. V milia *Savigny. de* L milia *cogitat Lenel
Edict.*[3] *p.* 69. 2) condemnanto *Wlassak.* 3) absolvunto *Wlassak.*
4) ierit *Eisele; sed cf. infra* § 183. 5) deposuisset V. 6) itagit V.
7) iudex *Hu.* id. iud. V. 8) condemnato n. r. V. condemnato, nisi restituat *Hu.* 9) reddita V.

---

§ 47. *cf. infra* 4, 60. QVA DE RE AGITVR] *cf. Cic. pro Mur.*
13, 28. EX FIDE BONA] *cf. Cic. de off.* 3, 17, 70 (*Iurispr.* I, 22).
EAMQVE DOLO MALO] *cf. D.* 44, 2, 22 (*Paul.* 480).
§ 48. *cf. I.* 4, 6, 32. *D.* 42, 1, 13, 1 (*Cels.* 58). 4, 8, 21, 3
(*Ulp.* 457). 42, 1, 6, 1 (*Ulp.* 1456). 38, 1, 37, 6 (*Paul.* 933).
sicut olim] *qua de re Gaius in folio deperdito post p.* 194 *egisse
videtur. cf. supra p.* 199 *not.* 15.

to this patron. If it does not so appear, exonerate him.'
The other formulas too which are listed under the
heading 'On summons to court' are actions framed on
the facts; for instance, that against a person who has
received a summons but failed to appear or to send a
guarantor* in court, and also against someone who
has used force to take away a person summoned.
Countless other formulas of this kind are set out on
the album* where the Edict is displayed. 47. There
are also certain cases in which the praetor sets out
actions framed both in law and on the facts, for
instance those on deposit and loan for use. The
formula which is drafted as follows is framed in law:
'Let a judge be appointed. Insofar as Aulus Agerius
deposited with Numerius Negidius a silver table
which is the subject of the action, let the judge
condemn Numerius Negidius to give to or to do for
Aulus Agerius whatever on that account in good faith
Numerius Negidius is under a duty to give to or do for
Aulus Agerius. If it does not so appear, exonerate.'
But the next formula, drafted as follows, is framed on
the facts: 'Let a judge be appointed. If it appears that
Aulus Agerius deposited a silver table with Numerius
Negidius and that the same was not returned to Aulus
Agerius by the bad faith of Numerius Negidius, let the
judge condemn Numerius Negidius to pay the value of
the matter to Aulus Agerius. If it does not so appear,
exonerate.' The formulas for actions on loan for use
are similar.

48. In all formulas which contain a condemnation,

nationem habent, ad pecuniariam aestimationem condemnatio[1] concepta est. itaque et si corpus aliquod
205 petamus, | uelut fundum, hominem, uestem, *aurum,*
t. s. argentum[2], iudex non ipsam rem condemnat *eum,* cum
quo actum est, sicut olim fieri solebat[3], *sed* aestimata
re pecuniam eum condemnat. 49. Condemnatio autem
uel certae pecuniae in formula proponitur uel incertae.
50. Certae pecuniae uelut in ea formula, qua certam
pecuniam petimus; nam illic ima parte formulae ita
est: IVDEX, NVMERIVM NEGIDIVM AVLO AGERIO SESTER-
TIVM X MILIA CONDEMNA.[4] SI NON PARET, ABSOLVE.[5]
51. Incertae uero condemnatio pecuniae duplicem significationem habet. est enim una cum[6] aliqua praefini-
tione, quae uulgo dicitur cum taxatione, uelut si incertum aliquid petamus; nam illic ima parte formulae
ita est: *EIVS,* IVDEX, NVMERIVM NEGIDIVM AVLO AGERIO
DVMTAXAT SESTERTIVM X MILIA CONDEMNA.[7] SI NON
PARET, ABSOLVE.[5] uel incerta est et[8] infinita, *uelut*
si rem aliquam a possidente nostram esse petamus, id
est, si in rem agamus uel ad exhibendum. nam illic
ita est: QVANTI *EA* RES *E*RIT, TANTAM PECVNIAM,
IVDEX, NVMERIVM NEGIDIVM AVLO AGERIO[9] CONDEMNA.[4]
SI NON PARET, ABSOLVITO. quid er*go* est? iudex,
si condemnet, certam pecuniam condemnare debet,
etsi certa pecunia in condemnatione posita non sit.

---

1) condemnation V.   2) aurum argentum *Hu.* argumentum V.   3) sicut — solebat *del. multi.*   4) condemnato
Wlassak.   5) absoluito *Wlassak.*   6) quae V.   7) condemnet V; condemnato *Wlassak*   8) est et] esset V.   9) Aulo
Agerio *Goeschen.* eidem (?) V.

---

§ 49. *cf. supra* 4, 43. *Cic. in Verr.* 2, 3, 21, 53; 54.
§ 50. *cf. Cic. pro Rosc. Com.* 5, 14. *Quintil. Inst. orat.*
4, 2, 6.
§ 51. *cf. supra* 3, 224. *Coll.* 2, 6, 1 (*Paul.* 882). *D.* 12,
3, 9 (*Iav.* 60). 38, 1, 39, 1 (*Paul.* 1144). *C.* 8, 38 (39), 3 (*a.* 290).
4, 49, 4 (*a.* 290). *I.* 4, 6, 32. *Cic. p. Tull.* 3, 7. *Fest. v.*
taxat p. 356 (*Bruns* II[7], 42). *Quintil. Decl.* 13. *lex Rubr. c.* 20
(*Bruns* 1[7], 97).

the condemnation is drafted in monetary terms. Therefore, if we are claiming some corporeal object, for instance, a farm, a slave, a garment, gold, silver, the judge does not condemn the defender to hand over the actual property, as was the custom in former times, but its estimated value in money. 49. The condemnation may be expressed in the formula in terms of a fixed sum or an indefinite sum. 50. A fixed sum is found, for instance, in the formula in which we seek a stated sum, for there the final part of the formula runs: 'Judge, condemn Numerius Negidius to pay ten thousand to Aulus Agerius. If it does not so appear, exonerate'. 51. Condemnation to pay an indefinite sum has two meanings. One of them involves a certain prior specification, commonly known as a limitation*, for instance, if we are seeking something indefinite. There the final part of the formula runs: 'Judge, condemn Numerius Negidius to pay not more than ten thousand to Aulus Agerius. If it does not so appear, exonerate.' Or there is an indefinite and unlimited action, for instance, if we are seeking some item of our own property from a possessor, that is to say, we are raising a real action or one for production. This runs as follows: 'Judge, condemn Numerius Negidius to pay the value of the matter to Aulus Agerius. If it does not so appear, exonerate.' What then? If the judge condemns him, he must condemn him to pay a fixed sum, even if a fixed sum is not set out in the condemnation. 52. The judge

52. Debet autem iudex attendere, *ut* cum certae pecuniae condemnatio posita sit, neque maioris neque minoris summa posita condemnet, alioquin litem suam facit; item si taxatio posita sit, ne pluris[1] condemnet quam taxatum sit; *alias* enim similiter litem suam facit. minoris autem damnare | ei permissum est. at si etiam 206
| ——————— *vv.* 1½ ——————— | qui formulam accipit, intendere debet, nec am*pli|us* ————————— certa condemnatione constringi ——————————— |
————————— *vv. 2* ——————————| usque uelit.

53. Si quis intentione plus conplexus fuerit[2], *causa cadit,* id est rem perdit, nec a praetore in integrum[3] restituitur[4], excep*tis* quibusdam casibus, in qui*bus* praetor non patitur | ——————— *vv. 2* ——————— |
53ᵃ. *Plus autem quattuor* | modis petitur: re[5], tempore, loco, causa. re, uel*ut si quis pro x* | milibus, quae ei debentur, xx milia petierit, *aut si is, cuius* | ex parte res esset, totam eam aut maiore ex par*te suam* | esse intender*it.* 53ᵇ. *Tempore, ueluti si quis ante diem uel*|ante *condicionem petierit.*[6] 53.ᶜ *Loco, ueluti si, quod certo loco* | dari promissum est, id *alio loco sine commemoratio*|ne eius loci petatur, uelut si *is, qui ita stipulatus fuerit:* EPHESI | DARE SPONDES? *deinde* Romae *pure intendat*

---

1) plures V.   2) fuit V.   3) integro V.   4) restituit V.
5) res V.   6) *cf. Enneccerus, Rechtsgeschäft* 354.

---

§ 52. *cf. Seneca de benef.* 3, 7, 5. *de clem.* 2, 7, 3. litem suam facit] *cf. I.* 4, 5 *pr. D.* 44, 7, 5, 4 = 50, 13, 6 (*Gai.* 506). 5, 1, 15, 1 (*Ulp.* 650).

§ 53. *cf. infra* 4, 56; 68; 131. *Paul.* 1, 10 = *Cons.* 5, 4. *Paul.* 2, 5, 3. *Fr. Vat.* 52; 53 (*Paul.* 991. 992). *Cons.* 5. *I.* 4, 6, 33. *D.* 11, 1, 1 *pr.* (*Call.* 66). 7, 3, 1, 4 (*Ulp.* 2548). 16, 2, 4 (*Paul.* 1645). *Plaut. Mostell.* 3, 1, 123 = 632. *Auct. ad Her.* 1, 12, 22. *Cic. de inv.* 2, 19, 57. *de orat.* 1, 36, 166 *sq. part. orat.* 28, 99. *pro Rosc. Com.* 4, 11. *Senec. ep.* 48, 10. *Quint. Inst.* 3, 6, 69. *Suet. Claud.* 14. *Fest. v. litis* p. 116 (*Bruns* II⁷, 12).

§ 53ᵃ. *cf. I.* 4, 6, 33 a. *D.* 6, 1, 8 (*Paul.* 238). *Paul.* 1, 13 b, 5 = *Cons.* 5, 5. *Euseb. Homil.* XI *de pascha* (*Max. bibl. patr. Lugd.* VI [*a.* 1577] *p.* 643 C).

should, however, be careful that when a condemnation for a fixed sum is set out he does not
condemn for either a larger or a smaller sum;
otherwise he makes the dispute his own*. Again, if a
limitation is set out, he may not condemn for more
than has been set, or else he makes the dispute his
own in the same way; he is allowed, however, to
condemn in a smaller sum. But if ... who accepts the
formula, must claim no more ... to be bound by a fixed
condemnation ... as far as he wishes.

53. If anyone includes an overclaim in his principal
pleading, his case falls, that is to say, he loses his
action; he will not get a decree from the praetor for
restoration to his original legal position, except in
certain cases, where the praetor does not allow ... 53a.
**There are four types of overclaim, in amount, time,
place or basis. Excess in amount happens, for
instance, if a debt of ten** thousand **is claimed as
twenty** thousand, **or when someone with a share
claims the whole or a larger share than he has. 53b.
Excess in time happens, for instance, if the claim is
made before it is due, or before a condition has
been satisfied. 53c. Excess in place happens, for
instance, if a promise to give in one place is
enforced without mention of the place appointed;**
for instance, **if someone stipulated: 'Do you
solemnly promise to give at Ephesus?' and then at
Rome pleads an unqualified 'ought to be given'.** ...

dari sibi oportere. | ———————— *v. 1* ——————— |
DARE MIHI OPORTERE ——————— *vv. 2½* ——————— |

207 petere, id est non adiecto loco. 53ᵈ. Causa plus petitur, uelut si quis in intentione tollat electionem debitoris, quam is[1] habet obligationis iure, uelut si quis
ita stipulatus sit: SESTERTIVM X MILIA AVT HOMINEM
STICHVM DARE SPONDES? deinde alterutrum eorum [ex
his] petat; nam quamuis petat, quod minus est, plus
tamen petere uidetur, quia potest aduersarius interdum
facilius id praestare, quod non petitur. similiter si
quis genus stipulatus sit, deinde speciem petat, uelut
si quis purpuram stipulatus sit generaliter, deinde
Tyriam specialiter petat; quin etiam licet uilissimam
petat, idem iuris est propter[2] eam rationem, quam
proxime diximus. idem iuris est, si quis generaliter
hominem stipulatus sit, deinde nominatim aliquem
petat, uelut Stichum, quamuis uilissimum. itaque sicut
ipsa stipulatio concepta est, ita et intentio formulae
concipi debet. 54. Illud satis apparet in incertis formulis plus peti non posse, quia cum certa quanti-
tas non petatur, sed QVIDQVID *PARET* aduersarium
DARE FACERE OPORTERE[3] intendatur[4], nemo potest
plus intendere. idem iuris est, et si in rem incertae
partis actio data sit, uelut talis[5]: QVANTAM PARTEM
PARET IN EO FVNDO, QVO DE[6] AGITVR, actoris ESSE.
quod genus actionis in paucissimis causis dari solet.
55. Item palam est, si quis aliud pro alio intenderit,

------

1) quam is *Goeschen.* quamuis V.　　2) papp V.
3) oporteret V.　　4) intendat V.　　5) tales V.　　6) quo de
Goeschen. quod V.

§ 54. *cf. Cic. pro Rosc. Com.* 4, 11.　*Paul.* 3, 8, 2.　*D.* 6,
1, 76, 1 (*Gai.* 156). 5, 4, 1, 5 (*Ulp.* 538). 6, 1, 5 *pr.* (*Ulp.* 549).
10, 3, 8, 1 (*Paul.* 394).
§ 55. *cf. I.* 4, 6, 35 *cum Theoph.* (*p.* 440 *Ferr.*).　*D.* 6, 1,
5, 5 (*Ulp.* 550). *Frontin. de controv. agror.* II (*Gromat. latin.*
ed. Lachm. 43, 26). si cognitor] *cf. infra* 4, 86.

to claim, that is, without adding the place. 53d. Someone overclaims in basis if, for instance, in his principal pleading he takes away the right of choice which the debtor has by virtue of the contract. For instance, **if someone has stipulated as follows: 'Do you solemnly promise to give either ten** thousand **or the slave Stichus?' and then claims one or other of them**. For even though he may be claiming the less valuable, he is regarded as overclaiming because his opponent can sometimes more easily produce the alternative which is not claimed. Similarly, if someone who has stipulated for a general category then makes a specific claim, for instance, if **someone having stipulated in general terms for 'purple' then claims Tyrian specifically**. Even if he claims the very cheapest thing, the rule is the same, for the reason that we have just stated. The rule is also the same if someone stipulates in general terms for a slave and then claims a particular one by name, for example, Stichus, even though he may be one of very little value. The principal pleading in the formula must therefore be drafted in the same terms as the stipulation. 54. It is quite clear that an overclaim is impossible in an indefinite formula; when a fixed amount is not being sought but the claim against the other party is for 'whatever it appears that he is under a duty to give or to do' no one can make an overclaim. The rule is the same if a real action is granted for an indefinite share, for instance: 'such part of the farm which is the subject of the action as appears to belong to the pursuer'. This class of action is in practice granted in a very small minority of cases. 55. Again, it is obvious that **if a pursuer's** principal pleading **claims the wrong thing he puts himself in no**

nihil eum periclitari eumque ex integro agere posse,
quia nihil ante uidetur egisse, uelut si is, qui hominem
Stichum | petere deberet, Erotem petierit, aut si quis 208
ex testamento dari[1] sibi oportere intenderit, cui ex
stipulatu debebatur[2], aut si cognitor aut procurator
intenderit sibi dari oportere. 56. Sed plus quidem
intendere, sicut supra diximus, periculosum est; minus
autem intendere licet. sed de reliquo intra eiusdem
praeturam agere non permittitur; nam qui ita agit,
per exceptionem excluditur, quae exceptio appellatur
litis diuiduae. 57. At si in condemnatione[3] plus positum[4] sit, quam oportet, actoris quidem[5] periculum
nullum est; sed *reus, cum* iniquam formulam acceperit,
in integrum restituitur, ut minuatur condemnatio. si
uero minus positum fuerit, quam oportet, hoc solum
consequitur *actor*, quod posuit; nam tota quidem res
in iudicium deducitur, constringitur autem condemna-
tionis fine, quam iudex egredi non potest. nec ex ea
parte praetor in integrum restituit; facilius enim reis
praetor succurrit quam actoribus. loquimur autem
exceptis minoribus xxv annorum; nam huius aetatis
hominibus in omnibus rebus lapsis praetor succurrit.
58. Si in demonstratione plus aut minus positum sit,
nihil in iudicium deducitur, et ideo res in integro
manet; et hoc est, quod dicitur falsa demonstratione
rem non perimi. 59. Sed sunt, qui putant minus recte
conprehendi, ut qui forte Stichum et Erotem *emerit,*

---

1) dare V.   2) deberedebatur V.   3) condemnationem V.
4) positum *Hollweg.* petitum V.   5) qā V.

---

§ 56. supra] 4, 53. minus] *cf. C.* 3, 10, 1, 3 (*a.* 486 *vel*
487). exceptio litis diuiduae] *cf. infra* 4, 122.
  § 57. positum] *cf. infra* 4, 68. constringitur] *cf. supra*
4, 52 a. *D.* 10, 3, 18 (*Iav.* 81). in integrum restituit] *cf. supra*
2, 163. 4, 53. *infra* 4, 125.
  § 58. *cf. supra* 4, 40; 55.
  § 59. *cf. D.* 19, 1, 33 (*Ulp.* 679). 13, 6, 17, 4 (*Paul.* 446). —
3, 3, 78, 1 (*Afr.* 57).

danger, and he can raise his action over again because he is not regarded as having brought any action before. **Suppose he should have claimed the slave Stichus, but claimed Eros, or he claimed that something ought to be given him under a will when it was due under a stipulation**, or a representative in court* or agent* claimed that something ought to be given to himself. 56. Note that, as we said above, it is risky to overclaim, yet it is lawful to claim less than is due; but in that case an action is not allowed to be raised for the remainder of the claim within the term of office of the same praetor. Someone who does raise such an action is barred by a defence*, which is described as the defence of action divided. 57. If the condemnation contains more than there should be, there is certainly no risk to the pursuer, but although the defender has accepted the unfair formula, he is restored to his original legal position, so that the amount of the condemnation may be reduced. If less is set out than there should be, however, the pursuer obtains only what he set out; the whole affair certainly is brought to trial, but it is narrowed to the limits of the condemnation which the judge cannot pass. Nor is he restored to his original legal position by the praetor on that account; for the praetor comes more readily to the assistance of defenders than pursuers. We speak, however, with the exception of people below the age of twenty-five, for the praetor comes to the assistance of men of that age in all cases where mistakes have been made. 58. If either more or less than is due is set out in the statement of facts alleged, nothing is brought to trial, and so the matter remains unaffected; this is the meaning of the maxim: a case is not lost by an incorrect statement of facts alleged. 59. There are, however, some people who think that less may correctly be covered. Perhaps someone bought both Stichus and Eros; he is regarded as rightly alleging:

recte uideatur[1] ita demonstrare: quod ego de te hominem Erotem emi, et si uelit, de Sticho alia formula
209   iterum[2] agat, quia uerum est eum, | qui duos emerit,
t. s.   singulos quoque emisse; idque ita maxime Labeoni[3]
uisum est. sed si is, qui unum emerit, de duobus
egerit, falsum demonstrat. idem et in aliis actionibus
est, uelut commodati et depositi. 60. Sed nos apud
quosdam scriptum inuenimus in actione depositi et
denique in ceteris omnibus, ex quibus damnatus unusquisque ignominia notatur, eum, qui plus quam oporteret demonstrauerit, litem perdere, uelut si quis una
re[4] deposita duas pluresue *se de*posuisse demonstrauerit, aut si is, cui pugno mala percussa est, in actione
iniuriarum etiam aliam partem corporis[5] percussam
sibi demonstrauerit; quod an debeamus credere uerius
esse, diligentius requiremus. certe cum duae sint depositi formulae, alia in ius concepta, alia in factum,
sicut supra quoque notauimus, et in ea quidem formula, quae in ius concepta est, initio res, de qua agitur, demonstratorio modo designetur, deinde inferatur
iuris inte*n*tio[6] his uerbis: QVIDQVID OB EAM REM
ILLVM ILLI DARE FACERE OPORTET, in ea[7] uero, quae
in factum conce*pta est, stat*im initio *intentionis*[8] alio
modo res, de qua agitur, designetur his uerbis: SI PA-
RET ILLVM APVD *ILLVM REM* ILLAM DEPOSVISSE, dubi-
tare non debemus, quin si quis in formula, quae in
factum composita est, plures res designauerit, quam
deposuerit, litem perdat, quia in intentione plus po*su*-|[9]

---

1) uidetur V.   2) iterum *Hu.* id V.   3) laticoni(?) V.
4) rei V.   5) corporalis V.   6) intentio *Boecking.* contentio V.
7) eam V.   8) *del. Lenel.*   9) *totam § 60 delet Beseler ZS* 46, 268.

---

§ 60. ignominia] *cf. infra* 4, 182. pugno mala percussa]
cf. Plaut. Asin. 2, 2, 104 = 371. *Senec. de benef.* 2, 35, 2.
iniuriarum] *cf. Coll.* 2, 6 (*Paul.* 882). *Suet. Vitell.* 7. supra]
4, 47. designetur] *cf. D.* 6, 1, 6 (*Paul.* 152). 47, 10, 7 *pr.* (*Ulp.*
1339). *Paul.* 2, 31, 22. *Cons.* 5, 2. alio modo] *cf. Cic. ad fam.*
13, 27, 1. *de fin.* 5, 29, 88.

'Insofar as I bought from you the slave Eros'. If he wishes, he can raise the action again with another formula concerning Stichus, because it is true that someone who has bought two slaves has also bought each of them. This is the opinion of Labeo in particular. But if someone who has bought one slave raises an action for two, his statement of facts is false. The same point arises in other actions as well, such as those on loan for use and deposit. 60. We find in the writings of some authorities that in an action on deposit and, in brief, in all other actions in which anyone who is condemned is branded with ignominy, someone who alleges more than there should be, loses his suit; for instance, if someone who deposited one article claims in his statement of facts alleged that he deposited two or more; or if, in an action for contempt, someone struck on the cheek in a brawl states that some other part of his body was struck as well. Let us inquire carefully into whether we should regard this as the truer view. It is certain that there are two formulas on deposit, one framed in law and the other on the facts, as we noted above; and in the formula framed in law the property which is the subject of the action is at the beginning designated in the statement of facts alleged, and then the principal pleading concludes with these words: 'Whatever there is a duty for him to give or do on that account', while in the formula framed on the facts the property which is the subject of the action is designated at the very outset of the principal pleading in another manner: 'If it appears that this man deposited this property with this defender'. From this we should have no doubt that if anyone in the formula framed on the facts designates more than he deposited, he loses his suit, because he is regarded as having overclaimed in the principal pleading.

isse uidetur.[1] ———————————————————————————— 210
t. s.
————————————————————————————————— |
211
t. s.

61. [2] ———————————————————————————— |
212
continetur, ut habita ratione eius, quod inuicem acto- t. s.

1) *sententiam Goeschen perfecit. in p. 210 et 211 fere nihil
legi potuit. quid perierit, aestimari potest ex eo, quod iam in
Iust. Inst. sequitur tit. de act.* (4, 6): § 36. Sunt praeterea
quaedam actiones, quibus non semper solidum, quod nobis
debetur, sed modo solidum consequimur, modo minus. ut ecce,
si in peculium filii seruiue agamus; nam si non minus in
peculio sit, quam persequimur, in solidum pater dominusue
condemnatur; si uero minus inuenitur, hactenus condemnat
iudex, quatenus in peculio sit; quemadmodum autem peculium
intellegi debeat, suo ordine proponemus (*cf. infra* § 72ᵃ *sq.*).
§ 37. Item si de dote iudicio mulier agat, placet hactenus
maritum condemnari debere, quatenus facere possit, id est,
quatenus facultates eius patiuntur. itaque si dotis quantitati
concurrant facultates eius, in solidum damnatur; si minus, in
tantum, quantum facere potest. propter retentionem quoque
dotis repetitio minuitur; nam ob impensas in res dotales factas
marito retentio concessa est, quia ipso iure necessariis sumpti-
bus dos minuitur, sicut ex latioribus Digestorum libris cogno-
scere liceat. § 38. Sed et si quis cum parente suo patronoue
agat, item si socius cum socio iudicio societatis agat, non plus
actor consequitur, quam aduersarius eius facere potest; idem
est, si quis ex donatione sua conueniatur. § 39. Compen-
sationes quoque oppositae plerumque efficiunt, ut minus quisque consequatur, quam ei debebatur; namque ex aequo et
bono habita ratione eius, quod inuicem actorem ex
eadem causa praestare oporteret, in reliquum eum,
cum quo actum est, condemnat, sicut iam dictum est.
§ 40, *quae pertinet ad bonorum cessionem, Iustinianus loco
deductionis* (§§ 65—68), *quae item decoctorum condicionem spectat,
posuisse et aliunde sumpsisse credendus est.* 2) *ad initium
huius paragraphi cf. Inst.* 4, 6, 30: In bonae fidei autem iudiciis libera potestas permitti uidetur iudici ex bono et aequo
aestimandi, quantum actori restitui debeat. in quo et illud
continetur, ut si quid inuicem actorem praestare oporteat, eo
compensato in reliquum is, cum quo actum est, condemnari
debeat.

§ 61. = *I.* 4, 6, 39; *cf. etiam* 4, 6, 30. *cf. Paul.* 2, 5, 3.

.... [From J. 4.6.36 onwards one can suggest the gist of the next two illegible pages. (36) There are also some actions in which we do not insist on the whole of what is due to us but sometimes obtain the whole and sometimes less. Suppose, for instance, that we bring an action in respect of the personal fund* of a son* in power or a slave. If the fund is as large as our claim, the father or owner is condemned for the whole amount. If it is less, the judge limits his condemnation to that amount. We will deal in the appropriate place with the question of how the personal fund ought to be assessed. (37) Again, if a woman* brings an action for her dowry, it is right that the husband should be condemned only to the limit of his ability to pay – that is, for as much as his wealth will bear. If his wealth equals the amount of the dowry, he is condemned for the whole sum; but if it comes to less, only to the limit of his ability. A claim to recover a dowry can also be reduced by a right of retention. Such a right is allowed to the husband for money expended on the dotal property; by operation of law a dowry is diminished by necessary expenditure on it. (38) If someone sues a parent or patron, or if a partner sues another in an action on partnership, he again obtains no more than the opponent can pay. The same where an action is brought against a donor for a gift. (39) Another reason a pursuer can end with less than he is owed is set-off. As has been said, – and J. here repeats the words of 4.6.30, which were taken from G. 4.61].

61. ... [In actions of good faith, however, the judge is seen to be allowed full discretion to work out the sum to be restored to the pursuer on the basis of what is fair and reasonable. This] **includes account being taken of the pursuer's own duties arising from the**

rem ex eadem causa praestare oporteret, in reliquum
eum, cum quo actum est, condemnare. **62.** Sunt autem
bonae fidei iudicia haec: ex empto uendito, locato con-
ducto, negotiorum gestorum, mandati, depositi, fiduciae,
pro socio, tutelae, rei uxoriae.[1] **63.** Liberum est
tamen iudici nullam omnino inuicem conpensationis
rationem habere; nec enim aperte formulae ue*r*bis
praecipitur, sed quia id bonae fidei iudicio conueniens
uidetur, id*eo* officio eius contineri creditur. **64.** Alia
causa est illius actionis, qua argentarius experitur.
nam is cogitur cum conpensatione agere, et ea con-
pensatio uerbis formulae exprimitur, adeo quidem, ut
statim[2] ab initio conpensatione facta minus intendat
sibi dari[3] oportere. ecce enim si sestertium[4] x milia
debeat Titio, atque ei XX debeantur, sic intendit: SI
PARET TITIVM SIBI X MILIA DARE OPORTERE AMPLIVS

---

1) *verba inde a* mandati *usque ad* rei uxoriae *in* V
per errorem bis sripta sunt.   2) statim *Hu.* itaque V, *vix
recte lectum. cf. V. I. R. s. v.* ab *p.* 57, 6.   3) dare V.
4) s̄. e. V.

---

§ 62. *cf. l.* 4, 6, 28. *D.* 17, 2, 38 *pr.* (*Paul.* 1734). *Cic. top.*
17, 66. *de off.* 3, 17, 70 (*Iurispr.* I, 22). *de nat. deor.* 3, 30, 74. *ad Attic.*
6, 1, 15. *lex Rubr. c.* 20 (*Bruns* I[7], 97). ex empto uendito]
cf. D. 19, 1, 11, 1 (*Ulp.* 930). 21, 1, 31, 20 (*Ulp.* 1782). *Cic. de
off.* 3, 16, 66. *Val. Max.* 8, 2, 1. locato conducto] *cf. C.* 4, 65,
17 (*a.* 290). negotiorum gestorum] *cf. D.* 44, 7, 5 (*Gai.* 506).
3, 5, 6 (*Paul.* 187). *C.* 2, 4, 3 (*a.* 223). 2, 18 (19), 18 (*a.* 293).
mandati] *cf. D.* 44, 7, 5 (*Gai.* 506). 17, 1, 10, 3 (*Ulp.* 909).
17, 1, 59, 1 (*Paul.* 1480). depositi] *cf. supra* 4, 47. *D.* 16, 3,
31 (*Tryph.* 31). 16, 3, 1, 23 (*Ulp.* 895). fiduciae] *cf. Cic. de
off.* 3, 15, 61. *ad fam.* 7, 12, 2. pro socio] *cf. D.* 17, 2, 52, 1
(*Ulp.* 922). 17, 2, 3, 3 (*Paul.* 493). rei uxoriae] *cf. Cic. de off.*
3, 15, 61. *Prob. Einsidl.* 9 (*Iurispr.* I, 89).
    § 63. *cf. D.* 13, 6, 18, 4 (*Gai.* 208). 16, 2, 7, 1 (*Ulp.* 813).
3, 5, 7, 2 (*Ulp.* 353). 27, 4, 1, 4 (*Ulp* 1034). *Sen. de ben.* 6, 4; 5.
    § 64. *cf. D. tituli* 16, 2 *leges has:* 2 (*Iul.* 840). 4 (*Paul.*
1645). 5 (*Gai.* 213). 8 (*Gai.* 214). 15 (*Iav.* 82). 18 (*Pap.* 454).
21 (*Paul.* 1273).

same grounds of action. Condemnation is for the balance. 62. Now the actions based on good faith are these: buying and selling, leasing and hiring, unsolicited administration, mandate, deposit, trust conveyance, **partnership, guardianship,** the action for a wife's property. 63. Now the judge is free to take no account whatever of reciprocal liability for set-off; for it is not something explicitly triggered by the wording of the formula. But because it is seen as appropriate to proceedings involving good faith, it is therefore believed to be within the scope of his duties. 64. Another ground for set-off is in a banker's special action. He is obliged to raise his action taking account of set-off, and this set-off is made explicit in the words of the formula, to the extent indeed that from the outset, having made his set-off, he ought to claim less than there is a formal duty to give him. Suppose he owes ten thousand to Titius and twenty thousand are owed to him, his pleading runs: 'If it appears that there is a duty for Titius to give me ten thousand more

QVAM IPSE TITIO DEBET.   65. Item bonorum emptor[1] cum deductione agere iube*tur*, *id est ut* in hoc solum aduersarius eius condemnetur, quod superest deducto eo, quod inuicem ei bonorum emptor defraudatoris nomine[2] debet.   66. Inter conpensationem autem, quae argentario opponitur, et deductionem, quae obicitur bonorum emptori, illa[3] differentia est, quod in conpensationem[4] hoc solum uocatur, quod eiusdem generis et naturae est; ueluti pecunia cum pecunia conpensatur[5], triticum cum tritico, uinum cum uino, adeo | ut quibusdam placeat[6] non omni modo uinum cum 213 uino aut triticum cum tritico conpensandum, sed ita si eiusdem naturae qualitatisque sit. in deductionem autem uocatur et quod non est eiusdem generis; itaque si[7] pecuniam petat bonorum emptor et inuicem frumentum aut uinum is debeat, deducto[8] quanti id erit, in reliquum experitur.   67. Item uocatur in deductionem[9] et id, quod in diem debetur; conpensatur autem hoc solum, quod praesenti die debetur. 68. Praeterea conpensationis[10] quidem ratio in intentione ponitur; quo fit, ut si facta conpensatione plus nummo uno intendat argentarius, causa cadat et ob id rem perdat. deductum[11] uero ad condemnationem ponitur, quo loco plus petenti periculum non interuenit, utique bonorum emptore agente, qui licet de certa pecunia agat, incerti tamen condemnationem concipit.

---

1) bonorum emptor] debe(?) V.   2) nomini V.   3) illae(?) V.
4) conpensatione V.   5) conpensetur V.   6) placet V
7) si uero V.   *aliquid excidisse putat Krueger.*   8) deductoiore(?) V.   9) deductione V.   10) conpensitationis V.
11) deductum O.   deductio V.

---

§ 65. *cf. supra* 3, 78 *sq.*; 81.   *Paul.* 2, 5, 3.   *D. tit.* 16, 2 *leges has:* 10, 1—3 (*Ulp.* 1426). 12 (*Ulp.* 1441). 14 (*Iav.* 68). *D.* 17, 2, 28 (*Paul.* 723).
§ 66. *cf. Paul.* 2, 5, 3.   *D.* 46, 8, 15 (*Paul.* 1206). *C.* 4, 34, 11 (*a.* 529).
§ 67. *cf. D.* 16, 2, 7 *pr.* (*Ulp.* 813).

than I owe him'. 65. Again, the buyer of a bankrupt estate is required to bring his action with a deduction; that is, his opponent is condemned to pay only what is available after the deduction of what in turn the buyer owes him in the name of the bankrupt. 66. There is this difference between the set-off which is imposed on the banker and the deduction applied to the buyer of a bankrupt estate; in set-off only things of the same class and type are invoked, for instance, money is set off against money, wheat against wheat, wine against wine, to such an extent that it is accepted by some authorities that set-off must be made not against any kind of wine or of wheat, but only that of the same type and quality. In deduction, however, things not of the same class are brought in. Therefore, if the buyer of a bankrupt estate seeks money and in turn owes corn or wine, its value is deducted and he goes to law for the balance. 67. Again, what is due on a specified future day is brought in for a deduction; set-off, however, is only applicable to what is due at the time of the trial. 68. Moreover, the calculation of the set-off is put in the principal pleading. As a result, once the set-off is made, if the banker claims even one penny more, the case falls and he accordingly loses his right. A deduction, however, is set out in the condemnation, at which point there is no risk to a pursuer who makes an overclaim. This is especially true for the buyer of a bankrupt estate who, though he may be raising an action for a fixed sum, still drafts the condemnation in indefinite terms.

69. Quia tamen superius mentionem habuimus de actione, qua in peculium filiorum familias seruorumque ageretur[1], opus est, ut de hac actione et de ceteris, quae eorundem[2] nomine in parentes dominosue dari solent[3], diligentius admoneamus. **70.** In primis itaque si iussu patris dominiue negotium gestum erit, in solidum praetor actionem in patrem dominumue comparauit, et recte, quia qui ita negotium gerit, magis patris[4] dominiue quam filii seruiue fidem sequitur.

214 **71.** Eadem ratione | comparauit duas alias actiones, exercitoriam et institoriam.[5] tunc autem exercitoria locum habet, cum pater dominusue filium seruumue magistrum naui[6] praeposuerit et quid cum eo eius rei gratia, cui praepositus fuerit[7],[negotium] gestum erit. cum enim ea quoque res ex uoluntate patris dominiue contrahi uideatur, aequissimum esse uisum est in solidum actionem dari; quin etiam licet extraneum quisque[8] magistrum naui[6] praeposuerit, siue seruum siue liberum, exercitoria[9] actio in eum redditur. ideo autem exercitoria[10] actio appellatur, quia exercitor uocatur is, ad quem cotidianus nauis quaestus peruenit. institoria[11] uero formula tum locum habet, cum quis tabernae aut cuilibet negotiationi filium seruumue suum uel[12] quemlibet extraneum, siue seruum siue liberum, praeposuerit et quid[13] cum eo eius rei gratia, cui praepositus est, contractum fuerit. ideo autem institoria[11] uocatur[14], quia qui tabernae praeponitur, institor[15] appel-

---

1) ageretur O. agatur V. agitur *Inst.*   2) in eorundem O.
3) solent V. licet O.   4) patros O.   5) institutoriam V.
6) nauis V.   7) fuerit] post(?) fuerit V.   8) ****que O. quis qua s V.
9) exercitoria O. tamen ea praetoria V.   10) autem exercitoria V.
exercitoria autem O.   11) institutoria V. O.   12) [suum] ue[l] O.
aut V.   13) quis O.   14) uocat V.   15) institor O. institutor V.

---

§ 69. = *I.* 4, 7 *pr.* superius] *cf. ad* § 60 *notata.*
§ 70. = *I.* 4, 7, 1. *cf. D. tit.* 15, 4. *C. Th. tit.* 2, 31.
C. I. tit. 4, 26. *D.* 4, 4, 3, 4 (*Ulp.* 398).
§ 71. *cf. I.* 4, 7, 2. *Paul.* 2, 6; 8. *D. tit.* 14, 1. 14, 3.
C. tit. 4, 25. *D.* 14, 6, 7, 11 (*Ulp.* 878).

69. We mentioned before the action about the personal fund of sons in power and slaves. Now we need to go into more detail about it and the other actions which are customarily given against parents* or owners in respect of the activities of these dependent persons. 70. First, therefore, **if someone deals with a dependent person on the order of his** father or **owner, the praetor** gives **an action against the** father or **owner for the full amount.** And rightly, **because the person so dealing relies more on the credit of the** father or **owner** than of the son or slave. 71. **For the same reason, the praetor** gives **two other actions, the exercitorian and the institorian. The former lies where the** father or **owner makes** a son or **a slave master of a ship and then there are dealings with him as master in the course of the ship's business.** For since such a contract appears to be made at the wish of the father or owner, the most equitable course seems to be to grant an action for the recovery of the full amount. What is more, even if someone appoints as master of a ship someone not in his power, whether slave or free, the exercitorian action will lie against him. **The action gets its name because the person in charge of the everyday business of a vessel is, in Latin, the 'exercitor'. The institorian formula lies where someone puts his son or slave or any** outsider, whether **slave** or **free, in charge of a shop or business of some kind, and then a contract is made with him in the course of his management. Here the name is from 'institor', the Latin for the manager of a shop.** This formula too is for the

latur.¹ quae *et* ipsa formula in solidum est. **72.** Praeterea tributoria quoque actio in patrem dominumue
constituta est, cum filius seruusue² in peculiari³ merce
sciente patre dominoue negotietur; nam si quid eius
rei gratia cum eo contra*ctum* fuerit, ita praetor⁴ ius
dicit, ut quidquid in *his* mercibus | ⁵erit, quod inde 215
receptum erit, id⁶ p*ater d*ominusue inter se, si quid debe- t. s.
bitur, et ceteros *creditores* pro rata portione distri-
buant⁷ et si *creditores* querantur minus sibi distri-
butum, quam opor*teret*, in id quod deest hanc eis
actionem pollicetur, *quae ut* diximus, tributoria uocatur. § 72ª. Est etiam de p*eculio et* de in rem uerso
actio a praetore constitu*ta*. *licet* enim negotium ita
gestum sit cu*m* filio ser*uoue, ut* neque uoluntas neque
consens*us* patris *dominiue inter*uenerit, si quid tam*en*
ex ea re, quae cum illis gesta est, in rem patris domi-
niue uersum sit, quatenus in rem eius uersum fuerit,
eate*nus datur actio.* [*uersum autem quid sit, eget plena*
interpret*atione*].⁸ *at si nihil sit uersum, praeto*r dat
actione*m* ᴅᴠᴍᴛᴀxᴀᴛ ᴅᴇ ᴘᴇᴄᴠʟɪᴏ, *et edictum u*titur his
uer*bis*. quod edi*ctum loquitur et de eo, qui dolo malo*
*peculium a*demerit. si igitur uerbi gratia ex ʜs · x,
quae seruus tuus a me *mutua accepit, creditori tuo*

---

1) appellat V.   2) constituta est, cum filius seruusue *bis
scripta in* V.   3) in peculiari quioptio (?) V. ex peculiari O.
in peculiari cuiusuis pretii *Hu*.   4) ita praetor V. praetor
ita O.   5) *cod.* V *paginae 215 fere nihil legi potest; lacuna
expletur codice Oxyrhynchico. cf. Levy, ZS.* 48, 536 *sq.*, *cuius
supplementis usus sum.* 6) ita O.   7) distribuunt O.   8) uersum autem — interpretatione *glossam esse censet Levy.*

---

§ 72. *cf. I.* 4, 7, 3.   *cf. infra* 4, 74.   *D. tit.* 14, 4. 14, 3,
11, 7 (*Ulp.* 828). in peculiari merce sciente patre dominoue
negotietur] *cf. D.* 15, 1, 27 *pr.* (*Gai.* 223). 14, 1, 1, 20
(*Ulp.* 818).

§ 72ª. *cf. I.* 4, 7, 4.   *cf. Paul.* 2, 9.   *D. tit.* 15, 1. 15, 2.
15, 3.   *C. tit.* 4, 26. voluntas] *cf. D.* 4, 9, 3, 3 (*Ulp.* 471).

recovery of the full amount. 72. Moreover, **the tributorian action** has also been provided against the father or **owner when a** son or **slave, with the knowledge of his** father or **owner, trades in goods from his personal fund. If a contract is made with him in that course of dealing, the law which the praetor lays down is that those goods and anything earned from them should be distributed in proportionate shares by the** father or **owner between himself, if anything is owed to him, and the other creditors**. If the creditors complain of having had less than what is due 'attributed' to them the praetor promises them this action to make up what is lacking. This, as we have said, is called the tributorian action. 72a. The praetor has also established an action **on the personal fund and on conversion to the owner's use**. Although there may be **some dealing** with a son or slave without either the **wish** or consent **of the** father or **owner, yet if something** from those dealings **is converted to the use of the** father or **owner**, then an action is given **to the extent** that it is so converted. [The exact meaning of converted needs full interpretation.] However, if nothing has been converted, the praetor gives an action for 'just so much as the personal fund', and the Edict uses these words. The words of the Edict apply also to someone who in bad faith diminishes a personal fund. **If** therefore, for example, **of the ten** thousand **which your slave receives** from me **as a loan, he pays five** thousand **to your creditor**, or buys

hs · v soluerit aut rem *necessariam, puta familiae cibaria,*
hs · v emerit et *reliqua v quolibet modo consumpserit,*
pro v quidem in solidum damnari debes, pro ceteris v
eatenus, quatenus in peculio sit. ex quo scilicet apparet, si
tota hs · x in rem tuam uersa fuerint, tota te hs · x consequi
posse; licet enim una est formula[1], *qua de peculio de-*
que eo, quod in rem (patris) domini(ue) uersum sit,
agitur, tamen duas habet condemnationes. itaque iudex,
apud quem ea formula[2] *agitur, ante dispicere solet, an*
in rem (patris) domini(ue) uersum sit, nec aliter ad
peculii aestimationem transit, quam si aut nihil in rem
(patris) domini(ue) uersum intellegatur aut non totum.
73. *Cum autem quaeritur, quantum in peculio sit, ante*

216
t. s. *de|ducitur,* quod patri dominoue quique in eius pote-
state sit, a filio seruoue debetur[3], et quod superest,
hoc solum peculium esse intellegitur. aliquando tamen
id, quod ei debet filius seruusue, qui in potestate patris dominiue sit, non deducitur ex peculio, uelut si
is, cui debet, in huius ipsius peculio sit. 74. Ceterum
dubium non est, quin et is, qui iussu patris dominiue
contraxit cuique exercitoria uel institoria[4] formula
competit, de peculio aut de in rem uerso agere possit;
sed nemo tam stultus erit, ut qui aliqua illarum actionum sine dubio solidum consequi possit, uel[5] in diffi-
cultatem[6] se deducat probandi[7] habere peculium eum,
cum quo contraxerit, exque eo peculio posse sibi satis
fieri uel id, quod persequitur, in rem patris dominiue
uersum esse. 74ᵃ. Is quoque, cui tributoria actio con-

---

1) actio *Inst.*   2) actione *Inst.*   3) debet V.   4) institutoria V.   5) uel *aptius collocaretur post* probandi.
6) difficultate V.   7) probando V.

---

§ 74. *cf. I.* 4, 7, 5. *supra* 4, 73. *D.* 14, 4, 9, 1 (*Ulp.* 847).
14, 5, 4, 5 (*Ulp.* 871).
§ 74ᵃ. *cf. D.* 14, 4, 11 (*Gai.* 219). supra] § 72 a.

necessities – say foodstuffs for the household – to the value of five thousand, and **uses the remaining five** thousand **in some other way, you should be condemned in the full amount for the first five** thousand, **for the other five** thousand **only up to the limit of the personal fund. Obviously, if all ten** thousand **had been converted to your use, I could sue you for the full amount. Although there is one** formula **for raising an action on the personal fund and on conversion to the use of the** father or **owner, yet there are two condemnations. The practice is for the judge before whom the action is raised to look first for conversion to the use of** father or **owner, and only to move to the valuation of the personal fund if it seems that nothing, or not the whole claim, has been so converted. 73. When the amount of the personal fund is investigated, a deduction has first to be made of what is owed by the** son or **slave to the** father or **owner or to a person in the power of the** father or **owner. Only the balance counts as the fund. Occasionally a** son's or **slave's debt to a person within the** father's or **owner's power is not deducted, for instance, if the creditor is himself part of the fund. 74. It is certainly true that someone who has contracted in reliance on the** father's or **owner's order and someone to whom the exercitorian or the institorian formula is available can also raise the action on personal fund and conversion.** But if **he can recover the full amount** without uncertainty by one of these actions, no one is going to be so **stupid** as to **subject himself to the difficulty of proving either that** the party with whom he contracted **has a fund** and that satisfaction can be made to him from that fund, or that what he claims **was converted to the use of the** father or **owner. 74a. One to whom the tributorian action is available can also raise the**

petit, de peculio uel de in rem uerso agere potest.
sed huic sane plerumque expedit hac potius actione
uti quam tributoria. nam in tributoria eius solius
peculii ratio habetur, quod in his mercibus est, in quibus negotiatur filius seruusue quodque inde receptum
erit, at in actione peculii[1], totius. et potest quisque
tertia forte aut quarta uel etiam[2] minore parte peculii
negotiari, maximam uero partem peculii in aliis[3] rebus habere; longe magis, si potest adprobari id, quod
dederit qui contraxit[4], in rem patris dominiue uersum
esse, ad hanc actionem transire debet; nam, ut supra
diximus, | eadem formula et de peculio et de in rem 217
uerso agitur.

75. Ex maleficio[5] filiorum familias seruorumque,
ueluti si furtum fecerint aut iniuriam commiserint,
noxales actiones proditae sunt, uti liceret patri dominoue aut litis aestimationem sufferre aut noxae dedere.
erat enim iniquum nequitiam eorum ultra ipsorum
corpora parentibus dominisue damnosam esse. 76. Constitutae sunt autem noxales actiones aut legibus aut
edicto praetoris: legibus, uelut furti lege XII tabularum, damni iniuriae lege[6] Aquilia; edicto praetoris,

---

1) de peculio peculii *Krueger coll. Dig.* 14, 4, 11.
2) et V.   3) alii V.   4) id — contraxit *del. Beseler.*
5) maleficiis *Inst. et infra* § 112; *sed* maleficio *est Gaianum:*
Dig. 44, 7, 4. 5. *infra* § 80.   6) uelut lege V.

---

§ 75. = *I.* 4, 8 *pr.*; 2 *fin. cf. supra* 1, 140. *Paul.* 2, 31, 7.
D. 9, 4, 1 (*Gai.* 72). 9, 4, 21 *pr.* (*Ulp.* 680). *C.* 3, 41, 2 (*a.* 239).
Fest. v. noxia p. 174 (*Bruns* II[7], 17). *Quint. Decl.* 4, 5. erat
enim iniquum] *cf. D.* 47, 2, 62 (61), 5 (*Afr.* 110). 9, 4, 2 *pr.*
(*Ulp.* 619). 39, 2, 7, 1 (*Ulp.* 1272). 2, 10, 2 (*Paul.* 155).
§ 76. = *I.* 4, 8, 4. lege XII tab.] 12, 2 (*Bruns* I[7], 39).
cf. D. 50, 16, 238, 3 (*Gai.* 445). 9, 4, 2, 1 (*Ulp.* 619). damni
iniuriae] *cf. D.* 9, 2, 27, 11 = *Coll.* 12, 7, 9 (*Ulp.* 623). *D.* 9,
4, 19 *pr.* (*Paul.* 370; *cf.* 368; 369; 371—373). iniuriarum] *cf.*
D. 47, 10, 17, 3 *sq.* (*Ulp.* 1360). ui bonorum raptorum] *cf. D*
47, 8, 2 *pr.* (*Ulp.* 1310; *cf.* 1317).

action on personal fund and conversion. For him it is generally advantageous to bring this latter action rather than the tributorian. For a **tributorian** action takes into account **only** that part of the personal fund **which was dealt with in the way of trade** by the son or slave, and what was earned from that, but in an action on the personal fund **account is taken of the whole fund. It can happen that a person's business dealings involve only a third or a quarter or even less of his fund, and that he keeps the** great **bulk of it invested elsewhere.** If it **can be proved** that what the third party handed over was **converted to the use of the** father or **owner,** he had far better transfer to this action; for, as we said above, the same formula is brought on personal fund and conversion.

75. **Noxal actions* lie when** sons in power and **slaves commit** a delict, **for instance, theft or contempt. These actions allow the** father or **owner either to pay the damages as assessed in money or to make noxal surrender. For it would be unjust to allow the wickedness of** sons or **slaves to inflict on** fathers or **owners any loss beyond their own value.** 76. **Some noxal actions were established by statute, some by the Edict of the praetor. Statutory instances are the action for theft under the Twelve Tables and for wrongful loss under the Aquilian Act. Examples from the praetor's Edict include**

uelut iniuriarum et ui bonorum raptorum. **77.** Omnes
autem noxales actiones caput[1] sequuntur. nam si filius
tuus seruusue noxam commiserit, quamdiu in tua potestate est, tecum est actio; si in alterius potestatem
peruenerit, cum illo incipit actio esse; si sui iuris coeperit esse, directa actio cum ipso est, et noxae deditio
extinguitur. ex diuerso quoque directa actio noxalis
esse incipit. nam si pater familias noxam commiserit
et is[2] se in adrogationem[3] tibi dederit aut seruus tuus
esse coeperit, *quod* quibusdam casibus accidere primo
commentario tradidimus, incipit tecum noxalis actio
esse, quae ante directa fuit. **78.** Sed si filius patri
aut seruus domino noxam commiserit, nulla actio
nascitur. nulla enim omnino inter me et eum, qui in
potestate mea est, obligatio nasci potest; ideoque et
218 si in alienam | potestatem peruenerit aut sui iuris esse
coeperit, neque cum ipso neque cum eo, cuius nunc
in potestate est, agi potest. unde quaeritur, si alienus
seruus filiusue noxam commiserit mihi et is postea
in mea esse coeperit potestate, utrum intercidat actio
an quiescat. nostri praeceptores intercidere putant,
quia in eum casum deducta sit, in quo ab initio[4] consistere non potuerit, ideoque licet exierit de mea po-

---

1) capita V.   2) his V.   · 3) adrogatione V.   4) ab
initio] actio(?) V. *cf. Dig.'* 5, 1, 11. 13, 6, 1, 2. 30, 41, 2. 47,
2, 17, 1.

---

§ 77. = *I.* 4, 8, 5. *cf. Paul.* 2, 31, 8; 9. *D.* 9, 4, 43
(*Pomp.* 191). 13, 6, 21, 1 (*Afr.* 107). 47, 2, 62 (61) *pr.*
(*Afr.* 110). 9, 4, 20 (*Gai.* 186). 9, 1, 1, 12 (*Ulp.* 608). 9, 4, 2, 1
(*Ulp.* 619).   16, 3, 1, 18 (*Ulp.* 893). 47, 1, 1, 2 *et* 47, 2, 41, 2
(*Ulp.* 2868). 47, 10, 17, 7 (*Ulp.* 1360). 2, 9, 2 *pr.* (*Paul.* 153).
4, 5, 7, 1 (*Paul.* 222). 47, 2, 18 (*Paul.* 1792). *C.* 3, 41, 1 (*a.* 223).
4, 14, 4 (*a.* 238). *Nov. Maiorian.* 7, 11. primo commentario]
§ 160.
   § 78. *cf. I.* 4, 8, 6. *D.* 47, 2, 65 (64) (*Ner.* 7). 9, 4, 37
(*Tryph.* 54). 47, 2, 17 (*Ulp.* 2735). 47, 2, 16 (*Paul.* 1773). 47,
2, 18 (*Paul.* 1792). *C.* 4, 14, 6 (*a.* 293).

contempt and robbery. 77. All noxal actions attach to the delinquent. If your son or slave commits a delict, the action lies against you so long as he remains within your power*. If he moves to another's power, the action then comes to lie against that other. If he becomes independent* he becomes directly liable himself, and the option of noxal surrender is extinguished. Conversely, it is possible for a direct action to become noxal. For if the head of a family commits a wrong, and then gives himself to you in adrogation or becomes your slave (which happens in some circumstances, as explained in the first commentary) the previously direct action now lies against you noxally. 78. If a son or a slave commits a wrong against his father or owner, no action arises. It is impossible for any obligation to come into being between me and someone in my power. This is so true that, even if he passes into the power of someone else or becomes independent, no action lies either against himself or against the person who now has power over him. From this the question arises: if another's slave or son commits a wrong against me and afterwards comes into my power, is the action extinguished or put into suspense? Our teachers think that it is extinguished, because it has been drawn into a situation in which, from the start, it cannot exist, and therefore, even if he moves out of my power, I

testate, agere me non posse. diuersae scholae auctores,
quamdiu in mea potestate sit, quiescere actionem
putant, quia[1] ipse mecum agere non possum, cum
uero exierit de mea potestate, tunc eam resuscitari.
79. Cum autem filius familias ex noxali causa mancipio datur, diuersae scholae auctores putant ter eum
mancipio dari debere, quia lege XII tabularum cautum
sit, *ne aliter filius de potestate patris*[2] exeat, quam si
ter fuerit mancipatus; Sabinus et Cassius ceterique
nostrae[3] scholae auctores sufficere unam mancipationem crediderunt et illas[4] tres legis XII tabularum ad
uoluntarias mancipationes pertinere.

80. Haec ita de his personis, quae in potestate
sunt, siue cx contractu siue ex *maleficio* earum *contro-
uersi*a[5] *sit*.[6] quod uero ad *eas* personas, quae in manu
mancipioue sunt, ita ius dicitur, ut cum ex *contra*ctu
earum ag*atur*[7], nisi ab eo, cuius iuri subiectae sint, in
solidum defendantur, bona, quae earum *fu*tura forent,
si *eius* iuri[8] subiectae non essent, ueneant. sed cum
resciss*a capitis deminutione cum iis*[9] imperio continenti
iud*icio* | agit*ur*[10], ————————————————　219
　　　　　　　　　　　　　　　　　　　　　　t. s

1) quae V.　　2) ne — patris *suppl. Goeschen.*　　3) nostris V.
4) illam(?) V.　　5) inomisia(?) V *ex lect. Bluhm.*　　6) esset V.
7) ageretur V.　　8) iure V.　　9) (resciss)a capitis - - iis
suppl. Hu.　　10) *initium paginae Hu. sic supplevit:* si aduersus eam actionem non defendantur, etiam cum ipsa muliere,
dum in mauu est, agi potest, quia tum tutoris auctoritas necessaria non est. sed cf. *Peters ZS.* 32, 240 *sq.* ''*haec fortasse
(nam in p.* 219 *nihil paene praeter paucula quaedam et incerta
legi potuit) ea statim exceperunt, quae habet Inst.* 4, 8 *pr., sed
tantum haecce:* 'Animalium nomine, quae ratione carent, si qua
lasciuia aut feruore aut feritate pauperiem fecerint, noxalis

§ 79. *cf. supra* 1, 140 *sq.*; 132; 135. *D.* 43, 29, 3, 4 (*Ulp.*
1616).
§ 80. *cf. supra* 3, 84. 4, 38. *Ulp.* 11, 27. *C.* 3, 6, 1 (*a.* 239).

17*

cannot sue. The authorities of the other school* think that so long as he is in my power the action is in suspense, because I cannot raise an action against myself, but that when he leaves my power it revives. 79. Now, when a son in power is mancipated for a wrong, the authorities of the other school think that he must be given in mancipation three times, because the Twelve Tables provide that a son leaves his father's power only if he has been mancipated three times; Sabinus and Cassius and the other authorities of our school believed that one mancipation is enough, and that the three laid down in the Twelve Tables apply to voluntary mancipations.

80. So much for contractual or delictual disputes concerning persons in power. As regards those persons who are in marital subordination* or in bondage* the law applied is that when a contractual action is raised against them, unless the person to whom they are subject defends them for the whole sum, any property which would be theirs if they were not subject to him is to be sold up. But when, disregarding their status-loss, an action is raised against them in a court dependent on magistral authority* .... [Too much is illegible for any restoration to be other than pure guesswork.] 81. What then? Although, as we have

220 ———————————— 81. *Quid*[1] | ergo *est?*[1] etiamsi * *, de
t. s. qua re modo diximus, quoque non permissum fuerit
ei mortuos homines dedere, tamen et si quis eum dederit, qui fato suo uita excesserit, aeque liberatur.[2]

82. Nunc admonendi sumus age*r*e nos aut nostro
nomine aut alieno, ueluti cognitorio, procuratorio, tu-
torio, curatorio, cum olim, quo tempore legis actiones
in usu fuissent, alieno nomine agere non liceret, praeterquam[3] ex certis[4] causis. 83. Cognitor autem certis

---

actio lege xii tabularum prodita est. quae animalia si noxae
dedantur, proficiunt reo ad liberationem, quia ita lex xii tab.
scripta est.' *non etiam cetera, quae ibi sequuntur, quae aliunde
assuta esse constat. Gaius contra post haec dixisse videtur illud
omnium noxalium actionum commune esse, quod si servus vel
animal ante litis contestationem mortuum sit, noxalis actio ex-
stinguatur (Dig. 9, 1, 1, 13. 9, 4, 39, 4. 9, 4, 26, 4). aliud iuris
esse, si post litis contestationem rei culpa moriatur (Dig. 9, 4, 16.
9, 2, 37, 1), quo casu ne mortuum quidem hominem noxae dare
ei licere. plane si is ab alio occidatur, aequum visum esse, ut
iudex, si reus actione, quam adversus illum ipse apiscitur, actori
cedere paratus sit, eum absolvat (Dig. 9, 1, 1, 16). reliqua
paginae pars fortasse controversiam tractabat nobis incognitam,
si animal noxium sine cuiusquam culpa post litem contestatam
periisset, utrum reus simpliciter an (quod verius sit) tum, si
quod inde superesset, noxae daret, liberaretur; eoque spectat § 81,
ad quam cf. Liv. 8, 39, 15. Zonar. 7, 26, 10."* Hu. — *revera
Gaium egisse de pauperie et de noxali actione servi filiique
nomine proposita et de servorum filiorumque etiam mortuorum
noxae deditione confirmatur codice Augustodunensi § 81 sq.*
1) suppl. Hu.   2) liberat V.   3) propequam V.
4) ex certis *Mommsen.* exceptis V.

---

§§ 82—102. cf. Paul. 1, 2; 3. Fr. Vat. 317—341.
§ 82. = I. 4, 10 pr. cum olim etc.] cf. D. 50, 17, 123 pr.
(Ulp. 488). C. 7, 1, 3 (Diocl. et Maximian.). certis causis] cf.
Cato ap. Fest. ep. v. vindiciae p. 376 (Bruns II⁷, 46). supra
4, 14. Fr. Vat. 324 (Ulp. 328). Liv. 3, 45, 2. Donat. ad
Terent. Adelph. 2, 1, 40.
§ 83. cf. Fr. Vat. §§ 318 sq. (Ulp. 302. 307). 329 (Pap.
409). Interpr. ad Cod. Th. 2, 12, 7. Fest. ep. v. cognitor p. 57
(Bruns II⁷, 5). Cic. pro Rosc. Com. 18, 53. Hor. sat. 2, 5, 38.
Ovid. Amor. 1, 12, 24. Liv. 39, 5, 2. Ps. Ascon. ad Cic. divin. 4, 11

said, he was not permitted to surrender dead men, yet if someone does surrender a person who has departed this life, he is likewise freed from liability.

82. **We should note that** we **can bring an action for** ourselves **or for someone else, for instance**, as a representative in court, **agent, guardian* or supervisor*. In earlier times**, when actions in the law were in use, **litigation in another's name was not allowed**, with the exception of certain specific cases. 83. The substitution of a representative in court is

uerbis in litem coram aduersario substituitur. nam
actor ita[1] cognitorem dat: QVOD EGO A TE[2] uerbi
gratia FVNDVM PETO, IN EAM REM LVCIVM TITIVM
TIBI COGNITOREM DO; aduersarius ita: QVIA TV A ME
FVNDVM PETIS, IN EAM REM TIBI PVBLIVM MEVIVM
COGNITOREM DO. potest, ut actor ita dicat: QVOD
EGO TECVM AGERE VOLO, IN EAM REM COGNITOREM
DO; aduersarius ita: QVIA TV MECVM AGERE VIS, IN
EAM REM COGNITOREM DO; nec interest, praesens an
absens cognitor detur. sed si absens datus fuerit,
cognitor ita erit, si cognouerit et susceperit officium
cognitoris. 84. Procurator uero nullis certis uerbis
in litem substituitur, sed ex solo mandato et absente
et ignorante aduersario constituitur; quin etiam sunt,
qui putant eum quoque procuratorem uideri, cui non
sit mandatum, si modo bona fide accedat ad negotium
et caueat ratam rem dominum habiturum; quamquam
et ille, cui mandatum *est*, plerumque satisdare debet, |
quia saepe mandatum initio litis in obscuro est et 221
postea apud iudicem ostenditur.[3] 85. Tutores autem
et curatores quemadmodum constituantur, primo commentario rettulimus. 86. Qui autem alieno nomine

---

1) ita *Goeschen.* ii V.   2) quod ego a te *Goeschen.*
qegeatē V.   3) quia — ostenditur *del. Eisele, Cognitur p.* 143 *sq.
totam paragraphum a Gaio abiudicat Frese. Cf. Donatuti, Arch.
giur.* 89, 240. *Solazzi, Ist. tutel.* 107.

p. 104 *Bait.* (*Bruns* II[7], 70). *Schol. Ambros. in Cic. Cat. p.* 370.
Gloss. lat.-graec. 102, 49 *Goetz:* cognitor ἔκδικος. *Isid. diff.*
1, 123. agere uolo] *cf. D.* 46, 8, 15 (*Paul.* 1206).
  § 84. *cf. I.* 4, 10, 1. *Paul.* 1, 3. *Fr. Vat.* 112 (*Paul.* 1519).
333 (*Pap.* 733). *Cons.* 3. *D.* 3, 3, 1 *pr.* (*Ulp.* 320). 46, 7, 3, 2
(*Ulp.* 1704). *C. Th.* 2, 12, 3 (*a.* 382). *C. I.* 2, 56 (57), 1 (*a.* 294).
Cic. pro Caec. 20, 57. *Brut.* 4, 17 *sq. top.* 10, 42. *Senec. de
benef.* 4, 12, 3. *Ps.-Ascon. ad Cic. divin.* 4, 11 (*Bruns* II[7], 70).
Isid. orig. 9, 3, 8. 9, 4, 35.
  § 85. = *I.* 4, 10, 2. *cf. supra* 1, 144 *sq.*
  § 86. *cf. supra* 4, 55.   *C.* 2, 12 (13), 9 (*Imp. Alex.?*).
Theoph. 4, 10, 2 (*p.* 458 *Ferr.*). *Cic. pro Rosc. Com.* 18, 53 *sq.*

made by specific words, said in court, in the presence of the other party. The pursuer appoints the representative in court as follows: 'Because I am claiming a farm, for example, from you, I appoint Lucius Titius to be my representative in court in this matter'. The other party replies: 'Because you are claiming the farm from me, I appoint Publius Mevius to be my representative in court for you in this matter'. The pursuer can say: 'Because I wish to raise an action against you, I appoint a representative in court in this matter', and the other party: 'Because you wish to raise an action against me, I appoint a representative in court in this matter'. It makes no difference either if the representative in court who is appointed is present or absent. If he is appointed in his absence, however, he shall act as representative in court only if he knowingly assumes the duties of that position. 84. The substitution of **an agent**, on the other hand, **is made without specific words said** in court: he is created by mandate alone, **even in the absence of the other party or without his knowledge**. There are, indeed, those who think that someone is also to be regarded as an agent even if he has no mandate, provided that he enters upon the proceedings in good faith, and that he gives security that his principal will ratify his actions. Nevertheless, generally even someone who has received a mandate must give security, because at the outset of the dispute the mandate is often obscure and only clarified subsequently before the judge. 85. We have described **in the first** commentary **the way in which guardians and supervisors are created**. 86. A person raising an action in another's name brings forward his

agit, intentionem quidem ex persona domini sumit,
condemnationem autem in suam personam conuertit.
nam si uerbi gratia L. Titius pro P.[1] Meuio agat, ita
formula concipitur: SI PARET NVMERIVM NEGIDIVM
PVBLIO MEVIO SESTERTIVM X MILIA DARE OPORTERE,
IVDEX, NVMERIVM NEGIDIVM LVCIO TITIO SESTERTIVM
X MILIA CONDEMNA.[2] SI NON PARET, ABSOLVE[3]; in rem
quoque si agat, intendit: PVBLII MEVII[4] REM ESSE EX
IVRE QVIRITIVM, et condemnationem in suam personam
conuertit. 87. Ab aduersarii quoque parte si interueniat
aliquis, cum quo actio constituitur, intenditur dominum DARE OPORTERE, condemnatio autem in eius
personam[5] conuertitur, qui iudicium acceperit; sed
cum in rem agitur, nihil in *in*tentione facit eius persona, cum quo agitur, siue suo nomine siue alieno
aliquis iudicio interueniat; tantum enim intenditur
rem[6] actoris esse.

88. Videamus nunc, quibus ex causis is, cum quo
agitur, uel hic, qui a*git, cogatur*[7] satisdare. 89. Igitur
si uerbi gratia in rem tecum agam[8], satis mihi dare[9]
debes; aequum enim uisum est *te*[10] *ideo*[11], quod interea
tibi rem, quae an ad te pertineat dubium est[12], possidere conceditur, cum satisdatione mihi[13] cauere, ut si
uictus sis nec rem[14] ipsam restituas nec litis aestimationem sufferas, sit mihi potestas aut tecum agendi
222 aut cum sponsoribus | tuis. 90. Multoque magis debes
satisdare mihi, si alieno nomine iudicium accipias.

---

1) pro P.] p̄l. V.   2) condemnato *Wlassak*.   3) absoluito
Wlassak.   4) PVBLII MEVII] p̄l utei. V.   5) persona V.   6) res V.
7) agit cogatur *Lachmann*. agat V.   8) agat V.   9) dari V.
10) *add. Goeschen*.   11) ideo *Hu.* de eo V.   12) est
Goeschen. eius V.   13) satisdatione mihi *Goeschen*. satis-
dationem V.   14) nec rem *Inst.* rem nec V.

---

§ 87. cf. Fr. Vat. 340, 1 ab Hu. restitutum.
§ 89. cf. I. 4, 11 pr. Paul. 1, 11, 1.
§ 90. cf. I. 4, 11 pr. Fr. Vat. 317 (inc. fr. 22). D. 3, 3,
53 (Ulp. 1392).

statement of claim in the person of his principal but takes the condemnation upon himself. Thus, if, for example, Lucius Titius is acting for Publius Mevius, the formula is framed as follows: 'If it appears that Numerius Negidius is under a duty to give Publius Mevius ten thousand, do you, judge, condemn Numerius Negidius in ten thousand to Lucius Titius. If it does not so appear, exonerate.' If it is a real action, he claims: 'That the thing belongs to Publius Mevius by quiritary right' but the condemnation is for himself. 87. On the other party's side also, if someone comes in to take up the action, the claim is made that the principal 'is under a duty to give', but the condemnation is made against the person who is before the court. When, however, it is a real action, the defender does not figure in the principal pleading – this applies whether someone is taking up the action in his own name or in another's – for the claim is only that the thing is the pursuer's.

88. Let us now see on what grounds the defender or the pursuer may be compelled to give security. 89. And so **if**, for example, I raise **a real action** against you, you **should give** me **security**; for, on the basis that you are granted interim possession of the property to which your right is in dispute, it is regarded as equitable for you to give me a guarantee with security **so that, should** you **lose the case and fail either to restore the actual property or** to pay **the court's valuation**, I shall **have the means of raising an action either against** you **or against** your personal sureties. 90. **All the more** ought you **to give** me **security** if you are **defending the action for a third party**. 91. But since there is a double form of

91. Ceterum cum in rem actio duplex sit, aut enim per formulam petitoriam agitur[1] aut per sponsionem, si quidem per formulam petitoriam agitur, illa stipulatio locum habet, quae appellatur IVDICATVM SOLVI, si uero per sponsionem, illa, quae appellatur PRO PRAEDE LITIS ET VINDICIARVM. **92.** Petitoria autem formula haec est, qua actor intendit rem suam esse. **93.** Per sponsionem uero hoc modo agimus: prouocamus aduersarium tali sponsione: SI HOMO, QVO DE AGITVR, EX IVRE QVIRITIVM MEVS EST, SESTERTIOS XXV NVMMOS[2] DARE SPONDES? deinde formulam edimus, qua[3] intendimus sponsionis summam nobis dari[4] oportere; qua formula ita demum uincimus, si probauerimus rem nostram[5] esse. **94.** Non tamen haec summa sponsionis exigitur. non enim poenalis est, sed praeiudicialis, et propter hoc solum fit, ut per eam de re iudicetur; unde etiam is, cum quo agitur[1], non restipulatur.[6] ideo autem appellata est PRO PRAEDE LITIS VINDICIARVM stipulatio, quia in locum praedium successit, quia[7] olim, cum lege agebatur, pro lite et uindiciis, id est pro re et fructibus, a possessore[8] petitori dabantur praedes. **95.** Ceterum si

---

1) agit V.   2) XXV NVMMOS] xx·unū·mor' V.   3) quia V.
4) dare V.   5) nostra V   6) restipulat V.   7) qui V.
8) possessoris V.

---

§§ 91—93. cf. supra 4, 1; 16.   Fr. Vat. 336 = Paul. 1, 3, 4.   Prob. 5, 22; 23 (Iurispr. I, 88).   Cic. Verr. 1, 45, 115; 116. 2, 12, 31.   formulam petitoriam] cf. I. 4, 15, 4. D. 6, 1, 36 pr. (Gai. 153).   IVDICATVM SOLVI] cf. I. 4, 11 pr. D. 4, 3, 39 (Gai. 364). 46, 7, 6 (Ulp. 1707). 46, 7, 9 (Ulp. 479). C. 2, 56 (57), 1, 3 (a. 294).   PRO PRAEDE L. E. V.] cf. Paul. 5, 9, 2.   D. 46, 1, 33 (Ulp. 1706). 5, 3, 5 pr. (Ulp. 478). 46, 7, 11 (Paul. 809).   46, 5, 2, 2 (Paul. 803).
§ 94. cf. supra 4, 13; infra 4, 165.   Cic. p. Quinct. 8, 30.
§ 95. centumuiros] cf. supra 4, 31.   per legis actionem] cf. Cic. Verr. 2, 1, 45, 115.   de orat. 1, 38, 175.   Valer. Prob. 5, 15 (Iurispr. I, 88).

real action, either by a petitory formula or by legal wager, if the action proceeds by the petitory formula there is scope for the stipulation 'that the judgment debt will be paid'; if, however, it is by wager, the stipulation is 'for a special surety for the suit and the claim'. 92. A petitory formula is one in which the pursuer claims that the property is his. 93. We proceed by wager in the following way: we challenge our opponent with the wager: 'If the slave who is the subject of the action is mine by quiritary right, do you solemnly promise to give twenty-five?' Then we set out the formula in which we claim that the amount of the wager ought to be given us. We only win our action with this formula if we prove that the property is ours. 94. The amount of the wager is not, however, what we seek to exact; it is not a penalty but a legal preliminary, and is made solely to provide a foundation for a judgment. For this reason the defender does not make a counter-stipulation. This is also why the stipulation is called 'for a special surety for the suit and the claim', because it has replaced the special sureties [who] formerly, in the days of the actions in the law, were given as special sureties by the possessor to the claimant for the suit and the claim, that is, for the property and its fruits. 95. But if

apud centumuiros agitur, summam sponsionis non per
formulam petimus, sed per legis actionem sacramento
∗ ∗ ∗ reo[1] prouocato; eaque sponsio sestertiorum CXXV
223 nummum fieri solet[2] | propter legem Crepereiam.[3]
96. Ipse autem, qui in rem agit, si suo nomine agat,
satis non dat. 97. Ac nec si per cognitorem quidem
agat[4], ulla[5] satisdatio uel ab ipso uel a domino
desideratur. cum enim certis et quasi sollemnibus
uerbis in locum domini substituatur cognitor, merito
domini loco habetur. 98. Procurator uero si agat,
satisdare iubetur[6] ratam rem dominum habiturum.
periculum enim est, ne iterum dominus de eadem re
experiatur; quod periculum *non* interuenit, si per
cognitorem actum fue*r*it, quia de qua re quisque per
cognitorem[7] egerit, de ea non magis amplius actionem
habet, quam si ipse egerit. 99. Tutores et curatores
eo modo, quo et procuratores, satisdare debere uerba
edicti faciunt; sed aliquando illis satisdatio remittitur.
100. Haec ita, si in rem agatur; si uero in personam,
ab actoris quidem parte, quando satisdari debeat,
quaerentes eadem repetemus, quae diximus in actione,
qua in rem agitur. 101. Ab eius uero parte, cum quo

---

1) possessore *Unterholzner*.   2) fieri solet *lectio incerta*.
3) Creperiam(?) V. 4) agatur *IIu*. 5) nulla(?) V.   6) iubet V.
7) *verba* actum—cognitorem *bis scripta in* V.

---

§ 96. = *I*. 4, 11 *pr*.
§ 97. *cf. supra* 4, 83. *Fr. Vat.* 317 (*inc. fr.* 22). *C*. 2,
56 (57), 1 (*a*. 294).
§ 98. *cf. I*. 4, 11 *pr. Fr. Vat.* 333 (*Pap.* 733). 336 = *Paul.*
1, 3, 4. *Cons.* 3. *D*. 46, 8, 22, 8 (*Iul*. 734). 3, 3, 33, 3 (*Ulp*. 333).
3, 3, 39, 1 (*Ulp*. 336). 44, 2, 11, 7 (*Ulp*. 1670). *Cic. ad Att*. 1, 8, 1.
§ 99. = *I*. 4, 11 *pr*. *cf. Theoph. ad h. l.* (*p*. 459 *Ferr*.).
uerba edicti] *cf. D*. 3, 3, 33, 3 (*Ulp*. 333). remittitur] *cf. D*.
26, 7, 23 (*Ulp*. 337). *C*. 5, 37, 13 (*a*. 243). 5, 37, 28, 3 (*a*. 531).
§ 100. = *I*. 4, 11, 1. *cf. supra* 4, 96.
§ 101. *cf. I*. 4, 11, 1; 5. *Fr. Vat.* 317 (*inc. fr.* 22). 336
= *Paul*. 1, 3, 4. *D*. 3, 3, 46, 2 (*Gai*. 84). 46, 7, 10 (*Mod*. 111).

the action is before the centumviral court, we claim the amount of the wager not by formula but by an action in the law by oath, having challenged the defender; because of the Crepereian Act the practice is for the wager to be the sum of one hundred and twenty-five sesterces. 96. **For his part, the pursuer in a real action** does **not give security if he** is **claiming on his own behalf.** 97. If the action is being brought by a representative in court, certainly no security is required either from him or from the principal. Since the representative in court is put in the place of his principal by fixed and, as it were, solemn words, he is rightly viewed as being in the place of the principal. 98. **An agent for the pursuer, however, is ordered to give security for ratification by his principal, because there is a risk that the principal may sue again on the same matter.** This risk does not occur if the action is brought by a representative in court because in any matter which anyone brings through such a representative, he no more has a further action than if he brought the first himself. 99. **The terms of the Edict** make **guardians and supervisors give security in the same manner as agents; but sometimes they** are **excused the giving of security.** 100. **These** are **the rules for real actions. For personal actions,** if we inquire when security should be given **on the pursuer's side,** we shall repeat **what we have already said about real actions.** 101. **On the defender's side, someone defending for a third**

agitur, si quidem alieno nomine[1] aliquis interueniat,
omni modo satisdari debet, quia nemo alienae rei sine
satisdatione defensor idoneus intellegitur; sed si quidem
cum cognitore agatur, dominus satisdare iubetur, si
uero cum procuratore, ipse procurator. idem et de
tutore et de curatore iuris est.[2] 102. Quod si proprio
nomine aliquis iudicium aliquid[3] accipiat | in per- 224
sonam, certis ex causis satisdare solet, quas ipse
praetor significat. quarum satisdationum duplex causa
est; nam aut propter genus actionis satisdatur[4] aut
propter personam[5], quia suspecta sit[6]: propter genus
actionis, uelut iudicati depensiue aut cum de moribus
mulieris agitur[7]; propter personam, uelut si cum eo
agitur, qui decoxerit cuiusue bona *a* creditoribus
possessa proscriptaue sunt, siue cum eo herede agatur, quem praetor suspectum aestimauerit.

103. Omnia autem iudicia aut legitimo iure consistunt aut imperio continentur.[8] 104. Legitima sunt

---

1) nomen V.   2) idem—est *del. Solazzi*.   3) *om. Inst.*
4) satisdaretur V.   5) propter personam] pro persona V.
6) *verba* propter genus—suspecta sit *bis scripta in* V.   7) agetur V.   8) continunt V.

50, 17, 166 (*Paul* 627).   *Cic. pro Quinct.* 7, 29.   *in Verr.* 2, 2,
24, 60.

§ 102. *cf. I.* 3, 11, 1.   *Fr. Vat.* 336 = *Paul.* 1, 3, 5.   *lex Iul.*
municip. 113 *sq.* (*Bruns* I[7], 108). iudicati depensiue] *cf. supra* 4,
25. *infra* 4, 186. de moribus] *cf. Ulp.* 6, 9; 12.   *D.* 23, 4, 5 *pr.*
(*Paul.* 1776). 24, 3, 15, 1 (*Paul.* 1766).   *C. Th.* 3, 13, 1 (*a.* 349).   *C. I.*
5, 17, 11, 2 (*a.* 533). 5, 13, 1, 5 (*a.* 530). qui decoxerit] *cf. lex Iul.*
municip. v. 114. 115 (*Bruns* I[7], 108). *de voce* decoquere *cf.*
Cic. Phil. 2, 18, 44.   *Val. Max.* 6, 9, 12.   *Plin. n. h.* 33, 133.
Senec. ep. 36, 5. cuiusue bona] *cf. supra* 3, 79.   *D.* 42, 5, 33, 1
(*Ulp.* 2371).   *Cic. pro Quinct.* 8, 30 *sq.   lex Iul. munic. v.* 116.
117 (*Bruns* I[7], 108). siue cum eo] *cf. D.* 42, 5, 31 (*Ulp.* 2265).
§ 103. *cf. supra* 1, 184. 3, 181. 4, 80.   *Ulp.* 11, 27.   *Cic.*
pro Flacc. 21, 50.
§ 104. intra—miliarium] *cf. Liv.* 3, 20, 7.   *Dio Cass.* 51,
19, 6. lege Iulia] *cf. supra* 4, 30.   *Gell.* 14, 2. anno et sex m.]
cf. Tac. ann. 6, 16. litem mori] *cf. D.* 46, 8, 8, 1 (*Ven.* 72).

party must give security in all events. Nobody defending a case other than his own is considered reliable without security given. If, however, the defence is being undertaken by a representative in court, it is the principal who is required to give security; if by an agent, that agent. The rule is the same for a guardian and a supervisor. 102. **With a defender joining issue* for himself in some personal action**, the practice is for him to give security in certain specific cases, as indicated by the praetor. There are two reasons for giving such security, for security is given either on account of the nature of the action or on account of the person, because he is suspect. It is on account of the nature of the action when, for instance, it is on a judgment debt or on expenditure, or when there is an action concerning a woman's morals. It is on account of the person when, for instance, the defender is insolvent or his estate has been seized by his creditors or advertised for sale, or if an heir defending an action is judged suspect by the praetor.

103. All courts are either based on statutory right or dependent on magistral authority. 104. Statutory courts* are defined as being in the City of Rome or

iudicia, quae in urbe Roma uel intra[1] primum urbis
Romae miliarium inter omnes ciues Romanos sub uno
iudice accipiuntur; eaque e lege Iulia iudicia*ria*, nisi
in anno et sex mensibus iudicata fuerint, expirant. et
hoc est, quod uulgo dicitur e lege Iulia litem anno
et sex mensibus mori. 105. Imperio uero continentur
recuperatoria[2] et quae sub uno iudice accipiuntur interueniente peregrini persona iudicis aut litigatoris; in
eadem[3] causa sunt, quaecumque extra primum urbis
Romae miliarium tam inter ciues Romanos[4] quam
inter peregrinos accipiuntur. ideo autem imperio contineri iudicia dicuntur, quia tamdiu ualent, quamdiu is,
qui ea praecepit, imperium habebit. 106. Et si quidem
imperio continenti iudicio actum[5] fuerit, siue in rem
225 siue in personam, siue ea formula, quae in fa|ctum
concepta est, siue ea, quae in ius habet intentionem,
postea nihilo minus ipso iure de eadem re agi potest;
et ideo necessaria est exceptio rei iudicatae uel in

---

1) inter(?) V.   2) recuperatoriae V.   3) eadem *Goeschen.*
ea V.   4) ciues Romanos] c. Romanum V.   5) proactum V.

44, 3, 2 (*Marcell.* 76).   5, 1, 32 (*Ulp.* 2048).   42, 8, 3, 1 (*Ulp.*
1451). 46, 5, 10 (*Ulp.* 2403). 4, 3, 18, 4 (*Paul.* 209). 9, 2, 30, 1
(*Paul.* 365). 46, 7, 2 (*Paul.* 789).

§ 105. recuperatoria] *cf. Fest. ep. v. reciperatio p.* 274
(*Bruns* II[7], 30). *infra* 4, 109; 141; 185. *D.* 42, 1, 36; 38 (*Paul.*
266. 267). *Plaut. Rud.* 5, 1, 2 = 1282. *Cic. div.* 17, 56. *in*
Verr. 2, 3, 11, 27 *sq.* 2, 3, 28, 69. *pro Tull.* 3, 7 *sq. pro Caec.*
1, 3 *sq. pro Flacco* 4, 11. 20, 47. *Liv.* 26, 48. 43, 2, 3. *Cic. de*
inv. 2, 20, 60. *Plin. ep.* 3, 20, 9. *Suet. Ner.* 17. *Vesp.* 3. *Domit.*
8. *Tac. ann.* 1, 74. *Gell.* 20, 1, 13 (*Iurispr.* I, 60; 100). *B. G.*
U. 611 (*Bruns* I[7], 198). *lex Lat. tab. Bant.* 4 (*Bruns* I[7], 53).
lex agr. 30 *sq.* (*Bruns* I[7], 79). *lex Iul. agr. c.* 55 (*Bruns* I[7], 95).
fragm. Atest. l. 15 (*Bruns* I[7], 101). *lex Urson. c.* 95 (*Bruns* I[7],
130). *edict. de aquaed. Venafr. l.* 66 (*Bruns* I[7], 251). *colleg.*
aquae l. 22 (*Bruns* I[7], 395). interueniente peregrini persona]
cf. Cic. pro Flacco 21, 50. *in Verr.* 2, 2, 13, 32. quamdiu *etc.*]
cf. D. 2, 1, 13 (*Ulp.* 2983). 5, 1, 49, 1 (*Paul.* 1458).

§ 106. *cf. supra* 3, 181. *infra* 4, 121; 123. *C.* 2, 26 (27), 1
(*a.* 231). *Cic. de orat.* 1, 37, 168.

within one mile of the City, between parties who are all Roman citizens, under a single judge. Under the Julian Act on judicial procedure, unless cases are brought to judgment within eighteen months, they expire. And so it is popularly said that under the Julian Act a suit dies within eighteen months. 105. Courts dependent on magistral authority are defined as those before assessors, or those which are under a single judge but involve a foreigner as judge or party. The same definition covers any courts beyond the first milestone from the City of Rome, whether in causes between Roman citizens or foreigners. They are described as dependent on magistral authority because they are only effective as long as the person who set them up holds authority. 106. If an action has been raised in a court dependent on magistral authority, whether a real or a personal action, and whether with a formula framed on the facts or with one where the principal pleading is framed in law, it is nevertheless possible as a matter of law subsequently to raise an action on the same matter; and so it is necessary to plead the defence of matter decided or carried to trial. 107. If, however, there has been a

iudicium deductae. **107.** Si[1] uero legitimo iudicio in personam actum sit ea formula, quae iuris ciuilis habet intentionem, postea ipso iure de eadem re agi non potest, et ob id exceptio superuacua est; si uero uel in rem uel in factum actum fuerit, ipso iure nihilo minus postea agi potest, et ob id exceptio necessaria est rei iudicatae uel in iudicium deductae. **108.** Alia causa fuit olim legis actionum. nam qua de re actum semel erat, de ea postea ipso iure agi non poterat; nec omnino ita, ut nunc, usus erat illis temporibus exceptionum. **109.** Ceterum potest ex lege quidem esse iudicium, sed legitimum non esse; et contra ex lege non esse, sed legitimum esse. nam si uerbi[2] gratia ex lege Aquilia uel Ollinia[3] uel Furia in prouinciis agatur, imperio continebitur iudicium; idemque iuris est, et si Romae apud recuperatores agamus uel apud unum iudicem interueniente peregrini persona; et ex diuerso si ex ea causa, ex qua nobis edicto praetoris datur actio, Romae sub uno iudice inter omnes ciues Romanos accipiatur iudicium, legitimum est.

110. Quo loco admonendi sumus eas quidem actiones, quae ex lege senatusue consultis proficiscuntur, perpetuo solere praetorem accommodare, | eas uero, 226 quae ex propria ipsius iurisdictione pendent, plerumque intra[4] annum dare. **111.** Aliquando tamen *et* per-

---

1) at(?) **V.**   2) uerbis **V.**   3) *fortasse corruptum.*
4) inter(?) **V.**

---

§ 108. *cf. supra* 4, 11; 30. *Cic. de domo* 29, 78. — *Terent. Phorm.* 2, 3, 56 *sq.* = 403. 2, 3, 72 = 419. *Cic. Lael.* 22, 85. *Donat. ad Adelph.* 2, 2, 24 = 233. *Andr.* 3, 1, 7 = 465. *Eunuch.* 1, 1, 9 = 54. *Serv. ad Aen.* 2, 424. *Quintil. Inst. orat.* 7, 6, 4. *Decl.* 266.

§ 109. ex lege Aquilia] *cf. supra* 4, 37. 3, 210 *sq.* Furia] *cf. supra* 3, 121. *Ulp. disp. fr. Argor.* 3 (*Iurispr.* I 498).

§§ 110. 111. *cf. I.* 4, 12 *pr. cum Theophilo* (*p.* 462 *Ferr.*). *D.* 4, 9, 7, 6 (*Ulp.* 629). 44, 7, 35 (*Paul.* 34). 40, 12, 24 *pr.*

personal action in a statutory court by a formula with its principal pleading based on state law, it is not possible as a matter of law subsequently to raise an action on the same matter, and therefore a defence is needless. However, after a real action or one framed on the facts, it is nevertheless possible as a matter of law subsequently to raise the action; therefore the defence of matter decided or carried to trial is necessary. 108. It was another case formerly with an action in the law. For once an action had been raised on anything, as a matter of law that could not be the subject of another action; nor was there in those times recourse at all to defences, as there is now. 109. But note that there can be a court based on statute which is not a statutory court; conversely it can be statutory but not based on statute. For example, if an action is brought under the Aquilian or Ollinian or Furian Acts in the provinces, the court will be dependent on magistral authority; the rule is the same if we raise an action in Rome before assessors, or before a single judge if a foreigner is involved. The other way round, if an action is granted to us in the Edict of the praetor in a case heard at Rome, under a single judge, between parties who are all Roman citizens, it is a statutory court.

110. **Here we should note that** it is the praetor's custom **to make available in perpetuity those actions based on statute or Senate resolution; actions which spring from his own jurisdiction, on the other hand**, he usually grants **within the year**. 111. **Sometimes, however**, he grants them **in**

petuo eas dat, uelut quibus[1] imitatur ius legitimum,
quales sunt eae, quas *bonorum*[2] *posse*ssoribus ceterisque,
qui heredis loco sunt, *accommodat.*[2] *furt*i quoque manifesti actio, quamuis ex ipsius praetoris iurisdictione
proficiscatur[3], perpetuo datur; et merito, cum pro capitali poena pecuniaria constituta sit.[4]

112. Non omnes *autem*[5] actiones, quae in aliquem
aut ipso iure *conpe*tunt aut a praetore dantur, etiam
in heredem aeque[6] conpetunt aut dari solent. est enim
certissima iuris regula ex maleficii*s*[7] poenales actiones
in heredem nec conpetere nec dari sole*re*, uelut furti,
ui bonorum raptorum, iniuriarum, damni iniuriae. sed
heredi ∗∗∗∗ dem[8] [uidelicet actoris] huiusmodi actiones competunt nec denegantur, excepta iniuriarum
actione et si qua alia similis inueniatur actio[9]. 113. Aliquando tamen *etiam* ex contractu actio neque heredi
neque in heredem conpetit. nam adstipulatoris heres

---

1) *suppl. Hu.*   2) *suppl. ex Inst.*   3) ∗∗∗ proficiscatur V.
4) sint V.   5) *suppl. Polenaar ex Inst.*   6) eaque(?) V.   7) ex
maleficiis *del. Beseler ZS* 46, 269.   8) *num* eiusdem?   9) et—
actio *del. Albertario.*

(*Paul.* 646).   *C. Th.* 4, 14, 1 = *C. J.* 7, 39, 3 (*a.* 424).   *Cic. partit.
orat.* 28, 99.   pro capitali poena] *cf. supra* 3, 189.
    § 112. = *I.* 4, 12, 1.   *cf. Theophil. ad h. l.* (*p.* 464 *Ferr.*).
D. 50, 17, 111, 1 (*Gai.* 73).   *supra* 4, 8.   *D.* 44, 7, 12 *et* 50,
17, 38 (*Pomp.* 742).   50, 17, 139 *pr.* (*Gai.* 49).   35, 2, 32 *pr.*
(*Maecian.* 42).   9, 3, 5, 5; 13 (*Ulp.* 689. 694).   42, 5, 9, 8 *et* 42,
5, 11 (*Ulp.* 1417).   47, 1, 1 *pr.*; 1 (*Ulp.* 2868).   47, 23, 8 (*Ulp.*
189).   50, 17, 87 (*Paul.* 1386).   50, 17, 164 (*Paul.* 647).   47, 7, 33
(*Paul.* 78).   *Cod. Herm. tit. Ex delictis defunctorum quemadmodum conveniantur successores. Cod. Iust. tit.* 4, 17.   *cf. etiam
D.* 39, 1, 22 (*Marcell.* 181).   excepta iniuriarum actione] *cf. D.*
35, 2, 32 *pr.* (*Maecian.* 42).   47, 10, 13 *pr.* (*Ulp.* 1346).   47, 1,
1, 1 (*Ulp.* 2868).   47, 10, 28 (*Ulp.* 2793).   2, 11, 10, 2 (*Paul.*
1073).   si qua alia similis] *cf. D.* 3, 6, 4 (*Gai.* 92).   11, 7, 9
(*Gai.* 325).   2, 4, 24 (*Ulp.* 264).   *cf. etiam* 24, 3, 15, 1 (*Paul.*
1766).   *C. Th.* 3, 13, 1 (*a.* 349).   8, 13, 1, 1 = *C. I.* 8, 55 (56),
7, 3 (*a.* 349).
    § 113. *cf. I.* 4, 12, 1.   *supra* 3, 114; 120.

perpetuity, for instance, those modelled on statutory right. **Among these are the ones which the praetor gives to estate-possessors and others equivalent to heirs. Similarly, the action on manifest theft is perpetual, despite the fact that it emanates from the praetor's jurisdiction**; and rightly so, since its money penalty replaces a capital* punishment.

112. **Not all actions which lie against a man as a matter of law or by praetorian grant equally descend against or are given against his heir. No rule is more certain than that penal actions arising from wrongs do not lie against** and are not given against **heirs, for instance, the actions for theft, things taken by force, contempt, and wrongful loss. But actions of this kind do descend to the heir [of the pursuer] and are not refused to him, with the exception of the action for contempt and any other action like it. 113. Sometimes, however, even an action arising from contract does not descend** either to or **against an heir.** The heir of an additional stipulator has no action, and further, the heir of a

non habet actionem, sed *et*[1] sponsoris et fidepromissoris heres non tenetur.

114. Superest, ut dispiciamus[2], si ante rem iudicatam is, cum quo agitur, post acceptum iudicium satisfaciat actori, quid officio iudicis conueniat, utrum absoluere an ideo potius damnare, quia iudicii accipiendi tempore in ea causa fuerit, ut damnari debeat. nostri praeceptores absoluere eum debere existimant; nec interesse[3], cuius generis sit[4] iudicium. et | hoc est, quod 22⁷ uolgo dicitur Sabino et Cassio placere omnia iudicia absolutoria esse. ——————————————[5] de bonae fidei[6] autem iudiciis idem sentiunt, quia in eiusmodi iudiciis liberum est officium iudicis. tantumdem *et* de *in* rem actionibus putant, quia *formulae uerb*is id ip*sum* exprimatur[7] —————— *vv.* 7 ————————————— | sunt etia*m* in personam tales actiones in quibus *ex*primitur[7] ——————————————————————
—————————— *vv.* 7 —————————— actum fuit.[8]

115. Sequitur, ut de exceptionibus dispiciamus.
116. Conparatae | sunt autem exceptiones defendendo- 2²
rum eorum[9] gratia, cum quibus agitur. saepe enim accidit, ut quis iure ciuili teneatur, sed iniquum sit eum iudicio condemnari. uelut *si* stipulatus sim a[10] te pecuniam tamquam credendi causa numeraturus nec

1) sed et *Hu.* set(?) V.   2) despiciamus V.   3) interest V.   4) fit V.   5) *ad sensum ita fere supple:* diuersae scholae auctoribus de strictis iudiciis contra placuit; *similiter Krueger.*   6) fideis V.   7) *suppl. Krueger; de frustulis vide apographum. cf. Gino Segré, Bull.* 41, 49 *sq.*   8) *sequitur linea vacua in* V.   9) reorum V.   10) ápa V.

§ 114. *cf. I.* 4, 12, 2. *supra* 3, 180. *I.* 4, 6, 31. *D.* 46, 3, 33, 1 (*Iul.* 699). 46, 7, 4 (*Iul.* 727). 39, 4, 5 *pr.* (*Gai.* 47). 3, 3, 73 (*Paul.* 1051). 4, 3, 25 (*Paul.* 212). *cf. etiam.* 45, 1, 84 (*Paul.* 807).
§ 115. = *I.* 4, 13 *pr.*
§ 116. *cf. I.* 4, 13 *pr.*; 1—3. *infra* 4, 119. *D.* 44, 1, 2 *pr.* (*Ulp.* 1650). 44, 4, 2, 3 (*Ulp.* 1678). 46, 2, 7 (*Pomp.* 715). *C. tit.* 4, 30. *Cic. partit. orat.* 28, 100

personal surety and of a surety* is not liable.

114. **It remains** for us to examine whether, **if the defender satisfies the pursuer before judgment** but after agreeing to the court, **the judge has an inherent duty to exonerate him**, or rather to condemn him, **because the facts at the time issue was joined justified condemnation**. Our teachers consider that he ought to exonerate him; and it does not matter what kind of court it is. **This is the meaning of the maxim**, accepted by Sabinus and Cassius: **Every trial allows exoneration.** [The authorities of the other school have a different opinion concerning trials based on the strict words of the law] but their views are the same for trials based on good faith, because in trials of this kind the judge exercises his discretion. They think that the same holds good for real actions, because that is expressly stated in the words of the formula ... there are also those personal actions in which it is expressly stated ... an action was brought.

115. **Next let us turn to defences.** 116. **These were developed for the benefit of defenders. For it often happens** that someone is liable at state law, but that it would be **unjust** for him to suffer condemnation in court. Suppose that I **have taken a stipulation from you in preparation for making you a loan of money and then I fail to give you the cash. I can definitely**

numerauerim. nam eam pecuniam a te peti posse
certum est. dare enim te oportet[1], cum ex stipulatu
tenearis[2]; sed quia iniquum est te eo nomine condemnari, placet per exceptionem doli mali te defendi debere. item si pactus fuero tecum, ne id, quod mihi
debeas, a te petam, nihilo minus id ipsum a[3] te petere
possum dari[4] mihi oportere, quia obligatio pacto con-
uento non tollitur; sed placet debere me petentem per
exceptionem pacti conuenti repelli. 117. In his quoque actionibus, quae *non* in personam[5] sunt, exceptiones locum habent. uelut si metu me co*e*geris aut dolo
induxeris, ut tibi rem aliquam[6] mancipio dem, tua
est[7]; sin[8] eam rem a me petas, datur mihi exceptio,
per[9] quam, si metus causa te fecisse uel dolo malo
arguero, repelleris. item si fundum litigiosum sciens
a non possidente emeris eumque a possidente petas,
opponitur tibi exceptio, per quam omni modo summo-
ueris. 118. Exceptiones autem alias in edicto praetor
habet propositas, alias causa cognita accommodat.
quae omnes uel ex legibus uel ex his, quae legis
uicem optinent, substantiam capiunt uel ex iurisdictione
229 praetoris proditae sunt. | 119. Omnes autem exceptiones
in contrarium concipiuntur, quam[10] adfirmat is, cum
quo agitur. nam si uerbi gratia reus dolo malo aliquid actorem facere dicat, qui forte pecuniam petit,
quam non numerauit, sic exceptio concipitur: SI IN EA
RE NIHIL DOLO MALO AVLI AGERII FACTVM SIT NEQVE

---

1) oporteret V.   2) tenearis *Inst.* teneris V.   3) ipsum
a V. ipso iure *Hu.*   4) dare V. *Hu.*   5) persona V.
6) aliqua V.   7) inan(?) V. *litterae* i *et* n *secunda incertae.*
8) *num* si uero?   9) pro V.   10) qui V.

---

§ 117. *cf. I.* 4, 13, 1; 4. fundum litigiosum] *cf. Fragm.
de iure fisci* § 8. *D.* 44, 6, 1, 1 (*Ulp.* 1691). 20, 3, 1, 2 (*Marcian.* 35). sciens] *cf. D.* 44, 6, 2 (*Ulp.* 1902). a non possidente]
cf. D. 44, 6, 1 (*Ulp.* 1691). 41, 2, 17 (*Ulp.* 1692).
    § 118. *cf. I.* 4, 13, 7.
    § 119. *cf. Cic. de inv.* 2, 20, 60.

make a claim against you for that money. You 'are under a duty to give' it; you are bound by virtue of the stipulation. But because it is unjust that you should be condemned on that account, it is agreed that you should defend yourself by the defence of deceit. Suppose that I have come to an agreement with you that I will not claim what you owe me, nevertheless I can claim that you 'are under a duty to give me', because an obligation is not discharged by simple agreement. It is, however, agreed that if I do sue, I can be defeated by the defence of agreement. 117. Defences are also found in real actions. For instance, if you compel me through intimidation or induce me through deceit to give you something by mancipation, it is yours. But if you sue me for it, I am granted a defence by which, if I prove that you acted deliberately with intimidation or deceit, you will be defeated. Again, if you knowingly buy a farm which is the subject of litigation from someone who is not the possessor and then sue for it from the possessor, you can be met with a defence by which you are barred entirely. 118. Some defences are set out by the praetor in his Edict, while he makes others available after having heard the case. All of them have their base either in a statute or in something with the status of a statute, or spring from the jurisdiction of the praetor. 119. All defences are drafted as a negative of what the defender is affirming. If, for example, the defender is stating that the pursuer has done something in bad faith, such as perhaps suing for money which he did not pay over, the defence is drafted as follows: 'If in this matter nothing either has been done or is being done by deceit on the part of Aulus Agerius'. Again, if he is stating that money is

FIAT; item si dicat[1] contra pactionem pecuniam peti,
ita concipitur exceptio: SI INTER AVLVM AGERIVM ET
NVMERIVM NEGIDIVM NON CONVENIT, NE EA PECVNIA
PETERETVR; et denique in ceteris causis similiter concipi solet, ideo scilicet, quia omnis[2] exceptio obicitur[3]
quidem a reo, sed ita formulae inseritur, ut condicio-
nalem faciat condemnationem, id est, ne aliter iudex
eum, cum quo agitur, condemnet, quam si nihil in ea
re, qua de agitur, dolo actoris factum sit; item ne
aliter iudex eum condemnet, quam si nullum pactum
conuentum de[4] non petenda pecunia factum fuerit.[5]

120. Dicuntur autem exceptiones aut peremptoriae
aut dilatoriae. 121. Peremptoriae sunt, quae perpetuo
ualent nec euitari possunt, uelut quod metus causa
aut dolo malo aut quod contra legem senatusue consultum[6] factum est aut quod res iudicata est uel in
iudicium deducta est, item . pacti conuenti, quod factum[7] est, ne omnino pecunia peteretur. 122. Dilatoriae
sunt exceptiones, quae ad tempus ualent, ueluti[8] illius
pacti conuenti, quod factum est uerbi gratia, ne intra
quinquennium peteretur; finito enim eo tempore |
[9] non habet locum exceptio. cui similis exceptio est 230
litis diuiduae et rei residuae. nam si quis partem rei
petierit et intra eiusdem praeturam reliquam partem

---

1) dicat *Goeschen.* dicat ut V. 2) omnes V. 3) obi-
gitur V. 4) conuentum de *Goeschen.* conuenite V.
5) fuerit *Goeschen.* erit V. 6) consulto V. 7) pactum V.
8) ūuis V. 9) *supra versum* 1 *huius paginae perpallidae
umbrae apparent litterarum quarundam, quae a Gaio alienae sunt.*

§ 120. *cf. I.* 4, 13, 8 (7). *D.* 44, 1, 3 (*Gai.* 63). 44, 1, 2, 4
(*Ulp.* 1650).
§ 121. *cf. I.* 4, 13, 9 (8). quod res iudicata est *etc.*] *cf.
supra* 4, 106. 3, 180. ne omnino *etc.*] *cf. supra* 4, 119. *infra*
4, 126.
§ 122. *cf. I.* 4, 13, 10 (9). *D.* 44, 1, 3 (*Gai.* 63). litis di-
uiduae] *cf. supra* 4, 56. *infra* 4, 131. *D.* 3, 3, 38 (*Ulp.* 1129).
rei residuae] *cf. C. Th.* 2, 18, 3 = *C. I.* 3, 1, 10 (*a.* 325).

being sued for contrary to an agreement, the defence is drafted: 'If no agreement exists between Aulus Agerius and Numerius Negidius that the money at issue should not be sued for'. To sum up, in other cases it is the practice to draft in similar terms, for the reason that any defence is, naturally, pleaded by the defender, but it is included in the formula so as to make the condemnation conditional. That is to say, the judge should only condemn the defender if the pursuer has done nothing by deceit in the matter which is the subject of the action; or again, the judge should condemn him only if there had been no agreement that the money should not be sued for.

120. **Defences are called either peremptory or dilatory.** 121. **Peremptory defences** are those which have permanent force and cannot be avoided, for instance, those **of intimidation, of deceit**, of something done contrary to a statute or a resolution of the Senate, or of matter decided or carried to trial, and also **of agreement, an agreement that in no circumstances would the money be sued for.** 122. **Dilatory defences are temporary**, for instance, that **of agreement, when the agreement was that the money should not be sued for within**, for example, **a five-year period; at the end of that time** the defence is not available. A similar defence is that of action divided and of matter remaining. If someone sues for a part of something and then, within the term of office of the same praetor, sues for the remainder, he is

petat, hac exceptione summouetur[1], quae appellatur
litis diuiduae; item si is, qui cum eodem plures lites
habebat, de quibusdam egerit, de quibusdam distulerit,
ut ad alios iudices eant[2], si intra eiusdem praeturam
de his, quas[3] distulerit, agat, per hanc exceptionem,
quae appellatur rei residuae, summouetur.[4] 123. Obseruandum est autem ei, cui dilatoria obicitur exceptio, ut differat actionem; alioquin si obiecta exceptione egerit, rem perdit; non enim post illud tempus,
quo integra re *eam*[5] euitare poterat, adhuc ei potestas
agendi superest re in iudicium deducta[6] et per exceptionem perempta.[7] 124. Non solum autem ex
tempore, sed etiam ex persona dilatoriae exceptiones
intelleguntur, quales sunt cognitoriae, uelut si is, qui
per edictum cognitorem dare non potest, per cognitorem agat, uel dandi quidem cognitoris ius habeat,
sed eum det, cui non licet cognituram suscipere. nam
si obiciatur exceptio cognitoria, si ipse talis erit[8], ut
ei non liceat cognitorem dare, ipse agere potest; si
uero cognitori non liceat cognituram suscipere[9], per
alium cognitorem aut per semet ipsum liberam habet
agendi potestatem, et tam hoc quam illo modo euitare
231 *potest*[10] exceptionem. quod si dissimulauerit eam[11]
et per cognitorem egerit, rem perdit. 125. Sed[12] per-

---

1) summoueatur V.   2) eant *Bluhme.* egant(?) V.
3) quas *Hu.* qua V.   4) summouet V.   5) *add. Hu.*
6) deductae V.   7) peremptae V.   8) erat V.   9) suscipe V.
10) *add. Goeschen.*   11) eam *Hollweg.* cum V.   12) sem V.

---

§ 123. *cf. I.* 4, 13, 10 (9) *cum Theoph.* (*p.* 468 *Ferr.*). *D.* 7,
3, 1, 4 (*Ulp.* 2548). *Auct. ad Herenn.* 1, 12, 22. *Cic. de inv.*
2, 19, 57; 58.
§ 124. *cf. I.* 4, 13, 11 (10). *Paul.* 1, 2, 1—3. *Fr. Vat.*
322 *sq.* (*Ulp.* 326—328). *D.* 44, 1, 3 (*Gai.* 63). 22, 3, 19, 2
(*Ulp.* 121). 44, 1, 2, 4 (*Ulp.* 1650). *Auct. ad Herenn.* 2, 13, 20.
Quintil. Inst. orat. 3, 6, 71. 4, 4, 6. 7, 1, 19 *sq.*
§ 125. *cf. supra* 4, 53; 57; 123. *C.* 7, 50, 2 (*a.* 294). 8,
35 (36), 8 (*a.* 294); 12 (*a.* 363); 13 (*a.* 415).

barred by the defence which is called 'of action divided'. Again, if someone who had a number of suits against the same defender pursued some of them and postponed others so that they might go before other judges, and in the same praetorship he then raises one of those which he had postponed, he is barred by the defence called 'of matter remaining'. 123. The pursuer who **is met by a dilatory defence** must take care **to postpone his action; otherwise, if he proceeds with it after the defence has been put forward**, he loses his case. For, once the matter has been **brought to trial** and lost by means of a defence, his ability to raise the action does not survive **until the time** at which he could have avoided the defence, had the matter remained in its original state. 124. **Dilatory defences** not only concern time limits but **also arise from the character of the parties, such as representational defences**. For instance, if someone who under the Edict cannot appoint a representative in court does raise his action through such a representative, or if someone, though having the right to appoint a representative in court, appoints someone who is not allowed to undertake representation. If a representational defence is put forward and the pursuer is a person who is not allowed to appoint a representative in court, he can raise the action himself; if the representative is not allowed to undertake representation in court, the pursuer can raise his action through another representative in court or in his own person and so, in one or the other way, he can avoid the defence. But if he dissembled and raised his action through the representative in court, he loses his case. 125. If a defender, through a

emptoria quidem exceptione si reus per errorem non
fuerit[1] usus, in integrum restituitur adiciendae exceptionis gratia. dilatoria uero si non fuerit[1] usus,
an in integrum restituatur[2], quaeritur.

126. Interdum euenit, ut exceptio, quae prima facie
iusta uideatur, inique noceat actori. quod cum accidit[3],
alia adiectione opus est adiuuandi actoris gratia. quae
adiectio replicatio uocatur, quia per eam replicatur
atque resoluitur uis exceptionis. nam si uerbi gratia
pactus sum tecum, ne pecuniam, quam mihi debes, a te
peterem, deinde postea in contrarium pacti sumus, id
est ut petere mihi liceat, et, si agam tecum, excipias
tu, ut ita demum mihi condemneris, si non conuenerit,
ne eam pecuniam peterem, nocet mihi exceptio pacti
conuenti; namque nihilo minus hoc uerum manet,
etiam si postea in contrarium pacti sumus; sed quia[4]
iniquum est me excludi exceptione, replicatio mihi
datur ex posteriore pacto hoc modo: ᴀᴠᴛ ꜱɪ[5] POSTEA
CONVENIT, VT MIHI EAM PECVNIAM PETERE LICERET.
126ᵃ. Item si argentarius pretium rei, quae in auctio-
nem uenerit, persequatur, obicitur ei exceptio, ut ita
demum emptor damnetur, si ei res, quam emerit, tradita est, et est iusta exceptio. sed si in auctione prae-

---

1) fuit V.   2) restituitur V.   3) accidat V.   4) qua V.
5) ᴀᴠᴛ ꜱɪ] si non V.

---

§ 126. = *I.* 4, 14 *pr.* *D.* 44, 1, 2, 2 (*Ulp.* 1650). 44, 1,
22, 1 (*Paul.* 2061). 2, 14, 27, 2 (*Paul.* 128). 44, 2, 24 (*Iul.* 128).
3, 3, 48 (*Gai.* 81). *C.* 8, 35 (36), 7 *et* 10 (*a.* 294).
§ 126ᵃ. argentarius coactor *memoratur D.* 40, 7, 40, 8
(*Scaev.* 107). *cf.* 46, 3, 88 (*Scaev.* 16). 5, 3, 18 *pr.* (*Ulp.* 513).
Acro et Porphyr. ad Hor. sat. 1, 6, 86. *Cic. pro Caec.* 6, 16.
pro Cluent. 64, 180. *pro Rab. Post.* 11, 30. *Senec. controv.*
praef. § 19 (*p.* 12 *ed. H. I. Mueller*). *Suet. Ner.* 5. *Vesp.* 1.
Quintil. Inst. orat. 11, 2, 24. *C. I. L.* V 8212. VI 1923. 8728
(= XI 3820). XI 3156 (*Dess.* 7929). 5285. XIV 2886 *etc. cf. lex*
metall. Vipasc. (*Bruns* I⁷, 289). *apochae Pompeian.* (*Bruns* I⁷,
355 *sqq*). *Pap. Straßb.* 79. si ei res *etc.*] *cf. D.* 19, 1, 25 (*Iul.*
713). 50, 16, 66 (*Ulp.* 1661). 44, 4, 5, 4 (*Paul.* 792).

mistake, fails to make use of a peremptory defence, he is restored to his original legal position in order to put it forward. If, however, he failed to make use of a dilatory defence, it is questioned whether he may be restored to his original legal position.

126. It happens sometimes that a plea of defence which on the face of it seems right would itself unjustly prejudice the pursuer. There then has to be an additional plea to assist the pursuer. This is called a replication, because by it the force of the plea in defence is turned back and undone. Suppose, for example, I **have agreed with** you **not to sue** you **for the money which** you **owe** me; **then, later, we make an agreement to the contrary effect,** that I may sue. If I **bring** my **action** and you rely **on the plea that** you **should be condemned only if there was no agreement not to sue, that plea of agreement prejudices** me; **for the plea of defence remains true, despite** our **subsequent agreement to the contrary. But because it is unjust** for me **to be defeated by the defence, a replication is allowed** me **based on the subsequent agreement,** in this form: 'Unless it was subsequently agreed that I may lawfully sue for the money'. 126a. Again, if a banker is seeking the price of an article which he sold at auction, a defence can be put forward that the buyer is only to be condemned if what he bought was delivered to him; this is a fair defence. But if it was stated in advance at the auction that the property

dictum est, ne ante emptori *res*[1] traderetur, quam si
232 pretium soluerit, replicatione | tali argentarius adiuua-
tur: AVT SI PRAEDICTVM EST, NE ALITER EMPTORI
RES TRADERETVR, QVAM SI PRETIVM EMPTOR[2] SOL-
VERIT. 127. Interdum autem euenit, ut rursus replicatio, quae prima facie iusta sit, inique reo noceat;
quod cum accidit[3], adiectione[4] opus est adiuuandi rei
gratia, quae duplicatio uocatur. 128. Et si rursus[5] ea
prima facie iusta uideatur, sed propter aliquam causam
inique actori noceat, rursus[6] adiectione opus est, qua
actor adiuuetur, quae[7] dicitur triplicatio. 129. Quarum
omnium adiectionum usum interdum etiam ulterius,
quam diximus, uarietas negotiorum introduxit.

130. Videamus etiam de praescriptionibus, quae
receptae sunt pro actore. 131. Saepe enim ex una
eademque obligatione aliquid iam praestari oportet,
aliquid in futura praestatione est, uelut cum in singulos
annos uel menses certam pecuniam stipulati fuerimus.
nam[8] finitis quibusdam annis aut mensibus huius quidem temporis pecuniam praestari oportet, futurorum
autem annorum sane quidem obligatio contracta intellegitur, praestatio uero adhuc nulla est; si ergo
uelimus id quidem, quod praestari oportet, petere et in

---

1) *suppl. Krueger.*   2) EMPTOR V. EMPTAE REI *Hu.*
3) accidat V.   4) alia adiectione *Hu. secundum Inst., ubi*
alia allegatione.   5) si rursus *Inst.*; si rursus si V. *num* rursus si?   6) rursus ex V.   7) quod V.   8) non V.

---

§§ 127—129. cf. D. 44, 1, 2, 3 (*Ulp.* 1650).
§ 127. = I. 4, 14, 1.
§ 128. = I. 4, 14, 2. cf. D. 27, 10, 7, 1 (*Iul.* 336).
§ 129. = I. 4, 14, 3.
§ 130. pro actore] cf. *infra* 4, 133. *Tertullian. de praescriptione haereticorum.*
§ 131. cf. D. 44, 2, 23 (*Ulp.* 65). 45, 1, 76, 1 (*Paul.* 285).
45, 1, 89 (*Paul.* 1172); 125 (*Paul.* 1282). *Prob. Einsidl.* 3 (E. R. A.
ea res agitur). *Cic. de orat.* 1, 37, 168. *Arnob.* 7, 31. ea scilicet formula] cf. *supra* 4, 41; 54.

would not be delivered to the buyer until he had paid the price, the banker has the benefit of this replication: 'Unless it was announced in advance that the property would not be delivered to the buyer unless he had paid the price'. 127. **It happens sometimes that a replication which may on the face of it be right would itself prejudice** the defender. **There then has to be an additional plea to assist** the defender. **This is called a duplication. 128. And if that in turn seems right on the face of it but would on some grounds unjustly prejudice the pursuer, there has to be an additional plea to assist the pursuer. This is called a triplication. 129. In practice, the diversity of human affairs sometimes prolongs all these exchanges even further than we have described.**

130. Let us now look at the preliminary clauses* which are admitted on behalf of the pursuer. 131. It often happens that, arising from one and the same obligation, there is a duty to produce something now and something in the future; for instance, when we have stipulated for a fixed sum to be paid each year or each month. At the end of each year or month there is a duty to produce the money due for this period, but it is also understood that there is an obligation contracted for future years, but performance is not yet due. If, therefore, we wish to sue for what is due and to

iudicium deducere, futuram uero obligationis praesta-
tionem in integro relinquere, necesse est, ut cum hac
praescriptione agamus: EA RES AGATVR, CVIVS REI
DIES FVIT.[1] alioquin si sine hac praescriptione egeri-
mus, ea scilicet formula, qua incertum petimus, | cuius 233
intentio his uerbis concepta est: QVIDQVID PARET t. 8.
NVMERIVM NEGIDIVM AVLO AGERIO DARE FACERE
OPORTERE, totam obligationem, id est etiam futuram, in
hoc iudicium deducimus, et quae ante tem|pus obligati

—————————————— *vv. 1¾* —————————————— |[2]

131ᵃ. Item si uerbi gratia ex empto agamus, *ut* nobis
fundu*s* mancipio detur, debemus *hoc modo*[3] praescri-
bere: EA RES AGATVR DE FVNDO MANCIPANDO, ut
postea, si uelimus uacuam possessionem nobis tradi,

| ——————————*vv. 1¼*—————————— |[4]

re sumus, totius illius iuris obligatio illa inc*e*rta actione:
QVIDQVID OB EAM REM NVMERIVM NEGIDIVM AVLO
AGERIO DARE FACERE OPORTET, *per intent*ionem con-
sumitur, ut postea nobis agere uolentibus de uacua
possessione tradenda nulla supersit actio. **132.** Praescriptiones *scilicet*[5] appellatas esse ab eo, quod *a*nte
formulas praescribuntur[6], plus quam manifestum est.
133. Sed his[7] quidem temporibus, sicut supra quoque

---

1) fuit *corr. ex* fiet V.　　2) *Kruegeri vestigia premens sic
fere suppleas:* quae ante tempus obligationis finitum in
iudicium deducitur, ex ea condemnatio fieri non potest neque
iterum de ea agi potest.　　3) hoc modo *suppl. Polenaar.*
4) *ad sensum sic fere suppleas:* contra debitorem eadem actione uti
possimus. alioquin si minus diligentes in ea. *similiter Polenaar.*　　5) scilicet *nos.* sic *Hu.* siq. (?) V　　6) prae-
scribentur V.　　7) sed iis *vel* si is V.

---

§ 131ᵃ. *cf. D.* 21, 1, 48, 7 (*Pomp.* 708).
§ 132. *cf. Charisius Gramm. Lat. ed. Keil* I, 235, 21.
§ 133. *cf. D.* 44, 1, 13 (*Iul.* 682). 44, 1, 16; 18 (*Afr.* 118).
10, 2, 1, 1 (*Gai.* 189). 5, 3, 25, 17 (*Ulp.* 526). 5, 3, 5, 2 (*Ulp.*
482). *C.* 3, 31, 12 *pr.* (a. 531). *Cic. de orat.* 1, 37, 168. — *D.* 47,
10, 7, 1 (*Ulp.* 1339). 47, 8, 2, 1 *et* 48, 2, 15 (*Ulp.* 1311). 48, 1, 4
(*Paul.* 554). *Cic. de inv.* 2, 20, 59; 60. supra] § 130.

bring it to trial without affecting future payment under the obligation, it is necessary to have this preliminary clause in our action: 'Let the action deal with what has reached its due date'. Otherwise, if we bring our action without this preliminary clause in a formula in which we sue for something indefinite, with the principal pleading framed in these words: 'Whatever it appears that Numerius Negidius is under a duty to give to or do for Aulus Agerius', we bring to trial the whole obligation, that is the future one also, and [an obligation brought to trial before its course has run cannot be grounds for a condemnation, nor can the action be raised again.] 131a. Again, if we raise an action, for example, on sale, to get a farm conveyed to us by mancipation, we should use a preliminary clause of this type: 'Let the action concern the mancipation of the farm', so that subsequently, if we wish vacant possession to be delivered to us, [we can have an action on the same sale against the seller. Otherwise, if we are careless in this] matter, in an action for something indefinite the obligation in respect of the whole of that right is completely used up by the principal pleading: 'For whatever on this account Numerius Negidius ought to give to or do for Aulus Agerius'; in this way, if subsequently we should wish to raise an action for delivery of vacant possession, no ground of action survives. 132. It is quite obvious that they are called preliminary clauses, in Latin 'praescriptiones', because they are written before the formulas. 133. But at this present time, as we have also noted above, all

notauimus, omnes praescriptiones ab actore proficiscun-
tur. olim autem quaedam et pro reo opponebantur,
qualis illa erat praescriptio: EA RES AGATVR, SI IN EA
RE[1] PRAEIVDICIVM HEREDITATI NON FIAT, quae nunc
in speciem exceptionis deducta est et locum habet,
cum petitor hereditatis alio genere iudicii praeiudicium
hereditati faciat, uelut cum singulas res pet*at*; est
234 enim iniquum per unius[2] ——— | ————————————
t. 8

235 134. . . . . in *inten*|tione formulae de *iure quaeritur*, id
non est, cui dari[3] oporteat[4]; et sane domino dari[3] oportet,
rescr.* quod seruus stipulatur; at in praescriptione de facto[5]
quaeritur, quod secundum naturalem significationem
uerum esse debet. 135. Quaecumque autem diximus
de seruis, eadem de ceteris quoque personis, quae
nostro iuri subiectae sunt, dicta intellegemus. 136. Item
admonendi sumus, si cum ipso agamus, qui incertum
promiserit[6], ita nobis formulam esse propositam, ut
praescriptio inserta sit formulae loco demonstrationis
hoc modo: IVDEX ESTO. QVOD AVLVS AGERIVS DE

1) *cf. Dig.* 10, 2, 1, 1.   2) *finem sententiae Krueger ad
sensum sic supplet:* per unius rei petitionem uniuersae hereditati praeiudicium fieri. *quae in sequenti folio fuerint, con-
iectura consequi non possumus.*   3) dare V.   4) oportet V.
5) facto *Savigny.* pacto V.   6) permisserit V

*) *pag.* 235 *et* 236 *folium est non rescriptum, extra codicem
Veronensem servatum, et iam anno* 1771 *a Maffeio, deinde
anno* 1816 *ab Hauboldo (in programmate Lipsiensi) et Savinio
(Zeitschr. f. gesch. RW.* III, 140—146 = *Verm. Schrift.* III,
169—174) *publici iuris factum, cuius imago delineata extat
ad calcem ed. Gösch. et apogr. Böcking.; posterioris pag. imaginem photographicam praebet apogr. Stud., utriusque paginae imaginem editio nova phototypica fol.* 128.

§§ 134. 135. *cf. I.* 3, 17, 2. *D.* 45, 1, 141 *pr.* (*Gai.* 513).
45, 1, 76 *pr.* (*Paul.* 285). 35, 1, 44 *pr.* (*Paul.* 1174).
§§ 136. 137. *cf. D.* 45, 1, 75 (*Ulp.* 675). 45, 1, 76, 1 (*Paul.* 285).

preliminary clauses originate with the pursuer. In former times certain of them were lodged by the defender, for example, this preliminary clause: 'Let the action take place, provided that the issue of the inheritance is not pre-judged'. This has now been made a kind of defence. It is relevant when a person suing for an inheritance in another type of court pre-judges the issue of the inheritance, for instance, when he sues for individual items; for it is unjust that by [suing for a single item one should pre-judge the whole inheritance. ... Then a long totally illegible passage.] ... 134. ... in the principal pleading of a formula there is a question of law, that is, to whom is there a duty to give? Certainly that for which a slave stipulates ought to be given to his owner. But in a preliminary clause the question is of fact, which should be verified in accordance with the natural meaning. 135. We are to understand that whatever we have said about slaves applies also to other persons subject to our control. 136. We must also note that, if we are raising an action against someone who has made an indefinite promise, the formula set out for us is as follows, inserting the preliminary clause in the formula in place of a statement of facts alleged, thus: 'Let X be judge. Insofar as Aulus Agerius has

NVMERIO NEGIDIO INCERTVM[1] STIPVLATVS EST,[2] CVIVS
REI DIES FVIT, QVIDQVID OB EAM REM NVMERIVM
NEGIDIVM AVLO *AGERIO* DARE FACERE OPORTET et
reliqua.[3] 137. At[4] si cum sponsore aut fideiussore
agatur[5], praescribi solet in persona quidem sponsoris
hoc modo: EA RES AGATVR[6], QVOD AVLVS AGERIVS
DE LVCIO TITIO INCERTVM STIPVLATVS EST, QVO NO-
MINE NVMERIVS NEGIDIVS SPONSOR EST, CVIVS REI
DIES FVIT; in persona uero fideiussoris: EA RES AGA-
TVR[5], QVOD NVMERIVS NEGIDIVS PRO LVCIO TITIO IN-
CERTVM FIDE SVA ESSE IVSSIT, CVIVS REI DIES FVIT[7];
deinde formula subicitur.[8]

138. Superest, ut de interdictis dispiciamus.

139. Certis igitur ex causis praetor aut proconsul
principaliter auctoritatem suam finiendis controuersiis
interponit.[9] quod tum maxime facit, cum de possessione aut quasi possessione[10] inter aliquos contenditur;
et in summa aut iubet aliquid fieri aut fieri prohibet.
formulae autem et uerborum[11] conceptiones, quibus in |
ea re utitur, interdicta de*cretaue uocantur*.[12] 140. Vo- 236
cantur autem decreta, cum fieri aliquid iubet, uelut non
cum praecipit, ut aliquid exhibeatur aut restituatur, res·
interdicta uero, cum prohibet fieri, uelut cum praecipit, ne sine uitio[13] possidenti uis fiat, neue in loco
sacro aliquid fiat. unde omnia interdicta aut restituto-

---

1) incerte V. 2) stipulatus est] stipem V. 3) reliq V.
4) at *Polenaar*. ā (*i. e.* aut) V. 5) agat V. 6) agetur V.
7) rei dies fuit *Goeschen*. heres defuit V. 8) subigitur V.
9) interponit *Caplick*. proponit V. 10) aut quasi possessione
del. Albertario, quod improbat Arangio-Ruiz. 11) et uerborum *Hu.* uerborum et V. 12) decretaue uocantur *suppl. Goeschen*. 13) sine uitio *Scipio Maffei*. debitio V.

§ 138. *cf. I.* 4, 15 *pr. Paul.* 5, 6. *D. tit.* 43, 1. *C. tit.* 8, 1.
§ 139. *cf. I.* 4, 15 *pr. D.* 39, 5, 27 (*Pap.* 354). 43, 8, 2, 5 (*Ulp.*
1492). *Fr. Vat.* 92. *Interpr. ad Paul.* 5, 6, 1. *Isid. orig.* 5, 25, 33
(*Bruns* II[7], 82). *Cic. pro Caec.* 13, 36. *lex Rubr. c.* 19 (*Bruns* I[7], 97).
§ 140. *cf. I.* 4, 15, 1. *infra* 4, 142. ne sine uitio] *cf. infra*
4, 148 *sq.* neue in loco sacro] *cf. D. tit.* 43, 6.

stipulated for something indefinite from Numerius Negidius, as to that which has fallen due, then, whatever on that account Numerius Negidius ought to give to or to do for Aulus Agerius', and so on. 137. If an action is brought against a personal surety or a guarantor*, it is the practice to use a preliminary clause; in the case of a personal surety it runs: 'Let the action concern this point: insofar as Aulus Agerius stipulated for something indefinite from Lucius Titius, on whose behalf Numerius Negidius is personal surety, in respect of what has fallen due', or in the case of a guarantor: 'Let the action concern this point: insofar as Numerius Negidius stood as guarantor for Lucius Titius for something indefinite, in respect of what has fallen due', and then the formula follows.

138. It remains for us to examine interdicts*.

139. In certain cases the praetor or proconsul directly interposes his authority in order to settle disputes. **He** does **this especially when the parties** are **arguing about possession or quasi-possession.** Briefly, he either **orders or prohibits something to be done**. The formulas and **sets of words** used for this are termed interdicts or decrees*. 140. They are called **decrees** when he orders something to be done, for instance, when he gives an instruction that something be produced or restored. But they are called interdicts when he forbids something to be done, for instance, when he gives an instruction that **no force is to be used against one possessing with no technical defect**, or that something should not be done **in a sacred place**. All interdicts are therefore termed **restitutory, exhibitory**, or **prohibitory**. 141. How-

ria aut exhibitoria aut prohibitoria uocantur. 141. Nec
tamen cum quid iusserit fieri aut fieri prohibuerit,
statim peractum[1] est negotium, sed ad iudicem re-
cuperatoresue itur et[2] ibi editis formulis quaeritur, an
aliquid aduersus praetoris edictum factum sit uel an
factum non sit, quod is fieri iusserit. et modo cum
poena agitur modo sine poena: cum poena, uelut cum
per sponsionem agitur[3], sine poena, uelut cum arbiter
petitur; et quidem ex prohibitoriis interdictis semper
per sponsionem agi solet, ex restitutoriis uero uel ex-
hibitoriis modo per sponsionem, modo per formulam
agitur, quae arbitraria uocatur.

142. Principalis igitur diuisio in eo est, quod aut
prohibitoria sunt interdicta aut restitutoria aut exhibitoria. 143. Sequens in eo est diuisio, quod uel adipiscendae possessionis causa conparata sunt uel retinendae[4] uel reciperandae. 144. Adipiscendae possessionis causa interdictum accommodatur bonorum possessori, cuius principium est QVORVM BONORVM; eiusque
uis et potestas haec est, ut quod quisque ex his bonis,
quorum possessio alicui data est[5], pro herede aut pro
237 possessore *possidet doloue fecit, quo minus*[6] | possideret,

---

1) proactum V.　　2) itur et *Hcise.* item et̄. (*i. e.* etiam) V.
3) agetur V.　　4) *post* retinendae *per errorem librarius addidit delevitque* possessionis causa interdictum.　　5) est si V.
6) possidet—quo minus *suppl. Hu. secundum Dig.* 43, 2, 1 *pr.*

---

§ 141. *cf. infra* 4, 162 *sq. Ulp. Inst. fr. Vindob.* 5. *Quintil.
Inst. or.* 2, 10, 5. 7, 5, 3. 12, 10, 70. recuperatoresue] *cf. supra*
4, 105. *Cic. pro Caec.* 8, 23.

§ 142. = *I.* 4, 15, 1 *init. D.* 43, 1, 1, 1 (*Ulp.* 1459). 42, 2,
6, 2 (*Ulp.* 2277). 43, 1, 2 *pr.* (*Paul.* 745). *supra* 4, 140.

§ 143. = *I.* 4, 15, 2. *Ulp. Instit. fr. Vindob.* 4. *D.* 43, 1,
2, 3 (*Paul.* 745). *Auson. griph.* 63 *sq.*

§ 144. = *I.* 4, 15, 3. *cf. supra* 3, 34. 2, 149. *D.* 43, 2, 1
(*Ulp.* 1460). 43, 1, 1 *pr.* (*Ulp.* 1459). 43, 2, 2 (*Paul.* 324). 43,
1, 2, 3 (*Paul.* 745). *C. Th. tit.* 4, 21. *C. I. tit.* 8, 2. pro herede
autem possidere *etc.*] *cf. D.* 41, 3, 33, 1 (*Iul.* 614). 5, 3, 11 *sq.*
(*Ulp.* 509. 511. 512. 513 1463). sciens—pertinere] *cf. D.* 5, 3,
20, 6 c (*Ulp.* 518).

ever, when he orders something to be done or forbids its being done, the business is not immediately settled; it goes to a judge or to assessors and there the question is asked in the formulas provided: has anything been done contrary to the praetor's Edict? or has something not been done that he had ordered? The action is sometimes penal, sometimes not; it is penal when, for instance, an action is raised by wager, non-penal when, for instance, an arbiter is applied for. The practice is that actions arising from prohibitory interdicts are always raised by wager, but those from restitutory or exhibitory interdicts are raised sometimes by wager, sometimes by a formula called discretionary.

142. **The** principal **classification, therefore, lies in whether interdicts are prohibitory, restitutory, or exhibitory.** 143. **The next classification is between those which are issued for obtaining, retaining, or recovering possession.** 144. **One to obtain possession is available to an estate-possessor**, which begins: **'of which estate'**, in Latin **'quorum bonorum'. Its force and effect is this. The praetor has awarded estate-possession to someone; as heir, or as bare possessor, another person is in possession of some of the assets from the estate** or has in bad faith brought it about that he is no longer

id ei, cui bonorum possessio data est, restituatur. pro
herede autem possidere uidetur tam is, qui heres est,
quam[1] is, qui putat se heredem esse; pro possessore
is[2] possidet, qui sine causa aliquam[3] rem hereditariam
uel etiam totam hereditatem sciens ad se non pertinere possidet. ideo autem adipiscendae possessionis
uocatur[4], quia[5] ei tantum utile est, qui nunc primum
conatur adipisci[6] rei possessionem; itaque si quis
adeptus possessionem amiserit, desinit ei id interdictum
utile esse. 145. Bonorum quoque emptori similiter
proponitur[7] interdictum, quod quidam possessorium
uocant. 146. Item ei, qui publica[8] bona emerit, eiusdem condicionis interdictum proponitur, quod appellatur sectorium, quod sectores uocantur, qui publice bona
mercantur.[9] 147. Interdictum quoque, quod appellatur
Saluianum, apiscendae possessionis *causa*[10] comparatum
est, eoque utitur dominus fundi de rebus coloni, quas
is pro[11] mercedibus fundi pignori futuras pepigisset.
148. Retinendae possessionis causa solet interdictum
reddi, cum ab utraque[12] parte de proprietate alicuius
rei controuersia est et ante quaeritur, uter ex litigatoribus possidere et uter petere debeat. cuius rei gratia

---

1) quae V.   2) his V.   3) aliquae V.   4) uocatur
interdictum *Inst.*   5) quia *Inst.* q V.   6) adipisce V.
7) proponit V.   8) publice *Baumbach.*   9) publice bona
mercantur *bis scriptum in* V.   10) *suppl. ex Inst.*   11) is pro
Inst. ἒ ipse V.   12) utroque V.

---

§ 145. *cf. supra* 3, 80. *D.* 41, 2, 16 (*Ulp.* 1649).
§ 146. *cf. supra* 3, 80. *Cic. pro Rosc. Am.* 36, 103. *in
Verr.* 2, 1, 20, 52. 2, 1, 23, 61 *cum Ps.-Ascon.* (*Bruns* II⁷, 72). *Phil.*
2, 26, 64. 2, 29, 71. *Cic. ap. Gell.* 13, 25, 6. *Non. p.* 432, 29.
p. 404, 9. *Fest. v. sectores p.* 337 (*Bruns* II⁷, 37). *Isid. orig.*
19, 19, 8. *Manil. Astron.* 5, 320.
§ 147. = *I.* 4, 15, 3. *cf. Theoph. ad h. l.* (*p.* 477 *Ferr.*).
D. 43, 1, 2, 3 (*Paul.* 745). *tit.* 43, 33. *C. tit.* 8, 9.
§§ 148. 149. = *I.* 4, 15, 4. *cf. supra* 4, 91. *infra* 4, 160.
Paul. 5, 6, 1. *D.* 43, 17, 1 *pr.*; 3 (*Ulp.* 1536). 43, 31, 1 *pr.* (*Ulp.*

in possession. **The interdict orders that those things be handed over to the person who has been awarded estate-possession. Possessing as heir** relates equally to someone who is heir and **someone who believes himself to be heir; possessing as bare possessor means holding some of the assets, or even the whole estate, without lawful grounds and in the knowledge that he is not entitled to the inheritance. The interdict is for obtaining possession, because it can only be used for getting possession for the first time. If someone has once had possession, and lost it, this interdict ceases to be of use.** 145. There is likewise available to the buyer of a bankrupt estate an interdict which some people call possessory. 146. Again, an interdict of the same type is available to a person who buys confiscated property; this is called divisory, because those who traffic in confiscated property are called dividers-up. 147. **The interdict known as Salvian is also for obtaining possession. This is used by a landowner to obtain things pledged by his tenant for the rent.**

148. **An interdict for retaining possession is customarily provided when two parties are in dispute about the ownership of some property, and the preliminary question is which of them is in possession and which must be pursuer.** For this purpose **are issued** the interdicts **'as you possess'**, in

comparata sunt VTI POSSIDETIS et VTRVBI. **149.** Et
quidem VTI[1] POSSIDETIS interdictum de fundi uel
aedium possessione[2] redditur, VTRVBI uero de rerum
mobilium possessione. **150.** Et si quidem de fundo uel
238 aedibus | interdicitur, eum potiorem esse praetor iubet,
qui eo tempore, quo interdictum redditur, nec ui nec
clam nec precario ab aduersario possideat; si uero de
re mobili, eum potiorem esse iubet, qui maiore parte
eius anni nec ui nec clam nec precario ab aduersario
possederit[3]; idque satis ipsis[4] uerbis interdictorum
significatur. **151.** Sed[5] in VTRVBI interdicto non solum
sua cuique[6] possessio prodest, sed etiam alterius, quam
iustum est ei accedere[7], uelut eius, cui heres extiterit,
eiusque, a quo emerit uel ex donatione aut dotis
nomine acceperit. itaque si nostrae possessioni iuncta
alterius iusta possessio exsuperat aduersarii possessionem, nos eo interdicto uincimus. nullam autem propriam possessionem habenti accessio temporis nec
datur nec dari potest. nam ei, quod nullum est, nihil
accedere potest. sed et si uitiosam habeat possessionem, id est aut ui aut clam aut precario ab aduersario
adquisitam, non datur accessio[8]; nam[9] ei *possessio*[10]
sua nihil prodest. **152.** Annus autem retrorsus numeratur. itaque si tu uerbi gratia VIII mensibus posse-

---

1) ut V.　　2) possessione *Inst.* possessioriis V. posses-
soriis controuersiis *Polenaar.*　　3) possederit *Hu.* possidet V.
4) ipsius V.　　5) si(?) V.　　6) qq V.　　7) accidere V.
8) naccessio V.　　9) n̄ (*i. e.* non) V.　　10) *add. Goeschen.*

1621). *Fest. ep. v. possessio p.* 233 (*Bruns* II[7], 24). *Cic. de rep.*
1, 13, 20.
§ 150. *cf. I.* 4, 15, 4a. *Fr. Vat.* 293, 1 (*a.* 293). 311
(*Paul.* 41).
§ 151. *cf. D.* 44, 3, 15 (*Ven.* 24). 44, 3, 14 (*Scaev.* 192).
41, 2, 13, 1—13 (*Ulp.* 1624). 50, 16, 65 (*Ulp.* 1623). 41, 2, 14
(*Paul.* 768). 44, 3, 16 (*Paul.* 1641).
§ 152. *cf. Paul.* 5, 6, 1. *D.* 50, 16, 156 (*Lic. Ruf.* 16).
Theoph. 4, 15, 4b (*p.* 479 *Ferr.*).

Latin **'uti possidetis',** and **'with which of the two',** in Latin **'utrubi'.** 149. **The interdict 'as you possess' is for disputes about land and buildings, the interdict 'with which of the two' for moveable property.** 150. If the interdict concerns land or buildings, the praetor lays down that the party with the superior claim is the one who, at the time the interdict was issued, was in possession **without force, stealth, or licence from his opponent.** If it concerns moveables, the party with the superior claim is the one who was **in possession for the greater part of the year in question without force, stealth, or licence from his opponent.** This is made quite clear in the actual wording of the interdicts. 151. But in the case of the interdict 'with which of the two' it is not his own possession alone that is advantageous to each party, but also another's possession which may lawfully be added to his, for instance, the possession of someone to whom he is heir, or of someone from whom he has bought the thing, or received it as gift or dowry. Therefore, if another person's lawful possession when joined to our own prevails over our opponent's possession, we win the action by this interdict. No addition of time is given to someone who has no possession of his own, nor can it be so given. To the man who has nothing, nothing can be added. Again, if he has defective possession, that is, acquired by force, or stealth, or licence from his opponent, no addition is given; for his possession does him no good. 152. We count time backwards for one year. Thus, if you were in possession, for example, for eight months and I

deris prioribus et ego VII posterioribus, ego potior
ero, quod trium priorum mensium possessio nihil tibi
in hoc interdicto prodest, quod alterius anni possessio
est. 153. Possidere autem uidemur non solum, si ipsi
possideamus, sed etiam si nostro nomine aliquis in
possessione[1] sit, licet is[2] nostro iuri[3] subiectus non
sit, qualis est colonus et inquilinus. per eos quoque,
apud quos deposuerimus aut quibus commodauerimus
aut quibus gratuitam habita|tionem praestiterimus[4], 239
ipsi possidere uidemur.[5] et hoc est, quod uolgo dicitur
retineri possessionem posse per quemlibet, qui nostro
nomine sit in possessione. quin etiam plerique putant
animo quoque *retine*ri possessio*nem, id est ut, quamuis
neque ipsi simus in possessione*[6] neque nostro nomine
alius, tamen si non relinquendae possessionis animo,
sed postea reuersuri inde discesserimus, retinere possessionem uideamur. apisci uero possessionem per
quos possimus, secundo commentario rettulimus; nec
ulla dubitatio est, quin animo possessionem apisci non
possimus.[7] 154. Reciperandae possessionis causa solet

---

1) possessionem V. 2) in V. 3) iure V. 4) praesti-
terimus] restituerimus aut quibus gratuitam habitationem V.
praestiterimus aut quibus usumfructum uel usum constitueri-
mus *Hu.* 5) deuimur V. 6) retineri — possessione *suppl.*
ex Inst. 7) possumus V.

---

§ 153. = *I.* 4, 15, 5. *cf. Paul.* 5, 2, 1. nostro nomine]
cf. D. 41, 2, 9 (*Gai.* 354). 43, 16, 1, 22 (*Ulp.* 1524). colonus]
cf. Cic. pro Caec. 32, 94. *D.* 41, 2, 25, 1 (*Pomp.* 286). 41,
2, 37 (*Marcian.* 40). deposuerimus] *cf. D.* 16, 3, 17, 1 (*Flor.*
11). commodauerimus] *cf. D.* 13, 6, 8 (*Pomp.* 438). gratuitam
habitationem] *cf. D.* 39, 5, 27 (*Pap.* 354). animo retineri] *cf.*
D. 41, 2, 27 (*Proc.* 18). 41, 2, 44, 2 (*Pap.* 306). 43, 16, 1, 25
(*Ulp.* 1525). 41, 2, 3, 7; 8; 11; 12 (*Paul.* 658). 41, 2, 30, 5
(*Paul.* 1871). *C.* 7, 32, 4 (a. 290). secundo commentario] 2, 89 *sq.*
nec ulla dubitatio] *cf. D.* 41, 2, 51 (*Iav.* 210). 41, 2, 3, 1 (*Paul.*
658). 41, 2, 8 = 50, 17, 153 (*Paul.* 752).
§ 154. = *I.* 4, 15, 6. *cf. Paul.* 5, 6, 3—8. *D.* 43, 16, 1 *pr.*
(*Ulp.* 1522). *C. Th. tit.* 4, 22. *C. I. tit.* 8, 4. *Cic. pro Caec.*

after that for seven, I shall have the superior claim because the first three months of your possession do you no good under this interdict, being reckoned as possession in a different year. 153. We **are regarded as possessing not only when** we ourselves **hold, but also when someone holds for** us, **even if he is not in** our **power, such as an agricultural or urban tenant.** We **are also regarded as** ourselves **having possession through people with whom** we **have deposited or to whom** we **have lent for use something,** or to whom we have granted free lodging. **That is what is meant by the** common **saying that** we **can retain possession through anyone who possesses on** our **behalf.** Indeed, many people **think that possession can be retained by intention alone; that is to say, even if** we **are not** ourselves **in possession and nobody is in possession on** our **behalf,** we **still possess, provided that** we **left without intending to give up possession and with the intention of coming back. As for obtaining possession through others,** we **have related in the second** commentary **who can do it for** us. **It is certainly impossible to obtain possession by intention.**

154. **An interdict for recovering possession is**

interdictum dari, si quis ex possessione ui deiectus
sit. nam ei proponitur interdictum, cuius principium
est VNDE TV ILLVM VI DEIECISTI, per quod is, qui
deiecit[1], cogitur ei restituere rei possessionem, si modo
is, qui deiectus est, nec ui nec clam nec precario *ab
eo*[2] possideret.[3] *nam*que eum, qui a me ui aut clam
aut precario possidet[4], inpune deicio[5]. 155. Interdum
tamen etsi eum ui deiecerim, qui a me ui aut clam
aut precario possideret, cogor ei restituere possessionem, uelut si armis eum ui deiecerim. nam[6] propter
atrocitatem delicti in tantum patior actionem, ut omni
modo debeam ei restituere possessionem.[7] armorum
autem appellatione non solum scuta et gladios et
galeas significari intellegemus, sed et fustes et la-
pides.

156. Tertia diuisio interdictorum in hoc est, quod
aut simplicia sunt aut duplicia. 157. Simplicia *sunt*,
[uelut][8] in quibus alter actor, alter reus est, qualia
sunt omnia restitutoria aut exhibitoria. namque actor
240 est, qui desiderat aut exhiberi aut restitui, reus is est,
a quo desideratur, ut exhibeat aut restituat. 158. Pro-
hibitoriorum autem interdictorum [interdum] alia duplicia[9], alia simplicia sunt. 159. Simplicia sunt, uelut
quibus prohibet praetor in loco sacro aut in flumine

---

1) deiecisti V.   2) ab eo *add. Hu.*   3) * * * de * (possidet?) V.   4) possideret V.   5) deicio *Fitting.* deici * V.
6) n̄ (*i. e.* non) V.   7) nam—possessionem *del. Beseler ZS* 47,
359 *et Albertario.*   8) uelut V *Inst.; del. Hu.*   9) duplici V

13, 37 *sq.* 31, 91 *sq. pro Tull.* 12, 29. 19, 44. *ad fam.* 7, **13,** 2.
de orat. 1, 10, 41. *Script. Hist. Aug. Pesc. Nig.* 2, 7.

§ 155. *cf. D.* 43, 16, **14** (*Pomp.* 743). 43, 16, 3, 2—12
(*Ulp.* 1533). *Cic. pro Caec.* 8. 23. 11, 33 *sq.* 31, 89 *sq. pro
Tullio fragm.* 1 (*demptum ex Victorin. p.* 209, 22 *ed. Halm*). *ad
fam.* 15, 16, 3. armorum appellatione *etc.*] = *I.* 4, 15, 6. *cf.
D.* 50, 16, 41 (*Gai.* 335). *Cic. pro Caec.* 21, 60.

§§ 156—159. = *I.* 4, 15, 7. *cf. D.* 43, 1, 2 *pr.* (*Paul.* 745).
in loco sacro] *cf. supra* 4, 140. in flumine publico] *cf. D.* 43,
13, 1 *pr.* (*Ulp.* 1516).

customarily granted where a person has been dispossessed by force. The interdict is available in his case which begins: 'From the place from which you dispossessed him by force', in Latin 'unde vi'. It compels the ejector to restore possession to the other, provided that the one dispossessed did not have possession by force, or stealth, or licence from him. For I can with impunity eject someone who possesses what is mine by force, stealth, or licence. 155. Sometimes, however, even if the person whom I have forcibly dispossessed was possessing from me by force, stealth or licence, I am compelled to restore possession to him, for instance, if I expelled him by force of arms. For by such gross wrongdoing I must in all circumstances submit to the action restoring possession to him. We are to understand by the term 'arms' not only shields and swords and helmets, but also sticks and stones.

156. The third classification of interdicts is that they are single or double. 157. In single interdicts one party is pursuer and the other is defender. All restitutory and exhibitory interdicts are of this kind. The pursuer is the party who wants the thing produced or handed over, the defender the one from whom these demands are made. 158. But with prohibitory interdicts some are double and some single. 159. Single examples are the praetor's prohibitions against activities on sacred land or in a public river or on its banks; there is a pursuer

publico ripaue eius aliquid facere reum.[1] nam actor est[2], qui desiderat, ne quid fiat, reus is, qui aliquid facere conatur. 160. Duplicia sunt uelut VTI POSSIDETIS interdictum et VTRVBI. ideo autem duplicia uocantur, quod par[3] utriusque litigatoris in his condicio est, nec quisquam praecipue reus uel actor intellegitur, sed unusquisque tam rei quam actoris partes sustinet; quippe praetor pari sermone cum utroque[4] loquitur. nam[5] summa conceptio eorum interdictorum haec est: VTI NVNC[6] POSSIDETIS, QVO MINVS ITA POSSIDEATIS, VIM FIERI VETO; item alterius: VTRVBI[7] HIC HOMO, DE QVO AGITVR, [APVD QVEM][8] MAIORE PARTE HVIVS ANNI FVIT, QVO MINVS IS EVM DVCAT, VIM FIERI VETO.

161. Expositis generibus interdictorum sequitur, ut de ordine et de exitu eorum dispiciamus; et incipiamus a simplicibus.[10] 162. Si igitur restitutorium uel exhibitorium interdictum redditur, uelut ut restituatur ei possessio, qui ui deiectus est, aut exhibeatur libertus, cui patronus operas indicere uellet, modo sine periculo res ad exitum perducitur, modo cum periculo. 163. Namque si arbitrum postulauerit is, cum quo

---

1) reum *Heffter.* eum V.   2) actor est *Inst.* actorum V. 3) piscar· V.   **4)** utrousque V.   5) non V.   6) nunc *Goeschen.* n. V.   7) VESTRVM *add. Lenel ex Theophilo.*   8) apud quem *ut glossema vocis* utrubi *del. Mommsen; cf. Ed. Fraenkel, Ztschr. Sav. Stiftg.* 54, 312.   9) maiore parte *Theophilus.* maiores partes V.   10) sinpublicibus V.

---

§ 160. ⚊ *I.* 4, 15, 7. *cf. supra* 4, 150. *D.* 43, 17, 3, 1 (*Ulp.* 1539). VTI POSSIDETIS] *cf. D.* 43, 16, 1 *pr.* (*Ulp.* 1522). *C.* 8, 6, 1 (*a.* 294). *Fest.* v. *possessio p.* 233 (*Bruns* II[7], 24). VTRVBI] *cf. D.* 43, 31, 1 *pr.* (*Ulp.* 1621). *Theoph.* 4, 15, 7 (*p.* 481 *Ferr.*).   § 161. *cf. Frontin. de contr. agr. p.* 16, 3. 44, 4 *ed. Lachm.*   § 162. *cf. supra* 4, 141; 157. exhibeatur libertus] *cf. D.* 38, 1, 13, 2 (*Ulp.* 1076). 43, 1, 2, 1 (*Paul.* 745).   § 163. *cf. Ulp. Inst. fragm.* 5, 2. *Cic. pro Tull.* 23, 53. *lex Rubr. c.* 22 *v.* 34 (*Bruns* I[7], 100). quanti ea res est] *cf. D.* 43, 24, 22, 2 (*Ven.* 17). 6, 1, 68 (*Ulp.* 2987). 43, 5, 3, 11 (*Ulp.* 1480). 43, 8, 2, 44 (*Ulp.* 1505). 43, 16, 1, 41 (*Ulp.* 1529). 43,

trying to stop the activity and a defender trying to do it. 159. **Double examples are 'as you possess' and 'with which of the two'. They are double because the position of both sides is the same; neither litigant can clearly be characterised as pursuer or defender; instead, both share each role.** The praetor, indeed, addresses each of them in the same words. The brief form of these interdicts is: 'As you now possess, I forbid the use of force against your possession', and of the other: 'With which of the two the slave, who is the subject of the action, was for the greater part of the past year, I forbid the other party to use force to remove him'.

161. Having set out the classes of interdicts, it remains for us to examine their **order and results**. Let us begin with single interdicts. 162. If, then, a restitutory or exhibitory interdict is granted, for instance, for the restoration of possession to someone dispossessed by force, or for the production of a freedman whose patron wishes to impose services, the result of the procedure may be either with or without risk. 163. If the defender demands an arbiter, he

²⁴¹
t. s. agitur, accipit formulam, quae appellatur | arbitraria,
et iudicis arbitrio si quid restitui uel exhiberi debeat,
id sine periculo exhibet[1] aut restituit et ita absolui-
tur[2]; quod si nec restituat neque exhibeat, quanti ea
res est, condemnatur.[3] sed et actor[4] sine poena experitur cum eo, quem[5] neque exhibere neque restituere
quicquam oportet[6], praeterquam si calumniae iudicium
ei oppositum fuerit[7] decimae partis. quamquam Proculo placuit non esse permittendum[8] calumniae iudicio
uti ei[9], qui arbitrum postulauerit, quasi hoc ipso con-
fessus uideatur restituere se uel exhibere debere. sed
alio iure utimur et recte; potius[10] enim ut modestiore
uia litiget[11], arbitrum quisque petit, quam quia con-
fitetur. 164. Ceterum[12] obseruare debet is, qui uult
arbitrum petere, ut statim petat, antequam ex[13] iure
exeat, [id est antequam a praetore discedat]; sero
enim petentibus non indulgetur.[14] 165. Itaque si arbitrum non petierit, sed tacitus de iure exierit, cum
periculo res ad exitum perducitur.[15] nam actor prouocat
aduersarium sponsione[16], quod[17] contra edictum praetoris non exhibuerit aut non restituerit; ille autem ad-

---

1) exhibeat V.   2) absoluit V.   3) condemnat V.
4) actores V.   5) quem *Hu.* q V.   6) oportet *Hu.* otere
V.   7) fuit V.   8) placuit non esse permittendum *Goudsmit.*
de V *cf. apographum.*   9) ei *Goudsmit.* eia V.   10) potius
Goudsmit. tius V.   11) litigiet V.   12) *suppl. Hu.*
13) *expectari de censet Kalb. sed cf. Probi Einsidlensis notam
infra citatam.*   14) indulgentur V.   15) pducit V.
16) sponsionem V.   17) *suppl. Krueger.* ni *Hu.*

24, 15, 7—12 (*Ulp.* 1600).   43, 26, 8, 4 (*Ulp.* 1609).   43, 1, 5
(*Paul.* 1860).   43, 3, 2, 2 (*Paul.* 747).   43, 16, 6 (*Paul.* 268).   43,
16, 15 (*Paul.* 1861).   calumniae iudicium] *cf. infra* 4, 175; 181.
    § 164. *cf. Prob. Einsidl.* 70: R. A. Q. E. I. E. restituas
antequam ex iure exeas.
    § 165. *cf. supra* 4, 141. *Cic. pro Caec.* 8, 23. 31, 91. 32,
92. *pro Tull.* 12, 30. 23, 53. *ad fam.* 7, 21. *Quintil. Inst. or*
7, 5, 3. *lex Rubr. c.* 22 (*Bruns* II⁷, 100).

accepts the formula called discretionary; if the judge's decision is that something should be restored or produced, he restores or produces it without risk and is thus exonerated. If, however, he should• fail to restore or produce it, he is condemned to pay the value of the property. The pursuer too comes under no penalty by raising an action against a person who is not under a duty to produce or restore anything, unless a charge of calumny is brought against him for one-tenth. Although Proculus held that a charge of calumny should be refused to someone who demands an arbiter, because he has, as it were, admitted openly that he ought to restore or produce, our law is different, and rightly so. For a party applies for an arbiter more to reduce the hazards of litigation than because he is admitting liability. 164. Someone wishing to apply for an arbiter must note, however, that he should apply immediately, before he leaves the pleading stage, [that is, while he is still before the praetor]; for no leave is granted to late applicants. 165. Therefore, if he does not apply for an arbiter but leaves the pleading stage in silence, the action then proceeds to its conclusion at his own risk. The pursuer challenges his opponent with a wager that he has failed, contrary to the praetor's Edict, to produce or to restore; and the defender stipulates for a counter-

uersus sponsionem aduersarii restipulatur; deinde actor
quidem sponsionis formulam edit aduersario, ille huic
inuicem restipulationis. sed actor sponsionis *formulae
subicit* et aliud iudicium de re restituenda uel ex-
hibenda, ut si sponsione uicerit, nisi ei res exhibeatur
aut restituatur[1], | ——————————————————————— 242
| ——————————————————————————————— t. s.
——————————————————————————————— 243
———————————————————————————————— t. s.

166. | [2] ————— [3] fructus licitando, is tantisper in pos- 244
sessione constituitur, si modo aduersario suo fructuaria
stipu*latione cau*erit, cuius uis et potestas haec est, ut
si contra eum *de possessione* pronun*tiatum fuerit, eam*
summam aduersario soluat. haec autem licendi contentio fructus licitatio uocatur, scilicet quia —————
————————————————— *vv.* 1½ ————————————— |
postea alter alterum sponsione prouocat, quod aduersus
edictum praetoris possidenti sibi uis facta sit[4], et
inuicem ambo restipulantur aduersus sponsionem:
————————————————————— [5] una inter eos sponsio item*que r*estipulatio un*a* ————————— ad eam fit.
| —————————————— *vv.* 2½ ————— 166ᵃ. —————[6]
iudex, apud quem de ea re agitur, illud scilicet requirit,

—————————

1) *Krueger sententiam Hollwegio duce sic perficit:* quanti
ea res erit, aduersarius ei condemnetur. 2) *p.* 244 *usque ad
v.* 13 *ter, a v.* 14 *ad* 24 *bis est scripta.* 3) *initium paginae
cum Kruegero sic expleas:* et qui superauerit. *transiit Gaius
in pagina antecedente, cuius praeter frustula minima nihil legi
potest, ad interdicta duplicia exponenda.* 4) est V. 5) *Hu.
suppl.:* uel stipulationibus iunctis duabus. *alii aliter.* 6) *initium paragraphi* 166ᵃ *Hu. sic restituere conatus est:* deinde
ab utroque editis formulis omnium sponsionum et restipula-
tionum, quas fieri placuit. *cf.* § 165.

—————————

§ 166. fructuaria stipulatione] *cf. D.* 45, 1, 4, 2 (*Paul.*
1841). cauerit] *cf. infra* 4, 167. sponsione *etc.*] *cf. Cic. pro
Caec.* 16. 45 *Quintil. Inst.* 7, 5, 3.
§ 166ᵃ. Cascelliano . . iudicio] *cf. D.* 43, 17, 3. 11 (*Ulp.*
1542).

wager. The pursuer then issues the formula of the wager to his opponent, who in turn serves his counter. The pursuer also combines with the formula for the wager a further suit for the restoration or production of the property; in this way, if he is successful with his wager, then unless the property is produced or restored to him, [his opponent will be condemned for its value. ... There follows an illegible passage and a page of repetitions; Gaius moved on to the discussion of double interdicts.]

166. ... by contending for the fruits, he is established in possession for just so long, provided that he has given a guarantee to his opponent about the fruits. Its force and effect is this. If judgment is given against him on possession, he pays that sum to his opponent. This dispute is called a contest for the fruits, doubtless because .... Subsequently one party challenges the other with a wager that, contrary to the praetor's Edict, violence has been done to him while in possession, and both in turn stipulate for a promise on the wager; [there may either be two linked stipulations] or one wager and one counter-stipulation between them ... happens to it. ... 166a. [Then it is agreed what should be done with all the wagers and counter-stipulations in the formulas each has put forward.] The judge before whom the action is being heard inquires into what the praetor included in the

quod praetor interdicto conplexus est, id est, uter eorum
eum fundum easue aedes per id tempus, quo interdictum[1]
redditur, nec ui nec clam nec precario possideret.
cum iudex id explorauerit et forte secundum me iudicatum sit, aduersarium mihi et sponsionis et restipulationis summas, quas cum eo feci, condemnat et
conuenienter me sponsionis[2] et restipulationis, quae
mecum factae sunt, absoluit; et hoc amplius si apud
aduersarium meum possessio *est*, quia[3] is fructus licitatione uicit, nisi restituat mihi possessionem, Cascel-
liano siue | secutorio iudicio condemnatur. 167. Ergo
is, qui fructus licitatione uicit, si non probat ad se
pertinere possessionem, sponsionis et restipulationis
et fructus licitationis summam[4] poenae nomine soluere
et praeterea possessionem restituere iubetur et hoc
amplius fructus, quos interea percepit, reddit; summa
enim[5] fructus licitationis non pretium est fructuum,
sed poenae nomine soluitur, quod quis alienam[6] possessionem per hoc tempus retinere et facultatem fruendi
nancisci conatus est. 168. Ille autem, qui fructus licitatione uictus est, si non probauerit ad se pertinere
possessionem, tantum sponsionis et restipulationis summam poenae nomine debet. 169. Admonendi tamen
sumus liberum esse ei, qui fructus licitatione uictus
erit, omissa fructuaria stipulatione, sicut Cascelliano
siue secutorio iudicio de *posses*sione reciperanda[7] experitur, ita *similiter*[8] de fructus licitatione agere. in
quam rem proprium iudicium conparatum est, quod
appellatur fructuarium, quo nomine actor iudicatum

---

1) interdicto V.   2) sponsiones V.   3) q̇ (*i. e.* quam) V
4) summas *Hu.*   5) *verba* fructus quos *usque ad* summa
enim *bis scripta in* V.   6) aliena nam V.   7) reciperandae V.   8) similiter *Hu.* s ✳ ✳ ✳ ✳ ✳ ✳ V.

---

§ 169. *cf. supra* 4, 166. *Polyb.* 32, 2, 8. iudicatum solui]
cf. supra 4, 91.

interdict; that is, which of the parties was in possession of the land or buildings, and not by force, stealth, or licence, at the time when the interdict was issued. When the judge has explored this and, let us say, judgment has been given in my favour, he condemns my opponent to pay the sums contained in the wager and the counter-stipulation which I made with him; he likewise exonerates me from the wager and counter-stipulation he made with me. Over and above this, if possession is with my opponent as a result of his success in the contest for the fruits, unless he restores possession to me, he is condemned in a Cascellian or consequential judgment. 167. Therefore, the winner of a contest for the fruits, if he fails to prove his claim to possession, is ordered to pay as penalty the sum total of the wager, the counter-stipulation and the contest for the fruits and, moreover, to restore possession. Over and above this, he has to return the fruits which he took in the meantime. The amount of the contest for the fruits is not the value of the fruits, but is paid by way of penalty because someone has attempted to retain another person's possession over this period and to acquire the opportunity of taking the fruits. 168. On the other hand, the party who loses the contest for the fruits, if he fails to prove his claim to possession, must pay by way of penalty only the sum of the wager and the counter-stipulation. 169. We must, however, notice that the party who loses the contest for the fruits, if the stipulation for the fruits was not taken, is free to raise his action on the contest for the fruits, just as he can proceed by a Cascellian or consequential action to recover possession. There is a special type of proceedings established for this purpose, which is called a fructuary action. In this the pursuer gets security for the payment of the amount adjudged.

solui[1] satis accipit.[2] dicitur autem et hoc iudicium secutorium, quod sequitur sponsionis uictoriam; sed non aeque Cascellianum uocatur.[3] **170.** Sed quia nonnulli interdicto reddito cetera ex interdicto facere nolebant atque ob id non poterat res expediri, praetor | in eam rem prospexit et comparauit interdicta, quae secundaria appellamus, quod secundo loco redduntur. quorum u*is et potesta*s haec est, ut qui cetera ex interdicto non faciat[4], uelut qui uim non faciat aut fructus non liceatur[5] aut qui fructus licitationis satis[6] non det[7] aut si sponsiones[8] non faciat[4] sponsionumue[9] iudicia non accipiat, siue possideat, restituat[10] aduersario possessionem, *siue non* possideat[11], uim illi possidenti non faciat. itaque etsi alias potue*rit* interdicto VTI POSSIDETIS uincere, si cetera ex interdicto *fecisset* ————————[12], tamen per interdictum secundarium u*in*|*citur.* ————— *vv. 4* —————

————— *Sabi*nus et Cassius secuti fuerint —————

————— *vv. 9* —————

————————— *vv. 24* ————— **171.** ——

pecuniaria poena modo iurisiurandi[13] religione *coercen* ———[14]. eaque praetor ——— ideo ——— aduersus in*fitiantes ex quibusdam* | causis dupli[15] actio constituitur, uelut si iudicati aut depensi aut damni

246 t. s.

247 t. s.

248 t. s.

---

1) iudicatum solui *Hu.* is V. 2) accipiatur V.
3) uocat V. 4) facit V. 5) licetur V. 6) sata V.
7) dat V. 8) sponsionibus V. 9) sponsionumue *Krueger.* sponsionisue V. 10) si restituat V. 11) possideant (?) V.
12) *suppl. Hu.:* si non fecit. 13) iurisiurando V. 14) *sensum supple ex Inst.* 4, 16 *pr.* 15) duplici V.

---

§ 170. *cf. D.* 41, 2, 52, 2 (*Ven.* 8). 50, 17, 155, 1 (*Paul.* 758). *Cic. pro Caec.* 16, 45. *ad fam.* 7, 13, 2. *Frontin. de controv. agr. p.* 44, 5 *ed. Lachm.*

§ 171. *cf. I.* 4, 16 *pr.*; 1. *supra* 4, 9; 13. *D.* 13, 5, 18, 2 (*Ulp.* 796). *Cic. pro Rosc. Com.* 4, 10. 5, 14. *de offic.* 3, 16, 65. *lex Rubr. c.* 21 (*Bruns* II[7], 99). *lex Iul. munic. v.* 40—45 (*Bruns* II[7], 104).

This is also called a consequential action, because it is a consequence of the successful wager, but it is not similarly called Cascellian. 170. But because some people, after the interdict had been issued, refused to perform the other things required by the interdict and therefore the action could not go ahead, the praetor gave thought to the matter and made available what are called secondary interdicts, because they are issued in the second place. Their force and effect is this. Someone who fails to perform the other things required by the interdict, for instance, who does no [formal act of] violence, or makes no offer for the fruits, or fails to give security for the contest for the fruits, or does not make the wagers, or does not accept the actions on the wagers, must, if he is in possession, restore possession to his opponent or, if he is not in possession, refrain from using violence on the possessor. In this way, even if he would otherwise be able to make successful use of the interdict 'as you possess', he may still be overcome by a secondary interdict if [he has failed to do] the other things required by the interdict. ... Sabinus and Cassius would have followed ....

171. [Gaius here turns to vexatious proceedings on the part of the defender.] ... are **compelled** [sometimes] **by a monetary penalty, sometimes by the sanctity of an oath ....** And these the praetor ... for that reason ... **in some actions the claim is doubled if the defender denies liability**, for instance, if an action is brought on a judgment debt, or on expenditure, or **for wrongful loss**, or for obligatory

iniuriae aut legatorum per damnationem relictorum[1]
nomine agitur. ex quibusdam causis sponsionem facere
permittitur, uelut de pecunia certa credita et pecunia
constituta, sed certae[2] quidem creditae pecuniae tertiae
partis, constitutae uero pecuniae partis dimidiae.
172. Quod si neque sponsionis neque dupli actionis periculum ei, cum quo agitur, iniungatur[3] ac ne statim
quidem ab initio pluris quam simpli sit actio, permittit praetor iusiurandum[4] exigere NON CALVMNIAE
CAVSA[5] INFITIAS IRE. unde quamuis heredes uel qui
heredum loco habentur ————[6] obligati sint[7], item
feminae[8] pupillique[9] eximantur[10] periculo sponsionis,
iubet tamen eos iurare. 173. Statim autem[11] ab initio
pluris quam simpli actio est uelut furti manifesti quadrupli, nec manifesti dupli, concepti et oblati tripli:
nam ex his causis et aliis quibusdam, siue quis neget[12]
siue fateatur, pluris quam simpli est actio.

174. Actoris quoque calumnia[13] coercetur modo
calumniae iudicio, modo contrario, modo iureiurando,
modo restipulatione. 175. Et quidem calumniae iudicium aduersus omnes actiones locum habet et est de-

---

1) relictum V.   2) certa V.   3) iniungatur *Lachmann.*
coniungatur V   4) iurisiurandum V.   5) causae V.
6) *ad* simplo tenus *vestigia ducere videntur Studemundio teste;
ex Bluhmii lectione fortasse conficere licet:* simpli nec amplius.
7) sunt V.   8) feminis V.   9) pupillisque V.   10) ex✳✳✳t
V.   11) autem *Inst.* aħ V.   12) negat V.   13) calumniae V

---

§ 172. *cf. I.* 4, 16, 1.   *D.* 10, 2, 44, 4 (*Paul.* 1740).   *C.* 2,
58 (59), 2 *pr.* (*a.* 531). *Nov.* 49, 3, 1 (*a.* 537). *Val. Prob.* 5, 11:
N. K. C. non calumniae causa.
§ 173. *cf. I.* 4, 16, 1. *supra* 3, 189—191.
§ 174. *cf. I.* 4, 16, 1. calumniae iudicio] *infra* 4, 175
—179. contrario] 4, 177. restipulatione] 4, 180.
§ 175. *cf. Cod. Herm. tit. De calumniat. ex Consult.* 6, 13
(*a.* 293).   *Theoph.* 4, 16, 1c (*p.* 483 *Ferr.*).   *Nov.* 112, 2 *pr.*
(*a.* 541). *Iustiniani edict.* 7, 5. *Cic. pro Cluent.* 59, 163. *Gell.*
14, 2, 8. *D.* 5, 1, 10 (*Ulp.* 362). 4, 3, 33 (*Ulp.* 2332). aduersus
adsertorem] *cf. Paul.* 5, 33, 7.

legacies. In certain cases it is permissible to make a wager, for instance, concerning a loan of money or on a money undertaking, but it is for a third part of the sum lent and a half of the money undertaking. 172. But if there is no risk to the defender either of a wager or of an action for twofold, nor even of an action which from the outset is for more than simple damages, the praetor allows an oath to be demanded: 'That you do not deny liability in order to be vexatious'. Even heirs and others in the position of heirs may be required to take this [even for simple damages]; again, women and independent children are free from the risk of a wager, but he orders them to swear an oath. 173. **Some actions lie from the outset for multiple damages, for instance, the action for manifest theft for fourfold or non-manifest for twofold**, and for theft by receiving and theft by planting threefold. **In these and in some others the defender is liable for more than single damages whether he denies or admits liability.**

174. **Vexatious proceedings on the part of the pursuer are** sometimes **checked** by an action for calumny, sometimes by a counter-action, sometimes by an oath, sometimes by a counter-stipulation. 175. An action for **calumny** is competent against all actions; it is for **one-tenth**, except against a claimant

cimae partis, *praeterquam quod*[1] aduersus adsertorem
tertiae partis est. **176.** Liberum est autem ei, cum
quo agitur, aut calumniae iudicium opponere aut
iusiurandum exigere NON CALVMNIAE CAVSA AGERE.
177. Contrarium autem iudicium ex certis causis con-
stitui*tur*, | uelut si iniuriarum agatur et si cum muliere **249**
eo nomine agatur, quod dic*atur*[2] uentris nomine in
possessionem missa dolo malo ad alium possessionem
transtulisse[3], et si quis eo nomine agat, quod dicat se
a praetore in possessionem missum ab alio quo ad-
missum non esse. sed aduersus iniuriarum quidem
actionem[4] decimae partis datur, aduersus uero duas
istas quintae. **178.** Seuerior autem coercitio est per
contrarium iudicium. nam[5] calumniae iudicio x. partis
nemo damnatur[6] nisi qui intellegit non recte se agere,
sed uexandi aduersarii gratia actionem instituit potius-
que ex iudicis errore uel iniquitate uictoriam sperat
quam ex causa ueritatis. calumnia enim in adfectu[7]
est, sicut furti crimen. contrario uero iudicio omni
modo damnatur actor, si causam non tenuerit, licet
aliqua[8] opinione inductus crediderit se recte agere.
179. Vtique autem ex quibus causis contrario iudicio
agi[9] potest, etiam calumniae iudicium locum habet;

---

1) praeterquam quod *suppl. Krueger; cf. supplementum*
apographi. 2) dicetur V. 3) transtulisset V. 4) actionis V. 5) non V. 6) damnetur V. 7) adfectum V.
8) alia V. 9) agere V.

---

§ 176. *cf. infra* 4, 179. *Paul.* 2, 1, 2. *D.* 10, 2, **44, 4**
(*Paul.* 1740). 12, 2, 34, 4 (*Ulp.* 760). 12, 2, 37 *et* 25, 2, 11, **1**
(*Ulp.* 961). 39, 1, 5, 14 (*Ulp.* 1268). 39, 2, 7 *pr.* (*Ulp.* 1271).
C. 4, 1, 9 (*a.* 294). *lex Rubr. c.* 20 (*Bruns* I[7], 97). *Cic. pro*
Rosc. Com. 1, 4.

§ 177. si iniuriarum] *cf. Paul.* 5, 4, 11. *D.* 47, 10, **43**
(*Gai.* 484). si cum muliere] *cf. D. tit.* 25, 5. quod dicat se a
praetore] *cf. D. tit.* 43, 4.

§ 178. *cf. D.* 48, 16, 1, 1; 3; 4 (*Marcian.* 287). *C.* 9, 46, **3**
(*Imp. Alex.*). furti] *cf. supra* 3, 197.

§ 179. *cf. supra* 4, 176.

of another's liberty when it is for one-third. 176. The defender is free either to raise an action for calumny, or to demand the taking of the oath: 'That the action is not brought vexatiously'. 177. A counter-action is laid down for certain specific cases, for instance, if there is an action for contempt, and if an action is brought against a woman because it is alleged that after she had been put in possession for the sake of her unborn child, she transferred that possession in bad faith to someone else, or if someone is bringing an action because he alleges that, after having been put in possession by the praetor, he was refused entry by the other party. One-tenth is granted in response to an action for contempt, for the latter two causes, one-fifth. 178. A counter-action imposes a more severe sanction. In a trial for calumny no one is condemned for the one-tenth unless, being aware that his case was not good, he began the action to vex his opponent, and in the hope of winning through the judge's error or injustice rather than by reason of the truth. For calumny, like the crime of theft, lies in the intention. In a counter-action, on the other hand, the pursuer is condemned anyway if he fails to make his case, even if he was led by some advice to believe that his case was good. 179. Anyhow, in those cases where a counter-action can be raised, an action for calumny is still competent; but only one of them can be brought. On

sed alterutro tantum[1] iudicio agere permittitur. qua
ratione si iusiurandum de calumnia[2] exactum fuerit,
quemadmodum calumniae iudicium non datur, ita et
contrarium non dari debet. 180. Restipulationis quoque poena ex certis causis fieri solet; et quemadmodum contrario iudicio omni modo condemnatur actor,
si causam non tenuerit, nec requiritur, an scierit non
recte se agere, ita etiam restipulationis poena omni |
250 modo damnatur actor, si uincere non potuerit. 181. Qui
autem restipulationis poenam patitur, ei neque calumniae iudicium opponitur neque iurisiurandi religio in-
iungitur[3]; nam[4] contrarium iudicium ex his causis
locum non habere palam est.

182. Quibusdam iudiciis damnati ignominiosi fiunt,
uelut furti, ui bonorum raptorum, iniuriarum, item
pro socio, fiduciae, tutelae, mandati, depositi. sed furti
aut ui *bonorum* raptorum aut iniuriarum non solum
damnati notantur ignominia, sed etiam pacti, ut[5] in
edicto praetoris scriptum est; et recte. plurimum enim
interest, utrum ex delicto aliquis an ex contractu debitor sit. nec tamen[6] ulla parte edicti id ipsum nominatim exprimitur, ut aliquis ignominiosus sit[7], sed[8]
qui prohibetur et pro alio postulare *et cognitorem*[9]

---

1) t͞m (*i. e.* tamen) V.   2) calumniae V.   3) religio
iniungitur] religioni iungitur V.   4) n̄ (*i. e.* non) V.
5) pacti ut] pactiit *aut* pactut V.   6) nec tamen *Krueger.*
nam (?) V.   7) esset V.   8) s * * * V.   9) * * gn * tor V.

---

§ 180. *cf. supra* 4, 13; 171.
§ 181. *cf. supra* 4, 171; 172; 163.
§ 182. *cf. supra* 4, 60. *I.* 4, 16, 2. *D.* 3, 2, 1 (*Ulp.* 277).
3, 2, 4, 5 (*Ulp.* 282). 50, 16, 42 (*Ulp.* 1368). 48, 1, 7 (*Macer* 29).
Fr. Vat. 322 *sq. Coll.* 10, 2, 4 (*Mod.* 9). *C. tit.* 2, 11 (12). *Cic.*
pro Rosc. Amerin. 38, 111 *sq.* 40, 116. *pro Rosc. Com.* 6, 16.
pro Caec. 3, 7. *pro Cluent.* 42, 119. *de orat.* 1, 36, 166. *Quin-*
til. Decl. 250. *lex Iul. munic.* (*Bruns* 1⁷, 107). *fragm. Atest.*
(*Bruns* 1⁷, 101). pacti] *cf. D.* 3, 2, 6, 3 (*Ulp.* 282). 3, 2, 5 (*Paul.*
140). 3, 2, 7 (*Paul.* 141). *C.* 2, 11 (12), 18 (*a.* 260). qui prohibe-
tur] *cf. Quintil. Inst.* 3, 6, 71; 75. 4, 4, 6. **7**, 1, 19; 20. 7, 5, 3.

this account, if an oath against calumny has been demanded, then just as an action for calumny is not granted, nor ought a counter-action be granted either. 180. In certain cases it is the practice for there to be a penalty on a counter-stipulation. Just as the pursuer who loses his case is anyway condemned in a counter-action, with no reference to whether he knew that his case was not good, so also, if he cannot win his action, is a pursuer in all cases condemned to the penalty on the counter-stipulation. However, a person who suffers the penalty on a counter-stipulation is not liable to an action for calumny, nor may the sanctity of an oath be imposed on him; it is obvious that a counter-action is not available in these cases.

182. **In some actions a condemned defender incurs disgrace, for instance, in theft, things taken by force, contempt**, and **also in actions on partnership**, on a trust-conveyance, **on guardianship, mandate and deposit. But in the actions for theft, things taken by force, or contempt, not only those condemned but also those who settle incur disgrace**, as is set out in the praetor's Edict. **This is quite right. The crucial question is whether a man's liability arises from wrongdoing or from contract.** It is not, however, set out anywhere explicitly in the praetor's Edict that a person shall incur disgrace; but someone who is forbidden to make a claim on behalf of another, to appoint a

dare procuratoremue habere, item *procuratorio* aut cognit*o*rio nomine iudicio interuenire, ignominiosus esse *dicitur*.

183. In summa sciendum est eum, qui cum aliquo consistere uelit, *in ius uocare*[1] oportere et eum, qui uocatus est, si non uenerit[2], poenam ex edicto praetoris committere. quasdam tamen personas sine[3] permissu praetoris in ius uocare non licet, uelut parentes patronos patronas[4], item liberos et parentes patroni patronaeue; et in eum[5], qui aduersus ea egerit, poena constituitur. 184. Cum autem in ius uocatus fuerit aduersarius neque eo die[6] finiri potuerit negotium, uadimonium ei faciendum est, id est ut promittat se certo die sisti. 185. Fiunt autem[7] uadimonia quibusdam ex causis pura, id est sine satisdatione, quibusdam cum satisdatione, | quibusdam iureiurando, quibus- 251 dam recuperatoribus suppositis, id est, ut qui non steterit, is protinus a recuperatoribus in summam[8] uadimonii condemnetur; eaque singula diligenter praetoris edicto significantur. 186. Et si quidem iudicati depensiue agetur, tanti fit[9] uadimonium, quanti ea res

---

1) in ius uocare *suppl. Hu.*   2) uenierit V.
3) siue V.   4) patronas patronos V.   5) eam V.   6) eo die] odie V.   7) ā (*i. e.* aut) V.   8) summa V.   9) fiat V.

---

§ 183. *cf. supra* 4, 46 *ibiq. cit.; adde D.* 2, 4, 6 (*Paul* 1915). 2, 4, 13 (*Mod.* 131). *C.* 2, 2, 2 (*a.* 239). 2, 2, 3 (*a.* 287).

§ 184. *cf. supra* 3, 224. *Varro de l. l.* 6, 74 (*Bruns* II[7], 57). *Cic. pro Quinct.* 5, 22. 6, 23; 25. 16, 51 *sq. pro Rosc. Com.* 13, 38. *Manil. Astron.* 1, 244. *Prob. Eins.* 63: V. F. I. uadimonium fieri iubere.

§ 185. *cf. D. tit.* 2, 8; 11. *Cic. ad Q. fratr.* 2, 13 (15), 3. *Ovid. amor.* 1, 12, 23. cum satisdatione] *cf. D.* 5, 1, 2, 6 (*Ulp.* 213). 50, 17, 110, 1 (*Paul.* 148). *Cornel. Nep. Attic.* 9, 4. *Porphyr. ad Hor. sat.* 1, 1, 11. iureiurando] *cf. D.* 2, 8, 16 (*Paul.* 150). recuperatoribus] *cf. supra* 4, 105.

§ 186. *cf. D.* 2, 10, 3, 4 (*Iul.* 28). 45, 1, 115 *pr.* (*Pap.* 79). 2, 11, 4, 5 (*Ulp.* 1657). iudicati] *cf. supra* 4, 9; 102; 171. depensi] *cf. supra* 3, 127. 4, 9; 102; 171.

representative in court, and to have an agent, as also to take part in an action as an agent or representative in court, is called disgraced.

183. To finish, you must know that someone who wishes to take proceedings against another ought to summon him to court; if the person summoned fails to appear, he makes himself liable to a penalty under the praetor's Edict. There are, however, certain persons who **may not be summoned to court** without the permission of the praetor, for instance, **parents, patrons, male and female, as also the descendants* and ascendants* of any patron, male and female. There is a penalty established** for any person who brings such an action. 184. When the defender has been summoned to court and the business cannot be finished on that day, a special undertaking* is required of him; that is, he promises to appear on a specified day. 185. Special undertakings occur in a variety of cases, sometimes unconditionally, that is, on the party's own promise without the giving of security, sometimes with security, sometimes by oath, sometimes by reference to assessors, that is, when someone failing to appear may at once be condemned by the assessors to pay the amount of his special undertaking. Each of these is made known in detail in the praetor's Edict. 186. If the action is on a judgment debt or on expenditure, the special undertaking is for the same amount as that sued for; in other cases, the

erit; si uero ex ceteris causis, quanti actor iurauerit
non[1] calumniae causa postulare sibi uadimonium pro-
mitti: nec tamen *pluris quam partis dimidiae nec*[2]
pluribus quam sestertium C milibus fit uadimonium.
itaque si centum milium res erit nec iudicati depensiue agetur[3], non plus quam sestertium quinquaginta
milium[4] fit uadimonium. 187. Quas autem personas
sine permissu praetoris inpune in ius uocare non possumus, easdem nec[5] uadimonio inuitas[6] obligare nobis[7]
possumus, praeterquam si praetor aditus permittat.

---

     1) nam (?) V   2) pluris — nec *suppl. Hu.*   3) ageretur
V.   4) milia V.   5) ne V.   6) inuicas V.   7) non V.

---

     § 187. *cf. supra* 4, 183. *D.* 2, 6, 2 (*Call.* 35). 2, 6, 1
(*Paul.* 87). 2, 6, 3 (*Paul.* 135). 2, 8, 2, 2 (*Ulp.* 266). *Plaut.*
Aulul. 2, 4, 40 = 319.

sum promised as a special undertaking is the amount in the oath of the pursuer that he is not making a vexatious claim. A special undertaking is not to exceed more than one half of the claim nor more than 100,000 sesterces; and so, if the action is for 100,000 sesterces, and it is not on a judgment debt nor on expenditure, the special undertaking is for no more than 50,000. 187. And we cannot, unless the praetor on application allows it, require a special undertaking against their will from those people whom we are unable without penalty to summon to court without the praetor's permission.

Vocabulary

This Vocabulary does not attempt to be comprehensive. The Outline of Contents should also be used to trace what Gaius says. The Vocabulary gives an explanation or elaboration of the translation adopted for particular Latin terms with which we, like the translators of Justinian's *Institutes*, found some difficulty. (We have, with their permission, adopted or adapted as necessary some of the explanations given in their Vocabulary to Justinian.) It also deals with technical terms which are not fully explained by Gaius himself. In general, we have adopted the terms used for Justinian in order to maintain consistency and bring out the debt owed to Gaius, as we mentioned in the Introduction. The reader should be warned that in the Vocabulary singular and plural, etc., do not always match, because we have preferred to cite the normal usage in each language rather than aim at literal grammatical translation, e.g. codicil is given for 'codicilli'. Certain Latin technical terms are listed at the end of this Vocabulary; these are the terms we thought the reader was most likely to meet in any further reading. Their alphabetical order includes words such as 'in'. We have not, however, listed those cases where we have resorted to anglicisation, e.g. the reader will find adrogation in the main part, but not 'adrogatio' in the Latin list.

Bold type is used to mark the words or terms featuring in the Vocabulary and its attached list; in this way cross-reference should be easy. We have also marked with an asterisk the first occurrence of the terms – not just single words – to be found in the Vocabulary as they appear in each Book of Gaius, that is, wherever the context was such that some further explanation might be required.

References in the form '1.87' are to the Book and numbered section of Gaius's *Institutes*; it seemed unnecessary to insert the normal 'G.' in the context. References to Justinian's *Institutes* are in the form 'J. 1.1.1' or 'J. 1.1pr'. The system of citation is explained more fully in the Vocabulary to the companion Justinian, but essentially the first number refers to the Book, the second to the Title (or chapter), and the third to the numbered section within the Title; the first section is always referred to as 'pr' and the next as '1' – like the British 'first floor'.

It has not been thought necessary to explain various things such as the priesthoods mentioned in 1.112, or gladiators in 3.146. Fuller information is readily available from such sources as the *Oxford*

Classical Dictionary; reference could also usefully be made to A. Berger's *Encyclopedic Dictionary of Roman Law*.

Acceptance, formal see **Formal acceptance**

Act see **Statute**

Action Most actions have an obvious name and function, such as 'action for theft', but not all.

Action of debt This translation of '**condictio**' is inspired by the old English form of action. Translation seemed preferable to anglicisation because 'condiction' sounded unnecessarily mysterious. 'Debt' implies owing in a wide enough sense to cover the many contractual and non-contractual causes for which the 'condictio' lay.

Action on expenditure 'Expenditure' attempts to render neatly the particular form of expenditure referred to, namely payment of the principal debt by a **personal surety**. It is frequently classed together with the action on a judgment debt (4.9).

Action in the law This translation of '**legis actio**' is intended to indicate both the formality of the old legal **procedure** and the fact that a 'legis actio' did not necessarily involve litigation. Adaptations of the forms used in litigation, such as the **vindication**, were also used for other purposes, especially in conveyance by **assignment in court**, and in the procedures for **adoption, emancipation**, and **manumission**. In the time of Gaius actions in the law as forms of litigation survived only in the **centumviral court** (4.31).

Noxal action A noxal action was given in respect of a delict (or tort) committed by a **son in power** or a slave. It lay against the **head of the family** who was obliged either to pay the penalty due or to surrender the wrongdoer to the victim. A son so surrendered was in **bondage**. (4.75-79; also 1.140)

Personal action The terms '**personal action**' and '**real action**' for 'actio **in personam**' and 'actio **in rem**' are convenient, but lose the sense of 'against' given by the Latin 'in'. A personal action lies against a specific person who is under an obligation to the **pursuer** as a result of contract, some relationship akin to contract (see **legacies**), or delict. That person is named in the **principal pleading** of the relevant **formula**. A real action is one which asserts in the principal pleading a legal relationship between the pursuer and a corporeal or incorporeal thing, typically ownership, as in a **vindication**. Normally the defender's name does not appear in the principal pleading, although of course it must in the **condemnation**.

Policy action The adjective 'utilis' in the expression '**actio utilis**' is difficult to translate. Such an action (like the similar 'action on the case', or '**actio in factum**', which is explained in the Vocabulary for Justinian's *Institutes* but is not a term used by Gaius) was given where the **praetor** extended the scope of an existing remedy on the basis of policy, or 'utilitas', where the situation fell within that policy but not within the letter of the law. 'Useful' or 'advantageous' are not words which convey this sense.

Real action, see **Personal action** (The word 'real' is used in a totally different sense in connection with parents and children, but the different context should prevent any confusion.)

Action for a wife's property is a literal translation of 'actio rei uxoriae' (only in 4.62), which allowed a widow or divorced woman to recover at least part of the value of her dowry. It is technically incorrect, however, because the husband was the actual owner of the dowry, although under a duty to return some or all of it according to circumstances. See also J. 4.6.37, referred to in 4.60, which uses the Justinianic term 'iudicium de dote'; Justinian substantially changed the law in this area.

Address ('oratio') see **Imperial legislation**

Adjudication see **Formula**

Adoption 'Adoptio' is the generic term for two forms of adoption, 'adoptio' in the narrower sense of adoption of someone in **paternal power**, and **adrogation** ('adrogatio') meaning adoption of an **independent** person, not in another's power. Modern law has no word for the latter form of adoption since the Roman distinction between dependent and independent people has not survived, hence the anglicisation 'adrogation'. 'Adoptio' involved **mancipation** of the person being adopted into **bondage**, followed by the adopting **head of the family's vindication** of him or her before a magistrate. Adrogation was originally performed before a **convocation of the people** ('comitia calata') under the presidency of the chief priest (or 'pontifex maximus'), and can be regarded as a legislative act (1.99 ff.) which was later performed through **imperial legislation**. The same convocation of the people under the chief priest was used in early times for making a will (2.101), because this, like adrogation, involved questions of religion affected by the deliberate continuance or termination of a family. Adoption brought the adoptee into a new **agnatic** family.

Adrogation see **Adoption**

Agent 'Agency' is a term to be used with caution in Roman law because a person who received a mandate was not an agent in the developed modern sense. The contract of mandate is therefore not called 'agency'. Nevertheless, people could act for others and, in particular, represent them in litigation. A representative in litigation who had been formally appointed was a '**cognitor**', which is translated as a **representative in court**; one not formally appointed was a '**procurator**', or **agent** (4.82-83). But 'procurator' can also mean something like **general agent**

and it is so translated where that seems more appropriate (1.18; 2.64).

Agnates Agnates are relatives through males, descended from a common male ancestor without any artificial break in the line of relationship, such as **emancipation**. People of either sex could be agnates, although the line could only be transmitted through males. If the common male ancestor, or **head of the family**, was still alive, the agnates were all in his **paternal power**. An agnatic relationship existed through **adoption** as fully as through blood. 'Consanguinei', siblings with the same father or adoptive father, are described as 'full agnates' (3.10). Agnates are linked with **clans**, and contrasted with **cognates**.

Album see **Praetor**

Answers see **Jurists**

'As' see **Money**

Ascendant **'Parens'** literally means ascendant, and it can apply to persons of either sex (1.59; 3.71). But Gaius uses the term more often to mean the **head of the family**, who is necessarily always male (1.65; 2.157).

Assessors see **Judge**

Assignment in court The form of **'in iure cessio'** is described in 2.24. It is translated as 'assignment in court' to reflect the fact that it is a form of conveyance sprung from the ancient **vindication** by **action in the law**. It could be used to transfer things capable of **mancipation**, but it was also used with appropriate modifications in **adoption** and **emancipation** (2.22; 4.16).

Assize see **Provinces**

Aulus Agerius and **Numerius Negidius** These are the stock names of pursuer and defender and it seemed pointless to translate them. They are a play on the words for 'to sue', 'agere', and 'to pay', 'numerare', while 'denying', 'negare', the claim.

Authorisation ('auctoritas') see **Guardianship; Statute**

Bankrupt estate Execution of a judgment (or enforcement of debts due to the state) was by sale of the debtor's whole **estate**, his 'bona', if he did not or could not pay up voluntarily. We have described the process (3.78-79) as 'sale of a bankrupt estate' (**'bonorum venditio'**) from the debtor's point of view, or as 'purchase of a bankrupt estate' (**'bonorum emptio'**) from the point of view of the **buyer of the bankrupt estate**, the '**bonorum emptor**'. The analogy with modern bankruptcy should not be pressed, but the term gives the right feel.

Bondage This is used to translate '**mancipium**' which is the (usually) temporary state involved in the **mancipation** used in the processes of **adoption** or **emancipation**; for a **son** transferred in consequence of a **noxal action**, the bondage meant real subjection, although in later classical law he could claim his freedom after he had worked off the penalty.

Bronze and scales This is a literal rendering of '**per aes et libram**', referring to the ceremony of **mancipation** described in 1.119. This represents the weighing out of a price by the acquirer, or the **property-purchaser** in a will, perhaps in copper, 'aes', rather than bronze, 'aeneum', used to describe the scales, but the Romans do not seem to have distinguished clearly between the pure metal and its compound.

Buyer of a bankrupt estate see **Bankrupt estate**

Capable of mancipation see **Mancipation**

Capital see **Status-loss**

Capitulated alien see **Manumission**

Case, in accordance with my (4.16) This translation of 'secundum suam causam' may be controversial, but there are occasions recognised in the *Oxford Latin Dictionary* where 'suus' is used with reference to a first-person subject.

Centumviral court see **Courts**

Champion ('vindex') see **Procedural security**

Child Roman law distinguished between three categories of children or young persons according to age, the 'infans', the 'impubes', and the 'minor viginti quinque annis' (our 'minor'). The 'infans' is a child who is literally too young to speak, but the name is applied by Gaius to one too young to have understanding (3.109); the translation 'very young child' seemed clear enough in the context. The 'impubes' is a child under the age of puberty, whether biological or legally fixed (1.196), who has a **guardian** if he or she is **independent**; the child is then called a **ward**. 'Child' is in general used for such a person, while one who has reached puberty is said to be 'of **full age**' or 'adult'. However, independent persons on reaching puberty might still need protection; they could have a **supervisor**, normally until the age of twenty-five. This area of the law had changed considerably by Justinian's time. Girls (**women**) over puberty in the time of Gaius would normally still have a guardian. '**Liberi**' also can be translated as 'children', meaning children of any age, particularly in relation to the **head of the family**; it also covers other **descendants**, especially in the context of succession. Where the masculine '**filius**' is used, it is not always clear whether the feminine 'filia' is to be understood, but 'child' has sometimes been used as an economical term to include both **sons** and daughters (1.29; 1.32a). 'Real' children are biological children as opposed to those by adoption (2.136).

Children, privilege of see **Privilege of children**

Claim ('vindiciae') see **Interdicts**

Clan 'Gens' often means 'people' or 'nation', as in the phrase **ius gentium** or in the reference to the Galatians in 1.55. In the field of succession, however, it refers to a group of families with a name in common, signifying a real or supposed genealogical connection. The translation 'clan' seemed appropriate, but the analogy with Irish or Scottish clans is not meant to be pressed.

Codicil This is a convenient translation of 'codicilli', but a Roman codicil was not necessarily an appendix to a **will**. It was an informal document which could create a **trust** or, if confirmed by will, could do anything a will could, except directly appoint an heir or disinherit.

Cognates 'Cognatio' is a general term for relationship (3.10), but cognates are blood relations through male or female lines, and including people who had left the agnatic family by **adoption** or **emancipation**. Since an **agnate** must also be within the class of cognates, someone adopted has cognatic ties with his new family as well as his old as long as the adoptive relationship lasts.

Compulsory heir see **Heir**

Condemnation see **Formula**

Conduct, obligation contracted by see **Obligation**

Contempt This translation of '**iniuria**' to refer to the delict of that name (3.220 ff) expresses what came to be the key-note of that very broad delict. It conceals the fact that 'iniuria' has an even broader sense and may simply mean 'a wrong' or 'wrongfully', as in 3.43 or 4.16 and particularly in the delict regulated by the Aquilian Act; in that context 'iniuria' acquired a different, specialised sense (3.211). The use of the same Latin term is undesirable, as the delicts are easily confused when their Latin names are used.

Contrived sale see **Mancipation; Marital subordination; Women**

Convocation of the people ('comitia calata') see **Adoption**

Court, assignment in see **Assignment in court**

Courts In the ordinary forms of **procedure** described by Gaius, the second stage, at which an issue based on a **formula** went before a **judge** for trial, is termed 'iudicium'; this can be translated either as 'court' or as 'trial' according to the context, and it can also mean the actual **action**. Gaius refers specifically to three kinds of 'iudicium', but he does not mention in terms the **'extraordinary procedure'**, procedure **'extra ordinem'**; this referred to the hearing of the whole case by one magistrate. **Trusts** were dealt with by this **special judicature** (2.278).

Centumviral court means literally 'the court of the hundred men', the 'centumviri', but the panel of judges thus referred to was never exactly one hundred, and the judges sat in divisions. The court had a very limited jurisdiction, dealing mainly with claims to inheritances or to guardianship; Pliny the Younger practised before it. It was the one court where **actions in the law** were still in use.

Courts dependent on magistral authority is the translation of 'iudicia imperio continentia', defined in relation to the **statutory courts**, 'iudicia legitima', in 4.104-105. The names relate to the basis for the existence of the court.

Decree ('decretum') see **Imperial legislation; Interdicts**

Defence 'Exceptio' is translated as 'defence'. It was a clause in the **formula** which allowed the defender to parry a claim made in the **pursuer's principal pleading** (4.116 ff). Particular defences mentioned are rendered as the defence 'of action divided' (4.56), 'of agreement' (3.179), 'of deceit', 'exceptio doli' (although **'dolus'** is sometimes rendered as 'bad faith'), 'of intimidation' (4.117), 'of matter decided or carried to trial' (3.181; 4.106), and 'matter remaining' (4.122). The reply which might be made to a defence by a pursuer, a 'replicatio', and subsequent exchanges (4.126-129) have simply been anglicised.

Descendants 'Liberi' in Latin commonly means 'children', although with no necessary implication of childhood, and may have this sense in particular contexts, such as the **privilege of children**, but Gaius often uses it, especially in the context of succession but not only there, to mean any descendants.

Edict see **Imperial legislation; Praetor**

Emancipation The release of someone from **paternal power** is called emancipation. It involved **status-loss**, although in one sense the position of the person emancipated is improved because he or she becomes **independent**. It broke **agnatic** (but not **cognatic**) relationships and reduced the emancipated person's rights in succession. The procedure involved **mancipation** and **manumission**.

Emperor The honorific title for a deceased emperor **'divus'**, literally 'deified' or 'divine', has been translated simply as 'emperor', for example, the Emperor Hadrian (1.7), although some religious and political meaning is lost. Of some significance in dating the *Institutes*, however, is the fact that Gaius refers to Antoninus Pius as 'divus' only in 2.195.

Equestrian order The **'equites'**, literally 'horsemen', were originally the cavalry of the Roman citizen army, and therefore came from the wealthiest class. There was no clear dividing line between leading members of the order and members of the Senate. Under the Empire, the status could be awarded by imperial grant. The imperial administration became increasingly the natural place for an equestrian career.

Estate The term 'bona', referring to a person's whole property, is usually translated as 'estate' although that term is also used to refer to an inheritance, as in modern parlance. However, **'in bonis'**, literally 'in the estate', has a special meaning when contrasted with **quiritary** ownership, as in 1.35; 2.88; 3.166. It there applies to someone who is not yet owner of a thing because he has not acquired title to it in the appropriate way, e.g. when a thing capable of **mancipation** was not mancipated. Until he acquires full title by **usucapion** he is not technically owner, but he is treated for most (but not all: 1.35) purposes as owner, and he can recover the thing if he loses possession of it by the Publician action mentioned in 4.36.

Estate-possession This translation of **'bonorum possessio'** is intended to have a technical ring to it, but to be compact enough for frequent repetition. 'Possession of goods' or 'of the estate' seemed either too informal or too cumbersome. 'Estate-possession' allows a neater version of the sub-forms 'estate-possession counter to the will' ('contra tabulas', 2.125; 3.41), and 'estate-possession in support of the will' ('secundum tabulas', 2.119; 3.34), and also 'effective estate-possession' and 'provisional estate-possession' ('cum re' and 'sine re' respectively, as in 2.148; 3.35).

Exonerate see **Formula**

Extraordinary procedure see **Courts; Procedure**

Family, head of see **Head of the family**

Foreigner This translation of '**peregrinus**' has been preferred to anglicisation because it is a more familiar word (except to bird-watchers); we still refer, however, to the Peregrine **praetor** because that title is so well known. For Gaius, however, 'foreigner' referred more to status than to domicile. As explained in the Introduction, the majority of the inhabitants of the Roman Empire were in his time still technically foreigners, that is, not Roman citizens. They could not use **state law**, whose rules were peculiar to Roman citizens, but most of the law of obligations and part of property law was open to them because it fell within the **law of all peoples**.

Formal acceptance '**Cretio**' is a formal declaration of the acceptance of an inheritance (2.166), but the Latin term is also used to express both the requirement in a **will** to make such a declaration and the time-limit within which it must be made. The Latin has been expanded accordingly (e.g. 2.164).

Formal trust ('**fiducia**') see **Real security; Women**

Formula In ordinary **procedure** the document in which the issue to be decided was set out was called in Latin the 'formula', and the name has been retained as neater than 'form of words'. The parts of the formula, that is, the main clauses from which a formula could be built up, are sufficiently explained by Gaius in 4.39 ff, although he deals with **defences** in 4.116 ff. '**Demonstratio**' is translated as **statement of facts alleged** but it is close to the Scottish 'condescendence'. '**Intentio**', which states the **pursuer**'s claim, whether in **personal** or **real actions**, is translated as **principal pleading**. (This, the normal use of 'claim' in the *Institutes*, is quite different from the archaic '**vindiciae**', which is mentioned under **interdicts**.) **Condemnation** is not ideal for 'condemnatio' because of its criminal overtones for the modern reader, but no better version seemed possible. **Exonerate**, however, is used for 'absolvere' to avoid any strengthening of the criminal suggestion; the Scottish 'assoilzie', derived from it, would have been closer but we feared it would be less generally comprehensible. Although **adjudication** seems sensible for 'adiudicatio', the essence of this clause was the awarding of actual property to one or the other party (4.42). 'Taxation', as in taxation of costs or of expenses, would be an exact translation of '**taxatio**' but it was felt to be technical and misleading because it is now used narrowly; **limitation** better indicates the function of the clause, which applied to the possible sum in the condemnation (4.51-52). It has nothing to do with the limitation of actions in the sense of a time-limit on proceedings. '**Praescriptio**' would be very misleading if anglicised because it too has nothing to do with time-limits on proceedings; it has been rendered as **preliminary clause**, but it has the specific function of narrowing the scope of the action before the court, as explained in 4.130 ff. See also **Courts; Praetor; Procedure**.

Freedman; Freedwoman see **Guardianship; Manumission**

Full age see **Child**

Fund, personal/military see **Personal fund**

General agent see **Agent**

Grant of freedom see **Manumission**

Guarantee; Guarantor see **Personal security; Procedural security**

Guarantor in court see **Procedural security**

Guardianship Classical Roman law knew two different classes of guardianship: 'tutela' of **independent children** under puberty and of **independent women** of any age – unless exempt – and 'cura', which applied to young persons over puberty but under twenty-five, to the insane, 'furiosi', and to spendthrifts, 'prodigi'. The relevant guardian is the 'tutor' or 'curator'. Both words are still familiar technical terms in some jurisdictions, such as Scotland, but to avoid any risk of confusion with teachers or those in charge of art galleries, we have used **guardian** and **supervisor** respectively. A child under guardianship is a 'pupillus' (or 'pupilla'). 'Pupil' is still the Scots technical term for a child under puberty but, to avoid confusion with the English usage referring to schools, we have translated by **ward**, although often 'child' is sufficient. In principle the guardian had to give his **authorisation** or 'auctoritas', to any act, such as incurring a debt or even accepting an inheritance, which might be prejudicial to the person under his control. This was much more strictly applied to children than to women, who are not called 'wards'. They could often compel authorisation, or change guardians by a **contrived sale** with a **formal trust**; in Gaius's day the only guardians with real control over a woman were **patrons** over their **freedwomen**, or the **head of the family** in the case of an **emancipated** daughter (2.122).

Head of the family The Latin terms covered by this phrase are 'paterfamilias', 'pater', and 'parens'. A literal translation – 'father of the family', 'father', or 'parent' – we felt to be inadequate because the 'head of the family' need not be father or parent but might be a more remote **ascendant**, or he might hold this position through **adoption**. Technically, slaves were counted within the 'family', but the term used in connection with them is 'dominus', 'owner'. The **power** of the head of the family, more specifically his **paternal power**, extended over all descendants, male and female, through the male line, that is, over the **agnatic** family. It also applied to those in **bondage** to him or a woman in **marital subordination**. Gaius uses the term 'paterfamilias' much less frequently than 'pater' or 'parens'; these latter two, on the other hand, can be used to describe a father or parent in the biological sense (1.59).

Heir Roman law distinguished three kinds of heir, the '**heres suus**' (or 'suus et necessarius' – 2.152), the 'heres necessarius', and the 'heres extraneus'. The first is the most difficult to translate because the literal meaning 'own heir' does not bear frequent repetition and does not at first glance make sense. The term **immediate heir** is meant to convey the sense that 'sui heredes' – the plural form – rank first on intestacy because they are in a way entitled even while the **head of the family** is still alive (2.157). **Compulsory** is used for 'necessarius'; see 2.153 ff. An '**extraneus**' is referred to as an **outside heir** or **outsider**; this refers to the fact that he is outside the deceased's **power**. An outsider could quite well be related to the deceased; an **emancipated** child was an outside heir. This meaning of someone outside a particular **power** explains why the term is sometimes translated in other contexts as 'third party' (e.g. 2.218, but not 2.95).

Immediate heir see **Heir**

Imperial legislation The emperors could make law in a number of ways. The generic term for these was '**constitutio**', but the traditional anglicisation 'constitution' is confusing because of the association with public law. 'Constitutio' is therefore translated as **pronouncement**, avoiding the oral ring of 'proclamation'. The commonest form of pronouncement was the '**rescriptum**', a written answer from the emperor which we have rendered as **written reply**. If the reply was appended to a petition, it was technically a 'subscriptio' (1.94), but we find Gaius using the broad term 'letter', 'epistula', as in 1.102 or 3.121. He also refers in 1.5 to '**decretum**' or judicial decision or **decree**, and to 'edictum', or **edict**, but there is no example of the former and only one (1.93) of the latter. When the emperor proposed legislation for enactment as a **resolution of the senate**, his draft is called an '**oratio**' or '**address**'. Not long after Gaius this came to be referred to as the formal source of law, but in his one example (2.285) the Senate's resolution is still quoted as the authority.

Independent ('sui iuris') see **Power**

Interdicts The name 'interdict' has been retained for 'interdictum' although the Roman interdict was not an exact equivalent of the Scottish interdict or English injunction. Issue of an interdict was in principle an exercise of a magistrate's authority, but it was normally a particular way of starting proceedings for protection of interests both public (4.140) and private. In private law the acquisition and protection of possession was the most important field of application. Even in the

actions in the law we find the **praetor** pronouncing on a **claim** ('**vindiciae**') to make a preliminary award of possession (4.16). ('Claim' here has a sense very different from the normal usage, which refers to a **principal pleading**.) The particular form of interdict described in 2.140 was a '**decretum**', which has been translated **decree**, although it is quite different from decree as a source of law (1.5) where the term means a judicial decision. In 4.139 Gaius makes the distinction between interdict (negative) and decree (positive), and then proceeds not to use it. Particular interdicts of great importance in private law were '**quorum bonorum**' (4.144), '**unde vi**' (4.154), '**uti possidetis**' and '**utrubi**' (4.148 ff), which have been translated as 'of which estate', 'from where by force', 'as you possess' and 'with which of the two' to try to indicate the original informality of the remedy.

Joinder of issue ('litis contestatio') see **Procedure**

Judge In the ordinary form of **procedure**, with its norm of the **statutory court**, the issue was usually heard out and decided by a single '**iudex**', whom we have translated as 'judge'. This is potentially very misleading because the Roman 'iudex' was not a professional lawyer or administrator but nearer to an unpaid, lay magistrate or a one-man jury. He was usually selected from a public list – **album** – of men qualified by their wealth. Some cases were heard before a panel of such judges who were then described as '**recuperatores**'; we have translated this as **assessors** because such a panel was regularly used where public interest was felt to be involved, as in cases of **contempt**. Gaius in 4.52 has one brief mention of the judge who **makes the dispute his own**, '**litem suam facere**', conduct which is described in J. 4.5pr as falling in the category of obligations as though from delict. In Gaius' example the judge fails to decide in accordance with the **formula**, but it is not clear what else was counted as such misconduct.

Jurists The experts in the law, 'prudentes' or 'iuris prudentes', from whose writings the Digest was compiled, have been given the unusual but traditional name of 'jurists'. The implication is of lawyers whose writings or whose opinions are influential in changing or creating the law, as opposed to the notary or law agent round the corner. That is partly why their **answers** or '**responsa**' (see 3.179 and 3.198) to queries put by anyone seeking legal advice, whether party, judge or magistrate, were authoritative; the other reason is that all such men of whom we know were eminent socially or through service to the state. It is not known whether Gaius himself was ranked as a jurist by his contemporaries, but he clearly identifies himself with one of the two **schools**, the Sabinians, whom he describes as 'our teachers' (1.196; 3.87), in opposition to the Proculians, whom he calls 'the authorities of the other school' (2.221; 3.141). The basis of the distinction between the two Schools is much debated. For '**veteres**', to Gaius the jurists of the

Republican period, the term **old lawyers** seemed sufficiently clear; to Justinian they were usually the classical jurists.

Latins see **Manumission**

Law None of the three terms '**ius civile**', '**ius gentium**', and '**ius naturale**' translates easily because of their implications and because of the suggestions triggered by literal renderings. **State law** for 'ius civile' tries to reflect the original meaning of law for 'citizens', as in 1.1. 'Civil law' is easily confused with civil law as opposed to criminal law. Neither 'civil' nor 'state law' is an altogether happy rendering when contrasted with the law developed through the **praetor**'s **edict**, the '**ius honorarium**' or 'praetorian law', or with law made by the later forms of **statute** (2.197). **Law of all peoples** for 'ius gentium' is somewhat less confusing than the more literal 'law of nations' which suggests public international law. The law of all peoples was really those rules and institutions of private law which the Romans regarded not as peculiar to themselves (state law) but as normal for any legal regime (1.52; 3.132). It could sometimes, however, come close to 'ius naturale', which we have translated as **law of nature**, or sometimes to the related phrase 'natural reason'; the difference is not clear, for example, in the classification of modes of acquisition in 2.65 (compare J. 2.1.11). This usage implies that there is a juridical law of nature existing independently of law made by man; it can, however, refer to the way the physical world is made up, to laws of nature such as gravity. This seems to be the thrust of 'natural' as used by Gaius in relation to children and other relatives (1.97; 3.31; 4.134). In relation to **children** we have preferred the term 'real' to identify the biological relationship, because a 'natural child' for us connotes illegitimacy, which was clearly not the meaning (1.97 and 1.55).

Law of all peoples see **Law**

Law of nature see **Law**

Lawyers, old see **Jurists**

Legacies In the time of Gaius different wording produced four different types of legacy, distinguished as 'proprietary' ('per vindicationem') because the legatee became proprietor of the thing bequeathed without a conveyance by the **heir** and so could immediately vindicate it; 'obligatory' ('per damnationem') because the heir was under an obligation to make the legacy over to the legatee; 'permissive' ('sinendi modo') because the legatee could be permitted to take the thing – while having a **personal action** if the heir did not allow him to take it; and 'preceptive' ('per praeceptionem'). The anglicisation of the last indicates that dispute over the circumstances in which it should be used

(2.217 ff) makes it difficult to suggest an appropriate version.

Legislation, imperial see **Imperial legislation**

Legal wagers see **Procedural security**

Limitation see **Formula**

Loan English does not distinguish between loan of a thing to be returned, in Latin '**commodatum**', and loan of a thing of which the equivalent is to be returned, in Latin '**mutuum**'. The former is normally translated 'loan for use' when it appears; it is not dealt with by Gaius in his discussion of obligations, although he does use it to provide examples of the use of the **formula**. 'Mutuum' is left as 'the loan called "mutuum" ' because the alternative 'loan for consumption' seemed indigestible when applied to money.

Make dispute his own see **Judge**

Mancipation The formal proceedings by **bronze and scales** were used for the transfer of things capable of mancipation, but also for the making of a will (2.102-107), the passing of **women** into **marital subordination** by **contrived sale**, and the bringing of people into **bondage**, which might be for the purpose of **adoption** or **emancipation**, or in consequence of a **noxal action**.
   Capable of mancipation There was a closed list of things in this category: slaves, land in Italy, animals used for transport and rustic praedial servitudes (1.120; 2.14a ff). Since they made cultivation possible, they were distinguished in early law by requiring formality in their transfer.

Manumission The term for freeing a slave is either left as an anglicisation or rendered **grant of freedom**, even in cases where the Latin uses neither 'grant' nor 'freedom'. Freeing a slave made him, in the time of Gaius, a citizen (with somewhat restricted rights), or a Junian **Latin** if there was a defect in the manumission, or a **capitulated alien** ('**dediticius**'), which was a special status for slaves of bad reputation. He or she was then described as a **freedman** or **freedwoman** ('**libertus**' or '**liberta**'; also 'libertinus' and 'libertina') and stood in a special relationship to the former owner, now the **patron**. 'Patron' is an appropriate translation because it has the correct overtones of continuing power over the freed person, including the power to do good. The patron had rights in succession to the freed person and would normally be the **guardian** of a freedwoman. Manumission by **rod** ('**vindicta**'), a fictitious **vindication** of liberty, was one of the formal methods which usually gave the freed slave citizenship; the rod is the same symbol of ownership as the 'festuca' in 4.16. A slave freed under a condition which was not yet fulfilled was a '**statuliber**'; although still a slave, he enjoyed some of the advantages of a free man, such as normal immunity from torture. The term manumission is also used for the release from **bondage** in the course of **emancipation**.

Marital subordination ('manus') see **Mancipation; Women**

Military fund see **Personal fund**

Money Sums of money mentioned in the *Institutes* are expressed either in 'asses' – an '**as**' was originally a weight rather than a coin, as appears, e.g., in the ceremony by **bronze and scales** – or in **sesterces**, silver coinage. The 'as' was also used in the law of succession; shares in an inheritance were expressed in duodecimal fractions of the **pound**, or 'as'. We have not translated these terms where the sum mentioned is simply given as an example. 'Uno nummo' is rendered 'for a penny'.

Natural law see **Law**

Noxal action see **Action**

Numerius Negidius see **Aulus Agerius**

Obligation contracted by conduct This translation of 'obligatio re contracta' brings out the symmetry of the series: contracts by words ('verbis'), by writing ('litteris'), by mere agreement ('consensu'), and by conduct ('re') – see 3.89. It also matches the description of delictual liability as arising 'ex re' in J. 4.1pr. Of the contracts in this category, Gaius deals expressly only with the **loan** called 'mutuum', which he links with the obligation to repay something paid by a debtor through mistake, but he describes the **formulas** for deposit and remarks on their similarity to those for loan for use; he also mentions pledge. The frequent translation 'real contract' is evasive and somewhat confusing.

Old lawyers see **Jurists**

Outside heir; Outsider see **Heir**

Parent see **Ascendant**

Paternal power ('patria potestas') see **Power**

Patrician see **Plebeian**

Patron see **Manumission**

Personal action see **Action**

Personal fund The 'peculium' which is thus translated belonged in law to the **head of the family** but was treated virtually as the property of the **son** or slave. 'Fund' suggests money, but it could consist of any property, such as land or a business (4.72). The law found ways to impose liability, usually limited, on the head of the family for the dealings of his dependants (4.69-74). The **military fund** ('peculium castrense') of a son was quite different in that he had full power to dispose of it, including leaving it by will (2.106); it consisted of pay for and acquisitions made on military service.

Personal security In the time of Gaius three kinds of **guarantee** by stipulation were distinguished according to the wording of the stipulation in which the guarantor gave a promise in support of an obligation incurred by the principal debtor (3.115 ff; 3.92). For the most modern of the three, the **'fideiussor'**, the modern term **guarantor** has been used. The older term 'surety' seemed appropriate for the older types of guarantor, the **'sponsor'** and the **'fidepromissor'**, who are distinguished, somewhat arbitrarily, as **personal surety** and **surety**. The promise of the 'sponsor', the **'sponsio'**, was a stipulation using the Latin word 'spondere', rendered as 'solemnly promise'; use of this was confined to citizens. While normally applying to a guarantee, such a solemn promise could be made by the principal debtor; this is the case in the **legal wagers** used in **procedural security**.

Personal surety see **Action on expenditure; Personal security**

Plebeians In early Rome plebeians had a social and legal status inferior to that of the **patricians**, although the basis of the distinction between the two groups is obscure. By the second century A.D., however, nearly all the leading families were technically plebeian, and such privileges as patricians still possessed were confined to the religious sphere. It was as early as 287 B.C. that the Hortensian Act was passed; this gave **statutes** of the plebeian assembly exactly the same force as **acts** passed by assemblies of the whole people.

Pledge see **Real security**

Policy action see **Action**

Pound see **Money**

Power The rights of the **head of the family**, biological or by **adoption**, over the persons and property of dependent members of the **agnatic** family and of his slaves are subsumed under **'potestas'**. This is rendered 'power' to indicate the extensive nature of these rights, which included the right to put to death as well as entitlement to virtually all property and contractual rights acquired by persons dependent on him; the head of the family was also liable to **noxal actions** for the delicts of **sons** or slaves. He had similar but lesser rights over those in **bondage** or in **marital subordination** to him. Someone, male or female, not in any such power is **independent ('sui iuris')**.

Paternal power ('patria potestas') is the fuller form of expression of the rights of the head of the family as **'paterfamilias'**, exercising his power over free persons; Gaius only uses the full term once (2.141). 'Dominica potestas' was the expanded term for the power of an owner, male or female, over his or her slaves.

Praetor The praetor was the magistrate responsible for the operation of the ordinary system of **procedure**, including the issuing of **interdicts**. One of his main functions was to decide whether a **formula** should be granted and when there was scope for a **policy action**. Developments of the law made in such ways are described as being of the **'ius honorarium'** or praetorian law. He set out the remedies promised in his **edict**, which was displayed in public on a white board or **album**; a similar public list, controlled by the praetor, existed of those eligible to serve as **judges**. Other magistrates could issue edicts concerning their sphere of office, and this was indeed one form of **imperial legislation**, but the legal importance of the Praetor's Edict justifies the capital. Although 'the praetor' in the singular is the normal usage, after 242 B.C. there were two, the Urban and the Peregrine; the latter had particular responsibility for litigation involving **foreigners**. Other praetors were also appointed with different responsibilities, such as the praetor with a **special judicature** relating to **trusts**, 'fideicommissarius' (2.278), but the Urban Praetor was always the senior.

Preliminary clause see **Formula**

Principal pleading see **Formula**

Privilege of children ('ius liberorum') 'Ius' is always a difficult word to translate, but in this context we are referring to the privileges granted under the legislation of Augustus which was aimed at increasing the citizen population. Some of the privileges related to succession. In general, the childless could take only half of what came to them by will or legacy, while the unmarried were unable to take at all. A free born female **patron** with the privilege of children was given a greater right in the estates of her **freedmen** and **freedwomen** (3.50). Men with this privilege were given preference in public life. Free born **women** who had borne three live children were exempted from **guardianship** while the same privilege was granted to freedwomen who had borne four since their **manumission**.

Procedural security One party to litigation had frequently to give a **guarantee** to the other that he or she would do or refrain from doing something. The guarantee was given by an oath or a promise, which might be supported by **personal security** of some sort. The technical terms are not easy to translate meaningfully because the institutions themselves were mostly somewhat archaic, and so the names chosen are rather arbitrary. For the guarantors called **'praedes'**, **special surety** seemed appropriate because 'surety' is rather an old-fashioned term. **Special undertaking** seemed clear enough for **'vadimonium'**, which appears in 3.224 and is explained in 4.184-185. **Guarantor in court** was chosen for **'vindex'** in the context of 4.46, but 'vindex' has a different sense in **procedure** by **action in the law**; therefore in 4.21 and 4.25 it is translated as **champion** because he himself acted to defend another's right. **'Sponsio'**, dealt with under **personal security**, was also a term for the promises (and counter-promises) with which the parties to litigation bound themselves.

Procedure In the time of Gaius the ordinary form of procedure was that by **formula**. It had almost entirely replaced the **actions in the law**, described in 4.12-29 and in practice only surviving in the **centumviral court** (4.31), but like them it consisted of two stages. In the first stage the legal issues were settled before the **praetor** – **'in iure'** – and set out in the formula. At this point there was said to be **'litis contestatio'**, which is translated as **joinder of issue**. The matter then went to the **judge** or judges – **'apud iudicem'** – for trial. Proceedings in courts outside the formulary system were described as **'extra ordinem'** or **extraordinary**. Such proceedings became normal during the third century, and formulas were abolished in the fourth; somewhat misleadingly, all the procedures found outside the formulary system are lumped together as **'cognitio'**, from 'causa cognita', taking cognisance of a case.

Pronouncement see **Imperial legislation**

Property-purchaser see **Bronze and scales**

Provinces The provinces were administrative areas of the Roman Empire; in the time of Gaius they did not include Italy. Governors of provinces were not only administrators and military commanders; they also exercised jurisdiction. In order to hear both civil and criminal causes they regularly went on circuit within the province and held gatherings ('conventus'); these we have translated as **assize**, although the modern term is associated rather more with criminal justice. Land in the provinces was subject to a tax called 'stipendium' in those provinces described as belonging to the Roman people and 'tributum' in provinces directly administered by the emperors. The names **stipendiary** and **tributary land** for provincial lands have been retained.

Pursuer see **Action, personal; Aulus Agerius**

Quiritary right 'Quirites' was one of the old names for Roman citizens. As the term 'ius Quiritium' appears in ancient formal claims, as in 2.24 or 4.16, it seemed best to retain the traditional 'quiritary right' or 'quiritary law' to suggest a slight archaism, as in a **vindication**. In the context of ownership a contrast is sometimes made between someone with bare quiritary right, who retains the formal title to something which someone else has in his **estate**, '**in bonis**' (1.54; 3.166). Quiritary right was **state law** and could be enjoyed only by a citizen or someone with '**commercium**', which is somewhat misleadingly translated as 'right of commerce' in 2.26 (as supplied), since it meant the ability to use state law and was not of great importance in most commercial transactions.

Real action see **Action, personal**

Real security Gaius does discuss real security, where a guarantee is made by giving the creditor some right over a thing, a 'res'. He refers incidentally to 'pignus', which is translated as **pledge** (e.g. 3.200). In this context he appears to have in mind only a case where possession of the thing is given to the creditor, but elsewhere he mentions the Salvian interdict relating to a landlord's security over his tenant's property without possession (4.147). The older '**fiducia**', in which ownership was transferred to the creditor subject to an obligation of good faith that he would reconvey it on payment of the debt, is normally rendered **trust** or **trust conveyance**. There is an inconvenient overlap with 'trust' as the translation for '**fideicommissum**', but the context should make clear which is meant. It is translated as 'formal trust' in the context of a **woman**'s **contrived sale** of herself for the purpose of changing her **guardian** or making a will (1.114). 'Fiducia' was also used for a sort of deposit for safe-keeping (2.60).

Rehabilitation No English equivalent recaptures the sense of 'return over the threshold' conveyed by the Latin '**postliminium**', which is briefly explained in 1.129. Rehabilitation indicates the central fact of recovery of rights when the captive resumed his former legal position after his return to Roman territory in honourable circumstances.

Religious things This translation is not an entirely satisfactory version of '**res religiosa**', but it does convey the idea that such things, e.g. graves, were subject to special rules because they were dedicated to the gods below (2.4); a '**res sacra**' was dedicated to the gods above. Both religious and **sacred things** were more the concern of divine (or sacral) than secular law, since neither could be owned by individuals.

Representative in court ('cognitor') see **Agent**

Resolution of the senate ('senatusconsultum') see **Statute**

Right, quiritary see **Quiritary right**

Rod see **Manumission; Vindication**

Sacred things see **Religious things**

Schools see **Jurists**

Security see **Personal/Procedural/Real security**

Senate resolution see **Statute**

Sesterces see **Money**

Son in power ('filius') see **Head of the family; Power**

Special judicature see **Courts; Praetor; Trusts**

Special surety see **Procedural security**

Special undertakings see **Procedural security**

State law see **Law**

Statement of facts alleged see **Formula**

Status-loss 'Capitis' or **'kapitis deminutio'** is literally the loss of a head, that is of a member of some body. A person suffers status-loss in the sense that he loses his or her previous status, even although the new status may be preferable, as might be the case with **emancipation**. 'Caput' in the sense of status also appears in the adjective **capital**; a capital penalty did not necessarily (particularly for the upper classes) involve loss of life, but rather loss of status.

Statute Roman law knew a number of forms of law-making which are comparable with modern statutes: **'leges'**, **'plebiscita'**, **'senatusconsulta'**, and **'constitutiones'**, all briefly explained in 1.3-5. 'Lex' is always translated as **'act'** when referring to a specific statute such as the Hortensian Act in 1.3; it seemed the natural English equivalent. 'Lex' is also used for the **Twelve Tables**, e.g. 1.132. Acts with two names or double names are hyphenated on the American model of the Taft-Hartley Act, e.g. the Julian-Plautian Act in 2.45. When the term is used more generally, 'statute' is often more convenient, especially as **plebeian statutes** are not distinguished from 'leges' after their first mention in 1.2-3, and are in fact cited as 'leges', e.g. the Aquilian Act in 2.210. Plebeian statutes are very different from what we now mean by plebiscites. These two forms of legislation fell into disuse during the first century A.D. **Resolutions of the senate** for 'senatusconsulta' – usually abbreviated to SCC, or SC in the singular – avoids anglicisation, although at the cost of length. Specific resolutions are given capitals, as with the Trebellian Resolution in 3.255. For the various forms of 'constitutio' see **Imperial legislation**. It is in the context of statute that we find the word '**auctoritas**' used to mean 'on the proposal of', e.g. 1.47, as well as an authorisation (1.3) that is not very different from a **guardian**'s.

Statutory court see **Courts**

Stipendiary land see **Provinces**

Subordination, marital see **Mancipation; Women**

Supervision ('cura'; 'curator') see **Guardianship**

Surety see **Personal security**

Token 'Arra' has been rendered as 'token' instead of the rather old-fashioned 'earnest'. In the time of Gaius 'arra' was normally a token of agreement rather than the substantial down-payment of Justinian's law.

Tributary land see **Provinces**

Trusts The normal institution translated as trust is the '**fideicommissum**', which is dealt with at length in Book 2. While there are marked differences from the modern trust, the term indicates the essential element. Originally it was indeed a matter of trust in the sense that no legal obligation was imposed (see J. 2.23.1), but in classical law matters arising from a trust were heard by a **praetor** with a **special judicature**. In Roman law a trust in this sense arose only in succession on death; it could not be constituted so as to take effect during the truster's lifetime. 'Trust' is also sometimes used for '**fiducia**'; see **Real security**.

Trust conveyance ('fiducia') see **Real security; Women**

Twelve Tables This early statement of existing law and custom, not really a code although sometimes referred to as such, dates from around 450 B.C.; it is often cited by Gaius, who had written a commentary on it. The Romans viewed it as the very basis of their law; 'statutory' ('**legitimus**') quite often refers to a provision springing from it. Only fragments have survived, in quotations by later writers.

Usucapion This unlovely word and the even more unlovely verb **usucapt** had to be retained for 'usucapio'. It is a form of what in modern law is called 'positive prescription', but such a translation would invite confusion with other usages of 'praescriptio', and even the cumbersome 'positive' does not give an indication of the great importance of this method of acquisition in Roman law. Failure to observe the formalities required for acquisition of things **capable of mancipation** could be cured by usucapion.

Veterans The word is the same as in the Latin but, unlike English usage, it implies completion of and honourable discharge from professional military service, whether with the legions or with other armed forces. Only legionaries were theoretically required to be Roman citizens on enlistment, but all troops normally received a grant of citizenship on honourable discharge (1.57), together with certain privileges, such as partial immunity from taxation.

Vindication The Latin verb 'vindicare' can simply mean 'claim', as in 3.94 or 3.217, but in most legal contexts 'vindicatio' means a **real action**, an action for assertion of ownership and other real rights, and also of **power**. The **principal pleading** of the **formula** simplifies the assertion made by the first claimant in the old **action in the law** (described in 4.16) to 'if it appears that the thing in question belongs to **Aulus Agerius** by **quiritary right**'. It was no longer necessary for the **pursuer** to touch the thing claimed with a **rod** symbolic of the ownership claimed. The vindication was a formality in conveyance by **assignment in court**.

Wagers, legal see **Procedural security**

Ward ('pupillus') see **Child; Guardianship**

Will 'Will' is the usual translation of 'testamentum'; it is also normally adequate for the fuller phrase 'tabulae testamenti' or 'tablets of the will', where 'tablets' means writing tablets. However, when Gaius talks in 2.151 about a testator 'cutting the thread holding the will together' or in 2.181 about substitutes being named separately, his words are not fully comprehensible unless it is realised that a will was normally written on waxed wooden boards, which were then tied together with thread and sealed by the witnesses. In this way the contents could not be read without opening the will, which in turn could not be done without disturbing the seals.

Women Certain terms relating to women require some explanation. In the time of Gaius, all **independent** women were in principle subject to **guardianship**, although he tells us that in many cases this was little more than a formality. Women with the **privilege of children** were exempt. A married woman did not fall into the guardianship of her husband, unless by deliberate arrangement or in the case of female slaves freed in order to marry their **patron**, and the property of the two parties in the normal 'free' marriage of classical law remained quite distinct. Marriage with **marital subordination** seems to have been rare in the time of Gaius; the Latin '**manus**' has been translated in this way because it was a concomitant of one form of marriage, not marriage itself. Unless entered into for sacral purposes (1.112) it was usually created by '**coemptio**', or **contrived sale**, so rendered because it was a fictitious sale contrived to bring about a legal consequence. This could also take place with a man other than a husband for the purpose of changing guardians or, earlier, making a will; in this case it was described as with a **formal trust**, '**fiducia**'. Entry into marital subordination on marriage carried an independent woman's property to her husband in the same way as **adrogation** carried it to the adopting **head of the family**, and similarly she acquired the rights of a daughter in the law of succession.

Written reply see **Imperial legislation**

Technical Latin terms

Actio utilis; – in factum see **Action, policy**
Apud iudicem see **Procedure**
Arra see **Token**
As, asses see **Money**
Auctor/auctoritas see **Guardianship; Statute**
Bonorum emptio/emptor/venditio see **Bankrupt estate**
Bonorum possessio see **Estate-possession**
Capitis deminutio see **State-loss**
Cessio in iure see **Assignment in court**
Coemptio see **Contrived sale; Women**
Cognitio see **Procedure**
Cognitor see **Agent**
Comitia calata see **Adoption**
Commercium see **Quiritary right**
Commodatum see **Loan**
Condictio see **Action of debt**
Constitutio see **Imperial legislation; Statute**
Cretio see **Formal acceptance**
Cura/curator see **Guardianship**
Decretum see **Imperial legislation; Interdicts**
Dediticius see **Manumission**
Demonstratio see **Formula**
Divus see **Emperor**
Dolus see **Defence**

Equites see **Equestrian order**
Exceptio see **Defence**
Extraneus see **Heir**
Extra ordinem see **Courts; Procedure**
Fideicommissum see **Trusts**
Fideiussor see **Personal security**
Fidepromissor see **Personal security**
Fiducia see **Real security; Trusts; Women**
Filius/filia familias see **Child**
Gens, gentes see **Clan; Law of all peoples**
Heres see **Heir**
Impubes see **Child**
In bonis see **Estate**
In iure see **Procedure**
In iure cessio see **Assignment in court**
Iniuria see **Contempt**
In personam see **Action, personal**
In rem see **Action, real**
Intentio see **Formula**
Iudex, iudices see **Judge**
Iudicia imperio continentia; – legitima see **Courts**
Ius civile see **Law**
Ius gentium see **Law**
Ius honorarium see **Law; Praetor**
Ius liberorum see **Privilege of children**
Ius naturale see **Law**
Ius quiritium see **Quiritary right**
Lex, leges see **Statute**
Legis actio see **Action in the law**
Legitimus see **Twelve Tables**
Liberi see **Child; Descendants**
Liberta/libertus see **Manumission**
Litem suam facere see **Judge**
Litis contestatio see **Procedure**
Mancipium see **Bondage**
Manus see **Women**
Mutuum see **Loan**
Oratio see **Imperial legislation**
Parens, parentes see **Ascendant**
Pater/paterfamilias see **Head of the family; Power**
Patria potestas see **Power**
Peculium; – castrense see **Personal fund**
Per aes et libram see **Bronze and scales**
Peregrinus see **Foreigner; Praetor**
Plebiscita see **Statute**
Postliminium see **Rehabilitation**
Potestas see **Power**

Praes, praedes see **Procedural security**
Praescriptio see **Formula**
Procurator see **Agent**
Pupillus see **Guardianship**
Quorum bonorum see **Interdicts**
Recuperatores see **Judge**
Rescriptum see **Imperial legislation**
Res mancipi see **Mancipation**
Res religiosa see **Religious things**
Res sacra see **Religious things**
Responsa see **Jurists**
Senatusconsulta (abbreviated as SCC) see **Statute**
Sponsio/sponsor see **Personal security; Procedural security**
Statuliber see **Manumission**
Suus heres, sui heredes see **Heir**
Sui iuris see **Power**
Taxatio see **Formula**
Testamentum see **Will**
Tutela/tutor see **Guardianship**
Unde vi see **Interdicts**
Uti possidetis see **Interdicts**
Utrubi see **Interdicts**
Vadimonium see **Procedural security**
Veteres see **Jurists**
Vindex see **Procedural security**
Vindiciae see **Interdicts**
Vindicta see **Manumission**

OUTLINE OF CONTENTS

CONSPECTVS RERVM.[1])

---

1) secundum Boeckingium, sed hic illic auctus et emen-
datus.

Outline of contents

I. THE LAW RELATING TO PERSONS

II. THE LAW RELATING TO THINGS

III. IVS QVOD AD ACTIONES PERTINET.

A. Actiones.

III. THE LAW RELATING TO ACTIONS

A. Actions